Pieces of The Personality Puzzle

Readings in Theory and Research

Second Edition

David C. Funder
University of California, Riverside

Daniel J. Ozer
University of California, Riverside

W · W · NORTON & COMPANY

New York · London

READINGS IN THEORY AND RESEARCH

SECOND EDITION

Printed in the United States of America
The text of this book is composed in Minion
with the display set in Matrix
Composition by PennSet, Inc.
Manufacturing by Maple-Vail
Book design by Jack Meserole

Library of Congress Cataloging-in-Publication Data

Pieces of the personality puzzle : readings in theory and research / [edited by] David C. Funder, Daniel J. Ozer.— 2nd ed.
p. cm.
Includes bibliographical references.
ISBN 0-393-97683-1 (pbk.)
1. Personality. I. Funder, David Charles. II. Ozer, Daniel J.

BF698 .P525 2001
155.2—dc21 00-052717

W. W. Norton & Company, Inc., 500 Fifth Avenue, New York, N.Y. 10110
http://www.wwnorton.com

W. W. Norton & Company Ltd., Castle House, 75/76 Wells Street, London W1T 3QT

2 3 4 5 6 7 8 9 0

CONTENTS

Part I

Research Methods 1

Part II

The Trait Approach to Personality 69

Part III

Biological Approaches to Personality 133

Part VI

Cross-cultural Approaches to Personality 349

Part VII

Behavioral and Social Learning Approaches to Personality 423

Part VIII

The Cognitive Approach to Personality 457

PREFACE

Theory and research in personality psychology address the ways in which people are different from one another, the relations between body and mind, how people think (consciously and unconsciously), what people want (consciously and unconsciously), and what people do. Personality is the broadest, most all-encompassing part of psychology.

This breadth of relevance is personality psychology's greatest attraction, but it also makes good work in this field difficult to do. Nearly all personality psychologists therefore choose to limit their approach in some way, by focusing on particular phenomena they deem of special interest and more or less neglecting everything else. A group of psychologists who focus on the same basic phenomena could be said to be working within the same "paradigm," or following the same "basic approach."

The articles in this book are organized by the basic approaches they follow. The first section presents articles that describe and discuss the research methods used by personality psychologists. The second section includes articles relevant to the "trait approach," which concentrates on the conceptualization and measurement of individual differences in personality. The third section presents articles that follow the biological approach and attempt to connect the biology of the body and nervous system with the processes of emotion, thought, and behavior. The fourth section presents classic and modern research from the psychoanalytic approach, which considers (among other things) unconscious processes of the mind ultimately based on the writings of Sigmund Freud. The fifth section presents some examples from the humanistic approach, which focuses on experience, free will, and the meaning of life. Articles in the sixth section consider the constancy and variability of personality across different cultures. Articles in the seventh section trace the way the behavioristic approach developed into social learning theory. The eighth and final section includes several articles that form the basis of and exemplify the modern social-cognitive approaches to personality.

There is no substitute for reading original work in a field to appreciate its content and its style. But assembling a book such as this does entail certain difficulties and requires strategic choices. We chose, first of all, to be representative rather than exhaustive in our coverage of the domain of personality psychology. While we believe the most important areas of personality are represented by an exemplar or two in what follows, no topic is truly covered in depth. We hope a reader who becomes seriously interested will use the reference sections that follow each article to guide his or her further reading.

A second choice was to search for articles most likely to be interesting to an audience that does *not* consist of professionally trained psychologists. At the same time, we tried to ensure that many of the most prominent personality psychologists of this century were represented. In some cases, this meant we chose a prominent psychologist's most accessible—rather than by some definition most "important"—writing.

A third decision—made reluctantly—was to excerpt nearly all of these articles. In their original form, most of the articles that follow are much longer. We tried to be judicious in our editing. We removed passages that would be incomprehensible to a nonprofessional reader, digressions, and treatments of issues beside the main point of each article. We have marked all changes to the original text; three asterisks centered on a blank line mark the omission of a complete paragraph or section, while three asterisks run into the text indicate that material within that paragraph has been omitted.

We probably should note one other thing that a reader might notice. Prior to about 1970, it was conventional practice to use the pronoun "he" to refer to both males and females. This practice is followed in some of the older selections of this text. Current guidelines of the American Psychological Association (APA, 1994) require that "he or she" or similar inclusive constructions be used.

Most articles have footnotes. A few of these are by the original authors (we have indicated which these are), but we deleted most other footnotes from the original articles. We added many footnotes of our own. These define bits of jargon, explain references to other research, and—when we couldn't help ourselves—provide editorial commentary.

Each section begins with an introduction that describes the articles to follow and lays out their sequence. Each article is preceded by a brief essay outlining what we see as its message and some issues we believe a reader should consider.

Finally, this volume contains a few surprises. The reader will find a passage from a novel, an excerpt from a 19th-century textbook in "physiognomy," and a satire about a place called "Nacirema." These were not written by psychologists, but we believe they are of interest and shed a unique light on their topic.

This book follows the same organization as Funder's (2001) textbook, *The Personality Puzzle* (2nd ed.), and some of the research referred to in that book can be found here. However, one does not need to use that text in conjunction with this one; the two books are largely independent and this one was designed to be useful with almost any textbook—or even by itself. This compilation includes representative writings in method, theory, and research—the three staples of any good personality course.

Acknowledgments

Many individuals helped with this project, in both its first and its current edition. For the first edition, useful suggestions came from Jana Spain of Highpoint University, Susan Krauss Whitbourne of the University of Massachusetts (Amherst), Andrew J. Tomarken of Vanderbilt University, and Brian C. Hayden of Brown University. Liz Suhay of W. W. Norton assembled the manuscript of the first edition, gathered copyright permissions, and performed many other necessary tasks with speed and good humor. April Lange, the editor of the first edition, patiently shepherded the book to completion and talked us out of several truly bad ideas. For the second edition, Mary Babcock copyedited a complex manuscript into a coherent product, along the way correcting many errors including a few she found in the first edition. With help from Rob Whiteside, Aaron Javsicas assembled the manuscript of this edition, gathering new copyright permissions and dealing with many other matters with good sense and dispatch. Jon Durbin was the editor who encouraged and oversaw the second edition. The original idea for a book of readings to accompany Funder's *Personality Puzzle* came from Don Fusting, a former Norton editor. We are grateful to all of these individuals, to the students and instructors who responded so positively to the first edition, and to the authors who graciously and generously allowed us to edit and reproduce their work.

PIECES OF

THE PERSONALITY PUZZLE

READINGS IN THEORY AND RESEARCH

SECOND EDITION

PART I

Research Methods

How do you learn something that nobody has ever known before? This is the question of "research methods," the strategies and techniques that are used to obtain new knowledge. The knowledge of interest for personality psychology is knowledge about people, so for this field the question of research methods translates into a concern with the ways in which one can learn more about a person. These include techniques for measuring an individual's personality traits as well as his or her thoughts, motivations, emotions, and goals.

Personality psychologists have a long tradition of being particularly interested in and sophisticated about research methods. Over the years, they have developed new sources of data, invented innovative statistical techniques, and even provided some important advances in the philosophy of science. The selections in this section address some critical issues that arise when considering the methods one might use to learn more about people.

The opening selection, by Dan McAdams, asks, "What do we know when we know a person?" The article presents an introduction to and comparison of the various conceptual units—ranging from traits to the holistic meaning of life—that personality psychologists have used to describe and understand people.

The second selection, by Jack Block, is an introduction to the longitudinal *method of personality research. In this method, the same people are studied over a sufficient length of time—many years—to provide a window into some of the important ways in which they develop. This research is extraordinarily difficult to do, but Block argues for its importance and outlines some vital considerations for how it should be conducted.*

The third selection, by Robert Rosenthal and Donald Rubin, concerns a particular statistic that is unavoidable by any reader of personality research—the correlation coefficient. Despite its ubiquity, this statistic is frequently misunderstood, and in particular, the effects it describes are often underestimated. For example, if someone tells you they have obtained a correlation between a trait and behavior equal to .32, is this big or little? For reasons Rosenthal and Rubin explain, the answer is "pretty big."

The fourth and fifth selections are two of the unquestioned, all-time classics of psychological methodology. They are absolutely required reading for any psychologist. The article by Lee Cronbach and Paul Meehl concerns "construct validity," or the issue of how one determines whether a test of personality (or any other attribute) really measures what it is supposed to. The article by Donald Campbell and Donald Fiske presents an important method, called the multitrait-multimethod matrix, for separating out the components of a measurement that reflect real properties of people, as opposed to properties of the instrument used to take the measurement. The sixth selection, by Harrison Gough, is also a classic, though perhaps a lesser-known one. It argues persuasively that test evaluation must go beyond the concerns outlined by Cronbach and Meehl and by Campbell and Fiske, and must include an effort to understand the psychological dynamics and the deeper psychological meaning of an individual's responses to a personality test.

Personality psychology is now moving away from its former nearly exclusive reliance on self-report personality assessments, to include other methods such as on-line coding of videotaped behavior. In the final selection, Samuel Gosling and his colleagues demonstrates how a comparison between self-reports and observers' reports of behavior can illustrate not only the relative validity of each kind of data but also interesting psychological processes, such as self-enhancement, that produce discrepancies between different sources of data.

What Do We Know When We Know a Person?

Dan P. McAdams

Personality psychology is all about understanding individuals better. In this first selection, the personality psychologist Dan McAdams asks one of the fundamental questions about this enterprise, which is: when we learn about a person, what is it we learn? He begins by describing the kind of personality psychology that nonpsychologists (or psychologists when off duty) frequently practice: discussing an individual that one has just met. In such discussions, the individual is often considered at several different levels, ranging from surface descriptions of behavior to inferences about deeper motivations.

The challenge for professional personality psychologists, McAdams argues, is to become at least as sophisticated as amateur psychologists by taking into account aspects of individuals at multiple levels. In his own work, McAdams collects life stories and tries to understand individuals in holistic terms. He is a critic of the more dominant approach that characterizes individuals in terms of their personality traits. However, in this well-balanced article we see McAdams attempt to integrate the various levels of personality description into a complete portrait of what we know when we know a person.

From *Journal of Personality, 63*, 365–396, 1995.

One of the great social rituals in the lives of middle-class American families is "the drive home." The ritual comes in many different forms, but the idealized scene that I am now envisioning involves my wife and me leaving the dinner party sometime around midnight, getting into our car, and, finding nothing worth listening to on the radio, beginning our traditional post-party postmortem. Summoning up all of the personological wisdom and nuance I can muster at the moment, I may start off with something like, "He was really an ass." Or adopting the more "relational" mode that psychologists such as Gilligan (1982) insist comes more naturally to women than men, my wife may say something like, "I can't believe they stay married to each other." It's often easier to begin with the cheap shots. As the conversation develops, however, our attributions become more detailed and more interesting. We talk about people we liked as well as those we found offensive. There is often a single character who stands out from the party—the person we found most intriguing, perhaps; or the one who seemed most troubled; maybe the one we would like to get to know much better in the future. In the scene I am imagining, let us call that person "Lynn" and let us consider what my wife and I might say about her as we drive home in the dark.

I sat next to Lynn at dinner. For the first 15 minutes, she dominated the conversation at our end of the table with her account of her recent trip to Mexico where she was doing research for an article to appear in a national magazine. Most of the people at the party knew that Lynn is a free-lance writer whose projects have taken her around the world, and they asked her many questions about her work and her travels. Early on, I felt awkward and intimidated in Lynn's presence. I have never been to Mexico; I was not familiar with her articles; I felt I couldn't keep up with the fast tempo of her account, how she moved quickly from one exotic tale to another. Add to this the fact that she is a strikingly attractive woman, about 40 years old with jet black hair, dark eyes, a seemingly flawless complexion, clothing both flamboyant and tasteful, and one might be able to sympathize with my initial feeling that she was, in a sense, "just too much."

My wife formed a similar first impression earlier in the evening when she engaged Lynn in a lengthy conversation on the patio. But she ended up feeling much more positive about Lynn as they shared stories of their childhoods. My wife mentioned that she was born in Tokyo during the time her parents were Lutheran missionaries in Japan. Lynn remarked that she had great admiration for missionaries "because they really believe in something." Then she remarked: "I've never really believed in anything very strongly, nothing to get real passionate about. Neither did my parents, except for believing in us kids. They probably believed in us kids too much." My wife immediately warmed up to Lynn for this disarmingly intimate comment. It was not clear exactly what she meant, but Lynn seemed more vulnerable now, and more mysterious.

I eventually warmed up to Lynn, too. As she and I talked about politics and our jobs, she seemed less brash and domineering than before. She seemed genuinely interested in my work as a personality psychologist who, among other things, collects people's life stories. She had been a psychology major in college. And lately she had been reading a great many popular psychology books on such things as Jungian archetypes, the "child within," and "addictions to love." As a serious researcher and theorist, I must confess that I have something of a visceral prejudice against many of these self-help, "New Age" books. Still, I resisted the urge to scoff at her reading list and ended up enjoying our conversation very much. I did notice, though, that Lynn filled her wine glass about twice as often as I did mine. She never made eye contact with her husband, who was sitting directly across the table from her, and twice she said something sarcastic in response to a story he was telling.

Over the course of the evening, my wife and I learned many other things about Lynn. On our drive home we noted the following:

1. Lynn was married once before and has two children by her first husband.
2. The children, now teenagers, currently live with her first husband rather than with her; she didn't say how often she sees them.
3. Lynn doesn't seem to like President Clinton and is very critical of his excessively "liberal" policies; but she admires his wife, Hillary, who arguably is more liberal in her views; we couldn't pin a label of conservative or liberal to Lynn because she seemed to contradict herself on political topics.
4. Lynn hates jogging and rarely exercises; she claims to eat a lot of "junk food"; she ate very little food at dinner.
5. Lynn says she is an atheist.
6. Over the course of the evening, Lynn's elegant demeanor and refined speech style seemed to give way to a certain crudeness; shortly before we left, my wife heard her telling an off-color joke, and I noticed that

she seemed to lapse into a street-smart Chicago dialect that one often associates with growing up in the toughest neighborhoods.

As we compared our notes on Lynn during the drive home, my wife and I realized that we learned a great deal about Lynn during the evening, and that we were eager to learn more. But what is it that we thought we now knew about her? And what would we need to know to know her better? In our social ritual, my wife and I were enjoying the rather playful exercise of trying to make sense of persons. In the professional enterprise of personality psychology, however, making sense of persons is or should be the very raison d'être of the discipline. From the time of Allport (1937) and Murray (1938), through the anxious days of the "situationist" critique (Bowers, 1973; Mischel, 1968), and up to the present, upbeat period wherein we celebrate traits[1] (John, 1990; Wiggins, 1996) while we offer a sparkling array of new methods and models for personality inquiry (see, for example, McAdams, 1994a; Ozer & Reise, 1994; Revelle, 1995), making sense of persons was and is fundamentally what personality psychologists are supposed to do, in the lab, in the office, even on the drive home. But how should we do it?

Making Sense of Persons

* * *

Since the time of Allport, Cattell, and Murray, personality psychologists have offered a number of different schemes for describing persons. For example, McClelland (1951) proposed that an adequate account of personality requires assessments of stylistic traits (e.g., extraversion, friendliness), cognitive schemes (e.g., personal constructs, values, frames), and dynamic motives (e.g., the need for achievement, power motivation). In the wake of Mischel's (1968) critique of personality dispositions, many personality psychologists eschewed broadband constructs such as traits and motives in favor of more domain-specific variables, like "encoding strategies," "self-regulatory systems and plans," and other "cognitive social learning person variables" (Mischel, 1973). By contrast, the 1980s and 1990s have witnessed a strong comeback for the concept of the broad, dispositional trait, culminating in what many have argued is a consensus around the five-factor model of personality traits (Digman, 1990; Goldberg, 1993; McCrae & Costa, 1996). Personality psychologists such as A. H. Buss (1989) have essentially proclaimed that personality *is traits* and only traits. Others are less sanguine, however, about the ability of the Big Five trait taxonomy in particular and the concept of trait in general to provide all or even most of the right stuff for personality inquiry (Block, 1995; Briggs, 1989; Emmons, 1993; McAdams, 1992, 1994b; Pervin, 1994).

Despite the current popularity of the trait concept, I submit that I will never be able to render Lynn "knowable" by relying solely on a description of her personality traits. At the same time, a description that failed to consider traits would be equally inadequate. Trait descriptions are essential both for social rituals like the post-party postmortem and for adequate personological inquiry. A person cannot be known without knowing traits. But knowing traits is not enough. Persons should be described on at least *three separate* and, at best, *loosely related levels* of functioning. The three may be viewed as levels of comprehending *individuality amidst otherness*—how the person is similar to and different from *some* (but not all) other persons. Each level offers categories and frameworks for organizing *individual differences* among persons. Dispositional traits comprise the first level in this scheme—the level that deals primarily with what I have called (McAdams, 1992, 1994b) a "psychology of the stranger."

[1]The reference here is to the "person-situation debate" that dominated personality psychology from 1968 to 1988. The debate was about whether the most important causes of behavior were properties of people or of the situations they find themselves in. The "situationist" viewpoint was that situations were more important. As McAdams notes, the eventual resolution of this controversy reaffirmed the importance—but not all-importance—of stable individual differences in personality (traits) as important determinants of behavior.

The Power of Traits

Dispositional traits are those relatively nonconditional, relatively decontextualized, generally linear, and implicitly comparative dimensions of personality that go by such titles as "extraversion," "dominance," and "neuroticism." One of the first things both I and my wife noticed about Lynn was her social dominance. She talked loudly and fast; she held people's attention when she described her adventures; she effectively controlled the conversation in the large group. Along with her striking appearance, social dominance appeared early on as one of her salient characteristics. Other behavioral signs also suggested an elevated rating on the trait of neuroticism, though these might also indicate the situationally specific anxiety she may have been experiencing in her relationship with the man who accompanied her to the party. According to contemporary norms for dinner parties of this kind, she seemed to drink a bit too much. Her moods shifted rather dramatically over the course of the evening. While she remained socially dominant, she seemed to become more and more nervous as the night wore on. The interjection of her off-color joke and the street dialect stretched slightly the bounds of propriety one expects on such occasions, though not to an alarming extent. In a summary way, then, one might describe Lynn, as she became known during the dinner party, as socially dominant, extraverted, entertaining, dramatic, moody, slightly anxious, intelligent, and introspective. These adjectives describe part of her dispositional signature.

How useful are these trait descriptions? Given that my wife's and my observations were limited to one behavioral setting (the party), we do not have enough systematic data to say how accurate our descriptions are. However, if further systematic observation were to bear out this initial description—say, Lynn were observed in many settings; say, peers rated her on trait dimensions; say, she completed standard trait questionnaires such as the Personality Research Form (Jackson, 1974) or the NEO Personality Inventory (Costa & McCrae, 1985)—then trait descriptions like these, wherein the individual is rated on a series of linear and noncontingent behavior dimensions, prove very useful indeed.

* * *

The Problem with Traits

It is easy to criticize the concept of trait. Trait formulations proposed by Allport (1937), Cattell (1957), Guilford (1959), Eysenck (1967), Jackson (1974), Tellegen (1982), Hogan (1986), and advocates of the Big Five have been called superficial, reductionistic, atheoretical, and even imperialistic. Traits are mere labels, it is said again and again. Traits don't explain anything. Traits lack precision. Traits disregard the environment. Traits apply only to score distributions in groups, not to the individual person (e.g., Lamiell, 1987). I believe that there is some validity in some of these traditional claims but that traits nonetheless provide invaluable information about persons. I believe that many critics expect too much of traits. Yet, those trait enthusiasts (e.g., A. H. Buss, 1989; Digman, 1990; Goldberg, 1993) who equate personality with traits in general, and with the Big Five in particular, are also claiming too much.

Goldberg (1981) contended that the English language includes five clusters of trait-related terms—the Big Five—because personality characteristics encoded in these terms have proved especially salient in human interpersonal perception, especially when it comes to the perennial and evolutionary crucial task of sizing up a stranger. I think Goldberg was more right than many trait enthusiasts would like him to be. Reliable and valid trait ratings provide an excellent "first read" on a person by offering estimates of a person's relative standing on a delimited series of general and linear dimensions of proven social significance. This is indeed crucial information in the evaluation of strangers and others about whom we know very little. It is the kind of information that strangers quickly glean from one another as they size one another up and anticipate future interactions. It did not take long for me to conclude that Lynn was high on certain aspects of Extraversion and moderately high on Neuroticism. What makes trait information like this so valuable is that it is comparative and relatively nonconditional. A highly extraverted person is generally more extraverted than most other people (comparative) and tends to be extraverted in a wide variety of settings (nonconditional), although by no means in all.

Consider, furthermore, the phenomenology of traditional trait assessment in personality psychology. In rating one's own or another's traits on a typical paper-and-pencil measure, the rater/subject must adopt an observational stance in which the target of the rating becomes an object of comparison on a series of linear and only vaguely conditional dimensions (McAdams, 1994c). Thus, if I were to rate Lynn, or if Lynn were to rate herself, on the Extraversion-keyed personality item "I am not a cheerful optimist" (from the NEO), I (or Lynn) would be judging the extent of Lynn's own "cheerful optimism" in comparison to the cheerful optimism of people I (or she) know or have heard about, or perhaps even an assumed average level of cheerful optimism of the rest of humankind. Ratings like these must have a social referent if they are to be meaningful. The end result of my (or her) ratings is a determination of the extent to which Lynn is seen as more or less extraverted across a wide variety of situations, conditions, and contexts, and compared to other people in general. There is, therefore, no place in trait assessment for what Thorne (1989) calls the conditional patterns of personality (see also Wright & Mischel, 1987). Here are some examples of conditional patterns: "My dominance shows when my competence is threatened; I fall apart when people try to comfort me; I talk most when I am nervous" (Thorne, 1989, p. 149). But to make traits into conditional statements is to rob them of their power as nonconditional indicators of general trends.

The two most valuable features of trait description—its comparative and nonconditional qualities—double as its two greatest limitations as well.[2] As persons come to know one another better, they seek and obtain information that is both noncomparative and highly conditional, contingent, and contextualized. They move beyond the mind-set of comparing individuals on linear dimensions. In a sense, they move beyond traits to construct a more detailed and nuanced portrait of personality, so that the stranger can become more fully known. New information is then integrated with the trait profile to give a fuller picture. My wife and I began to move beyond traits on the drive home. As a first read, Lynn seemed socially dominant (Extraversion) and mildly neurotic (Neuroticism). I would also give her a high rating on Openness to Experience; I would say that Agreeableness was probably medium; I would say that Conscientiousness was low to medium, though I do not feel that I received much trait-relevant information on Conscientiousness. Beyond these traits, however, Lynn professed a confusing set of political beliefs: She claimed to be rather conservative but was a big fan of Hillary Clinton; she scorned government for meddling in citizens' private affairs and said she paid too much in taxes to support wasteful social programs, while at the same time she claimed to be a pacifist and to have great compassion for poor people and those who could not obtain health insurance. Beyond traits, Lynn claimed to be an atheist but expressed great admiration for missionaries. Beyond traits, Lynn appeared to be having problems in intimate relationships; she wished she could believe in something; she enjoyed her work as a freelance writer; she was a good listener one on one but not in the large group; she expressed strong interest in New Age psychology; she seemed to think her parents invested too much faith in her and in her siblings. To know Lynn well, to know her more fully than one would know a stranger, one must be privy to information that does not

[2]This observation provides an example of Funder's First Law, which states that great strengths are often great weaknesses and, surprisingly often, the opposite is also true (Funder, 2001).

fit trait categories, information that is exquisitely conditional and contextualized.

Going beyond Traits: Time, Place, and Role

There is a vast and largely unmapped domain in personality wherein reside such constructs as motives (McClelland, 1961), values (Rokeach, 1973), defense mechanisms (Cramer, 1991), coping styles (Lazarus, 1991), developmental issues and concerns (Erikson, 1963; Havighurst, 1972), personal strivings (Emmons, 1986), personal projects (Little, 1989), current concerns (Klinger, 1977), life tasks (Cantor & Kihlstrom, 1987), attachment styles (Hazan & Shaver, 1990), conditional patterns (Thorne, 1989), core conflictual relationship themes (Luborsky & Crits-Christoph, 1991), patterns of self-with-other, domain-specific skills and talents (Gardner, 1993), strategies and tactics (D. M. Buss, 1991), and many more personality variables that are both linked to behavior (Cantor, 1990) and important for the full description of the person (McAdams, 1994a). This assorted collection of constructs makes up a second level of personality, to which I give the generic and doubtlessly inadequate label of *personal concerns.* Compared with dispositional traits, personal concerns are typically couched in motivational, developmental, or strategic terms. They speak to what people want, often during particular periods in their lives or within particular domains of action, and what life methods people use (strategies, plans, defenses, and so on) in order to get what they want or avoid getting what they don't want over time, in particular places, and/or with respect to particular roles.

What primarily differentiates, then, personal concerns from dispositional traits is the contextualization of the former within time, place, and/or role. Time is perhaps the most ubiquitous context. In their studies of the "intimacy life task" among young adults, Cantor, Acker, and Cook-Flanagan (1992) focus on "those tasks that individuals see as personally important and time consuming at particular times in their lives" (p. 644). In their studies of generativity across the adult life span, McAdams, de St. Aubin, and Logan (1993) focus on a cluster of concern, belief, commitment, and action oriented toward providing for the well-being of the next generation, a cluster that appears to peak in salience around middle age. Intimacy and generativity must be contextualized in the temporal life span if they are to be properly understood. By contrast, the traits of Extraversion and Agreeableness are easily defined and understood outside of time. They are not linked to developmental stages, phases, or seasons.

The temporal context also distinguishes traits on the one hand from motives and goals on the other. Motives, goals, strivings, and plans are defined in terms of future ends. A person high in power motivation wants, desires, strives for power—having impact on others is the desired end state, the temporal goal (Winter, 1973). To have a strong motive, goal, striving, or plan is to orient oneself in a particular way in time. The same cannot be readily assumed with traits. Extraversion is not naturally conceived in goal-directed terms. It is not necessary for the viability of the concept of extraversion that an extraverted person strive to obtain a particular goal in time, although of course such a person may do so. Extraverted people simply *are* extraverted; whether they try to be or not is irrelevant. The case is even clearer for neuroticism, for the commonsense assumption here is that highly neurotic people do not strive to be neurotic over time. They simply are neurotic. While dispositional traits may have motivational properties (Allport, 1937; McCrae & Costa, 1996), traits do not exist in time in the same way that motives, strivings, goals, and plans are temporally contextualized. To put it another way, I cannot understand Lynn's life in time when I merely consider her dispositional traits. Developmental and motivational constructs, by contrast, begin to provide me with the temporal context, the life embedded in and evolving over time.

Contextualization of behavior in place was a

major theme of the situationist critique in the 1970s (Frederiksen, 1972; Magnusson, 1971). The situationists argued that behavior is by and large local rather than general, subject to the norms and expectations of a given social place or space. Attempts to formulate taxonomies of situations have frequently involved delineating the physical and interpersonal features of certain kinds of prototypical behavioral settings and social environments, like "church," "football game," "classroom," and "party" (Cantor, Mischel, & Schwartz, 1982; Krahe, 1992; Moos, 1973). Certain domain-specific skills, competencies, attitudes, and schemas are examples of personality variables contextualized in place. For example, Lynn is both a very good listener in one-on-one conversations, especially when the topic concerns psychology, and an extremely effective storyteller in large groups, especially when she is talking about travel. When she is angry with her husband in a social setting, she drinks too much. The latter is an example of a conditional pattern (Thorne, 1989) or perhaps a very simple personal script. Some varieties of personal scripts and conditional patterns are contextualized in place and space: "When I am at home, I am unable to relax"; "When the weather is hot, I think about how miserable I was as a child, growing up in St. Louis"; "If I am lost in Chicago, I never ask for directions." To know a person well, it is not necessary to have information about all of the different personal scripts and conditional patterns that prevail in all of the different behavioral settings he or she will encounter. Instead, the personologist should seek information on the most salient settings and environments that make up the ecology of a person's life and investigate the most influential, most common, or most problematic personal scripts and conditional patterns that appear within that ecology (Demorest & Alexander, 1992).

Another major context in personality is social role. Certain strivings, tasks, strategies, defense mechanisms, competencies, values, interests, and styles may be role-specific. For example, Lynn may employ the defense mechanism of rationalization to cope with her anxiety about the setbacks she has experienced in her role as a mother. In her role as a writer, she may excel in expressing herself in a laconic, Hemingway-like style (role competence, skill) and she may strive to win certain journalistic awards or to make more money than her husband (motivation, striving). In the role of student/learner, she is fascinated with New Age psychology (interests). In the role of daughter, she manifests an insecure attachment style, especially with her mother, and this style seems to carry over to her relationships with men (role of lover/spouse) but not with women (role of friend). Ogilvie (Ogilvie & Ashmore, 1991) has developed a new approach to personality assessment that matches personality descriptors with significant persons in one's life, resulting in an organization of self-with-other constructs. It would appear that some of the more significant self-with-other constellations in a person's life are those associated with important social roles. Like social places, not all social roles are equally important in a person's life. Among the most salient in the lives of many American men and women are the roles of spouse/lover, son/daughter, parent, sibling, worker/provider, and citizen.

* * *

There is no compelling reason to believe that the language of nonconditional and decontextualized dispositions should work well to describe constructs that are situated in time, place, and role. Consistent with this supposition, Kaiser and Ozer (under review) found that personal goals, or what they term "motivational units," do not map onto the five-factor structure demonstrated for traits. Instead, their study suggests that the structure of personal goals may be more appropriately conceptualized in terms of various content domains (e.g., work, social). It seems reasonable, therefore, to begin with the assumption that an adequate description of a person should bring together contrasting and complementary attributional schemes, integrating dispositional insights with those obtained from personal concerns. To know Lynn well is to be able to describe her in ways that go significantly beyond the language of traits. This is not to suggest that Levels I and II are or must be completely unrelated to each other, that Lynn's extraversion, for example, has nothing to do with her personal career strivings. In personality psychology, linkages between constructs at these different levels should and will be investigated in research. But the linkages, if they indeed exist, should be established empirically rather than assumed by theorists to be true.

What Is Missing?

As we move from Level I to Level II, we move from the psychology of the stranger to a more detailed and nuanced description of a flesh-and-blood, in-the-world person, striving to do things over time, situated in place and role, expressing herself or himself in and through strategies, tactics, plans, and goals. In Lynn's case, we begin our very provisional sketch with nonconditional attributions suggesting a high level of extraversion and moderately high neuroticism and we move to more contingent statements suggesting that she seems insecurely attached to her parents and her husband, strives for power and recognition in her career, wants desperately to believe in something but as yet has not found it in religion or in spirituality, holds strong but seemingly contradictory beliefs about politics and public service, employs the defense of rationalization to cope with the frustration she feels in her role as mother, has interests that tend toward books and ideas rather than physical health and fitness, loves to travel, is a good listener one on one but not in groups, is a skilled writer, is a good storyteller, tells stories that are rambling and dramatic. If we were to continue a relationship with Lynn, we would learn more and more about her. We would find that some of our initial suppositions were naive, or even plain wrong. We would obtain much more information on her traits, enabling us to obtain a clearer and more accurate dispositional signature. We would learn more about the contextualized constructs of her personality, about how she functions in time, place, and role. Filling in more and more information in Levels I and II, we might get to know Lynn very well.

But I submit that, as Westerners living in this modern age, we would not know Lynn "well enough" until we moved beyond dispositional traits and personal concerns to a third level of personality. Relatedly, should Lynn think of herself only in Level I and Level II terms, then she, too, as a Western, middle-class adult living in the last years of the 20th century, would not know herself "well enough" to comprehend her own identity. The problem of identity is the problem of overall unity and purpose in human lives (McAdams, 1985). It is a problem that has come to preoccupy men and women in Western democracies during the past 200 years (Baumeister, 1986; Langbaum, 1982). It is not generally a problem for children, though there are some exceptions. It is probably not as salient a problem for many non-Western societies that put less of a premium on individualism and articulating the autonomous adult self, although it is a problem in many of these societies. It is not equally problematic for all contemporary American adults. Nonetheless, identity is likely to be a problem for Lynn, for virtually all people attending that dinner party or reading this article, and for most contemporary Americans and Western Europeans who at one time or another in their adult lives have found the question "Who am I?" to be worth asking, pondering, and worth working on.

Modern and postmodern democratic societies do not explicitly tell adults who they should be. At the same time, however, these societies insist that an adult should be someone who both fits in and is unique (Bellah, Madsen, Sullivan, Swidler, & Tipton, 1985). The self should be defined so that it is both separate and connected, individuated and integrated at the same time. These kinds of selves do not exist in prepackaged, readily assimilated form. They are not passed down from one generation to the next, as they were perhaps in simpler times. Rather, selves must be made or discovered as people become what they are to become in time. The selves that we make before we reach late adolescence and adulthood are, among other things, "lists" of characteristics to be found in Levels I and II of personality. My 8-year-old daughter, Amanda, sees herself as relatively shy (low Extraversion) and very caring and warm (high Agreeableness); she knows she is a good ice skater (domain-specific skill); she loves amusement parks (interests); and she has strong feelings of love and resentment toward her older sister (ambivalent attachment style, though she wouldn't call it that). I hazard to guess that these are a few items in a long list of things, including many that are not in the realm of personality proper ("I live in a white house"; "I go to Central School"), that make up Amanda's self-concept. A list of attributes from Levels I and II is not, however, an identity. Then again, Amanda is too young to have an identity because she is probably not able to experience unity and purpose as problematic in her life. Therefore, one can know Amanda very well by sticking to Levels I and II.

But not so for Lynn. As a contemporary adult, Lynn most likely can understand and appreciate, more or less, the problem of unity and purpose in her life. While the question of "Who am I?" may seem silly or obvious to Amanda, Lynn is likely to see the question as potentially problematic, challenging, interesting, ego-involving, and so on. For reasons that are no doubt physiological and cognitive, as well as social and cultural, it is in late adolescence and young adulthood that many contemporary Westerners come to believe that the self must or should be constructed and told in a manner that integrates the disparate roles they play, incorporates their many different values and skills, and organizes into a meaningful temporal pattern their reconstructed past, perceived present, and anticipated future (Breger, 1974; Erikson, 1959; McAdams, 1985). The challenge of identity demands that the Western adult construct a telling of the self that synthesizes synchronic and diachronic elements in such a way as to suggest that (*a*) despite its many facets the self is coherent and unified and (*b*) despite the many changes that attend the passage of time, the self of the past led up to or set the stage for the self of the present, which in turn will lead up to or set the stage for the self of the future (McAdams, 1990, 1993).

What form does such a construction take? A growing number of theorists believe that the only conceivable form for a unified and purposeful telling of a life is the story (Bruner, 1990; Charme, 1984; Cohler, 1982, 1994; Hermans & Kempen, 1993; Howard, 1991; Kotre, 1984; Linde, 1990; MacIntyre, 1984; Polkinghorne, 1988). In my own theoretical and empirical work, I have argued that identity is itself an internalized and evolving life story, or personal myth (McAdams, 1984, 1985, 1990, 1993, 1996). Contemporary adults create identity in their lives to the extent that the self can be told in a coherent, followable, and vivifying narrative that integrates the person into society in a productive and generative way and provides the person with a purposeful self-history that explains how the self of yesterday became the self of today and will become the anticipated self of tomorrow. Level III in personality, therefore, is the level of identity as a life story. Without exploring this third level, the personologist can never understand how and to what extent the person is able to find unity, purpose, and meaning in life. Thus what is missing so far from our consideration of Lynn is her very identity.

Misunderstandings About Level III

Lynn's identity is an inner story, a narration of the self that she continues to author and revise over time to make sense, for herself and others, of her own life in time. It is a story, or perhaps a collection of related stories, that Lynn continues to fashion to specify who she is and how she fits into the adult world. Incorporating beginning, middle, and anticipated ending, Lynn's story tells how she came to be, where she has been and where she may be going, and who she will become (Hankiss, 1981). Lynn continues to create and revise the story across her adult years as she and her changing social world negotiate niches, places, opportunities, and positions within which she can live, and live meaningfully.

What is Lynn's story about? The dinner party provided my wife and me with ample material to begin talking about Lynn's personality from the perspectives of Levels I and II. But life-story information is typically more difficult to obtain in a casual social setting. Even after strangers have sized each other up on dispositional traits and even after they have begun to learn a little bit about each others' goals, plans, defenses, strategies, and domain-specific skills, they typically have little to say about the other person's identity. By contrast, when people have been involved in long-term intensive relationships with each other, they may know a great deal about each others' stories, about how the friend or lover (or psychotherapy client) makes sense of his or her own life in narrative terms. They have shared many stories with each other; they have observed each other's behavior in many different situations; they have come to see how the other person sees life, indeed, how the other sees his or her own life organized with purpose in time.

Without that kind of intimate relationship with Lynn, my wife and I could say little of substance about how Lynn creates identity in her life. We left the party with but a few promising hints or leads as to what her story might be about. For example, we were both struck by her enigmatic comment about passionate belief. Why did she suggest that her parents believed too strongly in her and in her siblings? Shouldn't parents believe in their children? Has she disappointed her parents in a deep way, such that their initial belief in their children was proven untenable? Does her inability to believe passionately in things extend to her own children as well? It is perhaps odd that her ex-husband has custody of their children; how is this related to the narrative she has developed about her family and her beliefs? And what might one make of that last incident at the party, when Lynn seemed to lapse into a different mode of talking, indicative perhaps of a different persona, a different public self, maybe a different "character" or "imago" (McAdams, 1984) in her life story? One can imagine many different kinds of stories that Lynn might create to make sense of her own life—adventure stories that incorporate her exotic travels and her considerable success; tragic stories that tell of failed love and lost children; stories in which the protagonist searches far and wide for something to believe in; stories in which early disappointments lead to cynicism, hard-heartedness, despair, or maybe even hope. We do not know Lynn well enough yet to know what kinds of stories she has been working on. Until we can talk with some authority both to her and about her in the narrative language of Level III, we cannot say that we know her well at all. On the drive home, my wife and I know Lynn a little better than we might know a stranger. Our desire to know her much better than we know her now is, in large part, our desire to know her story. And were we to get to know her better and come to feel a bond of intimacy with her, we would want her to know our stories, too (McAdams, 1989).

* * *

References

Allport, G. W. (1937). *Personality: A psychological interpretation.* New York: Holt, Rinehart & Winston.

Baumeister, R. F. (1986). *Identity: Cultural change and the struggle for self.* New York: Oxford University Press.

Bellah, R. N., Madsen, R., Sullivan, W. M., Swidler, A., & Tipton, S. M. (1985). *Habits of the heart.* Berkeley: University of California Press.

Block, J. (1995). A contrarian view of the five-factor approach to personality description. *Psychological Bulletin.*

Bowers, K. S. (1973). Situationism in psychology: An analysis and critique. *Psychological Review, 80,* 307–336.

Breger, L. (1974). *From instinct to identity: The development of personality.* Englewood Cliffs, NJ: Prentice-Hall.

Briggs, S. R. (1989). The optimal level of measurement for personality constructs. In D. M. Buss & N. Cantor (Eds.), *Personality psychology: Recent trends and emerging directions* (pp. 246–260). New York: Springer-Verlag.

Bruner, J. S. (1990). *Acts of meaning.* Cambridge, MA: Harvard University Press.

Buss, A. H. (1989). Personality as traits. *American Psychologist, 44,* 1378–1388.

Buss, D. M. (1991). Evolutionary personality psychology. In M. R. Rosenzweig & L. W. Porter (Eds.), *Annual review of psychology* (Vol. 42, pp. 459–491). Palo Alto, CA: Annual Reviews.

Cantor, N. (1990). From thought to behavior: "Having" and "doing" in the study of personality and cognition. *American Psychologist, 45,* 735–750.

Cantor, N., Acker, M., & Cook-Flanagan, C. (1992). Conflict and preoccupation in the intimacy life task. *Journal of Personality and Social Psychology, 63,* 644–655.

Cantor, N., & Kihlstrom, J. F. (1987). *Personality and social intelligence.* Englewood Cliffs, NJ: Prentice-Hall.

Cantor, N., Mischel, W., & Schwartz, J. C. (1982). A prototype analysis of psychological situations. *Cognitive Psychology, 14,* 45–77.

Cattell, R. B. (1957). *Personality and motivation structure and measurement.* New York: Harcourt, Brace & World.

Charme, S. T. (1984). *Meaning and myth in the study of lives: A Sartrean perspective.* Philadelphia: University of Pennsylvania Press.

Cohler, B. J. (1982). Personal narrative and the life course. In P. Baltes & O. G. Brim, Jr. (Eds.), *Life span development and behavior* (Vol. 4, pp. 205–241). New York: Academic Press.

Cohler, B. J. (1994, June). *Studying older lives: Reciprocal acts of telling and listening.* Paper presented at annual meeting of the Society for Personology, Ann Arbor.

Costa, P. T., Jr., & McCrae, R. R. (1985). *The NEO Personality Inventory.* Odessa, FL: Psychological Assessment Resources.

Cramer, P. (1991). *The development of defense mechanisms.* New York: Springer-Verlag.

Demorest, A. P., & Alexander, I. E. (1992). Affective scripts as organizers of personal experience. *Journal of Personality, 60,* 645–663.

Digman, J. M. (1990). Personality structure: Emergence of the five-factor model. In M. R. Rosenzweig & L. W. Porter (Eds.), *Annual review of psychology* (Vol. 41, pp. 417–440). Palo Alto, CA: Annual Reviews.

Emmons, R. A. (1986). Personal strivings: An approach to personality and subjective well-being. *Journal of Personality and Social Psychology, 51,* 1058–1068.

Emmons, R. A. (1993). Current status of the motive concept. In K. H. Craik, R. Hogan, & R. N. Wolfe (Eds.), *Fifty years of personality psychology* (pp. 187–196). New York: Plenum.

Erikson, E. H. (1959). Identity and the life cycle: Selected papers. *Psychological Issues, 1*(1), 5–165.

Erikson, E. H. (1963). *Childhood and society* (2nd ed.). New York: Norton.

Eysenck, H. J. (1967). *The biological basis of personality.* Springfield, IL: Thomas.

Frederiksen, N. (1972). Toward a taxonomy of situations. *American Psychologist, 27,* 114–123.

Gardner, H. (1993). *Creating minds.* New York: Basic Books.

Gilligan, C. (1982). *In a different voice.* Cambridge, MA: Harvard University Press.

Goldberg, L. R. (1981). Language and individual differences: The search for universals in personality lexicons. In L. Wheeler (Ed.), *Review of personality and social psychology* (Vol. 2, pp. 141–166). Beverly Hills: Sage.

Goldberg, L. R. (1993). The structure of phenotypic personality traits. *American Psychologist, 48,* 26–34.

Guilford, J. P. (1959). *Personality.* New York: McGraw-Hill.

Hankiss, A. (1981). On the mythological rearranging of one's life history. In D. Bertaux (Ed.), *Biography and society: The life history approach in the social sciences* (pp. 203–209). Beverly Hills: Sage.

Havighurst, R. J. (1972). *Developmental tasks and education* (3rd ed.). New York: McKay.

Hazan, C., & Shaver, P. (1990). Love and work: An attachment-theoretical perspective. *Journal of Personality and Social Psychology, 59,* 270–280.

Hermans, H. J. M., & Kempen, H. J. G. (1993). *The dialogical self.* New York: Academic Press.

Hogan, R. (1986). *Hogan Personality Inventory manual.* Minneapolis: National Computer Systems.

Howard, G. S. (1991). Culture tales: A narrative approach to thinking, cross-cultural psychology, and psychotherapy. *American Psychologist, 46,* 187–197.

Jackson, D. N. (1974). *The Personality Research Form.* Port Huron, MI: Research Psychologists Press.

John, O. P. (1990). The "Big Five" factor taxonomy: Dimensions of personality in the natural language and in questionnaires. In L. Pervin (Ed.), *Handbook of personality theory and research* (pp. 66–100). New York: Guilford.

Kaiser, R. T., & Ozer, D. J. (under review). The structure of personal goals and their relation to personality traits. Manuscript under editorial review.

Klinger, E. (1977). *Meaning and void.* Minneapolis: University of Minnesota Press.

Kotre, J. (1984). *Outliving the self: Generativity and the interpretation of lives.* Baltimore: Johns Hopkins University Press.

Krahe, B. (1992). *Personality and social psychology: Toward a synthesis.* London: Sage.

Lamiell, J. T. (1987). *The psychology of personality: An epistemological inquiry.* New York: Columbia University Press.

Langbaum, R. (1982). *The mysteries of identity: A theme in modern literature.* Chicago: University of Chicago Press.

Lazarus, R. J. (1991). *Emotion and adaptation.* New York: Oxford University Press.

Linde, C. (1990). *Life stories: The creation of coherence* (Monograph No. IRL90-0001). Palo Alto, CA: Institute for Research on Learning.

Little, B. R. (1989). Personal projects analysis: Trivial pursuits, magnificent obsessions, and the search for coherence. In D. M. Buss & N. Cantor (Eds.), *Personality psychology: Recent trends and emerging directions* (pp. 15–31). New York: Springer-Verlag.

Loevinger, J. (1976). *Ego development.* San Francisco: Jossey-Bass.

Luborsky, L., & Crits-Christoph, P. (1991). *Understanding transference: The core conflictual relationship theme method.* New York: Basic Books.

MacIntyre, A. (1984). *After virtue.* Notre Dame: University of Notre Dame Press.

Magnusson, D. (1971). An analysis of situational dimensions. *Perceptual and Motor Skills, 32,* 851–867.

McAdams, D. P. (1984). Love, power, and images of the self. In C. Z. Malatesta & C. E. Izard (Eds.), *Emotion in adult development* (pp. 159–174). Beverly Hills: Sage.

McAdams, D. P. (1985). *Power, intimacy, and the life story: Personological inquiries into identity.* New York: Guilford.

McAdams, D. P. (1989). *Intimacy: The need to be close.* New York: Doubleday.

McAdams, D. P. (1990). Unity and purpose in human lives: The emergence of identity as a life story. In A. I. Rabin, R. A. Zucker, R. A. Emmons, & S. Frank (Eds.), *Studying persons and lives* (pp. 148–200). New York: Springer.

McAdams, D. P. (1992). The five-factor model in personality: A critical appraisal. *Journal of Personality, 60,* 329–361.

McAdams, D. P. (1993). *The stories we live by: Personal myths and the making of the self.* New York: Morrow.

McAdams, D. P. (1994a). *The person: An introduction to personality psychology* (2nd ed.). Fort Worth: Harcourt Brace.

McAdams, D. P. (1994b). A psychology of the stranger. *Psychological Inquiry, 5,* 145–148.

McAdams, D. P. (1994c). Can personality change? Levels of stability and growth in personality across the life span. In T. F. Heatherton & J. L. Weinberger (Eds.), *Can personality change?* (pp. 299–314). Washington, DC: American Psychological Association.

McAdams, D. P. (1996). Narrating the self in adulthood. In J. Birren, G. Kenyon, J. E. Ruth, J. J. F. Schroots, & T. Svensson (Eds.), *Aging and biography: Explorations in adult development.* New York: Springer.

McAdams, D. P., de St. Aubin, E., & Logan, R. L. (1993). Generativity among young, midlife, and older adults. *Psychology and Aging, 8,* 221–230.

McClelland, D. C. (1951). *Personality.* New York: Holt, Rinehart & Winston.

McClelland, D. C. (1961). *The achieving society.* New York: D. Van Nostrand.

McCrae, R. R., & Costa, P. T., Jr. (1996). Toward a new generation of personality theories: Theoretical contexts for the five-factor model. In J. S. Wiggins (Ed.), *The five-factor model of personality.* New York: Guilford.

Mischel, W. (1968). *Personality and assessment.* New York: Wiley.

Mischel, W. (1973). Toward a cognitive social-learning reconceptualization of personality. *Psychological Review, 80,* 252–283.

Moos, R. H. (1973). Conceptualization of human environments. *American Psychologist, 28,* 652–665.

Murray, H. A. (1938). *Explorations in personality.* New York: Oxford University Press.

Ogilvie, D. M., & Ashmore, R. D. (1991). Self-with-other representation as units of analysis in self-concept research. In R. A. Curtis (Ed.), *The relational self: Theoretical convergences in psychoanalysis and social psychology* (pp. 282–314). New York: Guilford.

Ozer, D. J., & Reise, S. P. (1994). Personality assessment. In L. W. Porter & M. R. Rosenzweig (Eds.), *Annual review of psychology* (Vol. 45, pp. 357–388). Palo Alto, CA: Annual Reviews.

Pervin, L. (1994). A critical analysis of current trait theory. *Psychological Inquiry, 5,* 103–113.

Polkinghorne, D. (1988). *Narrative knowing and the human sciences.* Albany, NY: SUNY Press.

Revelle, W. (1995). Personality processes. In L. W. Porter & M. R. Rosenzweig (Eds.), *Annual review of psychology* (Vol. 46, pp. 295–328). Palo Alto, CA: Annual Reviews.

Rokeach, M. (1973). *The nature of human values.* New York: Free Press.

Tellegen, A. (1982). *Brief manual for the Differential Personality Questionnaire.* Unpublished manuscript, University of Minnesota.

Thorne, A. (1989). Conditional patterns, transference, and the coherence of personality across time. In D. M. Buss & N. Cantor (Eds.), *Personality psychology: Recent trends and emerging directions* (pp. 149–159). New York: Springer.

Wiggins, J. S. (Ed.). (1996). *The five-factor model of personality.* New York: Guilford.

Winter, D. G. (1973). *The power motive.* New York: Free Press.

Wright, J. C., & Mischel, W. (1987). A conditional approach to dispositional constructs: The local predictability of social behavior. *Journal of Personality and Social Psychology, 53,* 1159–1177.

Studying Personality the Long Way

Jack Block

This article by Jack Block, one of the most respected personality psychologists of his generation, introduces a research project he has conducted for more than two decades that has addressed a wide variety of topics. It has used many different methods to study people—he calls them L, O, T, and S data—but its most important methodological aspect is that the study is longitudinal. *That is, Block's research follows a group of the same people over a span of their lives when important psychological development takes place. At the time this article was written, the individuals he and his wife Jeanne Block began studying at age 3 were past college age. In this excerpt, Block presents his argument for the longitudinal method as a uniquely useful technique for tackling such topics, the guiding principles behind the design of the Block Project—which are those that should guide any major longitudinal investigation—and a sampling of the many, many methods this project has used to assess important aspects of personality.*

From *Studying Lives Through Time: Personality and Development*, edited by D. C. Funder, R. D. Parke, C. Tomlinson-Keasey, and K. Widaman. (Washington, DC: American Psychological Association, 1993), pp. 9–41.

* * *

For various reasons, some of them overdetermined, it has seemed to me necessary to study people in the large, as they exist in their natural and real world, and the way and the why of their differences. And, to satisfyingly pursue this goal, the longitudinal study of personality development has seemed to me the compelled approach. By *longitudinal study*, I mean the close, comprehensive, systematic, objective, sustained study of individuals over significant portions of the life span. Such study permits unique and crucial scientific recognitions regarding human development and the factors influencing human development.

Longitudinal studies, once embarked on, perhaps inevitably become career investments of great personal significance and meaning to the investors. The commitment of self to so protracted a research enterprise runs the risk of distorting and subverting the subsequent scientific possibilities of the inquiry. It is also the case that such cathexis is required if the venture is to be carried through with care to a time of fruition and of harvest of what can be known in psychology no other way. No one longitudinal study will answer all the questions of developmental psychology, but also there is no alternative scientific approach that can begin to discern and disentangle the specific influential factors conjoining, interweaving, and reciprocating with each other as the individual reaches out to life, is enveloped by circumstance, and forges character. When we, as developmental or personality psychologists deign to observe a few conveniently accessible behaviors, here and there, now and then, for a moment or two, we are likely to be touching on or sampling rather little of the basis for comprehending a human life. It is the special merit of the longitudinal approach that by its scope, by its persistence, and by its analytical orientation toward the study of lives through time, it can perhaps permit a greater understanding of why it is people turn out as they do.

Aspirations for a Longitudinal Study of Personality Development

In 1968, my late wife, Jeanne, and I decided to initiate a longitudinal study of personality development. * * * We were moved to this commitment because we believed there was indeed an essential *coherence*, a deep structure to personality functioning and in personality development. Sure, it was crucial to recognize the ways in which the immediate environmental context influenced behavior, as personality psychologists Henry Murray (1938), Kurt Lewin (1946), Robert White (1959), and others earlier had observed. However, stimulus situations alone could not provide, we believed, a sufficient basis for understanding behavior. Human beings are not simply linear response systems effectively at the mercy of the situations they encounter. Besides making exquisite and unique discriminations, humans develop broad and adaptively functional, consistently applied generalizations. These constructed generalizations are shaped by a common evolutionary heritage, by modal perceptual and action patterns, and by commonly encountered environmental contingencies. Because of these constructed generalizations, individuals vary reliably and meaningfully and can be usefully dimensionalized or classified regarding the ways they perceive and react upon their world. We believed, 20 years ago, that the generally dismal state of empirical evidence for this proposition existed because, too often, the underlying coherence had not been sought well. In particular, we believed that consistency or continuity in behavior will not be found if one looks for expressions of personality consistency and continuity in ways that are conceptually obtuse or methodologically insufficient or empirically constrained. We thought we could do better and wanted to give it a try. We were by no means certain that, in our optimism, our faith would be fulfilled. We were certain, however, that those who would not try for coherence would not lead the way to understanding.

We sat down one evening to begin to list the desiderata for a longitudinal study of personality development. Gradually, as we thought about what had been done in the past and what we believed should be done in the future, we evolved a set of criterion dimensions in terms of which we planned our own effort.

Desiderata for a Longitudinal Study of Personality Development

1. *A longitudinal study should be an intentional rather than an accidental study, not a study begun for other reasons and only subsequently (and belatedly) declared to be a longitudinal study.* Some well-known longitudinal studies initially had not been conceived to be or to become long-term inquiries. Because of this lack of anticipation, various simple, obvious, crucial kinds of research planning and data gathering had not been done at the outset, the one and only time when planning could have been effective or certain kinds of data could have been gathered. I am not referring to deficiencies of research design or research implementation easily and unfairly identified by cheap and virtuous retrospective wisdom. Instead, I have in mind omissions of data collection and failures of research design that could have been known at the time to be attenuating or vitiating of later analyses and hoped-for understandings. Our study, therefore, was to be deliberately longitudinal. Of

course, intentionality did not prevent us from making our own mistakes, but it did permit us to avoid some important errors of the past.

2. *A longitudinal study should make public and communicable just what was done during the course of the study, how observations were made, how categories or numbers were generated, and how conclusions and interpretations were formulated.* We had observed that longitudinal investigators sometimes were carried away and infatuated by the aura of potential understanding that surrounds this well-regarded, if rarely used, approach. Too often, declamations and interpretations from longitudinal inquiries have been offered into the scientific literature on impressionistic and unspecifiable bases and, because of the positive aura surrounding longitudinal inquiry, have had unwarranted influence (see J. Block, 1981, for an account of one such unfortunate incident). Our longitudinal study, therefore, was to be one in which later psychologists could know what we had done, our rationales, the nature of our data and analyses, and the bases of our conclusions.

3. *A longitudinal study should be sufficiently extended in time so that developmental processes, continuities, and changes can be discerned.* Protracted, laborious, controlling of the researchers though a proper longitudinal study may be, there is not much point to a study so brief it cannot track development. Because of the cachet that now surrounds the term *longitudinal*, one sometimes encounters the oxymoron of "short-term longitudinal" studies. Our own plan and aspiration, therefore, was to conduct a long-term longitudinal study from early childhood (age 3 years) through the completion of high school (ages 17–18) and perhaps beyond. Although we viewed the then-incoming and increasingly popular emphasis on development throughout the life span to be salutary for those who had not earlier attained that important recognition, our own theoretical concerns were centered on the childhood and adolescent years, a time when personality development is relatively rapid and, as we believed, consequential.

4. *A longitudinal study should involve a sample of reasonable initial and continuing size, of reasonable relevance, and of both sexes seen a number of aptly selected times.* Given the diversity of personality development and the omnipresent noise in assessment measures, a sample size sufficient to permit discernment of relationships is crucial if this difficult game is to be worth the candle. Yet one cited longitudinal study involved a sample of 3 subjects that, when reassessed a final time 1 year later, showed a 33% attrition rate. Regarding sample relevance, in another longitudinal study the investigators apparently enlisted mothers from among their friends and friends of friends, with the consequence that 78% of their subjects came from Jewish, professional, urban, economically comfortable families. Certainly, one cannot aspire to a random or representative sample of subjects (representative of what, pray tell?) when close and continued study of development is being pursued, but certainly also, unusual, severely disproportionate subject selection that could well be relationship distorting is to be avoided. Other longitudinal researchers have considered subjects of only one sex, usually males; surely, this kind of exclusion is limiting of psychological understanding.

5. *A longitudinal study should have a conceptual or theoretically integrating rubric directing its doings and progression rather than be blandly or blindly eclectic.* In ranging widely in its coverage, a longitudinal study need not forsake theoretical pursuits. Indeed, the incisiveness and implicativeness of theoretical constructs are better seen when a wide array of behaviors can be evaluated. Jeanne and I had developed some large, organizing personality constructs, ego-control and ego-resiliency, during our thesis days at Stanford University and demonstrated their behavioral implications in a variety of concurrent circumstances. Our constructs seemed to relate in intrinsic ways to other constructs formulated and studied by other investigators, encouraging us to think we were onto something of appreciable theoretical and behavioral importance. However, our constructs (and related ones) had never been studied developmentally. Obviously, to deepen understanding it was crucial to do so. We wished, therefore, to see how

boys and girls over time evolved their personal systems for the modulation of motivations and the achievement of adaptive resourcefulness and perhaps to identify the environmental factors that differentially influenced these parameters of living. So we oriented our longitudinal study to examine developmentally our particular theoretical constructs.

6. *A longitudinal study should be comprehensive, intensive, systematic, and scientifically contemporary in coverage of its chosen conceptual domains.* Instead of being narrow and shallow, longitudinal inquiries should be broad and deep. They should involve *close psychological inquiry*, not just epidemiologically oriented surveys. Longitudinal studies are so rare that, although an already difficult research burden becomes even more difficult, a scientific responsibility is placed on the investigators to be catholic rather than parochial in designing and implementing their study. With broad and continuing assessments on the same set of subjects, there devolves the opportunity—which should not be missed—of relating within one sample research approaches customarily kept separate. Thereby, linkages among bodies of psychological research usually kept compartmentalized may possibly be established. The relationships, longitudinal or perhaps only concurrent, that subsequently may be discerned if there has been breadth of the research scan should have wide and cumulative import and speak to many psychological questions. Therefore, our longitudinal venture was to range widely in the constructs to be covered and was to be alert to current thinking and procedures in the ongoing field of personality development. We expected to spend appreciable time with each of our subjects during each assessment for, as Robert White once informally remarked, one must look at personality in order to study it.

7. *A longitudinal study should be methodologically competent and display craftsmanship in its implementation.* Methodological competence should not be taken to mean simply and only knowledge of statistics; psychologists often incorrectly make this equivalence. Rather, methodological competence should mean competence of several kinds, invoked sequentially, with the recognition that later analytical possibilities depend crucially on earlier sensible decisions appropriately implemented. Competence with sophisticated or at least pertinent statistical methods is certainly required in the ultimate effort to discern relationships. However, prior to the invocation of such methods, a proper longitudinal research design must have been employed so that, from one time to another or from one context to another, data can be known to be absolutely independent and the subsequently obtained relationships indisputably can be recognized as inferentially clean. Prior to these considerations of research design, the measures being used must achieve sufficient psychometric status in terms of reliability and consequent discriminating power. Elaborate statistical analysis of logically independent measures will fail or will issue dismayingly null findings unless the measures employed are dependable. Finally, prior to concerns regarding measure dependability, it is essential to worry about the construct validity of the measures being used: Do they have the sweet reasonability and the supporting nomological network they must have if they are to represent the constructs the psychologist has in mind? Historically, longitudinal studies have been methodologically innocent and therefore interpreted sinfully. Measures have been awarded auspicious but unearned labels, with the consequence that subsequently observed relationships have been portrayed in misleading ways. Aware of these different aspects of methodology and their logical sequence, we aspired, in our longitudinal effort, to a higher standard in this realm than previously had been achieved.

8. *A longitudinal study should seek to be innovative.* I mention this virtuous and grandiose aspiration, which modesty should perhaps cause me to conceal, to register my view that longitudinal studies often had been carried through in plodding, unthinking ways. Because head circumference was easy to measure, it was measured. In the home economics version of child psychology that prevailed prior to the 1950s, such parentally frowned-on behaviors as nail biting, eating prob-

lems, and enuresis were important topics and were longitudinally studied. Because the Rorschach Inkblot Test and the Thematic Apperception Test had become popular, they were administered. In short, a characteristic of previous longitudinal studies was that they brought together an agglomeration of readily available and unthought-about measures without much consideration being given to the concepts and issues to be studied and the necessary formulation of relevant assessment procedures bearing on these matters. A corollary of this passive, uncritical, atheoretical approach to longitudinal research is that when longitudinally studied subjects were followed up, it was too often the case that measures were reflexively, unthinkingly repeated *because they had been administered before* no matter how useless they had proved themselves to be or how age inappropriate they had become. We were determined to avoid such prosaicness in our longitudinal study. We therefore tried to seek out or create assessment procedures and concept-representing measures that were new, age appropriate, theoretically interesting, technically sound, and perhaps even elegant.

9. *A longitudinal study should be able to sustain the quality of the enterprise over the long period of time required.* An endemic disease of longitudinal studies seems to be that, after a time, they reach a point where they begin to falter, lose their vitality, and perhaps even their *raison d'être*. Staff demoralization occurs, and there is busyness without purpose. In part, this anomie may develop because the longitudinal idea takes so long before payoff. Also, some personnel replacements may be seeking a job rather than a purpose and so do not contribute to the necessary sense of meaning that must undergird the longitudinal enterprise. An especially troubling problem arises because longitudinal studies typically exist outside of academic departments and are supported by "soft" funds. In this insecure context, longitudinal researchers are hampered in their efforts to attract high-caliber research individuals for more than a few productive years. Understandably, such people must seize on ultimately more satisfying academic opportunities as they arise. Our longitudinal venture sought to forfend these problems by selecting and maintaining an intelligent, resourceful, dedicated cadre of professional staff, by encouraging an élan and group sense of meaning, by renewing and reinvigorating this small group over the years via carefully chosen replacements, and—perhaps primarily—by our very awareness that these problems could be expected to arise.

Taken altogether, these criteria for a longitudinal study represented a grandiose, quite adolescent ambition. I will not say that we achieved all of these worthy goals (indeed, I wish to be the first to criticize our enterprise), but these were the standards we set out for ourselves. I will leave to others and for another time the evaluation of how well we achieved our aspirations.

What, Indeed, Did We Do?

We began with 128 children from two nursery schools in Berkeley, a heterogeneous sample with regard to socioeconomic status, parental education, and ethnic background. Extensive individual assessments of these children were conducted at ages 3, 4, 5, 7, 11, 14, 18, and, most recently, at age 23. These time periods were selected for assessment because of our sense of when, developmentally, it would be most incisive to study our subjects. At age 23, we assessed 104 subjects. This small amount of subject attrition is due to the great attention we gave to motivating subjects and their parents, to repeated friendly contacts we initiated between assessment periods, to maintaining up-to-date records on subject locations, to paying the subjects a nominal sum for their participation once they entered adolescence, and to having the prescience to carry out such a study in the San Francisco Bay Area, from which there is a decided tendency not to move. Having interviewed just about all of our subjects during our most recent assessment, I have alerted them to our plans to see them again in their late 20s, after another eventful 5 years of life. * * *

During each of the eight assessment periods, every child (or adolescent or young adult) individually experienced an extensive battery of widely ranging procedures involving 10- or 11-hour-long sessions at ages 3 and 4, four or five longer sessions at ages 5 and 7, and six 2-hour (or longer) sessions at ages 11, 14, 18, and 23.

Various methodological or design principles guided our effort. We were oriented toward employing various kinds of data, not just life history, school, or demographic information (L-data); not just ratings of our subjects by teachers or parents or knowledgeable observers (O-data); not just formal experimental procedures or standardized tests (T-data); and not just questionnaires or other self-report techniques (S-data). Rather, we sought to include all (L-, O-, T-, and S-data) of these various approaches to generating useful data. Early on, we emphasized T-data in assessments because young children in their experimental and test behaviors rather directly express their motivations and characteristics. As our subjects moved into preadolescence and became "interiorized," we shifted to a greater use of S-data. Throughout our assessments, we collected various kinds of L-data information from the parents, school records, and the subjects themselves. And throughout the study we relied heavily on O-data, context-recognizing evaluations of our subjects at various ages, evaluations contributed by observers who had observed the subjects in diverse, often intimate situations, and often for appreciable periods of time.

We were also oriented toward the use of multiple measurements within each kind of data so as to achieve dependability and generalizability of our measures. Instead of measuring the fidgetiness of a child by a single behavioral time sample, we measured fidgetiness on a number of occasions and developed an averaged index, which, of course, displayed much better reliability and subsequent relations with other variables. When measures were not sensibly repeatable, such as when we sought to study a broad construct such as style of categorizing, we sampled the conceptual domain using diverse measures of categorizing, which we then composited so as to rise above the problem of method variance. When we relied on observer evaluations of personality or interactions, we relied on a composite judgment of several independent observers—never just one—encoded by the Q-sort method so as to ensure observer comparability in the way they used numbers and to lessen the influence of response sets.

In successive assessments we used entirely different crews of assessors so that absolute independence was maintained between the data gathered at these different times. The T-procedures that were specifically repeated, such as the Witkin Rod-and-Frame Test, were not influenceable by prior testing or were separated by enough time so that memory could not play a vitiating role.

We used various data-reduction procedures with the thousands of variables that accumulated (e.g., factor analysis, hierarchical regression analysis, the compositing of standard scores derived from variables all conceptually or empirically linked, the generation of prototype scores to reflect how well a constellation of obtained scores fits a conceptual standard). In our analyses, we were sensitive to the problem of chance significance and applied an early version of the bootstrap method (J. Block, 1960) to our results and also catalyzed a method developed by truly mathematical statisticians (Alemayehu & Doksum, 1990) to further deal with the data analysis problems besetting us. Our most persuasive way of analyzing data, however, was to seek for and to find convergence of relationships from different kinds of data sets and from different times of assessment.

Routinely, we analyzed our data for the two sexes separately. It is crucial to do so. When the same pattern of findings characterizes both boys and girls, both young men and young women, one has a cross-validated result. However, when, as happens surprisingly often, reliably different correlational patterns characterize the two sexes, a sex difference has been found that requires attention and thought. Over the years, I have been profoundly impressed by the differences between the sexes not so much in their respective mean levels on whatever is being measured as in the differences in the correlational *patterns* that characterize males as compared with females.

I now present an inundating listing (a sampling, really) of the measures and procedures and situations we imposed on our subjects over the years. The reader should not try to truly incorporate the meaning of the many measures so tersely mentioned; a sense of the scope and ambition of our effort is all that is needed.[1]

Thus, we used measures of activity level; delay of gratification; distractability; vigilance; exploratory behavior; motor inhibition (Simon Says!); susceptibility to priming; satiation and cosatiation; planfulness; curiosity; instrumental behavior when confronted by barriers or frustrations; dual focus (the ability to split attention); susceptibility to perceptual illusions; risk taking; level of aspiration; utilization of feedback; the Wechsler Intelligence Scale at ages 4, 11, and 18; the Raven Progressive Matrices; Piagetian measures of conservation; semantic retrieval; the Lowenfeld Mosaic Test; divergent thinking and other indexes of creativity; chained word association to index associative drift; various cognitive styles such as field dependence–independence, reflection–impulsivity, category breadth, and perceptual standards; sex role typing; egocentrism; physiognomic perception; incidental learning; the Stroop Color and Word Test; the Kogan Metaphor Test for metaphor comprehension; metaphor generation; short-term memory via digit span; memory for sentences; and memory for narrative stories; moral development; Loevinger's Washington University Sentence Completion Test to measure ego development; Kelly's Role Construct Repertory Test; skin conductance while lying, when startled, and recovery rate from startle; the phenomenology of emotions; Spivack and Shure's interpersonal problem-solving measure; free play at age 3 and free play again at age 11 (patterned after Erik Erikson's approach); self-concept descriptions; descriptions of ideal self, of mother, of father, and of sought-for love object; decision time and decision confidence in situations varying in the intrinsic difficulty of decision; enacting a standard set of expressive situations (videotaped); experience sampling for a week via a beeper; blood pressure and heart rate in response to a set of stressors; depressive realism; false consensus; health indexes; activity and interest indexes; long and intensive clinical interviews (videotaped) relating to, among other topics, adult attachment, ways of knowing and ego development, and core conflict relationship themes; Diagnostic Interview Schedule screening so as to connect with the revised third edition of the *Diagnostic and Statistical Manual of Mental Disorders* (*DSM-III-R*) classification system; and hundreds of questionnaire and inventory items relating to dozens of personality scales.

Both the mothers and fathers of our subjects also participated in the study in various ways, contributing several kinds of data over the years. We have information at various times of their child-rearing orientations, their self-descriptions, their characterizations of the child, their responses to a personality inventory, home interviews and characterizations of the home environment, and videotapes of their interactions with their child during the preschool years and also during early adolescence.

In assembling and administering this array of procedures, there was continual concern for the age appropriateness of the procedures used. Some measures of conceptual interest sensibly could be repeated in later years, such as the Rod-and-Frame Test, which we administered in six different assessments; others could not be, such as our procedure to measure delay of gratification by having nursery school children work for M&Ms. We were also attentive, as we went along, to the ongoing psychological literature, introducing into our assessments new topics and new measures that attracted our interest and to ensure continued

[1]The list of measures that follows is indeed inundating, as Block says. Even most psychologists would be unfamiliar with most of them. But this exhausting list does serve to illustrate how many different techniques exist for assessing different aspects of personality, and how many of them Block managed to include in his research project.

contemporaneity of our broad-gauge inquiry. I offer as an observation and not as a boast that there is not another sample in psychology so extensively and intensively assessed for so long a period.[2]

* * *

[2]The rest of this chapter, omitted here, surveyed some recent empirical results. Block and his co-workers have published numerous articles over the years that present results concerning a wide array of topics, from drug use and depression to delay of gratification and moral development.

References

Alemayehu, D., & Doksum, K. (1990). Using the bootstrap in correlation analysis, with applications to a longitudinal data set. *Journal of Applied Statistics, 17*, 357–368.

Block, J. (1960). On the number of significant findings to be expected by chance. *Psychometrika, 25*, 369–380.

Block, J. (1981). From infancy to adulthood: A clarification. *Child Development, 51*, 622–623.

Lewin, K. (1946). Behavior and development as a function of the total situation. In L. Carmichael (Ed.), *Manual of child psychology* (pp. 918–970). New York: Wiley.

Murray, H. A. (1938). *Explorations in personality*. New York: Oxford University Press.

White, R. W. (1959). Motivation reconsidered: The concept of competence. *Psychological Review, 66*, 297–333.

A Simple, General-Purpose Display of Magnitude of Experimental Effect

Robert Rosenthal and Donald B. Rubin

The most widely used statistic in personality psychology, the correlation coefficient, has been the source of considerable, needless confusion. An r of 1 (or −1) means that two variables are perfectly correlated, and an r of 0 means they are not correlated at all. But how should we interpret the r's in between, as most are?

Confusion has been engendered by a commonly taught practice of squaring correlations to yield the "percentage of variance explained" by the relationship. While this phrase sounds rather close to what one would want to know, it causes people to interpret correlations of .32, for example, as "explaining only 10% of the variance" (because .32 squared is about .10), which leaves 90% "unexplained." This does not make it sound like much has been accomplished.

In the next selection, psychologist Robert Rosenthal and statistician Donald Rubin team up to explain why this common calculation is misleading. In particular, they believe it causes strong effects, such as those indexed by correlations between .30 and .40, to seem smaller than they are. They introduce a simple technique of their own invention for illustrating the real size and importance of correlations. The "binomial effect size display" (BESD) allows correlation coefficients to be interpreted in terms of the percentage of correct classification or effective treatment they represent.

The basic calculation is even simpler than this article may make it sound. Look at Table 3.1 and assume an r of 0. This would yield an entry of 50 in each of the four cells. To see what a correlation of .32 looks like, divide 32 by 2, which gives you 16. Add the 16 to 50 and put this 66 in the upper left and lower right cells. Now subtract 16 from 50 and put 34 in the lower left and upper right cells. The rows and columns still each add up to 100, but now show what r = .32 looks like. It's easy! And it shows that a correlation between a treatment and an outcome, or between a predictor and a criterion, of a size of .32 would give you the right result almost twice as often as the wrong result.

The BESD is particularly important for personality psychology because most of the strongest relations between traits or between traits and behaviors are found to yield correlations between about .30 and .40. Rosenthal and Rubin show us that this means the prediction of one trait from another, or of a behavior on the basis of a trait, is usually more than twice as likely to be right as it is to be wrong.

From *Journal of Educational Psychology, 74*, 166–169, 1982.

* * *

Traditionally, behavioral researchers have concentrated on reporting significance levels of experimental effects. Recent years, however, have shown a welcome increase in emphasis on reporting the magnitude of experimental effects obtained (Cohen, 1977; Fleiss, 1969; Friedman, 1968; Glass, 1976; Hays, 1973; Rosenthal, 1978; Rosenthal & Rubin, 1978; Smith & Glass, 1977).

Despite the growing awareness of the importance of estimating sizes of effects along with estimating the more conventional levels of significance, there is a problem in interpreting various effect size estimators such as the Pearson *r*. For example, we found experienced behavioral researchers and experienced statisticians quite surprised when we showed them that the Pearson *r* of .32 associated with a coefficient of determination (r^2) of only .10 was the correlational equivalent of increasing a success rate from 34% to 66% by means of an experimental treatment procedure; for example, these values could mean that a death rate under the control condition is 66% but is only 34% under the experimental condition. We believe (Rosenthal & Rubin, 1979) that there may be a widespread tendency to underestimate the importance of the effects of behavioral (and biomedical) interventions (Mayo, 1978; Rimland, 1979) simply because they are often associated with what are thought to be low values of r^2.

The purpose of the present article is to introduce an intuitively appealing general purpose effect size display whose interpretation is perfectly transparent: the binomial effect size display (BESD). In no sense do we claim to have resolved the differences and controversies surrounding the use of various effect size estimators (e.g., Appelbaum & Cramer, 1974). Our display is useful because it is (a) easily understood by researchers, students, and lay persons; (b) applicable in a wide variety of contexts; and (c) conveniently computed.

The question addressed by BESD is: What is the effect on the success rate (e.g., survival rate, cure rate, improvement rate, selection rate, etc.) of the institution of a certain treatment procedure? It displays the change in success rate (e.g., survival rate, cure rate, improvement rate, selection rate, etc.) attributable to a certain treatment procedure. An example shows the appeal of our procedure.

In their meta-analysis of psychotherapy outcome studies, Smith and Glass (1977) summarized the results of some 400 studies. An eminent critic stated that the results of their analysis sounded the "death knell" for psychotherapy because of the modest size of the effect (Rimland, 1979). This modest effect size was calculated to be equivalent to an *r* of .32 accounting for "only 10% of the variance" (p. 192).

Table 3.1 is the BESD corresponding to an *r* of .32 or an r^2 of .10. The table shows clearly that it is absurd to label as "modest indeed" (Rimland, 1979, p. 192) an effect size equivalent to increasing the success rate from 34% to 66% (e.g., reducing a death rate from 66% to 34%).

Table 3.2 shows systematically the increase in success rates associated with various values of r^2 and *r*. Even so small an *r* as .20, accounting for only 4% of the variance, is associated with an increase in success rate from 40% to 60%, such as a reduction in death rate from 60% to 40%. The last column of Table 3.2 shows that the difference

TABLE 3.1

THE BINOMIAL EFFECT SIZE DISPLAY: AN EXAMPLE "ACCOUNTING FOR ONLY 10% OF THE VARIANCE"

Condition	Alive	Dead	Σ
Treatment	66	34	100
Control	34	66	100
Σ	100	100	200

TABLE 3.2

BINOMIAL EFFECT SIZE DISPLAYS CORRESPONDING TO VARIOUS VALUES OF r^2 AND r

		Success rate increased		
r^2	r	From	To	Difference in success rates
.01	.10	.45	.55	.10
.04	.20	.40	.60	.20
.09	.30	.35	.65	.30
.16	.40	.30	.70	.40
.25	.50	.25	.75	.50
.36	.60	.20	.80	.60
.49	.70	.15	.85	.70
.64	.80	.10	.90	.80
.81	.90	.05	.95	90
1.00	1.00	.00	1.00	1.00

in success rates is identical to r. Consequently the experimental success rate in the BESD is computed as $.50 + r/2$, whereas the control group success rate is computed as $.50 - r/2$. Cohen (1965) and Friedman (1968) have useful discussions of computing the r associated with a variety of test statistics, and Table 3.3 gives the three most frequently used equivalences.

We propose that the reporting of effect sizes can be made more intuitive and more informative by using the BESD. It is our belief that the use of the BESD to display the increase in success rate due to treatment will more clearly convey the real world importance of treatment effects than do the commonly used descriptions of effect size based on the proportion of variance accounted for. The

TABLE 3.3

COMPUTATION OF r FROM COMMON TEST STATISTICS

Test statistic	r^a given by
act	$\sqrt{\frac{t^2}{t^2 + df}}$
F^b	$\sqrt{\frac{F}{F + df\,(\text{error})}}$
$X^{2,c}$	$\sqrt{\frac{X^{\cdot}}{N}}$

[a] The sign of r should be positive if the experimental group is superior to the control group and negative if the control group is superior to the experimental group.
[b] Used only when df for numerator = 1 as in the comparison of two group means or any other contrast.
[c] Used only when df for $\chi^2 = 1$.

BESD is most appropriate when the variances within the two conditions are similar, as they are assumed to be whenever we compute the usual t test.

It might appear that the BESD can be employed only when the outcome variable is dichotomous and the mean outcome in one group is the same amount above .5 as the mean outcome in the other group is below .5. Actually, the BESD is often a realistic representation of the size of treatment effect when the variances of the outcome variable are approximately the same in the two approximately equal sized groups, as is commonly the case in educational and psychological studies.

* * *

References

Appelbaum, M. I., & Cramer, E. M. (1974). The only game in town. *Contemporary Psychology, 19*, 406–407.

Cohen, J. (1965). Some statistical issues in psychological research. In B. B. Wolman (Ed.), *Handbook of clinical psychology*. New York: McGraw-Hill.

Cohen, J. (1977). *Statistical power analysis for the behavioral sciences* (Rev. ed.). New York: Academic Press.

Fleiss, J. L. (1969). Estimating the magnitude of experimental effects. *Psychological Bulletin, 72*, 273–276.

Friedman, H. (1968). Magnitude of experimental effect and a

table for its rapid estimation. *Psychological Bulletin, 70,* 245–251.

Glass, G. V. (1976, April). *Primary, secondary, and meta-analysis of research.* Paper presented at the meeting of the American Educational Research Association, San Francisco.

Hays, W. L. (1973). *Statistics for the social sciences* (2nd ed.). New York: Holt, Rinehart & Winston.

Mayo, R. J. (1978). Statistical considerations in analyzing the results of a collection of experiments. *The Behavioral and Brain Sciences, 3,* 400–401.

Rimland, B. (1979). Death knell for psychotherapy? *American Psychologist, 34,* 192.

Rosenthal, R. (1978). Combining results of independent studies. *Psychological Bulletin, 85,* 185–193.

Rosenthal, R., & Rubin, D. B. (1978). Interpersonal expectancy effects: The first 345 studies. *The Behavioral and Brain Sciences, 3,* 377–386.

Rosenthal, R., & Rubin, D. B. (1979). A note on percent variance explained as a measure of the importance of effects. *Journal of Applied Social Psychology, 9,* 395–396.

Smith, M. L., & Glass, G. V. (1977). Meta-analysis of psychotherapy outcome studies. *American Psychologist, 32,* 752–760.

Construct Validity in Psychological Tests

Lee J. Cronbach and Paul E. Meehl

Lee Cronbach and Paul Meehl are two of the most prominent methodologists in the history of psychology. In the following classic selection, they team up to address the knotty question of "construct validity," which is, how do you know whether a test—such as a personality test—really measures what it is supposed to measure? As is mentioned in the opening paragraphs, the article was occasioned by very real concerns in the mid-1950s over the proper way to establish the validity of a test. This issue generated political heat both within and outside the American Psychological Association, the professional organization of many psychologists, because the tests that people take often have real consequences. They are used for selection in education and employment, for example. Thus, the degree to which a test is valid is more than an academic issue. Its resolution has real consequences for real people.

This article is a fairly difficult piece, but worth some effort. Psychologists who have been doing research for years can reread this article and learn something important that escaped them on previous readings. The essential points to glean from this article are that no single study or one source of data will ever sufficiently explain any important aspect of personality, and that psychological theory plays an essential role in developing an understanding of what any measure of personality really means. Multiple methods must always be employed, and the validation of a test will emerge only gradually from an examination of how different methods produce results that are sometimes the same and sometimes different. The present excerpt concludes with the important observation that the aim of construct validation is not to conclude that a test "is valid," but rather to assess its degree of validity for various purposes.

From *Psychological Bulletin, 52*, 281–302, 1955.

Validation of psychological tests has not yet been adequately conceptualized, as the APA Committee on Psychological Tests learned when it undertook (1950–54) to specify what qualities should be investigated before a test is published. In order to make coherent recommendations the Committee found it necessary to distinguish four types of validity, established by different types of research and requiring different interpretation. The chief innovation in the Committee's report was the term *construct validity*. This idea was first formulated by a subcommittee (Meehl and R. C. Challman) studying how proposed recommendations would apply to projective techniques, and later modified and clarified by the entire Committee (Bordin, Challman, Conrad, Humphreys, Super, and the present writers). The statements agreed upon by the Committee (and by committees of two other associations) were published in the *Technical Recommendations* (American Psychological Association, 1954). The present interpretation of construct validity is not "official" and deals with some areas where the Committee would probably not be unanimous. The present writers are solely responsible for this attempt to explain the concept and elaborate its implications.

Identification of construct validity was not an isolated development. Writers on validity during the preceding decade had shown a great deal of dissatisfaction with conventional notions of validity, and introduced new terms and ideas, but the resulting aggregation of types of validity seems only to have stirred the muddy waters. Portions of the distinctions we shall discuss are implicit in Jenkins's (1946) paper, Gulliksen (1950), Goodenough's (1950) distinction between tests as "signs" and "samples," Cronbach's (1949) separation of "logical" and "empirical" validity, Guilford's (1946) "factorial validity," and Mosier's (1947, 1951) papers on "face validity" and "validity generalization." Helen Peak (1953) comes close to an explicit statement of construct validity as we shall present it.

Four Types of Validation

The categories into which the *Recommendations* divide validity studies are: predictive validity, concurrent validity, content validity, and construct validity. The first two of these may be considered together as *criterion-oriented* validation procedures.

The pattern of a criterion-oriented study is familiar. The investigator is primarily interested in some criterion which he wishes to predict. He administers the test, obtains an independent criterion measure on the same subjects, and computes a correlation. If the criterion is obtained some time after the test is given, he is studying *predictive validity*. If the test score and criterion score are determined at essentially the same time, he is studying *concurrent validity*. Concurrent validity is studied when one test is proposed as a substitute for another (for example, when a multiple-choice form of spelling test is substituted for taking dictation), or a test is shown to correlate with some contemporary criterion (e.g., psychiatric diagnosis).

Content validity is established by showing that the test items are a sample of a universe in which the investigator is interested. Content validity is ordinarily to be established deductively, by defining a universe of items and sampling systematically within this universe to establish the test.

Construct validation is involved whenever a test is to be interpreted as a measure of some attribute or quality which is not "operationally defined." The problem faced by the investigator is, "What constructs account for variance in test performance?" Construct validity calls for no new scientific approach. Much current research on tests of personality (Child, 1954) is construct validation, usually without the benefit of a clear formulation of this process.

Construct validity is not to be identified solely by particular investigative procedures, but by the orientation of the investigator. Criterion-oriented validity, as Bechtoldt emphasizes (1951, p. 1245), "involves the *acceptance* of a set of operations as an adequate definition of whatever is to be measured." When an investigator believes that no criterion available in him is fully valid, he perforce becomes interested in construct validity because this is the only way to avoid the "infinite frustration" of relating every criterion to some more ultimate standard (Gaylord, unpublished manuscript). In content validation, *acceptance* of the universe of content as defining the variable to be measured is essential. Construct validity must be investigated whenever no criterion or universe of content is accepted as entirely adequate to define the quality to be measured. Determining what psychological constructs account for test performance is desirable for almost any test. Thus, although the MMPI was originally established on the basis of empirical discrimination between patient groups and so-called normals (concurrent validity), continuing research has tried to provide a basis for describing the personality associated with each score pattern. Such interpretations permit the clinician to predict performance with respect to criteria which have not yet been employed in empirical validation studies (cf. Meehl, 1954, pp. 49–50, 110–111).

> We can distinguish among the four types of validity by noting that each involves a different emphasis on the criterion. In predictive or concurrent validity, the criterion behavior is of concern to the tester, and he may have no concern whatsoever with the type of behavior exhibited in the test. (An employer does not care if a worker can manipulate blocks, but the score on the block test may predict something he cares about.) Content validity is studied when the tester *is* concerned with the type of behavior involved in the test performance. Indeed, if the test is a work sample, the behavior represented in the test may be an end in itself. Construct validity is ordinarily studied when the tester has no definite criterion measure of the quality with which he is concerned, and must use indirect measures. Here the trait or quality underlying the test is of central importance, rather than either the test behavior or the scores on the criteria (APA, 1954, p. 14).

Construct validation is important at times for every sort of psychological test: aptitude, achievement, interests, and so on. Thurstone's statement is interesting in this connection:

> In the field of intelligence tests, it used to be common to define validity as the correlation between a test score and some outside criterion. We have reached a stage of sophistication where the test-criterion correlation is too coarse. It is obsolete. If we attempted to ascertain the validity of a test for the second space-factor, for example, we would have to get judges [to] make reliable judgments about people as to this factor. Ordinarily their [the available judges'] ratings would be of no value as a criterion. Consequently, validity studies in the cognitive functions now depend on criteria of internal consistency . . . (Thurstone, 1952, p. 3).

Construct validity would be involved in answering such questions as: To what extent is this test of intelligence culture-free? Does this test of "interpretation of data" measure reading ability, quantitative reasoning, or response sets? How does a person with A in Strong Accountant, and B in Strong CPA, differ from a person who has these scores reversed?

Example of construct validation procedure. Suppose measure *X* correlates .50 with *Y*, the amount of palmar sweating induced when we tell a student that he has failed a Psychology I exam. Predictive validity of *X* for *Y* is adequately described by the coefficient, and a statement of the experimental and sampling conditions. If someone were to ask, "Isn't there perhaps another way to interpret this correlation?" or "What other kinds of evidence can you bring to support your interpretation?" we would hardly understand what he was asking because no interpretation has been made. These questions become relevant when the correlation is advanced as evidence that "test *X* measures anxiety proneness." Alternative interpretations are possible; e.g., perhaps the test measures "academic aspiration," in which case we will expect different results if we induce palmar sweating by economic threat. It is then reasonable to inquire about other *kinds* of evidence.

Add these facts from further studies: Test *X* correlates .45 with fraternity brothers' ratings on "tenseness." Test *X* correlates .55 with amount of intellectual inefficiency induced by painful electric shock, and .68 with the Taylor Anxiety scale. Mean *X* score decreases among four diagnosed groups in this order: anxiety state, reactive depression, "normal," and psychopathic personality. And palmar sweat under threat of failure in Psychology I correlates .60 with threat of failure in mathematics. Negative results eliminate competing explanations of the *X* score; thus, findings of negligible correlations between *X* and social class, vocational aim, and value-orientation make it fairly safe to reject the suggestion that *X* measures "academic aspiration." We can have substantial confidence that *X* does measure anxiety proneness if the current theory of anxiety can embrace the variates which yield positive correlations, and does not predict correlations where we found none.

* * *

The Relation of Constructs to "Criteria"

CRITICAL VIEW OF THE CRITERION IMPLIED An unquestionable criterion may be found in a practical operation, or may be established as a consequence of an operational definition. Typically, however, the psychologist is unwilling to use the directly operational approach because he is interested in building theory about a generalized construct. A theorist trying to relate behavior to "hunger" almost certainly invests that term with meanings other than the operation "elapsed-time-since-feeding." If he is concerned with hunger as a tissue need, he will not accept time lapse as *equivalent* to his construct because it fails to consider, among other things, energy expenditure of the animal.

In some situations the criterion is no more valid than the test. Suppose, for example, that we want to know if counting the dots on Bender-Gestalt figure five indicates "compulsive rigidity," and take psychiatric ratings on this trait as a criterion. Even a conventional report on the resulting correlation will say something about the extent and intensity of the psychiatrist's contacts and should describe his qualifications (e.g., diplomate status? analyzed?).

Why report these facts? Because data are needed to indicate whether the criterion is any good. "Compulsive rigidity" is not really intended to mean "social stimulus value to psychiatrists." The implied trait involves a range of behavior-dispositions which may be very imperfectly sampled by the psychiatrist. Suppose dot-counting does not occur in a particular patient and yet we find that the psychiatrist has rated him as "rigid." When questioned the psychiatrist tells us that the patient was a rather easy, free-wheeling sort: however, the patient *did* lean over to straighten out a skewed desk blotter, and this, viewed against certain other facts, tipped the scale in favor of a "rigid" rating. On the face of it, counting Bender dots may be just as good (or poor) a sample of the compulsive-rigidity domain as straightening desk blotters is.

Suppose, to extend our example, we have four tests on the "predictor" side, over against the psychiatrist's "criterion," and find generally positive correlations among the five variables. Surely it is artificial and arbitrary to impose the "test-should-predict-criterion" pattern on such data. The psychiatrist samples verbal content, expressive pattern, voice, posture, etc. The psychologist samples verbal content, perception, expressive pattern, etc. Our proper conclusion is that, from this evidence, the four tests and the psychiatrist all assess some common factor.

The asymmetry between the "test" and the so-designated "criterion" arises only because the terminology of predictive validity has become a commonplace in test analysis. In this study where a construct is the central concern, any distinction between the merit of the test and criterion variables would be justified only if it had already been shown that the psychiatrist's theory and operations were excellent measures of the attribute.

Inadequacy of Validation in Terms of Specific Criteria

The proposal to validate constructual interpretations of tests runs counter to suggestions of some others. Spiker and McCandless (1954) favor an operational approach. Validation is replaced by compiling statements as to how strongly the test predicts other observed variables of interest. To avoid requiring that each new variable be investigated completely by itself, they allow two variables to collapse into one whenever the properties of the operationally defined measures are the same: "If a new test is demonstrated to predict the scores on an older, well-established test, then an evaluation of the predictive power of the older test may be used for the new one." But accurate inferences are possible only if the two tests correlate so highly that there is negligible reliable variance in either test, independent of the other. Where the correspondence is less close, one must either retain all the separate variables operationally defined or embark on construct validation.

The practical user of tests must rely on constructs of some generality to make predictions about new situations. Test *X* could be used to predict palmar sweating in the face of failure without invoking any construct, but a counselor is more likely to be asked to forecast behavior in diverse or even unique situations for which the correlation of test *X* is unknown. Significant predictions rely on knowledge accumulated around the generalized construct of anxiety. The "Technical Recommendations" state:

> It is ordinarily necessary to evaluate construct validity by integrating evidence from many different sources. The problem of construct validation becomes especially acute in the clinical field since for many of the constructs dealt with it is not a question of finding an imperfect criterion but of finding any criterion at all. The psychologist interested in construct validity for clinical devices is concerned with making an estimate of a hypothetical internal process, factor, system, structure, or state and cannot expect to find a clear unitary behavioral criterion. An attempt to identify any one criterion measure or any composite as *the* criterion aimed at is, however, usually unwarranted (APA, 1954, pp. 14–15).

This appears to conflict with arguments for specific criteria prominent at places in the testing literature. Thus Anastasi (1950) makes many statements of the latter character: "It is only as a measure of a specifically defined criterion that a test can be objectively validated at all . . . To claim that a test measures anything over and above its criterion is pure speculation" (p. 67). Yet elsewhere this article supports construct validation. Tests can be profitably interpreted if we "know the relationships between the tested behavior . . . and other behavior samples, none of these behavior samples necessarily occupying the preeminent position of a criterion" (p. 75). Factor analysis with several partial criteria might be used to study whether a test measures a postulated "general learning ability." If the data demonstrate specificity of ability instead, such specificity is "useful in its own right in advancing our knowledge of behavior; it should not be construed as a weakness of the tests" (p. 75).

We depart from Anastasi at two points. She writes, "The validity of a psychological test should not be confused with an analysis of the factors which determine the behavior under consideration." We, however, regard such analysis as a most important type of validation. Second, she refers to "the will-o'-the-wisp of psychological processes which are distinct from performance" (Anastasi, 1950, p. 77). While we agree that psychological processes are elusive, we are sympathetic to attempts to formulate and clarify constructs which are evidenced by performance but distinct from it. Surely an inductive inference based on a pattern of correlations cannot be dismissed as "pure speculation."

SPECIFIC CRITERIA USED TEMPORARILY: THE "BOOTSTRAPS" EFFECT Even when a test is constructed on the basis of a specific criterion, it may ultimately be judged to have greater construct validity than the criterion. We start with a vague concept which we associate with certain observations. We then discover empirically that these observations covary with some other observation which possesses greater reliability or is more intimately correlated with relevant experimental changes than is the original measure, or both. For example, the notion of temperature arises because some objects feel hotter to the touch than others. The expansion of a mercury column does not have face validity as an index of hotness. But it turns out that (a) there is a statistical relation between expansion and sensed temperature; (b) observers employ the mercury method with good interobserver agreement; (c) the regularity of observed relations is increased by using the thermometer (e.g., melting points of samples of the same material vary little on the thermometer; we obtain nearly linear relations between mercury measures and pressure of a gas). Finally, (d) a theoretical structure involving unobservable microevents—the kinetic theory—is worked out which explains the relation of mercury expansion to heat. This whole process of conceptual enrichment begins with what in retrospect we see as an extremely fallible "criterion"—the human temperature sense. That original criterion has now been relegated to a peripheral position. We have lifted ourselves by our bootstraps, but in a legitimate and fruitful way.

Similarly, the Binet scale was first valued because children's scores tended to agree with judgments by schoolteachers. If it had not shown this agreement, it would have been discarded along with reaction time and the other measures of ability previously tried. Teacher judgments once constituted the criterion against which the individual intelligence test was validated. But if today a child's IQ is 135 and three of his teachers complain about how stupid he is, we do not conclude that the test has failed. Quite to the contrary, if no error in test procedure can be argued, we treat the test score as a valid statement about an important quality, and define our task as that of finding out what other variables—personality, study skills, etc.—modify achievement or distort teacher judgment.

Experimentation to Investigate Construct Validity

VALIDATION PROCEDURES We can use many methods in construct validation. Attention should particularly be drawn to Macfarlane's survey of these methods as they apply to projective devices (Macfarlane, 1942).

Group differences. If our understanding of a construct leads us to expect two groups to differ on the test, this expectation may be tested directly. Thus Thurstone and Chave validated the Scale for Measuring Attitude Toward the Church by showing score differences between church members and nonchurchgoers. Churchgoing is not *the* criterion of attitude, for the purpose of the test is to measure something other than the crude sociological fact of church attendance; on the other hand, failure to find a difference would have seriously challenged the test.

Only coarse correspondence between test and group designation is expected. Too great a correspondence between the two would indicate that the test is to some degree invalid, because members of the groups are expected to overlap on the test. Intelligence test items are selected initially on the basis of a correspondence to age, but an item that correlates .95 with age in an elementary school sample would surely be suspect.

Correlation matrices and factor analysis. If two tests are presumed to measure the same construct, a correlation between them is predicted. (An exception is noted where some second attribute has positive loading in the first test and negative loading in the second test; then a low correlation is expected. This is a testable interpretation provided an external measure of either the first or the second variable exists.) If the obtained correlation departs from the expectation, however, there is no way to know whether the fault lies in test A, test B, or the formulation of the construct. A matrix of intercorrelations often points out profitable ways of dividing the construct into more meaningful parts, factor analysis being a useful computational method in such studies.

Guilford (1948) has discussed the place of factor analysis in construct validation. His statements may be extracted as follows:

"The personnel psychologist wishes to know 'why his tests are valid.' He can place tests and practical criteria in a matrix and factor it to identify 'real dimensions of human personality.' A factorial description is exact and stable; it is economical in explanation; it leads to the creation of pure tests which can be combined to predict complex behaviors." It is clear that factors here function as constructs. Eysenck (1950) in his "criterion analysis," goes further than Guilford and shows that factoring can be used explicitly to test hypotheses about constructs.

Factors may or may not be weighted with surplus meaning. Certainly when they are regarded as "real dimensions" a great deal of surplus meaning is implied, and the interpreter must shoulder a substantial burden of proof. The alternative view is to regard factors as defining a working reference frame, located in a convenient manner in the "space" defined by all behaviors of a given type. Which set of factors from a given matrix is "most useful" will depend partly on predilections, but in essence the best construct is the one around which we can build the greatest number of inferences, in the most direct fashion.

Studies of internal structure. For many constructs, evidence of homogeneity within the test is relevant in judging validity. If a trait such as *dominance* is hypothesized, and the items inquire about behaviors subsumed under this label, then the hypothesis appears to require that these items be generally intercorrelated. Even low correlations, if consistent, would support the argument that people may be fruitfully described in terms of a generalized tendency to dominate or not dominate. The general quality would have power to predict behavior in a variety of situations represented by the specific items. Item-test correlations and certain reliability formulas describe internal consistency.

It is unwise to list uninterpreted data of this sort under the heading "validity" in test manuals, as some authors have done. High internal consistency may *lower* validity. Only if the underlying theory of the trait being measured calls for high item intercorrelations do the correlations support construct validity. Negative item-test correlations may support construct validity, provided that the items with negative correlations are believed irrelevant to the postulated construct and serve as suppressor variables (Horst, 1941, pp. 431–436; Meehl, 1945).

Study of distinctive subgroups of items within a test may set an upper limit to construct validity by showing that irrelevant elements influence scores. Thus a study of the PMA space tests shows that variance can be partially accounted for by a response set, tendency to mark many figures as similar (Cronbach, 1950). An internal factor analysis of the PEA Interpretation of Data Test shows that in addition to measuring reasoning skills, the test score is strongly influenced by a tendency to say "probably true" rather than "certainly true," regardless of item content (Damrin, 1952). On the other hand, a study of item groupings in the DAT Mechanical Comprehension Test permitted rejection of the hypothesis that knowledge about specific topics such as gears made a substantial contribution to scores (Cronbach, 1951).

Studies of change over occasions. The stability of test scores ("retest reliability," Cattell's "N-technique") may be relevant to construct validation. Whether a high degree of stability is encouraging or discouraging for the proposed interpretation depends upon the theory defining the construct.

More powerful than the retest after uncontrolled intervening experiences is the retest with experimental intervention. If a transient influence swings test scores over a wide range, there are definite limits on the extent to which a test result can be interpreted as reflecting the typical behavior of the individual. These are examples of experiments which have indicated upper limits to test validity: studies of differences associated with the examiner in projective testing, of change of score under alternative directions ("tell the truth" vs. "make yourself look good to an employer"), and of coachability of mental tests. We may recall Gulliksen's (1950) distinction: When the coaching is of a sort that improves the pupil's intellectual functioning in school, the test which is affected by the coaching has validity as a measure of intellectual functioning; if the coaching improves test taking but not school performance, the test which responds to the coaching has poor validity as a measure of this construct.

Sometimes, where differences between individuals are difficult to assess by any means other than the test, the experimenter validates by determining whether the test can detect induced intra individual differences. One might hypothesize that the Zeigarnik effect is a measure of ego involvement, i.e., that with ego involvement there is more recall of incomplete tasks. To support such an interpretation, the investigator will try to induce ego involvement on some task by appropriate directions and compare subjects' recall with their recall for tasks where there was a contrary induction. Sometimes the intervention is drastic. Porteus (1950) finds that brain-operated patients show disruption of performance on his maze, but do not show impaired performance on conventional verbal tests and argues therefrom that his test is a better measure of planfulness.

Studies of process. One of the best ways of determining informally what accounts for variability on a test is the observation of the person's process of performance. If it is supposed, for example, that a test measures mathematical competence, and yet observation of students' errors shows that erroneous reading of the question is common, the implications of a low score are altered. Lucas (1953) in this way showed that the Navy Relative Movement Test, an aptitude test, actually involved two different abilities: spatial visualization and mathematical reasoning.

Mathematical analysis of scoring procedures may provide important negative evidence on construct validity. A recent analysis of "empathy" tests is perhaps worth citing (Cronbach, 1955). "Empathy" has been operationally defined in many studies by the ability of a judge to predict what responses will be given on some questionnaire by a subject he has observed briefly. A mathematical argument has shown, however, that the scores depend on several attributes of the judge which enter into his perception of *any* individual, and that they therefore cannot be interpreted as evidence of his ability to interpret cues offered by particular others, or his intuition.

The Numerical Estimate of Construct Validity There is an understandable tendency to seek a "construct validity coefficient." A numerical statement of the degree of construct validity would be a statement of the proportion of the test score variance that is attributable to the construct variable. This numerical estimate can sometimes be arrived at by a factor analysis, but since present methods of factor analysis are based on linear relations, more general methods will ultimately be needed to deal with many quantitative problems of construct validation.

Rarely will it be possible to estimate definite "construct saturations," because no factor corresponding closely to the construct will be available. One can only hope to set upper and lower bounds to the "loading." If "creativity" is defined as something independent of knowledge, then a correlation of .40 between a presumed test of creativity and a test of arithmetic knowledge would indicate that at least 16 per cent of the reliable test variance is irrelevant to creativity as defined. Laboratory performance on problems such as Maier's "hatrack" would scarcely be an ideal measure of creativity, but it would be somewhat relevant. If its correlation with the test is .60, this permits a tentative estimate of 36 per cent as a lower bound. (The estimate is tentative because the test might overlap with the irrelevant portion of the laboratory measure.) The saturation seems to lie between 36 and 84 per cent; a cumulation of studies would provide better limits.

It should be particularly noted that rejecting the null hypothesis does not finish the job of construct validation (Kelly, 1954, p. 284). The problem is not to conclude that the test "is valid" for measuring the construct variable. The task is to state as definitely as possible the degree of validity the test is presumed to have.

* * *

References

American Psychological Association (1954). Technical recommendations for psychological tests and diagnostic techniques. *Psychological Bulletin Supplement, 51, Part 2,* 1–38.

Anastasi, A. (1950). The concept of validity in the interpretation of test scores. *Educational and Psychological Measurement, 10,* 67–78.

Bechtoldt, H. P. (1951). Selection. In S. S. Stevens (Ed.), *Handbook of experimental psychology* (pp. 1237–1267). New York: Wiley.

Child, I. L. (1954). Personality. *Annual Review of Psychology, 5,* 149–171.

Cronbach, L. J. (1949). *Essentials of psychological testing.* New York: Harper.

Cronbach, L. J. (1950). Further evidence on response sets and test design. *Educational and Psychological Measurement, 10,* 3–31.

Cronbach, L. J. (1951). Coefficient alpha and the internal structure of tests. *Psychometrika, 16,* 297–335.

Cronbach, L. J. (1955). Processes affecting scores on "understanding of others" and "assumed similarity." *Psychology Bulletin, 52,* 177–193.

Damrin, Dora E. (1952). A comparative study of information derived from a diagnostic problem-solving test by logical and factorial methods of scoring. Unpublished doctor's dissertation, University of Illinois.

Eysenck, H. J. (1950). Criterion analysis—an application of the hypothetico-deductive method in factor analysis. *Psychology Review, 57,* 38–53.

Gaylord, R. H. Conceptual consistency and criterion equivalence: a dual approach to criterion analysis. Unpublished manuscript (PRB Research Note No. 17). Copies obtainable from ASTIA-DSC, AD-21 440.

Goodenough, F. L. (1950). *Mental testing.* New York: Rinehart.

Guilford, J. P. (1946). New standards for test evaluation. *Educational and Psychological Measurement, 6,* 427–439.

Guilford, J. P. (1948). Factor analysis in a test-development program. *Psychology Review, 55,* 79–94.

Gulliksen, H. (1950). Intrinsic validity. *American Psychologist, 5,* 511–517.

Horst, P. (1941). The prediction of personal adjustment. *Social Science Research Council Bulletin,* No. 48.

Jenkins, J. G. (1946). Validity for what? *Journal of Consulting Psychology, 10,* 93–98.

Kelly, E. L. (1954). Theory and techniques of assessment. *Annual Review of Psychology, 5,* 281–311.

Lucas, C. M. (1953). Analysis of the relative movement test by a method of individual interviews. *Bureau Naval Personnel Res. Rep.,* Contract Nonr-694 (00), NR 151-13, Educational Testing Service, March 1953.

Macfarlane, J. W. (1942). Problems of validation inherent in projective methods. *American Journal of Orthopsychiatry, 12,* 405–410.

Meehl, P. E. (1945). A simple algebraic development of Horat's suppressor variables. *American Journal of Psychology, 58,* 550–554.

Meehl, P. E. (1954). *Clinical vs. statistical prediction.* Minneapolis: University of Minnesota Press.

Mosier, C. I. (1947). A critical examination of the concepts of face validity. *Educational and Psychological Measurement, 7,* 191–205.

Mosier, C. I. (1951). Problems and designs of cross-validation. *Educational and Psychological Measurement, 11,* 5–12.

Peak, H. (1953). Problems of objective observation. In L. Festinger and D. Katz (Eds.), *Research methods in the behavioral sciences* (pp. 243–300). New York: Dryden Press.

Porteus, S. D. (1950). *The Porteus maze test and intelligence.* Palo Alto: Pacific Books.

Spiker, C. C., & McCandless, B. R. (1954). The concept of intelligence and the philosophy of science. *Psychology Review, 61,* 255–267.

Thurstone, L. L. (1952). The criterion problem in personality research. *Psychometric Laboratory Report,* No. 78. Chicago: University of Chicago.

Convergent and Discriminant Validation by the Multitrait-Multimethod Matrix

Donald T. Campbell and Donald W. Fiske

If validity is not a simple property of a test, as Cronbach and Meehl argue, then what kinds of methods might be used to show that a particular measure has some degree of validity for a particular purpose? There are many possibilities, and Cronbach and Meehl briefly discussed a few of them. In the landmark paper that follows, the methodologists Donald Campbell and Donald Fiske propose that a "multitrait-multimethod matrix" of correlations provides especially useful information for examining construct validity. Their approach requires that one measure several different traits, each by several different methods. For example, sociability and impulsivity could each be assessed through self-descriptions and descriptions by peers. Once this kind of data is in hand, the correlations of each measure with all the others (the multitrait-multimethod matrix) can be examined. Measures of the same trait utilizing different methods (e.g., self- and peer-reports of sociability) should be positively correlated, demonstrating what Campbell and Fiske call "convergent" validity; and the self-reports of impulsivity and sociability should not be too strongly related to each other, despite their shared method of assessment ("discriminant validity"). Campbell and Fiske discuss the various kinds of information that might be gleaned from inspecting multitrait-multimethod matrices.

In the original version of this paper, Campbell and Fiske presented a number of previously published multitrait-multimethod matrices, and discussed the kinds of conclusions that each permitted. We have omitted this part of the article, because the data reported are now very old, and because the criteria used to evaluate multitrait-multimethod matrices have evolved considerably since the publication of this classic paper. More formal procedures using complex quantitative methods have replaced the informal rules described by Campbell and Fiske. These advanced methods (reviewed by Kenny & Kashy, 1992) *remove some of the arbitrariness inherent to the informal judgment scheme of Campbell and Fiske, but require that one impose a formal model of a particular kind. While at least one of us has deep reservations (Ozer, 1989; Ozer & Reise, 1994) about using multitrait-multimethod matrices as the sine qua non (a favorite phrase from high school Latin, meaning "without that, nothing") of validity assessment, there is no question that contemporary practice of validity assessment begins (but too often ends) with the use of Campbell and Fiske's multitrait-multimethod matrices.*

From *Psychological Bulletin, 56,* 81–105, 1959.

In the cumulative experience with measures of individual differences over the past 50 years, tests have been accepted as valid or discarded as invalid by research experiences of many sorts. The criteria suggested in this paper are all to be found in such cumulative evaluations, as well as in the recent discussions of validity. These criteria are clarified and implemented when considered jointly in the context of a multitrait-multimethod matrix. Aspects of the validational process receiving particular emphasis are these:

1. Validation is typically *convergent,* a confirmation by independent measurement procedures. Independence of methods is a common denominator among the major types of validity (excepting content validity) insofar as they are to be distinguished from reliability.

2. For the justification of novel trait measures, for the validation of test interpretation, or for the establishment of construct validity, *discriminant* validation as well as convergent validation is required. Tests can be invalidated by too high correlations with other tests from which they were intended to differ.

3. Each test or task employed for measurement purposes is a *trait-method unit,* a union of a particular trait content with measurement procedures not specific to that content. The systematic variance among test scores can be due to responses to the measurement features as well as responses to the trait content.

4. In order to examine discriminant validity, and in order to estimate the relative contributions of trait and method variance, *more than one trait* as well as *more than one method* must be employed in the validation process. In many instances it will be convenient to achieve this through a multitrait-multimethod matrix. Such a matrix presents all of the intercorrelations resulting when each of several traits is measured by each of several methods.

To illustrate the suggested validational process, a synthetic example is presented in Table 5.1. This illustration involves three different traits, each measured by three methods, generating nine separate variables. It will be convenient to have labels for various regions of the matrix, and such have been provided in Table 5.1. The reliabilities will be spoken of in terms of three *reliability diagonals,* one for each method. The reliabilities could also be designated as the monotrait-monomethod values. Adjacent to each reliability diagonal is the *heterotrait-monomethod* triangle. The reliability diagonal and the adjacent heterotrait-monomethod triangle make up a *monomethod block.* A *heteromethod block* is made up of a *validity* diagonal (which could also be designated as monotrait-heteromethod values) and the two *heterotrait-heteromethod* triangles lying on each side of it. Note that these two heterotrait-heteromethod triangles are not identical.

In terms of this diagram, four aspects bear upon the question of validity. In the first place, the entries in the validity diagonal should be significantly different from zero and sufficiently large to encourage further examination of validity. This requirement is evidence of convergent validity. Second, a validity diagonal value should be higher than the values lying in its column and row in the heterotrait-heteromethod triangles. That is, a validity value for a variable should be higher than the correlations obtained between that variable and any other variable having neither trait nor method in common. This requirement may seem so minimal and so obvious as to not need stating,

TABLE 5.1

A SYNTHETIC MULTITRAIT-MULTIMETHOD MATRIX

		Method 1			Method 2			Method 3		
	Traits	A_1	B_1	C_1	A_2	B_2	C_2	A_3	B_3	C_3
Method 1	A_1	(.89)								
	B_1	.51	(.89)							
	C_1	.38	.37	(.76)						
Method 2	A_2	*.57*	.22	.09	(.93)					
	B_2	.22	*.57*	.10	.68	(.94)				
	C_2	.11	.11	*.46*	.59	.58	(.84)			
Method 3	A_3	*.56*	.22	.11	*.67*	.42	.33	(.94)		
	B_3	.23	*.58*	.12	.43	*.66*	.34	.67	(.92)	
	C_3	.11	.11	*.45*	.34	.32	*.58*	.58	.60	(.85)

Note. The validity diagonals are the three sets of italicized values. The reliability diagonals are the three sets of values in parentheses. Each heterotrait-monomethod triangle is enclosed by a solid line. Each heterotrait-heteromethod triangle is enclosed by a broken line.

yet an inspection of the literature shows that it is frequently not met, and may not be met even when the validity coefficients are of substantial size. In Table 5.1, all of the validity values meet this requirement. A third common-sense desideratum is that a variable correlates higher with an independent effort to measure the same trait than with measures designed to get at different traits which happen to employ the same method. For a given variable, this involves comparing its values in the validity diagonals with its values in the heterotrait-monomethod triangles. For variables A_1, B_1, and C_1, this requirement is met to some degree. For the other variables, A_2, A_3 etc., it is not met and this is probably typical of the usual case in individual differences research, as will be discussed in what follows. A fourth desideratum is that the same pattern of trait interrelationship be shown in all of the heterotrait triangles of both the monomethod and heteromethod blocks. The hypothetical data in Table 5.1 meet this requirement to a very marked degree, in spite of the different general levels of correlation involved in the several heterotrait triangles. The last three criteria provide evidence for discriminant validity.

* * *

CONVERGENCE OF INDEPENDENT METHODS: THE DISTINCTION BETWEEN RELIABILITY AND VALIDITY Both reliability and validity concepts require that agreement between measures be demonstrated. A common denominator which most validity concepts share in contradistinction to reliability is that this agreement represents the convergence of independent approaches. The concept of independence is indicated by such phrases as "external variable," "criterion performance," "behavioral criterion" (American Psychological Association, 1954, pp. 13–15) used in connection with concurrent and predictive validity. For construct validity it has been stated thus: "Numerous successful predictions dealing with phenotypically diverse 'criteria' give greater weight to the claim of construct validity than do . . . predictions involving very similar behavior" (Cronbach & Meehl, 1955, p. 295). The importance of independence recurs in most discussions of proof. For example, Ayer, discussing a historian's belief about a past event, says "if these sources are numerous and independent, and if they agree with one another, he will be reasonably confident that their account of the matter is correct" (Ayer, 1956, p. 39). In discussing the manner in which abstract scientific concepts are tied to operations, Feigl speaks of their being "fixed" by "triangulation in logical space" (Feigl, 1958, p. 401).

Independence is, of course, a matter of degree, and in this sense, reliability and validity can be seen as regions on a continuum. (Cf. Thurstone, 1937, pp. 102–103.) Reliability is the agreement between two efforts to measure the same trait through maximally similar methods. Validity is represented in the agreement between two attempts to measure the same trait through maximally different methods. A split-half reliability is a little more like a validity coefficient than is an immediate test-retest reliability, for the items are not quite identical. A correlation between dissimilar subtests is probably a reliability measure, but is still closer to the region called validity.

Some evaluation of validity can take place even if the two methods are not entirely independent. In Table 5.1, for example, it is possible that Methods 1 and 2 are not entirely independent. If underlying Traits A and B are entirely independent, then the .10 minimum correlation in the heterotrait-heteromethod triangles may reflect method covariance. What if the overlap of method variance were higher? All correlations in the heteromethod block would then be elevated, including the validity diagonal. The heteromethod block involving Methods 2 and 3 in Table 5.1 illustrates this. The degree of elevation of the validity diagonal above the heterotrait-heteromethod triangles remains comparable and relative validity can still be evaluated. The interpretation of the validity diagonal in an absolute fashion requires the fortunate coincidence of both an independence of traits and an independence of methods, represented by zero values in the heterotrait-heteromethod triangles. But zero values could also occur through a combination of negative correlation between traits and positive correlation between methods, or the reverse. In practice, perhaps all that can be hoped for is evidence for relative validity, that is, for common variance specific to a trait, above and beyond shared method variance.

DISCRIMINANT VALIDATION While the usual reason for the judgment of invalidity is low correlations in the validity diagonal (e.g., the Downey Will-Temperament Test [Symonds, 1931, p. 337ff]) tests have also been invalidated because of too high correlations with other tests purporting to measure different things. The classic case of the social intelligence tests is a case in point. (See below and also Strang, 1930; R. Thorndike, 1936.) Such invalidation occurs when values in the heterotrait-heteromethod triangles are as high as those in the validity diagonal, or even where within a monomethod block, the heterotrait values are as high as the reliabilities. Loevinger, Gleser, and DuBois (1953) have emphasized this requirement in the development of maximally discriminating subtests.

When a dimension of personality is hypothesized, when a construct is proposed, the proponent invariably has in mind distinctions between the new dimension and other constructs already in use. One cannot define without implying distinctions, and the verification of these distinctions is an important part of the validational process. In discussions of construct validity, it has been expressed in such terms as "from this point of view, a low correlation with athletic ability may be just as important and encouraging as a high correlation with reading comprehension" (APA, 1954, p. 17).

THE TEST AS A TRAIT-METHOD UNIT In any given psychological measuring device, there are certain features or stimuli introduced specifically to represent the trait that it is intended to measure. There are other features which are characteristic of the method being employed, features which could also be present in efforts to measure other quite different traits. The test, or rating scale, or other device, almost inevitably elicits systematic variance in response due to both groups of features. To the extent that irrelevant method variance contributes to the scores obtained, these scores are invalid.

This source of invalidity was first noted in the "halo effects" found in ratings (E. Thorndike, 1920). Studies of individual differences among laboratory animals resulted in the recognition of "apparatus factors," usually more dominant than psychological process factors (Tryon, 1942). For paper-and-pencil tests, methods variance has been noted under such terms as "test-form factors" (Vernon, 1957, 1958) and "response sets" (Cronbach, 1946, 1950; Lorge, 1937). Cronbach has stated the point particularly clearly: "The assumption is generally made . . . that what the test measures is determined by the content of the items. Yet the final score . . . is a composite of effects resulting from the content of the item and effects resulting from the form of the item used" (Cronbach, 1946, p. 475). "Response sets always lower the logical validity of a test. . . . Response sets interfere with inferences from test data" (p. 484).

While E. L. Thorndike (1920) was willing to allege the presence of halo effects by comparing the high obtained correlations with common sense notions of what they ought to be (e.g., it was unreasonable that a teacher's intelligence and voice quality should correlate .63) and while much of the evidence of response set variance is of the same order, the clear-cut demonstration of the presence of method variance requires both several traits and several methods. Otherwise, high correlations between tests might be explained as due either to basic trait similarity or to shared method variance. In the multitrait-multimethod matrix, the presence of method variance is indicated by the difference in level of correlation between the parallel values of the monomethod block and the heteromethod blocks, assuming comparable reliabilities among all tests. Thus the contribution of method variance in Test A_1 of Table 5.1 is indicated by the elevation of r_{A1B1} above r_{A1B2}, i.e., the difference between .51 and .22, etc.

The distinction between trait and method is of course relative to the test constructor's intent. What is an unwanted response set for one tester may be a trait for another who wishes to measure acquiescence, willingness to take an extreme stand, or tendency to attribute socially desirable attributes to oneself (Cronbach, 1946, 1950; Edwards, 1957; Lorge, 1937).

* * *

Discussion

RELATION TO CONSTRUCT VALIDITY While the validational criteria presented are explicit or implicit in the discussions of construct validity (Cronbach & Meehl, 1955; APA, 1954), this paper is primarily concerned with the adequacy of tests as measures of a construct rather than with the adequacy of a construct as determined by the confirmation of theoretically predicted associations with measures of other constructs. We believe that before one can test the relationships between a specific trait and other traits, one must have some confidence in one's measures of that trait. Such confidence can be supported by evidence of convergent and discriminant validation. Stated in different words, any conceptual formulation of trait will usually include implicitly the proposition that this trait is a response tendency which can be observed under more than one experimental condition and that this trait can be meaningfully differentiated from other traits. The testing of these two propositions must be prior to the testing of other propositions to prevent the acceptance of erroneous conclusions. For example, a conceptual framework might postulate a large correlation between Traits A and B and no correlation between Traits A and C. If the experimenter then measures A and B by one method (e.g., questionnaire) and C by another method (such as the measurement of overt behavior in a situation test), his findings may be consistent with his hypotheses solely as a function of method variance common to his measures of A and B but not to C.

The requirements of this paper are intended to be as appropriate to the relatively atheoretical efforts typical of the tests and measurements field as to more theoretical efforts. This emphasis on validational criteria appropriate to our present atheoretical level of test construction is not at all incompatible with a recognition of the desirability of increasing the extent to which all aspects of a test and the testing situation are determined by explicit theoretical considerations, as Jessor and Hammond have advocated (Jessor & Hammond, 1957).

RELATION TO OPERATIONALISM Underwood (1957, p. 54) in his effective presentation of the operationalist point of view shows a realistic awareness of the amorphous type of theory with which most psychologists work. He contrasts a psychologist's "literary" conception with the latter's operational definition as represented by his test or other measuring instrument. He recognizes the importance of the literary definition in communicating and generating science. He cautions that the operational definition "may not at all measure the process he wishes to measure; it may measure something quite different" (1957, p. 55). He does not, however, indicate how one would know when one was thus mistaken.

The requirements of the present paper may be seen as an extension of the kind of operationalism Underwood has expressed. The test constructor is asked to generate from his literary conception or private construct not one operational embodiment, but two or more, each as different in research vehicle as possible. Furthermore, he is asked to make explicit the distinction between his new variable and other variables, distinctions which are almost certainly implied in his literary definition. In his very first validational efforts, before he ever rushes into print, he is asked to apply the several methods and several traits jointly. His literary definition, his conception, is now best represented in what his independent measures of the trait hold *distinctively* in common. The multitrait-multimethod matrix is, we believe, an important practical first step in avoiding "the danger . . . that the investigator will fall into the trap of thinking that because he went from an artistic or literary conception . . . to the construction of items for a scale to measure it, he has validated his artistic conception" (Underwood, 1957, p. 55). In contrast with the *single operationalism* now dominant in psychology, we are advocating a *multiple operationalism*, a *convergent operationalism* (Garner, 1954; Garner, Hake, & Eriksen, 1956), a *methodological triangulation* (Campbell, 1953, 1956), an *operational delineation* (Campbell, 1954), a *convergent validation.*

Underwood's presentation and that of this paper as a whole imply moving from concept to operation, a sequence that is frequent in science, and perhaps typical. The same point can be made, however, in inspecting a transition from operation to construct. For any body of data taken from a single operation, there is a subinfinity of interpretations possible; a subinfinity of concepts, or combinations of concepts, that it could represent. Any single operation, as representative of concepts, is equivocal. In an analogous fashion, when we view the Ames distorted room from a fixed point and through a single eye, the data of the retinal pattern are equivocal, in that a subinfinity of hexahedrons could generate the same pattern. The addition of a second viewpoint, as through binocular parallax, greatly reduces this equivocality, greatly limits the constructs that could jointly account for both sets of data. In Garner's (1954) study, the fractionation measures from a single method were equivocal—they could have been a function of the stimulus distance being fractionated, or they could have been a function of the comparison stimuli used in the judgment process. A multiple, convergent operationalism reduced this equivocality, showing the latter conceptualization to be the appropriate one, and revealing a preponderance of methods variance. Similarly for learning studies: in identifying constructs with the response data from animals in a specific operational setup there is equivocality which can operationally be reduced by introducing transposition tests, different operations so designed as to put to comparison the rival conceptualizations (Campbell, 1954).

Garner's convergent operationalism and our insistence on more than one method for measuring each concept depart from Bridgman's early position that "if we have more than one set of operations, we have more than one concept, and strictly there should be a separate name to correspond to each different set of operations" (Bridgman, 1927, p. 10). At the current stage of psychological progress, the crucial requirement is the demonstration of some convergence, not complete congruence, between two distinct sets of operations. With only one method, one has no way of distinguishing trait variance from unwanted method variance. When psychological measurement and conceptualization become better developed, it may well be appropriate to differentiate conceptually between Trait-Method Unit A_1 and Trait-Method Unit A_2, in which Trait A is measured by different methods. More likely, what we have called method variance will be specified theoretically in terms of a set of constructs. * * * It will then be recognized that measurement procedures usually involve several theoretical constructs in joint application. Using obtained measurements to estimate values for a single construct under this condition still requires comparison of complex measures varying in their trait composition, in something like a multitrait-multimethod matrix. Mill's joint method of similarities and differences still epitomizes much about the effective experimental clarification of concepts.

THE EVALUATION OF A MULTITRAIT-MULTIMETHOD MATRIX The evaluation of the correlation matrix formed by intercorrelating several trait-method units must take into consideration the many factors which are known to affect the magnitude of correlations. A value in the validity diagonal must be assessed in the light of the reliabilities of the two measures involved: e.g., a low reliability for Test A_2 might exaggerate the apparent method variance in Test A_1. Again, the whole approach assumes adequate sampling of individuals: The curtailment of the sample with respect to one or more traits will depress the reliability coefficients and intercorrelations involving these traits. While restrictions of range over all traits produce serious difficulties in the interpretation of a multitrait-multimethod matrix and should be avoided whenever possible, the presence of different degrees of restriction on different traits is the more serious hazard to meaningful interpretation.

Various statistical treatments for multitrait-multimethod matrices might be developed. We have considered rough tests for the elevation of a value in the validity diagonal above the comparison values in its row and column. Correlations between the columns for variables measuring the same trait, variance analyses, and factor analyses have been proposed to us. However, the development of such statistical methods is beyond the scope of this paper. We believe that such summary statistics are neither necessary nor appropriate at this time. Psychologists today should be concerned not with evaluating tests as if the tests were fixed and definitive, but rather with developing better tests. We believe that a careful examination of a multitrait-multimethod matrix will indicate to the experimenter what his next steps should be: it will indicate which methods should be discarded or replaced, which concepts need sharper delineation, and which concepts are poorly measured because of excessive or confounding method variance. Validity judgments based on such a matrix must take into account the stage of development of the constructs, the postulated relationships among them, the level of technical refinement of the methods, the relative independence of the methods, and any pertinent characteristics of the sample of Ss. We are proposing that the validational process be viewed as an aspect of an ongoing program for improving measuring procedures and that the "validity coefficients" obtained at any one stage in the process be interpreted in terms of gains over preceding stages and as indicators of where further effort is needed.

THE DESIGN OF A MULTITRAIT-MULTIMETHOD MATRIX The several methods and traits included in a validational matrix should be selected with care. The several methods used to measure each trait should be appropriate to the trait as conceptualized. Although this view will reduce the range of suitable methods, it will rarely restrict the measurement to one operational procedure.

Wherever possible, the several methods in one matrix should be completely independent of each other: there should be no prior reason for believing that they share method variance. This requirement is necessary to permit the values in the heteromethod-heterotrait triangles to approach zero. If the nature of the traits rules out such independence of methods, efforts should be made to obtain as much diversity as possible in terms of data-sources and classification processes. Thus, the classes of stimuli *or* the background situations, the experimental contexts, should be different. Again, the persons providing the observations should have different roles *or* the procedures for scoring should be varied.

Plans for a validational matrix should take into account the difference between the interpretations regarding convergence and discrimination. It is sufficient to demonstrate convergence between two clearly distinct methods which show little overlap in the heterotrait-heteromethod triangles. While agreement between several methods is desirable, convergence between two is a satisfactory minimal requirement. Discriminative validation is not so easily achieved. Just as it is impossible to prove the null hypothesis, or that some object does not exist, so one can never establish that a trait, as measured, is differentiated from all other traits. One can only show that this measure of Trait A has little overlap with those measures of B and C, and no dependable generalization beyond B and C can be made. For example, social poise could probably be readily discriminated from aesthetic interests, but it should also be differentiated from leadership.

Insofar as the traits are related and are expected to correlate with each other, the monomethod correlations will be substantial and heteromethod correlations between traits will also be positive. For ease of interpretation, it may be best to include in the matrix at least two traits, and preferably two sets of traits, which are postulated to be independent of each other.

In closing, a word of caution is needed. Many multitrait-multimethod matrices will show no convergent validation: no relationship may be found between two methods of measuring a trait. In this common situation, the experimenter should examine the evidence in favor of several alternative propositions: (a) Neither method is adequate for measuring the trait. (b) One of the two methods does not really measure the trait. (When the evidence indicates that a method does not measure the postulated trait, it may prove to measure some other trait. High correlations in the heterotrait-heteromethod triangles may provide hints to such possibilities.) (c) The trait is not a functional unity, the response tendencies involved being specific to the nontrait attributes of each test. The failure to demonstrate convergence may lead to conceptual developments rather than to the abandonment of a test.

* * *

References

American Psychological Association (1954). Technical recommendations for psychological tests and diagnostic techniques. *Psychological Bulletin Supplement, 51*, Part 2, 1–38.

Ayer, A. J. (1956). *The problem of knowledge*. New York: St Martin's Press.

Bridgman, P. W. (1927). *The logic of modern physics*. New York: Macmillan.

Campbell, D. T. (1953). *A study of leadership among submarine officers*. Columbus, OH: Ohio State University Research Foundation.

Campbell, D. T. (1954). Operational delineation of "what is learned" via the transposition experiment. *Psychological Review, 61*, 167–174.

Campbell, D. T. (1956). *Leadership and its effects upon the group*. Monograph No. 83. Columbus, OH: Ohio State University Bureau of Business Research.

Cronbach, L. J. (1946). Response sets and test validity. *Educational and Psychological Measurement, 6*, 475–494.

Cronbach, L. J. (1950). Further evidence on response sets and test design. *Educational and Psychological Measurement, 10*, 3–31.

Cronbach, L. J., & Meehl, P. E (1955). Construct validity in psychological tests. *Psychological Bulletin, 52*, 281–302.

Edwards, A. L. (1957). *The social desirability variable in personality assessment and research*. New York: Dryden.

Feigl, H. (1958). The mental and the physical. In H. Feigl, M. Scriven, & G. Maxwell (Eds.), *Minnesota studies in the philosophy of science*. Vol. II. *Concepts, theories and the mind-body problem*. Minneapolis: University of Minnesota Press.

Garner, W. R. (1954). Context effects and the validity of loudness scales. *Journal of Experimental Psychology, 48*, 218–224.

Garner, W. R., Hake, H. W., & Eriksen, C. W. (1956). Operationism and the concept of perception. *Psychological Review, 63*, 149–159.

Jessor, R., & Hammond, K. R. (1957). Construct validity and the Taylor Anxiety Scale. *Psychological Bulletin, 54*, 161–170.

Loevinger, J., Gleser, G. C., & DuBois, P. H. (1953). Maximizing the discriminating power of a multiple-score test. *Psychometrika, 18*, 309–317.

Lorge, I. (1937). Gen-like: Halo or reality? *Psychological Bulletin, 34*, 545–546.

Strang, R. (1930). Relation of social intelligence to certain other factors. *Schools and Sociology, 32*, 268–272.

Symonds, P. M. (1931). *Diagnosing personality and conduct.* New York: Appleton-Century.

Thorndike, E. L. (1920). A constant error in psychological ratings. *Journal of Applied Psychology, 4*, 25–29.

Thorndike, R. L. (1936). Factor analysis of social and abstract intelligence. *Journal of Educational Psychology, 27*, 231–233.

Thurstone, L. L. (1937). *The reliability and validity of tests.* Ann Arbor: Edwards.

Tryon, R. C. (1942). Individual differences. In F. A. Moss (Ed.), *Comparative Psychology.* (2nd ed., pp. 330–365) New York: Prentice-Hall.

Underwood, B. J. (1957). *Psychological research.* New York: Appleton-Century-Crofts.

Vernon, P. E. (1957). Educational ability and psychological factors. Address given to the Joint Education-Psychology Colloquium, University of Illinois, March 29, 1957.

Vernon, P. E. (1958). *Educational testing and test-form factors.* (Res. Bull. RB-58-3.) Princeton: Educational Testing Service.

Conceptual Analysis of Psychological Test Scores and Other Diagnostic Variables

Harrison G. Gough

What do you need to know to interpret an individual's score on a personality test? In the previous two selections, by Cronbach and Meehl and by Campbell and Fiske, we saw how it is important to know how the test correlates with other measures of personality. In the present, classic selection, Harrison Gough, developer of the California Psychological Inventory (CPI), argues that test interpretation must go further than that.

According to Gough, test interpretation occurs at three levels, which he calls primary, secondary, *and* tertiary. *Primary evaluation includes most of what was discussed in the previous two selections, such as assessing the degree to which a test correlates with other measures that it should be related to, and does not correlate with other measures that it should* not *be related to. In secondary evaluation, the psychologist attempts to understand the underlying psychological dimensions that the test measures and that produced the correlations observed during primary evaluation. In tertiary evaluation, according to Gough's most original and complex idea, a psychologist should gather data that allow for surprises. If a test turns out to correlate with some completely unexpected and seemingly unrelated behavior, this finding could be an important clue for understanding the meaning of the test score and the psychological dynamics of the person taking the test.*

Gough illustrates these three levels of test interpretation with an examination of the socialization scale of his CPI but is describing a process that could and probably should be applied to every new personality test. Up to the present day, however, most test developers use a more arms-length approach, evaluating tests in terms of correlations with other tests. The kind of in-depth understanding of the psychological dynamics underlying a test score that Gough believes is so important is sought only rarely.

From *Journal of Abnormal Psychology*, 70, 294–302, 1965.

The purpose of this paper is to offer a point of view concerning the meaning of measurement in psychology. Attention is centered on the use or application of such measures, and what they tell the interpreter about the individual who has been tested. Significant prior discussions of the validity issue in testing and diagnosis have sought to classify tests according to the criteria employed in their construction and evaluation (cf. Cronbach & Meehl, 1955), and to specify ways in which discriminations may be sharpened (cf. Campbell & Fiske, 1959). These emphases are important, but nevertheless do not touch on all of the significant facets of meaning subsumed under the concept of validity. The intention here is to present a different perspective, one which stresses the implications of any scale or variable when it is brought to bear upon the analysis of the individual case.

From this perspective, the practitioner in testing seeks variables which permit individuated descriptions of the subject who has been tested, forecasts of what he will say or do, and characterizations of the way in which others will react to him. The greater the range of such information, and the more accurate its specification, the greater the value of the instrument which produced it.

* * *

Two assumptions in this formulation are (*a*) that the purpose of the rest is to assess and/or forecast significant nontest behavior, and (*b*) that the test is intended ultimately for interpretation and analysis of the individual case. A third principle is that the organization and application of this knowledge can only be realized through the endeavors of the trained, professional practitioner.

Our problem in defining criteria of validity and meaning is therefore to keep in mind the needs of the clinician who will interpret the tests, and the individual case which provides the fundamental context for their application. This task is not easy, and it is not expected that all readers will agree with the solution attempted in this paper. It may even be that each practitioner must solve these issues for himself, or try to solve them, and that no single proposal can win general acceptance. The only warrant for the present effort, if this is true, is that even in disagreement the reader may be stimulated to new considerations and perhaps to a more logical and clinically meaningful personal perspective.

The Conceptual Model

Let us begin with a brief formulation of the conceptual model to be proposed, and after that move to more extended discussion of its components and to illustrative examples. This model is organized around three stages in the evaluative processes, that is, three foci of understanding which the interpreter must fully comprehend if he is to achieve an adequate conceptualization of a diagnostic variable. The first of these emphases may be designated the *primary evaluation.* The task here is to determine what criteria are principally relevant to the test, how well it predicts what it seeks to predict, measures what it purports to measure, or defines what it is intended to define. Most of what is said about test validity in textbooks and manuals may be classified under this first heading.

Secondary evaluation seeks to discover the psychological basis of measurement, to specify and clarify the meaning of that which is measured. A scale may forecast some important nontest behavior, such as the likelihood of improvement in psychotherapy, and thus meet the requirements of our primary evaluation; but the clinician needs to know more than this, he must know what it is that the scale reflects that leads to this favorable potentiality. The task is to uncover and hence illuminate the underlying psychological dimensionality that is inherent in any test or measure possessing primary utility. When we return for specific consideration of this topic I shall attempt to enumerate explicit steps which can be taken in pursuit of this psychological (to be distinguished from psychometric) understanding.

Tertiary evaluation is perhaps more difficult to define than the other two concepts. It is concerned with the justification for developing a particular measure, or for calling attention to a measure.

Part of this justification will come from the intrinsic significance of the primary aim of measurement, and part may come from the range of implications delineated in the secondary analysis. But additional and possibly even greater significance may come from the spectrum of life settings, beyond any envisaged under its primary validity, for which the technique has predictive and explanatory relevance.

An ability test might be developed with a primary goal of predicting success in school; on analysis, it is found that it does this satisfactorily, but perhaps no more so than many other such tests. Under secondary evaluation it is discovered that the key psychological variable which seems to be involved is the ability to reorganize and recombine perceptions and experiences, rather than the memory for facts and events which predominates in other devices. Our interest in this new test might now be heightening. But suppose that on the tertiary level we find, contrary to nearly all research with "ordinary" scholastic aptitude tests, that our new device appears to relate significantly to indices of creative and original endeavor, and that its forecasting efficiency becomes better and better as we move farther and farther away from the explicitly academic criteria in whose behalf it was initially constructed.

This kind of evidence is just what one seeks in the tertiary analysis; it is the kind of evidence which arouses the special interest of the clinician and which justifies his paying special attention to the instrument which possesses it.

Primary Evaluation

It might be useful to link the discussions of each of the three stages of analysis by offering observations of a single diagnostic variable under each heading. For this purpose I should like to utilize the So or "socialization" scale of the *California Psychological Inventory* (Gough, 1957). The CPI is a true-false objective inventory scaled for "folk concepts," that is, variables used for the description and analysis of personality in everyday life and in social interaction. It is theorized that such folk concepts, viewed as emergents from interpersonal behavior, have a kind of immediate meaningfulness and universal relevance which enhance their attractiveness as diagnostic concepts. Hopefully, diagnoses and forecasts of social behavior, if mediated by such concepts, will be more accurate and dependable than forecasts arrived at by way of other formulations.

* * *

* * * The primary validational task of the socialization scale is to locate individuals and groups along a continuum of asocial to social behavior, and to forecast the likelihood that any person will transgress whatever dividing line his own culture interposes between these two poles of the continuum. The phrase "his own culture" is used intentionally, because the folk concept theoretical basis of the inventory requires that its validity be demonstrated in other cultures than the one in which the sale is developed.

The So scale was first introduced in 1952 (Gough & Peterson, 1952). In 1960 a report was published (Gough, 1960b) which surveyed validational evidence obtained in the preceding 8-year period. For males, 25 samples involving 10,296 cases were considered, ranging from nominated "best citizens," through occupational samples of varying kinds, disciplinary problems, and county jail inmates, to incarcerated delinquents and felons. The biserial correlation for the dichotomy of more- versus less-socialized was +.73. For females, 16 samples totaling 10,560 subjects were studied, covering the same continuum of socialization; the biserial correlation here was +.78.[1]

Primary validation evidence for classification

[1]These are very high correlations. According to Rosenthal and Rubin's binomial effect size display (see reprint in the present volume), a correlation of .78 reflects an ability to correctly predict degree of socialization (high or low) 89 times out of 100. Some of the other correlations reported later in this article are near the more usually seen (but still impressive) level of about .40 (which would translate to 70 correct predictions out of 100).

of individuals along the full extent of the socialization continuum would appear adequate. The next question pertains to differentiation within zones or regions of the continuum. An interesting finding with respect to this question comes from the work of Vincent (1961) on unmarried mothers; for a sample of 232 women the biserial correlation between the So scale and the dichotomy of one illegitimate pregnancy versus two or more was +.83. Highly significant differences between recidivists and first offenders were found in studies of reformatory inmates (Donald, 1955) and juvenile offenders (Peterson, Quay, & Anderson, 1959).

Cross-cultural validation has been equally encouraging. For a sample of 203 institutionalized delinquents in India, tested in Hindi and Punjabi (Gough & Sandhu, 1964), the So scale correlated +.73 with court-assigned classifications of the severity of the offense. Just now we are reviewing data from Austria, Costa Rica, France, Germany, Italy, Japan, Puerto Rico, South Africa, and Switzerland, comparing delinquent versus nondelinquent samples of males and females. Nine countries are involved in this survey, and translations of the So scale into six languages: Afrikaans, French, German, Italian, Japanese, and Spanish. In every comparison the So scale has differentiated significantly between delinquents and nondelinquents; and, considering all samples, in no instances does the average for any sample of delinquents (no matter from which country or place) equal or exceed the lowest average score observed among the samples of nondelinquents.

* * *

The evidence just reviewed for the So scale is the kind of evidence we customarily expect on validity, and it is the kind of evidence which we must establish in our primary evaluation. The evaluation is primary because it comes first, and because there is no reason to follow a measure on into the realms of secondary and tertiary evaluation unless we are reasonably satisfied that its primary utility is established.

Secondary Evaluation

We are now ready to undertake a secondary evaluation of the So scale. Our aim here, to repeat, is to clarify the basis of measurement, that is, to determine what it is that the scale reveals about a person beyond the fact that he will probably behave in a more- or less-socialized manner. The four steps enumerated below are offered as aids in the accomplishing of this conceptual analysis.

Step 1. Review of the development of the measure, the procedures and samples used in its construction, its theoretical presuppositions and bases.

Step 2. Analysis of the components of the measure, its items, stimulus materials, and content.

Step 3. Determination of the relationships between the measure and (*a*) other measures already known and conceptualized, and (*b*) variables of self-evident importance such as sex, age, status, etc.

Step 4. Specification of the characterological and personological dispositions of individuals who obtain scores defined by the measure itself as diagnostically significant.

A primary evaluation will already have provided some of the information envisaged under Step 1, but other matters await consideration. Perhaps the most important of these is the conceptual basis of the measure. The So scale was initially conceived in the context of role theory. The less-socialized person was hypothesized to be less skillful in sensing and interpreting subtle and covert cues in social interaction, and hence less likely to evolve dependable and veridical internalized systems of control. Indirect evidence of such role-taking disability would be found in rule-breaking and rule-violating behavior, and direct evidence would be found in tests of the accuracy of role perspectives and interpersonal diagnosis.

In the construction of So, samples ranging from seriously delinquent through moderately delinquent to conventionally socialized were used, and item studies undertaken so as to identify those possessing validity for this continuum. The assumption here, the reader will recognize, is that one's manifest location along the socialization continuum will on the average provide a valid estimate of one's role-taking proficiency. Whether or not this assumption is true or partly true, a more direct test of the hypothesis is clearly needed.

To date, the most thorough check of this sort is found in a paper in 1957 by Reed and Cuadra. They studied 204 student nurses in a neuropsychiatric hospital. Each nurse described herself on the Gough Adjective Check List (ACL) (Gough, 1960a; Gough & Heilbrun, 1965) and then the other three nurses in a four-member group to which each was assigned. Next, each nurse attempted to guess how she would be described by her group. A point was earned for a predicted adjective if two of the three peers had, in fact, checked this word, and a total score was defined as the sum of these points. This score is therefore representative of the accuracy with which an individual senses the reactions of others to her, that is, of the degree to which she can take the role of the other and look upon self as an object. The correlation between the So scale and this social sensitivity index was +.41.

* * *

Recapitulating briefly the information under Step 1, we can say that the scale may be conceptualized from the role-taking perspective and that there is both direct and indirect evidence for its validity from this perspective.

Step 2 takes us into the content of the scale. Here we find that its 54 items are about equally distributed over two kinds of content. The first of these more or less directly embodies role-taking ideas, and may be instanced by these items: "Before I do something I try to consider how my friends will react to it," "I often think about how I look and what impression I am making upon others," and "I find it easy to 'drop' or 'break with' a friend."

The other group of items has more immediate relevance to deviant or rule-breaking behavior, this being justified by the aforementioned hypothesis that asocial deviation is itself an indicator of the role-taking disability. Examples of this second type of item are: "I have often gone against my parents' wishes," and "If the pay was right I would like to travel with a circus or carnival."

The task for the practitioner in this second step is to internalize the content of the scale, and by virtue of this intimate familiarity to enhance the insightfulness of the psychodynamic formulation which is being evolved. The clinician who has studied and restudied the Rorschach inkblots and the cards of the Thematic Apperception Test need not be told that this second step, the personal, intense, apperceptive, and empathic perusal of the stimulus materials included in the scale or instrument is one of compelling importance and significance. It is unfortunate indeed that this step, invariably taken by projective testers, is only occasionally taken by psychologists in the ranks of objective or structured testing.[2]

Step 3 concerns the relationships of the measure to other measures and to major categories of interpersonal variation. Perhaps the first question that should be asked of any test or scale being studied is "does it show a sex difference?" and the second "is it correlated with intelligence?" Among nondelinquent samples, both in the United States and elsewhere, the So scale does reveal a consistent sex difference of about half a standard deviation, with women scoring higher. One is tempted to say "as would be expected," as many would assert that women are in fact more law-abiding, more sensitive and perceptive, and more highly refined and elaborated in their role-taking. However, when attention is directed to delinquent and institution-

[2]The Rorschach and Thematic Apperception tests are "projective" tests, in which assessees' responses to ambiguous stimuli (inkblots, drawings) are interpreted. The CPI is an example of a structured test. Here Gough is suggesting that the deep understanding of assessees' responses routinely sought by users of projective tests also should be sought by users of structured tests. Even today, few users of structured tests do this.

alized samples, women tend to score a bit lower than their male counterparts.

Role-taking skill, if that is the underlying variable in the So scale, is probably correlated with intellect, but one would nonetheless hope that a personological measure could be defined which would be free of this particular component. The evidence seems to suggest that So is not correlated with intellectual ability. In seven or eight samples of fairly good size, varying with respect to age, educational level, etc., the correlations fall within a band of −.14 to +.10, with a median of close to .00.

* * *

Social status is another variable of interest. In several high schools the So scale yielded a median coefficient of +.11 with the Home Index (Gough, 1949), a measure of the socioeconomic status of the home and family background. Race differences have also been investigated, by Donald (1955) and Peterson et al. (1959) in the studies previously mentioned; in both instances Negro and white delinquents were *not* differentiated on the So scale.[3]

* * *

A great deal of information of this sort is offered in the CPI *Manual* (Gough, 1957), and may be consulted there by anyone wishing to push further into this third category. What has been presented is believed to be representative, and would seem to justify the conclusion that the So scale is a relatively independent variable, not contaminated by or unduly influenced by such factors as social desirability, status, anxiety, race, intellectual ability, or ego strength. Hence, it is not to be "explained" or "explained away" by such factors, but must be dealt with in its own right.

This leads us to Step 4, and a consideration of the immediate and direct personological implications of the scale. Although the previous steps are of interest to the clinician, and in fact vital if he wishes to reach a sophisticated and professional level of insight concerning any measure, it is the fourth step which comes closest to a direct delineation of the psychological meaning of a variable.

There are different ways of developing the information called for by this fourth step. One is the time-tested method of the individual clinician, who notes over the years of his practice what it is that characterizes patients scoring high or low on a particular test index—their defenses, their strengths, attitudes, self-conceptions, and stylistic predilections. The problem in this approach is that, even if valid, it takes years of patient accumulation of evidence before any sort of pattern begins to emerge. The need is for a faster and more efficient technique which retains the essential validity of the clinician's observations but shortens the time necessary to obtain them and to process them.

The personality assessment method, as practiced at the Institute of Personality Assessment and Research in Berkeley and at other centers, is exceedingly well adapted to do just this. Subjects come to the Institute in small numbers, and are studied intensively for 3 or 4 days by a panel of from 5 to 10 psychologists. Trait ratings, interviewers' formulations, *Q*-sort appraisals, and adjective check list descriptions are systematically gathered on all assessees. These sources of observational and diagnostic data may then be related back to the test scores of the assessees. The process is perhaps most clearly illustrated by ACL analyses, and only ACL data will therefore be drawn on in the discussion to follow.

Suppose 10 observers in assessment each complete a 300-word Gough Adjective Check List on an assessee. Any trait or quality which is above threshold in the eyes of the observer is checked, and any which is not is left blank. A convenient composite can be derived from these 10 individual descriptions simply by counting the number of times a word is checked, and treating that total as a score. Thus, if an assessee Adams is checked by all 10 observers as "alert" his score on this interpersonal quality or trait is 10; if 2 observers check him as "blustery" his score is 2; and if no one checks him as "charming" his score is zero. Ad-

[3]"Negro" was the conventional term in 1965 for referring to African Americans; here Gough is pointing to a *lack* of difference between blacks and whites on the So scale.

ams will in this way be assigned 300 scores, 1 for each adjective.

If a sample of assessees has been described by the same panel of observers, these adjectival scores may be treated correlationally. A test variable, for example, the So scale, may be correlated with each of the 300 words in this sample of assessees. Adjectives showing significant and positive correlations are those which tend to be used to characterize high scorers on the scale, and hence afford a conceptual starting point for a personological sketch of the high scorer. Likewise with adjectives showing significant and negative correlations with the scale: those are the words that are in fact differentially used to characterize low scorers and they afford a valid starting point for a personological formulation of the low scorer. I believe that this procedure is intrinsically valid, and that it offers an efficient and powerful method for the psychological analysis of any variable that can be dichotomized or quantified. * * *

This method of analysis has been applied five or six times to the So scale. I should like to draw on four of these analyses, one based on a sample of 295 adult males, a second on a sample of 80 university graduate students, a third on a sample of 51 college seniors, and the fourth a sample of 100 military personnel studied by Reed and Cuadra. The first two samples are male, the third female, and the fourth includes both males and females; in three samples the observations were contributed by psychologists who had studied the assessees, and in the last the descriptions were furnished by peers. The purpose in using all four samples is to overcome any limitations which might attach to a particular setting, use of professional versus peer evaluations, and to sex differences.

From these four independent analyses, those adjectives correlating in the same direction with the So scale in all four instances, and at a statistically significant level in at least two are presented below:

A. Adjectives used significantly more often to describe high scorers on the So scale.

calm	conventional	helpful
considerate	cooperative	moderate
modest	peaceable	unassuming
obliging	steady	
patient	trusting	

B. Adjectives used significantly more often to describe low scorers on the So scale.

affected	disorderly	irritable
arrogant	dissatisfied	rebellious
conceited	headstrong	restless
cynical	impatient	self-centered
defensive	impulsive	wary

A comment should be interjected here. Some psychologists, perhaps not given to thinking clinically, seem to be more bothered than helped by such a list of attributes. Such persons, one fears, are beyond the reach of the theoretical position being advocated in this paper. These adjectival clusters represent only the elements of clinical description, that is to say, protocol observations. From this starting point it is the interpreter's task to evolve an insightful diagnostic portrait of the high and low scorer on the scale, to render this evidence into an integrated formulation relevant for practice and understanding. The achievement of such a formulation requires all of the creativity that the interpreter can muster. But whatever its difficulty, the task must be attempted, for the elaboration of a psychological dynamic of the test variable is at the very heart of the conceptual analysis which is being illustrated.

Tertiary Evaluation

We come now to the third perspective, that of tertiary analysis. Is there any reason for paying attention to a scale or variable if one is not interested in its primary validational focus, that is, with respect to the So scale, in the problem of asocial versus socialized behavior?

Let us say that we grant that So can forecast asocial behavior with a surprisingly high degree of accuracy, and that it rests on a rather interesting theoretical and personological basis. Let us grant further that it is free of nuisance correlations with such variables as response sets, intellectual ability, and socioeconomic status. But if we are not working in a prison or juvenile hall, and if we are not concerned with identifying asocial dispositions, is there any other reason for studying this scale and for learning how to utilize it clinically? These are the questions met in the tertiary evaluation, questions which a systematic theory of test meaning must attempt to answer. We need to show, in other words, that the variable is in fact of significance in situations other than those encompassed by its domain of primary relevance.

For the So scale, three examples of such tertiary significance may be offered. The first comes from work on differential achievement among persons of unusually high intellectual talent. In 1955 a nationwide sample of high school and college students was surveyed (Gough, 1955), searching for correlates of differential academic achievement among students in the top 5% to 10% of the aptitude distribution. The one variable from the CPI which stood out above all others was the So scale: its correlations were significant for both sexes and at both educational levels. Superior achievement, as evidenced by grades, was associated with higher So scores. Note, in considering these results, that the So scale shows little or no correlation with grades if an unselected sample is studied. * * *

These findings led to the theoretical formulation that consistent use of high-level talent in the academic setting is more a matter of socialization and the cathexis[4] of approved goals and objectives than of achievement motivation per se, or of ambition as ordinarily defined and appraised, or of negative spurs such as anxiety and self-doubt.

This early study was followed by a much larger and more definitive analysis by Holland in 1959, in which freshman grades in college were forecast for a sample of 1,321 National Merit Scholarship corporation finalists. Holland found that the So scale gave valid forecasts of achievement as reflected in grades, and he also observed that the correlations for the So scale were two and three times as high as those for the Scholastic Aptitude Tests given after the finalists had already been selected.

Here, then, is one domain of functioning—academic achievement among the intellectually gifted—in which the So scale has a special significance and in which it can make a contribution which up to this time has been matched by no other variable.

A second example of a tertiary implication comes from studies of college graduation. It is known that only 40% to 50% of all students who begin college go on to graduation. This is a serious problem to educators, behavioral scientists, and everyone else. Would the So scale, administered at entry into college, be of any diagnostic value in identifying potential dropouts? The author is just finishing a large study of 3,242 students from seven classes in six colleges, in which CPI scales and Scholastic Aptitude Test scores are being compared on their forecasting efficiency. All test scores were obtained at the time of admission to college, and criteria on graduation versus dropping out were obtained 4 or more years later.

The aptitude test scores do not differeniate very well, contrary to the expectations of most psychologists. Such tests do predict GPA in college, but evidence is mounting that they bear less relationship to criteria of either rate of progress or survival (cf. Glimp & Whitla, 1964). The So scale, on the other hand, appears to be a useful predictor of graduation. Potential graduates achieve higher So scores at admission, and potential dropouts attain lower scores.

But is there an important social criterion on which persons with lower So scores excel? Certainly we should not expect or wish that in any and all situations the more conventional, more stringently self-regulated, and more interpersonally adaptable individual would do best. One such happy exception is found in the studies of creativity. Barron (1961) in his comparison of creative and journeyman writers found the former to score significantly lower on the So scale. MacKinnon (1961) in his study with Hall of 124 American

[4]"Cathexis" is a psychodynamic term referring to an emotional investment in or acceptance of something, in this case conventional achievement goals.

architects obtained the same findings. The most creative architects scored lowest on the So scale, the least creative scored highest, and the intermediate group on creativity occupied an intermediate point on the So distribution.

Conclusion

What is the purpose of the method of analysis presented in this paper? Its principal goal is to specify the kind of information and comprehension needed by the practitioner of testing. The position taken is that the user of any test must become intimately and fully familiar with all of the kinds of evidence sketched here for the So scale if he is to apply the instrument in a responsible and professional manner. Analysis of the conceptual problem into primary, secondary, and tertiary components may help him to keep straight what he must do, and may indicate the kinds of information he must discover and then assimilate. Out of all this he seeks to determine what it is that he can say about the individual who has been tested. The hope is to achieve a true, profound, and individual portrait of the person being appraised.

* * *

* * * This paper has dealt almost entirely with what one must do to arrive at an adequate comprehension of one component of one test; certainly it is evident that this is only a first step toward the kind of organized and insightful interpretation of profiles and test batteries which is the ultimate goal of the clinician in diagnosis. This inspiring and ultimate edifice of test usage, clearly, can only be constructed from building blocks of the highest quality; our need, therefore, is to delineate principles which can at each level contribute significantly to the generation of valid, dependable, and diagnostically relevant information.

References

Barron, F. (1961). Creative vision and expression in writing and painting. In *Proceedings of the Tahoe Conference on the Creative Person* (Part II, pp. 1–19). Berkeley, Calif.: Liberal Arts Department, University Extension, University of California.

Campbell, D. T., & Fiske, D. W. Convergent and discriminant validation by the multitrait-multimethod matrix. *Psychological Bulletin, 56,* 81–105.

Cronbach, L. J., & Meehl, P. E. (1955). Construct validity in psychological tests. *Psychological Bulletin, 52,* 281–302.

Donald, E. P. (1955). Personality scale analysis of new admission to a reformatory. Unpublished master's thesis, Ohio State University.

Glimp, F. L., & Whitla, D. K. (1964). Admissions and performance in college. *Harvard Alumni Bulletin, 66*(7), 304–309.

Gough, H. G. (1949). A short social status inventory. *Journal of Educational Psychology, 40,* 52–56.

Gough, H. G. (1955, September). Factors related to differential achievement among gifted persons. In P. A. Witty (Chm.), The gifted child. Symposium presented at the American Psychological Association, San Francisco.

Gough, H. G. (1957). *Manual for the California Psychological Inventory.* Palo Alto: Consulting Psychologists Press.

Gough, H. G. (1960a). The Adjective Check List as a personality assessment research technique. *Psychological Reports, 6,* 107–122.

Gough, H. G. (1960b). Theory and measurement of socialization. *Journal of Consulting Psychology, 24,* 23–30.

Gough, H. G., & Heilbrun, A. B., Jr. (1965). *Manual for the Adjective Check List.* Palo Alto: Consulting Psychologists Press.

Gough, H. G., & Peterson, D. R. (1952). The identification and measurement of predispositional factors in crime and delinquency. *Journal of Consulting Psychology, 16,* 207–212.

Gough, H. G., & Sandhu, H. S. (1964). Validation of the CPI Socialization scale in India. *Journal of Abnormal and Social Psychology, 68,* 544–547.

Holland, J. L. (1959). The prediction of college grades from the California Psychological Inventory and the Scholastic Aptitude Test. *Journal of Educational Psychology, 50,* 135–142.

MacKinnon, D. W. (1961). Creativity in architects. In *Proceedings of the Tahoe Conference on the Creative Person* (Part V, pp. 1–24). Berkeley, Calif.: Liberal Arts Department, University Extension, University of California.

Peterson, D. R., Quay, H. C., & Anderson, A. C. (1959). Extending the construct validity of a socialization scale. *Journal of Consulting Psychology, 23,* 182.

Reed, C. F., & Cuadra, C. A. (1957). The role-taking hypothesis in delinquency. *Journal of Consulting Psychology, 21,* 386–390.

Vincent, C. (1961). *Unmarried mothers.* New York: Free Press of Glencoe.

Do People Know How They Behave? Self-Reported Act Frequencies Compared with On-line Codings by Observers

Samuel D. Gosling, Oliver P. John, Kenneth H. Craik, and Richard W. Robins

Self-reports of personality and behavior are by far the most commonly used method of personality assessment. As we saw in the earlier selections by McAdams and by Block, however, other methods are available as well. One particularly interesting possibility is to observe directly the behavior of research participants and record on videotape what they do. The use of such a method immediately raises interesting questions, such as, What is the relationship between behavior as recorded on-line and behavior as reported by the person being observed?

This selection reports data that address this question directly, comparing self-reports of behavior with counts of these same behaviors as recorded off of videotaped interactions. As the data quickly reveal, such a comparison raises issues that go beyond a mere methodological comparison of self-reports and observers' ratings. Some of the discrepancies illustrate interesting psychological processes such as self-enhancement *(striving to appear in a more favorable light than is objectively justifiable) and personality traits such as* narcissism *(the disposition to habitually practice self-enhancement).*

Which illustrates a still broader point: Discrepancies between sources of data about personality often are more than merely errors to be explained away. They can be clues to interesting and important psychological processes that deserve research attention.

From *Journal of Personality and Social Psychology, 74,* 1397–1349, 1998.

"You interrupted my mother at least three times this morning" exclaims Roger. "That's not true," responds Julia, "I only interrupted her *once*!" And so the discussion continues. Disagreements about who did and did not do what are commonplace in social interactions. When such disagreements arise, whom should we believe? Perhaps Julia was distorting the truth to paint a favorable picture of herself. Alternatively, Roger may remember that Julia interrupted his mother, when really the conversation was interrupted by a telephone call; or perhaps Julia was so caught up with what she was trying to say that she did not notice that Roger's mother had not finished speaking. When caught in such situations, many of us, convinced that we are right, wish that somehow past events had been recorded on videotape so that we could triumphantly rewind the tape and reveal the veracity of our own reports. Unfortunately, in everyday life, no such video is available.

In the present study, however, we compared individuals' reports of their behavior with observer codings of their behavior from videotapes. Specifically, participants interacted in a 40-min group discussion task and then reported how frequently they had performed a set of acts. Observers later coded (from videotapes) the frequency with which each participant had performed each act. Thus, this design allowed us to compare retrospective act frequency reports by the self with on-line act frequency codings by observers.[1] Specifically, we examined whether individuals can accurately report how they behaved in a specific situation, and when and why their reports are discrepant from observer codings of their behavior. Understanding the processes that lead to accurate judgments about act performances is fundamental to the study of social perception.

* * *

The present research examined the following questions. First, to what extent do people agree about how often an act occurred? For example, do Julia's self-reports of her behavior agree with Roger's reports of her behavior, and will Roger agree with other observers about Julia's behavior? Second, what makes an act easy to judge? That is, are there some attributes or properties intrinsic to a given act that influence the degree to which both self and observer agree about its occurrence? Third, do people accurately report what they did in a particular situation? For example, did Julia really interrupt Roger's mother only once? Fourth, are self-reports of specific acts biased by a motive to self-enhance, and are some individuals more likely to self-enhance than others? For example, does Julia tend to exaggerate her desirable behaviors?

The present research builds on recent investigations of the determinants of agreement and accuracy in personality judgments. For example, John and Robins (1993, 1994) and Kenny (1994) found observer–observer agreement in trait judgments to be consistently higher than self–observer agreement. Furthermore, Funder and Colvin (1988) and John and Robins (1993) found trait properties, such as observability, social desirability, and location within the five-factor model (FFM) of personality structure (John, 1990), to be related to observer–observer and self–observer agreement in trait judgments. Finally, John and Robins (1994) found that self-judgments at the trait level are influenced by self-enhancement bias, which in turn is associated with individual variations in narcissism. Ozer and Buss (1991) have begun to address issues of this kind at the level of act frequency reports. They showed, for example, that agreement between retrospective observer and self act frequency reports is higher for acts associated with Extraversion but lower for acts associated with Agreeableness.

The present study extends this line of inquiry by examining determinants of agreement and accuracy using on-line act reports by observers and retrospective act reports by the self. On-line observer reports warrant study because in aggregated form they represent an important criterion for act occurrence. Retrospective self-reports warrant study because the self is an ever-present monitor of act occurrence and because the self enjoys a distinctive and, in certain respects, privileged vantage point for interpreting the nature of acts as they are performed. At the same time, however, self-reports are vulnerable to self-enhancement and other biases. Below we formulate hypotheses

[1]By *on-line codings*, we mean that observers coded and recorded acts as they occurred rather than relying on memory.—Authors

based on self-concept theory and previous research in the act and trait domains.

How Well Do People Agree About How Often an Act Occurred?

Two types of agreement can be distinguished: agreement between observers (observer–observer agreement) and agreement between observers and the targets' own self-reports of their behavior (self–observer agreement). Bem (1967, 1972) and other cognitive-informational self-theorists have argued that individuals perceive their own behavior in much the same way as external observers do: the way individuals perceive themselves should, therefore, correspond closely with the way they are perceived by others. This view suggests that self and observer reports of act frequencies should show substantial convergence, especially when the reports concern an interaction situation that is brief and clearly delimited.

In contrast, studies of global trait judgments (Funder & Colvin, 1997; John & Robins, 1993; Kenny, 1994) and evaluations of task performance (John & Robins, 1994) have shown that the self is a unique judge: Self-judgments tend to agree less with observer judgments than observers agree with each other. On the basis of this research, we predicted that self–observer agreement on act frequency reports would be lower than observer–observer agreement (Hypothesis 1).

Do Acts Differ in How Much Individuals Agree About Act Frequencies?

What makes an act easy to judge? To address this question, Ozer and Buss (1991) asked spouses to report how frequently they had performed a set of acts over the previous 3 months. Agreement between spouses varied across acts and depended on a number of properties of the acts. For example, spouses showed relatively high levels of agreement about acts related to Extraversion (e.g., "I danced in front of a crowd") but relatively little agreement about acts related to Agreeableness (e.g., "I let someone cut into the parking space I was waiting for"). The Ozer and Buss study provides insights into act properties that might moderate interjudge agreement. Several studies have identified properties of traits that influence agreement, including the observability of trait-relevant behaviors, the social desirability of the trait, and the Big Five content domain of the trait judged. If acts are indeed the building blocks of personality, then the properties affecting agreement about traits may also affect agreement about acts, and findings for acts should therefore parallel those for traits.

Thus, drawing on trait research, we made the following predictions about acts. First, we predicted higher observer–observer and self–observer agreement for acts that are easily observed (Funder & Dobroth, 1987; John & Robins, 1993; Kenrick & Stringfield, 1980; Ozer & Buss, 1991) (Hypothesis 2a). Some acts refer to psychological events or processes within the mind of the actor that may not be directly observable (e.g., "I appeared cooperative in order to get my way"), whereas other acts are more easily observed from an external vantage point (e.g., "I sat at the head of the table"). Highly observable acts will be more salient to observers (who focus on visible behaviors) than to the self-perceiver, for whom internal experiences (e.g., intentions and motives) are also available (Funder, 1980). Whereas observable behavior is, in principle, available to both observer and self, less observable aspects of an act (such as intentions) are available primarily to the self and are potentially more salient than observable aspects of the act (Robins & John, 1997b; White & Younger, 1988). Thus, it seems unlikely that all acts can be coded with high reliability by even the most conscientious observers.

Second, we predicted higher agreement for acts that occur frequently (Funder & Colvin, 1991; Ozer & Buss, 1991) (Hypothesis 2b). If an act has a low base rate of occurrence, then observers are more likely to miss it over the course of an interaction. Moreover, on psychometric grounds, low base-rate acts will have less variance across targets, which will tend to reduce correlations between observers. Both observability and base rate involve informational factors that might limit agreement about act performances.

We also expected motivational factors to play a role. In particular, we predicted that agreement would be related to the social desirability of the act (Hypothesis 2c). However, trait research provides conflicting evidence about whether this relation will be linear or curvilinear. That is, Funder and Colvin (1988) and Hayes and Dunning (1997) found a positive linear relation, with higher agreement for more desirable traits. In contrast, the two studies reported by John and Robins (1993) showed a curvilinear relation, with higher agreement for evaluatively neutral traits and lower agreement for evaluatively extreme traits (either highly undesirable or highly desirable). The present study will examine the effects of desirability and evaluativeness on agreement in the act domain.

Fourth, extrapolating from earlier findings, we predicted higher agreement for acts related to Extraversion (Funder & Colvin, 1988; John & Robins, 1993; Kenny, 1994; Norman & Goldberg, 1966; Ozer & Buss, 1991) and lower agreement for acts related to Agreeableness (John & Robins, 1993) (Hypothesis 2d).

How Accurate Are Self-Reports of Act Frequency?

The accuracy of self-perception has been a longstanding concern in psychology (see Robins & John, 1997a, for a review). Many theorists are less than sanguine about the ability of people to perceive their behavior objectively. Hogan (1996), for example, spoke of the "inevitability of human self-deception" (p. 165), and Thorne (1989) observed that "due to self-deception, selective inattention, repression, or whatever one wishes to call lack of self-enlightenment, self-views may be less accurate than outsiders' views" (p. 157).

Assessing the accuracy of self-reports requires a criterion—a measure of "reality" against which self-perceptions can be compared. Given the absence of a single objective standard for evaluating the accuracy of global personality traits, the social consensus (i.e., aggregated trait ratings by others) has often been used as an accuracy criterion (e.g., Funder, 1995; Hofstee, 1994; Norman & Goldberg, 1966; Robins & John, 1997a). For example, much research on the accuracy of self-reports has compared self-ratings with judgments provided by peers (John & Robins, 1994; Kolar, Funder, & Colvin, 1996). However, some researchers have been skeptical of reports by such informants and have instead emphasized the need for direct behavioral observation (e.g., Kenny, 1994, p. 136). Hence, the present research focused on observer codings of act frequencies from videotapes in a specific interaction task. These codings provide a more objective measure of the behavioral reality in the task and can therefore serve as a criterion to evaluate accuracy and bias in self-reports of behavior in this task (Funder, 1995; Kenny, 1994; Robins & John, 1997b). We expected self-reported act frequencies to reflect, at least in part, the observed "reality" of participants' behavioral conduct. Thus, we predicted that the self-reports would show levels of accuracy similar to those found in trait research (Hypothesis 3). However, we did not expect the accuracy correlations to be uniformly high, so we also examined the properties of acts that might explain why accuracy is higher for some behaviors than for others.

Are Self-Reports of Act Frequency Biased?

Do individuals overreport socially desirable acts to enhance their self-views? Most self-concept theorists assume that people are motivated to maintain and enhance their feelings of self-worth (e.g., Allport, 1937; Greenwald, 1980; James, 1890; Rogers, 1959; Tesser, 1988). According to Taylor and Brown (1988, 1994) and others, most individuals have "positive illusions" about themselves, presumably stemming from the basic motive toward self-enhancement. Several studies have examined positive illusions by comparing self-reports to observer ratings of global personality traits, such as friendly and outgoing (Campbell & Fehr, 1990; Colvin, Block, & Funder, 1995; Lewinsohn, Mischel, Chaplin, & Barton, 1980). This research on trait ratings shows that, on average, individuals perceive themselves somewhat more positively than they are perceived by others. If these positive illusions extend to perceptions of specific behaviors, then we would also expect individuals to show a self-enhancement bias in their act reports.

* * *

Illusory self-enhancement is sometimes described as if it is present in all normal, psychologically healthy individuals: Taylor (1989) concluded that "normal human thought is marked not by accuracy but by positive self-enhancing illusions" (p. 7); Paulhus and Reid (1991) emphasized that "the healthy person is prone to self-deceptive positivity" (p. 307); and Greenwald and Pratkanis (1984) believed that self-enhancing biases pervade the "self-knowledge of the average normal adult of (at least) North American culture" (p. 139). However, John and Robins (1994) found self-enhancement bias in only 60% of their participants who evaluated their performance in a group discussion task more positively than did a group of independent observers. This finding raises the question of whether some individuals are particularly prone to positive illusions. As noted by John and Robins, the most theoretically relevant construct is narcissism. The *Diagnostic and Statistical Manual of Mental Disorders* (4th ed.; *DSM-IV*) criteria for the narcissistic personality include a grandiose sense of self-importance, a tendency to exaggerate accomplishments and talents, and an expectation to be recognized as "extraordinary" even without appropriate accomplishments (American Psychiatric Association, 1994). Research suggests that narcissistic individuals respond to threats to their self-worth by perceiving themselves more positively than is justified (Gabriel, Critelli, & Ee, 1994; John & Robins, 1994) and by denigrating others (Morf & Rhodewalt, 1993). Narcissists may be particularly prone to positively distorted self-evaluations because their inflated sense of self-importance is easily threatened. Thus, we predicted that narcissistic individuals will show more self-enhancement bias than non-narcissistic individuals in their act frequency self-reports (Hypothesis 4).

Method

Participants Ninety Masters of Business Administration (MBA) students (41 women, 49 men) volunteered to participate in a personality and managerial assessment program. Because of technical problems, the videotapes of 2 participants were unusable; thus, the final N was 88. Their median age was 29 years, and on average they had more than 3 years of postcollege work experience. We collected data from two samples: 54 participants (26 women) in Sample 1 and 36 participants (15 women) in Sample 2.

Group Discussion Task The group discussion task we used is a standardized exercise commonly used to assess managerial performance (e.g., Howard & Bray, 1988; Thornton & Byham, 1982). The task simulates a committee meeting in a large organization. Participants were randomly assigned to mixed-sex groups, with 6 members in each. Participants were told that the purpose of the meeting was to allocate a fixed amount of money to 6 candidates for a merit bonus. Each participant was assigned the role of supervisor of one candidate and was instructed to present a case for that candidate at the meeting; participants were seated at a round table and no leader was assigned. Participants received a realistic written summary of the employment backgrounds of all candidates, including salary, biographical information, and appraisals of prior job performance, and were given 10 min to review this information. They were instructed to start the meeting by each giving a 3- to 5-min presentation on the relative merits of their candidate. The groups had 40 min to reach consensus on how to allocate the merit bonuses. Instructions emphasized two goals: (a) obtain a large bonus for the candidate they represented and

(b) help the group achieve a fair overall allocation of the bonus money. Thus, effective performance required behaviors that promoted the achievement of both goals. To permit subsequent coding of act frequencies, the task was videotaped with cameras mounted unobtrusively on the walls and focused on each participant's face and upper body.

SELECTION OF ACTS We studied a total of 34 acts (20 acts in Sample 1 and 14 acts in Sample 2). * * * We selected 20 acts * * * that seemed likely to occur in our task (e.g., "Target issued orders that got the group organized"). In Sample 2, five psychologists familiar with the group discussion task generated a second set of 14 acts that refer to easily observable behaviors and occur often in this task (e.g., "Target outlined a set of criteria for determining how to allocate the money").

SELF-REPORTS OF ACT FREQUENCY Immediately after completing the task, participants reported how frequently they had performed each act during the group discussion. The acts were worded in the first person (e.g., "I persuaded the others to accept my opinion on the issue"). * * * We used a 4-point scale referring to the actual frequency of acts performed (0 = *not at all*, 1 = *once*, 2 = *two or three times*, 3 = *more than three times*).

VIDEO-BASED OBSERVER CODINGS OF ACT FREQUENCY In Sample 1, four observers viewed the videotaped behavior of each participant and coded the frequencies of each of the 20 acts. In Sample 2, a second set of four observers coded the additional 14 acts for each participant. Both sets of observers were students at the same university but unacquainted with the videotaped participants. Acts were worded in the third person (e.g., "Target persuaded the others to accept his/her opinion on the issue"). Before viewing the videotapes, the observers watched four practice videotapes (which were not used in this research) to familiarize themselves with typical behavioral repertoires and the way the acts were manifested in the task.

* * * The four observers coded participants' act frequencies with reasonable reliability; across the 34 acts, the average coefficient alpha reliability of the composited ratings was .69 (*SD* = .29).[2]

INDEPENDENT VARIABLES: PROPERTIES OF ACTS For each of the 34 acts, we measured four properties hypothesized to influence interjudge agreement and accuracy and bias in self-reported act frequencies.

Observability. Two facets of observability were rated by eight judges who were familiar with the group discussion task: *Noticeability* was defined by how well the act stands out from the stream of behavior (α = .89), and *high inferential content* was the degree of inference about internal thoughts and motivations required for an observer to be sure that the act has occurred (α = .96).[3] * * * We standardized both variables, reverse scored high inferential content, and combined the two ratings into one overall measure of observability. The most observable act was "Target reminded the group of their time limit"; the least observable act was "Target took the opposite point of view just to be contrary."

Social desirability. Using a 9-point scale (Hampson, Goldberg, & John, 1987), the judges also rated how socially desirable it was to perform each act in the group discussion. The mean ratings were used as an index of each act's desirability

[2]"Reliability" in this context refers to the statistical stability of the averaged observers' ratings. This number is higher to the degree that (a) the different observers agree in their ratings and (b) there is a large number of observers. With four observers being averaged here, a composite reliability of .69 is good but not excellent. Other reliabilities reported later (e.g., of act properties) were higher, as you will see.

[3]The Greek letter α is a conventional label for the reliability (stability) of a personality scale. A scale is more reliable to the degree that (a) its items correlate with each other and (b) it has more items. Reliability in this sense is a necessary but not sufficient condition for validity.

(α = .94). The most desirable act was "Target settled the dispute among other members of the group"; the least desirable act was "Target yelled at someone." Evaluativeness was measured by folding the 9-point scale such that 1 and 9 were recoded as 4, 2 and 8 were recoded as 3, and so on.

Base rate. The base rate of an act was the number of times the act was performed by any participant, on the basis of the observer codings. This index was computed separately for each observer and then composited; the mean alpha (averaged across the two sets of observers) was .83. The act with the highest base rate was "Target expressed her/his agreement with a point being made by another member of the group"; the act with the lowest base rate was "Target monopolized the conversation." * * *

Big Five personality domain. Acts in the group discussion task tend to be overt behaviors that are either interpersonal (e.g., negotiation and persuasion) or task-oriented (setting goals and organizing group activities; Bass, 1954). In terms of the Big Five personality domains, the interpersonal domains of Extraversion and Agreeableness and the task-focused domain of Conscientiousness were most relevant. In contrast, the other two Big Five domains (Neuroticism, Openness to Experience) refer primarily to an individual's covert experiences. Three expert judges rated the prototypicality of each act for each of the Big Five domains, with low ratings indicating the act was unrelated to that Big Five domain and high ratings indicating the act was highly related to either high or low pole. For example, the Extraversion rating for each act ranged from 0 (*act is unrelated to Extraversion or Introversion*) to 4 (*act is extremely prototypical of Extraversion or Introversion*). The alpha reliabilities of their composite judgments were high for Extraversion (.81), Agreeableness (.86), and Conscientiousness (.88) and somewhat lower for Neuroticism (.67) and Openness to Experience (.62). There were no prototypical examples of the Neuroticism and Openness to Experience domains. All acts had their highest mean prototypicality values on Extraversion, Agreeableness, or Conscientiousness, and therefore only these three Big Five domains will be examined in our analyses. "Target laughed out loud" was the most prototypical act for the Extraversion domain, "Target took the opposite point of view just to be contrary" for (low) Agreeableness, and "Target reminded the group of their time limit" for Conscientiousness. We used these continuous prototypicality ratings in our correlational analyses. * * *

NARCISSISM We used the 33-item version of the Narcissistic Personality Inventory (NPI; α = 70; Raskin & Terry, 1988) to assess participants' level of narcissism. The NPI is the best validated self-report measure of overt narcissism for nonclinical populations (Raskin & Terry, 1988; see also Hendin & Cheek, 1997) and has been shown to predict psychologists' ratings of narcissism (e.g., John & Robins, 1994).

DEPENDENT VARIABLES

Interjudge agreement: Observer–observer and self–observer agreement. To assess how much the observers agreed about the frequency of each act, we computed the correlation (across participants) between each pair of observers' video-based codings. We then averaged the resulting six pairwise observer–observer correlations. This index reflects the average observer–observer agreement for each act.

To assess how much self and observer agreed about the frequency of each act, we computed the correlation (across participants) between the self-reports and video-based codings by each of the four observers. We then averaged the resulting four dyadic self–observer correlations. This index reflects the average agreement between self and a single observer and is therefore directly comparable to the dyadic observer–observer agreement index.

Accuracy and bias in self-reported acts. To assess accuracy and bias, we used the aggregated video-based observer codings as a behavior-based criterion measure of act frequency. Accuracy was defined by the correlation (computed across participants) between self-reports of act frequency and the observer criterion for act frequency. Bias was defined by the discrepancy between each participant's self-report and the observer criterion; positive values indicate that participants overreported how frequently they performed the act, and negative values indicate they underreported how frequently they performed the act. Bias can be computed both at the aggregate level (i.e., do individuals, on average, overreport or underreport some acts more than others?) and at the level of the individual person (i.e., do some persons overreport or underreport an act more than others?). Both accuracy and bias were computed separately for each act.

The dependent variables were computed separately for the acts in each sample. However, because the findings were similar in both samples, analyses across acts used the whole set of 34 acts.

Results and Discussion

Do Observers Agree More with Each Other Than They Do with the Self? We first tested Hypothesis 1, which predicts that observer–observer agreement would be higher than self–observer agreement. Across the 34 acts, observer–observer agreement (M = .40, SD = .25) was significantly higher than self–observer agreement (M = .19, SD = .19), as shown by a t test for paired samples, $t(33) = 5.2$, $p < .001$, one-tailed.[4] This effect held for 83% of the acts. In short, two observers generally agreed more about an act's frequency than did the self and an observer. * * *

We also found that acts eliciting high levels of observer–observer agreement also tended to elicit high self–observer agreement; the correlation between the two agreement indices across the 34 acts was .65, closely replicating the .64 value reported by John and Robins (1993) for trait ratings. In other words, when two observers agree about an act (or a trait), self and observer are also likely to agree.

What Makes an Act Easy to Judge? Effects of Observability, Social Desirability, Base Rate, and Big Five Domain The level of agreement varied substantially across acts, ranging from −.08 to .88 for observer–observer agreement, and from −.12 to .62 for self–observer agreement. Why are some acts judged more consensually than others? To address this question, we correlated the act properties with observer–observer and self–observer agreement across the 34 acts. These across-act correlation coefficients are given in Table 7.1. As predicted by Hypotheses 2a, 2b, and 2c, observability, social desirability, and base rate of the acts were all positively and substantially correlated with both observer–observer and self–observer agreement. The observability effect is consistent with Ozer and Buss's (1991) research on acts, as well as with Funder and Dobroth's (1987) and John and Robins's (1993) research on traits. The positive linear relation between social desirability and agreement is consistent with Funder and Dobroth (1987) and Hayes and Dunning (1997). However, we did not find the evaluativeness effect reported by John and Robins, who found that both extremely negative and extremely positive traits elicit lower levels of agreement. In summary, acts that were observable, desirable, and occurred relatively frequently were judged with relatively more agreement than acts that were difficult to observe, undesirable, and relatively infrequent.

Table 7.1 also shows the correlation between Big Five content domain and interjudge agreement. These correlations are generally consistent with Hypothesis 2d. Self–observer agreement correlated positively with act prototypically for both

[4] M is the mean and SD is the standard deviation. The p-level reported implies that a difference of the size found would occur less than 1 time in 1,000 if there really is no difference between the two kinds of agreement.

TABLE 7.1

CORRELATIONS BETWEEN ACT PROPERTIES AND INTERJUDGE AGREEMENT ON ACT FREQUENCY REPORTS (COMPUTED ACROSS THE 34 ACTS)

Act properties	Observer–observer agreement	Self–observer agreement
Observability	.38*	.34*
Base rate	.44*	.35*
Desirability	.52*	.46*
Evaluativeness	−.14	−.06
Prototypicality for Big Five domain		
Extraversion	.08	.32*
Agreeableness	−.27†	−.51*
Conscientiousness	.20	.38*

Note. Numbers in this table are correlations computed across the 34 acts. For example, the correlation of .38 between observability and observer–observer agreement indicates that more observable acts tended to elicit higher levels of agreement than less observable acts. Similarly, the correlation of −.51 between Agreeableness and self–observer agreement indicates that acts from the Agreeableness domain (i.e., prototypical examples of either Agreeableness or Disagreeableness) tended to elicit lower levels of self–observer agreement than acts unrelated to Agreeableness.
† $p < .10$ (marginally significant). * $p < .05$.

Extraversion and Conscientiousness and negatively with prototypicality for Agreeableness, indicating that self–observer agreement was higher for acts from the Extraversion and Conscientiousness domains and lower for acts from the Agreeableness domain. The same pattern was found for observer–observer agreement, but the correlations did not reach conventional levels of significance. These findings are generally consistent with previous research in both the act and trait domains. However, there were two differences. First, we did not find the Extraversion effect for observer–observer agreement found in several previous studies (e.g., John & Robins, 1993; Kenny, 1994). Second, we found a Conscientiousness effect for self–observer agreement that has not been found in previous research.

* * *

HOW ACCURATE ARE SELF-REPORTS OF ACT FREQUENCY? To examine accuracy, we correlated the self-reported act frequencies with the aggregated observer codings. Across all 34 acts, the mean correlation was .24 ($SD = .26$). However, this value underestimates the accuracy of the self-reports because for some acts the video-based observer codings were not highly reliable. Thus, as a fairer test, we considered only those 12 acts that observers coded with high reliability (i.e., those with an alpha above .80). Consistent with Hypothesis 3, the self-reports showed a significant level of accuracy, with a mean correlation of .40 ($SD = .26$; see Table 7.2).

However, the accuracy correlations varied considerably even within this subset of highly reliable acts, ranging from a high of .72 to a low of .03. Table 7.2 presents the Big Five classifications of these 12 acts. The 4 acts with the highest accuracy correlations (mean $r = .61$) were all from the Extraversion domain, whereas the 5 acts with the lowest accuracy correlations (mean $r = .16$) were all from the Agreeableness domain; the 3 Conscientiousness acts fell in between, with a mean r of .44.

* * *

INDIVIDUAL DIFFERENCES IN SELF-ENHANCEMENT BIAS * * * Now we turn to the question of whether certain kinds of individuals give biased reports of their behavior. To establish the existence of such individual differences, we examined for each desirable act the percentage of individuals whose self-reported act frequencies were greater than, less than, and the same as the observer codings. Averaging the percentages across the 15 desirable acts, 57% of the participants overreported (i.e., showed self-enhancement bias), 24% underreported (i.e., self-diminishment bias), and 19% were exactly accurate. That is, 43% of the participants failed to show the general self-enhancement effect (Taylor & Brown, 1988). Clearly, then, individuals show substantial differences in self-

TABLE 7.2

THE 12 MOST RELIABLY CODED ACTS (α > .80) RANKED BY THEIR SELF–OBSERVER VALIDITY

Act	Big Five domain	Self–observer validity
Told joke to lighten tense moment	E	.72
Made humorous remark	E	.60
Took charge of things at the meeting	E	.57
Laughed out loud	E	.52
Outlined set of steps thought group should follow	C	.45
Pointed out the distinction between a merit bonus and salary increase	C	.45
Reminded group of time limit	C	.41
Said was willing to lower the money recommending for our candidate	A	.32
Expressed agreement with another group member	A	.31
Pointed out possible effects on employee morale	A	.08
Interrupted someone else	A	.07
Suggested they give some money to every candidate	A	.03
M		.40
SD		.26

Note. The act descriptions have been slightly abbreviated. All acts are desirable (i.e., rated above 6 on the 9-point social desirability scale) except "Interrupted someone else," which was undesirable (mean desirability = 2.8), and "Laughed out loud," which was relatively neutral (mean desirability = 5.6). E = Extraversion; A = Agreeableness; C = Conscientiousness.

perception bias, suggesting that the self-enhancement tendency should not be treated as a general law of social behavior (John & Robins, 1994).

To test the prediction that narcissism will predict these individual differences in self-enhancement, we computed a self-enhancement index based on the degree to which participants overreported their desirable acts plus the degree to which they underreported their undesirable acts. Consistent with Hypothesis 4, the NPI correlated .27 ($p < .05$) with this self-enhancement index. Analyses of individual acts revealed that narcissists were particularly inclined to overreport desirable acts such as "I took charge of things at the meeting" and "I made an argument that changed another person's mind." The tendency for narcissistic individuals to exaggerate the frequency with which they performed desirable acts provides further support for the link between narcissism and positive illusions about the self (John & Robins, 1994).

General Discussion

This research addressed a fundamental question about self-perception: Do people know how they acted in a particular situation? We compared individuals' reports of how frequently they performed a set of acts with observer codings of their behavior from videotapes. We found that for some acts there is a clear consensus about how often the act occurred whereas for other acts individuals simply do not agree. We explored several factors that might account for these differences and found that individuals tend to agree about acts that are observable, desirable, frequently occurring, and are from the Extraversion and Conscientiousness (rather than the Agreeableness) domains. We also examined how accurately people report on their behavior and whether their reports are positively biased. We found that individuals' recollections of their behavior showed some correspondence with codings of their behavior, but the degree of correspondence varied systematically across acts. Finally, we found a general tendency toward self-enhancement bias in the act self-reports, but the degree of bias depended on both the individual act and the individual person. Specifically, self-enhancement was greatest for acts that were highly desirable and difficult to observe and for persons who were particularly narcissistic.

What can these findings tell us about the disagreement between Julia and Roger regarding how many times she had interrupted his mother that morning? First, we can expect less agreement between self and other, Julia and Roger, than between Roger and another observer. Second, however, for both Julia and Roger, the amount of agreement will depend on the specific act being monitored; we would expect relatively low agreement because "interrupting another person" is an undesirable and disagreeable act. Third, given that act self-reports are susceptible to self-enhancement bias, we would expect Julia to underestimate how often she had in fact interrupted Roger's mother, especially if she has narcissistic tendencies. In short, our analysis suggests that their disagreement may resist easy resolution.

We now move beyond the rather specific context of Julia and Roger's disagreement and turn to the wider implications of the findings. * * *

Comparison of Act and Trait Research on Agreement and Accuracy

* * *

* * * There appear to be both similarities and differences between agreement on acts and agreement on traits. Clearly, an important avenue for future research concerns the psychological roots of these similarities and differences. Such research will need to take into account differences in the way act and trait judgments are made. One might expect judges to agree more about acts than about general personality traits because many acts are directly observable (Buss & Craik, 1980, 1983; Kenny, 1994), whereas traits represent summary impressions of multiple-act occurrences. Thus, trait inferences require first perceiving specific behaviors and then abstracting them into trait ascriptions. On the other hand, agreement may be higher for traits because trait inferences are typically based on a diverse set of relevant behavioral episodes. The broader observational base of traits means that observers are less likely to miss all of the many trait-relevant behaviors than they are to miss a specific performance of a single act. For example, it would be perfectly plausible for some judges to miss an instance of the specific act of "interrupting someone." It is less plausible that a judge will miss all disagreeable behaviors in the situation (including, among others, "interrupting someone," "loudly correcting someone's mistake," and "insisting on having the last word"). The present findings indicate higher observer–observer agreement for acts than for trait ratings by peers, thus suggesting that the greater observability of acts may outweigh the greater breadth of traits in determining agreement among observers.

In addition, act and trait reports may differ because they derive from two different forms of memory. Specific behaviors are encoded in episodic memory whereas representations of traits are encoded in semantic memory (Klein & Loftus, 1993). Consequently, judgments about acts require recall of specific behavioral instances (i.e., episodic memory) and are likely to proceed through a different cognitive process than judgments about traits, which require retrieval of abstract, generalized information about a person (i.e., semantic memory). One implication of this distinction is that self-perception bias may occur either at the initial stage of encoding behavior into episodic memory or at the stage when memories of specific acts are generalized into semantic knowledge as trait representations (e.g., by selectively attending to desirable episodic memories). The present findings imply the former—that act perceptions themselves are biased. Thus, self-judgments about traits may be biased just because self-judgments about acts are biased. Clearly, however, our findings do not exclude the possibility that bias also exists when semantic knowledge about the self is formed. In summary, understanding the processes by which perceptions of act occurrences are translated into trait judgments will help elucidate the factors that cause accuracy and bias in personality impressions.

* * *

IMPLICATIONS FOR ACT-BASED TRAIT ASSESSMENT The present study has some implications for the feasibility and practice of act-based personality assessment using both on-line and retrospective act frequency reports. Our findings for on-line act reports showed levels of interobserver agreement that were reasonably high for the majority of acts, and, indeed, slightly higher than that obtained for trait ratings. These results support the feasibility of this fundamental mode of act-based trait assessment. Furthermore, Borkenau and Ostendorf (1987) studied a situation similar to that used in this research and found substantial accuracy for retrospective observer act reports. Finally, it is important to keep in mind that our findings focus on reports of single acts and do not benefit from aggregation across acts. Thus, reliability and validity of both on-line observer and retrospective self-reports would be substantially higher for the multiple-act indices advocated by the AFA (Cheek, 1982).

However, the present findings suggest some limitations of retrospective self-reports as surrogates for on-line codings of act frequency. Although we found some degree of correspondence between self-reports and aggregated on-line act reports by observers, the more salient finding was the great variability in self–observer agreement across acts. For some acts, self-reports appear to correspond with the on-line observer codings (i.e., Extraversion) but for other acts self-reports do not (i.e., Agreeableness). Furthermore, our results indicate that the operation of self-enhancement bias, previously found for trait ratings, cannot be avoided at the act report level. Finally, unlike observer reports, self-reports of acts have the intrinsic limitation that aggregation across "multiple selves" is not possible (Hofstee, 1994).

* * *

The present findings suggest that some practical challenges remain to be overcome to fully implement the AFA and realize its envisioned theoretical potential. For example, valid retrospective self-reports are difficult to obtain for acts related to Agreeableness, results consistent with those reported by Ozer and Buss (1991). These findings for acts parallel those for trait ratings, thus indicating that the problem may reside not with act monitoring per se but rather with the distinctiveness of self–other perspectives in this behavioral domain. Thus, the implications of these findings pertain not just to AFA assessment methods but more generally to method effects in construct validation (e.g., Ozer, 1989). In particular, researchers should specify what kinds of method effects should be expected given the conceptual definition of the particular trait construct in question.

* * *

In conclusion, a greater understanding of when and why individuals can accurately report what they and others did in a situation should be the goal of further psychological research. Not only can such research inform studies that use observer and self-report methods, but it can also illuminate the processes that underlie disagreements in such domains as romantic relationships, conflict resolution, and negotiation.

References

Allport, G. W. (1937). *Personality: A psychological interpretation.* New York: Holt.

American Psychiatric Association. (1994). *Diagnostic and statistical manual of mental disorders* (4th ed.). Washington, DC: Author.

Bass, B. (1954). The leaderless group discussion. *Psychological Bulletin, 51*, 465–492.

Bem, D. J. (1967). Self-perception: An alternative interpretation of cognitive dissonance phenomena. *Psychological Review, 74*, 183–200.

Bem, D. J. (1972). Self-perception theory. In L. Berkowitz (Ed.), *Advances in experimental social psychology* (Vol. 6, pp. 1–62). New York: Academic Press.

Borkenau, P., & Ostendorf, F. (1987). Retrospective estimates of act frequencies: How accurately do they reflect reality? *Journal of Personality and Social Psychology, 52*, 626–638.

Botwin, M. D., & Buss, D. M. (1989). Structure of act-report data: Is the five-factor model of personality recaptured? *Journal of Personality and Social Psychology, 56*, 988–1001.

Buss, D. M., & Craik, K. H. (1980). The frequency concept of disposition: Dominance and prototypically dominant acts. *Journal of Personality, 48,* 379–392.

Buss, D. M., & Craik, K. H. (1983). The act frequency approach to personality. *Psychological Review, 90,* 105–126.

Campbell, J. D., & Fehr, B. (1990). Self-esteem and perceptions of conveyed impressions: Is negative affectivity associated with greater realism? *Journal of Personality and Social Psychology, 58,* 122–133.

Cheek, J. M. (1982). Aggregation, moderator variables, and the validity of personality tests: A peer rating study. *Journal of Personality and Social Psychology, 43,* 1254–1269.

Colvin, C. R., Block, J., & Funder, D. C. (1995). Overly positive self-evaluations and personality: Negative implications for mental health. *Journal of Personality and Social Psychology, 68,* 1152–1162.

Funder, D. C. (1980). On seeing ourselves as others see us: Self–other agreement and discrepancy in personality ratings. *Journal of Personality, 48,* 473–493.

Funder, D. C. (1995). On the accuracy of personality judgment: A realistic approach. *Psychological Review, 102,* 652–670.

Funder, D. C., & Colvin, C. R. (1988). Friends and strangers: Acquaintanceship, agreement, and the accuracy of personality judgment. *Journal of Personality and Social Psychology, 55,* 149–158.

Funder, D. C., & Colvin, C. R. (1991). Explorations in behavioral consistency: Properties of persons, situations, and behaviors. *Journal of Personality and Social Psychology, 60,* 773–794.

Funder, D. C., & Colvin, C. R. (1997). Congruence of self and others' judgments of personality. In R. Hogan, J. A. Johnson, & S. R. Briggs (Eds.), *Handbook of personality psychology* (pp. 617–647). New York: Academic Press.

Funder, D. C., & Dobroth, K. M. (1987). Differences between traits: Properties associated with interjudge agreement. *Journal of Personality and Social Psychology, 52,* 409–418.

Gabriel, M. T., Critelli, J. W., & Ee, J. S. (1994). Narcissistic illusions in self-evaluations of intelligence and attractiveness. *Journal of Personality, 62,* 143–155.

Greenwald, A. G. (1980). The totalitarian ego: Fabrication and revision of personal history. *American Psychologist, 35,* 603–618.

Greenwald, A. G., & Pratkanis, A. R. (1984). The self. In R. S. Wyer & T. K. Srull (Eds.), *Handbook of social cognition* (Vol. 3, pp. 129–178). Hillsdale, NJ: Erlbraum.

Hampson, S. E., Goldberg, L. R., & John, O. P. (1987). Category-breadth and social-desirability values for 573 personality terms. *European Journal of Personality, 1,* 241–258.

Hayes, A. F., & Dunning, D. (1997). Construal processes and trait ambiguity: Implications for self–peer agreement in personality judgment. *Journal of Personality and Social Psychology, 72,* 664–677.

Hendin, H. M., & Cheek, J. M. (1997). Assessing hypersensitive narcissism: A reexamination of Murray's Narcissism scale. *Journal of Research in Personality, 31,* 588–599.

Hofstee, W. K. B. (1994). Who should own the definition of personality? *European Journal of Personality, 8,* 149–162.

Hogan, R. (1996). A socioanalytic perspective on the five-factor model. In J. S. Wiggins (Ed.), *The five-factor model of personality: Theoretical perspectives* (pp. 163–179). New York: Guilford Press.

Howard, A., & Bray, D. W. (1988). *Managerial lives in transition: Advancing age and changing times.* New York: Guilford Press.

James, W. (1890). *The principles of psychology.* Cambridge, MA: Harvard University.

John, O. P. (1990). The "Big Five" factor taxonomy: Dimensions of personality in the natural language and in questionnaires. In L. A. Pervin (Ed.), *Handbook of personality: Theory and research* (pp. 66–100). New York: Guilford Press.

John, O. P., & Robins, R. W. (1993). Determinants of interjudge agreement on personality traits: The Big Five domains, observability, evaluativeness, and the unique perspective of the self. *Journal of Personality, 61,* 521–551.

John, O. P., & Robins, R. W. (1994). Accuracy and bias in self-perception: Individual differences in self-enhancement and the role of narcissism. *Journal of Personality and Social Psychology, 66,* 206–219.

Kenny, D. A. (1994). *Interpersonal perception: A social relations analysis.* New York: Guilford Press.

Kenrick, D. T., & Stringfield, D. O. (1980). Personality traits and the eye of the beholder: Crossing some traditional philosophical boundaries in the search for consistency in all of the people. *Psychological Review, 87,* 88–104.

Klein, S. B., & Loftus, J. (1993). The mental representation of trait and autobiographical knowledge about the self. In T. K. Srull & R. S. Wyer, Jr. (Eds.), *Advances in social cognition* (Vol. 5, pp. 1–49). Hillsdale, NJ: Erlbaum.

Kolar, D. W., Funder, D. C., & Colvin, C. R. (1996). Comparing the accuracy of personality judgments by the self and knowledgeable others. *Journal of Personality, 64,* 311–337.

Lewinsohn, P. M., Mischel, W., Chaplin, W., & Barton, R. (1980). Social competence and depression: The role of illusory self-perceptions. *Journal of Abnormal Psychology, 89,* 203–212.

Morf, C. C., & Rhodewalt, F. (1993). Narcissism and self-evaluation maintenance: Explorations in object relations. *Personality and Social Psychology Bulletin, 19,* 668–676.

Norman, W. T., & Goldberg, L. R. (1966). Raters, ratees, and randomness in personality structure. *Journal of Personality and Social Psychology, 4,* 681–691.

Ozer, D. J. (1989). Construct validity in personality assessment. In D. M. Buss & N. Cantor (Eds.), *Personality psychology: Recent trends and emerging directions* (pp. 224–234). New York: Springer-Verlag.

Ozer, D. J., & Buss, D. M. (1991). Two views of behavior: Agreement and disagreement among marital partners. In D. J. Ozer, J. M. Healy, Jr., & A. J. Stewart (Eds.), *Perspectives in personality* (Vol. 3, pp. 91–106). London: Jessica Kingsley.

Paulhus, D. L., & Reid, D. B. (1991). Enhancement and denial in socially desirable responding. *Journal of Personality and Social Psychology, 60,* 307–317.

Raskin, R., & Terry, H. (1988). A principal-components analysis of the Narcissistic Personality Inventory and some further evidence of its construct validity. *Journal of Personality and Social Psychology, 54,* 890–902.

Robins, R. W., & John, O. P. (1997a). The quest for self-insight: Theory and research on accuracy and bias in self-perception. In R. Hogan, J. Johnson, & S. Briggs (Eds.), *Handbook of personality psychology* (pp. 649–679). New York: Academic Press.

Robins, R. W., & John, O. P. (1997b). Self-perception, visual perspective, and narcissism: Is seeing believing? *Psychological Science, 8*, 37–42.

Rogers, C. R. (1959). A theory of therapy, personality, and interpersonal relations, developed in the client-centered framework. In S. Koch (Ed.), *Psychology: A study of a science* (Vol. 3, pp. 185–256). New York: McGraw-Hill.

Taylor, S. E. (1989). *Positive illusions: Creative self-deception and the healthy mind.* New York: Basic Books.

Taylor, S. E., & Brown, J. (1988). Illusion and well-being: A social psychological perspective on mental health. *Psychological Bulletin, 103*, 193–210.

Taylor, S. E., & Brown, J. (1994). Positive illusions and well-being revisited: Separating fact from fiction. *Psychological Bulletin, 116*, 21–27.

Tesser, A. (1988). Toward a self-evaluation maintenance model of social behavior. In L. Berkowitz (Ed.), *Advances in experimental social psychology* (Vol. 21, pp. 181–227). New York: Academic Press.

Thorne, A. (1989). Conditional patterns, transference, and the coherence of personality across time. In D. M. Buss & N. Cantor (Eds.), *Personality psychology: Recent trends and emerging directions* (pp. 149–159). New York: Springer-Verlag.

Thornton, G. C., & Byham, W. C. (1982). *Assessment centers and managerial performance.* San Diego, CA: Academic Press.

White, P. A., & Younger, D. (1988). Differences in the ascription of transient internal states to self and other. *Journal of Experimental Social Psychology, 24*, 292–309.

PART II

The Trait Approach to Personality

People are not all the same. They think differently, feel differently, and act differently. This fact raises an important question: What is the best way to describe enduring psychological differences among persons? The purpose of the trait approach to personality psychology is to attempt to answer this question. The ordinary language of personality—found in any dictionary—consists of terms like "sociable" and "anxious" and "dominant." The goal of many researchers who follow the trait approach is to transform this everyday language into a scientifically valid technology for describing individual differences in personality that can be used for predicting behavior and, more importantly, for understanding what people do and how they feel.

This section begins with a brief excerpt from a novel that illustrates how a person (in this case, a fictional one) can be described vividly in trait terms. In the second selection, the person widely recognized as the founder of modern personality psychology, Gordon Allport, describes what he thinks a personality trait is and why it is important.

The third selection takes the opposite tack. It is an excerpt from a book by Walter Mischel that was read widely as a frontal assault on the very existence of personality. Although Allport anticipated many of Mischel's criticisms, the book had widespread impact and inspired numerous rebuttals. One of the shortest of these rebuttals is the fourth selection, by Jack Block. This article briefly and elegantly describes the uncertain connection between behavior and personality and the reasons why variability in the first does not necessarily imply inconsistency in the second. The fifth selection, by Douglas Kenrick and David Funder, sums up the lessons learned from the controversy over the existence of personality, which not only include the conclusion that "traits exist," but also concern the circumstances under which personality is most likely to be seen clearly.

The sixth and seventh selections return to the Allportian theme of using traits to understand behavior. Mark Snyder introduces the concept of "self-

monitoring" to examine the differences between people who do and those who do not adjust their expressive behavior to match the situation they find themselves in. The seventh and final selection, by Robert McCrae and Paul Costa Jr., argues that a wide swath of the personality domain is encompassed by five broad traits (extraversion, neuroticism, openness, agreeableness, and conscientiousness), and they suggest that these traits describe the "basic tendencies" that underlie all of human personality.

From *The Last Hurrah*

Edwin O'Connor

The first selection in this section is an excerpt from Edwin O'Connor's famous political novel, The Last Hurrah. *The passage describes the mayor's impression of the personality of his disappointing son. It provides a vivid demonstration of how trait terms are used in daily life—there is certainly nothing unusual about a person thinking about another in this way. It also shows how useful such terms can be. A few well-chosen words link the son's personality traits to his typical behaviors, and these are sufficient to convey a clear impression of what he is like. It seems likely that if you were actually to meet the mayor's son, you would recognize him, and you might even be able to predict what he would do under a wide range of circumstances.*

In the terminology used by Block in his article in Part I, the father's impressions of his son constitute O data (judgments by an observer). And as O data often do, these impressions have their own consequences. The father may not be right about his son's personality, but his beliefs no doubt have a profound effect on their relationship. Finally, notice that even though this selection describes the son from the father's viewpoint, it tells you nearly as much about the father as it does about the son.

From *The Last Hurrah* (Boston: Little, Brown, 1956), pp. 17–19.

On the way out he thought suddenly of his son; he stopped and said to the maid, "Has Francis come downstairs yet?"

"No sir. I think he's still asleep."

A growing boy needs his rest, Skeffington thought sardonically; the only question was whether or not Francis Jr., at the age of thirty-seven, might properly qualify as a growing boy. For years Skeffington had been baffled and badly disappointed by his only son. Francis Jr. was virtually a physical duplicate of his father—the resemblance was so astonishing that Skeffington, looking at his son in recent years, could only groan at the unkind mockery of the mnemonic shell, smiling emptily at him across the dinner table. For some important if not quite definable ingredient had been omitted from the boy's makeup; he had been a pleasant, well-mannered, lazy youngster who had grown placidly into manhood without betraying a sign of ambition or, indeed, of intelligence. He had skinned through high school, preparatory school, college, and law school, gaining in this educational passage but a single distinction: in his junior year at college he had been voted Best Dancer in his class. It was an honor that Skeffington had failed to appreciate.

"I've sired a featherhead," he had said to his wife. "A waltzing featherhead. Or am I doing the boy an injustice? Perhaps he fox-trots as well."

"Ah, Frank, you expect too much," she had replied. A gentle woman, she knew and in part shared his disappointment in the boy, yet she had kept herself the buffer between the uncomprehending father and the smiling phantom son. "You want him to be like you and the simple fact of it is he can't be. It's not fair to expect it of him."

He had shrugged. "I don't expect it. I merely expect him to be like some recognizable adult. He's not like me, he's not like you, he's not like anybody. Possibly he's a throwback: a throwback to some dancing ancestor. He claims he wants to be a lawyer; do you suppose he plans to dance his way into court?"

She had persisted. "He's very young yet, after all. It's much too early to pass judgment. And he *is* a good boy; that's no small thing, surely?"

"He's good, he's moral, he's likable," he had agreed, "but he's also a puffball. No weight at all. Twenty-one years old, and everybody still calls him Junior; they'll call him Junior when he's ninety. I don't find that particularly encouraging, Kate."

She had returned to a long-cherished ambition. "I don't know, I always thought that one day he might surprise us all by going to the seminary. He still might, I suppose. I wish he would; I think he'd be happy there."

"Well, he's made a grand start," Skeffington had said dryly. "I understand the seminaries want only the best dancers. No, Kate, the boy will go through law school. He'll go through without too much trouble, I think I can promise you that; the good Dean Gillis is a fine old-fashioned scholar with a healthy respect for his own skin. Then when he gets through he'll get a place in a decent firm; it's barely possible I may have something to do with that, too. But what's to happen to him after I'm gone I haven't the least idea. Maybe he'll be all right as long as his legs hold out."

Now, sixteen years later, Skeffington's bleak prediction for the most part had been fulfilled. At thirty-seven, his son, unmarried, still danced: he could be seen nightly at any one of the city's numerous nightclubs in the company of any one of a number of young women who danced well, laughed immoderately, and were remarkably similar in appearance. He was a thoroughly agreeable, well-tailored man, with a face as unlined as that of a child, who perhaps drank a bit more with the passing of each year, but whose behavior had remained untouched by scandal or disgrace. He was by occupation a practicing attorney, although the practice was largely limited to routine and undemanding labors in the offices of the city's Corporation Counsel, a department of government which had been for some years under Skeffington's control. And, by friend and foe alike, he was still called Junior.

Now that you have finished reading about Junior, you can see how this passage exemplifies not only what the trait approach includes but also what it leaves out. Traits provide a view from the outside only. We have a vivid impression of how the son appears to others, but we have learned nothing about his *opinions of his father, his goals in life, his emotional experience, his values, his fears, or anything else that is part of what could be considered his "inner life." It can be useful to keep in mind what a trait approach to personality—and O data in particular—can and cannot do.*

What Is a Trait of Personality?

Gordon W. Allport

The trait section of this reader now really begins, with a classic statement by the original and still perhaps most important trait theorist. What Sigmund Freud is to psychoanalysis, Gordon Allport is—almost—to trait psychology.

In this selection, Allport offers one of the earliest—and still one of the best—psychological definitions of a personality trait. This article was written for a conference held in 1929, when the modern field of personality psychology was just beginning to be formed. Allport's fundamental contribution, in efforts like this paper, was to take the study of normal variations in personality out of the exclusive hands of novelists, dramatists, theologians, and philosophers and to begin to transform it into a scientific discipline.

Especially considering how old this article is, it is remarkable to observe how many modern issues it anticipates, and how cogently it addresses them. These issues include the person-situation debate (see the upcoming selection by Mischel), the issue of whether a trait is a cause or just a summary of behavior (Allport says it is a cause), and the distinction between focusing on how traits are structured within a single individual (now called the idiographic approach) and focusing on how traits distinguish between people (now called the nomothetic approach). Almost 70 years after it was written, this article still has much to say to the modern field of personality psychology.

From *Journal of Abnormal and Social Psychology, 25*, 368–372, 1931.

At the heart of all investigation of personality lies the puzzling problem of the nature of the unit or element which is the carrier of the distinctive behavior of a man. *Reflexes* and *habits* are too specific in reference, and connote constancy rather than consistency in behavior; *attitudes* are ill defined, and as employed by various writers refer to determining tendencies that range in inclusiveness from the *Aufgabe* to the *Weltanschauung*;[1] *dispositions* and *tendencies* are even less definitive. But *traits*, although appropriated by all manner of writers for all manner of purposes, may still be salvaged, I think, and limited in their

[1]With these German words, Allport is describing the range from the specific tasks an individual must perform (*Aufgabe*) to his or her entire view of the world (*Weltanschauung*).

reference to a certain definite conception of a generalized response-unit in which resides the distinctive quality of behavior that reflects personality. Foes as well as friends of the doctrine of traits will gain from a more consistent use of the term.

The doctrine itself has never been explicitly stated. It is my purpose with the aid of eight criteria to define *trait*, and to state the logic and some of the evidence for the admission of this concept to good standing in psychology.

1. A trait has more than nominal existence. A trait may be said to have the same kind of existence that a habit of a complex order has. Habits of a complex, or higher, order have long been accepted as household facts in psychology. There is no reason to believe that the mechanism which produces such habits (integration, *Gestaltung*, or whatever it may be) stops short of producing the more generalized habits which are here called traits of personality.

2. A trait is more generalized than a habit. Within a personality there are, of course, many independent habits; but there is also so much integration, organization, and coherence among habits that we have no choice but to recognize great systems of interdependent habits. If the habit of brushing one's teeth can be shown, statistically or genetically, to be unrelated to the habit of dominating a tradesman, there can be no question of a common trait involving both these habits; but if the habit of dominating a tradesman can be shown, statistically or genetically, to be related to the habit of bluffing one's way past guards, there is the presumption that a common trait of personality exists which includes these two habits. Traits may conceivably embrace anywhere from two habits to a legion of habits. In this way, there may be said to be major, widely extensified traits and minor, less generalized traits in a given personality.

3. A trait is dynamic, or at least determinative. It is not the stimulus that is the crucial determinant in behavior that expresses personality; it is the trait itself that is decisive. Once formed a trait seems to have the capacity of directing responses to stimuli into characteristic channels. This emphasis upon the dynamic nature of traits, ascribing to them a capacity for guiding the specific response, is variously recognized by many writers. The principle is nothing more than that which has been subscribed to in various connections by Woodworth, Prince, Sherrington, Coghill, Kurt Lewin, Troland, Lloyd Morgan, Thurstone, Bentley, Stern, and others.[2] From this general point of view traits might be called "derived drives" or "derived motives." Whatever they are called they may be regarded as playing a motivating role in each act, thus endowing the separate adjustments of the individual to specific stimuli with that *adverbial* quality that is the very essence of personality.

* * *

4. The existence of a trait may be established empirically or statistically. In order to know that a person has a *habit* it is necessary to have evidence of repeated reactions of a constant type. Similarly in order to know that an individual has a trait it is necessary to have evidence of repeated reactions which, though not necessarily constant in type, seem none the less to be consistently a function of the same underlying determinant. If this evidence is gathered casually by mere observation of the subject or through the reading of a case-history or biography, it may be called empirical evidence.

More exactly, of course, the existence of a trait may be established with the aid of statistical techniques that determine the degree of coherence among the separate responses. Although this employment of statistical aid is highly desirable, it is not necessary to wait for such evidence before speaking of traits, any more than it would be necessary to refrain from speaking of the habit of bit-

[2]This is an all-star list of important psychologists and scientists at the time this article was written. Of these, Kurt Lewin and Allport himself had the most lasting influence on personality psychology.

ing fingernails until the exact frequency of the occurrence is known. Statistical methods are at present better suited to intellective than to conative functions, and it is with the latter that we are chiefly concerned in our studies of personality.[3]

5. Traits are only relatively independent of each other. The investigator desires, of course, to discover what the fundamental traits of personality are, that is to say, what broad trends in behavior do exist independently of one another. Actually with the test methods and correlational procedures in use, completely independent variation is seldom found. In one study expansion correlated with extroversion to the extent of +.39, ascendance with conservatism, +.22, and humor with insight, +.83, and so on. This overlap may be due to several factors, the most obvious being the tendency of the organism to react in an integrated fashion, so that when concrete acts are observed or tested they reflect not only the trait under examination, but also simultaneously other traits; several traits may thus converge into a final common path. It seems safe, therefore, to predict that traits can never be completely isolated for study, since they never show more than a relative independence of one another.

In the instance just cited, it is doubtful whether humor and insight (provided their close relationship is verified in subsequent studies) represent distinct traits. In the future perhaps it may be possible to agree upon a certain magnitude of correlation below which it will be acceptable to speak of *separate* traits, and above which *one* trait only will be recognized. If one trait only is indicated it will presumably represent a broadly generalized disposition. For example, if humor and insight cannot be established as independent traits, it will be necessary to recognize a more inclusive trait, and name it perhaps "sense of proportion."

6. A trait of personality, psychologically considered, is not the same as moral quality. A trait of personality may or may not coincide with some well-defined, conventional, social concept. Extroversion, ascendance, social participation, and insight are free from preconceived moral significance, large because each is a word newly coined or adapted to fit a psychological discovery. It would be ideal if we could in this way find our traits first and then name them. But honesty, loyalty, neatness, and tact, though encrusted with social significance, *may* likewise represent true traits of personality. The danger is that in devising scales for their measurement we may be bound by the conventional meanings, and thus be led away from the precise integration as it exists in a given individual. Where possible it would be well for us to find our traits first, and then seek devaluated terms with which to characterize our discoveries.

7. Acts, and even habits, that are inconsistent with a trait are not proof of the non-existence of the trait. The objection most often considered fatal to the doctrine of traits has been illustrated as follows: "An individual may be habitually neat with respect to his person, and characteristically slovenly in his handwriting or the care of his desk."[4]

In the first place this observation fails to state that there are cases frequently met where a constant level of neatness is maintained in all of a person's acts, giving unmistakable empirical evidence that the trait of neatness is, in some people at least, thoroughly and permanently integrated. All people must not be expected to show the same

[3]"Conative functions" here refer to motivation; at the time this was written statistical methods of psychological measurement (psychometrics) had been used exclusively for the measurement of intellectual skills, not motivation or personality. Over the following decades, this situation changed and psychometrics became a foundation of modern personality psychology.

[4]This comment anticipates the "person-situation" debate that flared up in 1968, almost 40 years later, with the publication of a book by Walter Mischel (excerpted in a following selection). Interestingly, the inconsistency of neatness, almost exactly as Allport here describes it, *was* used as an argument against the doctrine of traits in an even later article by Mischel and Peake (1982).

degree of integration in respect to a given trait. *What is a major trait in one personality may be a minor trait, or even nonexistent in another personality.*[5]

In the second place, we must concede that there may be opposed integrations, i.e., contradictory traits, in a single personality. The same individual may have a trait *both* of neatness *and* of carelessness, of ascendance *and* submission, although frequently of unequal strength.

In the third place there are in every personality instances of acts that are unrelated to existent traits, the product of the stimulus and of the attitude of the moment. Even the characteristically neat person may become careless in his haste to catch a train.

But to say that not all of a person's acts reflect some higher integration is not to say that no such higher integrations exist.

8. A trait may be viewed either in the light of the personality which contains it, or in the light of its distribution in the population at large. Each trait has both its unique and its universal aspect. In its unique aspect, the trait takes its significance entirely from the role it plays in the personality as a whole. In its universal aspect, the trait is arbitrarily isolated for study, and a comparison is made between individuals in respect to it. From this second point of view traits merely extend the familiar field of the psychology of individual differences.

There may be relatively few traits, a few hundred perhaps, that are universal enough to be scaled in the population at large; whereas there may be in a single personality a thousand traits distinguishable to a discerning observer. For this reason, after a scientific schedule of universal traits is compiled, there will still be the field of *artistic* endeavor for psychologists in apprehending correctly the subtle and unique traits peculiar to one personality alone, and in discovering the *pattern* which obtains *between* these traits in the same personality.

---

[5]This comment—that not all traits apply to all people—was developed into an important article many years later by the psychologists Daryl Bem and Andrea Allen (1974).

Consistency and Specificity in Behavior

Walter Mischel

The "book that launched a thousand rebuttals" is Walter Mischel's (1968) Personality and Assessment. *This book, widely perceived as an all-out frontal assault on the existence of personality traits and the viability of personality psychology, touched off the "person-situation debate," which lasted 20 years. Put briefly, the debate was over this issue: For determining what an individual does, which is more important, stable aspects of his or her personality, or the situation he or she happens to be in at the time? You have already seen that Allport's view, which is the traditional view of the trait approach, is that personality is an important determinant of behavior. Mischel's view is that people act very differently in different situations, to the point that characterizing them in terms of broad personality traits may be neither meaningful nor useful.*

The next selection is drawn from one of the key chapters of Mischel's book. In it, Mischel argues that inconsistency in behavior is the rule rather than the exception. He surveys, very briefly, a large number of studies that attempted to find strong relationships between what individuals did in one situation and what they did in another. In Mischel's view, such studies generally have failed. Specifically, Mischel assumes that if the relationship between behaviors in two different situations yields a correlation coefficient of less than about .30, not enough of the variance in behavior has been explained to make it useful to assume that both behaviors are affected by the same underlying personality trait. Of course, the selection by Rosenthal and Rubin in Part I provides a different—and more optimistic—interpretation of a correlation of about .30.

Although the field of personality and what Allport called the "doctrine of traits" ultimately survived the Mischelian onslaught, the book and this chapter remain important landmarks in the recent history of personality psychology. First, the ideas presented in this chapter had a powerful effect on the viewpoint of many psychologists within and outside the field of personality, an effect that more than 25 years later has still not dissipated. To this day, a surprising number of psychologists "don't believe in personality." Second and even more important, with the words you are about to read Mischel forced the field of personality into an agonizing reappraisal of some of its most basic and cherished assumptions. Although these assumptions can be said to have survived, their close reexamination was on the whole potentially beneficial for our understanding of personality (see the selection by Kenrick and Funder later in this section).

From *Personality and Assessment* (New York: Wiley, 1968), pp. 13–39.

For more than 50 years personality psychologists have tried to measure traits and states in order to discover personality structure and dynamics. There has been an enormous effort to investigate the reliability and, more recently, the validity of the results. This chapter examines some of the evidence for the assumption of generalized personality traits and states. Empirically, the generality of a trait is established by the associations found among trait indicators. The evidence consists of obtained correlations between behaviors measured across similar situations. Data that demonstrate strong generality in the behavior of the same person across many situations are critical for trait and state personality theories; the construct of personality itself rests on the belief that individual behavioral consistencies exist widely and account for much of the variance in behavior. Most definitions of personality hinge on the assumption that an individual's behavior is consistent across many stimulus conditions (e.g., Sanford, 1963).

Data on the generality-specificity of behavior usually fall under the rubric of "reliability" and are separated from "validity" evidence. This distinction between reliability and validity is not very sharp. Both reliability and validity are established by demonstrating relations between responses to various stimulus conditions. The stimulus conditions are the particular measures and settings used to sample responses. *Reliability* concerns the congruence among responses measured under maximally *similar* stimulus conditions (Campbell, 1960; Campbell & Fiske, 1959). *Validity*, in contradistinction to reliability, requires convergence between responses to maximally *different*, independent stimulus conditions or measures.[1] The distinction between reliability and validity research depends chiefly on judgments about the degree of similarity among the stimuli used to evoke responses with the particular eliciting techniques or tests employed. For example, correlations among two similar tests, or of two forms of one test, or of the same test administered to the same person on different occasions, all are taken as reliability evidence; correlations among more dissimilar tests, on the other hand, are interpreted as validity data. This chapter is concerned mainly with reliability evidence and evaluates the behavioral consistencies obtained under relatively similar stimulus conditions. We shall look at several kinds of data, first examining the consistency of intellectual variables and then turning to measures of personality. Throughout this chapter some of the empirical evidence for the cross-situational generality of behavior will be reviewed in order to assess more concretely the appropriateness of the trait assumptions which have had such a marked impact on the field.

* * *

Personality Variables

* * *

Personality variables have been examined thoroughly to determine individual consistencies with respect to particular dimensions or dispositions. The following personality dimensions are repre-

[1]Our reading of Cronbach and Meehl and of Campbell and Fiske (see Part I) suggests that validity implies something much more than, and sometimes much different from this simple characterization. Validity concerns the convergence between patterns of data that are theoretically predicted and those that are empirically obtained. The patterns are not necessarily simple consistency of the sort Mischel describes.

sentative of those attracting most theoretical and research interest during the last decade, and some of the evidence for their consistency is examined. It will become apparent rapidly that the generality of these dispositions usually is far less than that found for cognitive and intellectual variables.[2]

ATTITUDES TOWARD AUTHORITY AND PEERS The belief that an individual has generalized attitudes toward classes of persons pervades clinical, diagnostic, and research practice. This belief is reflected in the common assumption that problems of sibling rivalry repeat themselves in peer relations, and that attitudes toward parental figures are mirrored in reactions to diverse authority figures throughout life and toward the psychotherapist in particular. Psychologists of many theoretical orientations often agree that persons develop highly generalized attitudes toward authority. Freud, Piaget, and Rogers, among others, all posit that reactions toward authority originate in the family situation and manifest themselves as broadly generalized attitudes expressed in many contexts toward superiors in later social situations. As Piaget puts it:

> Day to day observation and psycho-analytic experience show that the first personal schemas are afterward generalised and applied to many people. According as the first inter-individual experiences of the child who is just learning to speak are connected with a father who is understanding or dominating, loving or cruel, etc., the child will tend (even throughout life if these relationships have influenced his whole youth) to assimilate all other individuals to this father schema. (Piaget, 1951, p. 207)

These assumptions have been subjected to a rare and extensive test by Burwen and Campbell (1957). Burwen and Campbell studied a large sample of Air Force personnel by means of interviews, TAT,[3] description of self and others, judgments of photos, and autobiographical inventories, as well as an attitude survey and sociometric questionnaire.[4] Through each of these techniques, where possible, attitudes were scored toward own father, symbolic authority (e.g., in responses to pictures of older persons on the TAT), immediate boss, immediate peers, and symbolic peers. The topics or attitude objects and the measures for scoring attitudes toward authority on each are summarized below:

Topic	*Measures*
Father	Interview; description of self and others; autobiographical inventory
Symbolic authority	Interview; TAT (scored globally); TAT (scored objectively); judgments of photos (of older persons); attitude survey
Boss	Interview; description of self and others; autobiographical inventory; sociometric questionnaire

Similar measures were used to score attitudes toward real and symbolic peers.

The interjudge reliability of all ratings on each instrument was adequately high, and scores were available on twenty variables. Their intercorrelations revealed, first of all, the major impact of stimulus similarity or "method variance": for three quarters of all the variables the highest correlations occurred between measures of different attitudes based on the *same* instrument. When these method-produced correlations were disre-

[2]In a section of this chapter that has been omitted, Mischel acknowledged that cognitive and intellectual variables, such as IQ and cognitive style, are relatively consistent over time and across situations.

[3]The TAT is the Thematic Apperception Test, in which a person looks at a picture (e.g., of a person working at a desk) and makes up a story about what is going on. This story can then be scored in various ways, most commonly as to the motivations that it reveals.

[4]A sociometric questionnaire is one in which members of a group are asked about their impressions of or feelings about one another.

TABLE 10.1

MEAN CORRELATIONS AMONG ATTITUDES MEASURED BY DIFFERENT METHODS

Attitude toward		F	SA	B	P	SP
Father	F	.35	.12	.03	.06	.08
Symbolic authority	SA		.15	.08	.10	.06
Boss	B			.09	.13	.03
Peer	P				.22	.07
Symbolic peer	SP					.01

(Adapted from Burwen & Campbell, 1957, p. 26.)

garded, there was little evidence for generality of attitudes either toward authority or toward peers. Attitudes toward father, symbolic authority, and boss were no more highly correlated with each other than they were with attitudes toward real or symbolic peers, and all correlations tended to be low.

Table 10.1 shows the average of transformed correlations between attitude topics, eliminating those based on the same instrument. Of the correlations between different measures of attitude toward a *single* type of authority figure, only among attitudes toward father and among attitudes toward peers are there any indications that independent methods tap a specific attitude focus at least to some extent. Even these associations among different measures of attitudes toward the same type of authority were very modest, being .35 for father and .22 for peers. Attitude toward *different* types of authority figures showed no consistency at all. For example, attitude toward one's father correlated .03 with attitude toward one's boss. The authors appropriately concluded that:

> Evidence for a generalized attitude toward authority which encompasses attitudes toward father, symbolic authority, and boss is totally negative, suggesting the need for reconsideration of the applicability of commonly held theory in this area. (Burwen & Campbell, 1957, p. 31)

MORAL BEHAVIOR Psychodynamic theory has emphasized the role of the "superego" as an internalized moral agency that has a critical role in the regulation of all forms of conduct and in the control of impulses. Theorizing regarding the superego has focused on the way in which authority figures and their values become "incorporated" during the course of socialization. It has been assumed that as a result of this process the child adopts parental standards and controls as his own. There is no doubt that in the course of development most children acquire the capacity to regulate, judge, and monitor their own behavior even in the absence of external constraints and authorities. An important theoretical issue, however, is the consistency of these self-regulated patterns of conduct and self-control.

In the extraordinarily extensive and sophisticated Character Education Inquiry, more than thirty years ago,[5] thousands of children were exposed to various situations in which they could cheat, lie, and steal in diverse settings, including the home, party games, and athletic contexts (Hartshorne & May, 1928; Hartshorne, May, & Shuttleworth, 1930).

Although moral conduct was relatively inconsistent, the children showed substantial consistency in their self-reported opinions and thoughts about moral issues elicited on paper-and-pencil tests administered in the classroom. High correlations also were found between various forms of these paper-and-pencil tests. However, if children took alternate equivalent forms of the same tests

[5]That is, more than 30 years before this book was published in 1968.

in diverse social settings—such as at home, in Sunday school, at club meetings, as well as in the classroom—the correlations of their scores among situations were reduced to about .40. The investigators concluded that children vary their opinions to "suit the situation" (Hartshorne, May, & Shuttleworth, 1930, p. 108) and do not have a generalized code of morals.

The specificity of responses, and their dependence on the exact particulars of the evoking situation, was keenly noted by Hartshorne and May (1928). For example:

> . . . even such slight changes in the situation as between crossing out A's and putting dots in squares are sufficient to alter the amount of deception both in individuals and in groups. (p. 382)

To illustrate further from their data, copying from an answer key on one test correlated .696 with copying from a key on another test, and cheating by adding on scores from a speed test correlated .440 with adding on scores on another speed test. However, copying from a key on one test correlated only .292 with adding on scores. Moreover, the average intercorrelations among four classroom tests was only .256 (Hartshorne & May, 1928, p. 383). The more the situation changed the lower the correlations became. The average correlation between four classroom tests and two out-of-classroom tests (contests and stealing) was .167. The lying test given in the classroom averaged .234 with the other classroom tests but only .061 with the two out-of-classroom deception tests (p. 384).

* * *

The observations that Hartshorne and May reported for the relative specificity of moral behavior accurately foreshadowed the findings that emerged from later research on other behavioral consistencies. Response specificity of the kind emphasized by Hartshorne and May is also reflected, for example, in the finding that questionnaires dealing with attitudes and hypothetical matters may correlate with other questionnaires but are less likely to relate to non-self-report behavior (Mischel, 1962). In one study, children were asked questions about whether or not they would postpone immediate smaller rewards for the sake of larger but delayed outcomes in hypothetical situations. Their answers in these hypothetical delay of reward situations were found to relate to other questionnaires dealing with trust and a variety of verbally expressed attitudes. What they said, however, was unrelated to their actual delay of reward choices in real situations (Mischel, 1962). Likewise, measures eliciting direct nonverbal behavior may relate to other behavioral indices in the same domain but not to questionnaires. Thus real behavioral choices between smaller but immediately available gratifications, as opposed to larger but delayed rewards, correlated significantly with such behavioral indices as resistance to temptation, but not with self reports on questionnaires (Mischel, 1962).

Moral guilt also has been studied utilizing projective test[6] responses. For example, in a study with teenage boys (Allinsmith, 1960) moral feelings were inferred from the subjects' projective story completions in response to descriptions of various kinds of immoral actions. The findings led Allinsmith to the view that a person with a truly generalized conscience is a statistical rarity. Johnson (1962) also found that moral judgments across situations tend to be highly specific and even discrepant.

Recent research on moral behavior has concentrated on three areas: moral judgment and verbal standards of right and wrong (e.g., Kohlberg, 1963); resistance to temptation in the absence of external constraint (e.g., Aronfreed & Reber, 1965; Grinder, 1962; MacKinnon, 1938; Mischel & Gilligan, 1964); and post-transgression indices of remorse and guilt (e.g., Allinsmith, 1960; Aronfreed, 1961; Sears, Maccoby, & Levin, 1957; Whiting, 1959). These three areas of moral behavior turn out to be either completely independent or at best only minimally interrelated (Becker, 1964; Hoffman, 1963; Kohlberg, 1963). Within each area

[6]A projective test is one in which a subject is shown an ambiguous stimulus (e.g., an inkblot, a TAT picture) and asked for his or her interpretation. The subject's answer is assumed to be a "projection" of some aspect of his or her underlying psychology.

specificity also tends to be the rule. For example, an extensive survey of all types of reactions to transgression yielded no predictable relationships among specific types of reaction (Aronfreed, 1961). Similarly, Sears and his coworkers (1965, chapter 6) did not find consistent associations among various reactions to transgression. Thus the data on moral behavior provide no support for the widespread psychodynamic belief in a unitary intrapsychic moral agency like the superego, or for a unitary trait entity of conscience or honesty. Rather than acquiring a homogeneous conscience that determines uniformly all aspects of their self-control, people seem to develop subtler discriminations that depend on many considerations.

SEXUAL IDENTIFICATION, DEPENDENCY, AND AGGRESSION It is widely assumed in most dynamic and trait theories that people develop firm masculine or feminine identifications early in life. These stable identifications, in turn, are believed to exert pervasive effects on what the person does in many diverse situations (e.g., Kohlberg, 1966). There is, of course, no doubt that boys and girls rapidly learn about sex differences and soon recognize their own gender permanently. A much less obvious issue is the extent to which children develop highly consistent patterns of masculine or feminine "sex-typed" behavior. This question has received considerable research attention. The chief strategy has involved studying the associations among different indicators of masculine and feminine sex-typed behavior.

Dependency and aggression often serve conceptually as behavioral referents for sex typing, with boys expected to be more aggressive and girls more dependent. In dependency research, although Beller's (1955) correlations ranged from .48 to .83 for teacher ratings of five dependency components in nursery school children, it is likely that a "halo" effect spuriously inflated the teachers' ratings.[7] Mann (1959) obtained ratings of 55 two-minute observations of 41 nursery school children in free play on six kinds of dependency behavior. He found only 1 of 15 intercorrelations among components of dependency significant. Likewise, observations of nursery school children revealed that the frequencies of "affection seeking" and "approval seeking" were unrelated (Heathers, 1953).

Sears (1963) extensively studied the intercorrelations between five categories of dependency behavior in preschool girls and boys. The five categories were: *negative attention seeking*, e.g., attention getting by disruption or aggressive activity; *positive attention seeking*, as in seeking praise; nonaggressive *touching or holding*; *being near*, e.g., following a child or teacher; and *seeking reassurance*. The frequency of these behaviors was carefully and reliably scored by observing the children at nursery school with an extensive time-sampling procedure. Each child was observed in free play for a total of 7 to 10 hours. The intercorrelations among the five dependency categories for 21 boys and 19 girls are shown in Table 10.2. Note that only 1 of the 20 correlations reached statistical significance since for 20 degrees of freedom correlations of .423 and .537 would have been needed to reach significance at the .05 and .01 levels respectively.[8]

* * *

Some support for sex differences in the generality of particular patterns of sex-typed behaviors comes in the form of more (and stronger) intercorrelations for girls than boys on five observation measures of dependency (Sears, 1963), whereas the reverse holds for aggression, with more intercorrelations among aggression variables for boys than for girls (Lansky, Crandall, Kagan, & Baker, 1961; Sears, 1961). However, individuals discriminate sharply between situations. The specificity of aggressive behavior, for example, is documented in a study of highly aggressive boys by Bandura (1960). Parents who punished aggression

[7]A "halo effect" occurs when a rater's global positive or negative evaluation of a target person affects all of her or his ratings.

[8]The .05 and .01 significance levels are conventional criteria by which findings are judged not to have occurred merely by chance.

TABLE 10.2

INTERCORRELATIONS AMONG DEPENDENCY MEASURES[a]

Measures		I	II	III	IV	V
Negative attention	I		.06	.10	.15	.37
Reassurance	II	.24		.25	.19	.26
Positive attention	III	.23	.11		.11	.03
Touching and holding	IV	.01	.11	.16		.71
Being near	V	.03	.12	.14	.13	

(Adapted from Sears, 1963, p. 35.)
[a]Girls above diagonal, boys below.

in the home, but who simultaneously modeled aggressive behavior and encouraged it in their sons' peer relationships, produced boys who were nonaggressive at home but markedly aggressive at school.

RIGIDITY AND TOLERANCE FOR AMBIGUITY If individuals did develop strongly consistent character structures that channelized them in stable ways, it would be important to identify these syndromes. One of the most thoroughly studied personality patterns is the "authoritarian personality." Intolerance for ambiguity attracted considerable interest as a characteristic of the authoritarian personality (Adorno, Frenkel-Brunswik, Levinson, & Sanford, 1950), and a voluminous literature was devoted to elaborating its correlates.

Several behavioral signs have been used as the referents for intolerance for ambiguity. These signs include resistance to reversal of apparent fluctuating stimuli, early selection and adherence to one solution in perceptually ambiguous situations, seeking for certainty, rigid dichotomizing into fixed categories, premature closure, and the like. In one study, an extensive battery of tests to measure intolerance of ambiguity was designed and administered (Kenny & Ginsberg, 1958). Only 7 of the 66 correlations among intolerance of ambiguity measures reached significance and the relationship for 2 of these was opposite to the predicted direction. Moreover, the measures in the main failed to correlate with the usual questionnaire indices of authoritarianism submissiveness as elicited by a form of the California *F* scale.

Closely related to authoritarianism, "rigidity" is another personality dimension that has received much attention as a generalized trait (Chown, 1959; Cronbach, 1956). In one study (Applezweig, 1954), among 45 correlations between behaviors on six measures of rigidity (including arithmetic problems, Rorschach,[9] and *F* scale), 22 were negative, 21 were positive, and 2 were zero; only 3 of the 45 correlations were significant and 2 of these were negative. Likewise, Pervin's (1960) data on five noninventory performance measures of rigidity, including the water-jars problems, provide generally low associations and suggest that "individuals may be rigid in one area of personality functioning and not in another" and that "rigidity is not a general personality characteristic" (p. 394). The conclusion that rigidity is not a unitary trait is also supported by the modest intercorrelations between measures obtained by Wrightsman and Baumeister (1961) and by the specificity found earlier by Maher (1957).

* * *

Thus investigators frequently measure and describe a purportedly general dimension of behavior only to discover later that it has dubious consistency. As a result the popular dimensions of personality research often wax and wane almost like fashions. Research on the generality of the be-

[9]The Rorschach is the famous projective test in which subjects are asked what they see in blots of ink.

havioral indices of personality dimensions has generated its own truisms. Over and over again the conclusions of these investigations, regardless of the specific content area, are virtually identical and predictable. The following paragraph, from Applezweig's (1954) own summary, is essentially interchangeable with those from a plethora of later researches on the generality of many different traits:

> The following conclusions appear to be justified:
> (a) There is no general factor of rigidity among a number of so-called measures of rigidity; the interrelationships of these measures appear to vary with the nature of the tests employed and the conditions of test administration as well as behavioral determinants within S's.[10]
> (b) Scores obtained by an individual on any so-called measure of rigidity appear to be a function not only of the individual, but also of the nature of the test and the conditions of test administration. (Applezweig, 1954, p. 228)

* * *

CONDITIONABILITY Classical learning formulations place great emphasis on conditioning as a basic process in learning. Consequently psychologists with an interest in both learning and individual differences have been especially interested in studying conditionability as a personality dimension. In spite of a great deal of research, however, there is no evidence for the existence of a general factor or trait of "conditionability" in either classical or operant conditioning paradigms.

Correlations among different measures and types of conditioning tend to be low or zero (e.g., Bunt & Barendregt, 1961; Campbell, 1938; Davidson, Payne, & Sloane, 1964; Eysenck, 1965; Franks, 1956; Lovibond, 1964; Moore & Marcuse, 1945; Patterson & Hinsey, 1964). Moore and Marcuse (1945) noted many years ago that "the concept of good or poor conditioners must always be with reference to a specific response." Reviewing the literature two decades later, Eysenck (1965) points out that correlations between conditionability measures depend on specific peripheral factors (sweat glands in the hand, pain sensitivity of the cornea). He also notes that even if these sources were eliminated correlations would still be affected by situational circumstances such as the sequence and massing of stimuli, the scheduling of reinforcement, the strength of CS and UCS,[11] temporal intervals, and so on.

The evidence that learning variables like conditionability are unitary traitlike entities is no more convincing than the data for the consistency of personality traits couched in any other theoretical language. Whenever individual differences are elicited, however, the failure to demonstrate impressive reliability does not preclude the existence of extensive correlations with other response measures (e.g., Franks, 1961).

MODERATOR VARIABLES Wallach (1962) and Kogan and Wallach (1964) have called attention to the fact that "moderator variables" may influence the correlations found in research on behavioral consistency. By moderator variables Wallach and Kogan mean interactions among several variables that influence the correlations obtained between any one of the variables and other data. For example, correlations between two response patterns may be found for males, but not for females, or may even be positive for one sex but negative for the other. Thus, if the correlations between two response patterns are examined for both sexes combined, the different relations that might be obtained if each sex were taken into account separately could become obscured. Similarly, relations between two measures might be positive for children with high IQ but negative for those with low IQ. In other words, there are complex interactions so that the relations between any two variables depend on several other variables.

By analyzing their data to illuminate higher-

---

[10]The abbreviation S's refers to subjects (now usually called "participants").

[11]The abbreviation CS means conditioned stimulus; UCS means unconditioned stimulus. In learning experiments, the stimuli employed, of either type, may vary in intensity or strength.

order interactions of this kind, these investigators have been able to demonstrate significant associations among various measures of risk taking, and between risk taking and other variables. The resulting associations of course apply only to some subjects under a few conditions. This strategy of searching for interactions holds some promise. Since the interactions are obtained post hoc rather than predicted, however, considerable interpretative caution must be observed. Otherwise the analysis of the same data for many interactions provides many additional chances to obtain seemingly statistically significant results that actually monopolize on chance. That is, more "significant" associations occur by chance when more correlations are computed.

TEMPORAL STABILITY So far, our discussion of consistency has focused on relationships among a person's behaviors across situations sampled more or less at the same time. Equally important, however, are data that examine how stable the individual's behavior remains in any one particular domain when he is reassessed at later times.

Results from the Fels Longitudinal Study give some typical examples of the stability of a person's behavior patterns over time (Kagan & Moss, 1962). The overall findings suggest some significant consistency between childhood and early adulthood ratings of achievement behavior, sex-typed activity, and spontaneity for both sexes. For certain other variables, like dependency, some consistency was found for one sex but not the other. Thus the rated dependency of girls at age six years to ten years correlated .30 with their adult dependence on family; the comparable correlation for boys was near zero. In the same longitudinal study of middle class subjects the most highly significant positive associations were found between ratings of achievement and recognition strivings obtained at various periods of childhood and in early adulthood (Kagan & Moss, 1962; Moss & Kagan, 1961). Children who were rated as showing strong desires for recognition also tended to be rated as more concerned with excellence and with the attainment of high self-imposed standards when they were interviewed as young adults. Some of the many correlations between achievement strivings in childhood and comparable adult preoccupation with attaining excellence were exceptionally high, in several instances reaching the .60 to .70 range.

Apart from ratings the motive or need to achieve ("*n* Ach") has also been studied most extensively by scoring the subject's achievement imagery in the stories he tells to selected TAT cards. For example, if the person creates stories in which the hero is studying hard for a profession and aspires and strives to improve himself and to advance in his career, the story receives high *n* Ach scores. This technique, developed thoroughly by McClelland and his associates (1953), has become the main index of the motive to achieve and to compete against standards of excellence. As a result considerable attention has been devoted to studying the stability of this need by comparing *n* Ach scores obtained from the same individuals at different times. Moss and Kagan (1961) reported a stability coefficient of .31 for their sample over a 10-year period from adolescence to adulthood. They also reported a 3-year stability coefficient of .32 for TAT achievement themes obtained at ages 8 and 11 (Kagan & Moss, 1959). However, the correlation between *n* Ach at age 8 and at age 14 was only .22; the correlation between *n* Ach at age 11 and at 14 years was a nonsignificant .16.

The stability of achievement motivation was also studied closely for shorter time intervals with other samples of people. Birney (1959) reported a coefficient of only .29 for *n* Ach on equivalent picture forms administered to college students within six months. He concluded that ". . . the *n* Ach measure is highly situational in character . . ." (p. 267). Similarly, a significant but modest coefficient of .26 was reported for a 9-week test-retest study with college students (Krumboltz & Farquhar, 1957). Higher correlations ranging from .36 to .61 have been found for shorter time intervals of 3 weeks to 5 weeks (Haber & Alpert, 1958; Morgan, 1953). Reviewing a great deal of information from many studies, Skolnick (1966a, b) reported extensive correlations between diverse adolescent and adult measures. Many correlations reached significance, especially for achievement and power imagery indices, although the associations tended to be extremely complicated and most often of modest magnitude.

Just as with consistency across situations, stability over time tends to be greatest for behaviors associated with intelligence and cognitive processes (e.g., Bloom, 1964; Gardner & Long, 1960; Kagan & Moss, 1962; Moss & Kagan, 1961). Most notably, extremely impressive stability over long time periods has been found for certain cognitive styles. Retest correlations on Witkin's rod-and-frame test (RFT), for example, were as high as .92 for time intervals of a few years (Witkin, Goodenough, & Karp, 1967). A time lapse of 14 years was the lengthiest interval sampled in their longitudinal study. Even after such a long period, the stability correlation for boys tested with the RFT at age 10 and retested at age 24 was .66. Data of this kind demonstrate genuine durability in aspects of cognitive and perceptual functioning.

A representative illustration of temporal stability comes from studies of behavior during interviews. Reasonable stability has been demonstrated for certain interaction patterns during interviews. These patterns were measured by an interaction chronograph devised to record selected temporal aspects of verbal and gestural behavior (e.g., Matarazzo, 1965; Saslow, Matarazzo, Phillips, & Matarazzo, 1957). In these studies the interviewer followed a standardized pattern of behavior, including systematic periods of "not responding," "interrupting," and other variations in style. The subject's corresponding behavior was scored on formal dimensions such as the frequency of his actions, their average duration, and the length of his silences. The results indicated that these interactions are highly stable across short time periods (such as 1-week retests) when the interviewer's behavior remains fixed. The same interactions, however, were readily and predictably modifiable by planned changes in the interviewer's behavior.

The trait-descriptive categories and personality labels with which individuals describe themselves on questionnaires and trait-rating scales seem to be especially long lasting. E. L. Kelly (1955) compared questionnaire trait self-descriptions obtained almost 20 years apart. During the years 1935–1938 several personality questionnaires were administered to 300 engaged couples, and most of them were retested with the same measures in 1954. The questionnaires included the Strong Vocational Interest Blank, the Allport-Vernon values test, and the Bernreuter personality questionnaire, among others. Self-reports of attitudes about marriage were highly unstable ($r < .10$), but the stability coefficients for self-descriptions of interests, of economic and political values, of self-confidence and sociability were high. The coefficients for these areas of self-reported traits ranged from about .45 to slightly over .60, indicating impressive stability, considering the long temporal delay between assessments.

As another example, the test retest correlations on the California Psychological Inventory scales for high school students retested after 1 year, and for a sample of prisoners retested after a lapse of 7 to 21 days, were also high (Gough, 1957). In general, trait self-descriptions on many personality questionnaires show considerable stability (Byrne, 1966). Studies of the semantic differential also suggest that the meanings associated with semantic concepts may be fairly stable (Osgood, Suci, & Tannenbaum, 1957).

Research on the temporal stability of personal constructs evoked by Kelly's Role Construct Repertory Test (Reptest) also indicates considerable consistency in constructs over time (Bonarius, 1965). For example, a retest correlation of .79 was found for constructs after a 2-week interval (Landfield, Stern, & Fjeld, 1961). * * * Thus the trait categories people attribute to themselves and others may be relatively permanent, and may be more enduring than the behaviors to which they refer.

Implications

The data on cross-situational consistency and stability over time reviewed in this chapter merely provide representative examples from an enormous domain. The results indicate that correlations across situations tend to be highest for cognitive and intellectual functions. Moreover, behaviors sampled in closely similar situations generally yield the best correlations. Considerable stability over time has been demonstrated for some domains, and again particularly for ability and cognitive measures. Self-descriptions on trait dimensions also seem to be especially consistent even over very long periods of time.

As early as 1928 Hartshorne and May surprised psychologists by showing that the honesty or moral behavior of children is not strongly consistent across situations and measures. The Hartshorne and May data were cited extensively but did not influence psychological theorizing about the generality of traits. Similar evidence for behavioral specificity across situations has been reported over and over again for personality measures since the earliest correlational studies at the turn of the century. Considerable specificity has been found regularly even for syndromes like attitudes toward authority, or aggression and dependency, whose assumed generality has reached the status of a cliché in psychological writings.

The interpretation of all data on behavioral consistency is affected of course by the criteria selected. Consistency coefficients averaging between .30 and .40, of the kind obtained by Hartshorne and May, can be taken either as evidence for the relative specificity of the particular behaviors or as support for the presence of underlying generality. Indeed, the Hartshorne and May data have been reinterpreted as evidence for generality in children's moral behavior, at least across related situations (Burton, 1963). Similarly, McGuire (1968) reviewed data on the consistency of suggestibility, persuasibility, and conformity and concluded that each has the status of a generalized, although "weak," trait. McGuire noted the tenuousness of the evidence, since the data consisted mostly of low but positive correlations which often reached the .05 statistical confidence level, sometimes did not, and which never accounted for more than a trivial proportion of the variance.[12]

There is nothing magical about a correlation coefficient, and its interpretation depends on many considerations. The accuracy or reliability of measurement increases with the length of the test. Since no single item is a perfect measure, adding items increases the chance that the test will elicit a more accurate sample and yield a better estimate of the person's behavior. Second, a test may be reliable at one score level but unreliable at another. That is, the accuracy of the test is not necessarily uniform for different groups of people; a test that yields reliable achievement scores for 10-year-old children may be so difficult for 7-year-olds that they are reduced to guessing on almost all items. Moreover, different items within the same test do not necessarily yield uniformly reliable information (Cronbach, 1960). The interpretation of reliability coefficients is influenced by the relative homogeneity or heterogeneity in the tested behavior range of the sample of subjects. For example, if an ability test is given to a more or less uniformly bright group of college students, very slight errors in measurement could obscure actual individual differences. Any one set of observations provides merely a sample of behavior whose meaning may be confounded by numerous errors of measurement.

These and similar statistical considerations (Cronbach, 1960) caution us to interpret the meaning of particular coefficients with care. In spite of methodological reservations, however, it is evident that the behaviors which are often construed as stable personality trait indicators actually

[12]Mischel is here following the common practice of squaring a correlation to yield the percent of variance "explained" (see the selection by Rosenthal and Rubin in Part I). Thus a correlation of .30 is said to explain 9% of the variance (.30 squared being .09) and a correlation of .40 is said to explain 16% of the variance (.40 squared being .16). Mischel regards these percentages as "trivial." But recall that Rosenthal and Rubin (Part I) demonstrated that a correlation of .32 yields correct classification twice as often as incorrect classification.

are highly specific and depend on the details of the evoking situations and the response mode employed to measure them.

* * *

It is important to distinguish clearly between "statistically significant" associations and equivalence. A correlation of .30 easily reaches statistical significance when the sample of subjects is sufficiently large, and suggests an association that is highly unlikely on the basis of chance. However, the same coefficient accounts for less than 10 percent of the relevant variance. Statistically significant relationships of this magnitude are sufficient to justify personality research on individual and group differences. It is equally plain that their value for making statements about an individual is severely limited. Even when statistically significant behavioral consistencies are found, and even when they replicate reliably, the relationships usually are not large enough to warrant individual assessment and treatment decisions except for certain screening and selection purposes.

It is very easy to misunderstand the meaning of the findings on behavioral consistency and specificity surveyed in this chapter. It would be a complete misinterpretation, for instance, to conclude that individual differences are unimportant.[13] To remind oneself of their pervasive role one need merely observe the differences among people's responses to almost any complex social stimulus under most supposedly uniform laboratory conditions. The real questions are not the existence of differences among individuals but rather their nature, their causes and consequences, and the utility of inferring them for particular purposes and by particular techniques.

Consistency coefficients of the kind reviewed in this chapter are only one of several types of data pertinent to an appropriate evaluation of the empirical status of the main trait and state approaches to personality. It would be premature therefore to attempt to draw conclusions at this point. Sophisticated dispositional personality theories increasingly have come to recognize that behavior tends to change with alterations in the situations in which it occurs. They note, however, that the same basic underlying disposition (or "genotype") may manifest itself behaviorally in diverse ways in different situations so that heterogeneous behaviors can be signs of the same underlying trait or state. According to this argument, the dependent person, for example, need not behave dependently in all situations; indeed his basic dependency may show itself in diverse and seemingly contradictory overt forms. Although fundamentally dependent, he may, for instance, try to appear aggressively independent under some circumstances, and even may become belligerent and hostile in other settings in efforts to deny his dependency. Similarly, and in accord with psychodynamic theorizing, seemingly diverse acts may be in the service of the same underlying motivational force. For example, a person's overtly liberal political behavior and his overt social conservativism, although apparently inconsistent, may actually both be understandable as expressions of a more fundamental motive, such as his desire to please and win approval and recognition. These arguments for basic consistencies that underlie surface diversity are theoretically defensible, but they ultimately depend, of course, on supporting empirical evidence.

* * *

[13]Despite this disclaimer, the book from which this excerpt is drawn *was* widely interpreted as arguing—even proving—that stable individual differences in personality are unimportant.

References

Adorno, I. W., Frenkel-Brunswik, Else, Levinson, D. J., & Sanford, R. N. (1950). *The authoritarian personality.* New York: Harper.

Allinsmith, W. (1960). The learning of moral standards. In D. R. Miller & G. E. Swanson (Eds.), *Inner conflict and defense* (pp. 141–176). New York: Holt.

Applezweig, Dee G. (1954). Some determinants of behavioral rigidity. *Journal of Abnormal and Social Psychology, 49,* 224–228.

Aronfreed, J. (1961). The nature, variety, and social patterning of moral responses to transgression. *Journal of Abnormal and Social Psychology, 63,* 223–240.

Aronfreed, J. (1964). The origin of self-criticism. *Psychological Review, 71,* 193–218.

Aronfreed, J., & Reber, A. (1965). Internalized behavioral suppression and the timing of social punishment. *Journal of Personality and Social Psychology, 1,* 3–16.

Bandura, A. (1960). Relationship of family patterns to child behavior disorders. Progress Report, U.S.P.H. Research Grant M-1734, Stanford University.

Becker, W. C. (1964). Consequences of different kinds of parental discipline. In M. L. Hoffman & Lois W. Hoffman (Eds.), *Review of child development research* (Vol. 1, pp. 169–208). New York: Russell Sage Foundation.

Beller, E. K. (1955). Dependency and independence in young children. *Journal of Genetic Psychology, 87,* 25–35.

Birney, R. C. (1959). The reliability of the achievement motive. *Journal of Abnormal and Social Psychology, 58,* 266–267.

Bloom, R. S. (1964). *Stability and change in human characteristics.* New York: Wiley.

Bonarius, J. C. J. (1965). Research in the personal construct theory of George A. Kelly: Role Construct Repertory Test and basic theory. In B. A. Maher (Ed.), *Progress in experimental personality research* (Vol. 2, pp. 1–46). New York: Academic Press.

Bunt, A. van de, & Barendregt, J. T. (1961). Inter-correlations of three measures of conditioning. In J. T. Barendregt (Ed.), *Research in psychodiagnostics.* The Hague: Mouton.

Burton, R. V. (1963). Generality of honesty reconsidered. *Psychological Review, 70,* 481–499.

Burwen, L. S., & Campbell, D. T. (1957). The generality of attitudes toward authority and nonauthority figures. *Journal of Abnormal and Social Psychology, 54,* 24–31.

Byrne, D. (1966). *An introduction to personality.* Englewood Cliffs, N. J.: Prentice-Hall.

Campbell, A. A. (1938). The interrelations of two measures of conditioning in man. *Journal of Experimental Psychology, 22,* 225–243.

Campbell, D. T. (1960). Recommendations for APA test standards regarding construct, trait, or discriminant validity. *American Psychologist, 15,* 546–553.

Campbell, D., & Fiske, D. (1959). Convergent and discriminant validation by the multitrait-multimethod matrix. *Psychological Bulletin, 56,* 81–105.

Chown, Sheila M. (1959). Rigidity—A flexible concept. *Psychological Bulletin, 56,* 195–223.

Cronbach, L. J. (1956). Assessment of individual differences. *Annual Review of Psychology, 7,* 173–196.

Cronbach, L. J. (1960). *Essentials of psychological testing* (2nd ed.) New York: Harper.

Davidson, P. O., Payne, R. W., & Sloane, R. B. (1964). Introversion, neuroticism, and conditioning. *Journal of Abnormal and Social Psychology, 68,* 136–148.

Eysenck, II. J. (1965). Extraversion and the acquisition of eyeblink and GSR conditioned responses. *Psychological Bulletin, 63,* 258–270.

Franks, C. M. (1956). Conditioning and personality: A study of normal and neurotic subjects. *Journal of Abnormal and Social Psychology, 52,* 143–150.

Franks, C. M. (1961). Conditioning and abnormal behaviour. In H. J. Eysenck (Ed.), *Handbook of abnormal psychology* (pp. 457–487). New York: Basic Books.

Gardner, R. W., & Long, R. I. (1960). The stability of cognitive controls. *Journal of Abnormal Social Psychology, 61,* 485–487.

Gough, H. G. (1957). *Manual for the California Psychological Inventory.* Palo Alto, Calif: Consulting Psychologists Press.

Grinder, R. E. (1962). Parental childrearing practices, conscience, and resistance to temptation of sixth-grade children. *Child Development, 33,* 803–820.

Haber, R. N., & Alpert, R. (1958). The role of situation and picture cues in projective measurement of the achievement motive. In J. W. Atkinson (Ed.), *Motives in fantasy, action, and society* (pp. 644–663). Princeton: Van Nostrand.

Hartshorne, H., & May, M. A. (1928). *Studies in the nature of character.* Vol. I., *Studies in deceit.* New York: Macmillan.

Hartshorne, H., May, M. A., & Shuttleworth, F. K. (1930). *Studies in the nature of character.* Vol. 3, *Studies in the organization of character.* New York: Macmillan.

Heathers, G. (1953). Emotional dependence and independence in a physical threat situation. *Child Development, 24,* 169–179.

Hoffman, M. L. (1963). Child rearing practices and moral development: Generalizations from empirical research. *Child Development, 34,* 295–318.

Johnson, R. C. (1962). A study of children's moral judgments. *Child Development, 33,* 327–354.

Kagan, J., & Moss, H. A. (1959). Stability and validity of achievement fantasy. *Journal of Abnormal and Social Psychology, 58,* 357–364.

Kagan, J., & Moss, H. A. (1962). *Birth to maturity: A study in psychological development.* New York: Wiley.

Kelly, E. L. (1955). Consistency of the adult personality. *American Psychologist, 10,* 659–681.

Kenny, D. T., & Ginsberg, Rose. (1958). The specificity of intolerance of ambiguity measures. *Journal of Abnormal and Social Psychology, 56,* 300–304.

Kogan, N., & Wallach, M. A. (1964). *Risk taking: A study in cognition and personality.* New York: Holt, Rinehart & Winston.

Kohlberg, L. (1963). The development of children's orientations toward a moral order: I. Sequence in the development of moral thought. *Vita Humana, 6,* 11–33.

Kohlberg, L. (1966). A cognitive-developmental analysis of children's sex-role concepts and attitudes. In Eleanor E. Maccoby (Ed.), *The development of sex differences* (pp. 25–55). Stanford: Stanford University Press.

Krumboltz, J. D., & Farquhar, W. W. (1957). Reliability and validity of the *n*-Achievement test. *Journal of Consulting Psychology, 21,* 226–228.

Landfield, A. W., Stern, M., & Fjeld, S. (1961). Social conceptual processes and change in students undergoing psychotherapy. *Psychological Reports, 8,* 63–68.

Lansky, L. M., Crandall, V. J., Kagan, J., & Baker, C. T. (1961). Sex differences in aggression and its correlates in middle-class adolescents. *Child Development, 32,* 45–58.

Lovibond, S. H. (1964). Personality and conditioning. In B. A. Maher (Ed.), *Progress in experimental personality research* (pp. 115–168). Vol. 1. New York: Academic Press.

MacKinnon, D. W. (1938). Violation of prohibitions. In H. A. Murray, *Explorations in personality* (pp. 491–501). New York: Oxford University Press.

Maher, B. A. (1957). Personality, problem solving, and the Einstellung effect. *Journal of Abnormal and Social Psychology, 54,* 70–74.

Mann, R. D. (1959). A review of the relationships between personality and performance in small groups. *Psychological Bulletin, 56,* 241–270.

Matarazzo, J. D. (1965). The interview. In B. B. Wolman (Ed.), *Handbook of clinical psychology* (pp. 403–450). New York: McGraw-Hill.

McClelland, D. C., Atkinson, J. W., Clark, R. A., & Lowell, E. I. (1953). *The achievement motive.* New York: Appleton-Century-Crofts.

McGuire, W. J. (1968). Personality and susceptibility to social influence. In E. F. Borgatta & W. W. Lambert (Eds.), *Handbook of personality theory and research* (pp. 1130–1187). Chicago: Rand McNally.

Mischel, W. (1962). Delay of gratification in choice situations. NIMH Progress Report, Stanford University.

Mischel, W., & Gilligan, C. (1964). Delay of gratification, motivation for the prohibited gratification, and responds to temptation. *Journal of Abnormal and Social Psychology, 69,* 411–417.

Moore, A. U., & Marcuse, F. I. (1945). Salivary, cardiac and motor indices of conditioning in two sows. *Journal of Comparative Psychology, 38,* 1–16.

Morgan, H. H. (1953). Measuring achievement motivation with "picture interpretations." *Journal of Consulting Psychology, 17,* 289–292.

Moss, H. A., & Kagan, J. (1961). Stability of achievement and recognition seeking behaviors from early childhood through adulthood. *Journal of Abnormal and Social Psychology, 62,* 504–518.

Osgood, C. E., Suci, G. J., & Tannenbaum, P. H. (1957). *The measurement of meaning.* Urbana: University of Illinois Press.

Patterson, G. R., & Hinsey, W. C. (1964). Investigations of some assumptions and characteristics of a procedure for instrumental conditioning in children. *Journal of Experimental Child Psychology, 1,* 111–122.

Pervin, L. A. (1960). Rigidity in neurosis and general personality functioning. *Journal of Abnormal and Social Psychology, 61,* 389–395.

Piaget, J. (1951). *Play, dreams, and imitation in childhood.* New York: Norton.

Sanford, N. (1963). Personality: Its place in psychology. In S. Koch (Ed.), *Psychology: A study of a science.* Vol. 5 (pp. 488–592). New York: McGraw-Hill.

Saslow, G., Matarazzo, J. D., Phillips, Jeanne S., & Matarazzo, Ruth C. (1957). Test-retest stability of interaction patterns during interviews conducted one week apart. *Journal of Abnormal and Social Psychology, 54,* 295–802.

Sears, R. R. (1961). Relation of early socialization experiences to aggression in middle childhood. *Journal of Abnormal and Social Psychology, 63,* 466–492.

Sears, R. R. (1963). Dependency motivation. In M. R. Jones (Ed.), *Nebraska symposium on motivation* (pp. 25–64). Lincoln: University of Nebraska Press.

Sears, R. R., Maccoby, Eleanor E., & Levin, H. (1957). *Patterns of child rearing.* Evanston, IL: Row, Peterson.

Sears, R. R., Rau, Lucy, & Alpert, R. (1965). *Identification and child rearing.* Stanford, CA: Stanford University Press.

Skolnick, Arlene. (1966a). Motivational imagery and behavior over twenty years. *Journal of Consulting Psychology, 30,* 463–478.

Skolnick, Arlene. (1966b). Stability and interrelations of thematic test imagery over 20 years. *Child Development, 37,* 389–396.

Wallach, M. A. (1962). Commentary: Active-analytical vs. passive-global cognitive functioning. In S. Messick & J. Ross (Eds.), *Measurement in personality and cognition* (pp. 199–215). New York: Wiley.

Whiting, J. W. M. (1959). Sorcery, sin, and the superego. A cross-cultural study of some mechanisms of social control. In M. R. Jones (Ed.), *Nebraska symposium on motivation* (pp. 174–195). Lincoln: University of Nebraska Press.

Witkin, H. A., Goodenough, D. R., & Karp, S. A. (1967). Stability of cognitive style from childhood to young adulthood. *Journal of Personality and Social Psychology, 7,* 291–300.

Wrightsman, L. S., Jr., & Baumeister, A. A. (1961). A comparison of actual and paper-and-pencil versions of the Water Jar Test of Rigidity. *Journal of Abnormal and Social Psychology, 63,* 191–198.

ous in retrospect but, Kenrick and Funder point out, it took the field of personality a surprisingly long time to realize how important they are.

Notice that this article originally appeared in 1988, exactly 20 years after the publication of Mischel's influential book. The article attempted not just to sum up the lessons learned from the person-situation controversy, but to declare the war over. In the years since 1988, the field of personality largely has turned its attention to other issues.

From *American Psychologist, 43,* 23–34, 1988.

* * *

Whether we are acting as professional psychologists, as academic psychologists, or simply as lay psychologists engaging in everyday gossip, the assumption that people have "traits" (or enduring cross-situational consistencies in their behavior) provides a basis for many of our decisions. When a clinical or counseling psychologist uses a standard assessment battery, he or she assumes that there is some degree of trait-like consistency in pathological behavior to be measured. When an organizational psychologist designs a personnel selection procedure, he or she assumes that consistent individual differences between the applicants are there to be found. When an academic psychologist teaches a course in personality, he or she must either assume some consistency in behavior or else face a bit of existential absurdity for at least 3 hours a week. Likewise, a good portion of our courses on clinical and developmental psychology would be unimaginable unless we assumed some cross-situational consistency. Even in everyday lay psychology, our attempts to analyze the behaviors of our friends, relatives, and co-workers are riddled with assumptions about personality traits.

Despite the wide appeal of the trait assumption, personality psychologists have been entangled for some time in a debate about whether it might be based more on illusion than reality (e.g., Alker, 1972; Allport, 1966; Argyle & Little, 1972; Bem, 1972; Block, 1968, 1977; Bowers, 1973; Epstein, 1977, 1979, 1980; Fiske, 1974; Gormly & Edelberg, 1974; Hogan, DeSoto, & Solano, 1977; Hunt, 1965; Magnusson & Endler, 1977; Mischel, 1968, 1983; West, 1983). Murmurs of the current debate could be heard more than 40 years ago (Ichheisser, 1943), but the volume increased markedly after Mischel's (1968) critique, and things have not quieted down yet (Bem, 1983; Epstein, 1983; Funder, 1983; Kenrick, 1986; Mischel, 1983; Mischel & Peake, 1982, 1983). Of late, discussants have begun to express yearning to end what some see as an endless cycle of repeating the same arguments. Mischel and Peake (1982) and Bem (1983), for instance, both use the term *déjà vu* in the titles of recent contributions, suggesting that they feel as if they have been here before. Other commentators maintain that the debate has been a "pseudo-controversy" (Carlson, 1984; Endler, 1973) that never should have occurred in the first place.

However fatiguing it may now seem to some of its erstwhile protagonists, the debate over the alleged inconsistency of personality has been more than an exercise in sophistry. In the course of the nearly two decades since Mischel's (1968) critique, a number of provocative hypotheses have been put forward, along with a host of studies to evaluate them. Platt (1964) and Popper (1959), among others, maintained that science typically progresses through the accumulation of negative information—that is, by eliminating hypotheses that data suggest are no longer tenable. From this perspective, it may be worth taking a look back at the hypotheses suggested during the consistency controversy, this time in the improved light shed by two decades of research. In this light, the debate can be seen as an intellectually stimulating chapter in the history of the discipline, replete with useful lessons for professionals who include assessment in their repertoire.

The "Pure Trait" Model and Its Alternatives

Discussions of the "person versus situation" debate traditionally begin with the "pure trait" model (Alston, 1975; Argyle & Little, 1972; Mischel, 1968): that people show powerful, unmodulated consistencies in their behavior across time and diverse situations. This position has been attacked frequently over the years. However, it is really just a "straw man," and even traditional personality researchers find it unacceptable (see, e.g., Allport, 1931, 1966; Block, 1977; Hogan et al., 1977; Jackson, 1983; Wiggins, 1973; Zuroff, 1986). Complete invariance in behavior is associated more with severe psychopathology than with "normal" behavior.

If the consensus rejects the "pure trait" position, then what can replace it? Several alternative hypotheses have been advanced over the years. These hypotheses differ with regard to four issues, which can be arranged into a logical hierarchy:

1. Consensus versus solipsism. Are traits merely idiosyncratic constructs that reside solely inside the heads of individual observers, or can observers reach agreement in applying trait terms?

2. Discriminativeness versus generality. If observers can agree with one another in ascribing traits to targets, is it simply because they apply a nondiscriminative "one size fits all" approach?

3. Behavior versus labeling. If observers can agree with one another, and can also differentiate between who is low or high on a given trait, does this occur because they really observe behavior? Or do they merely provide their judgments based on superficial stereotypes, targets' self-presentations, or other socially assigned labels?

4. Internal versus external locus of causal explanation. If observers can agree with one another and can distinguish individual differences on the basis of *actual behavior* of the people they are observing, are the causes of these consistencies located within each person or within his or her situation and role?

Each of these issues depends on the resolution of those earlier in the list. For instance, if observers cannot agree with one another about who has which traits, there is no point in going on to debate whether traits have a behavioral basis. Ultimately, assumptions about traits must pass the tests of consensus, discriminativeness, behavioral foundation, and internality. We will discuss seven hypotheses that assume that traits fail one or more of these tests. In Table 12.1, we list the hypotheses in terms of the four hierarchical issues just discussed. As can be seen, the hypotheses can be arranged more or less in order of their pessimism regarding the existence of (consensually verifiable, discriminative, internal) traitlike consistencies.

We will consider each hypothesis in its purest form and, for the moment, disregard the various qualifications that have sometimes been attached to each. Placing each hypothesis in bold relief allows us to assess it most clearly, and philosophers of science tell us that we learn most when hypotheses are stated in such a way as to allow disproof (e.g., Platt, 1964; Popper, 1959). Moreover, each of these hypotheses has, at some time, actually been stated in its bold form. In 1968, for instance, one social psychologist argued that

> the prevalent view that the normal behavior of individuals tends toward consistency is misconceived [and the research evidence] . . . strongly suggests that consistency, either in thought or action, does not constitute the normal state of affairs. (Gergen, 1968, pp. 305–306)

TABLE 12.1

Hierarchy of Hypotheses From the Person-Situation Controversy, Arranged From Most to Least Pessimistic

Critical assumptions	Hypotheses
Solipsism over consensus	1. Personality is in the eye of the beholder.
Consensus without discrimination	2. Agreement between raters is an artifact of the semantic structure of the language used to describe personality.
	3. Agreement is an artifact of base-rate accuracy (rater's tendency to make similar guesses about what people in general are like).
Discriminative consensus without behavioral referents	4. Differential agreement is an artifact of the shared use of invalid stereotypes.
	5. Observers are in cahoots with one another; that is, their agreement results from discussion rather than accurate observation.
Differential agreement about behavior without internal traits	6. Raters see targets only within a limited range of settings and mistake situational effects for traits.
	7. Compared with situational pressures, cross-situational consistencies in behavior are too weak to be important.

In the same year, a behavioral psychologist stated that "I, for one, look forward to the day when personality theories are regarded as historical curiosities" (Farber, 1964, p. 37).

Such extreme pessimism was clearly unwarranted. The data available now, more than two decades later, argue strongly against all seven of the hypotheses in Table 12.1. However, it would be a mistake to presume, as some personologists seem to do, that the issues raised by the "situationists" were merely diversions from the true path that can now be safely disregarded. We have learned, in the course of the debate, about a number of sources of distortion in trait judgments. These not only are of interest in their own right but are useful to personality assessment professionals, whose main goal may be to eliminate as much clutter from their path as possible.

Hypothesis 1: Personality Is in the Eye of the Beholder The first and most pessimistic hypothesis that must be considered is that our perceptions of personality traits in our friends, acquaintances, and selves might be largely or exclusively by-products of the limitations and flaws of human information processing. Although no personality researcher has ever advocated that personality exists solely in the head and not in the external world, social psychologists such as Gergen (1968) and behavioral analysts such as Farber (1964) have done so. Moreover, the issue lies in the logical path of any further inquiries into the origin of trait attributions.

Social psychologists have often emphasized how personality impressions can arise in the absence of supporting evidence in the real world:

> Unwitting evidence provided by countless personality psychologists shows how objectively low or nonexistent covariations (between personality and behavior) can be parlayed into massive perceived covariations through a priori theories and assumptions. (Nisbett & Ross, 1980, p. 109)

> The personality theorists' (and the layperson's) conviction that there are strong cross-situational consistencies in behavior may be seen as merely another instance of theory-driven covariation assessments operating in the face of contrary evidence. (Nisbett & Ross, 1980, p. 112)

Research relevant to the "eye of the beholder" hypothesis has mainly consisted of (a) demonstrations of various "errors" in the way that people process social information, or (b) claims that different judges rating the same personality rarely agree with each other or with the person being rated.

The demonstrations of error (for reviews, see Nisbett & Ross, 1980; Ross, 1977) establish that information given to subjects in laboratory settings is frequently distorted. People tend to jump to conclusions, biasing their judgments and their memories on the basis of their "implicit personality theories" (Schneider, 1973) or "scripts" (Abelson, 1976; Schank & Abelson, 1977). Studies of these attributional errors clearly demonstrate that people have biased expectations and that they routinely go beyond the information they are given.

However, for two reasons such studies do not establish that personality resides solely in the eye of the beholder. First, some of the errors are more a product of the unusual experimental situation than of a fundamentally biased cognitive process (cf. Block, Weiss, & Thorne, 1979; Trope, Bassok, & Alon, 1984). More important, the existence of judgmental biases does not necessarily imply the existence of mistakes. The expectations and biases demonstrated in laboratory tasks are, in principle, liable to lead to correct judgments in the real world (Funder, 1987). Many demonstrations of this principle can be found in the field of visual perception, where a useful rule of thumb underlies every "optical illusion" (Gregory, 1971). The "Ponzo" or "railroad lines" illusion, for example, produces errors in the lab but correct judgments when applied to three-dimensional reality. In the field of social perception, even the "fundamental attribution error" will lead to correct judgments to the extent that real people actually are somewhat consistent in their behavior. In short, demonstrations of laboratory errors are not informative, one way or the other, as to whether the associated judgmental biases lead mostly to mistakes or correct judgments in real life (see also McArthur & Baron, 1983).

A different line of support for the "eye of the beholder" hypothesis has been the belief that people generally do not agree with each other in their judgments of the same personality. For example, Dornbusch, Hastorf, Richardson, Muzzy, and Vreeland (1965) found that the constructs children in a summer camp used to describe personality were more a function of the person doing the ratings than they were of the person being rated. Such studies do show that people have individually preferred constructs for thinking about others. But these judgmental idiosyncrasies must be interpreted in the light of frequent findings that (a) when raters and ratees get a chance to know one another, their ratings come to agree with each other more (Funder & Colvin, 1987; Norman & Goldberg, 1966), and (b) when common rating categories are imposed on raters, their judgments will show substantial agreement in orderings of individual targets (e.g., Amelang & Borkenau, 1986; Bem & Allen, 1974; Cheek, 1982; Funder, 1987; Funder & Dobroth, 1987; Kenrick & Braver, 1982; Koretzky, Kohn, & Jeger, 1978; McCrae, 1982; Mischel & Peake, 1982).

Table 12.2 demonstrates some fairly typical

TABLE 12.2

Interrater Correlations From Recent Trait Studies

Trait	Kenrick & Stringfield (1980) (n = 71)	Kenrick & Stringfield (1980) Obs[a] (n = 34)	Funder & Dobroth (1987) (n = 69)	Dantchik (1985) (n = 92)	Dantchik (1985) Obs[a] (n = 36)	Cheek (1982) 1/2/3[b] (n = 81)	Cheek (1982) Obs[a] (n = 40)	McCrae (1982) (n = 139)	Paunonen & Jackson (1985) (n = 90)	Mischel & Peake (1982) (n = 63)
Intellectance	.17	.04	.36	.40	.52		.36	.50	.53	
Likability	.35	.52	.41	.14	.14	.22/.33/.39	.49	.47	.57	
Self-control	.26	.26	.25	.19	.47	.27/.40/.47	.64	.48	.67	.52
Sociability	.40	.55	.34	.46	.53	.43/.53/.59	.46	.53	.74	
Adjustment	.23	.43	.23	.38	.40	.22/.25/.27		.58	.48	
Dominance	.35	.41	.40	.58	.61			.52	.60	
M	.29	.37	.34	.37	.45	.29/.38/.44	.50	.51	.59	.52
	(.53)[c]	(.67)		(.51)	(.64)					

Note. The trait labels used here are based on Hogan's (1982) terminology, and we have used roughly equivalent scales from studies that did not use those exact terms (denoting the major "factors" usually found in trait rating studies).

[a] Data from subjects who rated their behaviors on a given dimension as publicly observable (Obs).

[b] Data based on 1, 2, and 3 judges, respectively.

[c] Figures in parentheses are corrected for attenuation.

findings in the area. In each of these studies, adult targets rated their own personalities and were also rated by more than one person who knew them well (parents, spouses, housemates, or friends). Correlations represent agreement about the same person by different raters who filled out the scales independently. Studies on the left side of the table used single-item scales (Funder & Dobroth, 1987; Kenrick & Stringfield, 1980); Dantchik (1985) and Cheek (1982) used 5-item and 3-item scales, respectively; and the studies to the right used lengthier scales with better established psychometric properties. It is clear that the use of reliable rating scales leads to high agreement regarding a target's personality, but even single-item scales can produce consistently positive (and statistically significant) levels of agreement.[1] * * *

[1]Most rating scales consist of a total score computed across the ratings of several or more individual items. The more the ratings of these different items within a scale tend to agree with each other, the more reliable the total scale is. More reliable scales tend to yield larger correlations with other variables. Single-item scales, by contrast, usually produce lower correlations.

A consideration of this first hypothesis has taught us something about when the eyes of different beholders will behold different characteristics in the persons at whom they are looking. For instance, when rating strangers, observers will be quite happy to make attributions about what the strangers are like but will show little consensus (Funder & Colvin, 1987; Monson, Keel, Stephens, & Genung, 1982; Passini & Norman, 1966). So, although strangers' ratings provide an excellent domain for the study of bias (Fiske & Taylor, 1984), it is probably futile to expect them to manifest much validity. However, when observers are well acquainted with the person they are judging, they nevertheless do manage to see something on which they can agree. The findings of consensus (such as those in Table 12.2) are sufficient to rule out the radical hypothesis that personality resides solely in the eye of the beholder.

* * *

Hypothesis 2: Agreement Is Due to Semantic Generalization The first hypothesis, in its radical form, considered traits to be idiosyncratic constructions of the individual perceiver. The second hypothesis concedes that there is consensus in the use of trait terms but views that agreement as due simply to shared delusions based on common linguistic usage. According to the semantic generalization hypothesis, as soon as one judgment about another person is made, many other judgments follow based on nothing more than implicit expectations about which words "go together." Anyone judged as "friendly" may also be judged as "empathic," "altruistic," and "sincere" because the concepts are semantically linked, even though the component behaviors themselves may not be so linked. For instance, "helping others in distress" and "contributing to charities" (behavioral components of "altruism") may not be correlated with "smiling a lot" and "talking to strangers" (behavioral components of "friendliness"), but judges who see evidence of "smiling a lot" might still infer "altruism," at least sometimes incorrectly. Shweder (1975) argued that shared preconceptions about "what goes with what" affected judgments so pervasively as to raise the question "How relevant is an individual differences theory of personality?" (See also D'Andrade, 1974.) Bourne (1977) went even further, suggesting that trait ratings might not reflect "anything more than raters' conceptual expectancies about which traits go together" (p. 863).

* * *

It is crucial to realize, as Block, Weiss, and Thorne (1979) pointed out, that semantic generalization cannot explain how different judges agree on attributing a *single* trait to a target person (as research such as that in Table 12.2 shows they do). To take a well-known example, the Passini and Norman (1966) study has been cited as evidence that trait ratings are based on "nothing more" than semantic similarity judgments. Indeed, Passini and Norman's data yielded a similar factor structure for ratings of friends and for ratings of strangers (who had been observed only briefly).[2] Because the strangers had very little time to observe one another, it is clear that an implicit personality theory guided their judgments. However, this issue of the relationships between trait words is completely orthogonal to the question of accuracy in application of any one of those words. Passini and Norman's subjects not only reached significant agreement about which trait applied to which person but they also agreed more about friends' ratings than about strangers' (see also Funder & Colvin, 1987; Norman & Goldberg, 1966).

In light of such arguments, Shweder and D'Andrade (1979) seem to have reversed their earlier claim that semantic generalization negates the importance of judgments of individual differences. Although semantic structure might tell us to expect "friendly" to go with "altruistic" and not with "aggressive," it does not tell us whether we should apply the term more strongly to Walter or Seymour or Daryl. We must seek further for an adequate explanation of findings like those in Table 12.2.

HYPOTHESIS 3: AGREEMENT IS DUE TO BASE-RATE ACCURACY According to this hypothesis, interrater agreement is an artifact of the highly stable base rates that many traits have in the population at large. For example, the trait "needs to be with other people" characterizes most of us, whereas "has murderous tendencies" characterizes few. If one is trying to describe someone one does not know, therefore, one can achieve a certain degree of "accuracy" just by rating the first trait higher than the second. The base-rate hypothesis, like the semantic structure hypothesis, allows for consensus between observers but regards their judgments as indiscriminate. "Accuracy" of this sort might reflect knowledge about what people in general are like, what Cronbach (1955) called "stereotype accuracy," but does not necessarily reflect any knowledge specific to the person being described.

The base-rate accuracy problem helps us un-

---

[2]This reference to "factor structure" means that the different traits on which raters judged others tended to be correlated with each other in a similar manner whether the targets of judgment were close acquaintances or strangers. For example, people rated high on "talkativeness" also tend to be rated high on "friendliness," whether these people are well known to the rater or not.

derstand phenomena such as the "Barnum effect" (Ulrich, Stachnik, & Stainton, 1963), reflected in widespread acceptance of generalized descriptions such as, "You have a strong need for other people to like you and for them to admire you."[3] Questions of when and for whom base-rate accuracy becomes an issue are interesting ones. For example, a recent study by Miller, McFarland, and Turnbull (1985) found that Barnum statements are more likely to be accepted by subjects when the statements refer to attributes that are publicly observable and flattering. However, to argue that base-rate accuracy is a basis for doubting whether we "can . . . describe an individual's personality" (Bourne, 1977) takes things too far. The base-rate accuracy hypothesis, like the semantic similarity hypothesis, can explain how judges reach consensus but not how they distinguish *between* the targets they judge. To take a simple case, imagine that a group of sorority sisters rates one another on a dichotomous item (as either "friendly" or "unfriendly"). If "friendly" is chosen over "unfriendly" 9 out of 10 times, there could be a very high percentage of "agreement," in terms of overlapping judgments, even if there were absolutely no agreement about who the 10th, unfriendly person is. But if there is truly no agreement about individual targets, correlations calculated between judges will show no relationship at all. So base-rate accuracy cannot explain the results of interrater studies such as those in Table 12.2 either (cf. Funder, 1980a; Funder & Colvin, 1987; Funder & Dobroth, 1987).

Summarizing thus far, we may say that whatever role solipsism and glittering generality play as noise in personality assessment, a signal of consensus and discrimination comes through. Can that signal be explained without acceding to the existence of trait-like consistencies in behavior? The answer is still yes, and in at least three ways.

HYPOTHESIS 4: AGREEMENT IS DUE TO STEREOTYPES BASED ON OBVIOUS (BUT ERRONEOUS) CUES None of the arguments considered so far can account for interjudge agreement about the differences between people. One hypothesis that does is this: Perhaps agreement about peers is due to shared (but incorrect) stereotypes based on one or another readily accessible (e.g., physical) cues. Many such stereotypes come to mind: physical types (athlete, fat person, dumb blonde), racial and ethnic stereotypes, and so forth. Judges might share cultural stereotypes and so "agree" about burly, obese, or blond targets regardless of whether there were any corresponding consistencies in the targets' behavior.

Note that this hypothesis is very different from the sort of "stereotype accuracy" discussed under Hypothesis 3. That hypothesis referred to the possibility of indiscriminate responding based on raters' common preconceptions about what *everybody* is like. Hypothesis 4 refers to consensual agreement about traits that are *differentially* assigned to others. None of the first three hypotheses requires the observer to really "observe" anything distinctive about the person he or she is describing. This hypothesis, however, does require that the observer at least take a look at the target person—but assumes that the observer hardly looks much further than the end of his or her nose, just enough to assign the target person to a general category.

Such categorical stereotypes undoubtedly exist, but this does not mean we cannot become more accurate after getting to know someone beyond their "surface" categorization. Raters will try to make "reasonable" (i.e., stereotypic) guesses in the absence of real behavioral information. But as we mentioned earlier, their ratings increasingly converge as they actually observe the person's behavior (e.g., Funder & Colvin, 1987; Monson, Tanke, & Lund, 1980; Moskowitz & Schwarz, 1982; Norman & Goldberg, 1966; Passini & Norman, 1966).

---

[3]The "Barnum effect" was named for the circus promoter P. T. Barnum, who is said to have claimed "there's a sucker born every minute." In demonstrations of this effect a group of people are all given descriptions of their personalities that include phrases such as "you have a strong need for other people to like you." People often report that the descriptions are remarkably accurate, but in reality they were all given the same description!

The data that are most difficult for the stereotype hypothesis to explain are relationships between judgments and independent, objective behavioral measurements. For example, parents and teachers can provide general personality descriptions of children that not only agree with each other but also predict the children's "delay of gratification" behavior, measured in minutes and seconds, in a lab situation that none of the raters have ever seen (Bem & Funder, 1978; Funder, Block, & Block, 1983; Mischel, 1984). Other examples include Funder's studies of personality correlates of attributional style (1980b), attitude change (1982), and social acuity (Funder & Harris, 1986b); Gormly and Edelberg's (1974) work on aggression; Moskowitz and Schwarz's (1982) work on dominance; and Alker and Owen's (1977) research on reactions to stressful events. This sort of predictive capability must arise from something beyond the use of invalid stereotypes.

Although the existence of stereotypes does not negate the existence of traits, it is useful to consider how stereotypes and personality traits interact. For example, physical attractiveness may actually lead one to become more friendly, via self-fulfilling prophecies (Goldman & Lewis, 1977; Snyder, Tanke, & Berscheid, 1977). Likewise, burly males really are more aggressive (Glueck & Glueck, 1956), probably because aggressiveness has a higher payoff for a muscular youth than it does for a skinny or flabby one.

In sum, although stereotypes may be informative about the genesis of some traits, and may account for judgments of strangers, the findings that observers agree more with one another after they have gotten to know the target and the correlations between ratings and independent assessments of behavior rule out the possibility that interrater agreement is due solely to the use of shared stereotypes based on superficial cues.

HYPOTHESIS 5: AGREEMENT IS DUE TO DISCUSSION BETWEEN OBSERVERS We just considered evidence that observers agree with each other better when they know the target person well. Is this because acquaintances have had more time to observe the relevant behaviors and hence are more truly accurate than strangers? Perhaps not. It could be argued that observers ignore the truly relevant nonverbal behaviors of a target person but are attentive to the target's verbalizations about himself or herself and come to regard the target as the target does for that reason (cf. Funder, 1980a; Funder & Colvin, 1987). Alternatively, observers might get together and discuss the target (McClelland, 1972), agree on his or her reputation, and then inform the target about how to regard himself or herself (as in the classical "looking glass self" formulations of C. H. Cooley, 1902).

The research cited earlier, showing how ratings of personality traits can predict behavior in unique settings, strongly suggests that such explicit "negotiation" is not all that underlies interjudge agreement. Moreover, several researchers have found that agreement between parents "back home" and peers at college is about as good as that among peers or among parents (Bem & Allen, 1974; Kenrick & Stringfield, 1980). Likewise, Koretzky et al. (1978) found respectable agreement between judges from different settings. In that study, the various settings were all within the same (mental) institution, but the Kenrick and Stringfield (1980) study was conducted in an isolated college town in Montana and used parents who often lived several hundred miles away from campus and were unlikely to have met the peers (whose home towns may have been hundreds of miles in the opposite direction), much less to have had intimate discussions with them about their children's traits.

Findings of higher agreement on traits that relate to observable behaviors (such as "friendliness" as opposed to "emotionality") are also relevant here. Kenrick and Stringfield (1980) found that "observable" traits are reported with better agreement than "unobservable" ones. * * * Related findings are reported by Amelang and Borkenau (1986), Cheek (1982), Funder and Colvin (1987), Funder and Dobroth (1987), and McCrae (1982) and in two unpub-

havioral instance from another single behavioral instance.

Those who would respond to this list by claiming that they "knew it all along" may or may not be guilty of hindsight bias (Fischoff, 1975). But they should at least acknowledge that many of us did not know these principles all along and needed the light generated by controversy to open our eyes. For instance, the apparently "obvious" insight that we should not rely on ratings made by strangers can help us understand why some of the data on clinical assessment (e.g., Goldberg & Werts, 1966; Golden, 1964; Soskin, 1959) have been so disappointing, and the awareness that traits will not show up in overpowering situations has led to a dramatic reassessment of failures to find "consistency" in brief laboratory observations. Likewise, if these issues and that of the unreliability of single behavioral instances were so obvious, one is left to wonder why the field responded so strongly to Mischel's (1968) critique. "Déjà vu" may be an accurate description of our current situation after all, because the term actually refers to the *illusion* that one has previously experienced something that is really new.

One side effect of the person-situation debate has been an intensification of the antagonism between personality and social psychology. Social psychologists have historically focused on situational determinants of behavior and were therefore quite willing to join with behavioral clinicians in the situationist attack on personality (Hogan & Emler, 1978; Kenrick & Dantchik, 1983). Personologists share a very different set of assumptions, and the two subdisciplines have sometimes seemed intent on defining each other out of existence (Kenrick, 1986). To continue such separation between the two fields would be a mistake. Many exciting developments are beginning to emerge at the interface of social and personality psychology. For instance, research that combines personality with biology suggests a vast array of questions about the connection between personality traits and social interaction (Kenrick, 1987; Kenrick & Trost, 1987; Sadalla, Kenrick, & Vershure, 1987). And research on the accuracy of interpersonal judgment draws equally on both personality and social psychology (Funder, 1987; Funder & Colvin, 1987; Funder & Dobroth, 1987).

Houts, Cook, and Shadish (1986) made a strong case that science best progresses through multiple and mutually critical attempts to understand the same problem. When camps with strongly opposing sets of biases manage to come to some level of agreement, we may be more confident of the validity of the conclusions that are agreed upon. Viewed in this light, the controversy stimulated by the situationist attack on personality may be seen more as a life-giving transfusion than as a needless bloodletting.

References

Abelson, R. P. (1976). A script theory of understanding, attitude, and behavior. In J. Carroll & J. Payne (Eds.), *Cognition and social behavior* (pp. 33–45). Hillsdale, NJ: Erlbaum.

Abelson, R. P. (1985). A variance explanation paradox: When a little is a lot. *Psychological Bulletin, 97*, 129–133.

Alker, H. A. (1972). Is personality situationally specific or intrapsychically consistent? *Journal of Personality, 40*, 1–16.

Alker, H. A., & Owen, D. W. (1977). Biographical, trait, and behavioral-sampling predictions of performance in a stressful life setting. *Journal of Personality and Social Psychology, 35*, 717–723.

Allport, G. W. (1931). What is a trait of personality? *Journal of Abnormal and Social Psychology, 25*, 368–372.

Allport, G. W. (1966). Traits revisited. *American Psychologist, 21*, 1–10.

Alston, W. P. (1975). Traits, consistency, and conceptual alternatives for personality theory. *Journal for the Theory of Social Behavior, 5*, 17–48.

Amabile, T. M., & Kabat, L. G. (1982). When self-description contradicts behavior: Actions do speak louder than words. *Social Cognition, 1*, 311–335.

Amelang, M., & Borkenau, P. (1986). The trait concept: Current theoretical considerations, empirical facts, and implications for personality inventory construction. In A. Angleitner & J. S. Wiggins (Eds.), *Personality assessment via questionnaire* (pp. 7–24). Berlin: Springer-Verlag.

Argyle, M., & Little, B. R. (1972). Do personality traits apply to social behavior? *Journal for the Theory of Social Behavior, 2*, 1–35.

Bem, D. J. (1972). Constructing cross-situational consistencies in behavior: Some thoughts on Alker's critique of Mischel. *Journal of Personality, 40*, 17–26.

Bem, D. J. (1983). Further *déjà vu* in the search for cross situational consistency: A reply to Mischel and Peake. *Psychological Review, 90*, 390–393.

Bem, D. J., & Allen, A. (1974). On predicting some of the

people some of the time: The search for cross-situational consistencies in behavior. *Psychological Review, 81*, 506–520.

Bem, D. J., & Funder, D. C. (1978). Predicting more of the people more of the time: Assessing the personality of situations. *Psychological Review, 85*, 485–501.

Block, J. (1968). Some reasons for the apparent inconsistency of personality. *Psychological Bulletin, 70*, 210–212.

Block, J. (1977). Advancing the science of personality: Paradigmatic shift or improving the quality of research? In D. Magnusson & N. S. Endler (Eds.), *Personality at the crossroads: Current issues in interactional psychology* (pp. 37–63). Hillsdale, NJ: Erlbaum.

Block, J., Buss, D. M., Block, J. M., & Gjerde, P. F. (1981). The cognitive style of breadth of categorization: The longitudinal consistency of personality correlates. *Journal of Personality and Social Psychology, 40*, 770–779.

Block, J., von der Lippe, A., & Block, J. H. (1973). Sex-role and socialization patterns: Some personality concomitants and environmental antecedents. *Journal of Consulting and Clinical Psychology, 41*, 321–341.

Block, J., Weiss, D. S., & Thorne, A. (1979). How relevant is a semantic similarity interpretation of personality ratings? *Journal of Personality and Social Psychology, 37*, 1055–1074.

Bourne, E. (1977). Can we describe an individual's personality? Agreement on stereotype versus individual attributes. *Journal of Personality and Social Psychology, 35*, 863–872.

Bowers, K. S. (1973). Situationism in psychology: An analysis and critique. *Psychological Review, 80*, 307–336.

Bryan, J., & Walbek, N. (1970). Impact of words and deeds concerning altruism upon children. *Child Development, 41*, 747–757.

Carlson, R. (1984). What's social about social psychology? Where's the person in personality research? *Journal of Personality and Social Psychology, 35*, 1055–1074.

Cheek, J. M. (1982). Aggregation, moderator variables, and the validity of personality tests: A peer-rating study. *Journal of Personality and Social Psychology, 43*, 1254–1269.

Cooley, C. H. (1902). *Human nature and the social order.* New York: Scribner's.

Cronbach, L. J. (1955). Processes affecting scores on "understanding of others" and "assumed similarity." *Psychological Bulletin, 52*, 177–193.

Dahlstrom, W. G. (1972). *Personality systematics and the problem of types.* Morristown, NJ: General Learning Press.

D'Andrade, R. G. (1974). Memory and the assessment of behavior. In H. M. Blalock (Ed.), *Measurement in the social sciences* (pp. 159–186). Chicago: Aldine-Atherton.

Dantchik, A. (1985). *Idiographic approaches to personality assessment.* Unpublished master's thesis, Arizona State University, Tempe.

Dornbusch, S. M., Hastorf, A. H., Richardson, S. A., Muzzy, R. E., & Vreeland, R. S. (1965). The perceiver and perceived: Their relative influence on categories of interpersonal perception. *Journal of Personality and Social Psychology, 1*, 434–440.

Eaton, W. D., & Enns, L. R. (1986). Sex differences in human activity level. *Psychological Bulletin, 100*, 19–28.

Endler, N. S. (1973). The person vs. situation: A pseudo issue? *Journal of Personality, 41*, 287–303.

Epstein, S. (1977). Traits are alive and well. In D. Magnusson & N. S. Endler (Eds.), *Personality at the crossroads: Current issues in interactional psychology* (pp. 83–98). Hillsdale, NJ: Erlbaum.

Epstein, S. (1979). The stability of behavior: I. On predicting most of the people much of the time. *Journal of Personality and Social Psychology, 37*, 1097–1126.

Epstein, S. (1980). The stability of behavior: II. Implications for psychological research. *American Psychologist, 35*, 790–806.

Epstein, S. (1983). The stability of confusion: A reply to Mischel and Peake. *Psychological Review, 90*, 390–393.

Epstein, S., & O'Brien, E. J. (1985). The person-situation debate in historical and current perspective. *Psychological Bulletin, 98*, 513–537.

Farber, I. E. (1964). A framework for the study of personality as a behavioral science. In P. Worchel & D. Bryne (Eds.), *Personality change* (pp. 3–37). New York: Wiley.

Fischoff, B. (1975). Hindsight does not equal foresight: The effect of outcome knowledge on judgment under uncertainty. *Journal of Experimental Psychology: Human Perception and Performance, 1*, 288–299.

Fiske, D. W. (1974). The limits for the conventional science of personality. *Journal of Personality, 42*, 1–11.

Fiske, D. W. (1979). Two worlds of psychological phenomena. *American Psychologist, 34*, 733–739.

Fiske, S., & Taylor, S. (1984). *Social cognition.* New York: Random House.

Funder, D. C. (1980a). On seeing ourselves as others see us: Self-other agreement and discrepancy in personality ratings. *Journal of Personality, 48*, 473–493.

Funder, D. C. (1980b). The "trait" of ascribing traits: Individual differences in the tendency to trait ascription. *Journal of Research in Personality, 14*, 376–385.

Funder, D. C. (1982). On assessing social psychological theories through the study of individual differences: Template matching and forced compliance. *Journal of Personality and Social Psychology, 43*, 100–110.

Funder, D. C. (1983). Three issues in predicting more of the people: A reply to Mischel and Peake. *Psychological Review, 90*, 283–289.

Funder, D. C. (1987). Errors and mistakes: Evaluating the accuracy of social judgment. *Psychological Bulletin, 101*, 75–90.

Funder, D. C., Block, J., & Block, J. H. (1983). Delay of gratification: Some longitudinal personality correlates. *Journal of Personality and Social Psychology, 44*, 1198–1213.

Funder, D. C., & Colvin, C. R. (1987). *Friends and strangers: Acquaintanceship, agreement, and the accuracy of personality judgment.* Manuscript submitted for publication.

Funder, D. C., & Dobroth, J. M. (1987). Differences between traits: Properties associated with interjudge agreement. *Journal of Personality and Social Psychology, 52*, 409–418.

Funder, D. C., & Harris, M. J. (1986a). Experimental effects and person effects in delay of gratification. *American Psychologist, 41*, 476–477.

Funder, D. C., & Harris, M. J. (1986b). On the several facets of personality assessment: The case of social acuity. *Journal of Personality, 54*, 528–550.

Funder, D. C., & Ozer, D. J. (1983). Behavior as a function of the situation. *Journal of Personality and Social Psychology, 44*, 107–112.

Gergen, K. J. (1968). Personal consistency and the presentation of self. In C. Gordon & K. J. Gergen (Eds.), *The self in social interaction* (pp. 299–308). New York: Wiley.

Glueck, S., & Glueck, E. (1956). *Physique and delinquency*. New York: Harper & Row.

Goldberg, L. R., & Werts, C. E. (1966). The reliability of clinician's judgments: A multitrait-multimethod approach. *Journal of Consulting Psychology, 30*, 199–206.

Golden, M. (1964). Some effects of combining psychological tests on clinical inferences. *Journal of Consulting Psychology, 28*, 440–446.

Golding, S. L. (1978). Toward a more adequate theory of personality: Psychological organizing principles. In H. London (Ed.), *Personality: A new look at metatheories* (pp. 69–96). New York: Wiley.

Goldman, W., & Lewis, P. (1977). Beautiful is good: Evidence that the physically attractive are more socially skilled. *Journal of Experimental Social Psychology, 13*, 125–130.

Gormly, J., & Edelberg, W. (1974). Validity in personality trait attributions. *American Psychologist, 29*, 189–193.

Gregory, R. L. (1971). Visual illusions. In R. C. Atkinson (Ed.), *Contemporary psychology* (pp. 167–177). San Francisco: W. H. Freeman.

Hogan, R. (1982). A socioanalytic theory of personality. In R. A. Dienstbier & M. M. Page (Eds.), *Nebraska symposium on motivation* (Vol. 30, pp. 55–89). Lincoln: University of Nebraska Press.

Hogan, R., DeSoto, C. B., and Solano, C. (1977). Traits, tests, and personality research. *American Psychologist, 32*, 255–264.

Hogan, R. T., & Emler, N. P. (1978). The biases in contemporary social psychology. *Social Research, 45*, 478–534.

Houts, A. C., Cook, T. D., & Shadish, W. R. (1986). The person-situation debate: A critical multiplist perspective. *Journal of Personality, 54*, 52–105.

Hunt, J. McV. (1965). Traditional personality theory in the light of recent evidence. *American Scientist, 53*, 80–96.

Ichheisser, G. (1943). Misinterpretations of personality in everyday life and the psychologist's frame of reference. *Character and Personality, 12*, 145–160.

Jackson, D. N. (1983). Some preconditions for valid person perception. In M. P. Zanna, E. T. Higgins, & C. P. Herman (Eds.), *Consistency in social behavior: The Ontario Symposium* (pp. 251–279). Hillsdale, NJ: Erlbaum.

James, W. (1890). *Principles of psychology* (Vol. 1). London: Macmillan.

Kenny, D. A., & La Voie, L. (1984). The social relations model. In L. Berkowitz (Ed.), *Advances in experimental social psychology* (Vol. 18, pp. 141–182). Orlando, FL: Academic Press.

Kenrick, D. T. (1986). How strong is the case against contemporary social and personality psychology? A response to Carlson. *Journal of Personality and Social Psychology, 50*, 839–844.

Kenrick, D. T. (1987). Gender, genes, and the social environment. In P. C. Shaver & C. Hendrick (Eds.), *Review of personality and social psychology: Vol. 7. Sex and gender* (pp. 14–43). Beverly Hills, CA: Sage.

Kenrick, D. T., & Braver, S. L. (1982). Personality: Idiographic and nomothetic! A rejoinder. *Psychological Review, 89*, 182–186.

Kenrick, D. T., & Dantchik, A. (1983). Interactionism, idiographics, and the social psychological invasion of personality. *Journal of Personality, 51*, 286–307.

Kenrick, D. T., & Stringfield, D. O. (1980). Personality traits and the eye of the beholder: Crossing some traditional philosophical boundaries in the search for consistency in all of the people. *Psychological Review, 87*, 88–104.

Kenrick, D. T., Stringfield, D. O., Wagenhals, W. L., Dahl, R. H., & Ransdell, H. J. (1980). Sex differences, androgyny, and approach responses to erotica: A new variation on the old volunteer problem. *Journal of Personality and Social Psychology, 40*, 1039–1056.

Kenrick, D. T., & Trost, M. R. (1987). A biosocial theory of heterosexual relationships. In K. Kelley (Ed.), *Males, females, and sexuality: Theory and research* (pp. 59–100). Albany: State University of New York Press.

Koretzky, M. B., Kohn, M., & Jeger, A. M. (1978). Cross-situational consistency among problem adolescents: An application of the two-factor model. *Journal of Personality and Social Psychology, 36*, 1054–1059.

Magnusson, D., & Endler, N. S. (Eds.). (1977). *Personality at the crossroads: Current issues in interactional psychology*. Hillsdale, NJ: Erlbaum.

McArthur, L. Z., & Baron, R. M. (1983). Toward an ecological theory of social perception. *Psychological Review, 90*, 215–235.

McCall, M., Linder, D. E., West, S. G., & Kenrick, D. T. (1985). *Some cautions on the template-matching approach to assessing person/environment interactions*. Unpublished manuscript, Arizona State University, Tempe.

McClelland, D. C. (1972). Opinions reflect opinions: So what else is new? *Journal of Consulting and Clinical Psychology, 38*, 325–326.

McCrae, R. R. (1982). Consensual validation of personality traits: Evidence from self-reports and ratings. *Journal of Personality and Social Psychology, 43*, 293–303.

McGowen, J., & Gormly, J. (1976). Validation of personality traits: A multicriteria approach. *Journal of Personality and Social Psychology, 34*, 791–795.

Miller, D. T., McFarland, C., & Turnbull, W. (1985). *Pluralistic ignorance: Its causes and consequences*. Paper presented at the annual meeting of the Eastern Psychological Association, Boston.

Mischel, W. (1968). *Personality and assessment*. New York: Wiley.

Mischel, W. (1983). Alternatives in the pursuit of the predictability and consistency of persons: Stable data that yield unstable interpretations. *Journal of Personality, 51*, 578–604.

Mischel, W. (1984). Convergences and challenges in the search for consistency. *American Psychologist, 39*, 351–364.

Mischel, W., & Peake, P. K. (1982). Beyond *déjà vu* in the search for cross-situational consistency. *Psychological Review, 89*, 730–755.

Mischel, W., & Peake, P. K. (1983). Some facets of consistency: Replies to Epstein, Funder, and Bem. *Psychological Review, 90*, 394–402.

Monson, T. C., Keel, R., Stephens, D., & Genung, V. (1982). Trait attributions: Relative validity, covariation with behavior, and prospect of future interaction. *Journal of Personality and Social Psychology, 42*, 1014–1024.

Monson, T. C., Tanke, E. D., & Lund, J. (1980). Determinants of social perception in a naturalistic setting. *Journal of Research in Personality, 14,* 104–120.

Monson, T. C., & Snyder, M. (1977). Actors, observers, and the attribution process: Toward a reconceptualization. *Journal of Experimental Social Psychology, 13,* 89–111.

Moskowitz, D. S. (1982). Coherence and cross-situational generality in personality: A new analysis of old problems. *Journal of Personality and Social Psychology, 43,* 754–768.

Moskowitz, D. S., & Schwarz, J. C. (1982). Validity comparison of behavior counts and ratings by knowledgeable informants. *Journal of Personality and Social Psychology, 42,* 518–528.

Newcomb, T. M., Koenig, K. E., Flacks, R., & Warwick, D. P. (1967). *Persistence and change: Bennington College and its students after twenty-five years.* New York: Wiley.

Nisbett, R. E., & Ross, L. D. (1980). *Human inference: Strategies and shortcomings of social judgment.* New York: Prentice-Hall.

Norman, W. T., & Goldberg, L. R. (1966). Raters, ratees, and randomness in personality structure. *Journal of Personality and Social Psychology, 4,* 681–691.

Ozer, D. J. (1985). Correlation and the coefficient of determination. *Psychological Bulletin, 97,* 307–315.

Passini, F. T., & Norman, W. T. (1966). A universal conception of personality structure? *Journal of Personality and Social Psychology, 4,* 44–49.

Paunonen, S. V., & Jackson, D. N. (1985). Idiographic measurement strategies for personality and prediction: Some unredeemed promissory notes. *Psychological Review, 92,* 486–511.

Platt, J. R. (1964). Strong inference. *Science, 146,* 347–353.

Popper, K. (1959). *The logic of scientific discovery.* New York: Basic Books.

Price, R. H., & Bouffard, D. L. (1974). Behavioral appropriateness and situational constraint as dimensions of social behavior. *Journal of Personality and Social Psychology, 30,* 579–586.

Rausch, M. L. (1977). Paradox, levels, and junctures in person-situation systems. In D. Magnusson & N. S. Endler (Eds.), *Personality at the crossroads* (pp. 287–304). Hillsdale, NJ: Erlbaum.

Romer, D., & Revelle, W. (1984). Personality traits: Fact or fiction? A critique of the Shweder and D'Andrade systematic distortion hypothesis. *Journal of Personality and Social Psychology, 47,* 1028–1042.

Rosenthal, R., & Rubin, D. B. (1979). A note on percent variance explained as a measure of the importance of effects. *Journal of Applied Social Psychology, 9,* 385–396.

Rosenthal, R., & Rubin, D. B. (1982). A simple, general purpose display of magnitude of experimental effect. *Journal of Educational Psychology, 74,* 166–169.

Ross, L. (1977). The intuitive psychologist and his shortcomings: Distortions in the attribution process. In L. Berkowitz (Ed.), *Advances in experimental social psychology* (Vol. 10, pp. 174–221). New York: Academic Press.

Sadalla, E. K., Kenrick, D. T., & Vershure, B. (1987). Dominance and heterosexual attraction. *Journal of Personality and Social Psychology, 52,* 730–738.

Sarason, I. G., Smith, R. E., & Diener, E. (1975). Personality research: Components of variance attributable to the person and the situation. *Journal of Personality and Social Psychology, 32,* 199–204.

Schank, R. C., & Abelson, R. P. (1977). *Scripts, plans, goals, and understanding.* Hillsdale, NJ: Erlbaum.

Schneider, D. (1973). Implicit personality theory: A review. *Psychological Bulletin, 79,* 294–309.

Schutte, N. A., Kenrick, D. T., & Sadalla, E. K. (1985). The search for predictable settings: Situational prototypes, constraint, and behavioral variation. *Journal of Personality and Social Psychology, 49,* 121–128.

Shweder, R. A. (1975). How relevant is an individual-difference theory of personality? *Journal of Personality, 43,* 455–485.

Shweder, R. A., & D'Andrade, R. G. (1979). Accurate reflection or systematic distortion: A reply to Block, Weiss, and Thorne. *Journal of Personality and Social Psychology, 37,* 1075–1084.

Snyder, M., & Ickes, W. (1985). Personality and social behavior. In G. Lindzey & E. Aronson (Eds.), *Handbook of social psychology* (3rd ed., Vol. 2, pp. 883–948). Reading, MA: Addison-Wesley.

Snyder, M., Tanke, E. D., & Berscheid, E. (1977). Social perception and interpersonal behavior: On the self-fulfilling nature of social stereotypes. *Journal of Personality and Social Psychology, 35,* 656–666.

Soskin, W. F. (1959). Influence of four types of data on diagnostic conceptualization in psychological testing. *Journal of Abnormal and Social Psychology, 58,* 69–78.

Trope, Y., Bassok, M., & Alon, E. (1984). The questions lay interviewers ask. *Journal of Personality, 52,* 90–106.

Ulrich, R. E., Stachnik, T. J., & Stainton, N. R. (1963). Student acceptance of generalized personality interpretations. *Psychological Reports, 13,* 831–834.

Wachtel, P. (1973). Psychodynamics, behavior therapy, and the implacable experimenter: An inquiry into the consistency of personality. *Journal of Abnormal Psychology, 82,* 324–334.

Wade, T. C., & Baker, T. B. (1977). Opinions and use of psychological tests: A survey of clinical psychologists. *American Psychologist, 32,* 874–882.

West, S. G. (1983). Personality and prediction: An introduction. *Journal of Personality, 51,* 275–285.

Wiggins, J. S. (1973). *Personality and prediction: Principles of personality assessment.* Reading, MA: Addison-Wesley.

Zuroff, D. C. (1986). Was Gordon Allport a trait theorist? *Journal of Personality and Social Psychology, 51,* 993–1000.

Self-Monitoring of Expressive Behavior

Mark Snyder

As the person-situation debate began to be resolved, researchers again turned their attention to interesting and consequential psychological processes that could be addressed through personality assessment. The following selection, by the influential social-personality psychologist Mark Snyder, concerns expressive behavior.

An important part of social interaction is the way we express our feelings and attitudes to one another. Snyder points out that such expressive behavior could have two sources. First, one could simply act the way one feels in a "what you see is what you get" manner. Or, second, one could adjust what one expresses with great sensitivity to the current social context. In other words, expressive behavior can be affected by both the person and the situation.

Snyder hypothesized that these two possible influences on expressive behavior vary in their relative importance to different individuals. Some people, high on the trait Snyder calls "self-monitoring" (SM), sensitively adjust their expressive behavior to match what is appropriate and socially useful in the particular situational context. Others, low on SM, do not adjust their behavior so much and instead are relatively likely to express their feelings, attitudes, and personality through their behavior regardless of the situation they find themselves in.

Snyder's SM scale is short and clearly written (see Table 13.1). Take a moment, before you read the article, and answer its questions yourself. Then you will be able to compute your own score and compare your own style of social and expressive behavior with those of the people discussed in this article.

We would not be responsible editors if we did not mention that in the ensuing years the SM scale produced a small controversy of its own. In a sense it became a victim of its own success. As dozens and perhaps hundreds of studies were done using this scale, it gradually became less clear what it really measured. For example, some researchers concluded that it measured not one trait but three—extraversion, acting ability, and "other-directedness" (concern with the opinions of others, Briggs & Cheek, 1986, 1988). Snyder responded that the construct was still valid and its key findings held despite these concerns (Snyder & Gangestad, 1986). The controversy was never completely settled, and many personality psychologists remain somewhat wary of this scale and its psychometric properties.

The bottom line, though, is that the construct and scale of SM reintroduced an important topic—the study of expressive behavior—into personality psychology. Moreover, as illustrated in this article, scores on SM have been shown to be relevant to interesting behaviors and relevant group memberships (e.g., being an actor or mental patient). Despite some technical complications, the SM scale remains an interesting and useful way to identify one way in which people differ.

From *Journal of Personality and Social Psychology, 30,* 526–537, 1974.

A common observation in literature and cultural folklore has been that certain nonlanguage behaviors, such as voice quality, body motion, touch, and the use of personal space, appear to play a prominent role in communication. Furthermore, laboratory and field research clearly indicates that much information about a person's affective states, status and attitude, cooperative and competitive nature of social interaction, and interpersonal intimacy is expressed and accurately communicated to others in nonverbal expressive behavior (e.g., Ekman, 1971; Hall, 1966; Mehrabian, 1969; Sommer, 1969).

Much interest in nonverbal expressive behavior stems from a belief that it may not be under voluntary control and might function as a pipeline or radarscope to one's true inner "self" (e.g., Freud, 1905/1959). Although nonverbal behavior may often escape voluntary attempts at censorship (Ekman & Friesen, 1969), there have been numerous demonstrations that individuals can voluntarily express various emotions with their vocal and/or facial expressive behavior in such a way that their expressive behavior can be accurately interpreted by observers (e.g., Davitz, 1964). In fact, some social observers have proposed that the ability to manage and control expressive presentation is a prerequisite to effective social and interpersonal functioning. Thus Goffman (1955) has likened social interaction to a theatrical performance or "line" of verbal and nonverbal self-expressive acts which are managed to keep one's line appropriate to the current situation. Such self-management requires a repertoire of face-saving devices, an awareness of the interpretations which others place on one's acts, a desire to maintain social approval, and the willingness to use this repertoire of impression management tactics. Within the more restricted domain of facial expressions of emotional affect, Ekman (1971) has suggested that individuals typically exercise control over their facial expressions to intensify, deintensify, neutralize, or mask the expression of a felt affect, according to various norms of social performance.

There are, however, striking and important individual differences in the extent to which individuals can and do monitor their self-presentation, expressive behavior, and nonverbal affective display. Clearly, professional stage actors can do what I cannot. Politicians have long known how important it is to wear the right face for the right constituency. LaGuardia learned the expressive repertoires of several different cultures in New York and became, "chameleon-like," the son of whatever people he was facing. Yet little research has directly concerned such individual differences in the self-control of expressive behavior. At best, some dispositional correlates[1] of spontaneous and

---

[1]A "dispositional correlate" is a trait found to be related to a particular behavior.

natural expression of emotion have been reported (e.g., Buck, Savin, Miller, & Caul, 1972; Davitz, 1964).

A CONCEPT OF SELF-MONITORING OF EXPRESSIVE BEHAVIOR How might individual differences in the self-control of expressive behavior arise? What might be the developmental, historical, and current motivational origins of self-control ability and performance? Perhaps some individuals have learned that their affective experience and expression are either socially inappropriate or lacking. Such people may *monitor* (observe and control) their self-presentation and expressive behavior. The goals of self-monitoring may be (a) to communicate accurately one's true emotional state by means of an intensified expressive presentation; (b) to communicate accurately an arbitrary emotional state which need not be congruent with actual emotional experience; (c) to conceal adaptively an inappropriate emotional state and appear unresponsive and unexpressive; (d) to conceal adaptively an inappropriate emotional state and appear to be experiencing an appropriate one; (e) to appear to be experiencing some emotion when one experiences nothing and a nonresponse is inappropriate.

An acute sensitivity to the cues in a situation which indicate what expression or self-presentation is appropriate and what is not is a corollary ability to self-monitoring. One such set of cues for guiding self-monitoring is the emotional expressive behavior of other similar comparison persons in the same situation.

There is some evidence of an acute version of this process. When persons are made uncertain of their emotional reactions, they look to the behavior of others for cues to define their emotional states and model the emotional expressive behavior of others in the same situation who appear to be behaving appropriately (Schachter & Singer, 1962).

On the other hand, persons who have not learned a concern for appropriateness of their self-presentation would not have such well-developed self-monitoring skills and would not be so vigilant to social comparison information about appropriate patterns of expression and experience. This is not to say that they are not emotionally expressive or even that they are less so than those who monitor their presentation. Rather, their self-presentation and expressive behavior seem, in a functional sense, to be controlled from within by their affective states (they express it as they feel it) rather than monitored, controlled, and molded to fit the situation.

SELF-MONITORING AND CONSISTENCY IN EXPRESSION: BETWEEN MODALITIES AND ACROSS SITUATIONS Do people, as Freud (1905/1959) believed, say one thing with their lips and another with their fingertips? More specifically, what governs the consistency between expression in different channels of expression, such as vocal and facial, and the consistency between nonverbal and verbal expression? The self-monitoring approach provides one perspective on differences and consistencies across channels of expression, including verbal self-presentation.

It is likely that when one is monitoring, various channels are monitored differentially, and perhaps some forgotten. Thus, what may be communicated by one channel may differ from what is communicated by another. For example, I may cover my sadness by putting on a happy face but forget to use a happy voice.

Ekman and Friesen (1969, 1972) have demonstrated with psychiatric patients and student nurses that in deception situations people are more likely to monitor their facial than body presentation, with the result that the deception is more likely to be detected from an examination of body cues than facial cues. Thus, the information encoded in monitored channels should differ from that encoded in nonmonitored channels. However, it is likely that great consistency characterizes that set of channels of expressive (verbal or nonverbal) behaviors which are simultaneously monitored according to the same criteria. Furthermore, self-monitored expressive behavior should vary more from situation to situation than nonmonitored expressive behavior. Self-monitoring individuals should be most likely to monitor and control their expression in situations which contain reliable cues to social appropriateness. Thus, such a person would be more likely to laugh at a comedy when watching it with amused peers than when watching it alone. The laughing behavior of the non-self-monitoring person should be more invariant across those two situations and more related to how affectively amused he himself actually is. The expressive behavior of self-monitoring individuals should be more reflective of an internal affect state when it is generated in a situation with minimal incentives for, and cues to, self-monitoring.

The cross-situational variability of the self-monitoring versus the consistency of the non-self-monitoring individuals is similar to the "traits versus situations" issue: Is behavior controlled by situational factors and hence predictable from characteristics of the surrounding situation, or is it controlled by internal states and dispositions which produce cross-situational consistency and facilitate prediction from characteristics of the person, measures of internal states, or dispositions (Mischel, 1968; Moos, 1968, 1969)? Bem (1972) has proposed that the issue be redirected from an "either traits or situations for all behavior of all people" debate to a search for moderating variables which would allow the specification for an individual of equivalence classes of situations and responses across which he monitors his behavior with respect to a particularly central self-concept. In these areas he would show traitlike cross-situational and interresponse mode consistency; in others he would not. In the domain of expressive behavior, individual differences in self-monitoring are a moderating variable which identifies individuals who demonstrate or fail to demonstrate consistency across channels of expression and between situations differing in monitoring properties.

In Search of a Measure of Individual Differences in Self-Monitoring

* * *

Self-monitoring would probably best be measured by an instrument specifically designed to discriminate individual differences in concern for social appropriateness, sensitivity to the expression and self-presentation of others in social situations as cues to social appropriateness of self-expression, and use of these cues as guidelines for monitoring and managing self-presentation and expressive behavior. Accordingly, an attempt was made to transpose the self-monitoring concept into a self-report scale which reliably and validly measures it.

The convergence between diverse methods of measuring self-monitoring was examined according to the strategy of construct validation (Cronbach & Meehl, 1955). To demonstrate discriminant validity (Campbell & Fiske, 1959), comparisons were made between self-monitoring and need for approval in the prediction of each external criterion in the validation strategy.[2] Need for approval was chosen for these critical comparisons. * * *

Construction of the Self-Monitoring Scale

Forty-one true–false self-descriptive statements were administered to 192 Stanford University undergraduates. The set included items which describe (a) concern with the social appropriateness of one's self-presentation (e.g., "At parties and social gatherings, I do not attempt to do or say things that others will like"); (b) attention to social comparison information as cues to appropriate self-expression (e.g., "When I am uncertain how to act in social situations, I look to the behavior of others for cues"); (c) the ability to control and modify one's self-presentation and expressive behavior (e.g., "I can look anyone in the eye and tell a lie with a straight face [if for a right end]"); (d) the use of this ability in particular situations (e.g., "I may deceive people by being friendly when I really dislike them"); and (e) the extent to which the respondent's expressive

[2]The two basic methodological articles referred to in this sentence are excerpted in Part I. It is nearly impossible to introduce a new personality scale without making reference to Cronbach-Meehl and Campbell-Fiske.

behavior and self-presentation are cross-situationally consistent or variable (e.g., "In different situations and with different people, I often act like very different persons").

The individual items were scored in the direction of high self-monitoring. For approximately half the items, agreement was keyed as high SM; for the remainder, disagreement was keyed as high SM.

An item analysis was performed to select items to maximize internal consistency.

* * *

The 25 items of the SM are presented in Table 13.1.

CORRELATIONS WITH OTHER SCALES Correlations between the SM and related but conceptually distinct individual differences measures provide some evidence for its discriminant validity.[3] There is a slight negative relationship ($r = -.1874$, $df = 190$, $p < .01$)[4] between the SM and the Marlowe-Crowne Social Desirability Scale (M-C SDS, Crowne & Marlowe, 1964). Individuals who report that they observe, monitor, and manage their self-presentation are unlikely to report that they engage in rare but socially desirable behaviors.

There is a similarly low negative relationship ($r = -.2002$, $df = 190$, $p < .01$) between the SM and the Minnesota Multiphasic Personality Inventory Psychopathic Deviate scale. High-SM subjects are unlikely to report deviant psychopathological behaviors or histories of maladjustment.

There is a small and nonsignificant negative relationship ($r = -.25$, $df = 24$, *ns*) between the SM and the *c* scale of the Performance Style Test (e.g., Ring & Wallston, 1968). The *c* scale was designed to identify a person who is knowledgeable about the kind of social performance required in a wide range of situations and who seeks social approval by becoming whatever kind of person the situation requires. He is literally a chameleon. Clearly the SM and *c* do not identify the same individuals.

The SM was also found to be unrelated to Christie and Geis's (1970) Machiavellianism ($r = -.0931$, $df = 51$, *ns*), Alpert-Haber (1960) Achievement Anxiety Test ($r = +.1437$, $df = 51$, *ns*), and Kassarjian's (1962) inner-other directedness ($r = -.1944$, $df = 54$, *ns*).

It thus appears that SM is relatively independent of the other variables measured.

* * *

Validation: Self-Monitoring, Stage Actors, and Psychiatric Ward Patients

* * * [One] means of establishing the validity of an instrument is by predicting how predetermined groups of individuals would score when the instrument is administered to them. According to this strategy, SM scores of criterion groups chosen to represent extremes in self-monitoring were compared with the unselected sample of Stanford University undergraduates.

PROFESSIONAL STAGE ACTORS Groups of individuals known to be particularly skilled at controlling their expressive behavior (e.g., actors, mime artists, and politicians) should score higher on the SM than an unselected sample. The SM was administered to a group of 24 male and female dramatic actors who were appearing in professional productions at Stanford and in San Francisco.

Their average score on the SM was 18.41 with a standard deviation of 3.38. This is significantly higher than the mean SM score for the Stanford sample ($t = 8.27$, $df = 555$, $p < .001$).[5]

[3]"Discriminant validity," discussed by Campbell and Fiske in Part I, means that a scale is not redundant with other, preexisting measures. Here Snyder has decided to contrast SM with a widely used measure of "social desirability," to ensure that the SM construct is different and new.

[4]In these analyses, *r* is the correlation coefficient, *df* is the degrees of freedom (here, the number of participants minus 2), and *p* is the "significance," or probability that a correlation of the magnitude obtained would be found if the population value were zero.

[5]The *t* statistic reported here is a standard method for evaluating the difference between two means.

TABLE 13.1

INSTRUCTIONS, ITEMS, AND SCORING KEY, INDEXES FOR THE SELF-MONITORING SCALE[a]

Item and scoring key[b]

1. I find it hard to imitate the behavior of other people. (F)
2. My behavior is usually an expression of my true inner feelings, attitudes, and beliefs. (F)
3. At parties and social gatherings, I do not attempt to do or say things that others will like. (F)
4. I can only argue for ideas which I already believe. (F)
5. I can make impromptu speeches even on topics about which I have almost no information. (T)
6. I guess I put on a show to impress or entertain people. (T)
7. When I am uncertain how to act in a social situation, I look to the behavior of others for cues. (T)
8. I would probably make a good actor. (T)
9. I rarely need the advice of my friends to choose movies, books, or music. (F)
10. I sometimes appear to others to experiencing deeper emotions than I actually am. (T)
11. I laugh more when I watch a comedy with others than when alone. (T)
12. In a group of people I am rarely the center of attention. (F)
13. In different situations and with different people, I often act like very different persons. (T)
14. I am not particularly good at making other people like me. (F)
15. Even if I am not enjoying myself, I often pretend to be having a good time. (T)
16. I'm not always the person I appear to be. (T)
17. I would not change my opinions (or the way I do things) in order to please someone else or win their favor. (F)
18. I have considered being an entertainer. (T)
19. In order to get along and be liked, I tend to be what people expect me to be rather than anything else. (T)
20. I have never been good at games like charades or improvisational acting. (F)
21. I have trouble changing my behavior to suit different people and different situations. (F)
22. At a party I let others keep the jokes and stories going. (F)
23. I feel a bit awkward in company and do not show up quite so well as I should. (F)
24. I can look anyone in the eye and tell a lie with a straight face (if for a right end). (T)
25. I may deceive people by being friendly when I really dislike them. (T)

Note. T = true; F = false; SM = Self-monitoring scale.

[a] Directions for Personal Reaction Inventory were: The statements on the following pages concern your personal reactions to a number of different situations. No two statements are exactly alike, so consider each statement carefully before answering. If a statement is *TRUE* or *MOSTLY TRUE* as applied to you, blacken the space marked *T* on the answer sheet. If a statement is *FALSE* or *NOT USUALLY TRUE* as applied to you, blacken the space marked *F*. Do not put your answers on this test booklet itself.

It is important that you answer as frankly and as honestly as you can. Your answers will be kept in the strictest confidence.

[b] Items keyed in the direction of high SM.

Thus, stage actors do score higher than nonactors on the SM. Actors probably do have particularly good self-control of their expressive behavior and self-presentation while on stage. It is not clear that actors are any more concerned about monitoring their expressive presentation in other situations.

Hospitalized Psychiatric Ward Patients

The behavior of hospitalized psychiatric patients is less variable across situations than that of "normals." Moos (1968) investigated the reactions of patients and staff in a representative sample of daily settings in a psychiatric inpatient ward in order to assess the relative amount of variance accounted for by settings and individual differences. The results indicated that for patients, individual differences accounted for more variance than setting differences; whereas for staff, individual differences generally accounted for less variance than setting differences. One interpretation of this finding is that psychiatric ward patients are unable or unwilling to monitor their social behavior and self-presentation to conform to variations in contingencies of social appropriateness between situations. In fact, diagnoses of "normal" and "psychopathological" may be closely related to cross-situational plasticity or rigidity (Cameron, 1950). Moos (1969) has reported that situational factors play an increasingly potent role in the behavior of institutionalized individuals as therapy progresses.

Accordingly, it was expected that a sample of hospitalized psychiatric ward patients should score lower on the SM than nonhospitalized normals.

The SM was administered to 31 male hospitalized psychiatric patients at the Menlo Park Veterans Administration Hospital. Their psychiatric diagnoses varied, and most had been previously institutionalized. Each patient's cumulative length of hospitalization varied from several months to several years.

The average SM score for this group was 10.19 with a standard deviation of 3.63. This is significantly lower than the mean SM score for the Stanford sample ($t = 3.44$, $df = 562$, $p < .001$).

Validation: Self-Monitoring and the Expression of Emotion

If the SM discriminates individual differences in the self-control of expressive behavior, this should be reflected behaviorally. In a situation in which individuals are given the opportunity to communicate an arbitrary affective state by means of nonverbal expressive behavior, a high-SM individual should be able to perform this task more accurately, easily, and fluently than a low SM.

Method

Subjects: Expression of Emotion. Male and female students whose SM scores were above the 75th percentile (SM > 15) or below the 25th percentile (SM < 9) were recruited by telephone from the pool of pretested introductory psychology students. In all, 30 high-SM and 23 low-SM subjects participated in the study and received either course credit or $1.50.

Procedure: Expression of Emotion. Each subject was instructed to read aloud an emotionally neutral three-sentence paragraph (e.g., "I am going out now. I won't be back all afternoon. If anyone calls, just tell him I'm not here.") in such a way as to express each of the seven emotions anger, happiness, sadness, surprise, disgust, fear, and guilt or remorse using their vocal and facial expressive behavior. The order of expression was determined randomly for each subject. The subject's facial and upper-body expressive behavior was filmed and his voice tape-recorded. It was suggested that he imagine he was trying out for a part in a play and wanted to give an accurate, convincing, natural, and sincere expression of each emotion—one that someone listening to the tape or watching the film would be able to understand as the emotion the subject had been instructed to express. The procedure is similar to one used by Levitt (1964).

These filmed and taped samples of expressive behavior were scored by judges who indicated which of the seven emotions the stimulus person

TABLE 13.2

SM AND ACCURACY OF EXPRESSION OF EMOTION: NAIVE JUDGES

Stimulus	High-SM judge		Low-SM judge	
	Face	Voice	Face	Voice
High SM (n = 30)				
M[a]	3.353	4.047	3.196	3.564
Variance	.718	.636	1.117	1.769
Low SM (n = 23)				
M	2.518	2.957	2.493	3.094
Variance	1.348	.982	1.479	2.102

Note. SM = Self-monitoring scale.
[a] Average accuracy computed for each stimulus across all judges who rated him and then averaged across n stimulus persons; range = 0–7.

was expressing. Accuracy of the judges was used as a measure of the expressive self-control ability of the stimulus subjects.

Judgments of Expressive Behavior: Subjects. The films and tapes of expressive behavior were scored by a group of 20 high-SM (SM > 15, or top 25%) and 13 low-SM (SM < 9, or bottom 25%) naive judges who were paid $2.00 an hour.

Judgments of Emotional Expressive Behavior: Procedure. Judges participated in small groups of both high- and low-SM judges who watched films for approximately one fourth of the subjects in the expression experiment and listened to the tapes of approximately another one fourth of the subjects. For each stimulus segment, judges indicated which of the seven emotions had been expressed.

RESULTS AND DISCUSSION

Accuracy of Expression and SM Scores. Accuracy of the judges in decoding the filmed and taped expressive behavior for each stimulus person was used as a measure of his self-control of expressive behavior ability. For each of the 53 subjects in the expression task, the average accuracy of his judges was computed separately for films and tapes and high- and low-SM judges. Table 13.2 represents these accuracy scores as a function of stimulus (expresser) SM scores, facial or vocal channel of expression, and judge SM score for naive judges. Each stimulus person expressed seven emotions. Therefore, mean accuracy scores can range from 0 to 7.

* * *

The following pattern of results emerges. Individuals who scored high on the SM were better able to communicate accurately an arbitrarily chosen emotion to naive judges than were individuals who scored low on the SM. That is, judges were more often accurate in judging both the facial and vocal expressive behavior generated in this emotion communication task by high-SM stimuli than by low-SM stimuli ($F = 11.72$, $df = 1/51$, $p < .01$).[6] For both high- and low-SM stimuli, accuracy was greater in the vocal than the facial channel ($F = 19.12$, $df = 1/153$, $p < .001$). Finally, there was a tendency for high-SM judges to be better judges of emotion than low-SM judges ($F = 1.69$, $df = 1/153$, $p < .25$). In addition, high-SM judges may have been more differentially sensitive to the expressive behavior of high- and low-SM stimuli. That is, the difference in accuracy for judging high-SM and low-SM stimuli for high-SM judges was greater than the corresponding difference for low-SM judges. However, once again the differences are not significant ($F = 2.41$, $df = 1/153$, $p < .25$).

* * *

Conclusions

Individuals differ in the extent to which they monitor (observe and control) their expressive behav-

[6]The analysis of variance and F statistics reported here are another way of evaluating mean differences. If you are not familiar with this statistic, don't worry; Snyder is just showing that the means of the high- and low-SM groups are different from each other on a variety of measures of nonverbal accuracy.

ior and self-presentation. Out of a concern for social appropriateness, the self-monitoring individual is particularly sensitive to the expression and self-presentation of others in social situations and uses these cues as guidelines for monitoring and managing his own self-presentation and expressive behavior. In contrast, the non-self-monitoring person has little concern for the appropriateness of his presentation and expression, pays less attention to the expression of others, and monitors and controls his presentation to a lesser extent. His presentation and expression appear to be controlled from within by his experience rather than by situational and interpersonal specifications of appropriateness.

* * *

References

Alpert, R., & Haber, R. N. (1960). Anxiety in academic achievement situations. *Journal of Abnormal and Social Psychology, 61,* 207–215.

Bem, D. J. (1972). Constructing cross-situational consistencies in behavior: Some thoughts on Alker's critique of Mischel. *Journal of Personality, 40,* 17–26.

Buck, R., Savin, V. J., Miller, R., & Caul, W. F. (1972). Nonverbal communication of affect in humans. *Journal of Personality and Social Psychology, 23,* 362–371.

Cameron, N. W. (1950). Role concepts in behavior pathology. *American Journal of Sociology, 55,* 464–467.

Campbell, D. J., & Fiske, D. W. (1959). Convergent and discriminant validation by the multitrait-multimethod matrix. *Psychological Bulletin, 56,* 81–105.

Christie, R., & Geis, F. L. (1970). *Studies in Machiavellianism.* New York: Academic Press.

Cronbach, L. J., & Meehl, P. E. (1955). Construct validity in psychological tests. *Psychological Bulletin, 52,* 281–302.

Crowne, D. P., & Marlowe, D. (1964). *The approval motive.* New York: Wiley.

Davitz, J. R. (Ed.) (1964). *The communication of emotional meaning.* New York: McGraw-Hill.

Ekman, P. (1971). Universals and cultural differences in facial expressions of emotion. In J. Cole (Ed.), *Nebraska Symposium on Motivation: 1971.* Lincoln, NE: University of Nebraska Press.

Ekman, P., & Friesen, W. V. (1969). Nonverbal leakage and clues to deception. *Psychiatry, 32,* 88–105.

Ekman, P., & Friesen, W. V. (1972). Judging deception from the face or body. Paper presented at the meeting of the Western Psychological Association, Portland, OR.

Freud, S. (1959). Fragment of an analysis of a case of hysteria. In *Collected Papers* (Vol. 3). New York: Basic Books, 1959. (Original work published 1905)

Goffman, E. (1955). On face work: An analysis of ritual elements in social interaction. *Psychiatry, 18,* 213–221.

Hall, E. T. (1966). *The hidden dimension.* Garden City, NY: Doubleday.

Kassarjian, W. M. (1962). A study of Riesman's theory of social character. *Sociometry, 25,* 213–230.

Levitt, E. A. (1964). The relationship between abilities to express emotional meanings vocally and facially. In J. R. Davitz (Ed.), *The communication of emotional meaning.* New York: McGraw-Hill.

Mehrabian, A. (1969). Significance of posture and position in the communication of attitude and status relationship. *Psychological Bulletin, 71,* 359–372.

Mischel, W. (1968). *Personality and assessment.* New York: Wiley.

Moos, R. H. (1968). Situational analysis of a therapeutic community milieu. *Journal of Abnormal Psychology, 73,* 49–61.

Moos, R. H. (1969). Sources of variance in responses to questionnaires and in behavior. *Journal of Abnormal Psychology, 74,* 403–412.

Ring, K., & Wallston, K. (1968). A test to measure performance styles in interpersonal relations. *Psychological Reports, 22,* 147–154.

Schachter, S., & Singer, J. (1962). Cognitive, social, and physiological determinants of emotional state. *Psychological Review, 69,* 379–399.

Sommer, R. (1969). *Personal space.* Englewood Cliffs, NJ: Prentice-Hall.

A Five-Factor Theory of Personality

Robert R. McCrae and Paul T. Costa Jr.

More than 60 years ago, Gordon Allport and one of his students did a count of trait words in an unabridged dictionary and came up with 17,953 (Allport & Odbert, 1936)! Personality psychologists have not made up tests to measure all of these, but it is safe to estimate that at least a couple of thousand different personality traits have been investigated by one researcher or another. It is reasonable to wonder whether all these different traits are strictly necessary. Can we reduce the vast number of trait terms in the language and the research literature down to an essential few? If so, this would be an important accomplishment, for it would vastly simplify the task of personality assessment and go a long way toward making it possible to compare the research of different psychologists.

In recent years, the personality psychologists Robert McCrae and Paul Costa Jr. have argued that the "Big Five" traits of personality are the truly essential ones. They call these traits extraversion, neuroticism, openness to experience, agreeableness, and conscientiousness. Not everybody believes these traits are important (see Block, 1995, for one vigorous dissent), but many psychologists find the Big Five to be a useful—if not all-encompassing—common framework for the conceptualization of individual differences in personality. As Ozer and Reise (1994) stated, the Big Five can serve a useful purpose as the "latitude and longitude" along which the thousands of possible personality traits can be located.

In the last article in this section McCrae and Costa present the latest wrinkle in their thinking about the Big Five, which is that these traits are useful not only for describing personality but also for explaining it. They present a theory of personality that presents the Big Five traits as the "basic tendencies" that underlie all of personality, and include a figure that shows how these tendencies interact with culture, situations, the self-concept, and behavior.

The research and theorizing relevant to the Big Five—pro and con—continue to be lively, and the final chapter on this topic has not yet been written. In the meantime, it is worth pondering two questions. First, how much of human personality can be encompassed by five basic traits—is anything important left out? And second, are these traits simply descriptions of personality, or are they the actual causes?

From *Handbook of Personality: Theory and Research* (2nd ed.), edited by L. A. Pervin and O. P. John (New York: Guilford, 1999), pp. 139–153.

Empirical and Conceptual Bases of a New Theory

In a narrow sense, the Five-Factor Model (FFM) of personality is an empirical generalization about the covariation of personality traits. As Digman and Inouye (1986) put it, "If a large number of rating scales is used and if the scope of the scales is very broad, the domain of personality descriptors is almost completely accounted for by five robust factors" (p. 116). The five factors, frequently labeled Neuroticism (N), Extraversion (E), Openness (O), Agreeableness (A), and Conscientiousness (C), have been found not only in the peer rating scales in which they were originally discovered (Tupes & Christal, 1961/1992) but also in self-reports on trait descriptive adjectives (Saucier, 1997), in questionnaire measures of needs and motives (Costa & McCrae, 1988), in expert ratings on the California Q-Set (Lanning, 1994), and in personality disorder symptom clusters (Clark & Livesley, 1994). Much of what psychologists mean by the term *personality* is summarized by the FFM, and the model has been of great utility to the field by integrating and systematizing diverse conceptions and measures.

In a broader sense, the FFM refers to the entire body of research that it has inspired, amounting to a reinvigoration of trait psychology itself. Research associated with the FFM has included studies of diverse populations (McCrae, Costa, del Pilar, Rolland, & Parker, 1998), often followed over decades of the lifespan (Costa & McCrae, 1992c); employed multiple methods of assessment (Funder, Kolar, & Blackman, 1995); and even featured case studies (Costa & McCrae, 1998b; McCrae, 1993–94). * * * After decades of floundering, personality psychology has begun to make steady progress, accumulating a store of replicable findings about the origins, development, and functioning of personality traits (McCrae, 1992).

But neither the model itself nor the body of research findings with which it is associated constitutes a theory of personality. A theory organizes findings to tell a coherent story, to bring into focus those issues and phenomena that can and should be explained. * * * Five-Factor Theory (FFT; McCrae & Costa, 1996) represents an effort to construct such a theory that is consistent with current knowledge about personality. In this chapter we summarize and elaborate it.

* * *

Assumptions About Human Nature The trait perspective, like every psychological theory, is based on a set of assumptions about what people are like and what a theory of personality ought to do. Most of these assumptions—for example, that explanations for behavior are to be sought in the circumstances of this life, not karma from a previous one—are implicit. FFT explicitly acknowledges four assumptions about human nature (cf. Hjelle & Siegler, 1976)—*knowability, rationality, variability*, and *proactivity*; all of these appear to be implicit in the standard enterprise of trait research.

Knowability is the assumption that personality is a proper object of scientific study. In contrast to some humanistic and existential theories that celebrate human freedom and the irreducible uniqueness of the individual, FFT assumes that there is much to be gained from the scientific study of personality in individuals and groups.

* * *

Rationality is the assumption that, despite errors and biases (e.g., Robins & John, 1997), people are in general capable of understanding themselves and others (Funder, 1995). In this respect, psychology is an unusual science. Physicians would not ask their patients to estimate their own white blood cell count, because patients could not be expected to possess such information. But trait psychologists routinely—and properly—ask people how sociable or competitive or irritable they are and interpret the answers (suitably aggregated and normed) as meaning what they say. Psychologists are able to do this because with respect to personality traits, laypersons are extraordinarily sophisticated judges who employ a trait language evolved over centuries to express important social judgments (cf. Saucier & Goldberg, 1996).

* * *

Variability asserts that people differ from each other in psychologically significant ways—an obvious premise for differential psychology. Note, however, that this position sets trait theories apart from all those views of human nature, philosophical and psychological, that seek a single answer to what human nature is really like. Are people basically selfish or altruistic? Creative or conventional? Purposeful or lazy? Within FFT, those are all meaningless questions; *creative* and *conventional* define opposite poles of a dimension along which people vary.

Proactivity refers to the assumption that the locus of causation of human action is to be sought in the person. It goes without saying that people are not absolute masters of their destinies, and that (consistent with the premise of variability) people differ in the extent to which they control their lives. But trait theory holds that it is worthwhile to seek the origins of behavior in characteristics of the person. People are neither passive victims of their life circumstances nor empty organisms programmed by histories of reinforcements. Personality is actively involved in shaping people's lives.

* * *

A Universal Personality System

Personality traits are individual difference variables; to understand them and how they operate, it is necessary to describe personality itself, the dynamic psychological organization that coordinates experience and action. * * *

COMPONENTS OF THE PERSONALITY SYSTEM The personality system [shown in Figure 14.1] consists of components that correspond to the definitions of FFT and dynamic processes that indicate how these components are interrelated—the basic postulates of FFT. The definitions would probably seem reasonable to personologists from many different theoretical backgrounds; the postulates distinguish FFT from most other theories of personality and reflect interpretations of empirical data.

The core components of the personality system, indicated in rectangles, are designated as *basic tendencies, characteristic adaptations*, and the *self-concept* (actually a subcomponent of characteristic adaptations, but one of sufficient interest to warrant its own box). The elliptical peripheral components, which represent the interfaces of personality with adjoining systems, are labeled *biological bases, external influences*, and the *objective biography*. Figure 14.1 can be interpreted cross-sectionally as a diagram of how personality operates at any given time; in that case the external influences constitute the situation, and the objective biography is a specific instance of behavior, the output of the system. Figure 14.1 can also be interpreted longitudinally to indicate personality development (in basic tendencies and characteristic adaptations) and the unfolding of the life course (objective biography).

It may be helpful to consider some of the substance of personality to flesh out the abstractions in Figure 14.1. Table 14.1 presents some examples. For each of the five factors, an illustrative trait is identified in the first column of the table. The intrapsychic and interpersonal adaptations that develop over time as expressions of these facet traits are illustrated in the second column, and the third column mentions an instance of behavior from an individual characterized by the high or low pole of the facet.

At present, FFT has relatively little to say about

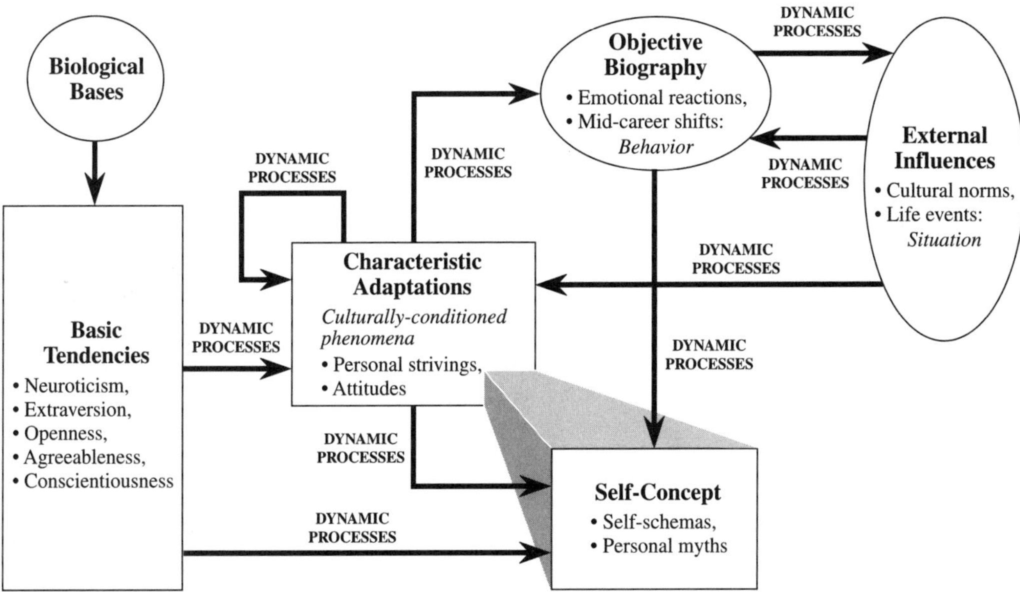

Figure 14.1. A representation of the five-factor theory personality system. Core components are in rectangles; interfacing components are in ellipses. Adapted from McCrae and Costa (1996).

the peripheral components of the personality system. Biological bases certainly include genes and brain structures, but the precise mechanisms—developmental, neuroanatomical, or psychophysiological—are not yet specified. Similarly, FFT does not detail types of external influences or aspects of the objective biography. Like most theories of personality, FFT presumes that "situation" and "behavior" are more or less self-evident.

What FFT does focus attention on is the distinction between basic tendencies (abstract psychological potentials) and characteristic adaptations (their concrete manifestations). Somewhat similar distinctions have been made by others—for example, in the familiar contrast of genotypic and phenotypic traits (Wiggins, 1973/1997) and in McAdams's (1996) distinction between Level 1 and Level 2 personality variables. FFT, however, insists on a distinction that other theories usually make only in passing, and it assigns traits exclusively to the category of basic tendencies. In FFT, traits are not patterns of behavior (Buss & Craik, 1983), nor are they the plans, skills, and desires that lead to patterns of behavior (Johnson, 1997). They are directly accessible neither to public observation nor to private introspection. Instead, they are deeper psychological entities that can only be *inferred* from behavior and experience. Self-reports of personality traits are based on such inferences, just as observer ratings are.

Although it smacks of obfuscation, there are good reasons to uncouple personality traits from the more observable components of personality. Characteristic adaptations—habits, attitudes, skills, roles, relationships—are influenced both by basic tendencies and by external influences. They are *characteristic* because they reflect the enduring psychological core of the individual, and they are *adaptations* because they help the individual fit into the ever-changing social environment. Characteristic adaptations and their configurations inevitably vary tremendously across cultures,

TABLE 14.1

SOME EXAMPLES OF FFT PERSONALITY SYSTEM COMPONENTS

Basic tendencies	Characteristic adaptations	Objective biography
Neuroticism		
N3: Depression (a tendency to experience dysphoric effect—sadness, hopelessness, guilt)	Low self-esteem, irrational perfectionistic beliefs, pessimistic attitudes	"Betty" (very high N3) feels guilty about her low-prestige job (Bruehl, 1994).
Extraversion		
E2: Gregariousness (a preference for companionship and social stimulation)	Social skills, numerous friendships, enterprising vocational interests, participation in sports, club memberships	J.-J. Rousseau (very low E2) leaves Paris for the countryside (McCrae, 1996).
Openness to Experience		
O4: Actions (a need for variety, novelty, and change)	Interest in travel, many different hobbies, knowledge of foreign cuisine, diverse vocational interests, friends who share tastes	Diane Ackerman (high O4) cruises the Antarctic (McCrae, 1993–1994).
Agreeableness		
A4: Compliance (a willingness to defer to others during interpersonal conflict)	Forgiving attitudes, belief in cooperation, inoffensive language, reputation as a pushover.	Case 3 (very low A4) throws things at her husband during a fight (Costa & McCrae, 1992b).
Conscientiousness		
C4: Achievement Striving (strong sense of purpose and high aspiration levels)	Leadership skills, long-term plans, organized support network, technical expertise	Richard Nixon (very high C4) runs for President (Costa & McCrae, 2000).

families, and portions of the lifespan. *But personality traits do not:* The same five factors are found in all cultures studied so far (McCrae & Costa, 1997); parent–child relations have little lasting effect on personality traits (Rowe, 1994; see also Fraley, 1998, on the precipitous drop in the continuity of attachment); and traits are generally stable across the adult lifespan (McCrae & Costa, 1990). These well-replicated empirical generalizations make sense only if personality traits are insulated from the direct effects of the environment. Human nature is proactive because personality traits are endogenous basic tendencies (McCrae, Costa, Ostendorf, et al., 1998).

OPERATION OF THE SYSTEM The welter of arrows in Figure 14.1 indicate some of the most important paths by which personality components interact. The plural *processes* is used because many quite distinct processes may be involved in each pathway. For example, the arrow from objective biography to self-concept implies that we learn who we are in part from observing what we do. But interpreting what we have done may involve social comparison, selective attention, defensive denial, implicit learning, or any number of other cognitive-affective processes. * * *

One implication is that personality theories that posit a small handful of key dynamic processes (repression, learning, self-actualization, getting ahead and getting along) are unlikely to prove adequate. Another is that psychologists who prefer to study processes instead of traits—"doing" instead of "having" (Cantor, 1990)—face the challenging prospect of identifying the most important of these many processes to study. There is as yet nothing like an adequate taxonomy of processes, and although evolutionary theory points to certain adaptive functions for which mechanisms must presumably have evolved, the evolutionary significance of much of human behavior is not clear (Buss, Haselton, Shackelford, Bleske, & Wakefield, 1998). FFT acknowledges the issue of multiple dynamic processes and specifies important categories of processes that share a common function in the organization of the personality system. It does not, however, detail the specifics. A complete theory of personality will ultimately include subtheories that elaborate on such specific topics (cf. Mayer, 1998).

Table 14.2 lists the 16 postulates originally proposed to specify how the personality system operates (McCrae & Costa, 1996). They are intended to be empirically testable, and in fact most of them are based on a body of empirical literature. Although it may generate novel predictions, FFT was designed primarily to make understandable what was already known.

The most radical of these postulates is 1b, *Origin*, which flatly declares that traits are endogenous basic tendencies. This postulate is based chiefly on results from studies of behavior genetics, which consistently point to a large role played by genetic factors and little or no role for common environmental factors (Riemann, Angleitner, & Strelau, 1997). Future research may well force some modification of this postulate; culture (McCrae, Yik, Trapnell, Bond, & Paulhus, 1998) or birth order (Sulloway, 1996) may be shown to affect trait levels. But as stated, Postulate 1b parsimoniously summarizes most of what is now known and offers a clear alternative to most older theories of personality, which emphasize the importance of culture and early life experience in forming personality. Today, even clinicians have begun to recognize that the standard environmental theories of personality are inadequate (Bowman, 1997).

Postulates 1b and 1d recently inspired a novel twin study (Jang, McCrae, Angleitner, Riemann, & Livesley, 1998). FFT clearly implies that N, E, O, A, and C are heritable, a claim long since supported in the cases of N and E, and more recently with respect to O, A, and C (Loehlin, McCrae, Costa, & John, 1998; Riemann, Angleitner, & Strelau, 1997). But are the specific facet traits that define the five factors also specifically heritable; or are they better interpreted as characteristic adaptations, the environmentally molded forms in which the heritable factors are manifested? One could easily suppose that people inherit only a global tendency to be Open to Experience and become open to Aesthetics, or to Ideas, or to Values as a result of individual learning experiences. But behavior genetic analyses of specific facet scores (from which the variance accounted for by the five factors had been partialled) showed that in almost all cases, specific variance was significantly heritable. It appears that the genetic blueprint for personality includes detailed specifications of dozens, perhaps hundreds, of traits.

Postulate 1c is also ripe for minor revision. At the time it was proposed, there was little convincing evidence of systematic personality change after age 30. Newer analyses, especially cross-cultural analyses (McCrae, Costa, Lima, et al., 1999), suggest that cross-sectional decreases in N, E, and O and increases in A and C continue at a very modest pace throughout adulthood. Strikingly similar results from cross-cultural studies of adult age differences in personality do, however, strongly support the basic idea that change in the level of personality traits is part of an intrinsic, endogenous maturational process that belongs in the category of basic tendencies.

* * *

Postulate 2a states the obvious claim that traits affect the way one adapts to the world. A recent example is found in analyses of the need for closure (Kruglanski & Webster, 1996). This tendency to "seize" the first credible answer and to "freeze" on one's initial decisions was shown to be strongly inversely related to Openness to Experience. It is easy to imagine the paths by which such habits of thought might develop:

> Lacking a need for change and uncertainty, closed people come to prefer a simple, structured, familiar world. Through experience they discover that tradition, conventionality, and stereotypes offer tried-and-true answers that they can adopt without much thought. They begin to think of themselves as con-

TABLE 14.2

FIVE-FACTOR THEORY POSTULATES

1. Basic tendencies

- 1a. *Individuality.* All adults can be characterized by their differential standing on a series of personality traits that influence patterns of thoughts, feelings, and actions.
- 1b. *Origin.* Personality traits are endogenous basic tendencies.
- 1c. *Development.* Traits develop through childhood and reach mature form in adulthood; thereafter they are stable in cognitively intact individuals.
- 1d. *Structure.* Traits are organized hierarchically from narrow and specific to broad and general dispositions; Neuroticism, Extraversion, Openness to Experience, Agreeableness, and Conscientiousness constitute the highest level of the hierarchy.

2. Characteristic adaptations

- 2a. *Adaptation.* Over time, individuals react to their environments by evolving patterns of thoughts, feelings, and behaviors that are consistent with their personality traits and earlier adaptations.
- 2b. *Maladjustment.* At any one time, adaptations may not be optimal with respect to cultural values or personal goals.
- 2c. *Plasticity.* Characteristic adaptations change over time in response to biological maturation, changes in the environment, or deliberate interventions.

3. Objective biography

- 3a. *Multiple determination.* Action and experience at any given moment are complex functions of all those characteristic adaptations that are evoked by the situation.
- 3b. *Life course.* Individuals have plans, schedules, and goals that allow action to be organized over long time intervals in ways that are consistent with their personality traits.

4. Self-concept

- 4a. *Self-schema.* Individuals maintain a cognitive–affective view of themselves that is accessible to consciousness.
- 4b. *Selective perception.* Information is selectively represented in the self-concept in ways that (i) are consistent with personality traits; and (ii) give a sense of coherence to the individual.

5. External influences

- 5a. *Interaction.* The social and physical environment interacts with personality dispositions to shape characteristic adaptations and with characteristic adaptations to regulate the flow of behavior.
- 5b. *Apperception.* Individuals attend to and construe the environment in ways that are consistent with their personality traits.
- 5c. *Reciprocity.* Individuals selectively influence the environment to which they respond.

6. Dynamic processes

- 6a. *Universal dynamics.* The ongoing functioning of the individual in creating adaptations and expressing them in thoughts, feelings, and behaviors is regulated in part by universal cognitive, affective, and volitional mechanisms.
- 6b. *Differential dynamics.* Some dynamic processes are differentially affected by basic tendencies of the individual, including personality traits.

Note. Adapted from McCrae & Costa (1996).

> servative, down-to-earth people, and they seek out like-minded friends and spouses who will not challenge their beliefs. Thus, basic tendencies of closedness develop into preferences, ideologies, self-construals, and social roles; these characteristic adaptations habitualize, legitimatize, and socially support a way of thinking that expresses a high need for closure. (Costa & McCrae, 1998a, p. 117)

According to FFT, the personality system represented in Figure 14.1 is a universal of human nature. All people have basic tendencies, characteristic adaptations, and a self-concept, and they are related to biology and to society in the same basic ways. FFT adopts this system as a framework for explaining the operation of personality; it does not explain why the system exists. Various hypotheses might be offered, most probably based on Darwinian evolution (Buss, 1991); rudimentary forms of this system might be seen in animals (Gosling & John, in press). More formally, the FFT personality system includes the two features that characterize many dynamic systems: a distinctive core that is preserved, and mechanisms for adapting to a changing environment. Species that did not reproduce or adapt to their environments are now extinct; personality traits that did not endure over time and transcend situational influences would never have been recognized in lay lexicons or psychological theories.

Individual Differences in Personality

Consider as a thought experiment the possibility of a utopian community—call it Walden Three—based on the findings of trait psychology. Because individual differences can lead to misunderstanding and conflict (McCrae, 1996), its founders decide to people their society with clones from a single individual; to ensure happiness, they choose an adjusted extravert (Costa & McCrae, 1980). We will let medical ethicists and social philosophers debate the wisdom of this plan and turn our attention to the consequences for personality psychology.

In one respect nothing will have changed. The personality system is universal, and the denizens of Walden Three would still have needs, plans, skills, habits, relationships; they would still interact with the world in ways that external observers would recognize as reflecting their sociability and emotional stability—they would be happy people.

But personality psychologists who attempted to study them by the usual methods would reach startling conclusions. Except for error of measurement, everyone would score the same on every personality scale, and with no variance there could be no covariance. Traits would appear to have no longitudinal stability, no heritability, no five-factor structure. Indigenous psychologists might conclude that traits were a myth, and if asked, residents of Walden Three would probably attribute their behavior solely to situational causes ("Why did you go to that party?" "I was invited!").

What this thought experiment demonstrates is the curious relation of trait psychology to individual differences. On the one hand, it might be argued that personality psychology is not about individual differences; it is about how basic tendencies of a certain class affect thoughts, feelings, and actions. Employers seek conscientious employees not because they differ from lazy and careless employees, but because they work hard and well (Barrick & Mount, 1991). On the other hand, it is only the existence of individual differences in personality that reveals that hard work and carefulness are in part the result of heritable and enduring dispositions. Variation in personality traits across individuals is the ultimate natural experiment that illuminates the workings of personality.

* * *

Five-Factor Theory and the Individual

Although it is doubtless true that every person is in some respects like no other person (Kluckhohn & Murray, 1953), FFT (like most personality theories) has nothing to say about this aspect of the person. It is, from a scientific perspective, error variance. This most emphatically does not mean that personality is irrelevant to understanding the individual.

In the typical application in clinical or personnel psychology, the individual case is understood by inferring personality traits from one set of indicators and using the resulting personality profile to interpret a life history or predict future adjustment. This is not circular reasoning, because if valid personality measures are used, the traits identified carry surplus meaning that allows the interpreter to go beyond the information given (McCrae & Costa, 1995b). If respondents tell us that they are cheerful and high-spirited, we detect Extraversion and can guess with better-than-chance accuracy that they will be interested in managerial and sales positions. However, it would be much harder to predict their current occupation: Just as the theory of evolution is better at explaining how existing species function than it is at predicting which species will evolve, so personality profiles are more useful in understanding a life than in making specific predictions about what a person will do. This is not a limitation of FFT; it is an intrinsic feature of complex and chaotic systems.

Postulate 3a, *Multiple determination*, points out that there is rarely a one-to-one correspondence between characteristic adaptations and behaviors; the same is of course equally true for the traits that underlie characteristic adaptations. Consequently, interpreting individual behaviors even when the personality profile is well known is a somewhat speculative art. Consider the case of Horatio, Lord Nelson (Costa & McCrae, 1998b; Southey, 1813/1922). In the course of his campaigns against Napoleon's France, he spent many months defending the woefully corrupt court of Naples against a democratic insurrection that had been encouraged by the French. Why would so heroic a figure take on so shabby a task?

We know from a lifetime of instances that Nelson was a paragon of dutifulness, and we might suspect that he was simply following orders—certainly he would have rationalized his conduct as devotion to the war against France. But we also know that Nelson was fiercely independent in his views of what constituted his duty: "I always act as I feel right, without regard to custom" (Southey, 1813/1922, p. 94). He might equally well have supported the insurrection and won its allegiance to the English cause.

We should also consider another trait Nelson possessed: He was excessively low in modesty. Great as his naval achievements were, he never failed to remind people of them. His sympathies were thus with the aristocracy, and he was flattered by the court of Naples, which ultimately named him Duke Di Bronte.

Together, diligence (C), independence (O), and vanity (low A) go far to explain this episode of behavior.

To be sure, there are other factors, including Nelson's relationship to the English ambassador's wife, Lady Hamilton (Simpson, 1983). That notorious affair itself reflects Nelson's independence and vanity, but seems strikingly incongruent with his dutifulness. At the level of the individual, the operations of personality traits are complex and often inconsistent (a phenomenon Mischel and Shoda, 1995, have recently tried to explain).

THE SUBJECTIVE EXPERIENCE OF PERSONALITY A number of writers (e.g., Hogan, 1996) have suggested that the FFM does not accurately represent personality as it is subjectively experienced by the individual. Daniel Levinson dismissed the whole enterprise of trait psychology as a concern for trivial and peripheral aspects of the person (Rubin, 1981). McAdams (1996) has referred to it as the "psychology of the stranger," because standing on the five factors is the sort of thing one would want to know about a stranger to whom one has just been introduced. Ozer (1996) claims that traits are personality as seen from the standpoint of the other, not the self.

We believe this last position represents a slight confusion. Individuals, who have access to private thoughts, feelings, and desires, and who generally have a more extensive knowledge of their own history of behavior, have a quite different perspective on their own traits than do external observers. What they nonetheless share with others is the need to infer the nature of their own traits and to express their inference in the comparative language of traits. We have no direct intuition of our trait profile; we can only guess at it from its manifestations in our actions and experience. (One possible reason for the increasing stability of personality as assessed by self-reports from age 20 to age 30—see Siegler et al., 1990—is that we continue to learn about ourselves in this time period.)

The fact that traits must be inferred does not, however, mean that they are or seem foreign. When adults were asked to give 20 different answers to the question "Who am I?," about a quarter of the responses were personality traits, and many others combined trait and role characteristics (e.g., "a loving mother"). Traits seem to form an important component of the spontaneous self-concept (McCrae & Costa, 1988); even children use trait terms to describe themselves (Donahue, 1994).

Sheldon, Ryan, Rawsthorne, and Ilardi (1997) brought a humanistic perspective to this issue by assessing sense of authenticity in individuals as they occupied different social roles. They also asked for context-specific self-reports of personality (e.g., how extraverted respondents were as students and as romantic partners). They found that individuals who described themselves most consistently across roles also claimed the highest feelings of authenticity. They concluded that "more often than not, one's true self and one's trait self are one and the same" (p. 1392).

Conclusion

* * *

Historically, personality psychology has been characterized by elaborate and ambitious theories with only the most tenuous links to empirical findings, and theorists have often been considered profound to the extent that their visions of human nature departed from common sense. Freud's glorification of the taboo, Jung's obscure mysticism, Skinner's denial of that most basic experience of having a mind—such esoteric ideas set personality theorists apart from normal human beings and suggested they were privy to secret knowledge. By contrast, FFT is closely tied to the empirical findings it summarizes, and its vision of human nature, at least at the phenotypic level, is not far removed from folk psychology. If that makes it a rather prosaic Grand Theory, so be it. What matters is how far it takes us in understanding that endlessly fascinating phenomenon, personality.

References

Barrick, M. R., & Mount, M. K. (1991). The Big Five personality dimensions and job performance: A meta-analysis. *Personnel Psychology, 44,* 1–26.

Bowman, M. (1997). *Individual differences in posttraumatic response: Problems with the adversity–distress connection.* Mahwah, NJ: Erlbaum.

Bruehl, S. (1994). A case of borderline personality disorder. In P. T. Costa, Jr., & T. A. Widiger (Eds.), *Personality disorders and the five-factor model of personality* (pp. 189–197). Washington, DC: American Psychological Association.

Buss, D. M. (1991). Evolutionary personality psychology. *Annual Review of Psychology, 42,* 459–491.

Buss, D. M., & Craik, K. H. (1983). The act frequency approach to personality. *Psychological Review, 90,* 105–126.

Buss, D. M., Haselton, M. G., Shackelford, T. K., Bleske, A. L. & Wakefield, J. C. (1998). Adaptations, exaptations, and spandrels. *American Psychologist, 53,* 533–548.

Cantor, N. (1990). From thought to behavior: "Having" and "doing" in the study of personality and cognition. *American Psychologist, 45,* 735–750.

Clark, L. A., & Livesley, W. J. (1994). Two approaches to identifying dimensions of personality disorder: Convergence on the five-factor model. In P. T. Costa Jr. & T. A. Widiger (Eds.), *Personality disorders and the five-factor model of personality* (pp. 261–278). Washington, DC: American Psychological Association.

Costa, P. T., Jr., & McCrae, R. R. (1980). Influence of extraversion and neuroticism on subjective well-being: Happy and unhappy people. *Journal of Personality and Social Psychology, 38,* 668–678.

Costa, P. T., Jr., & McCrae, R. R. (1988). From catalog to classification: Murray's needs and the five-factor model. *Journal of Personality and Social Psychology, 55,* 258–265.

Costa, P. T., Jr., & McCrae, R. R. (1992a). *Revised NEO Personality Inventory (NEO-PI-R) and NEO Five-Factor Inventory (NEO-FFI) professional manual.* Odessa, FL: Psychological Assessment Resources.

Costa, P. T., Jr., & McCrae, R. R. (1992b). Trait psychology comes of age. In T. B. Sonderegger (Ed.), *Nebraska Symposium on Motivation: Psychology and aging* (pp. 169–204). Lincoln: University of Nebraska Press.

Costa, P. T., & McCrae, R. R. (1998a). Trait theories of personality. In D. F. Barone, M. Hersen, & V. B. V. Hasselt (Eds.), *Advanced personality* (pp. 103–121). New York: Plenum Press.

Costa, P. T., Jr., & McCrae, R. R. (1998b). Six approaches to the explication of facet-level traits: Examples from conscientiousness. *European Journal of Personality, 12*, 117–134.

Costa, P. T., Jr., & McCrae, R. R. (2000). Theories of personality and psychopathology: Approaches derived from philosophy and psychology. In H. I. Kaplan & B. J. Saddock (Eds.), Kaplan & Saddock's *Comprehensive textbook of psychiatry* (7th ed.) Philadelphia: Lippincott, Williams & Wilkins.

Digman, J. M., & Inouye, J. (1986). Further specification of the five robust factors of personality. *Journal of Personality and Social Psychology, 50*, 116–123.

Donahue, E. M. (1994). Do children use the Big Five, too? Content and structural form in personality description. *Journal of Personality, 62*, 45–66.

Fraley, R. C. (1998). *Attachment continuity from infancy to adulthood: Meta-analysis and dynamic modeling of developmental mechanisms.* Unpublished manuscript, University of California, Davis.

Funder, D. C. (1995). On the accuracy of personality judgment: A realistic approach. *Psychological Review, 102*, 652–670.

Funder, D. C., Kolar, D. C., & Blackman, M. C. (1995). Agreement among judges of personality: Interpersonal relations, similarity, and acquaintanceship. *Journal of Personality and Social Psychology, 69*, 656–672.

Gosling, S. D., & John, O. P. (in press). Personality dimensions in non-human animals: A cross-species review. *Current Directions in Psychological Science.*

Hjelle, L. A., & Siegler, D. J. (1976). *Personality: Theories, basic assumptions, research and applications.* New York: McGraw-Hill.

Hogan, R. (1996). A socioanalytic perspective on the five-factor model. In J. S. Wiggins (Ed.), *The five-factor model of personality: Theoretical perspectives* (pp. 163–179). New York: Guilford Press.

Jang, K. L., McCrae, R. R., Angleitner, A., Riemann, R., & Livesley, W. J. (1998). Heritability of facet-level traits in a cross-cultural twin study: Support for a hierarchical model of personality. *Journal of Personality and Social Psychology, 74*, 1556–1565.

Johnson, J. A. (1997). Units of analysis for the description and explanation of personality. In R. Hogan, J. A. Johnson, & S. R. Briggs (Eds.), *Handbook of personality psychology* (pp. 73–93). New York: Academic Press.

Kluckhohn, C., & Murray, H. A. (1953). Personality formation: The determinants. In C. Kluckhohn, H. A. Murray, & D. M. Schneider (Eds.), *Personality in nature, society, and culture* (pp. 53–67). New York: Knopf.

Kruglanski, A. W., & Webster, D. M. (1996). Motivated closing of the mind: "Seizing" and "freezing." *Psychological Review, 103*, 263–283.

Lanning, K. (1994). Dimensionality of observer ratings on the California Adult Q-Set. *Journal of Personality and Social Psychology, 67*, 151–160.

Loehlin, J. C., McCrae, R. R., Costa, P. T., Jr., & John, O. P. (1998). Heritabilities of common and measure-specific components of the Big Five personality factors. *Journal of Research in Personality, 32*, 431–453.

Mayer, J. D. (1998). A systems framework for the field of personality. *Psychological Inquiry, 9*, 118–144.

McAdams, D. P. (1996). Personality, modernity, and the storied self: A contemporary framework for studying persons. *Psychological Inquiry, 7*, 295–321.

McCrae, R. R. (1992). The five-factor model: Issues and applications [Special issue]. *Journal of Personality, 60*(2).

McCrae, R. R. (1993–1994). Openness to Experience as a basic dimension of personality. *Imagination, Cognition and Personality, 13*, 39–55.

McCrae, R. R. (1996). Social consequences of experiential openness. *Psychological Bulletin, 120*, 323–337.

McCrae, R. R., & Costa, P. T., Jr. (1988). Age, personality, and the spontaneous self-concept. *Journal of Gerontology: Social Sciences, 43*, S177–S185.

McCrae, R. R., & Costa, P. T., Jr. (1990). *Personality in adulthood.* New York: Guilford Press.

McCrae, R. R., & Costa, P. T., Jr. (1995b). Trait explanations in personality psychology. *European Journal of Personality, 9*, 231–252.

McCrae, R. R., & Costa, P. T., Jr. (1996). Toward a new generation of personality theories: Theoretical contexts for the five-factor model. In J. S. Wiggins (Ed.), *The five-factor model of personality: Theoretical perspectives* (pp. 51–87), New York: Guilford Press.

McCrae, R. R., & Costa, P. T., Jr. (1997). Personality trait structure as a human universal. *American Psychologist, 52*, 509–516.

McCrae, R. R., Costa, P. T., Jr., del Pilar, G. H., Rolland, J. P., & Parker, W. D. (1998). Cross-cultural assessment of the five-factor model: The Revised NEO Personality Inventory. *Journal of Cross-Cultural Psychology, 29*, 171–188.

McCrae, R. R., Costa, P. T., Jr., Lima, M. P., Simóes, A., Ostendorf, F., Angleitner, A., Marusic, I., Bratko, D., Caprara, G. V., Barbaranelli, C., Chae, J. H., & Piedmont, R. L. (1999). Age differences in personality across the adult lifespan: Parallels in five cultures. *Development Psychology 35*, 466–477.

McCrae, R. R., Costa, P. T., Jr., Ostendorf, F., Angleitner, A., Hrebickova, M., Avia, M. D., Sanz, J., Sánchez-Bernardos, M. L., Kusdil, M. E., Wood-field, R., Saunders, P. R., & Smith, P. B. (1998). *Nature over nurture: Temperament, personality, and lifespan development.* Unpublished manuscript. Gerontology Research Center.

McCrae, R. R., Yik, M. S. M., Trapnell, P. D., Bond, M. H., & Paulhus, D. L. (1998). Interpreting personality profiles across cultures: Bilingual, acculturation, and peer rating studies of Chinese undergraduates. *Journal of Personality and Social Psychology 74*, 1041–1058.

Mischel, W., & Shoda, Y. (1995). A cognitive–affective system theory of personality: Reconceptualizing situations, dispositions, dynamics, and invariance in personality structure. *Psychological Review, 102*, 246–268.

Ozer, D. J. (1996). The units we should employ. *Psychological Inquiry, 7*, 360–363.

Riemann, R., Angleitner, A., & Strelau, J. (1997). Genetic and environmental influences on personality: A study of twins reared together using the self-and peer report NEO-FFI scales. *Journal of Personality, 65*, 449–475.

Robins, R. W., & John, O. P. (1997). Effects of visual perspective and narcissism on self-perceptions: Is seeing believing? *Psychological Science, 8*, 37–42.

Rowe, D. C. (1994). *The limits of family influence: Genes, experience, and behavior.* New York: Guilford Press.

Rubin, Z. (1981). Does personality really change after 20? *Psychology Today, 15,* 18–27.

Saucier, G. (1997). Effects of variable selection on the factor structure of person descriptors. *Journal of Personality and Social Psychology, 73,* 1296–1312.

Saucier, G., & Goldberg, L. R. (1996). The language of personality: Lexical perspectives on the five-factor model. In J. S. Wiggins (Ed.), *The five-factor model of personality: Theoretical perspectives* (pp. 21–50). New York: Guilford Press.

Sheldon, K. M., Ryan, R. M., Rawsthorne, L. J., & Ilardi, B. (1997). Trait self and true self: Cross-role variation in the Big-Five personality traits and its relations with psychological authenticity and subjective well-being. *Journal of Personality and Social Psychology, 73,* 1380–1393.

Siegler, I. C., Zonderman, A. B., Barefoot, J. C., Williams, R. B., Jr., Costa, P. T., Jr., & McCrae, R. R. (1990). Predicting personality in adulthood from college MMPI scores: Implications for follow-up studies in psychosomatic medicine. *Psychosomatic Medicine, 52,* 644–652.

Simpson, C. (1983). *Emma: The life of Lady Hamilton.* London: The Bodley Head.

Southey, R. (1922). *Life of Nelson.* New York: Dutton. (Original work published 1813)

Sulloway, F. J. (1996). *Born to rebel: Birth order, family dynamics, and creative lives.* New York: Pantheon Books.

Tupes, E. C., & Christal, R. E. (1992). Recurrent personality factors based on trait ratings. *Journal of Personality, 60,* 225–251. (Original work published 1961)

Wiggins, J. S. (1997). In defense of traits. In R. Hogan, J. A. Johnson, & S. R. Briggs (Eds.), *Handbook of personality psychology* (pp. 97–115). San Diego: Academic Press. (Original work presented 1973)

PART III

Biological Approaches to Personality

The field of biology has made remarkable progress over the past century, particularly in the past few decades. It was only natural, therefore, for personality psychologists to begin to use biology to help them understand the roots of important human behaviors. A biological psychology of personality that has developed is based upon four different areas of biology and therefore comprises four rather different approaches.

One approach relates the anatomy of the brain to personality. Work in this area, perhaps the oldest field of biological psychology, began by cataloging the ways in which accidental brain damage affected behavior and has proceeded in recent years to the use of sophisticated techniques such as fMRI (functional magnetic resonance imaging). A second approach, very active today, relates the physiology of the nervous system to personality. This approach can be traced back to the ancient Greeks, who proposed that "humors" or bodily fluids influenced personality. Modern research addresses the complex interactions still being discovered between neurotransmitters, hormones, and behavior. A third approach, called behavioral genetics, studies the way individual differences in personality are inherited from one's parents and shared among family members. Finally, a fourth approach applies Darwin's theory of evolution—a foundation of all of modern biology—to understand the behavioral propensities of the human species.

The readings in this section sample all of these approaches. Be forewarned: some of these articles contain a fair amount of technical detail that is not really part of psychology at all. You will read about neurohormonal assays and even the kind of paste used to attach an electrode to a subject's hand. These details are included to provide a flavor of this enterprise and for your reference. But the general principles concerning the relationships between biological markers and psychological characteristics are what matter. Even among psychologists, only a few researchers develop—or need to develop—a real expertise in all of these details.

The section begins with a chapter, more than a century old, that describes the ancient humoral theory of personality and proposes a "modern"—as of the mid 19th century—modification. The next selection, by James Dabbs Jr. and his colleagues, describes research on the association between a "humor" of modern interest—testosterone—and aggressive or, as they call it, "rambunctious" behavior by members of college fraternities. Next, Kenneth Blum and his colleagues summarize some very recent research on "reward deficiency syndrome," a behavioral pattern they believe underlies a wide range of behaviors from drug addiction to compulsive gambling. They deploy recently developed techniques of molecular genetics and brain imaging in a search for the biological substrate of this syndrome.

Behavioral genetics is introduced in the next selection by Thomas Bouchard Jr. Bouchard reviews the current evidence that many personality traits have a substantial heritable component. Next, a selection by Robert Plomin describes a particularly important conclusion from research in behavioral genetics, that the aspects of family environment shared by siblings has a surprisingly small influence on the way their personality ultimately develops.

The evolutionary biology of personality is illustrated in the sixth and seventh selections. David Buss and his co-workers describe research that measures gender differences in jealousy through self-report and *physiological indicators, and provide an evolutionarily based account of their results. Then Margo Wilson and Martin Daly describe what they see as the evolutionary basis of "uxoricide," the propensity to kill one's spouse in a jealous rage. The evolutionary approach of Buss, Wilson, Daly, and others comes under fire in the next selection, by Alice Eagly and Wendy Wood, which argues that the cause of sex differences in behavior is to be found in social structure rather than evolutionarily derived biological mechanisms.*

The final section, by Daryl Bem, illustrates what may be the wave of the future for biological approaches to personality. Bem introduces a theory of sexual orientation that explains this important personality characteristic as a result of a complex interplay between predisposing biological factors, basic biological mechanisms, and a child's and adolescent's social interactions in a sexually polarized society. Other theories of sexual development are likely to appear in the future to compete with Bem's. Even more important, we may begin to see other complete theories of complex phenomena, such as violence, extraversion, jealousy, and even wife beating, that move step-by-step from genes to temperament to early experience to interaction with society.

Figure 15.6 Silas Wright.

ends with a stern and reckless disregard of their own and others' physical welfare. Nothing can turn them aside from their purpose; and they attain success by means of energy and perseverance rather than by forethought or deep scheming. They are men of the field rather than of the closet—men with whom to think and to feel is to act. As speakers, they make use of strong expressions, emphasize many words, and generally hit the nail with a heavy blow.

In its typical form, the motive temperament is less proper to woman than to man, but there are several modifications of it which give much elegance and beauty to the female figure.

The first is that in which the bones, except those of the pelvis, are proportionally small, which gives the figure additional delicacy and grace. This conformation, while it adds to the beauty of the female figure, detracts from the strength and consequently the beauty of the masculine form. The Diana of Grecian sculpture furnishes a fine example of the motive temperament thus modified.

The second modification is that in which the ligaments and the articulations which they form are proportionally small, which corrects the tendency to angularity which is characteristic of this temperament, and tends to round the contour of the joints. This will be particularly observable in the wrists and ankles.

The third modification of this temperament is that which presents proportionally shorter bones, and, except around the pelvis, smaller and more rounded muscles, affording less strongly marked reliefs and more of that rounded plumpness essential to the highest style of female beauty. In this characteristic, it approaches the vital temperament, to which this modification is allied.

In accordance with the law of homogeneousness, we find, on examining this temperament more closely, that it is characterized in details, as well as in general form, by length. The face is oblong, the head high, the nose long and prominent, and all the features correspond. This structure indicates great power and activity in some particular direction, but lack of breadth or comprehensiveness.

* * *

II. The Vital Temperament As this temperament depends upon the preponderance of the vital or nutritive organs, which occupy the great cavities of the trunk, it is necessarily marked by a breadth and thickness of body proportionally greater, and a stature and size of limbs proportionally less than the motive temperament. Its most striking physical characteristic is *rotundity.* The face inclines to roundness; the nostrils are wide; the neck rather short; the shoulders broad and rounded; the chest full; the abdomen well developed; the arms and legs plump but tapering, and terminating in hands and feet relatively small. The complexion is generally florid; the countenance smiling; the eyes light; the nose broad, and the hair soft, light, and silky.

In a woman of this temperament (which seems to be peculiarly the temperament of woman), the shoulders are softly rounded, and owe any breadth they may possess rather to the expanded chest, with which they are connected, than to the bony or muscular size of the shoulders themselves; the bust is full and rounded; the waist, though sufficiently marked, is, as it were, encroached upon by the plumpness of the contiguous parts; the haunches are greatly expanded; the limbs tapering; the feet and hands small, but plump; the complexion, depending on nutrition, has the rose and the lily so exquisitely blended that we are surprised that it should defy the usual operations of the elements; and there is a profusion of soft, and fine flaxen or auburn hair. The whole figure is plump, soft and voluptuous. This temperament is not so common among American women as could be desired.

Persons of this temperament have greater vigor, but less density and toughness of fiber than those in whom the motive predominates. They love fresh air and exercise, and must be always doing something to work off their constantly accumulating stock of vitality; but they generally love play better than hard work.

Mentally, they are characterized by activity, ardor, impulsiveness, enthusiasm, versatility, and sometimes by fickleness. They are distinguished by elasticity rather than firmness, and possess more diligence than persistence, and more brilliancy than depth. They are frequently violent and passionate, but are as easily calmed as excited; are generally cheerful, amiable, and genial; always fond of good living, and more apt than others to become addicted to the excessive use of stimulants. Their motto is *dum vivimus, vivamus*—let us live while we live. There is great enjoyment to them in the mere sense of being alive—in the consciousness of animal existence. The English furnish some of the best examples of the vital temperament. Our illustration gives a good idea of it so far as its outlines are concerned.

* * *

III. The Mental Temperament The mental temperament, depending upon the brain and nervous system, is characterized by a slight frame; a head relatively large, an oval or a pyriform face; a high, pale forehead; delicate and finely chiseled features; bright and expressive eyes; slender neck; and only a moderate development of the chest. The whole figure is delicate and graceful, rather than striking or elegant. The hair is soft, fine, and not abundant or very dark; the skin soft and delicate in texture; the voice somewhat high-keyed, but flexible and varied in its intonations; and the expression animated and full of intelligence.

Figure 15.7 Prof. Tholuck.

Women in whom this temperament predominates, though often very beautiful, lack the rounded outlines, the full bosom, and the expanded pelvis, which betoken the highest degree of adaptation to the distinctive offices of the sex.

The mental temperament indicates great sensitiveness, refined feelings; excellent taste; great love of the beautiful in nature and art; vividness of conception; and intensity of emotion. The thoughts are quick, the senses acute, the imagination lively and brilliant, and the moral sentiments active and influential.

This is the literary, the artistic, and especially the poetic temperament.

There is at the present day, in this country especially, an excessive and morbid development of this temperament which is most inimical to health, happiness, and longevity. It prevails particularly among women (to whom even in its normal predominance it is less proper than the preced-

are drawn to certain fraternities, and certain environments (such as fraternity houses) make testosterone levels higher.

Finally, notice how the research on the behavioral correlates of testosterone is squarely in the tradition of theorizing about bodily "humors" and temperament, such as exemplified in the previous selection by Wells. Here, the humor is testosterone and the behavior is aggressiveness. The technology is modern and the data much better, but the basic idea—substances in the body explain why people behave as they do—is ancient.

From *Personality and Individual Differences, 20,* 157–161, 1996.

Introduction

The character of groups arises from their circumstances and history. It also arises from the nature of the people who belong to the groups. People are social and biological creatures, and among the qualities that affect their behavior in groups is the hormone testosterone.

Testosterone in animals is related to aggression, dominance, and sexual activity (Archer, 1988; Lesher, 1978). In people it is related to dominance (Gladue, Boechler, & McCaul, 1989), aggression (Archer, 1991), libido (Booth & Dabbs, 1993; Morris, Udry, Kahn-Dawood, & Dawood, 1987; Sherwin, Gelfand, & Brender, 1985), sensation seeking (Daitzman & Zuckerman, 1980), drug abuse (Dabbs & Morris, 1990), low educational achievement (Dabbs, 1992; Kirkpatrick, Campbell, Wharry, & Robinson, 1993), and marital discord and divorce (Booth & Dabbs, 1993). The picture is one of excess and delinquency, although Dabbs and Ruback (1988) found high testosterone college students engaging and likeable.

Testosterone can be regarded as a characteristic of groups as well as of individuals. Mean testosterone levels differ across occupations (Dabbs, 1992; Dabbs, de La Rue, & Williams, 1990a; Schindler, 1979). Because people affiliate with others similar to themselves (Buss, 1985), we might expect them to have testosterone levels like those of their friends and associates. When individuals join together into groups, their shared conversations and social activities should intensify their preexisting characteristics. Testosterone is important in the lives of young men, and it is plausibly related to the kind of groups to which they belong. Relationships between testosterone and group behavior could be studied in friendship groups, civic clubs, or college fraternities.

The present study dealt with college fraternities. Fraternities are allowed a large latitude of behavior on most campuses, and there is room for individual members to shape the overall tone of the fraternity. The present study was initiated by Hargrove's (1991) observation that *Ss*[1] from a fraternity known for good behavior and high grades appeared somewhat low in testosterone, although she had no comparative data from other fraternities. Hargrove hypothesized that, consistent with findings about other occupations including the ministry (Dabbs et al., 1990a), low testosterone fraternities would be more intellectually oriented and socially responsible than high testosterone fraternities. Based on this hypothesis and the studies cited above, we expected higher testosterone groups to be wilder and more rambunctious and lower testosterone groups to be more docile and well-behaved. The present study address two specific questions: Do fraternities differ among themselves in mean testosterone level? If they do, what best describes the behavior associated with these differences?

---

[1]Following the format of the journal in which this article originally appeared, *Ss* stands for subjects, or research participants.

Method

We examined five fraternities at the one university and seven fraternities at another. At the first university there were 26 fraternities, and interfraternity council members helped us identify those most similar to and those most different from the one studied by Hargrove (1991). This resulted in two sets of fraternities, containing two and three fraternities each. We labeled the first set, which included Hargrove's original fraternity, "responsible," and we labeled the second set "rambunctious." At the second university there were 31 fraternities. We were unable to group these clearly, but a university official helped us identify a diverse set of seven that represented a range of popularity, social skill, academic achievement, and university rule violations.

A female researcher visited each fraternity in the hour before noon on a weekday. She contacted a fraternity officer and offered $75 for a set of saliva samples from approx. 20 members. The officer recruited *Ss*, each of whom chewed a stick of sugar-free gum and deposited 3 ml saliva into a 20-ml polyethylene vial. The samples were stored frozen until assayed. While *Ss* collected saliva samples, the officer completed a questionnaire that asked about the fraternity's current grade point average; its number of parties and community service projects during the past year; and its number of academic awards, sports awards, interfraternity council awards, and national fraternity awards during the past two years.

Photographs of *Ss* and the researcher's notes provided other information. At the first university three judges, blind as to testosterone scores, examined the photographs of all members of the five fraternities appearing in the university yearbook. Each judge scored each picture as smiling or not, with a smile defined as "an apparent smile with teeth showing." The task was not difficult, and all judges agreed on 99% of the photographs. Each fraternity was assigned a score representing the proportion of its members the judges agreed were smiling. At the second university, the yearbook did not contain individual student photographs, and smiling was scored differently. Two judges counted smiles in fraternity group pictures that appeared in the yearbook, and two judges visited the fraternity houses and counted smiles in composite membership photographs hanging there. There was 100% agreement between the judges. Each fraternity was assigned a mean score combining the proportion smiling in the yearbook and the proportion smiling in the house photograph. All smile proportion scores, including the separate yearbook and house scores at the second university, were transformed from proportions to arcsin values prior to any statistical treatment.

Salivary testosterone levels were determined using an in-house radioimmunoassay procedure with ^{125}I-testosterone tracer and charcoal separation (Dabbs, 1990). Testosterone concentrations in saliva and serum are highly correlated, and the day-to-day reliability of salivary testosterone measurements is about $r = 0.64$ (Dabbs, 1990), approximately the same as the reliability of serum measurements (Gutai, Dai, La Porte, & Kuller, 1988). * * *

Results

UNIVERSITY ONE We analyzed testosterone scores from the first university using a two factor (Fraternity and Set) analysis of variance, with 98 *Ss* in five Fraternities nested in two Sets. Mean testosterone level was significantly higher in the rambunctious than the responsible set (14.3 vs 12.3 ng/dL), $F(1, 93) = 6.59$, $P < 0.05$. Differences in testosterone among fraternities within the sets was not significant, $F < 1.0$.

Questionnaire responses and yearbook smile scores were analyzed using *t*-tests, with the fraternities treated as five *Ss* in two groups. Rambunctious fraternities had more parties (33.0 vs 10.5 each), $t(3) = 3.68$, $P < 0.05$, lower grade point averages (2.5 vs 2.9), $t(3) = 5.03$, $P < 0.05$, fewer academic awards (0.0 vs 2.5), $t(3) = 6.71$, $P < 0.01$, fewer community service projects (0.3 vs 3.0), $t(3) = 6.20$, $P < 0.01$, and fewer members smiling in yearbook photographs (34 vs 62%), $t(3) = 3.61$, $P < 0.05$, than responsible fraternities.[2]

The researcher's notes indicated the fraternities differed in other ways. Fraternities in the rambunctious set more often ignored letters of inquiry or failed to return telephone calls. When the researcher arrived at their houses, all they needed to comply was an offer of money. One fraternity officer listened to her request and translated it for his brothers: "Hey guys, want to spit for a keg?" Two of the three houses were decorated in spartan fashion, with furniture in disrepair, as with a sofa supported by three legs and a brick. The third house, according to the housemother, was "only standing because it was constructed of steel and concrete." (Note: As of the time of publication, two of the three rambunctious fraternities had been banned from campus for misbehavior.)

Fraternities in the responsible set were more deliberate and considerate. One postponed participating to discuss the researcher's request at a chapter meeting, and the other telephoned her advisor long distance to make sure the request was legitimate. The responsible fraternities were polite when she visited. They invited her to have a seat and offered her something to eat or drink. Rambunctious fraternities were slower to respond to her arrival, letting her stand unattended, unfed, and apparently unwanted.

UNIVERSITY TWO At the second university we had no clear basis for clustering fraternities into sets, and we analyzed the data using one-way analysis of variance, which 142 *Ss* nested in seven fraternities. The fraternities differed significantly among themselves in testosterone, $F(6, 135) = 2.64$, $P < 0.05$. Their mean scores, ordered from low to high, were 10.3, 10.5, 11.2, 11.5, 11.6, 12.1 and 14.0 ng/dL. In comparisons among specific fraternities, Neuman–Keuls tests indicated that the highest fraternity was significantly different from the two lowest fraternities.

Contrary to the difference between two sets of fraternities at the first university, questionnaires completed by fraternity officers did not differentiate significantly among the seven fraternities at the second university. However, as at the first university, more smiling was associated with lower levels of testosterone. The correlation between proportion of members smiling and mean testosterone level across the seven fraternities was $r = -0.78$, 5 d.f.,[3] $P < 0.05$. The proportion smiling ranged from 55% in the fraternity with the lowest testosterone level to 35% in the fraternity with the highest level.

The researcher's notes revealed behavioral differences between fraternities that the Neuman–Keuls tests found significantly different in testosterone, the highest one and the two lowest ones. The highest fraternity was rough to a degree beyond rambunctiousness. The notes, stated, "I felt as if I'd been thrown to the lions. Very good looking, pumped up. No manners. They'd walk around without shirts, belch. 'Macho meatheads' is very fitting." The two lowest fraternities shared a common friendliness, though they differed in social skill. The notes on one of the two stated, "They talked a lot about computers and calculus. Very mild-mannered. They were nice, and we all sat around and talked while waiting for more people. Not great socially or good looking. Discussed their difficulty finding girls." The notes on the other stated, "These guys were nice and cooperative. Their house was well kept, and everyone was neatly dressed (preppy). One guy went upstairs and recruited other members of the fraternity to come spit."

Discussion

At both universities there were significant mean differences in testosterone among fraternities. At

[2]The *t*'s and *F*'s reported in this article are derived from *t*-tests and the analysis of variance, respectively, both of which yield *p*-values, which are estimates of the probability that between-group differences of the magnitude found would appear, by chance, if no such differences existed.

[3]The abbreviation d.f. represents degrees of freedom, which is related to N or the number of participants.

both universities there was less smiling in higher testosterone fraternities. At the first university, fraternities with higher testosterone levels were lower in academic achievement and community service and less friendly, as revealed by questionnaire measures and reactions to the researcher. Although they smiled less they had more parties, reminiscent of Barratt's (1993) description of impulsive aggressive individuals, high in gregariousness but low in warmth. At the second university, members of the highest testosterone fraternity were boisterous and macho, and members of the lowest testosterone fraternities were attentive and helpful. Testosterone was not related to academic achievement or community service at the second university.

Inconsistencies between the universities in the relationship of testosterone to academic achievement and community service present a puzzle. We spent more time identifying extreme fraternities at the first university, which may account for our finding of differences in socially responsible behavior there. However, we did examine a diverse set of fraternities at the second university, and we think that different cultures at the two universities may have led to different correlates of testosterone. The second university placed more emphasis on engineering and less on service and altruistic activities. To obtain descriptions of the two universities, we examined *The Insider's Guide to Colleges* (Yale Daily News, 1991). According to this source, the second university had half as many students as the first. It accepted fewer applicants (69 vs 79%), and its students had higher mean SAT scores (1190 vs 1080). It had fewer degree-granting programs (4 vs 12), and its academic pressure was more intense. It was located near the heart of a city, and more of its students came from urban backgrounds.

At the larger and more heterogenous first university, there was more room for students of varied abilities and more time for students to express values of community, altruism, and responsibility. The university was in a small town in a rural setting. The community depended upon help from students to get things done, while the urban community around the other university was relatively independent of student participation.

We would expect the more diverse academic and civic activities at the first university to allow more room for the play of individual differences. Low testosterone *S*s were friendly at both universities, but only at the first was their friendliness translated into what we called more socially responsible behavior. We suspect that university differences moderated the positive effects of low testosterone, analogous to the way in which social control forces can moderate violent and antisocial aspects of high testosterone (Dabbs & Morris, 1990; Udry, 1990). We think that while high testosterone fraternities are rambunctious, low-testosterone fraternities are not necessarily responsible. "Well-behaved vs rambunctious" may be better than "responsible vs rambunctious" to describe the underlying dimension that characterized the differences between fraternities.

We have several caveats regarding the present findings. There was undoubtedly some error in the information provided by fraternity officers. We cannot know that testosterone caused the behavioural differences we found, although we are unaware of studies showing causation in the opposite direction, in which behavioral differences like those we observed cause differences in testosterone. And finally, smiles may be something other than a measure of friendliness. There is literature on the enjoyment reflected in smiles (Ekman, Davidson, & Friesen, 1990) and on emotional feeling vs social context as determinants of smiles (Hess, Banse, & Kappas, 1995), but there is little information on whether people who smile are more friendly in other ways. People smile for many reasons, including a desire to ingratiate themselves to others (DePaulo, 1992). In the present findings we have taken smiling to indicate friendliness, and we suggest that friendliness provides a link between smiling and low testosterone. Consistent with this notion about friendliness, Hargrove (1991) found low testosterone *S*s more generous than high testosterone *S*s in judging their peers. At the other end of the friendliness continuum, there is considerable evidence linking high testosterone to hostile and antisocial behavior (Booth & Dabbs, 1993; Dabbs, Carr, Frady, & Riad, 1995; Dabbs & Morris, 1990) and thus, one might expect, to lower levels of smiling.

It is somewhat surprising to find differences in testosterone among fraternities, given the paucity of other testosterone findings with college students. Questionnaire studies have seldom found personality measures related to testosterone (Dabbs, Hopper, & Jurkovic, 1990b), though Harris and Rushton (1993) found testosterone in college students related to high aggression and low pro-social behavior, when they treated aggression and pro-social behavior as latent variables defined by several indicators. The present findings suggest mean testosterone level can be regarded as a significant characteristic of a fraternity. It is possible that testosterone has more effect in groups than in individuals, as small individual tendencies accumulate into large group tendencies. Observing groups rather than individuals may be a way of making more visible the effects of testosterone.

Findings with fraternities may extend beyond the college campus. Many groups are central to modern life, and groups can have distinct and lasting natures. An acquaintance explained to one of the present authors when she moved to a new city, "Marian, this town is just like any other. The Rotarians own it, the Kiwanians raise money for it, and the Lions just enjoy it." These stereotypes fitted with her own knowledge of stuffy Rotary balls and luncheons where Lions threw rolls at their speakers. Fraternity members are like young Rotarians, Kiwanians, or Lions in training, waiting to take their place in the grown-up clubs when they leave the university. The hormones of individuals may shape the culture of groups.

References

Archer, J. (1988). *The behavioral biology of aggression.* Cambridge: Cambridge University Press.

Archer, J. (1991). The influence of testosterone on human aggression. *British Journal of Psychology, 82,* 1–28.

Barratt, E. S. (1993). Defining impulsive aggression. Unpublished manuscript, University of Texas Medical Branch at Galveston.

Booth, A., & Dabbs, J. M., Jr. (1993). Testosterone and men's marriages. *Social Forces, 72,* 463–477.

Buss, D. M. (1985). Human mate selection. *American Scientist, 73,* 47–51.

Dabbs, J. M., Jr. (1990). Salivary testosterone measurements: Reliability across hours, days, and weeks. *Physiology and Behavior, 48,* 83–86.

Dabbs, J. M., Jr. (1992). Testosterone and occupational achievement. *Social Forces, 70,* 813–824.

Dabbs, J. M., Jr. Carr, T. S., Frady, R. L., & Riad, J. K. (1995). Testosterone, crime, and misbehavior among 692 male prison inmates. *Personality and Individual Differences, 18,* 627–633.

Dabbs, J. M., Jr., de La Rue, D., & Williams, P. M. (1990a). Testosterone and occupational choice: Actors, ministers, and other men. *Journal of Personality and Social Psychology, 59,* 1261–1265.

Dabbs, J. M., Jr., Hopper, C. H., & Jurkovic, G. J. (1990b). Testosterone and personality among college students and military veterans. *Personality and Individual Differences, 11,* 1263–1269.

Dabbs, J. M., Jr., & Morris, R. (1990). Testosterone, social class, and antisocial behavior in a sample of 4,462 men. *Psychological Science, 1,* 209–211.

Dabbs, J. M., Jr., & Ruback, R. B. (1988). Saliva testosterone and personality of male college students. *Bulletin of the Psychonomic Society, 26,* 244–247.

Daitzman, R., & Zuckerman, M. (1980). Disinhibitory sensation seeking, personality and gonadal hormones. *Personality and Individual Differences, 1,* 103–110.

DePaulo, B. M. (1992). Nonverbal behavior and self-presentation. *Psychological Bulletin, 111,* 203–243.

Ekman, P., Davidson, R., & Friesen, W. V. (1990). Emotional expression and brain physiology II: The Duchenne smile. *Journal of Personality and Social Psychology, 58,* 342–353.

Gladue, B. A., Boechler, M., & McCaul, K. D. (1989). Hormonal response to competition in human males. *Aggressive Behavior, 15,* 409–422.

Gutai, J. P., Dai, W. S., LaPorte, R. E., & Kuller, L. H. (1988). The reliability of sex hormone measurements in men for epidemiologic research. Unpublished manuscript, University of Pittsburgh.

Hargrove, M. F. (1991). An investigation of personality correlates of testosterone using peer perceptions. Unpublished Master's Thesis, Georgia State University.

Harris, J. A., & Rushton, J. P. (1993). Salivary testosterone and aggression and altruism. Unpublished manuscript, University of Western Ontario.

Hess, U., Banse, R., & Kappas, A. (1995). Implicit audience and solitary smiling revisited. *Journal of Personality and Social Psychology, 69,* 280–288.

Kirkpatrick, S. W., Campbell, P. S., Wharry, R. E., & Robinson, S. L. (1993). Saliva testosterone in children with and without learning disabilities. *Physiology and Behavior, 53,* 583–586.

Lesher, A. I. (1978). *An introduction to behavioral endocrinology.* New York: Oxford.

Morris, N. M., Udry, J. R., Kahn-Dawood, F., & Dawood,

M. Y. (1987). Marital sex frequency and midcycle female testosterone. *Archives of Sexual Behavior, 16*, 27–37.

Schindler, G. L. (1979). Testosterone concentration, personality patterns, and occupational choice in women. *Dissertation Abstracts International, 40*, 1411A (University Microfilms No. 79–19, 403).

Sherwin, B. B., Gelfand, M. M., & Brender, W. (1985). Androgen enhances sexual motivation in females: A prospective, crossover study of sex steroid administration in the surgical menopause. *Psychosomatic Medicine, 47*, 339–351.

Udry, J. R. (1990). Biosocial models of adolescent behavior problems. *Social Biology, 37*, 1–10.

Yale Daily News (1991). *The insider's guide to the colleges, 1991* (17th ed.). New Haven: Yale Daily News.

Reward Deficiency Syndrome

Kenneth Blum, John G. Cull, Eric R. Braverman, and David E. Comings

Advances in molecular biology and human genetics will surely affect our understanding of personality in the coming years. The next selection is one of the first examples of a research program that is beginning to capitalize on this potential, and is a good illustration of what the state of the art in biological research relevant to personality looks like. Very recent research has moved beyond the humoral-like approach, such as that used in the previous selection concerning testosterone, to using techniques of molecular genetics and recordings of electrical activity in the brain. Kenneth Blum and his colleagues have identified what they believe is a wide-ranging behavior pattern, which they call "reward deficiency syndrome," and pursued its biological correlates. In this article, they claim that drug addiction, obesity, alcoholism, and even compulsive gambling may have a common genetic and physiological basis.

An important part of this research is purely biological and involves the development of molecular techniques to identify differences in DNA between people who do and those who do not have the genes believed to be important. Although the description of this part of the research may be difficult to understand for someone who has not recently taken a course in molecular biology, we include it in the selection because it is an important part of Blum's contribution to psychology. So do not be concerned if you do not understand all of the technical terms or cannot follow the nature of Blum's exact procedure; these are included just to provide a sense of the flavor of the new enterprise of combining molecular biology and psychology.

The psychological side of this research addresses the degree to which addiction, obesity, Tourette's syndrome, compulsive gambling, and other behaviors may have a common psychological basis. Further understanding in this area, therefore, will depend equally on the development of new microbiological technologies and on improvement of the thoroughness and sophistication of the behavioral measures employed.

From *American Scientist, 84*, 132–146, 1996.

In 1990 one of us published with his colleagues a paper suggesting that a specific genetic anomaly was linked to alcoholism (Blum et al., 1990). Unfortunately it was often erroneously reported that they had found the "alcoholism gene," implying that there is a one-to-one relation between a gene and a specific behavior. Such misinterpretations are common—readers may recall accounts of an "obesity gene," or a "personality gene." Needless to say, there is no such thing as a specific gene for alcoholism, obesity or a particular type of personality. However, it would be naive to assert the opposite, that these aspects of human behavior are not associated with any particular genes. Rather the issue at hand is to understand how certain genes and behavioral traits are connected.

In the past five years we have pursued the association between certain genes and various behavioral disorders. In molecular genetics, an *association* refers to a statistically significant incidence of a genetic variant (an allele) among genetically unrelated individuals with a particular disease or condition, compared to a control population. In the course of our work we discovered that the genetic anomaly previously found to be associated with alcoholism is also found with increased frequency among people with other addictive, compulsive or impulsive disorders. The list is long and remarkable—it comprises alcoholism, substance abuse, smoking, compulsive overeating and obesity, attention-deficit disorder, Tourette's syndrome[1] and pathological gambling.

We believe that these disorders are linked by a common biological substrate, a "hard-wired" system in the brain (consisting of cells and signaling molecules) that provides pleasure in the process of rewarding certain behavior. Consider how people respond positively to safety, warmth and a full stomach. If these needs are threatened or are not being met, we experience discomfort and anxiety. An inborn chemical imbalance that alters the intercellular signaling in the brain's reward process could supplant an individual's feeling of well being with anxiety, anger or a craving for a substance that can alleviate the negative emotions. This chemical imbalance manifests itself as one or more behavioral disorders for which one of us (Blum) has coined the term "reward deficiency syndrome."

This syndrome involves a form of sensory deprivation of the brain's pleasure mechanisms. It can be manifested in relatively mild or severe forms that follow as a consequence of an individual's biochemical inability to derive reward from ordinary, everyday activities. We believe that we have discovered at least one genetic aberration that leads to an alteration in the reward pathways of the brain. It is a variant form of the gene for the dopamine D_2 receptor, called the A_1 allele. This is the same genetic variant that we previously found to be associated with alcoholism. In this review we shall look at evidence suggesting that the A_1 allele is also associated with a spectrum of impulsive, compulsive and addictive behaviors. The concept of a reward deficiency syndrome unites these disorders and may explain how simple genetic anomalies give rise to complex aberrant behavior.

The Biology of Reward

The pleasure and reward system in the brain was discovered by accident in 1954. The American psychologist James Olds was studying the rat brain's alerting process, when he mistakenly placed the electrodes in a part of the limbic system, a group of structures deep within the brain that are generally believed to play a role in emotions. When the brain was wired so that the animal could stimulate this area by pressing a lever, Olds found that the rats would press the lever almost nonstop, as many as 5,000 times an hour. The animals would stimulate themselves to the exclusion of everything else except sleep. They would even endure tremendous pain and hardship for an

[1]Tourette's syndrome is a neurological condition that produces involuntary tics such as blinking, jumping, or coughing or can even cause people to bark, yelp, or shout obscenities.

opportunity to press the lever. Olds had clearly found an area in the limbic system that provided a powerful reward for these animals.

Research on human subjects revealed that the electrical stimulation of some areas of the brain (the medial hypothalamus) produced a feeling of quasi-orgasmic sexual arousal (Olds & Olds, 1969). If certain other areas of the brain were stimulated, an individual experienced a type of light-headedness that banished negative thoughts. These discoveries demonstrated that pleasure is a distinct neurological function that is linked to a complex reward and reinforcement system (Hall, Bloom, & Olds 1977).

During the past several decades research on the biological basis of chemical dependency has been able to establish some of the brain regions and neurotransmitters involved in reward. In particular it appears that the dependence on alcohol, opiates and cocaine relies on a common set of biochemical mechanisms (Cloninger, 1983; Blum et al., 1989). A neuronal circuit deep in the brain involving the limbic system and two regions called the nucleus accumbens and the globus pallidus appears to be critical in the expression of reward for people taking these drugs (Wise & Bozarth, 1984). Although each substance of abuse appears to act on different parts of this circuit, the end result is the same: Dopamine is released in the nucleus accumbens and the hippocampus (Koob & Bloom, 1988). Dopamine appears to be the primary neurotransmitter of reward at these reinforcement sites.

Although the system of neurotransmitters involved in the biology of reward is complex, at least three other neurotransmitters are known to be involved at several sites in the brain: serotonin in the hypothalamus, the enkephalins (opioid peptides) in the ventral tegmental area and the nucleus accumbens, and the inhibitory neurotransmitter GABA in the ventral tegmental area and the nucleus accumbens (Stein & Belluzi, 1986; Blum, 1989). Interestingly, the glucose receptor is an important link between the serotonergic system and the opioid peptides in the hypothalamus. An alternative reward pathway involves the release of norepinephrine in the hippocampus from neuronal fibers that originate in the locus coeruleus.

In a normal person, these neurotransmitters work together in a cascade of excitation or inhibition—between complex stimuli and complex responses—leading to a feeling of well being, the ultimate reward, (Cloninger, 1983; Stein & Belluzi, 1986; Blum & Koslowski, 1990). In the cascade theory of reward, a disruption of these intercellular interactions results in anxiety, anger and other "bad feelings" or in a craving for a substance that alleviates these negative emotions. Alcohol, for example, is known to activate the norepinephrine system in the limbic circuitry through an intercellular cascade that includes serotonin, opioid peptides and dopamine. Alcohol may also act directly through the production of neuroamines that interact with opioid receptors or with dopaminergic systems (Alvaksinen et al., 1984; Blum & Kozlowski, 1990). In the cascade theory of reward, genetic anomalies, prolonged stress or long-term abuse of alcohol can lead to a self-sustaining pattern of abnormal cravings in both animals and human beings.

* * *

Support for the cascade theory of alcoholism in human beings is found in a series of clinical trials. When amino-acid precursors of certain neurotransmitters (serotonin and dopamine) and a drug that promotes enkephalin activity were given to alcoholic subjects, the individuals experienced fewer cravings for alcohol, a reduced incidence of stress, an increased likelihood of recovery and a reduction in relapse rates (Brown et al., 1990; Blum & Tractenberg, 1988; Blum, Briggs, & Tractenberg, 1989). Furthermore, the notion that dopamine is the "final common pathway" for drugs such as cocaine, morphine and alcohol is supported by recent studies by Jordi Ortiz and his associates at Yale University School of Medicine and the University of Connecticut Health Services Center. These authors demonstrated that the chronic use of cocaine, morphine or alcohol re-

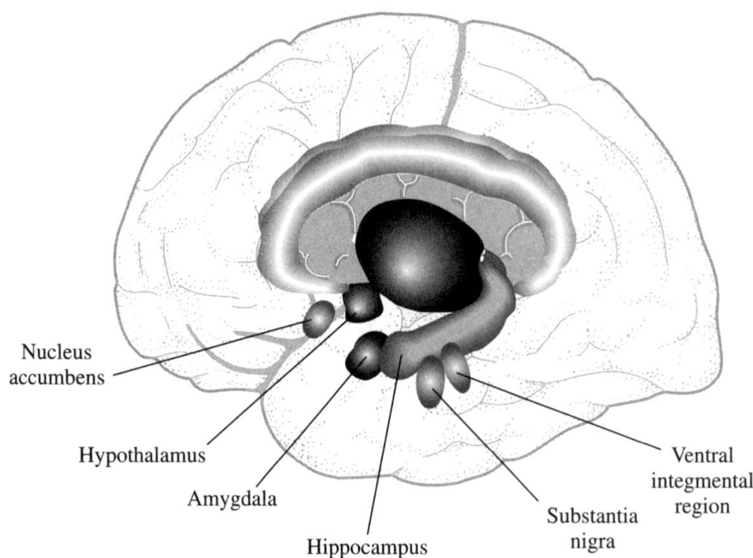

Figure 17.1 Structures deep within the limbic system play a crucial role in the expression of emotions and the activity of the reward system of the brain. The experience of pleasure and the modulation of reward are based on a reward "cascade," a chain of neurons within the limbic system that interact through various signaling molecules, or neurotransmitters. The authors propose that a biochemical deficiency in one or more of these neurons or signaling molecules can supplant an individual's feeling of well-being with anxiety, anger or a craving for a substance that can alleviate the negative emotions.

sults in several biochemical adaptations in the limbic dopamine system. They suggest that these adaptations may result in changes in the structural and functional properties of the dopaminergic system.

We believe that the biological substrates of reward that underlie the addiction to alcohol and other drugs are also the basis for impulsive, compulsive and addictive disorders comprising the reward deficiency syndrome.

Alcoholism and Genes

An alteration in any of the genes that are involved in the expression of the molecules in the reward cascade might predispose an individual to alcoholism. Indeed, the evidence for a genetic basis to alcoholism has accumulated steadily over the past five decades. The earliest report comes from studies of laboratory mice by the American psychologist L. Mirone in 1952. Mirone found that, given a choice, certain mice preferred alcohol to water. Gerald McLearn at the University of California at Berkeley took this a step farther by producing an inbred mouse (the C57 strain) that had a marked preference for alcohol. The alcohol-preferring C57 strain bred true through successive generations—it was the first clear indication that alcoholism has a genetic basis (McLearn & Rodgers, 1959).

The first evidence that alcoholism has a genetic basis in human beings came in 1972 when scientists at the Washington University School of Medicine in St. Louis found that adopted children whose biological parents were alcoholics were more likely to have a drinking problem than those born to nonalcoholic parents (Schuckit, Goodwin, & Winokur, 1972). In 1973 Goodwin and Winokur, working at the Psykologisk Institut in Copenhagen, studied 5,483 men in Denmark who had been adopted in early childhood. They found that the sons born to alcoholic fathers were three

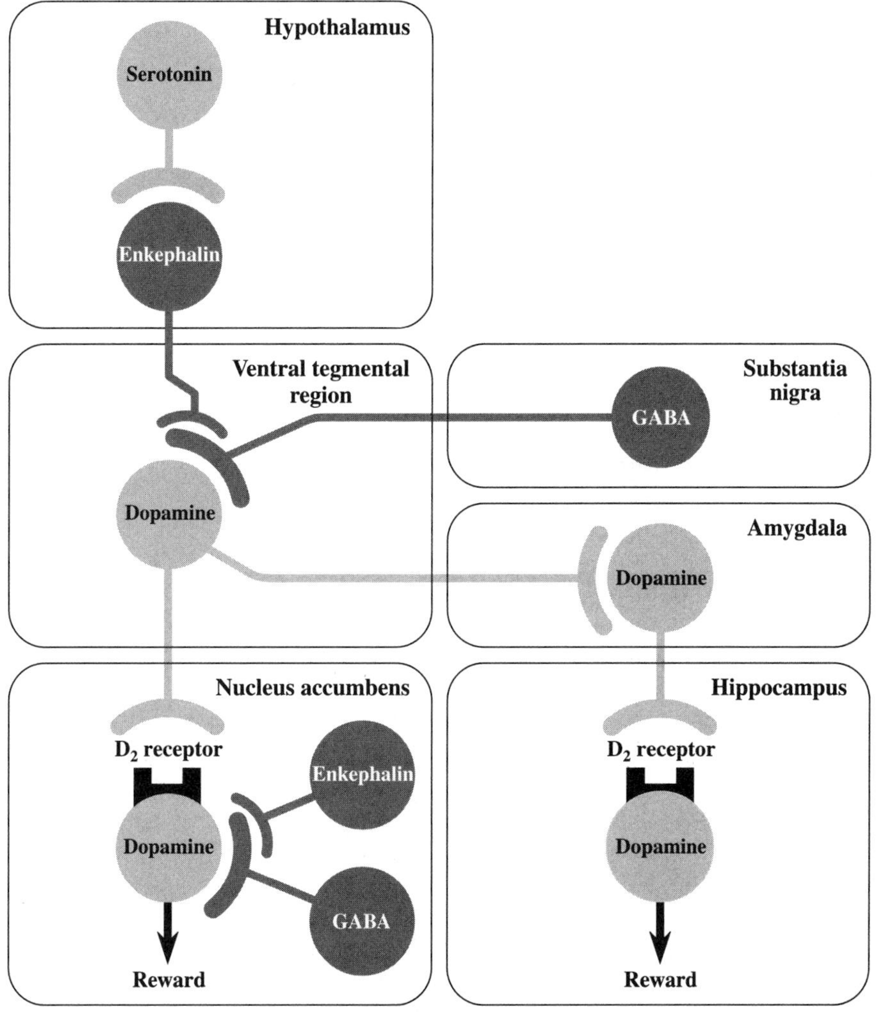

Figure 17.2 Reward cascade in the limbic system consists of excitatory *(light gray)* and inhibitory *(dark gray)* connections between neurons that are modulated by neurotransmitters. The activation of the dopamine D_2 receptor by dopamine on the cell membranes of neurons in the nucleus accumbens and the hippocampus is hypothesized by the authors to be the "final common pathway" of the reward cascade. If the activity of the dopamine D_2 receptor is deficient, the activity of neurons in the nucleus accumbens and the hippocampus is decreased, and the individual experiences unpleasant emotions or cravings for substances that can provide temporary relief by releasing dopamine. Alcohol, cocaine and nicotine are known to promote the release of dopamine in the brain. A simplified version of the cascade is presented here. Disorders of the cells and molecules in the "upstream" part of the cascade may also disrupt the normal activity of the reward system. The cascade begins with the excitatory activity of serotonin-releasing neurons in the hypothalamus. This causes the release of the opioid peptide met-enkephalin in the ventral tegmental area, which inhibits the activity of neurons that release the inhibitory neurotransmitter gamma-aminobutyric acid (GABA). The disinhibition of dopamine-containing neurons in the ventral tegmental area allows them to release dopamine in the nucleus accumbens and in certain parts of the hippocampus, permitting the completion of the casade.

times more likely to become alcoholic than the sons of nonalcoholic fathers.

* * *

The opportunity to investigate a ninth genetic marker arose after Olivier Civelli of the Vollum Institute at Oregon University cloned and sequenced the gene for one form of the dopamine D_2 receptor. The D_2 receptor is one of at least five physiologically distinct dopamine receptors (D_1, D_2, D_3, D_4 and D_5) found on the synaptic membranes of neurons in the brain (Sibley & Monsma, 1992). Previous studies had established that D_2 receptors are expressed in neurons within the cerebral cortex and the limbic system, including the nucleus accumbens, the amygdala and the hippocampus. Because these are the same areas of the brain (with the exception of the cortex) that are believed to be involved in the reward cascade, Civelli's work provided the opportunity to investigate an important molecular candidate for genetic aberrations among alcoholics.

The technique we used to distinguish between the D_2 receptor genes of alcoholics and those of nonalcoholics relies on the detection of restriction-fragment-length polymorphisms (RFLPs). This approach involves the use of DNA-cutting enzymes (restriction endonucleases) that cleave the DNA molecule at specific nucleotide sequences. If there are genetic differences between two individuals such that a restriction enzyme cuts their DNA along different points in (or near) a gene, the resulting fragments of their genes will be of different lengths. These differing fragments, or polymorphisms, are recognized by the use of a radioactively labeled DNA probe—in this case a short sequence of the D_2 receptor gene—that binds to a complementary DNA sequence on the fragments. Radiolabeled fragments of different lengths signify a difference in the cleavage sequence recognized by the restriction enzyme (Grandy et al., 1989).

The restriction enzyme (*Taq* 1) cuts the nucleotide sequence at a site just outside the coding region for the D_2 receptor gene. This produces the *Taq 1A* polymorphisms. To date there are four *Taq 1A* alleles known, the A_1, A_2, A_3 and A_4 alleles. The A_3 and A_4 alleles are rare, whereas the A_2 allele is found in nearly 75 percent of the general population and the A_1 allele in about 25 percent of the population.

In 1990 we used the *Taq* I enzyme to search for *Taq* IA polymorphisms in the DNA[2] extracted from the brains of deceased alcoholics and a control population of nonalcoholics. The results were striking: In our sample of 35 alcoholics we found that 69 percent had the A_1 allele and 31 percent had the A_2 allele. In 35 nonalcoholics we found that 20 percent had the A_1 allele and 80 percent had the A_2 allele.

* * *

Further evidence for the role of biology in alcoholism comes from efforts to find electrophysiological markers that might indicate a predisposition to the addictive disorder. One such marker is the latency and the magnitude of the positive 300-millisecond (P300) wave, an indicator of the general electrical activity of the brain that is evoked by a specific stimulus such as a tone. It turns out that abnormalities in the electrical activity of the brain are evident in the young sons of alcoholic fathers. Their P300 waves are markedly reduced in amplitude compared to the P300 waves of the sons of nonalcoholic fathers. These results raised the question as to whether this deficit had been transferred from father to son and whether this deficit would predispose the son to substance abuse in the future (Begleiter, Porjexa, Bihari, & Kissin, 1984).

Experiments carried out since then have answered both questions. The alcoholic fathers had the same P300-wave deficit seen in their sons, and the sons showed increased drug-seeking behaviors (including alcohol and nicotine) compared to the sons of nonalcoholic fathers. Moreover, the sons of alcoholic fathers had an atypical neurocognitive

[2]Here the authors are referring to a molecular genetics technique they helped develop that is described in more detail in sections of the paper not included in this edited verson.

profile (Whipple, Parker, & Noble, 1988). It now appears that children with P300 abnormalities are more likely to abuse drugs and tobacco in later years (Berman, Whipple, Fitch, & Noble, 1993).

* * *

Drug Addiction and Smoking

Cocaine can bring intense, but temporary, pleasure to the user. The aftermath is addiction and severe psychological and physiological harm. Various psychosocial theories have been advanced to account for the abuse of cocaine and other illicit drugs. In contrast to alcoholism, where growing empirical evidence is implicating hereditary factors, relatively little has been known about the genetics of human cocaine dependence. However, some recent studies have suggested that hereditary factors are involved in the use and abuse of cocaine and other illicit drugs.

Studies of adopted children, for example, show that a biological background of alcohol problems in the parents predicts an increased tendency toward illicit drug abuse in the children (Cadoret, Froughton, O'Gorman, & Heywood, 1986). Similarly, family studies of cocaine addicts show a high percentage of first- or second-degree relatives who have been diagnosed as alcoholics (Miller, Gold, Belkin, & Klaher, 1989; Wallace, 1990).

Behavioral anomalies such as conduct disorder (in which children violate social norms and the rights of others) and antisocial personality (the adult equivalent of conduct disorder) are often found to be associated with alcohol and drug problems. Several investigators have noted that sociopathic behavior in children predicts a tendency toward antisocial personality behavior, alcohol abuse and drug problems later in life. An analysis of 40 studies showed a strong positive correlation between alcoholism and drug abuse, between alcoholism and antisocial personality, and between drug abuse and antisocial personality (Schubert et al., 1988).

Although there is little known about the genetics of cocaine dependence, extensive scientific data are available on the effects of cocaine on brain chemistry. The current view is that the system that uses dopamine in the brain plays an important role in the pleasurable effects of cocaine. In animals, for example, the principal location where cocaine takes effect is the dopamine D_2 receptor gene on chromosome 11 (Koob & Bloom, 1988). Recently George Koob and his colleagues of the Scripps Research Institute in La Jolla, California, found evidence suggesting that the dopamine D_3 receptor gene is a primary site of cocaine effects. The exact effect of cocaine on gene expression is unknown. However, we do know that D_2 receptors are decreased by chronic cocaine administration, and this may induce severe craving for cocaine and possibly cocaine dreams (Volkow et al., 1993).

A recent study by Ernest Noble of the University of California at Los Angeles and Blum found that about 52 percent of cocaine addicts have the A_1 allele of the dopamine D_2 receptor gene, compared to only 21 percent of nonaddicts. The prevalence of the A_1 allele increases significantly with three risk factors: parental alcoholism and drug abuse; the potency of the cocaine used by the addict (intranasal versus "crack" cocaine); and early-childhood deviant behavior, such as conduct disorder. In fact, if the cocaine addict has three of these risk factors, the prevalence of the A_1 allele rises to 87 percent. These findings suggest that childhood behavioral disorders may signal a genetic predisposition to drug or alcohol addiction (Noble et al., 1993).

* * *

Although not viewed in the same light as the use of cocaine and other illicit drugs, cigarette smoking is another form of chemical addiction. Most attempts to stop smoking are associated with withdrawal symptoms typical of the other chemical addictions. Although environmental factors may be important determinants of cigarette use, there is strong evidence that the acquisition of the smoking habit and its persistence are strongly influenced by hereditary factors.

Of particular significance are studies of iden-

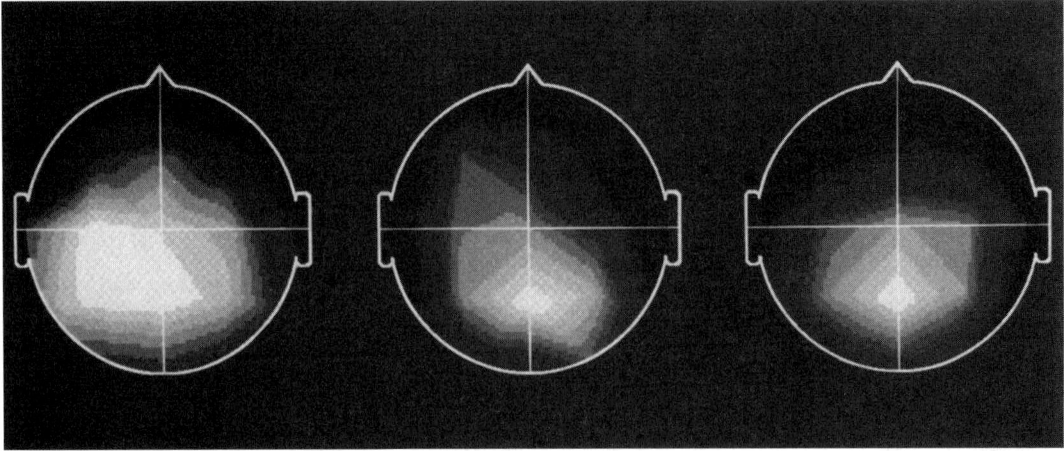

Figure 17.3 Differences in the electrical activity of the brain are evident in the latency and the magnitude of the Positive 300 millisecond (P300) wave of evoked potentials in individuals who carry the A_1 allele for the dopamine D_2 receptor gene. In normal individuals *(left)* the P300 wave typically occurs between 300 and 330 milliseconds and has a high amplitude (about 10 microvolts). In certain brain disorders associated with the neurotransmitters dopamine and acetylcholine the latency of the P300 wave increases and its magnitude diminishes. Here an obese patient *(middle)* with a A_1/A_2 heterozygous genotype displays a normal latency but a decreased magnitude (about seven microvolts) of the P300 wave. An alcoholic patient *(right)* with a homozygous A_1/A_1 genotype displays an abnormally long latency (364 milliseconds) and a decreased magnitude (about six microvolts). Previous studies have shown that the young sons of alcoholic fathers have an abnormally delayed latency of the P300 wave, which is a predictor of adolescent substance abuse. (Photography courtesy of the authors.)

tical twins, which show that when one twin smokes, the other tends to smoke. This is not the case in nonidentical twins. In one twin study, Dorit Carmelli of the Stanford Research Institute and her associates examined a national sample of male twins who were veterans of World War II. A unique aspect of this study was that the twins were surveyed twice, once in 1967–68 and again 16 years later. This allowed an examination of genetic factors in all aspects of smoking—initiation, maintenance and quitting. In general, whatever happened to one identical twin happened to the other—including the long-term pattern of not smoking, smoking and then quitting smoking. The absence of these similarities in a control population of nonidentical twins suggests a strong biogenetic component in smoking behavior (Swan et al., 1990).

Animal studies have suggested that the dopaminergic pathways of the brain may be involved. For example, the administration of nicotine to rodents disturbs dopamine metabolism in the reward centers of the brain to a greater extent than does the administration of alcohol.

With this in mind, one of us (Comings) and his colleagues investigated the incidence of the A_1 allele in a population of Caucasian smokers. These smokers did not abuse alcohol or other drugs, but had made at least one unsuccessful attempt to stop smoking. It turned out that 48 percent of the smokers carried the A_1 allele. The higher the prevalence of the A_1 allele, the earlier had been the age of onset of smoking, the greater the amount of smoking and the greater the difficulty experienced in attempting to stop smoking. In another sample of Caucasian smokers and non-smokers, Noble and his colleagues found that the prevalence of the A_1 allele was highest in current smokers, lower in those who had stopped smoking and lowest in those who had never smoked (Noble et al., 1994).

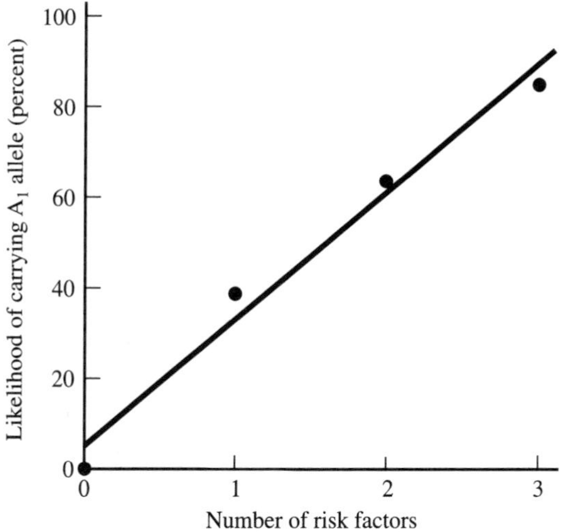

Figure 17.4 Likelihood of carrying the A_1 allele increases as the number of risk factors increases among cocaine-dependent people. Three risk factors are especially significant: parental alcoholism and drug abuse, the potency of the cocaine used by the addict (intranasal versus "crack" cocaine), and early childhood deviant behavior, such as conduct disorder. The study included 49 subjects (Noble et al., 1993).

Compulsive Bingeing and Gambling

Obesity is a disease that comes in many forms. Once thought to be primarily environmental, it is now considered to have both genetic and environmental components. In a Swedish adoption study, for example, the weight of the adult adoptees was strongly related to the body-mass index of the biological parents *and* to the body-mass index of the adoptive parents. The links to both genetic and environmental factors were dramatic. Other studies of adoptees and twins suggest that heredity is an important contributor to the development of obesity, whereas childhood environment has little or no influence. Moreover, the distribution of fat around the body has also been found to have heritable elements. The inheritance of subcutaneous fat distribution is genetically separable from body fat stored in other compartments (among the viscera in the abdomen, for example). It has been suggested that there is evidence for both single and multiple gene anomalies (Bouchard, 1995).

* * *

The complexity of compulsive eating disorders suggests that more than one defective gene is involved. Indeed, the relation between compulsive overeating and drug and alcohol addiction is well documented (Krahn, 1991; Newman & Gold, 1992). Neurochemical studies show that pleasure-seeking behavior is a common denominator of addiction to alcohol, drugs and carbohydrates (Blum et al., 1990). Alcohol, drugs and carbohydrates all cause the release of dopamine in the primary reward area of the brain, the nucleus accumbens. Although the precise localization and specificity of the *pleasure-inducing* properties of alcohol, drugs and food are still debated, there is general agreement that they work through the dopaminergic pathways of the brain. Other studies suggest the involvement of at least three other neurotransmitters serotonin, GABA and the opioid peptides.

* * *

Pathological gambling—in which an individual becomes obsessed with the act of risking money or possessions for greater "payoffs"—occurs at a rate of less than two percent in the general population. Although it is the most socially acceptable of the behavioral addictions, pathological gambling has many affinities to alcohol and drug abuse. Clinicians have remarked on the similarity between the aroused euphoric state of the gambler and the "high" of the cocaine addict or substance abuser. Pathological gamblers express a distinct craving for the "feel" of gambling; they develop tolerance in that they need to take greater risks and make larger bets to reach a desired level of excitement, and they experience withdrawal-like symptoms (anxiety and irritability) when no "action" is available (Volberg & Steadman, 1988). Indeed, there is a typical course of progression through four stages of the compulsive-gambling syndrome: winning, losing, desperation and hopelessness—a series not uncommon to other addictive behaviors.

Might the dopamine pathways in the brain be involved with pathological gambling? A recent study of Caucasian pathological gamblers found that 50.9 percent carried the A_1 allele of the dopamine D_2 receptor (Comings et al., 1996b). The more severe the gambling problem, the more likely it was that the individual was a carrier of the A_1 allele. Finally, in a population of males with drug problems who were also pathological gamblers the incidence of the A_1 allele rose to 76 percent.

Attention-Deficit Disorder

This disorder is most commonly found among school-age boys, who are at least four times more likely to express the symptoms than are young girls. These children have difficulty applying themselves to tasks that require a sustained mental effort, they can be easily distracted, they may have difficulty remaining seated without fidgeting and they may impulsively blurt out answers in the classroom or fail to wait their turn. Although normal children occasionally display these symptoms, attention-deficit disorder is diagnosed when the behavior's persistence and severity impede the child's social development and education.

Early speculation about the causes of attention-deficit disorder focused on potential sources of stress within the child's family, including marital discord, poor parenting, psychiatric illness, alcoholism or drug abuse. It has become progressively clear, however, that stress within the family cannot explain the incidence of the disorder. There is now little doubt that the disorder has a genetic basis.

Evidence in support of this notion comes from patterns of inheritance in the families of children with the disorder and from studies of identical twins. For example, consider instances in which full siblings and half-siblings (who have only half of the genetic identity of full siblings) are both raised in the same family environment. If the behavioral symptoms of attention-deficit disorder were "learned" in the family, then the incidence of the disorder should be the same for full siblings as it is for half-siblings. In fact, half-siblings of children with attention-deficit disorder have a significantly lower frequency of the disorder than full siblings (Lopez, 1965). In another study, investigators found that if one identical twin had attention-deficit disorder, there was a 100 percent probability that the other also had the disorder. In contrast, the incidence of concordance among non-identical twins was only 17 percent. This result has been supported by two other independent studies of identical twins (Willerman, 1973). Finally, one of us (Comings) and his coworkers found that the A_1 allele of the dopamine D_2 receptor gene was present in 49 percent of the children with attention-deficit disorder compared to only 27 percent of the controls (Coming et al., 1991).

Some other recent work has linked attention-deficit disorder with another impulsive disorder: Tourette syndrome. More than 100 years ago the French neurologist Giles de la Tourette described a condition that was characterized by compulsive swearing, multiple muscle tics and loud noises. He found that the disorder usually appeared in children between 7 to 10 years old, with boys more likely to be affected than girls. Tourette suggested that the condition might be inherited.

In the early 1980s one of us (Comings) and his colleagues studied 246 families in which at least one member of the family had Tourette disorder. The study indicated that virtually all cases of Tourette syndrome are genetic (Comings et al.,

1991). Subsequent studies also found that there was a high incidence of impulsive, compulsive, addictive, mood and anxiety disorders on both sides of the affected individual's family (Comings & Comings, 1987). The A_1 allele was implicated in a recent report showing that nearly 45 percent of the people diagnosed with Tourette disorder carried the aberrant gene (Comings et al., 1991). Moreover, the A_1 allele had the highest incidence among people who had the severest manifestations of the disorder.

As mentioned earlier, Tourette syndrome appears to be tightly coupled to attention-deficit disorder. In studies of the two disorders, it was found that 50 to 80 percent of the people with Tourette syndrome also had attention-deficit disorder. Furthermore, an increased number of relatives of individuals with Tourette disorder also had attention-deficit/hyperactivity disorder (Knell & Comings, 1993). It now appears that Tourette syndrome is a complex illness that may include attention-deficit disorder, conduct disorder, obsessive, compulsive and addictive disorders and other related disorders. The close coupling between these disorders has led one of us (Comings) to propose that Tourette syndrome is a severe form of attention-deficit disorder (Comings & Comings, 1989; Comings, 1995).

* * *

The Dopamine D_2 Receptor

* * *

Why would carriers of the A_1 allele be predisposed to the spectrum of disorders associated with the reward deficiency syndrome? Individuals having the A_1 allele have approximately 30 percent fewer D_2 receptors than those with the A_2 allele (Noble et al., 1991). Since the D_2 receptor gene controls the production of these receptors, the finding suggests that the A_1 allele is responsible for the reduction in receptors. In some way that we do not yet understand, carrying the A_1 allele reduces the expression of the D_2 gene compared to carrying the A_2 allele. Perhaps a regulatory site for the D_2 receptor gene is affected in A_2 carriers.

Fewer numbers of dopamine D_2 receptors in the brains of A_1 allele carriers may translate into lower levels of dopaminergic activity in those parts of the brain involved in reward. A_1 carriers may not be sufficiently rewarded by stimuli that A_2 carriers find satisfying. This may translate into the persistent cravings or stimulus-seeking behavior of A_1 carriers. Moreover, because dopamine is known to reduce stress, individuals who carry the A_1 allele may have difficulty coping with the normal pressures of life. In response to stress or cravings, A_1 carriers may turn to other substances or activities that release additional quantities of dopamine in an attempt to gain temporary relief. Alcohol, cocaine, marijuana, nicotine and carbohydrates (like chocolate) all cause the release of dopamine in the brain and bring about a temporary relief of craving. These substances can be used singly, in combination or to some extent interchangeably.

* * *

Treatment

* * *

There is reason to believe that a pharmacological approach could help people with reward deficiency syndrome. It is tempting to speculate that the pharmacological sensitivity of alcoholics to dopaminergic agonists (bromocriptine, bupropion and n-propylnor-apomorphine) may be partly determined by the individual's D_2 genotype. We predict that A_1 carriers should be pharmacologically more responsive to D_2 agonists, especially in the treatment of alcoholics or stimulant-dependent people. At least one study has already shown that the direct microinjection of the D_2 agonist n-propylnor-apomorphine into the rat nucleus accumbens significantly suppresses the animal's symptoms after the withdrawal of opiates (Harris & Aston-Jones, 1994).

* * *

These findings provide an important rationale for DNA testing to detect genetic variants for the D_2 receptor or other dopamine-related genetic variants in the tertiary treatment of alcoholism. Unlike certain other complex disorders, such as

Alzheimer's disease, the early identification and treatment of alcohol and drug abuse can occasionally alter the devastating course of these addictions. Consider the successes of self-help programs such as Alcoholics Anonymous and Narcotics Anonymous, psychopharmacological adjunctive therapy, neuroregulation or brain-wave training and electrophysiological stimulation. Identifying individuals with the A_1 allele offers the possibility of helping individuals before alcoholism or substance abuse affects their lives. We foresee the possibility for better treatment, new forms of prevention and the removal of the social stigma attached not only to alcoholism but also to related "reward-seeking" behaviors comprising the reward deficiency syndrome.

References

Alvaksinen, M. N., Saano, V., Juvonene, H., Huhtikangas, A., & Gunther, J. (1984). Binding of beta-carbolines and tetrahydroisoquinolines by opiate receptors of the d-type. *Acta Pharmacologica et Toxicologica, 55*, 380–385.

Begleiter, H. B., Porjexa, Bihari, B., & Kissin, B. (1984). Event-related brain potentials in boys at risk for alcoholism. *Science, 225*, 1493–1496.

Berman, S. M., Whipple, S. C., Fitch, R. J., & Noble, E. P. (1993). P300 in boys as a predictor of adolescent substance use. *Alcohol, 10*, 69–76.

Blum, K. (1989). A commentary on neurotransmitter restoration as a common mode of treatment for alcohol, cocaine and opiate abuse. *Integrative Psychiatry, 6*, 199–204.

Blum, K., Briggs, A. H., & Trachtenberg, M. C. (1989). Ethanol ingestive behavior as a function of central neurotransmission. *Experientia, 46*, 444–452.

Blum, K. & Kozlowski, G. P. (1990). Ethanol and neuromodulator interactions: A cascade model of reward. *Progress in Alcohol Research, 2*, 131–149.

Blum, K., Noble, E. P., Sheridan, P. J., Montgomery, A., Ritchie, T., Jagadeeswaran, P., Nogami, H., Briggs, A. H., & Cohn, J. B. (1990). Allelic association of human dopamine D2 receptor gene in alcoholism. *Journal of the American Medical Association, 263*, 2055–2060.

Blum, K., & M. C. Trachtenberg. 1988. Neurogenic deficits caused by alcoholism: Restoration by SAAVE™. *Journal of Psychoactive Drugs, 20*, 297–312.

Blum, K., Trachtenberg, M. C., Elliott, C. E., Dingler, M. L., Sexton, R. L., Samuels, A. I., & Cataldie, L. (1989). Enkephalinase inhibition and precursor amino acid loading improves inpatient treatment of alcohol and polydrug abusers: Double-blind placebo-controlled study of the nutritional adjunct SAAVE™. *Alcohol, 5*, 481–493.

Bouchard, C. (1995). Genetics of obesity: An update on molecular markers. *International Journal of Obesity, 19* (Supplement 3), S10–S13.

Brown, R. J., Blum, K., & Trachtenberg, M. C. (1990). Neurodynamics of relapse prevention: A neuronutrient approach to outpatient DUI offenders. *Journal of Psychoactive Drugs, 22*, 173–187.

Cadoret, R. J., Froughton, E., O'Gorman, T., & Heywood, E. (1986). An adoption study of genetic and environmental factors in drug abuse. *Archives of General Psychiatry, 43*, 1131–1136.

Cloninger, C. R. (1983). Genetic and environmental factors in the development of alcoholism. *Journal of Psychiatric Treatment Evaluation, 5*, 487–496.

Comings, D. E. (1995). Tourette syndrome: A hereditary neuropsychiatric spectrum disorder. *Annals of Clinical Psychiatry, 6*, 235–247.

Comings, B. G., & Comings, D. E. (1987). A controlled study of Tourette syndrome. V. Depression and mania. *American Journal of Human Genetics, 41*, 804–821.

Comings, D. E., & Comings, B. G. (1989). A controlled family history study of Tourette syndrome I. Attention deficit hyperactivity disorder, learning disorders and dyslexia. *Journal of Clinical Psychiatry, S1*, 275–280.

Comings, D. E., Comings, B. G., Muhleman, D., Deitz, G., Shahbahrami, B., Tast, D., Knell, E., Kocsis, P., Baumgarten, R., Kovacs, B. W., Levy, D. L., Smith, M., Kane, J. M., Lieberman, J. A., Klein, D. N., MacMurray, J., Tosk, J., Sverd, J., Gysin, R., & Flanagan, S. (1991). The dopamine D_2 receptor locus as a modifying gene in neuropsychiatric disorders. *Journal of the American Medical Association, 266*, 1793–1800.

Comings, D. E., Rosenthal, R. J., Leiseur, H. R., Rugle, L., Muhleman, D., Chiu, C., Dietz, F., & Gane, R. (1996b). The molecular genetics of pathological gambling. The DRD2 gene. *Pharmacogenetics* (in press).

Grandy, D. K., Lih, M., Allen, L., Bunzow, J. R., Marchionni, M., Makam, H., Reed, L., Magenis, R. E., & Civelli, D. (1989). The human dopamine D2 receptor gene is located on chromosome 11 at q22–q23 and identified as Taq I RLFP. *American Journal of Human Genetics, 45*, 778–785.

Hall, R. D., Bloom, F. E., & Olds, J. (1977). Neuronal and neurochemical substrates of reinforcement. *Neuroscience Research Program Bulletin, 15*, 131–314.

Harris, G. C., & Aston-Jones, G. (1994). Involvement of D2 dopamine receptors in then ucleus accumbens in the opiate withdrawal syndrome. *Nature, 371*(6493), 155–157.

Knell, E., & Comings, D. E. (1993). Tourette syndrome and attention deficit hyperactivity disorder: Evidence for a genetic relationship. *Journal of Clinical Psychiatry, 54*, 331–337.

Koob, G. F., & Bloom, F. E. (1988). Cellular and molecular mechanisms of drug dependence. *Science, 242*, 715–723.

Krahn, D. (1991). The relationship of eating disorders and substance abuse. *Journal of Studies on Alcohol, 3*, 239–253.

Lopez, R. (1965). Hyperactivity in twins. *Canadian Psychological Association, 10*, 421–426.

McLearn, G. E., & Rodgers, D. A. (1959). Differences in alcohol preferences among inbred strains of mice. *Quarterly Journal of Studies on Alcohol, 20*, 691–695.

Miller, N. S., Gold, M. S., Belkin, B. M., & Klaher, A. L. (1989). The diagnosis of alcohol and cannabis dependence in cocaine dependents and alcohol dependence in their families. *British Journal of Addiction, 84*, 1491–1498.

Newman, M. M., & Gold, M. S. (1992). Preliminary findings

of patterns of substance abuse in eating. *American Journal of Drugs and Alcohol Abuse, 18,* 207–211.

Noble, E. P., Blum, K., Khalsa, M. E., Ritchie, T., Montgomery, A., Wood, R. C., Fitch, R. J., Ozkaragoz, T., Sheridan, P. J., Anglin, M. D., Paredes, A., Treiman, L. J., Sparks, R. S. (1993). Allelic association of the D2 dopamine receptor gene with cocaine dependence. *Drug and Alcohol Dependence, 83,* 271–285.

Noble, E. P., Blum, K., Ritchie, T., Montgomery, A., & Sheridan, P. J. (1991). Allelic association of the D2 dopamine receptor gene with receptor binding characteristics in alcoholism. *Archives of General Psychiatry, 48,* 648–654.

Noble, E. P., Jeor, S. T., Ritchie, T., Svndulko, K., Jeor, S. C., Fitch, R. J., Brunner, R. L., & Sparkes, R. S. (1994) D2 dopamine receptor gene and cigarette smoking: A reward gene? *Medical Hypothesis, 42,* 257–260.

Olds, M. E., & Olds, J. (1969). Effects of lesions in medical forebrain bundle on self-stimulation behavior. *American Journal of Physiology, 217,* 1253–1264.

Schubert, D. S. P., Wolf, A. W., Paterson, M. B., Grande, T. P., & Pendleton, L. (1988). A statistical evaluation of the literature regarding the associations among alcoholism, drug abuse and antisocial personality disorder. *International Journal of Addiction, 23,* 797–808.

Schuckit, M. A., Goodwin, D. W., & Winokur, G. (1972). A study of alcoholism in half-siblings. *American Journal of Psychiatry, 128,* 1132–1136.

Sibley, D., & Monsma, F. J. (1992). Molecular biology of dopamine receptors. *Trends in Pharmacological Sciences, 13,* 61–69.

Stein, L., & Belluzzi, J. D. (1986). Second messenger, natural rewards, and drugs of abuse. *Clinical Neuropharmacology, 9*(Suppl. 4), 205–209.

Swan, G. E., Carmelli, D., Rosenman, R. H., Fabsitz, R. R., & Christian, J. C. (1990). Smoking and alcohol consumption in adult male twins: Genetic heritability and shared environmental influence. *Journal of Substance Abuse, 2,* 39–50.

Volberg, R. A., & Steadman, H. J. (1988). Refining prevalence estimates of pathological gambling. *American Journal of Psychiatry, 145,* 502–505.

Volkow, N. D., Fowler, J. S., Wang, G.-J., Hitzemann, R., Logan, J., Shlyer, D., Dewey, S., & Wolf, A. P. (1993). Decreased dopamine D2 receptor availability is associated with reduced frontal metabolism in cocaine abusers. *Synapse, 14,* 169–177.

Wallace, B. C. (1990). Crack cocaine smokers as adult children of alcoholics. The dysfunctional family link. *Journal of Substance Abuse Treatment, 7,* 89–100.

Whipple, S. C., Parker, E. S., & Noble, E. P. (1988). An atypical neurocognitive profile in alcoholic fathers and their sons. *Journal of Studies in Alcohol, 49,* 240–244.

Willerman, L. (1973). Activity level and hyperactivity in twins. *Child Development, 44,* 288–293.

Wise, R. A., & Bozarth, M. A. (1984). Brain reward circuitry: Four circuit elements "wired" in apparent series. *Brain Research Bulletin, 291,* 265–273.

Genes, Environment, and Personality

Thomas J. Bouchard Jr.

We have seen that modern research on the anatomy and physiology of personality can be traced back to the ancient Greek physicians. The other important area of research on the biology of personality has a different and more recent foundation, the late-19th-century writings of Charles Darwin. Darwin's theory of evolution has a strong influence on modern research on the genetic inheritance of personality. This research itself has two threads. One pursues quantitative studies of the extent to which individual differences in personality are affected by genetic as opposed to environmental factors; and the other tries to bring Darwinian evolutionary theorizing to bear in explaining behavioral propensities in the modern human race.

The next selection, by one of the most prominent practitioners of research in "behavioral genetics," Thomas Bouchard, provides a brief review of the evidence concerning the inheritance of personality. (Selections later in this section will address the evolutionary angle.) Drawing on the five-factor model of personality we saw espoused in the selection by Costa and McCrae in Part II, Bouchard reviews evidence that all five of these basic traits have substantial "heritabilities." That is, monozygotic twins are more similar on these traits than are dizygotic twins, which implies that part of the basis of these traits is genetic.

As Bouchard notes, the news that personality is influenced by one's genes has not always been welcomed by other psychologists. But research of the sort summarized in this article establishes convincingly that genes are important for personality, and this finding will not be wished away. On the other hand, it is important to remember that a high heritability does not mean a trait is determined by genetics alone; all organisms must grow up in an environment, and even if this environment is simply a stage for "genetic actors," it is hard to imagine how Julius Caesar *would play on the set of "Gilligan's Island." The role that a gene plays in development could have completely different effects in two different environments. Bouchard notes correctly that much remains to be learned about the complex interplay of our genes in our environments.*

Notice also that although genetic analysis has come in for some unfair criticism, Bouchard himself takes an extreme position on the other side. When he says that the effect of variation of environments on personality "may even turn out to be the equivalent of noise," he is saying the environment in which a child grows up may not matter at all. This conclusion runs at variance with decades of research in developmental psychology, and many psychologists remain unwilling to accept it.

From *Science, 264,* 1700–1701, 1994.

The idea that genetic factors influence behavior, including personality, is very old. The most compelling evidence has always been, as Darwin (1871–1967) noted, the successful domestication of animals:

> So in regard to mental qualities, their transmission is manifest in our dogs, horses and other domestic animals. Besides special tastes and habits, general intelligence, courage, bad and good tempers, etc., are certainly transmitted.

Unlike genetic influences on the intelligence quotient, which have been studied continuously since the time of Galton a century ago, the study of genetic influences on personality has had a much briefer history. Although Galton discussed genetic influence on personality, the lack of reliable and valid measures of personality qualities hampered progress. In addition, until recently, psychologists could not agree on which were the important traits of personality. Currently there is a modest consensus that five broad traits or "super factors" are necessary to describe personality—extraversion, neuroticism, conscientiousness, agreeableness, and openness (Goldberg, 1993) (see Table 18.1).

Until the early 1980s, the evidence for genetic influence on personality derived almost exclusively from twin studies that utilized very modest sample sizes and measured different variables. Heritability was estimated as twice the difference between the correlation for identical or monozygotic (MZ) twins and that for fraternal or dizygotic (DZ) twins. The typical conclusion was that about 50% of the observed variance in personality is due to genetic factors (Nichols, 1978). The influence on personality of the shared home environment (estimated as twice the DZ correlation minus the MZ value) was concluded to be small or even negligible. These simple equations make a number of assumptions, including (1) on average DZ twins share half as many genes in common by descent as MZ twins, (2) the genes act additively, and (3) MZ and DZ twins experience the same shared environmental influences. If the assumptions are correct, the difference between the two types of twins reflects one half the genetic influence on the trait being studied.

The conclusion that 50% of the variation in personality is genetic was not universally embraced. Many psychologists questioned that MZ and DZ twins experience the same home environment and ascribed much of the greater similarity of MZ twins over DZ twins to more similar environmental treatment of the MZ than the DZ twins. It also seemed implausible to psychologists that being reared in the same home would have so little influence on sibling similarity. Consequently these findings were not generally accepted outside of behavioral genetics.

In recent years, three trends have converged to transform our understanding of genetic and environmental influences on personality traits. First, studies of twins reared together with very large sample sizes, in some instances over 2,000 pairs of each sex and zygosity, have been carried out. Second, data have been gathered from monozygotic and dizygotic twins reared apart (MZA and DZA), as well as from both biological and adoptive families. Third, powerful methods of model fitting have been introduced that allow full utilization of the available information and statistical testing of competing hypotheses (Eaves, Eysenck, & Martin, 1989; Neale & Cardon, 1992).

Figure 18.1 compares the results of the early

TABLE 18.1

FIVE MAIN DETERMINANTS OF PERSONALITY

Extraversion: Surgency, Introversion-Extraversion (–), Dominance, *Positive Emotionality*	
Is outgoing, decisive, persuasive, and enjoys leadership roles	Is retiring, reserved, withdrawn, and does not enjoy being the center of attention
Neuroticism: Anxiety, Emotional Stability (–), Stress Reactivity, *Negative Emotionality*	
Is emotionally unstable, nervous, irritable, and prone to worry	Quickly gets over upsetting experiences, stable, and not prone to worries and fears
Conscientiousness: Conformity, Dependability, Authoritarianism (–), *Constraint*	
Is planful, organized, responsible, practical, and dependable	Is impulsive, careless, irresponsible, and cannot be depended upon
Agreeableness: Likability, Friendliness, Pleasant, *Aggression (–)*	
Is sympathetic, warm, kind, good-natured, and will not take advantage of others	Is quarrelsome, aggressive, unfriendly, cold, and vindictive
Openness: Culture, Intellect, Sophistication, Imagination, *Absorption*	
Is insightful, curious, original, imaginative, and open to novel experiences and stimuli	Has narrow interests, is unintelligent, unreflective, and shallow

Negative signs indicate trait names that characterized the opposite end of the dimension. The italic trait terms indicate the Multidimensional Personality Questionnaire factors or scales used to measure these five characteristics in the Minnesota study of twins reared apart.

twin studies, an analysis of an extremely large data set assembled by Loehlin (1992), and our own analysis of MZA (n = 59) and DZA (n = 47)[1] data from the Minnesota study of twins reared apart (MISTRA) and MZT (n = 522) and DZT (n = 408) twins from the Minnesota Twin Registry (Bouchard, Lykken, McGue, Segal, & Tellegen, 1990). The Loehlin analysis yields an estimated genetic influence of 42% (with a sizable contribution from nonadditive genetic factors—influences that are configural and not inherited in a simple additive manner) and a very modest contribution of the shared environment. The most parsimonious fit to the Minnesota data is a simple additive genetic model for all five traits with an estimate of genetic influence of 46%. Addition of nonadditive genetic and shared environmental parameters do not, however, significantly change the fit of the model, and those data are shown in the figure for comparison with the Loehlin analysis. Both approaches yield estimates of genetic influence of just over 40% and modest estimates of shared environmental influence (7%). Of the remaining variance, about half is due to nonshared environmental influences and half to error of measurement. Thus, about two thirds of the reliable variance in measured personality traits is due to genetic influence.

The early studies of twins appear to have only slightly overestimated the degree of genetic influence on personality variation, and the main contribution of the more sophisticated recent analyses is that some of the genetic influence seems to be due to nonadditive genetic variance for all five traits. All three analyses yield quite small estimates of shared environmental influence. This is now a well-replicated finding in behavior genetics, and

[1] *n* refers to the number of subjects or, in this case, the number of twin-pairs.

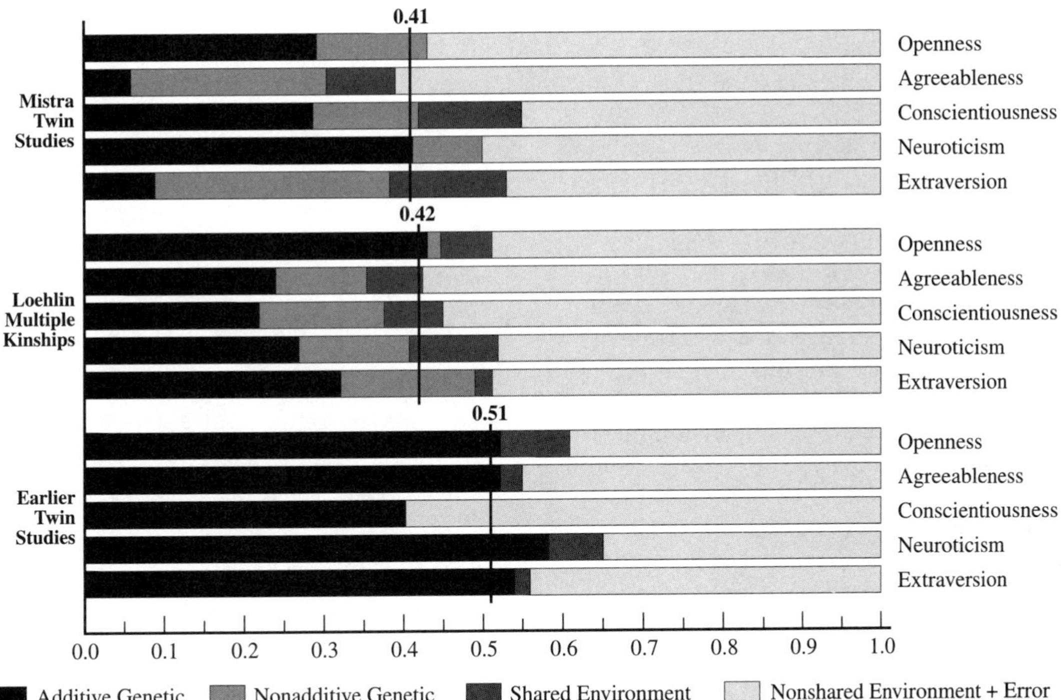

Figure 18.1 Sources of variation in personality in three sets of data. Percentages of variance accounted for by various genetic and environmental influences in personality traits. The solid lines indicate the mean Falconer heritability for the twin data from earlier studies and the mean broad heritability from model fitting for the other data sets.

its implications are straightforward. The similarity we see in personality between biological relatives is almost entirely genetic in origin. If we wish to study environmental influences on personality development in families, we must look for influences that operate differentially among children in the same family (Rowe, 1994).

However, simply demonstrating that systematic differences in treatment within the family exist does not suffice to prove that such treatments explain personality differences. First, the treatment may have no effect. For example, differences in socialization due to birth order exist, but contrary to widespread belief (Hoffman, 1991), they do not influence personality. Second, as Lytton (1990) has demonstrated, the differential behavior of children is often the cause of differential parental behavior rather than a consequence. Third, arguments as to the purported importance of environmental factors in shaping personality, though superficially plausible, often fail to stand up to scrutiny when subjected to quantitative analysis. Consider physical attractiveness. It is often argued that because twins reared apart are similar in physical attractiveness they must be treated alike, and therefore this is an important source of their similarity in personality (Hoffman, 1991; Ford, 1993). The problem with this argument is that physical attractiveness is so poorly correlated with personality traits that, when numbers are fit to the model implied by the argument, it can explain only a trivial portion of the similarity between MZA twins (Rowe, 1994). In truth, how nontraumatic environmental determinants influence the normal range of variance in adult personality remains largely a mystery. This variation may even turn out to be the equivalent of noise (Molenar, Boomsma, & Dolan, 1993).

Current thinking holds that each individual picks and chooses from a range of stimuli and events largely on the basis of his or her genotype and creates a unique set of experiences—that is, people help to create their own environments (Scarr, 1992). This view of human development does not deny the existence of inadequate and debilitating environments nor does it minimize the role of learning. Rather, it views humans as dynamic creative organisms for whom the opportunity to learn and to experience new environments amplifies the effects of the genotype on the phenotype. It also reminds us of our links to the biological world and our evolutionary history. This brings us to the core problem of the genetics of personality—the function of the variation in personality traits. The purpose of this variation is undoubtedly rooted in the fact that humans have adapted to life in face-to-face groups (sociality). Unraveling the role human individual differences play in evolution is the next big hurdle (Buss, 1993), and its solution will turn the behavior genetics of human personality from a descriptive discipline to an explanatory one.

References

Bouchard, T. J., Jr., Lykken, Dt. T., McGue, M., Segal, N. L., & Tellegen, A. (1990). Sources of human psychological differences: The Minnesota study of twins reared apart. *Science, 250*, 223–228.

Buss, D. M. (1993). Strategic individual differences: The evolutionary psychology of selection, evocation, and manipulation. In T. J. Bouchard, Jr., & P. Propping (Eds.), *Twins as a tool of behavioral genetics* (pp. 121–137). Chichester, England: Wiley.

Darwin, C. (1967). *The descent of man and selection in relation to sex.* New York: Modern Library. (Original work published 1871)

Eaves, L. J., Eysenck, H. J., & Martin, N. G. (1989). *Culture and personality: An empircal approach.* New York: Academic Press.

Ford, B. D. (1993). Emergenesis: An alternative and a confound. *American Psychologist, 48*, 1294.

Goldberg, L. R. (1993). The structure of phenotype personality traits. *American Psychologist, 48*, 26–34.

Hoffman, L. W. (1991). The influence of the family environment on personality: Accounting for sibling differences. *Psychological Bulletin, 110*, 187–203.

Loehlin, J. C. (1992). *Genes and environment in personality development.* Newbury Park, CA: Sage.

Lytton, H. (1990). Child effects: Still unwelcome? *Developmental Psychology, 26*, 705–709.

Molenar, P. C. M., Boomsma, D. I., & Dolan, C. V. (1993). A 3rd source of developmental differences. *Behavior Genetics, 23*, 519–524.

Neale, M. C., & Cardon, L. R. (Eds.). (1992). *Methodology for genetic studies of twins and families.* Boston: Kluwer Academic.

Nichols, R. C. (1978). Twin studies of ability, personality, and interests. *Homo, 29*, 158–173.

Rowe, D. (1994). *The limits of family influence: Genes, experience, and behavior.* New York: Guilford.

Scarr, S. (1992). Developmental theories for the 1990s: Development and individual differences. *Child Development, 63*, 1–19.

Environment and Genes: Determinants of Behavior

Robert Plomin

According to many behavioral geneticists, a major finding of their research concerns not genetics so much as the environment: Their results seem to indicate that the part of the family environment that is shared by siblings growing up together does not make them similar to each other. In the following selection, the prominent behavioral genetics researcher Robert Plomin describes this finding, its basis, and some of its implications.

As Plomin notes, the proposal that the shared family environment is unimportant remains controversial. There are several reasons why. First, many psychologists were trained to be environmental determinists, believing that how you turn out depends critically on how you were raised—and that children in the same family tend to be raised in the same way. Second, at least some findings from developmental psychology seem to contradict the conclusion from behavioral genetics research. For example, the number of siblings in a child's family has been shown by the developmentalist Arnold Sameroff to be a risk factor in development—a child growing up in a family with more than four children is more likely to develop problems in intellectual and social development (Barocas, Seifer, & Sameroff, 1985; Sameroff & Seifer, 1995). Yet the number of siblings is a "shared environment" variable that is equivalent for all the children in a family! The large literature on child development and the more recent and smaller literature on the developmental psychology of behavioral genetics have still not successfully integrated seemingly contradictory findings like these.

A third reason for controversy is the fact that, as Plomin himself has noted, nearly all behavioral genetics studies rely on self-report questionnaires as their measures of behavioral outcome. Perhaps the seemingly contradictory findings in the literature will be reconciled when behavioral genetics research begins to be conducted using a wider range of measures, including direct observations of behavior, life outcomes, and peers' reports of personality. Until that happens, many findings from behavioral genetics are likely to remain both intriguing and perplexing.

From *American Psychologist, 44,* 105–111, 1989.

* * *

Environmental Influences Do Not Make Children in the Same Family Similar

Children growing up in the same family are not very similar. Sibling correlations are about .40 for cognitive abilities and about .20 for personality, and sibling concordances for psychopathology are typically less than 10%.[1] In other words, siblings show greater differences than similarities for the major domains of psychology. What is more, behavioral genetic research has shown that nearly all of the sibling resemblance found in these domains is due to heredity shared by siblings rather than to shared family environment. By no means do these findings imply that environmental influences—or more specifically, family environmental influences—are unimportant. Rather, the data imply that environmental influences important to behavioral development operate in such a way as to make children in the same family different from one another. That is, environmental influences do not operate on a family-by-family basis but rather on an individual-by-individual basis. They are specific to each child rather than general for an entire family.

IMPORTANCE OF NONSHARED ENVIRONMENT The case for the importance of so-called nonshared environmental influences was presented in a target article in *Behavioral and Brain Sciences*, which was published with 32 commentaries (Plomin & Daniels, 1987). One of several results that converge on the conclusion that shared family environment is unimportant is the correlation for adoptive "siblings," genetically unrelated children adopted early in life into the same adoptive families. Their resemblance cannot be due to shared heredity, and thus their resemblance directly assesses the importance of environmental influence shared by children growing up in the same family. Results are clear in showing little influence of shared environment. For personality, adoptive sibling correlations are about .05 on average. Genetically unrelated individuals adopted together show no-greater-than-chance resemblance for psychopathology. For cognitive abilities, although adoptive siblings are similar in childhood (correlations of about .25), by adolescence, their correlations are near zero, suggesting that the long-term impact of shared family environment is slight (Plomin, 1988).

The importance of nonshared environmental factors suggests the need for a reconceptualization of environmental influences that focuses on experiential differences between children in the same family. That is, many environmental factors differ across families; these include socioeconomic status, parental education, and child-rearing practices. However, to the extent that these environmental factors do not differ between children growing up in the same family, they do not influence behavioral development. The critical question becomes, Why are children in the same family so different from one another? The key to unlock this riddle is to study more than one child per family. This permits the study of experiential differences within a family and their association with differences in outcome. Because heredity contributes to differences between siblings, sibling differences in experiences might reflect as well as affect differences in their behavior. Behavioral genetic methods are useful in addressing this issue. For example, because members of identical twin pairs do not differ genetically, one approach is to relate behavioral differences within pairs of identical twins to their experiential differences.

SOURCES OF NONSHARED ENVIRONMENTAL INFLUENCES What are these nonshared environmental influences that are so important in development? They need not be mysterious: Any environmental factor that has been studied in the traditional family-by-family manner can be reconsidered in terms of experiential differences within a family, as

---

[1]These correlational statistics are described in the selection by Rosenthal and Rubin in Part I. A "concordance" is a statistic that reflects the probability of one sibling developing a disorder if the other one does.

long as environmental measures are specific to each child in the family. For example, differential parental behavior toward their two children could create or magnify differences between the children. Even small differences in relative parental affection within the family might have large effects on differences in siblings' outcomes. Siblings' perceptions of differences in treatment may be important even if their perceptions are not veridical. In addition to differential treatment within the family, family composition variables such as birth order and gender differences might contribute to sibling differences. Experiences outside the family could also play a role; for example, siblings in the same family often have nonoverlapping friends. These are systematic sources of nonshared environment. It is also possible that nonsystematic factors such as accidents and illnesses and other idiosyncratic experiences initiate differences between siblings that, when compounded over time, make children in the same family different, perhaps in unpredictable ways.

So far, research on this new topic indicates that siblings in the same family experience considerably different environments in terms of parental treatment and their interaction with one another and with their peers. Evidence is beginning to accumulate that these differential experiences are systematically related to sibling differences in developmental outcomes. Although the first few steps have been taken toward identifying specific sources of nonshared environment, much remains to be learned. Answers to the question, Why are children in the same family so different from one another? are not only answers to the question about sibling differences. Their importance is far more general: understanding the environmental origins of individual differences in development.

Nature and Nurture

Behavioral genetics is likely to make other contributions to understanding environmental processes in development. For example, the special 1979 issue of *American Psychologist* on children included a behavioral genetic article that discussed an important implication of the fact that family members share heredity as well as family environment: Measured environmental influences in families "are not solely environmental but confound heredity with environment and are causally ambiguous with respect to the direction of effects" (Willerman, 1979, p. 925). Recent research has shown that heredity can affect measures of the family environment (Plomin, Pedersen, McClearn, Nesselroade, & Bergeman, 1988; Rowe, 1981, 1983a) and that heredity can also mediate associations between measures of the family environment and developmental outcomes of children (Plomin, Loehlin, & DeFries, 1985). Other examples of the usefulness of behavioral genetic strategies for understanding environmental influences include the analysis of genotype-environment interaction (differential effects of environments on children with different genetic propensities) and genotype-environment correlation (the extent to which children receive or create environments correlated with their genetic propensities; Plomin, 1986; Scarr & McCartney, 1983).

The move away from a rigid adherence to environmental explanations of behavioral development to a more balanced perspective that recognizes genetic as well as environmental sources of individual differences must be viewed as healthy for the social and behavioral sciences. The danger now, however, is that the swing from environmentalism will go too far. During the 1970s, I found I had to speak gingerly about genetic influence, gently suggesting heredity might be important in behavior. Now, however, I more often have to say, "Yes, genetic influences are significant and substantial, but environmental influences are just as important." This seems to be happening most clearly in the field of psychopathology, where evidence of significant genetic influence has led to a search for single genes and simple neurochemical triggers at the expense of research on its psychosocial origins. It would be wonderful if some simple, and presumably inexpensive, biochemical cure could be found for schizophrenia. However, this happy outcome seems highly unlikely given that schizophrenia is as much influenced by environmental factors as it is by heredity.

Furthermore, genetic effects on behavior are polygenic and probabilistic, not single-gene and deterministic. The characteristics in the pea plant that Mendel studied and a few diseases such as Huntington's disease and sickle-cell anemia are due to single genes that have their effects regardless of the environment or the genetic background of the individual. The complexity of behaviors studied by psychologists makes it unlikely that such a deterministic model and the reductionistic approach that it suggests will pay off. There is as yet no firm evidence for a single-gene effect that accounts for a detectable amount of variation for any complex behavior. For example, earlier reports of a major gene effect for spatial ability have not been replicated, a recent suggestion of a major gene effect for spelling disability has been questioned, and the widely publicized major gene effects for schizophrenia and manic-depressive psychosis may be limited to particular families.

The complex interplay between environment and genes is most apparent in the case of development. For example, the lowly roundworm has become distinguished by being the first multicelled organism to have the developmental fate of each of its 959 adult cells mapped from the initial fertilized egg, by having the complete wiring diagram of the nervous system worked out, and by having many of its 2,000 genes mapped. Despite these tremendous advances, we have learned little about the genetics of development except to appreciate its complexity. Clearly, development is not coded in DNA in the same way that the triplet code determines the amino acid sequence of proteins. The point is that a reductionistic, deterministic view is not likely to be a profitable way to think about genetic effects on behavioral development in the roundworm, and certainly not in children.

As the pendulum swings from environmentalism, it is important that the pendulum be caught midswing before its momentum carries it to biological determinism. Behavioral genetic research clearly demonstrates that both nature and nurture are important in human development.

References

Plomin, R. (1986). *Development, genetics, and psychology*. Hillsdale, NJ: Erlbaum.

Plomin, R. (1988). The nature and nurture of cognitive abilities. In R. J. Sternberg (Ed.), *Advances in the psychology of human intelligence* (Vol. 4, pp. 1–33). Hillsdale, NJ: Erlbaum.

Plomin, R., & Daniels, D. (1987). Why are children in the same family so different from each other? *Behavioral and Brain Sciences, 10*, 1–16.

Plomin, R., Loehlin, J. C., & DeFries, J. C. (1985). Genetic and environmental components of "environmental" influences. *Developmental Psychology, 21*, 391–402.

Plomin, R., Pedersen, N. L., McClearn, G. E., Nesselroade, J. R., & Bergeman, C. S. (1988). EAS temperaments during the last half of the life span: Twins reared apart and twins reared together. *Psychology and Aging, 3*, 43–50.

Rowe, D. C. (1981). Environmental and genetic influences on dimensions of perceived parenting: A twin study. *Developmental Psychology, 17*, 203–208.

Rowe, D. C. (1983a). A biometrical analysis of perceptions of family environment: A study of twin and singleton sibling kinships. *Child Development, 54*, 416–423.

Scarr, S., & McCartney, K. (1983). How people make their own environments: A theory of genotype ∩ environment effects. *Child Development, 54*, 424–435.

Willerman, L. (1979). Effects of families on intellectual development. *American Psychologist, 34*, 923–929.

Sex Differences in Jealousy: Evolution, Physiology, and Psychology

David M. Buss, Randy J. Larsen, Drew Westen, and Jennifer Semmelroth

The essence of Darwin's theory of evolution is that those traits that are associated with successful reproduction will be increasingly represented in succeeding generations. For this reason, the obvious place to look for an evolutionarily based influence on behavior is in the area of sex. It is unsurprising, therefore, that as the evolutionary biology of personality has grown into an active research area in its own right, sex has come in for special attention.

The following article is a collaboration of several personality psychologists led by David Buss, one of the leaders in the application of evolutionary theory to personality. It derives hypotheses about the different approaches to mating that evolutionary theory would expect to be manifest by women and by men. In a nutshell, evolutionary considerations would lead one to expect men to be particularly worried that "their" children might have been fathered by other men, and therefore to be prone to sexual jealousy. Women, however, are not doubtful about their maternity but rather about the possibility that their mates might not continue to provide resources and protection for their children. They would, therefore, be more prone to emotional jealousy.

The next step taken by Buss and his co-workers is to test this hypothesis in a sample of undergraduates, presenting each with scenarios designed to trigger emotional and sexual jealousy. Not only are the expected sex differences found, but physiological indices of emotional arousal, such as heart rate, yield results that are consistent with the feelings that the subjects report.

The final paragraphs of this article acknowledge that these findings might be the result of cultural conditioning, not a process biologically built in through evolution. Nonetheless, Buss et al. point out that their results were predicted by their evolutionary theorizing, not merely explained after they were obtained. This fact does not prove their theory, but does give it added plausibility.

From *Psychological Science*, 3, 251–255, 1992.

* * *

In species with internal female fertilization and gestation, features of reproductive biology characteristic of all 4,000 species of mammals, including humans, males face an adaptive problem not confronted by females—uncertainty in their paternity of offspring. Maternity probability in mammals rarely or never deviates from 100%. Compromises in paternity probability come at substantial reproductive cost to the male—the loss of mating effort expended, including time, energy, risk, nuptial gifts, and mating opportunity costs. A cuckolded male also loses the female's parental effort, which becomes channeled to a competitor's gametes. The adaptive problem of paternity uncertainty is exacerbated in species in which males engage in some postzygotic parental investment (Trivers, 1972). Males risk investing resources in putative offspring that are genetically unrelated.

These multiple and severe reproductive costs should have imposed strong selection pressure on males to defend against cuckoldry. Indeed, the literature is replete with examples of evolved anticuckoldry mechanisms in lions (Bertram, 1975), bluebirds (Power, 1975), doves (Erickson & Zenone, 1976), numerous insect species (Thornhill & Alcock, 1983), and nonhuman primates (Hrdy, 1979). Since humans arguably show more paternal investment than any other of the 200 species of primates (Alexander & Noonan, 1979), this selection pressure should have operated especially intensely on human males. Symons (1979); Daly, Wilson, and Weghorst (1982); and Wilson and Daly (1992) have hypothesized that male sexual jealousy evolved as a solution to this adaptive problem (but see Hupka, 1991, for an alternative view). Men who were indifferent to sexual contact between their mates and other men presumably experienced lower paternity certainty, greater investment in competitors' gametes, and lower reproductive success than did men who were motivated to attend to cues of infidelity and to act on those cues to increase paternity probability.

Although females do not risk maternity uncertainty, in species with biparental care they do risk the potential loss of time, resources, and commitment from a male if he deserts or channels investment to alternative mates (Buss, 1988; Thornhill & Alcock, 1983; Trivers, 1972). The redirection of a mate's investment to another female and her offspring is reproductively costly for a female, especially in environments where offspring suffer in survival and reproductive currencies without investment from both parents.

In human evolutionary history, there were likely to have been at least two situations in which a woman risked losing a man's investment. First, in a monogamous marriage, a woman risked having her mate invest in an alternative woman with whom he was having an affair (partial loss of investment) or risked his departure for an alternative woman (large or total loss of investment). Second, in polygynous marriages, a woman was at risk of having her mate invest to a larger degree in other wives and their offspring at the expense of his investment in her and her offspring. Following Buss (1988) and Mellon (1981), we hypothesize that cues to the development of a deep emotional attachment have been reliable leading indicators to women of potential reduction or loss of their mate's investment.

Jealousy is defined as an emotional "state that is aroused by a perceived threat to a valued relationship or position and motivates behavior aimed at countering the threat. Jealousy is 'sexual' if the valued relationship is sexual" (Daly et al., 1982, p. 11; see also Salovey, 1991; White & Mullen, 1989). It is reasonable to hypothesize that jealousy involves physiological reactions (autonomic arousal) to perceived threat and motivated action to reduce the threat, although this hypothesis has not been examined. Following Symons (1979) and Daly et al. (1982), our central hypothesis is that the events that activate jealousy physiologically and psychologically differ for men and women because of the different adaptive problems they have faced over human evolutionary history in mating contexts. Both sexes are hypothesized to be distressed over both sexual and emotional infidelity, and previous findings bear this out (Buss, 1989). However, these two kinds of infidelity should be weighted differently by men and women. Despite the importance of these hypothesized sex differences, no systematic scientific work has been directed toward verifying or falsifying their existence (but for suggestive data, see Francis, 1977; Teismann & Mosher, 1978; White & Mullen, 1989).

Study 1: Subjective Distress Over a Partner's External Involvement

This study was designed to test the hypothesis that men and women differ in which form of infidelity—sexual versus emotional—triggers more upset and subjective distress, following the adaptive logic just described.

METHOD After reporting age and sex, subjects ($N = 202$ undergraduate students) were presented with the following dilemma:

> Please think of a serious committed romantic relationship that you have had in the past, that you currently have, or that you would like to have. Imagine that you discover that the person with whom you've been seriously involved became interested in someone else. What would distress or upset you more (*please circle only one*):
>
> (A) Imagining your partner forming a deep emotional attachment to that person.
>
> (B) Imagining your partner enjoying passionate sexual intercourse with that other person.
>
> Subjects completed additional questions, and then encountered the next dilemma, with the same instructional set, but followed by a different, but parallel, choice:
>
> (A) Imagining your partner trying different sexual positions with that other person.
>
> (B) Imagining your partner falling in love with that other person.

RESULTS Shown in Figure 20.1 are the percentages of men and women reporting more distress in response to sexual infidelity than emotional infidelity. The first empirical probe, contrasting distress over a partner's sexual involvement with

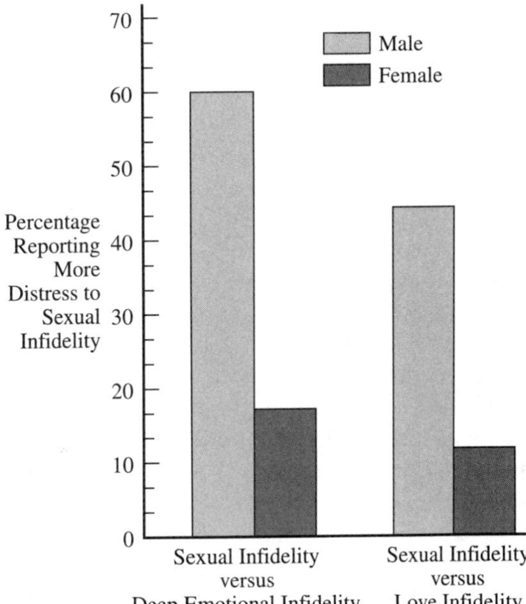

Figure 20.1 Reported comparisons of distress in response to imagining a partner's sexual or emotional infidelity. The panel shows the percentage of subjects reporting more distress to the sexual infidelity scenario than to the emotional infidelity (left) and the love infidelity (right) scenarios.

distress over a partner's deep emotional attachment, yielded a large and highly significant sex difference ($\chi^2 = 47.56$, $df = 3$, $p < .001$).[1] Fully 60% of the male sample reported greater distress over their partner's potential sexual infidelity; in contrast, only 17% of the female sample chose that option, with 83% reporting that they would experience greater distress over a partner's emotional attachment to a rival.

This pattern was replicated with the contrast between sex and love. The magnitude of the sex difference was large, with 32% more men than women reporting greater distress over a partner's

[1]This "chi-square" statistic is a test for the randomness of arrangement of outcomes into categories, *df* refers to the degrees of freedom in the design, and the *p* is the "significance," or probability that a χ^2 this large would have been produced by chance if the population value were 0.

sexual involvement with someone else, and the majority of women reporting greater distress over a partner's falling in love with a rival ($\chi^2 = 59.20$, $df = 3$, $p < .001$).

Study 2: Physiological Responses to a Partner's External Involvement

Given the strong confirmation of jealousy sex linkage from Study 1, we sought next to test the hypotheses using physiological measures. Our central measures of autonomic arousal were electrodermal activity (EDA), assessed via skin conductance, and pulse rate (PR). Electrodermal activity and pulse rate are indicators of autonomic nervous system activation (Levenson, 1988). Because distress is an unpleasant subjective state, we also included a measure of muscle activity in the brow region of the face—electromyographic (EMG) activity of the *corrugator supercilii* muscle. This muscle is responsible for the furrowing of the brow often seen in facial displays of unpleasant emotion or affect (Fridlund, Ekman, & Oster, 1987). Subjects were asked to image two scenarios in which a partner became involved with someone else—one sexual intercourse scenario and one emotional attachment scenario. Physiological responses were recorded during the imagery trials.

SUBJECTS Subjects were 55 undergraduate students, 32 males and 23 females, each completing a 2-hr laboratory session.

PHYSIOLOGICAL MEASURES Physiological activity was monitored on the running strip chart of a Grass Model 7D polygraph and digitized on a laboratory computer at a 10-Hz rate, following principles recommended in Cacioppo and Tassinary (1990).

Electrodermal activity. Standard Beckman Ag/AgCl surface electrodes, filled with a .05 molar NaCl solution in a Unibase paste, were placed over the middle segments of the first and third fingers of the right hand. A Wheatstone bridge applied a 0.5-V voltage to one electrode.

Pulse rate. A photoplethysmograph was attached to the subject's right thumb to monitor the pulse wave. The signal from this pulse transducer was fed into a Grass Model 7P4 cardiotachometer to detect the rising slope of each pulse wave, with the internal circuitry of the Schmitt trigger individually adjusted for each subject to output PR in beats per minute.

Electromyographic activity. Bipolar EMG recordings were obtained over the *corrugator supercilii* muscle. The EMG signal was relayed to a wide-band AC-preamplifier (Grass Model 7P3), where it was band-pass filtered, full-wave rectified, and integrated with a time constant of 0.2 s.[2]

PROCEDURE After electrode attachment, the subject was made comfortable in a reclining chair and asked to relax. After a 5-min waiting period, the experiment began. The subject was alone in the room during the imagery session, with an intercom on for verbal communication. The instructions for the imagery task were written on a form which the subject was requested to read and follow.

Each subject was instructed to engage in three separate images. The first image was designed to be emotionally neutral: "Imagine a time when you were walking to class, feeling neither good nor bad, just neutral." The subject was instructed to press a button when he or she had the image clearly in mind, and to sustain the image until the experimenter said to stop. The button triggered the computer to begin collecting physiological data for 20 s, after which the experimenter instructed the subject to "stop and relax."

The next two images were infidelity images,

[2]The preceding paragraphs are a detailed technical description of state-of-the-art techniques for measuring autonomic arousal, for the use of researchers who might want to replicate these results.

one sexual and one emotional. The order of presentation of these two images was counterbalanced. The instructions for sexual jealousy imagery were as follows: "Please think of a serious romantic relationship that you have had in the past, that you currently have, or that you would like to have. Now imagine that the person with whom you're seriously involved becomes interested in someone else. *Imagine you find out that your partner is having sexual intercourse with this other person.* Try to feel the feelings you would have if this happened to you."

The instructions for emotional infidelity imagery were identical to the above, except the italicized sentence was replaced with "*Imagine that your partner is falling in love and forming an emotional attachment to that person.*" Physiological data were collected for 20 s following the subject's button press indicating that he or she had achieved the image. Subjects were told to "stop and relax" for 30 s between imagery trials.

TABLE 20.1

Means and Standard Deviations on Physiological Measures During Two Imagery Conditions

Measure	Imagery type	Mean	SD
	Males		
EDA	Sexual	1.30	3.64
	Emotional	−0.11	0.76
Pulse rate	Sexual	4.76	7.80
	Emotional	3.00	5.24
Brow EMG	Sexual	6.75	32.96
	Emotional	1.16	6.60
	Females		
EDA	Sexual	−0.07	0.49
	Emotional	0.21	0.78
Pulse rate	Sexual	2.25	4.68
	Emotional	2.57	4.37
Brow EMG	Sexual	3.03	8.38
	Emotional	8.12	25.60

Note. Measures are expressed as changes from the neutral image condition. EDA is in microsiemen units, pulse rate is in beats per minute, and EMG is in microvolt units.

Results

Physiological scores. The following scores were obtained: (a) the amplitude of the largest EDA response occurring during each 20-s trial; (b) PR in beats per minute averaged over each 20-s trial; and (c) amplitude of EMG activity over the *corrugator supercilii* averaged over each 20-s trial. Difference scores were computed between the neutral imagery trial and the jealousy induction trials. Within-sex *t* tests revealed no effects for order of presentation of the sexual jealousy image, so data were collapsed over this factor.

Jealousy induction effects. Table 20.1 shows the mean scores for the physiological measures for men and women in each of the two imagery conditions. Differences in physiological responses to the two jealousy images were examined using paired-comparison *t* tests for each sex separately for EDA, PR, and EMG. The men showed significant increases in EDA during the sexual imagery compared with the emotional imagery ($t = 2.00$, $df = 29$, $p < .05$).[3] Women showed significantly greater EDA to the emotional infidelity image than to the sexual infidelity image ($t = 2.42$, $df = 19$, $p < .05$). A similar pattern was observed with PR. Men showed a substantial increase in PR to both images, but significantly more so in response to the sexual infidelity image ($t = 2.29$, $df = 31$, $p < .05$). Women showed elevated PR to both images, but not differentially so. The results of the *corrugator* EMG were similar, although less strong. Men showed greater brow contraction to the sexual infidelity image, and women showed the opposite pattern, although results with this nonautonomic measure did not reach significance

[3]The *t* statistic here indicates that given the number of subjects (related to *df*) in this sample, the data obtained would have occurred less than 5% of the time if there were no sex differences.

($t = 1.12$, $df = 30$, $p < .14$, for males; $t = -1.24$, $df = 22$, $p < .12$, for females). The elevated EMG contractions for both jealousy induction trials in both sexes support the hypothesis that the affect experienced is negative.

* * *

Discussion

The results of the empirical studies support the hypothesized sex linkages in the activators of jealousy. Study 1 found large sex differences in reports of the subjective distress individuals would experience upon exposure to a partner's sexual infidelity versus emotional infidelity. Study 2 found a sex linkage in autonomic arousal to imagined sexual infidelity versus emotional infidelity; the results were particularly strong for the EDA and PR. * * *

These studies are limited in ways that call for additional research. First, they pertain to a single age group and culture. Future studies could explore the degree to which these sex differences transcend different cultures and age groups. Two clear evolutionary psychological predictions are (a) that male sexual jealousy and female commitment jealousy will be greater in cultures where males invest heavily in children, and (b) that male sexual jealousy will diminish as the age of the male's mate increases because her reproductive value decreases. Second, future studies could test the alternative hypotheses that the current findings reflect (a) domain-specific psychological adaptations to cuckoldry versus potential investment loss or (b) a more domain-general mechanism such that any thoughts of sex are more interesting, arousing, and perhaps disturbing to men whereas any thoughts of love are more interesting, arousing, and perhaps disturbing to women, and hence that such responses are not specific to jealousy or infidelity. Third, emotional and sexual infidelity are clearly correlated, albeit imperfectly, and a sizable percentage of men in Study 1 reported greater distress to a partner's emotional infidelity. Emotional infidelity may signal sexual infidelity and vice versa, and hence both sexes should become distressed at both forms (see Buss, 1989). Future research could profitably explore in greater detail the correlation of these forms of infidelity as well as the sources of within-sex variation.

Within the constraints of the current studies, we can conclude that the sex differences found here generalize across both psychological and physiological methods—demonstrating an empirical robustness in the observed effect. The degree to which these sex-linked elicitors correspond to the hypothesized sex-linked adaptive problems lends support to the evolutionary psychological framework from which they were derived. Alternative theoretical frameworks, including those that invoke culture, social construction, deconstruction, arbitrary parental socialization, and structural powerlessness, undoubtedly could be molded post hoc to fit the findings—something perhaps true of any set of findings. None but the Symons (1979) and Daly et al. (1982) evolutionary psychological frameworks, however, generated the sex-differentiated predictions in advance and on the basis of sound evolutionary reasoning. The recent finding that male sexual jealousy is the leading cause of spouse battering and homicide across cultures worldwide (Daly & Wilson, 1988a, 1988b) offers suggestive evidence that these sex differences have large social import and may be species-wide.

References

Alexander, R. D., & Noonan, K. M. (1979). Concealment of ovulation, parental care, and human social evolution. In N. Chagnon & W. Irons (Eds.), *Evolutionary biology and human social behavior* (pp. 436–453). North Scituate, MA: Duxbury.

Bertram, B. C. R. (1975). Social factors influencing reproduction in wild lions. *Journal of Zoology*, *177*, 463–482.

Buss, D. M. (1988). From vigilance to violence: Tactics of mate retention. *Ethology and Sociobiology*, *9*, 291–317.

Buss, D. M. (1989). Conflict between the sexes: Strategic interference and the evocation of anger and upset. *Journal of Personality and Social Psychology*, *56*, 735–747.

Cacioppo, J. T., & Tassinary, L. G. (Eds.). (1990). *Principles of psychophysiology: Physical, social, and inferential elements.* Cambridge, England: Cambridge University Press.

Daly, M., & Wilson, M. (1988a). Evolutionary social psychology and family violence. *Science*, *242*, 519–524.

Daly, M., & Wilson, M. (1988b). *Homicide.* Hawthorne, NY: Aldine.

Daly, M., Wilson, M., & Weghorst, S. J. (1982). Male sexual jealousy. *Ethology and Sociobiology, 3,* 11–27.

Erickson, C. J., & Zenone, P. G. (1976). Courtship differences in male ring doves: Avoidance of cuckoldry? *Science, 192,* 1353–1354.

Francis, J. L. (1977). Toward the management of heterosexual jealousy. *Journal of Marriage and Family Counseling, 10,* 61–69.

Fridlund, A., Ekman, P., & Oster, J. (1987). Facial expressions of emotion. In A. Siegman & S. Feldstein (Eds.), *Nonverbal behavior and communication* (pp. 143–224). Hillsdale, NJ: Erlbaum.

Hrdy, S. B. G. (1979). Infanticide among animals: A review, classification, and examination of the implications for the reproductive strategies of females. *Ethology and Sociobiology, 1,* 14–40.

Hupka, R. B. (1991). The motive for the arousal of romantic jealousy: Its cultural origin. In P. Salovey (Ed.), *The psychology of jealousy and envy* (pp. 252–270). New York: Guilford Press.

Levenson, R. W. (1988). Emotion and the autonomic nervous system: A prospectus for research on autonomic specificity. In H. Wagner (Ed.), *Social psychophysiology: Theory and clinical applications* (pp. 17–42). London: Wiley.

Mellon, L. W. (1981). *The evolution of love.* San Francisco: W. H. Freeman.

Power, H. W. (1975). Mountain bluebirds: Experimental evidence against altruism. *Science, 189,* 142–143.

Salovey, P. (Ed.). (1991). *The psychology of jealousy and envy.* New York: Guilford Press.

Symons, D. (1979). *The evolution of human sexuality.* New York: Oxford University Press.

Teismann, M. W., & Mosher, D. L. (1978). Jealous conflict in dating couples. *Psychological Reports, 42,* 1211–1216.

Thornhill, R., & Alcock, J. (1983). *The evolution of insect mating systems.* Cambridge, MA: Harvard University Press.

Trivers, R. (1972). Parental investment and sexual selection. In B. Campbell (Ed.), *Sexual selection and the descent of man, 1871–1971* (pp. 136–179). Chicago: Aldine.

White, G. L., & Mullen, P. E. (1989). *Jealousy: Theory, research, and clinical strategies.* New York: Guilford Press.

Wilson, M., & Daly, M. (1992). The man who mistook his wife for a chattel. In J. Barkow, L. Cosmides, & J. Tooby (Eds.), *The adapted mind: Evolutionary psychology and the generation of culture.* New York: Oxford University Press.

Male Sexual Proprietariness and Violence Against Wives

Margo I. Wilson and Martin Daly

The preceding selection provided an evolutionary explanation of the causes of jealousy; the following selection provides an evolutionary explanation of one of its effects. Margo Wilson and Martin Daly, two Canadian researchers on interpersonal conflict and violence, propose that thousands of years of evolutionary processes have produced modern men so concerned about the sexual ownership of their mates that they may physically harm and even kill their wives to prevent other men from taking possession of them. (In an interesting twist of evolutionary logic, they suggest that the seemingly self-defeating behavior—from a reproductive point of view—of killing one's own wife is the result of the necessity of maintaining a credible threat that one's wife will *be killed if she strays.)*

This article presents a set of ideas that are provocative to say the least. It takes a phenomenon, here called "uxoricide," that is usually considered due to a variety of poor social conditions and criminal psychopathology and describes it as a built-in element of the male behavioral repertoire. This account may disturb some readers.

If you find yourself disturbed, inspired, offended, or just intrigued by this and the previous selection, you might want to do further reading in evolutionary biology. In fact, the editors of your reader have misgivings about several aspects of this paper, particularly its explanation of why spouses are sometimes killed. The crucial missing piece in Wilson and Daly's explanation is any description of a psychological mechanism by which ancient evolutionary history could influence contemporary behavior. Rather than focusing exclusively on the behavioral outcome of uxoricide, they might have done better to concentrate on the rage of a jealous husband, much as Buss and his co-workers (in the previous selection) concentrated on the experience of jealousy.

The issues raised by this article are stimulating, thought-provoking, and illustrate the ambitious reach of evolutionary personality psychology. A good place to begin further reading would be the references at the end of this and the preceding selection. The issues raised by an evolutionary approach are not simple, wide differences of opinion exist, and it takes some study to be in a position to be able to make up one's own mind intelligently for oneself.

From *Current Directions in Psychological Science*, 5, 2–7, 1996.

There is a cross-culturally ubiquitous connection between men's sexual possessiveness and men's violence (Wilson & Daly, 1992, 1993). We have studied accounts of uxoricides (wife killings) from a broad range of societies, and find that male sexual proprietariness—broadly construed to encompass resentment both of infidelity and of women's efforts to leave marriages—is everywhere implicated as the dominant precipitating factor in a large majority of cases (Daly & Wilson, 1988). The discovery of wifely infidelity is viewed as an exceptional provocation, likely to elicit a violent rage, both in societies where such a reaction is considered a reprehensible loss of control and in those where it is considered a praiseworthy redemption of honor. Indeed, such a rage is widely presumed to be so compelling as to mitigate the responsibility of even homicidal cuckolds.

Battered women nominate "jealousy" as the most frequent motive for their husbands' assaults, and their assailants commonly make the same attribution (Wilson & Daly, 1992, 1993; Daly & Wilson, 1988). Moreover, assaulted wives often maintain that their husbands are not only violently jealous about their interactions with other men, but are so controlling as to curtail contacts with female friends and family. In a 1993 national survey, Statistics Canada interviewed more than 8,000 women currently residing with male part-

TABLE 21.1

Association Between Violence Against Wives and Husbands' Autonomy-Limiting Behaviors, According to a National Probability Sample of Canadian Wives (Wilson et al., 1995)

	History of violence against wife		
Statement	Serious violence *N* = 286	Relativity minor only *N* = 1,039	None *N* = 6,990
"He is jealous and doesn't want you to talk to other men"	39	13	4
"He tries to limit your contact with family or friends"	35	11	2
"He insists on knowing who you are with and where you are at all times"	40	24	7
"He calls you names to put you down or make you feel bad"	48	22	3
"He prevents you from knowing about or having access to the family income, even if you ask"	15	5	1

Note. Table entries are the percentages of respondents affirming that each item applied to their husbands. Violence was categorized as "serious" or "relatively minor" on the basis of the alleged assaultive acts; the validity of this distinction is supported by sample interviews indicating that an injury that required medical attention occurred in 72% of the incidents that met the "serious" criterion versus 18% of the "relatively minor" violent incidents.

ners. In addition to answering questions about their experiences of violence, the women indicated whether five statements about autonomy-limiting aspects of some men's behavior applied to their husbands. Autonomy-limiting behavior was especially likely to be attributed to those husbands who were also reported to have behaved violently, and women who had experienced relatively serious or frequent assaults were much more likely to affirm each of the five statements than were women who had experienced only lesser violence (Table 21.1) (Wilson, Johnson, & Daly, 1995). These and other data suggest that unusually controlling husbands are also unusually violent husbands. Rather than being one of a set of alternative controlling tactics used by proprietary men, wife assault appears to go hand in hand with other tactics of control.

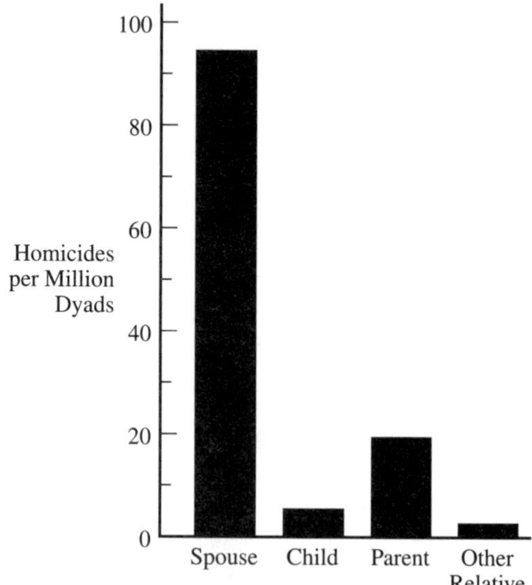

Figure 21.1 Homicide victimization rates characteristic of different categories of co-residing relatives (considering only adults as potential perpetrators) in the city of Detroit, 1972 (Daly & Wilson, 1988).

Evolutionary Psychology, Intrasexual Competition, and Marital Alliance

Why should sexually proprietary feelings be linked with violence in this way? Although it is often supposed that wives are assaulted mainly because they are accessible, legitimate targets when men are frustrated or angry, mere opportunity cannot account for the differential risk of violent victimization within households. Wives are far more likely than other relatives to be murdered by an adult in their household (Figure 21.1) (Daly & Wilson, 1988). Wife assault has distinct motives. We propose that a satisfactory account of the psychological links between male sexual proprietariness and violence will depend on an understanding of the adaptive problems that men have faced in the course of human evolutionary history and the ways in which the psyche is organized to solve them. Those adaptive problems include both the risk of losing the wife, a valued reproductive resource, to a rival and the risk of directing paternal investments to another man's child (Wilson & Daly, 1992, 1993).

Adaptations are organismic attributes that are well "designed," as a result of a history of natural selection, to achieve functions that promoted reproductive success in ancestral environments (Williams, 1966). Because organisms can usefully be analyzed into numerous distinct parts with complementary functions, investigation in the life sciences is almost invariably conducted in the shadow of (often inexplicit) adaptationist ideas. Sound hypotheses about what the heart or lungs or liver are "for" were essential first steps for investigating their physiology, for example. Psychological research is similarly (and equally appropriately) infused with adaptationist premises.

The goal of psychological science is and always has been the discovery and elucidation of psychological adaptations. Evolutionary thinking can help. By paying explicit attention to adaptive significance and selective forces, evolutionists are better able to generate hypotheses about which developmental experiences and proximate causal cues are likely to affect which aspects of behavior, and what sorts of contingencies, priorities, and combinatorial information-processing algorithms are likely to be instantiated in the architecture of the mind (Tooby & Cosmides, 1992; Buss, 1995;

Daly & Wilson, 1995, in press). Psychological constructs from self-esteem to color vision to sexual jealousy are formulated at a level of abstraction intended to be of panhuman (cross-cultural) generality. If these things exist and are complexly structured and organized, they almost certainly evolved to play some fitness-promoting role in our ancestors' lives. But although psychologists usually recognize that the phenomena they study have utility, jealousy in particular has often been dismissed as a functionless epiphenomenon or pathology. In light of what is known about evolution by selection, this is scarcely plausible.

In a sexual population, all the males are engaged in a *zero-sum game* in which the paternal share of the ancestry of all future generations is divided among them, while the females are engaged in a parallel contest over the maternal share of that ancestry. In a fundamental sense, then, one's principal competitors are same-sex members of one's own species. But although it is true for both females and males that selection entails a zero-sum competitive contest for genetic posterity, the evolutionary consequences are not necessarily similar in the two sexes. In particular, *sexual selection* (the component of selection that is attributable to differential access to mates) is generally of differential intensity, leading to a variety of sexually differentiated adaptations for intrasexual competition (Andersson, 1994).

In most mammals, the variance in male fitness is greater than the variance in female fitness, with the result that male mammals are generally subject to more intense sexual selection than females, and that the psychological and morphological attributes that have evolved for use in intrasexual competition are usually costlier and more dangerous in males than in females. The human animal is no exception to these generalizations, and rivalry among men is a ubiquitous and sometimes deadly source of conflict. Where homicide rates are high, most victims are men, and their killers are mainly unrelated male acquaintances; the predominant motive is not robbery, but some sort of interpersonal conflict, especially a status or "face" dispute, with an overt element of sexual rivalry apparent in a substantial minority of the cases (Daly & Wilson, 1988). Of course, killing often oversteps the bounds of utility, but the circumstances under which dangerous violence is used in these cases bespeak its more typical functionality in its much more numerous nonlethal manifestations. And although the principal victims of men's lethal assaults are other men, violence is a coercive social tool that can be used on women, too, including wives.

From a selectionist perspective, the marital relationship has special properties. The fitnesses of genetic relatives overlap in proportion to genealogical proximity, a situation that engenders selection for altruistic and cooperative inclinations toward kin. Mates share genetic interests, too, but their solidarity is more fragile. By reproducing together, a monogamous couple may attain a state in which all exigencies affect their fitnesses identically, a situation conducive to consensus and harmony. However, the correlation between their expected fitnesses can be abolished or even rendered negative if one or both betray the relationship (Daly & Wilson, 1995, in press).

Is it reasonable to propose the existence of an evolved social psychology specific to the marital relationship? Certainly, marital alliance is neither a sporadically distributed cultural option nor a modern discovery or invention, like agriculture or writing. Women and men everywhere enter into socially recognized unions, with a set of complementary sex-specific entitlements and obligations predicated on the complementarity of female and male sexual and reproductive roles, and they have done so for many millennia. We therefore expect that there are certain fundamental, universal sources of marital conflict, reflecting situations in which one marriage partner could have gained fitness in ancestral human environments at the other partner's expense. These situations would include conflicts over equity of contributions to the couple's joint endeavors (work sharing), over each partner's nepotistic interest in the welfare of his or her distinct kindred (in-law disputes), over asymmetrical temptations to abandon the union, and over sexual infidelity. In a pair-forming, biparental species, most of these conflicts can apply both ways, but the potential effects of infidelity are an exception: Males, unlike females, can be cuckolded and unwittingly invest their parental efforts in the service of rivals' fitness.

* * *

Undetected cuckoldry poses a major threat to a man's fitness, but for women the threat is slightly different: that a husband's efforts and resources will be diverted to the benefit of other women and their children. It follows that the arousal of men's and women's proprietary feelings toward their mates is likely to have evolved to be differentially attuned to distinct cues indicative of the sex-specific threats to fitness in past environments. Diverse evidence on feelings, reactions, and cultural practices supports the hypothesis that men are more intensely concerned with sexual infidelity per se and women more intensely concerned with the allocation of their mates' resources, affection, and attentions (Wilson & Daly, 1992, 1993; Buss, Larsen, Western, & Semmelroth, 1992).

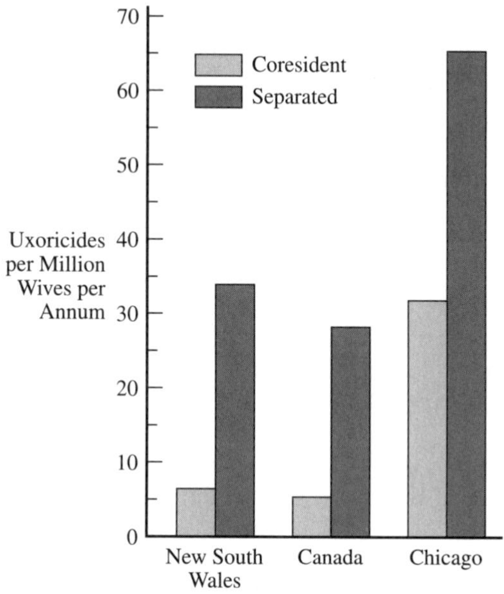

Figure 21.2 Rates of uxoricides perpetrated by registered-marriage husbands, for coresiding versus estranged couples in New South Wales (NSW), Australia (1968–1986); Canada (1974–1990); and Chicago (1965–1989) (Wilson et al., in press).

Contingent Cuing of Male Sexual Proprietariness and the Epidemiology of Violence Against Wives

If sexual proprietariness is aroused by cues of threats to sexual monopoly, and if use of violence is contingent on cues of its utility (including tolerable costs), then variations within and between societies in the frequency and severity of violence against wives may be largely attributable to variations in such cues (Wilson & Daly, 1992, 1993). Those relevant to the arousal of sexual proprietariness are likely to include cues of pressure from potential rivals and cues of one's partner's fertility and attractiveness to those rivals. Regarding the former issue, we would expect a husband to be sensitive to indicators of the local intensity of male competition and sexual poaching, and to indicators of the status, attractiveness, and resources of potential rivals relative to himself. Being part of a relatively large age cohort may also be expected to intensify male-male competition, especially if same-age women are unavailable; thus, cohort-size effects on intrasexual rivalry and hence on the coercive constraint of women may be especially evident where age disparities at marriage are large. Parameters like relative cohort size, local marital instability, and local prevalence of adultery clearly cannot be cued simply by stimuli immediately present, but must be induced from experience accumulated over large portions of the life span.

If men's violence and threats function to limit female autonomy, husbands may be motivated to act in these ways in response to probabilistic cues that their wives may desert them. Women who actually leave their husbands are often pursued, threatened, and assaulted; separated wives are even killed by their husbands at substantially higher rates than wives who live with their husbands (Figure 21.2) (Wilson, Daly, & Scheib, in press). The elevation of uxoricide risk at separation is even more severe than the contrasts in Figure 21.2 suggest because the rate denominators include all separated wives regardless of the duration of separation, whereas when separated wives are killed, it is usually soon after separation. Of course, the temporal association between separation and violence does not necessarily mean that the former caused the latter; however, many husbands who have killed their wives had explicitly threatened to do so should their wives ever leave, and explain their behavior as a response to the intolerable stimulus of their wives' departure.

Why are men ever motivated to pursue and kill women who have left them? Such behavior is spiteful in that it is likely to impose a net cost on its perpetrator as well as its victim, and therefore challenges the evolutionary psychological hypothesis that motives and emotions are organized in such a way as to promote the actors' interests. Moreover, if the adaptive function of the motivational processes underlying violence against wives resides in retaining and controlling one's mate, as we have suggested, killing is all the more paradoxical. The problem is akin to that of understanding vengeance (Daly & Wilson, 1988). A threat is an effective social tool, and usually an inexpensive one, but it loses its effectiveness if the threatening party is seen to be bluffing, that is, to be unwilling to pay the occasional cost of following through when the threat is ignored or defied. Such vengeful follow-through may appear counter-productive—a risky or expensive act too late to be useful—but effective threats cannot "leak" signs of bluff and may therefore have to be sincere. Although killing an estranged wife appears futile, threatening one who might otherwise leave can be self-interested, and so can pursuing her with further threats, as can advertisements of anger and ostensible obliviousness to costs.

Evolutionary psychologists have predicted and confirmed that men are maximally attracted to young women as sexual and marital partners (Symons, 1995). This fact suggests that sexual proprietariness will be relatively intensely aroused in men married to younger women, and young wives indeed incur the highest rates of both lethal (Daly & Wilson, 1988; Wilson et al., 1995, in press) (Figure 21.3) and nonlethal violence by husbands. (It might be suggested that male sexual jealousy cannot be an evolved adaptation because men remain sexually jealous of postmenopausal or otherwise infertile women, but adaptations can have evolved only to track ancestrally informative cues of fertility and not fertility itself. In a modern society with contraception, improved health, and diverse cosmetic manipulations, postmenopausal women are likely to exhibit fewer cues of age-related declining reproductive value than still-fertile women in ancestral societies; Symons, 1995.)

There are several reasons to suppose that husbands may be relatively insecure in their proprietary claims in de facto marriages, which have higher rates of dissolution and a weaker or more ambiguous legal status than registered unions. And, indeed, wives in de facto marital unions in Canada incur an eight times greater risk of uxoricide and a four times greater risk of nonlethal assault by husbands (Wilson et al., 1995). However, registered and de facto unions differ in many ways, and the higher risk of uxoricide and assault in the latter may be due to a complex combination of factors, including youth, poverty, parity, and the presence of stepchildren (Daly & Wilson, 1988, 1995, in press; Wilson et al., 1995); whether adultery and desertion are greater sources of conflict in de facto unions than in registered unions is unknown. Demographic risk markers such as type of marital union and age are undoubtedly correlated with several variables that may be more directly causal to the risk of violence; elucidation of their relative roles awaits further research. However, it was the logic of evolution by selection which suggested to us that these demographic variables are likely correlates of breaches of sexual exclusivity and hence of violence.

Evolution by selection offers a framework for the development of hypotheses about the functional design of motivational-emotional-cognitive subsystems of the mind such as male sexual proprietariness, providing hints about proximate causal cues, modulated expression, attentional priorities, and perceptual and informational processing. We have argued that the development and modulation of male sexual proprietariness is con-

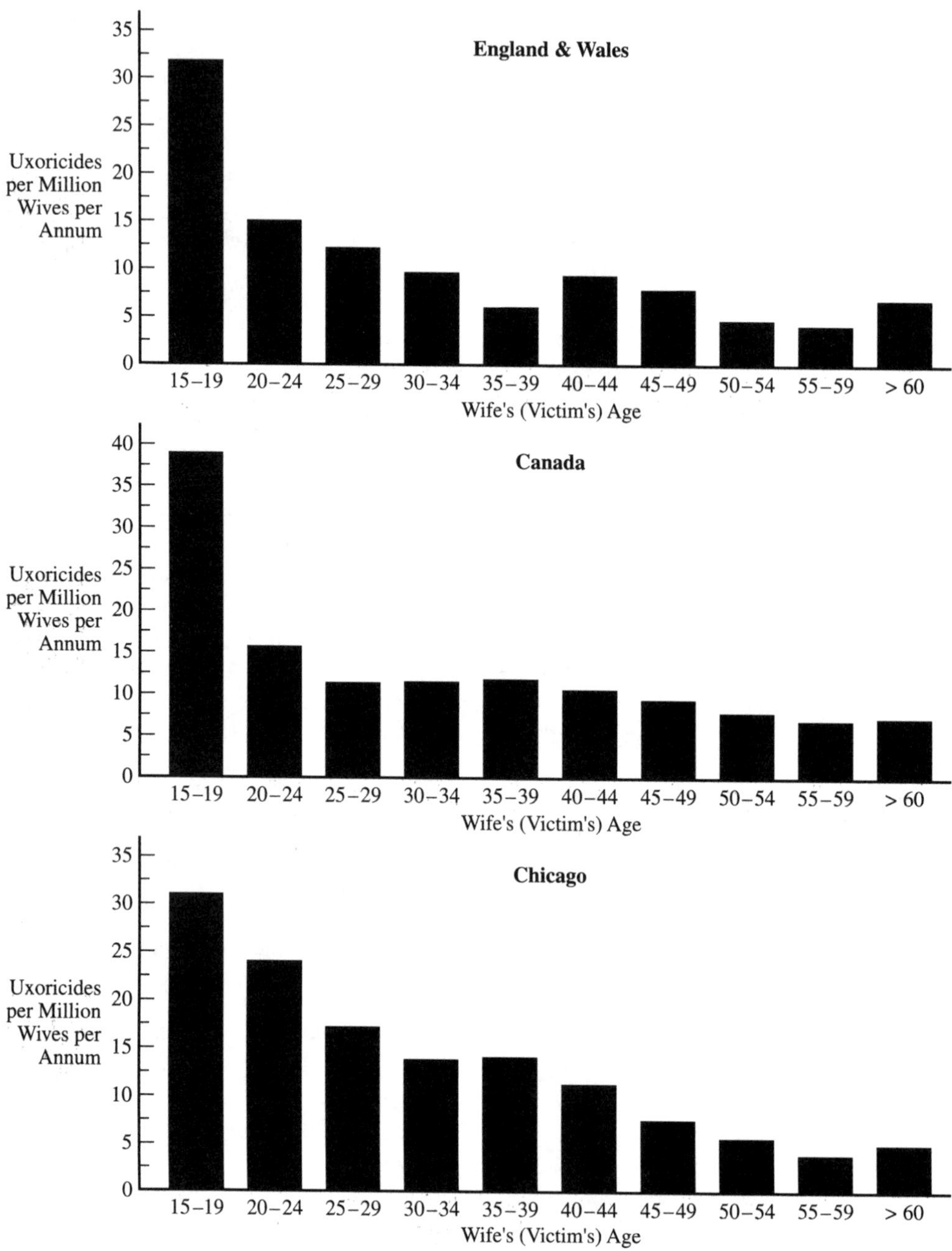

Figure 21.3 Uxoricide rates as a function of the victim's age, in England and Wales (1977–1990), Canada (1974–1990), and Chicago (1965–1989) (Wilson et al., in press).

tingent on ecologically valid cues of threats to a sexually exclusive relationship. The link between male sexual proprietariness and violent inclinations has presumably been selected for because violence and threat work to deter sexual rivals and limit female autonomy. (This is not to say that violent capacities and inclinations were not also subject to selection pressures in other contexts, including intergroup warfare and hunting.) The expression of male sexual proprietariness, including violent manifestations, will depend not only on the presence and incidence of ecologically valid cues, but also on community, family, and person-specific factors that are likely to affect the thresholds and other parameter settings of the psychological mechanisms involved.

References

Andersson, M. (1994). *Sexual selection.* Princeton, NJ: Princeton University Press.

Buss, D. M. (1995). Evolutionary psychology: A new paradigm for psychological science. *Psychological Inquiry, 6,* 1–30.

Buss, D. M., Larsen, R. J., Westen, D., & Semmelroth, J. (1992). Sex differences in jealousy: Evolution, physiology, and psychology. *Psychological Science, 3,* 251–255.

Daly, M., & Wilson, M. I. (1988). *Homicide.* Hawthorne, NY: Aldine de Gruyter.

Daly, M., & Wilson, M. I. (1995). Discriminative parental solicitude and the relevance of evolutionary models to the analysis of motivational systems. In M. Gazzaniga (Ed.), *The Cognitive Neurosciences* (pp. 1269–1286). Cambridge, MA: MIT Press.

Daly, M., & Wilson, M. I. (in press). Evolutionary psychology and marital conflict: The relevance of stepchildren. In D. M. Buss & N. Malamuth (Eds.), *Sex, Power, Conflict: Feminist and Evolutionary Perspectives.* New York: Oxford University Press.

Symons, D. S. (1995). Beauty is in the adaptations of the beholder: The evolutionary psychology of human female sexual attractiveness. In P. R. Abramson & S. D. Pinkerton (Eds.), *Sexual Nature/Sexual Culture* (pp. 80–119). Chicago: University of Chicago Press.

Tooby, J., & Cosmides, L. (1992). The psychological foundations of culture. In J. H. Barkow, L. Cosmides, & J. Tooby (Eds.), *The Adapted Mind* (pp. 19–136). New York: Oxford University Press.

Williams, G. C. (1966). *Adaptation and Natural Selection.* Princeton, NJ: Princeton University Press.

Wilson, M. I., & Daly, M. (1992). The man who mistook his wife for a chattel. In J. H. Barkow, L. Cosmides, & J. Tooby (Eds.), *The Adapted Mind* (pp. 289–322). New York: Oxford University Press.

Wilson, M. I., & Daly, M. (1993). An evolutionary psychological perspective on male sexual proprietariness and violence against wives. *Violence & Victims, 8,* 271–294.

Wilson, M. I., Daly, M., & Scheib, J. (in press). Femicide: An evolutionary psychological perspective. In P. A. Gowaty (Ed.), *Evolutionary Biology and Feminism.* New York: Chapman and Hall.

Wilson, M. I., Johnson, H., & Daly, M. (1995). Lethal and nonlethal violence against wives. *Canadian Journal of Criminology, 37,* 331–361.

The Origins of Sex Differences in Human Behavior: Evolved Dispositions Versus Social Roles

Alice H. Eagly and Wendy Wood

The increasing fame and popularity of evolutionary explanations of behavior such as seen in the previous two selections have been accompanied by an increasing amount of criticism. Not all critics offer alternative explanations of their own, however. Alice Eagly and Wendy Wood, to their credit, do have an explanation of widespread sex differences in behavior that is different from the evolutionary account. Their alternative, which they call "social structural theory," is that it is the structure of society rather than biological evolution that determines differences between what men and women desire and view as important. So the next selection offers both a critique of some evolutionary reasoning and an alternative framework for understanding some important data.

Although Eagly and Wood believe that evolutionary theorizing about personality is mostly wrong, to some degree the evolutionary and structural approaches address different data, rather than necessarily being incompatible. Evolutionary theorists such as Buss, Daly, and Wilson explain the components of sex differences that seem to be universal across cultures, whereas social structural theory addresses the components that vary. Thus, in the data that are reinterpreted in this article, Buss (who gathered the data) focused on how the direction *of the sex difference was the same in all cultures, whereas Eagly and Wood address how the* degree *of difference differs across cultures. Both components are clearly important and perhaps deserve to be examined together in an integrated approach.*

Eagly and Wood's article can be read as an argument for social change. If, as they maintain, sex differences in behavior are a function of social structure, then if society can be changed, behavioral change will soon follow. The evolutionary account of these differences can be taken to imply that things will not be so simple, because any changes in social structure will interact with and perhaps in some cases be resisted by innate biological preferences, propensities, and mechanisms.

From *American Psychologist*, 54, 408–423, 1999.

As more research psychologists have become willing to acknowledge that some aspects of social behavior, personality, and abilities differ between women and men (e.g., Eagly, 1995; Halpern, 1997), their attention has begun to focus on the causes of these differences. Debates about causes center, at least in part, on determining what can be considered the basic or ultimate causes of sex differences. Theories of sex differences that address causes at this level are termed in this article *origin theories* (Archer, 1996). In such theories, causation flows from a basic cause to sex-differentiated behavior, and biological, psychological, and social processes mediate the relation between the basic cause and behavior. In this article, we consider two types of origin theories: One of these implicates evolved psychological dispositions, and the other implicates social structure. Evolutionary psychology, as illustrated in the work of Buss (1995a), Kenrick and Keefe (1992), and Tooby and Cosmides (1992), thus represents the first type of origin theory, and social psychological theories that emphasize social structure represent the second type of origin theory (e.g., Eagly, 1987; Eagly, Wood, & Diekman, in press; Lorenzi-Cioldi, 1998; Ridgeway, 1991; West & Zimmerman, 1987; Wiley, 1995).

In the origin theory proposed by evolutionary psychologists, the critical causal arrow points from evolutionary adaptations to psychological sex differences. Because women and men possess sex-specific evolved mechanisms, they differ psychologically and tend to occupy different social roles. In contrast, in the social structural origin theory, the critical causal arrow points from social structure to psychological sex differences. Because men and women tend to occupy different social roles, they become psychologically different in ways that adjust them to these roles.

One important feature is shared by these two origin theories: Both offer a functional analysis of behavior that emphasizes adjustment to environmental conditions. However, the two schools of thought differ radically in their analysis of the nature and timing of the adjustments that are most important to sex-differentiated behavior. Evolutionary psychologists believe that females and males faced different pressures in primeval environments and that the sexes' differing reproductive status was the key feature of ancestral life that framed sex-typed adaptive problems. The resolutions of these problems produced sex-specific evolved mechanisms that humans carry with them as a species and that are held to be the root cause of sex-differentiated behavior. Although evolutionary psychologists readily acknowledge the abstract principle that environmental conditions can influence the development and expression of evolved dispositions, they have given limited attention to variation of sex differences in response to individual, situational, and cultural conditions (e.g., Archer, 1996; Buss, 1995b; Buss & Kenrick, 1998). For example, Buss (1998, p. 421) emphasized "universal or near-universal sex differences" in preferences for long-term mates.

Social structuralists maintain that the situations faced by women and men are quite variable across societies and historical periods as social organization changes in response to technological, ecological, and other transformations. From a social structural perspective, a society's division of labor between the sexes is the engine of sex-differentiated behavior, because it summarizes the social constraints under which men and women carry out their lives. Sex differences are viewed as accommodations to the differing restrictions and opportunities that a society maintains for its men and women, and sex-differentiated behavior is held to be contingent on a range of individual, situational, and cultural conditions (see Deaux & LaFrance, 1998). Despite this emphasis on the social environment, social structuralists typically acknowledge the importance of some genetically mediated sex differences. Physical differences between the sexes, particularly men's greater size and strength and women's childbearing and lactation, are very important because they interact with shared cultural beliefs, social organization, and the

Author's note. Thanks are extended to David Buss for making available for reanalysis data from his 37 cultures study (Buss, 1989b; Buss et al., 1990).

demands of the economy to influence the role assignments that constitute the sexual division of labor within a society and produce psychological sex differences (Eagly, 1987; Wood & Eagly, 1999).

These thumbnail sketches of these two origin theories should make it clear that this debate about the origins of sex differences cannot be reduced to a simple nature-versus-nurture dichotomy. Both evolutionary psychology and social structural theory are interactionist in the sense that they take both biological and environmental factors into account, but they treat these factors quite differently. Evolutionary psychology views sex-specific evolved dispositions as psychological tendencies that were built in through genetically mediated adaptation to primeval conditions; the theory treats contemporary environmental factors as cues that interact with adaptations to yield sex-typed responses. Social structural theory views sex-differentiated tendencies as built in through accommodation to the contemporaneous sexual division of labor; in this approach, physical differences between the sexes serve as one influence on role assignment.

* * *

To illustrate the contrasting approaches of evolutionary psychology and social structural theory, we first present and discuss each theory. Then we examine their predictions concerning the criteria men and women use in selecting mates. This domain of behavior has been central to evolutionary theorizing about human sex differences (e.g., Buss & Schmitt, 1993; Kenrick & Keefe, 1992), and the cross-cultural findings available in this area provide an opportunity to examine empirically some of the predictions of evolutionary and social structural analyses.

Evolutionary Psychology as an Origin Theory of Sex Differences

From the perspective of evolutionary psychology, human sex differences reflect adaptations to the pressures of the differing physical and social environments that impinged on females and males during primeval times (Buss, 1995a; Tooby & Cosmides, 1992). Evolutionary psychologists thus label the environment that produced a species' evolved tendencies as its environment of evolutionary adaptedness (EEA; Cosmides, Tooby, & Barkow, 1992; Symons, 1979, 1992; Tooby & Cosmides, 1990b). They loosely identify the Pleistocene era as the human EEA and generally assume that it was populated by hunter–gatherer groups. To the extent that males and females faced different adaptive problems as they evolved, the two sexes developed different strategies to ensure their survival and to maximize their reproductive success. The resolutions to these problems produced evolved psychological mechanisms that are specific to each problem domain and that differ between women and men.

Although humans' evolved mechanisms developed in response to the types of problems consistently encountered by their ancestors and thus are presumed to be universal attributes of humans, environmental input affects how these mechanisms develop in individuals and how they are expressed in behavior (e.g., Buss & Kenrick, 1998). Because culture influences developmental experiences and patterns current situational input, culture is in principle important to the expression of adaptive mechanisms (Tooby & Cosmides, 1992). However, evolutionary psychologists have devoted relatively little attention to the interaction between such broader attributes of the social and cultural environment and the evolved mechanisms that may underlie sex differences. The contextual factors that have interested them generally relate directly to these hypothesized mechanisms. For example, Buss and Schmitt (1993) maintained that the characteristics that people seek in mates depend, not only on their sex, but also on whether they are engaging in short-term or long-term mating. Because of a relative neglect of broader social context, evolutionary psychologists have generated little understanding of how variation in sex-differentiated behavior arises from developmental factors and features of social structure and culture (for an exception, see Draper & Harpending, 1982).

The aspect of evolutionary theory that has been applied most extensively to sex differences is the theory of sexual selection initially proposed by Darwin (1871) and further developed by Trivers (1972). In the evolutionary psychologists' rendition of these views, sex-typed features of human behavior evolved through male competition and female choice of mates. Because women constituted the sex that devoted greater effort to parental investment, they were a limited reproductive resource for men, who were the less investing sex. Women were restricted in the number of children they could propagate during their life span because of their investment through gestating, bearing, and nursing their children; men did not have these restrictions. Men therefore competed for access to women, and women chose their mates from among the available men. As the more investing sex, women were selected for their wisdom in choosing mates who could provide resources to support their parenting efforts. Women's preferences for such men, in turn, produced sexual selection pressures on men to satisfy these criteria.

Proponents of sexual selection theory argue that sex differences in parental investment favored different strategies for reproductive success for men and women and consequently established different adaptive mechanisms governing mating behavior (Buss, 1996; Kenrick, Trost, & Sheets, 1996). It was to men's advantage in terms of fitness outcomes to "devote a larger proportion of their total mating effort to short-term mating than do women" (Buss & Schmitt, 1993, p. 205)—that is, to be relatively promiscuous. Women, in contrast, benefited from devoting a smaller proportion of their effort to short-term mating and a larger proportion to long-term mating. Also, because of women's concealed fertilization, men were unable to determine easily which children could proffer the fitness gains that follow from genetic relatedness. Men ostensibly adapted to this problem of paternity uncertainty by exerting sexual control over women and developing sexual jealousy and a motive to control women's sexuality (Daly & Wilson, 1998).

According to evolutionary psychologists (e.g., Buss, 1995b; Buss & Kenrick, 1998), sex differences in numerous psychological dispositions arose from differing fitness-related goals of women and men that followed from their contrasting sexual strategies. Because men competed with other men for sexual access to women, men's evolved dispositions favor violence, competition, and risk taking. Women in turn developed a proclivity to nurture and a preference for long-term mates who could support a family. As a result, men strived to acquire more resources than other men in order to attract women, and women developed preferences for successful, ambitious men who could provide resources.

Critical to some of evolutionary psychologists' claims about sex differences is the assumption that ancestral humans living in the EEA had a hunter–gatherer socioeconomic system (e.g., Buss, 1995b; Cosmides et al., 1992; DeKay & Buss, 1992). The idea of a division of labor in which men hunted while women gathered suggests sex-differentiated pressures linked to survival and reproduction. Such an ancestral division of labor might have favored men who were psychologically specialized for hunting and women who were specialized for gathering. For example, cognitive abilities could have been affected, with men acquiring the superior spatial skills that followed from ancestral hunting, and women acquiring the superior spatial location memory that followed from ancestral gathering (e.g., Geary, 1995; Silverman & Phillips, 1998).

Various mediating processes are implied in evolutionary psychology models of behavioral sex differences. The first and most important involves some means of retaining effective adaptations in human design and perpetuating them over time. Thus, sex-differentiated psychological mechanisms and developmental programs, like other adaptations, are "genetic, hereditary, or inherited in the sense that . . . their structured design has its characteristic form because of the information in our DNA" (Tooby & Cosmides, 1990a, p. 37; see also Buss, Haselton, Shackelford, Bleske, & Wakefield, 1998; Crawford, 1998). Some evolutionary accounts also emphasize that genetic factors trigger biochemical processes that mediate psychological sex differences, especially by means of sex differences in hormone production (e.g., Daly & Wilson, 1983; Geary, 1995, 1996). In addition, sex-typed evolved mechanisms are translated into behavioral sex differences by various cognitive and affective processes. Establishing these links requires theoretical understanding and empirical documentation of the range of processes by which the genetic factors implicated in innate dispositions might affect human behavior (e.g., Collear & Hines, 1995).

Buss and Kenrick (1998) described evolutionary psychology's approach to understanding sex differences as a "metatheory" and summarized it as follows: "Men and women differ in domains where they faced different adaptive problems over human evolutionary history" (p. 994). These theorists thus derive sex differences from heritable adaptations built into the human species. Because these differences are assumed to follow from evolutionary adaptations, they are predicted to occur as central tendencies of male versus female behavior. Human behavior would thus be characterized by a deep structure of sex-differentiated dispositions, producing similar, albeit not identical, behavioral sex differences in all human societies.

CRITIQUE OF THE EVOLUTIONARY ORIGIN THEORY A number of questions can be raised about evolutionary psychology's account of the origins of sex differences. One consideration is that evolutionary analyses have generally identified adaptations by relying on "informal arguments as to whether a presumed function is served with sufficient precision, economy, efficiency, etc. to rule out pure chance as an adequate explanation" (Williams, 1966, p. 10). Explanations that reflect this approach consist of an analysis of the functional relations served by a particular psychological mechanism, along with the construction of a convincing story about how the adaptation might have made an efficient contribution to genetic survival or to some other goal contributing to reproduction in the EEA. These explanations serve as hypotheses that require additional validation and thus can be useful for initiating scientific research.

In developing these analyses of the possible functions of behaviors, evolutionary scientists face special challenges in distinguishing adaptations from other possible products of evolution—for example, features that were random or that had utility for one function but were subsequently coopted to fulfill a new function (see Buss et al., 1998; Gould, 1991; Williams, 1966). Moreover, the products of evolution must be distinguished from the products of cultural change. Behaviors that provide effective solutions to problems of reproduction and survival can arise from inventive trial-and-error among individuals who are genetically indistinguishable from other members of their living groups; such beneficial behaviors are then imitated and transmitted culturally.

An understanding of humans' primeval environment might help validate evolutionary hypotheses because adaptations evolved as solutions to past environmental challenges. Various bodies of science have some relevance, including observational studies of other primates, the fossil record, and ethnographic studies. However, models of human nature constructed from the behavior of nonhuman primates do not yield a uniform picture that reflects key features of sex differences in modern human societies (see Fedigan, 1986: Strier, 1994; Travis & Yeager, 1991). Similarly ambiguous concerning sex differences are the models of early human social conditions that paleontologists and paleoanthropologists have developed from fossil evidence. Anthropologists continue to debate fundamental points—for example, whether hunting of dangerous prey might have emerged during the period that is usually identified as the human EEA (e.g., Potts, 1984; Rose & Marshall, 1996). As a consequence, assumptions that certain traits were adaptive and consequently are under genetic control cannot be firmly supported from analyzing attributes of the EEA. Moreover, early human societies likely took a wide variety of forms during the period when the species was evolving toward its modern anatomical form (Foley, 1996). Variability in social organization is consistent with observations of more contemporary hunter–gatherer societies, which show great diversity in their social organization (Kelly, 1995). For example, studies of power relations between the sexes across diverse cultures show variability in the extent to which men control women's sexuality (Whyte, 1978), although evolutionary psychologists have assumed that this control is a defining feature of male–female relations. Therefore, because the EEA likely encompassed a variety of conditions, tracing humans' evolution requires understanding of the timing, social organization, and ecological circumstances of multiple periods of adaptation (Foley, 1996). The ambiguity and complexity of the relevant scientific findings leave room for evolutionary psychologists to inadvertently transport relatively modern social conditions to humans' remote past by inappropriately assuming that the distinctive characteristics of contemporary relations between the sexes were also typical of the EEA.

Given the difficulty of knowing the functions of behaviors and the attributes of the EEA, other types of scientific evidence become especially important to validating the claims of evolutionary psychologists. The most convincing evidence that a behavioral pattern reflects an adaptation would be that individuals who possessed the adaptation enjoyed a higher rate of survival and reproduction than individuals who did not possess it. However, such evidence is difficult, if not impossible, to produce. Because humans' evolved mechanisms emerged in relation to past selection pressures, present reproductive advantage does not necessarily reflect past advantage, and evolutionary psychologists have warned against relying on measures of current reproductive success to validate hypothesized adaptations (Buss, 1995a; Tooby & Cosmides, 1992). In the absence of evidence pertaining to reproductive success, scientists might document the genetic inheritance of postulated mechanisms and the processes by which genetic factors result in sex differences in behavior. However, for the psychological dispositions considered in this article, such evidence has not been produced. Instead, the scientific case for these sex-differentiated evolved dispositions rests on tests of evolutionary psychologists' predictions concerning the behavior of men and women in contemporary societies (e.g., Buss & Schmitt, 1993; Kenrick & Keefe, 1992). We evaluate some of these predictions in this article.

Social Structural Theory as an Origin Theory of Sex Differences

A respected tradition in the social sciences locates the origins of sex differences, not in evolved psychological dispositions that are built into the human psyche, but in the contrasting social positions of women and men. In contemporary American society, as in many world societies, women have less power and status than men and control fewer resources. This feature of social structure is often labeled gender hierarchy, or in feminist writing it may be called patriarchy. In addition, as the division of labor is realized in the United States and many other nations, women perform more domestic work than men and spend fewer hours in paid employment (Shelton, 1992). Although most women in the United States are employed in the paid workforce, they have lower wages than men, are concentrated in different occupations, and are thinly represented at the highest levels of organizational hierarchies (Jacobs, 1989; Reskin & Padavic, 1994; Tomaskovic-Devey, 1995). From a social structural perspective, the underlying cause of sex-differentiated behavior is this concentration of men and women in differing roles.

The determinants of the distribution of men and women into social roles are many and include the biological endowment of women and men. The sex-differentiated physical attributes that influence role occupancy include men's greater size and strength, which gives them priority in jobs demanding certain types of strenuous activity, especially activities involving upper body strength. These physical attributes of men are less important in societies in which few occupational roles require these attributes, such as postindustrial societies. Also important in relation to role distributions are women's childbearing and in many societies their activity of suckling infants for long periods of time; these obligations give them priority in roles involving the care of very young children and cause conflict with roles requiring extended absence from home and uninterrupted activity. These reproductive activities of women are less important in societies with low birthrates, less reliance on lactation for feeding infants, and greater reliance on nonmaternal care of young children.

In general, physical sex differences, in interaction with social and ecological conditions, influence the roles held by men and women because certain activities are more efficiently accomplished by one sex. The benefits of this greater efficiency can be realized when women and men are allied in cooperative relationships and establish a division of labor. The particular character of the activities that each sex performs then determines its placement in the social structure (see Wood & Eagly, 1999). As historians and anthropologists have argued (e.g., Ehrenberg, 1989; Harris, 1993; Lerner, 1986; Sanday, 1981), men typically specialized in activities (e.g., warfare, herding) that yielded greater status, wealth, and power, especially as societies became more complex. Thus, when sex differences in status emerged, they tended to favor men.

The differing distributions of men and women into social roles form the basis for a social structural metatheory of sex differences, just as evolutionary theory provides a metatheory. The major portion of this social structural theory follows from the typical features of the roles of men and women. Thus, the first metatheoretical principle derives from the greater power and status that tends to be associated with male-dominated roles and can be succinctly stated as follows: Men's accommodation to roles with greater power and status produces more dominant behavior, and women's accommodation to roles with lesser power and status produces more subordinate behavior (Ridgeway & Diekema, 1992). Dominant behavior is controlling, assertive, relatively directive and autocratic, and may involve sexual control. Subordinate behavior is more compliant to social influence, less overtly aggressive, more cooperative and conciliatory, and may involve a lack of sexual autonomy.

The second metatheoretical principle follows from the differing balance of activities associated with the typical roles of each sex. Women and men seek to accommodate sex-typical roles by acquiring the specific skills and resources linked to successful role performance and by adapting their social behavior to role requirements. A variety of sex-specific skills and beliefs arise from the typical family and economic roles of men and women, which in many societies can be described as resource provider and homemaker. Women and men seek to accommodate to these roles by acquiring role-related skills, for example, women learning domestic skills such as cooking and men learning skills that are marketable in the paid economy. The psychological attributes and social behaviors associated with these roles have been characterized in terms of the distinction between communal and agentic characteristics (Bakan, 1966; Eagly, 1987). Thus, women's accommodation to the domestic role and to female-dominated occupations favors a pattern of interpersonally facilitative and friendly behaviors that can be termed communal. In particular, the assignment of the majority of child rearing to women encourages nurturant behaviors that facilitate care for children and other individuals. The importance of close relationships to women's nurturing role favors the acquisition of superior interpersonal skills and the ability to communicate nonverbally. In contrast, men's accommodation to the employment role, especially to male-dominated occupations, favors a pattern of assertive and independent behaviors that can be termed agentic (Eagly & Steffen, 1984). This argument is not to deny that paid occupations show wide variation in the extent to which they favor more masculine or feminine qualities. In support of the idea that sex-differentiated behaviors are shaped by paid occupations are demonstrations that to the extent that occupations are male dominated, they are thought to require agentic personal qualities. In contrast, to the extent that occupations are female dominated, they are thought to require communal personal qualities (Cejka & Eagly, 1999; Glick, 1991).

In social structural theories, differential role occupancy affects behavior through a variety of mediating processes. In social role theory (Eagly, 1987; Eagly et al., in press), an important mediating process is the formation of gender roles by which people of each sex are expected to have characteristics that equip them for the tasks that they typically carry out. These expectations encompass the preferred or desirable attributes of men and women as well as their typical attributes. Gender roles are emergents from the productive work of the sexes; the characteristics that are required to perform sex-typical tasks become stereotypic of women or men. To the extent that women more than men occupy roles that demand communal behaviors, domestic behaviors, or subordinate behaviors for successful role performance, such tendencies become stereotypic of women and are incorporated into a female gender role. To the extent that men more than women occupy roles that demand agentic behaviors, resource acquisition behaviors, or dominant behaviors for successful role performance, such tendencies become stereotypic of men and are incorporated into a male gender role. Gender roles facilitate the activities typically carried out by people of each sex. For example, the expectation that women be other-oriented and compassionate facilitates their nurturing activities within the family as well as their work in many female-dominated occupations (e.g., teacher, nurse, social worker).

People communicate gender-stereotypic expectations in social interaction and can directly induce the targets of these expectations to engage in behavior that confirms them (e.g., Skrypnek & Snyder, 1982; Wood & Karten, 1986). Such effects of gender roles are congruent with theory and research on the behavioral confirmation of stereotypes and other expectancies (see Olson, Roese, & Zanna, 1996). Gender-stereotypic expectations can also affect behavior by becoming internalized as part of individuals' self-concepts and personalities (Feingold, 1994). Under such circumstances, gender roles affect behavior through self-regulatory processes (Wood, Christensen, Hebl, & Rothgerber, 1997). The individual psychology that underlies these processes is assumed to be the maximization of utilities. People perceive these utilities from the rewards and costs that emerge in social interaction, which takes place within the constraints of organizational and societal arrangements.

* * *

In summary, in social structural accounts, women and men are differently distributed into social roles, and these differing role assignments can be broadly described in terms of a sexual division of labor and a gender hierarchy. This division of labor and the patriarchal hierarchy that sometimes accompanies it provide the engine of sex-differentiated behavior because they trigger social and psychological processes by which men and women seek somewhat different experiences to maximize their outcomes within the constraints that societies establish for people of their sex. Sex differences in behavior thus reflect contemporaneous social conditions.

* * *

Sex Differences in Mate Selection Criteria Predicted From Evolutionary Psychology and Social Structural Theory

One reasonable area for comparing the predictive power of the evolutionary and the social structural origin theories of sex differences is human mating behavior, especially the criteria that people use for selecting mates. Evolutionary predictions have been articulated especially clearly for mating activities, and these behaviors can also be used to test a social structural perspective. Furthermore, empirical findings concerning mate selection preferences have been well-established for many years in the literature on the sociology of the family (e.g., Coombs & Kenkel, 1966). Powers's (1971) summary of 30 years of research concluded that at least in the United States, women generally prefer mates with good earning potential, whereas men prefer mates who are physically attractive and possess good domestic skills. Furthermore, women typically prefer a mate who is older than them, whereas men prefer a mate who is younger. Feingold's (1990, 1991, 1992a) meta-analyses of studies drawn from various research paradigms established that the sex differences in valuing potential mates' earning potential and physical attractiveness are robust, despite sex similarity on most criteria for selecting mates. Subsequent research based on a national probability sample of single adults provided further confirmation of the sex differences in age preferences as well as in valuing earning potential and physical attractiveness (Sprecher, Sullivan, & Hatfield, 1994).

Evolutionary psychologists have adopted mate preferences as signature findings of their analysis. Women's valuing of mates' resources and men's valuing of mates' youth and physical attractiveness are thought to arise from the different parental investment of the sexes that was outlined in Trivers's (1972) sexual selection theory. It is commonly argued that women, as the more investing sex, seek mates with attributes that can support their parenting efforts. However, human mate selection does not follow a strict version of Trivers's males-compete-and-females-choose model, because among humans, selection is a product of the behavior of both sexes, a process Darwin (1871) called "dual selection." In Buss's (1989a) account, male choice derives from women's time-limited reproductive capacity and the tendency for men to seek mates with attributes that suggest such capacity. In Kenrick and Keefe's (1992) account, men and women are both selective about potential mates and both invest heavily in offspring but with different kinds of resources. In particular, "males invest relatively more indirect resources (food, money, protection, and security), and females invest relatively more direct physiological resources (contributing their own bodily nutrients to the fetus and nursing child)" (Kenrick & Keefe, 1992, p. 78). As a result, women prefer mates who can provide indirect resources, and men prefer healthy mates with reproductive potential.

In contrast, from a social structural perspective, the psychology of mate selection reflects people's effort to maximize their utilities with respect to mating choices in an environment in which these utilities are constrained by societal gender roles as well as by the more specific expectations associated with marital roles. Consistent with these ideas, Becker's (1976) economic analysis of mating decisions characterized marriage as occurring between utility-maximizing men and women who can reach an equilibrium with a variety of types of exchanges, including, for example, an exchange between men's wages and women's household production and other attributes such as education and beauty. This cost–benefit analysis of mating appears even on occasion in the writings of evolutionary scientists. For example, Tattersall (1998) maintained that behavioral regularities, such as sex differences in mate selection criteria, are as likely to be due to rational economic decisions as to inherited predispositions, and Hrdy (1997) wrote that "a woman's preference for a wealthy man can be explained by the simple reality that . . . males monopolize ownership of productive resources" (p. 29).

The outcomes that are perceived to follow from mating decisions depend on marital and family arrangements. To the extent that women and men occupy marital and family roles that entail different responsibilities and obligations, they should select mates according to criteria that reflect these divergent responsibilities and obligations. Consider, for example, the family system based on a male provider and a female domestic worker. This system became especially pronounced in industrial economies and is still prevalent in many world societies. To the extent that societies have this division of labor, women maximize their outcomes by seeking a mate who is likely to be successful in the economic, wage-earning role. In turn, men maximize their outcomes by seeking a mate who is likely to be successful in the domestic role.

The sex differences in the preferred age of mates also can be understood as part of the general tendency of men and women to seek partners likely to provide a good fit to their society's sexual division of labor and marital roles. Specifically, the marital system based on a male breadwinner and a female homemaker favors the age gap in marriage. Marriageable women who are younger than their potential mates tend to have lesser wages, social status, and education and knowledge than women who are the same age as potential mates. With the combination of a younger, less experienced woman and an older, more experienced man, it would be easier to establish the power differential favoring men that is normative for marital roles defined by a male breadwinner and a female domestic worker (Lips, 1991; Steil, 1997). Moreover, compared with somewhat older women, young women lack independent resources and therefore are more likely to perceive that their utilities are maximized in the domestic worker role. In complementary fashion, older men are more likely to have acquired the economic resources that make them good candidates for the provider role. The older man and younger woman thus fit more easily than same-age partners into the culturally expected pattern of breadwinner and homemaker.

Cross-cultural Evidence for Sex Differences in Mate Preferences Evolutionary psychologists' predictions that women select for resources and older age and men for attractiveness and younger age have been examined cross-culturally. Buss's (1989a; Buss et al., 1990) impressive study in 37 cultures of the characteristics that people desire in mates suggested that consistent with evolutionary psychology, these sex differences in mate preferences emerged cross-culturally. Similarly, Kenrick and Keefe (1992) examined the preferred ages of mates in five countries and across various time periods in the 20th century and concluded that all provided evidence of sex differences in these preferences. Specifically, for dating and marriage, women preferred older men and men preferred younger women, although men's preferences were moderated by their age, with teenage boys preferring girls of similar age.

On the basis of these investigations, evolutionary accounts have emphasized the cross-cultural commonality in women's preference for resources and older age and men's preference for attractiveness and younger age. According to Buss (1989a) and Tooby and Cosmides (1989), uniformity across diverse cultures and social circumstances suggests powerful sex-differentiated evolved mechanisms that reflect an innate, universal human nature. Kenrick and Keefe (1992) also argued that "invariance across cultures is evidence that supports a species-specific, rather than a culture-specific, explanation" (p. 76).

Despite evidence for cross-cultural commonality in sex differences in mate selection criteria, these investigations also yielded evidence for cultural variation. For example, Kenrick and Keefe (1992) found that the preference for younger wives was evident among Philippine men of all ages, but only among older men (i.e., age 30 or over) in the United States. However, the simple existence of uniformity or variability does not provide a definitive test of either the evolutionary or the social structural origin theory. Although evolutionary psychologists emphasize uniformity and social structural theorists emphasize variability, both perspectives have some power to explain both of these cross-cultural patterns. To account for uniformity, social structuralists can point to similarities in the sexual division of labor in the studied societies and can argue that these similarities produce these relatively invariant sex differences. As Buss (1989a) noted, his 37 cultures, which were drawn from 33 nations, were biased toward urbanized cash-economy cultures, with 54% from Europe and North America. Furthermore, respondents selected from each society tended to be young, comparatively well-educated, and of relatively high socioeconomic status. To the extent that these societies similarly defined the roles of women and men and that the respondents were similarly placed in these societies' social structures, commonality in the sex differences that follow from social structure should characterize these societies.

To account for cross-cultural variability, both evolutionary and social structural origin theories recognize that developmental processes and social factors that are unique to each society direct behavior in ways that can yield variability in sex differences across cultures. Beyond this insight that some evidence of cross-cultural variability would not surprise theorists in either camp, the particular pattern of cross-cultural variation provides an informative test of the mechanisms underlying sex differences. Specifically, the social structural argument that a society's sexual division of labor and associated gender hierarchy are responsible for sex differences in social behavior yields predictions concerning cross-cultural variability in mate preferences.

In the nations included in Buss et al.'s (1990) cross-cultural sample, whose economies ranged from agrarian to postindustrial, some cultures were still strongly marked by this division of labor between the provider and domestic worker, whereas other cultures had departed from it. In advanced economies like the United States, women have entered the paid labor force and spend a smaller proportion of their time in domestic labor (Haas, 1995; Shelton, 1992). Although the tendency for men to increase their hours of domestic work is much more modest, the lives of men and women become more similar with greater gender equality. Therefore, people of both sexes should lessen their emphasis on choosing mates whose value is defined by their fit to the division between domestic work and wage labor. Even in postindustrial economies such as the United States, however, the sex-typed division of labor remains in modified form, with men devoting longer hours than women to wage labor and women devoting longer hours to domestic work (e.g., Ferree, 1991; Presser, 1994; Shelton, 1992). Therefore, the social structural prediction is that the sex differences in mate selection criteria that follow from the male-female division of labor should be substantially weakened in societies characterized by greater gender equality, albeit they should still be present to the extent that complete equality has not been achieved.

REANALYSIS OF BUSS ET AL.'S (1990) 37 CULTURES DATA To evaluate whether the division of labor within a society could explain the mate preferences of men and women, we reanalyzed Buss et al.'s (1990) 37 cultures data. Our efforts focused on men's tendencies to select wives for domestic skill and younger age and women's tendencies to select husbands for earning capacity and older age. To test the hypothesis that a higher level of gender equality lessens these sex differences, we represented societies' gender equality in terms of archival data available from the United Nations (United Nations Development Programme, 1995).

Buss et al. (1990) derived the data on criteria for selecting mates from questionnaire measures of preferences for a wide range of characteristics that might be desired in a mate: (a) One instrument obtained rankings of a set of 13 characteristics according to "their desirability in someone you might marry" (p. 11); (b) the other instrument obtained ratings on a 4-point scale of each of 18 characteristics on "how important or desirable it would be in choosing a mate" (p. 11). Buss et al. represented each culture by the male and female respondents' mean ranking of each of the 13 male selection criteria and by their mean rating of each of the 18 criteria. A separate question inquired about preferences for a spouse's age. The data that we reanalyzed consisted of mean preferences for each culture.

Our reanalysis confirmed Buss et al.'s (1990) conclusion that women placed more value than men on a mate's wage-earning ability. Furthermore, consistent with the greater domestic responsibility of women than men in most cultures, men valued *good cook and housekeeper* more than women did, a sex difference that has received little attention from evolutionary psychologists. When the sex differences in the mean preference ratings were averaged across the cultures, this difference was of comparable magnitude to those obtained on the attributes most strongly emphasized by evolutionary psychologists. Specifically, in both the rating and ranking data, the criteria of *good earning capacity, good housekeeper and cook*, and *physically attractive* produced the largest sex differences. The appropriateness of focusing on the criteria pertaining to earning ability and domestic skill within Buss et al.'s data was also supported by the good agreement across the ranking and rating data sets for sex differences in the valuation of the qualities of financial prospect, $r(33) = .76$, $p < .001$, and domestic skill, $r(33) = .68$, $p < .001$, whereas the agreement in the valuation of physical attractiveness was poorer, $r(33) = .34$, $p < .05$.[1] In addition, as Buss et al. reported, the sex difference in the preferred age of mates was fully intact in the 37 cultures data.

Additional evidence for the social structural predictions emerged when we evaluated the pattern of sex differences in preferences across societies. Consistent with the division of labor principle, a substantial relation emerged between the sex difference in valuing a spouse's domestic skills and the sex difference in valuing a spouse's capacity to provide a good income. Specifically, on the basis of the ranking measure, the sex differences in the good earning capacity criterion and the good housekeeper criterion were correlated across the cultures, $r(33) = .67$, $p < .001$. On the basis of the rating measure, the sex differences in the financial prospect criterion and the housekeeper–cook criterion were also correlated, $r(35) = .38$, $p < .05$. These positive correlations indicate that to the extent that women more than men reported seeking a mate who is a good breadwinner, men more than women reported seeking a mate who is a good homemaker. In addition, the sex difference in the preferred age of one's spouse bore a positive relation to the sex difference in preference for a good earner, $r(33) = .34$, $p < .05$ for the ranking data, and $r(35) = .32$, $p < .06$ for the rating data. Similarly, the sex difference in preferred age bore a positive relation to the sex difference in preference for a good housekeeper and cook, $r(33) = .58$, $p < .001$ for the ranking data, and $r(35) = .60$, $p < .001$ for the rating data. These relationships show that to the extent that the sex difference in the preferred age of spouses was large, women more than men preferred mates who were good providers and men more than women preferred mates who were good domestic workers. The division of labor provides the logic of all of these relationships: Women who serve in the domestic role are the complement of men who serve as breadwinners, and the combination of older husbands and younger wives facilitates this form of marriage.

Analysis of gender equality. To test our hypothesis that sex differences in mate preferences erode to the extent that women and men are similarly placed in the social structure, we sought cross-national indicators of gender equality. Among the many such indicators compiled by United Nations researchers, the most direct indicator of gender equality is the aggregate Gender Empowerment Measure, which represents the extent to which women participate equally with men in economic, political, and decision-making roles (United Nations Development Programme, 1995). This index increases as (a) women's percentage share of administrative and managerial jobs and professional and technical jobs increases, (b) women's percentage share of parliamentary seats rises, and (c) women's proportional share of earned income approaches parity with men's.

The Gender-Related Development Index is another useful indicator of societal-level gender equality provided by United Nations researchers. It increases with a society's basic capabilities to provide health (i.e., greater life expectancy), educational attainment and literacy, and wealth, but imposes a penalty for gender inequality in these capabilities (United Nations Development Programme, 1995). Whereas this measure reflects equality in basic access to health care, education and knowledge, and income, the Gender Empowerment Measure is a purer indicator of equal participation in economic and political life.

In the set of 37 cultures, the Gender Empowerment Measure and the Gender-Related Development Index were correlated, $r(33) = .74$,

[1] r is the correlation coefficient, the number in parentheses is the degrees of the freedom (in this case the number of participants minus 2), and p is the significance, or probability that an r this large would have been found by chance alone if the population value were in fact 0.

TABLE 22.1

CORRELATIONS OF MEAN RANKINGS AND RATINGS OF MATE SELECTION CRITERIA WITH UNITED NATIONS INDEXES OF GENDER EQUALITY FOR BUSS ET AL.'S (1990) 37 CULTURES SAMPLE

	Ranked criteria		Rated criteria	
Mate selection criterion and rater	Gender Empowerment Measure (n = 33)	Gender-Related Development Index (n = 34)	Gender Empowerment Measure (n = 35)	Gender-Related Development Index (n = 36)
Good earning capacity (financial prospect)				
Sex difference	–.43*	–.33†	–.29†	–.23
Women	–.29	–.18	–.49**	–.42**
Men	.24	.27	–.40*	–.36*
Good housekeeper (and cook)				
Sex difference	–.62***	–.54**	–.61***	–.54**
Women	.04	–.01	.11	–.07
Men	–.46**	–.42*	–.60***	–.61***
Physically attractive (good looks)				
Sex difference	.13	–.12	.20	.18
Women	.14	.34†	–.45**	–.25
Men	.20	.28	–.33†	–.14

Note. The criteria were described slightly differently in the ranking and the rating tasks: The ranking term is given first, with the rating term following in parentheses. Higher values on the gender equality indexes indicate greater equality. For the preferences of women or men, higher values of the mean rankings and ratings of mate selection criteria indicate greater desirability in a mate; therefore, a positive correlation indicates an increase in the desirability of a criterion as gender equality increased, and a negative correlation indicates a decrease. Sex differences in these preferences were calculated as female minus male means for good earning capacity and male minus female means for good housekeeper and physically attractive. A positive correlation thus indicates an increase in the sex difference as gender equality increased, and a negative correlation indicates a decrease in the sex difference.
†$p < .10$. *$p < .05$. **$p < .01$. ***$p < .001$.

$p < .001$, and both of these indexes were moderately correlated with general indexes of human development and economic development. One limitation of the indexes of gender equality is that they are based on data from the early 1990s. Because Buss et al.'s (1990) data were collected in the mid-1980s, these indexes are from a slightly later time period, but the relative positions of the cultures should remain approximately the same.

To examine the relation between societal gender equality and mate preferences, we calculated the correlations of these indexes with the sex differences in valuing a mate as a breadwinner and as a domestic worker—the two criteria most relevant to the traditional division of labor. These correlations for the ranking and the rating data, which appear in Table 22.1, are generally supportive of the social structural predictions. As the Gender Empowerment Measure increased in value, the tendency decreased for women to place greater emphasis than men on a potential spouse's earning capacity, although the correlation with the rated criterion was relatively weak. Also, as the Gender Empowerment Measure increased, the tendency decreased for men to place greater emphasis than women on a potential spouse's domestic skills. As expected in terms of the Gender-Related Development Index's less direct

TABLE 22.2

CORRELATIONS OF MEAN PREFERRED AGE DIFFERENCE BETWEEN SELF AND SPOUSE WITH UNITED NATIONS INDEXES OF GENDER EQUALITY FOR BUSS ET AL.'S (1990) 37 CULTURES SAMPLE

Rater	Gender Empowerment Measure (n = 35)	Gender-Related Development Index (n = 36)
Sex difference	−.73***	−.70***
Women	−.64***	−.57***
Men	.70***	.70***

Note. Higher values on the gender equality indexes indicate greater equality. Positive ages indicate preference for an older spouse, and negative ages indicate preference for a younger spouse. Therefore, for the preferences of women, a negative correlation indicates a decrease in the tendency to prefer an older spouse as gender equality increased, whereas for the preferences of men, a positive correlation indicates a decrease in the tendency to prefer a younger spouse. Because the sex difference in preferred age was calculated as female minus male mean preferred spouse age in relation to self, a negative correlation indicates a decrease in the sex difference in preferred age as gender equality increased.

***$p < .001$.

representation of the similarity of the roles of women and men, its correlations with these sex differences were somewhat weaker.

The preference data for each sex reported in Table 22.1 provide insight into these sex-difference findings. For good housekeeper and cook, the correlations for both the rating data and the ranking data indicated that as gender equality increased, men decreased their interest in choosing mates for their skill as domestic workers, and women showed no change in this preference. In contrast, for good earning capacity, as gender equality increased, women decreased their emphasis on mates' earning potential in the rating data (although nonsignificantly in the ranking data). However, men's preferences for good earning capacity are more difficult to interpret because their relations to gender equality were inconsistent across the ranking and rating measures. Inconsistencies between the two measures may reflect that rankings are judgments of the relative importance of the criteria in relation to the others in the list, whereas ratings are judgments of the absolute importance of the different criteria.

As shown in Table 22.2, examination of preferences for a spouse's age showed that as gender equality increased, women expressed less preference for older men, men expressed less preference for younger women, and consequently the sex difference in the preferred age of mates became smaller. These relations suggest that sex differences in age preferences reflect a sex-differentiated division of labor.

* * *

Preference for physical attractiveness. As also shown in Table 22.1, correlations between the sex difference in valuing potential mates' physical attractiveness and the United Nations indexes of gender equality were low and nonsignificant. These findings are not surprising, because this mate selection criterion does not mirror the division between wage labor and domestic labor in the manner that earning potential, domestic skill, and age do. Nevertheless, under some circumstances, physical attractiveness may be part of what people exchange for partners' earning capacity and other attributes.

Assuming that attractiveness is sometimes exchanged for other gains, the social structural perspective offers possibilities for understanding its value. Research on the physical attractiveness stereotype has shown that attractiveness in both sexes conveys several kinds of meaning—especially social competence, including social skills, sociability, and popularity (Eagly, Ashmore, Makhijani, & Longo, 1991; Feingold, 1992b). Therefore, men's greater valuing of attractiveness might follow from the greater importance of this competence in women's family and occupational roles, including women's paid occupations in postindustrial societies (Cejka & Eagly, 1999; Lippa, 1998), and the consequent inclusion of this competence in the female gender role. If women's roles demand greater interpersonal competence in societies with greater and lesser gender equality, the tendency for men to place greater value on mates' attractiveness would not covary with indexes that assess equality.

Another possibility is that the value of attractiveness stems from its perceived association with the ability to provide sexual pleasure. This idea receives support from research showing that attractiveness conveys information about sexual warmth (Feingold, 1992b). If so, men might seek sexiness in a mate in all societies, in addition to attributes such as domestic skill, whose importance varies with the society's level of gender equality. Given that the female gender role often includes sexual restraint and lack of sexual autonomy, women may place less emphasis on sexiness in mates than men do.

It is less certain that physical attractiveness conveys information about women's fertility, as should be the case if men's preference for attractiveness in mates developed because attractiveness was a cue to fertility (Buss, 1989a; Jones, 1995; Singh, 1993). It seems reasonable that perceptions of attractiveness and potential fertility would covary even in contemporary data, but these relations have proven to be inconsistent (e.g., Cunningham, 1986; Tassinary & Hansen, 1998). Moreover, Singh's (1993) research on judgments of female figures that varied in weight and waist-to-hip ratio suggested three somewhat independent groupings of attributes: health, attractiveness, and sexiness; capacity and desire for children; and youth.

Although little is known about the relation between women's attractiveness and their actual fecundity, Kalick, Zebrowitz, Langlois, and Johnson (1998) found that facial attractiveness in early adulthood was unrelated to number of children produced or to health across the life span. Although the few participants in their sample who did not marry were less attractive than those who did marry, once the nonmarried were excluded, physical attractiveness was unrelated to the number of children produced by male or female participants. Kalick et al. (1998) concluded that "any relation between attractiveness and fecundity was due to mate-selection chances rather than biological fertility" (p. 10). Of course, as we noted in our critique of evolutionary psychology in this article, proponents of the theory do not predict that hypothesized evolved dispositions, such as men's preference for physically attractive partners, would necessarily be related to current reproductive success. Evolutionary psychologists argue instead that actual fertility in modern societies may bear little relation to the factors indicative of reproductive success in the EEA.

In summary, several aspects of the findings from Buss et al.'s (1990) 37 cultures study are compatible with the social structural origin theory of sex differences. The idea that the extremity of the division between male providers and female homemakers is a major determinant of the criteria that people seek in mates fits with the observed covariation between men placing more emphasis than women on younger age and domestic skill and women placing more emphasis than men on older age and earning potential. The lessening of these sex differences with increasing gender equality, as represented by the United Nations indexes, is consistent with our claim that these sex differences are by-products of a social and family structure in which the man acts as a provider and the woman acts as a homemaker. More ambiguous are the sex differences in valuing mates' physical attractiveness. Without evidence that men's greater valuing of attractiveness follows from one or more specific mechanisms, the simple absence of a relation between gender equality and sex differences in valuing attractiveness in our reanalysis does not advance the claims of evolutionary psychology or the social structural theory. Convincing evidence for either interpretation has yet to be generated. However, with respect to the other sex differences emphasized by evolutionary psychologists, their cross-cultural patterning suggests that they arise from a particular economic and social system.

* * *

Conclusion

Considered at the level of a general metatheory of sex differences, social structural theories provide alternative explanations of the great majority of the general predictions about sex-differentiated social behavior that have been featured in evolutionary psychology. Because the central tendencies of sex differences (see Eagly, 1995; Halpern, 1997; Hyde, 1996) are readily encompassed by both of these perspectives, neither the evolutionary metatheory nor the social structural metatheory is convincingly substantiated by a mere noting of the differences established in the research literature. It is far too easy to make up sensible stories about how these differences might be products of sex-differentiated evolved tendencies or the differing placement of women and men in the social structure. This overlap in general main-effect predictions calls for more refined testing of the two theoretical perspectives, and each perspective is associated with numerous more detailed predictions and empirical tests.

Certainly there are many possibilities for distinguishing between the two approaches with appropriate research designs (see Jackson, 1992). Evolutionary psychologists have been especially resourceful in obtaining cross-cultural data intended to support their claims of invariance across cultures in sex-differentiated behavior. To be maximally informative about social structural factors, cross-cultural research should be systematically designed to represent cultures with differing forms of social organization and levels of gender equality. In addition, a variety of other research methods, including experiments and field studies, can yield tests of predictions that emerge from evolutionary and social structural perspectives.

Although this article contrasts social structural explanations of sex differences with those based on evolutionary psychology, social structural analyses may be generally compatible with some evolutionary perspectives, as we noted in the introductory section of this article. Our argument that sex differences in behavior emerge primarily from physical sex differences in conjunction with influences of the economy, social structure, ecology, and cultural beliefs is potentially reconcilable with theories of coevolution by genetic and cultural processes (Janicki & Krebs, 1998). Our position is also sympathetic to the interest that some evolutionary biologists and behavioral ecologists have shown in the maintenance of behavioral patterns from generation to generation through nongenetic, cultural processes (e.g., Sork, 1997). However, despite our acknowledgement of the importance of some evolved genetic influences on the behavior of women and men, an implicit assumption of our approach is that social change emerges, not from individuals' tendencies to maximize their inclusive fitness, but instead from their efforts to maximize their personal benefits and minimize their personal costs in their social and ecological settings.

One test of the evolutionary psychology and social structural origin theories of sex differences lies in the future—that is, in the emerging postindustrial societies in which the division between men's wage labor and women's domestic labor is breaking down. Notable is the increase in women's paid employment, education, and access to many formerly male-dominated occupations. Accompanying these changes is a marked attitudinal shift toward greater endorsement of equal opportunity for women in the workplace and role-sharing in the home (e.g., Simon & Landis, 1989; Spence & Hahn, 1997; Twenge, 1997). Nonetheless, occupational sex segregation is still prevalent with women concentrated in occupations that are thought to require feminine qualities and with men in occupations thought to require masculine qualities (Cejka & Eagly, 1999; Glick, 1991). Given that occupational distributions currently take this form and that the homemaker–provider division of labor remains weakly in place, social structuralists would not predict that sex differences in behavior should have already disappeared. Instead, to the extent that the traditional sexual division between wage labor and domestic labor disappears and women and men become similarly distributed into paid occupations, men and women should converge in their psychological attributes.

References

Archer, J. (1996). Sex differences in social behavior: Are the social role and evolutionary explanations compatible? *American Psychologist, 51*, 909–917.

Bakan, D. (1966). *The duality of human existence: An essay on psychology and religion*. Chicago: Rand McNally.

Becker, G. S. (1976). *The economic approach to human behavior*. Chicago: University of Chicago Press.

Buss, D. M. (1989a). Sex differences in human mate preferences: Evolutionary hypotheses tested in 37 cultures. *Behavioral and Brain Sciences, 12*, 1–14.

Buss, D. M. (1989b). Toward an evolutionary psychology of human mating. *Behavioral and Brain Sciences, 12*, 39–49.

Buss, D. M. (1995a). Evolutionary psychology: A new paradigm for psychological science. *Psychological Inquiry, 6*, 1–30.

Buss, D. M. (1995b). Psychological sex differences: Origins through sexual selection. *American Psychologist, 50*, 164–168.

Buss, D. M. (1996). The evolutionary psychology of human social strategies. In E. T. Higgins & A. W. Kruglanski (Eds.), *Social psychology: Handbook of basic principles* (pp. 3–38). New York: Guilford Press.

Buss, D. M. (1998). The psychology of human mate selection: Exploring the complexity of the strategic repertoire. In C. Crawford & D. L. Krebs (Eds.), *Handbook of evolutionary psychology: Ideas, issues, and applications* (pp. 405–429). Mahwah, NJ: Erlbaum.

Buss, D. M., et al. (1990). International preferences in selecting mates: A study of 37 cultures. *Journal of Cross-Cultural Psychology, 21*, 5–47.

Buss, D. M., Haselton. M. G., Shackelford, T. K., Bleske, A. L., & Wakefield, J. C. (1998). Adaptations, exaptations, and spandrels. *American Psychologist, 53*, 533–548.

Buss, D. M., & Kenrick, D. T. (1998). Evolutionary social psychology. In D. T. Gilbert, S. T. Fiske, & G. Lindzey (Eds.). *The handbook of social psychology* (4th ed., Vol. 2, pp. 982–1026). Boston: McGraw-Hill.

Buss, D. M., & Schmitt, D. P. (1993). Sexual strategies theory: An evolutionary perspective on human mating. *Psychological Review, 100*, 204–232.

Cejka, M. A., & Eagly, A. H. (1999). Gender-stereotypic images of occupations correspond to the sex segregation of employment. *Personality and Social Psychology Bulletin, 25*, 413–423.

Collear, M. L., & Hines, M. (1995). Human behavioral sex differences: A role for gonadal hormones during early development? *Psychological Bulletin, 118*, 55–107.

Coombs, R. H., & Kenkel, W. F. (1966). Sex differences in dating aspiration and satisfaction with computer-selected partners. *Journal of Marriage and the Family, 28*, 62–66.

Cosmides, L., Tooby, J., & Barkow, J. H. (1992). Introduction: Evolutionary psychology and conceptual integration. In J. H. Barkow, L. Cosmides, & J. Tooby (Eds.). *The adapted mind: Evolutionary psychology and the generation of culture* (pp. 3–15). New York: Oxford University Press.

Crawford, C. (1998). The theory of evolution in the study of human behavior: An introduction and overview. In C. Crawford & D. L. Krebs (Eds.), *Handbook of evolutionary psychology: Ideas, issues, and applications* (pp. 3–41). Mahwah, NJ: Erlbaum.

Cunningham, M. R. (1986). Measuring the physical in physical attractiveness: Quasi-experiments on the sociobiology of female facial beauty. *Journal of Personality and Social Psychology, 50*, 925–935.

Daly, M., & Wilson, M. (1983). *Sex, evolution, and behavior* (2nd ed.). Boston: Grant Press.

Daly, M., & Wilson, M. (1998). The evolutionary social psychology of family violence. In C. Crawford & D. L. Krebs (Eds.), *Handbook of evolutionary psychology: Ideas, issues, and applications* (pp. 431–456). Mahwah, NJ: Erlbaum.

Darwin, C. (1871). *The descent of man and selection in relation to sex*. London: Murray.

Deaux, K., & LaFrance, M. (1998). Gender. In D. T. Gilbert, S. T. Fiske, & G. Lindzey (Eds.), *The handbook of social psychology* (4th ed., Vol. 1, pp. 788–827). Boston: McGraw-Hill.

DeKay, W. T., & Buss. D. M. (1992). Human nature, individual differences, and the importance of context: Perspectives from evolutionary psychology. *Current Directions in Psychological Science, figure 1*, 184–189.

Draper, P., & Harpending, H. (1982). Father absence and reproductive strategy: An evolutionary perspective. *Journal of Anthropological Research, 38*, 255–273.

Eagly, A. H. (1987). *Sex differences in social behavior: A social-role interpretation*. Hillsdale, NJ: Erlbaum.

Eagly, A. H. (1995). The science and politics of comparing women and men. *American Psychologist, 50*, 145–158.

Eagly, A. H., Ashmore, R. D., Makhijani, M. G., & Longo, L. C. (1991). What is beautiful is good, but . . . : A meta-analytic review of research on the physical attractiveness stereotype. *Psychological Bulletin, 110*, 109–128.

Eagly, A. H., & Steffen, V. J. (1984). Gender stereotypes stem from the distribution of women and men into social roles. *Journal of Personality and Social Psychology, 46*, 735–754.

Eagly, A. H., Wood, W., & Diekman, A. (in press). Social role theory of sex differences and similarities: A current appraisal. In T. Eckes & H. M. Trautner (Eds.), *The developmental social psychology of gender*. Mahwah, NJ: Erlbaum.

Ehrenberg, M. (1989). *Women in prehistory*. London: British Museum Publications.

Fedigan, L. M. (1986). The changing role of women in models of human evolution. *Annual Review of Anthropology, 15*, 25–66.

Feingold, A. (1990). Gender differences in effects of physical attractiveness on romantic attraction: A comparison across five research paradigms. *Journal of Personality and Social Psychology, 59*, 981–993.

Feingold, A. (1991). Sex differences in the effects of similarity and physical attractiveness on opposite-sex attraction. *Basic and Applied Social Psychology, 12*, 357–367.

Feingold, A. (1992a). Gender differences in mate selection preferences: A test of the parental investment model. *Psychological Bulletin, 112*, 125–139.

Feingold, A. (1992b). Good-looking people are not what we think. *Psychological Bulletin, 111*, 304–341.

Feingold, A. (1994). Gender differences in personality: A meta-analysis. *Psychological Bulletin, 116*, 429–456.

Ferree, M. M. (1991). The gender division of labor in two-earner marriages: Dimensions of variability and change. *Journal of Family Issues, 12*, 158–180.

Foley, R. (1996). The adaptive legacy of human evolution: A search for the environment of evolutionary adaptedness. *Evolutionary Anthropology, 4*, 194–203.

Geary, D. C. (1995). Sexual selection and sex differences in spatial cognition. *Learning and Individual Differences, 7*, 289–301.

Geary, D. C. (1996). Sexual selection and sex differences in mathematical abilities. *Behavioral and Brain Sciences, 19*, 229–284.

Glick, P. (1991). Trait-based and sex-based discrimination in occupational prestige, occupational salary, and hiring. *Sex Roles, 25*, 351–378.

Gould, S. J. (1991). Exaptation: A crucial tool for an evolutionary psychology. *Journal of Social Issues, 47*, 43–65.

Haas, L. L. (1995). Household division of labor in industrial societies. In B. B. Ingoldsby & S. Smith (Eds.), *Families in multicultural perspective: Perspectives on marriage and the family* (pp. 268–296). New York: Guilford Press.

Halpern, D. F. (1997). Sex differences in intelligence: Implications for education. *American Psychologist, 52*, 1091–1102.

Harris, M. (1993). The evolution of human gender hierarchies: A trial formulation. In B. D. Miller (Ed.), *Sex and gender hierarchies* (pp. 57–79). New York: Cambridge University Press.

Hrdy, S. B. (1997). Raising Darwin's consciousness: Female sexuality and the prehominid origins of patriarchy. *Human Nature, 8*, 1–49.

Hyde, J. S. (1996). Where are the gender differences? Where are the gender similarities? In D. M. Buss & N. M. Malamuth (Eds.), *Sex, power, conflict: Evolutionary and feminist perspectives*. New York: Oxford University Press.

Jackson, L. A. (1992). *Physical appearance and gender: Sociobiological and sociocultural perspectives*. Albany: State University of New York Press.

Jacobs, J. A. (1989). *Revolving doors: Sex segregation and women's careers*. Stanford, CA: Stanford University Press.

Janicki, M. G., & Krebs, D. L. (1998). Evolutionary approaches to culture. In C. Crawford & D. L. Krebs (Eds.), *Handbook of evolutionary psychology: Ideas, issues, and applications* (pp. 163–207), Mahwah, NJ: Erlbaum.

Jones, D. (1995). Sexual selection, physical attractiveness, and facial neoteny: Cross-cultural evidence and implications. *Current Anthropology, 36*, 723–748.

Kalick, S. M., Zebrowitz, L. A., Langlois, J. H., & Johnson, R. M. (1998). Does human facial attractiveness honestly advertise health? Longitudinal data on an evolutionary question. *Psychological Science, 9*, 8–13.

Kelly, R. L. (1995). *The foraging spectrum: Diversity in hunter–gatherer lifeways*. Washington, DC: Smithsonian Institution Press.

Kenrick, D. T., & Keefe, R. C. (1992). Age preferences in mates reflect sex differences in human reproductive strategies. *Behavioral and Brain Sciences, 15*, 75–91.

Kenrick, D. T., Trost, M. R., & Sheets, V. L. (1996). Power, harassment, and trophy mates: The feminist advantages of an evolutionary perspective. In D. M. Buss & N. M. Malamuth (Eds.), *Sex, power, and conflict: Evolutionary and feminist perspectives* (pp. 29–53). New York: Oxford University Press.

Lemer, G. (1986). *The creation of patriarchy*. New York: Oxford University Press.

Lippa, R. (1998). Gender-related individual differences and the structure of vocational interests: The importance of the "people-things" dimension. *Journal of Personality and Social Psychology, 74*, 996–1009.

Lips, H. M. (1991). *Women, men, and power*. Mountain View, CA: Mayfield.

Lorenzi-Cioldi, F. (1998). Group status and perceptions of homogeneity. In W. Stroebe & M. Hewstone (Eds.), *European review of social psychology* (Vol. 9, pp. 31–75). Chichester, England: Wiley.

Olson, J. M., Roese, N. J., & Zanna, M. P. (1996). Expectancies. In E. T. Higgins & A. W. Kruglanski (Eds.), *Social psychology: Handbook of basic principles* (pp. 211–238). New York: Guilford.

Potts, R. (1984). Home bases and early hominids. *American Scientist, 72*, 338–347.

Powers, E. A. (1971). Thirty years of research on ideal mate characteristics: What do we know? *International Journal of Sociology of the Family, 1*, 207–215.

Presser, H. B. (1994). Employment schedules among dual-earner spouses and the division of household labor by gender. *American Sociological Review, 59*, 348–364.

Reskin, B. F., & Padavic, I. (1994). *Women and men at work*. Thousand Oaks, CA: Pine Forge Press.

Ridgeway, C. L. (1991). The social construction of status value: Gender and other nominal characteristics. *Social Forces, 70*, 367–386.

Ridgeway, C. L., & Diekema, D. (1992). Are gender differences status differences? In C. L. Ridgeway (Ed.), *Gender, interaction, and inequality* (pp. 157–180). New York: Springer-Verlag.

Rose, L., & Marshall, F. (1996). Meat eating, hominid sociality, and home bases revisited. *Current Anthropology, 37*, 307–338.

Sanday, P. R. (1981). *Female power and male dominance: On the origins of sexual inequality*. New York: Cambridge University Press.

Shelton, B. A. (1992). *Women, men and time: Gender differences in paid work, housework, and leisure.* New York: Greenwood Press.

Silverman, I., & Phillips, K. (1998). The evolutionary psychology of spatial sex differences. In C. Crawford & D. L. Krebs (Eds.), *Handbook of evolutionary psychology: Ideas, issues, and applications* (pp. 595–612). Mahwah, NJ: Erlbaum.

Simon, R. J., & Landis, J. M. (1989). The polls—A report: Women's and men's attitudes about a woman's place and role. *Public Opinion Quarterly, 53,* 265–276.

Singh, D. (1993). Adaptive significance of female physical attractiveness: Role of waist-to-hip ratio. *Journal of Personality and Social Psychology, 65,* 293–307.

Skrypnek, B. J., & Snyder, M. (1982). On the self-perpetuating nature of stereotypes about women and men. *Journal of Experimental Social Psychology, 18,* 277–291.

Sork, V. L. (1997). Quantitative genetics, feminism, and evolutionary theories of gender differences. In P. A. Gowaty (Ed.), *Feminism and evolutionary biology: Boundaries, intersections, and frontiers* (pp. 86–115). New York: Chapman & Hall.

Spence, J. T., & Hahn, E. D. (1997). The Attitudes Toward Women Scale and attitude change in college students. *Psychology of Women Quarterly, 21,* 17–34.

Sprecher, S., Sullivan, Q., & Hatfield, E. (1994). Mate selection preferences: Gender differences examined in a national sample. *Journal of Personality and Social Psychology, 66,* 1074–1080.

Steil, J. M. (1997). *Marital equality: Its relationship to the well-being of husbands and wives.* Thousand Oaks, CA: Sage.

Strier, K. B. (1994). Myth of the typical primate. *Yearbook of Physical Anthropology, 37,* 233–271.

Symons, D. (1979). *The evolution of human sexuality.* New York: Oxford University Press.

Symons, D. (1992). On the use and misuse of Darwinism in the study of human behavior. In J. H. Barkow, L. Cosmides, & J. Tooby (Eds.), *The adapted mind: Evolutionary psychology and the generation of culture* (pp. 137–159). New York: Oxford University Press.

Tassinary, L. G., & Hansen, K. A. (1998). A critical test of the waist-to-hip-ratio hypothesis of female physical attractiveness. *Psychological Science, 9,* 150–155.

Tattersall, I. (1998). *Becoming human: Evolution and human uniqueness.* New York: Harcourt Brace.

Tomaskovic-Devey, D. (1995). Sex composition and gendered earnings inequality: A comparison of job and occupational models. In J. A. Jacobs (Ed.), *Gender inequality at work* (pp. 23–56). Thousand Oaks, CA: Sage.

Tooby, J., & Cosmides, L. (1989). The innate versus the manifest: How universal does universal have to be? *Behavioral and Brain Sciences, 12,* 36–37.

Tooby, J., & Cosmides, L. (1990a). On the universality of human nature and the uniqueness of the individual: The role of genetics and adaptation. *Journal of Personality, 58,* 17–67.

Tooby, J., & Cosmides, L. (1990b). The past explains the present: Emotional adaptations and the structure of ancestral environments. *Ethology and Sociobiology, 11,* 375–424.

Tooby, J., & Cosmides, L. (1992). The psychological foundations of culture. In J. H. Barkow, L. Cosmides, & J. Tooby (Eds.), *The adapted mind: Evolutionary psychology and the generation of culture* (pp. 19–136). New York: Oxford University Press.

Travis, C. B., & Yeager, C. P. (1991). Sexual selection, parental investment, and sexism. *Journal of Social Issues, 47*(3), 117–129.

Trivers, R. (1972). Parental investment and sexual selection. In B. Campbell (Ed.), *Sexual selection and the descent of man: 1871–1971* (pp. 136–179). Chicago: Aldine.

Twenge, J. M. (1997). Attitudes toward women, 1970–1995: A meta-analysis. *Psychology of Women Quarterly, 21,* 35–51.

United Nations Development Programme. (1995). *Human development report 1995.* New York: Oxford University Press.

West, C., & Zimmerman, D. H. (1987). Doing gender. *Gender & Society, 1,* 125–151.

Whyte, M. K. (1978). *The status of women in preindustrial societies.* Princeton, NJ: Princeton University Press.

Wiley, M. G. (1995). Sex category and gender in social psychology. In K. S. Cook, G. A. Fine, & J. S. House (Eds.). *Sociological perspectives on social psychology* (pp. 362–386). Boston: Allyn & Bacon.

Williams, G. C. (1966). *Adaptation and natural selection: A critique of some current evolutionary thought.* Princeton, NJ: Princeton University Press.

Wood, W., Christensen, P. N., Hebl, M. R., & Rothgerber, H. (1997). Conformity to sex-typed norms, affect, and the self-concept. *Journal of Personality and Social Psychology, 73,* 523–535.

Wood, W., & Eagly, A. H. (1999). *Social structure and the origins of sex differences in social behavior.* Manuscript in preparation.

Wood, W., & Karten, S. J. (1986). Sex differences in interaction style as a product of perceived sex differences in competence. *Journal of Personality and Social Psychology, 50,* 341–347.

Exotic Becomes Erotic: A Developmental Theory of Sexual Orientation

Daryl J. Bem

Despite the rapid and impressive gains made by biological approaches to personality in recent years, some observers have found the results disappointing, for a couple of reasons. First, biological approaches to psychological issues too often have become reductionistic—treating the identification of a gene associated with a behavior as a complete explanation, for example, or even concluding that behavior and personality are "nothing but" by-products of a bioneurological system best explained in terms of anatomy and physiology. A second and related criticism of biological approaches is that they generally limit themselves to positing a biological cause on one hand, a psychological result on the other hand, and then showing that the two are connected. As we have seen, the biological cause might be testosterone, cortisol, one's DNA, or the evolutionary history of the species. And the behavioral result might be violence, overreaction to stress, one's degree of extraversion, or the murder of one's wife!

Although such demonstrations of connections between biology and behavior are interesting and useful, they typically leap over all the processes in between—the traditional domain of psychology. For example, what does it feel like to be a high-testosterone prison inmate, and how does that feeling affect your motivations? What is it, exactly, that develops in the DNA of two extraverted twins, and how does that interact with their early experiences to produce the people they eventually become? And what really goes on the mind of a wife murderer? These are the kinds of questions many people—including psychologists—expect psychology to address. But, as we have seen, biological approaches to personality typically neither answer nor ask questions like these.

The real potential for a biological approach to psychology, therefore, is for it to be integrated with psychological and social factors in a way that leads all the way and step by step from genetically based predeterminants, on the one hand, to important behavioral outcomes on the other. Such integration is yet rare, but a superb example is provided by the final selection in this section. The well-known social and personality psychologist Daryl Bem tackles the issue of sexual orientation—what makes a person turn out to be heterosexual or homosexual.

Although this article contains a wide range of interesting commentary on many issues, the heart of the theory is portrayed in a simple fashion in Figure 23.1. Notice how the development of sexual orientation begins with genes, prenatal hormones, and other purely biological variables. These variables produce the basic personality styles, evident in early childhood, called temperaments. These temperaments in turn lead to preferences and aversions to different kinds of activities. Since our gender-polarized society sees rough-and-tumble play as appropriate for boys but more sedate activities as appropriate for girls, the activity preferences of a given child quickly become identified as either appropriate or inappropriate to his or her gender. Depending on which kind of activities one prefers, one associates with either same-sex or opposite-sex peers, leading in turn to a viewing of the nonassociated sex as mysterious or, in Bem's term, "exotic." A basic biological mechanism then engages, which leads stimuli seen as exotic to become endowed with erotic appeal. Finally, one has eroticized either the opposite or same sex, and thus become either heterosexual or homosexual.

Bem's theory may be right or it may be wrong. Although he arrays an impressive amount of evidence in its favor, new theories as complex as this one have a small chance of being correct in their entirety. But the most important aspect of the theory is how it points the way for biological personality psychology in general. Unlike so many other biologically based explanations, Bem's is complete. Rather than leaping over the gap between biology and behavior, it explains how each link in a complex chain leads to an important attribute of the person.

From *Psychological Review, 103*, 320–335, 1996.

* * *

The question "What causes homosexuality?" is both politically suspect and scientifically misconceived. Politically suspect because it is so frequently motivated by an agenda of prevention and cure. Scientifically misconceived because it presumes that heterosexuality is so well understood, so obviously the "natural" evolutionary consequence of reproductive advantage, that only deviations from it are theoretically problematic. Freud himself did not so presume: "[Heterosexuality] is also a problem that needs elucidation and is not a self-evident fact based upon an attraction that is ultimately of a chemical nature" (1905/1962, pp. 11–12).

Accordingly, this article proposes a developmental theory of erotic/romantic attraction that provides the same basic account for both opposite-sex and same-sex desire—and for both men and women. In addition to finding such parsimony politically, scientifically, and aesthetically satisfying, I believe that it can also be sustained by the evidence.

The academic discourse on sexual orientation is currently dominated by the biological essentialists—who can point to a corpus of evidence linking sexual orientation to genes, prenatal hormones, and brain neuroanatomy—and the social constructionists—who can point to a corpus of historical and anthropological evidence showing that the very concept of sexual orientation is a culture-bound notion (De Cecco & Elia, 1993). The personality, clinical, and developmental theorists who once dominated the discourse on this topic have fallen conspicuously silent. Some have probably become closet converts to biology because they cannot point to a coherent corpus of evidence that supports an experience-based account of sexual orientation. This would be understandable; experience-based theories have not fared well empirically in recent years.

The most telling data come from an intensive, large-scale interview study conducted in the San Francisco Bay Area by the Kinsey Institute for Sex Research (Bell, Weinberg, & Hammersmith, 1981a). Using path analysis to test several developmental hypotheses,[1] the investigators compared approximately 1,000 gay men and lesbians with 500 heterosexual men and women. The study (hereinafter, the San Francisco study) yielded virtually no support for current experience-based accounts of sexual orientation. With respect to the classical psychoanalytic account, for example,

> our findings indicate that boys who grow up with dominant mothers and weak fathers have nearly the same chances of becoming homosexual as they would if they grew up in "ideal" family settings. Similarly, the idea that homosexuality reflects a failure to resolve boys' "Oedipal" feelings during childhood receives no support from our study. Our data indicate that the connection between boys' relationships with their mothers and whether they become homosexual or heterosexual is hardly worth mentioning. . . . [Similarly,] we found no evidence that prehomosexual girls are "Oedipal victors"—having apparently usurped their mothers' place in the fathers' affections. . . . [Finally,] respondents' identification with their opposite-sex parents while they were growing up appears to have had no significant impact on whether they turned out to be homosexual or heterosexual. (pp. 184, 189)

More generally, no family variables were strongly implicated in the development of sexual orientation for either men or women.[2]

The data also failed to support any of several possible accounts based on mechanisms of learning or conditioning, including the popular layperson's "seduction" theory of homosexuality. In particular, the kinds of sexual encounters that would presumably serve as the basis for such learning or conditioning typically occurred after, rather than before, the individual experienced the relevant sexual feelings. Gay men and lesbians, for example, had typically not participated in any "advanced" sexual activities with persons of the same sex until about 3 years after they had become aware of same-sex attractions. Moreover, they neither lacked opposite-sex sexual experiences during their childhood and adolescent years nor found them unpleasant.

And finally, there was no support for "labeling" theory, which suggests that individuals might adopt a homosexual orientation as a consequence of being labeled homosexual or sexually different by others as they were growing up. Although gay men and lesbians were, in fact, more likely to report that they had been so labeled, the path analysis revealed the differential labeling to be the result of an emerging homosexual orientation rather than a cause of or even a secondary contributor to it.

But before we all become geneticists, biopsychologists, or neuroanatomists, I believe it's worth another try. In particular, I believe that the theoretical and empirical building blocks for a coherent, experience-based developmental theory of sexual orientation are already scattered about in the literature. What follows, then, is an exercise in synthesis and construction—followed, in turn, by analysis and deconstruction.

Overview of the Theory

The theory proposed here claims to specify the causal antecedents of an individual's erotic or romantic attractions to opposite-sex and same-sex persons. In particular, Figure 23.1 displays the proposed temporal sequence of events that leads to sexual orientation for most men and women in a gender-polarizing culture like ours—a culture that emphasizes the differences between the sexes

---

[1]"Path analysis" is a statistical technique that evaluates numerous correlations in complex data sets to try to disentangle cause and effect.

[2]This is reminiscent of Plomin's conclusion, in the earlier selection, that shared family experience has a small impact on development.

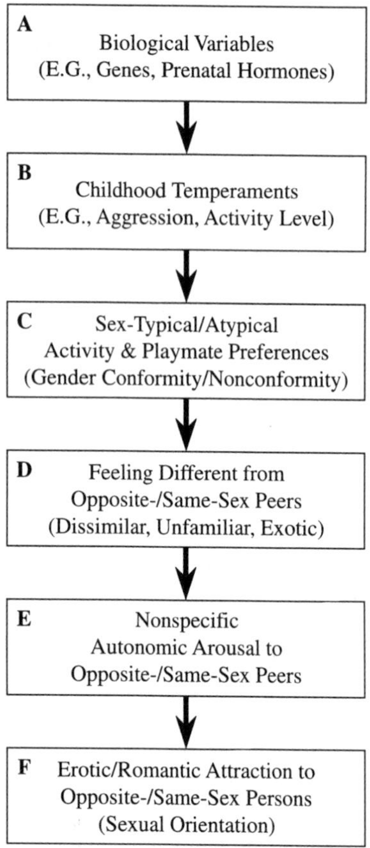

Figure 23.1 The temporal sequence of events leading to sexual orientation for most men and women in a gender-polarizing culture.

by pervasively organizing both the perceptions and realities of communal life around the male-female dichotomy (S. Bem, 1993). The sequence begins at the top of the figure with biological variables (labeled **A**) and ends at the bottom with erotic/romantic attraction (**F**).

A → B. Biological variables such as genes or prenatal hormones do not code for sexual orientation per se but for childhood temperaments, such as aggression or activity level.

B → C. A child's temperaments predispose him or her to enjoy some activities more than others. One child will enjoy rough-and-tumble play and competitive team sports (male-typical activities); another will prefer to socialize quietly or play jacks or hopscotch (female-typical activities). Children will also prefer to play with peers who share their activity preferences; for example, the child who enjoys baseball or football will selectively seek out boys as playmates. Children who prefer sex-typical activities and same-sex playmates are referred to as gender conforming; children who prefer sex-atypical activities and opposite-sex playmates are referred to as gender nonconforming.

C → D. Gender-conforming children will feel different from opposite-sex peers, perceiving them as dissimilar, unfamiliar, and exotic. Similarly, gender-nonconforming children will feel different—even alienated—from same-sex peers, perceiving them as dissimilar, unfamiliar, and exotic.

D → E. These feelings of dissimilarity and unfamiliarity produce heightened autonomic arousal. For the male-typical child, it may be felt as antipathy or contempt in the presence of girls ("girls are yucky"); for the female-typical child, it may be felt as timidity or apprehension in the presence of boys. A particularly clear example is provided by the "sissy" boy who is taunted by male peers for his gender nonconformity and, as a result, is likely to experience the strong autonomic arousal of fear and anger in their presence. Although girls are punished less than boys for gender nonconformity, a "tomboy" girl who is ostracized by her female peers may feel similar, affectively toned arousal in their presence. The theory claims, however, that every child, conforming or nonconforming, experiences heightened, nonspecific autonomic arousal in the presence of peers from whom he or she feels different. In this modal case, the arousal will not necessarily be affectively toned or consciously felt.

E → F. Regardless of the specific source or affective tone of the childhood autonomic arousal, it is transformed in later years into erotic/romantic attraction. Steps **D → E** and **E → F** thus encompass specific psychological mechanisms that transform exotic into erotic (**D → F**). For brevity, the entire sequence outlined in Figure 23.1 will be referred to as the EBE (Exotic Becomes Erotic) theory of sexual orientation.

As noted above, Figure 23.1 does not describe

TABLE 23.1

PERCENTAGE OF RESPONDENTS REPORTING GENDER-NONCONFORMING PREFERENCES AND BEHAVIORS DURING CHILDHOOD

Response	Men		Women	
	Gay (n = 686)	Heterosexual (n = 337)	Lesbian (n = 293)	Heterosexual (n = 140)
Had not enjoyed sex-typical activities	63	10	63	15
Had enjoyed sex-atypical activities	48	11	81	61
Atypical sex-typed (masculinity/femininity)	56	8	80	24
At least half of childhood friends were of the opposite sex	42	13	60	40

Note. Percentages have been calculated from the data given in Bell, Weinberg, and Hammersmith (1981b, pp. 74–75, 77). All chi-square comparisons between gay and heterosexual subgroups are significant at $p < .0001$.

an inevitable, universal path to sexual orientation but the modal path followed by most men and women in a gender-polarizing culture like ours. Individual variations, alternative paths, and cultural influences on sexual orientation are discussed in the final sections of the article.

Evidence for the Theory

Evidence for EBE theory is organized into the following narrative sequence: Gender conformity or nonconformity in childhood is a causal antecedent of sexual orientation in adulthood (**C → F**). This is so because gender conformity or nonconformity causes a child to perceive opposite or same sex peers as exotic (**C → D**), and the exotic class of peers subsequently becomes erotically or romantically attractive to him or her (**D → F**). This occurs because exotic peers produce heightened autonomic arousal (**D → E**) which is subsequently transformed into erotic/romantic attraction (**E → F**). This entire sequence of events can be initiated, among other ways, by biological factors that influence a child's temperaments (**A → B**), which, in turn, influence his or her preferences for gender-conforming or gender-nonconforming activities and peers (**B → C**).

GENDER CONFORMITY OR NONCONFORMITY IN CHILDHOOD IS A CAUSAL ANTECEDENT OF SEXUAL ORIENTATION (C → F) In a review of sex-role socialization in 1980, Serbin asserted that "there is no evidence that highly sex-typed children are less likely to become homosexual than children showing less extreme sex-role conformity" (p. 85).

Well, there is now. In the San Francisco study, childhood gender conformity or nonconformity was not only the strongest but the only significant childhood predictor of later sexual orientation for both men and women (Bell et al., 1981a). As Table 23.1 shows, the effects were large and significant. For example, gay men were significantly more likely than heterosexual men to report that as children they had not enjoyed boys' activities (e.g., baseball and football), had enjoyed girls' activities (e.g., hopscotch, playing house, and jacks), and had been nonmasculine. These were the three variables that defined gender nonconformity in the study. Additionally, gay men were more likely than heterosexual men to have had girls as childhood friends. The corresponding comparisons between lesbian and heterosexual women were also large and significant. Moreover, the path analyses implied that gender conformity or nonconformity in childhood was a causal antecedent of later sexual orientation for both men and women—with the usual caveat that even path analysis cannot "prove" causality.

It is also clear from the table that relatively more women than men had enjoyed sex-atypical activities and had opposite-sex friends during childhood. (In fact, more heterosexual women than gay men had enjoyed boys' activities as children—61% versus 37%, respectively.) As I suggest later, this might account, in part, for differences between men and women in how their sexual orientations are distributed in our society.

The San Francisco study does not stand alone. A meta-analysis of 48 studies with sample sizes ranging from 34 to 8,751 confirmed that gay men and lesbians were more likely to recall gender-nonconforming behaviors and interests in childhood than were heterosexual men and women (Bailey & Zucker, 1995). The differences were large and significant for both men and women, ranging (in units of standard deviation) from 0.5 to 2.1 across studies, with means of 1.31 and 0.96 for men and women, respectively. As the authors noted, "these are among the largest effect sizes ever reported in the realm of sex-dimorphic behaviors" (p. 49).[3]

Prospective studies have come to the same conclusion. The largest of these involved a sample of 66 gender-nonconforming and 56 gender-conforming boys with a mean age of 7.1 years (Green, 1987). The researchers were able to assess about two thirds of each group in late adolescence or early adulthood, finding that about 75% of the previously gender-nonconforming boys were either bisexual or homosexual compared with only one (4%) of the gender-conforming boys. In six other prospective studies, 63% of gender-nonconforming boys whose sexual orientations could be ascertained in late adolescence or adulthood had homosexual orientations (Zucker, 1990). Unfortunately, there are no prospective studies of gender-nonconforming girls.

This body of data has led one researcher in the field to assert that the link between childhood gender nonconformity and an adult homosexual orientation "may be the most consistent, well-documented, and significant finding in the entire field of sexual-orientation research and perhaps in all of human psychology" (Hamer & Copeland, 1994, p. 166). That may be a bit hyperbolic—Hamer is a molecular geneticist, not a psychologist—but it is difficult to think of other individual differences (besides IQ or sex itself) that so reliably and so strongly predict socially significant outcomes across the life span, and for both sexes, too. Surely it must be true.

GENDER CONFORMITY AND NONCONFORMITY PRODUCE FEELINGS OF BEING DIFFERENT FROM OPPOSITE AND SAME-SEX PEERS, RESPECTIVELY (C → D) EBE theory proposes that gender-conforming children will come to feel different from their opposite-sex peers and gender-nonconforming children will come to feel different from their same-sex peers. To my knowledge, no researcher has ever asked children or adults whether they feel different from opposite-sex peers, probably because they expect the universal answer to be yes. The San Francisco researchers, however, did ask respondents whether they felt different from same-sex peers in childhood. They found that 71% of gay men and 70% of lesbian women recalled having felt different from same-sex children during the grade-school years, compared with 38% and 51% of heterosexual men and women, respectively ($p < .0005$ for both gay/heterosexual comparisons).

When asked in what way they felt different, gay men were most likely to say that they did not like sports; lesbians were most likely to say that they were more interested in sports or were more masculine than other girls. In contrast, the hetero-

[3]In other words, these differences are as large or larger than sex differences in general usually are.

sexual men and women who had felt different from their same-sex peers in childhood typically cited differences unrelated to gender. Heterosexual men tended to cite such reasons as being poorer, more intelligent, or more introverted. Heterosexual women frequently cited differences in physical appearance.

Finally, the data showed that the gender-nonconforming child's sense of being different from same-sex peers is not a fleeting early experience but a protracted and sustained feeling throughout childhood and adolescence. For example, in the path model for men, gender nonconformity in childhood was also a significant predictor of feeling different for gender reasons during adolescence (which was, in turn, a significant predictor of a homosexual orientation). Similarly, the statistically significant difference between the lesbians and heterosexual women in feeling different from same-sex peers during childhood remained significant during adolescence. This is, I believe, why sexual orientation displays such strong temporal stability across the life course for most individuals.

Exotic Becomes Erotic (D → F) The heart of EBE theory is the proposition that individuals become erotically or romantically attracted to those who were dissimilar or unfamiliar to them in childhood. We have already seen some evidence for this in Table 23.1: Those who played more with girls in childhood, gay men and heterosexual women, preferred men as sexual/romantic partners in later years; those who played more with boys in childhood, lesbian women and heterosexual men, preferred women as sexual/romantic partners in later years. As we shall now see, however, the links between similarity and erotic/romantic attraction are complex.

Similarity and complementarity. One of the most widely accepted conclusions in social psychology, cited in virtually every textbook, is that similarity promotes interpersonal attraction and that complementarity ("opposites attract") does not.

For example, the vast majority of married couples in the United States are of the same race and religion, and most are significantly similar in age, socioeconomic class, educational level, intelligence, height, eye color, and even physical attractiveness (Feingold, 1988; Murstein, 1972; Rubin, 1973; Silverman, 1971). In one study, dating couples who were the most similar were the most likely to be together a year later (Hill, Rubin, & Peplau, 1976). In a longitudinal study of 135 married couples, spouses with similar personalities reported more closeness, friendliness, shared enjoyment in daily activities, marital satisfaction, and less marital conflict than less similar couples (Caspi & Herbener, 1990). In contrast, attempts to identify complementarities that promote or sustain intimate relationships have not been very successful (Levinger, Senn, & Jorgensen, 1970; Strong et al., 1988). Marital adjustment among couples married for up to 5 years was found to depend more on similarity than on complementarity (Meyer & Pepper, 1977).

But there is an obvious exception: sex. Most people choose members of the opposite sex to be their romantic and sexual partners. It is an indication of how unthinkingly heterosexuality is taken for granted that authors of articles and textbooks never seem to notice this quintessential complementarity and its challenge to the conclusion that similarity produces attraction. They certainly don't pause to ponder why we are not all gay or lesbian.

The key to resolving this apparent paradox is also a staple of textbooks: the distinction between liking and loving or between companionate and passionate love (Berscheid & Walster, 1974; Brehm, 1992). The correlation among dating or engaged couples between liking their partners and loving them is only .56 for men and .36 for women (Rubin, 1973). Both fiction and real life provide numerous examples of erotic attraction between two incompatible people who may not even like each other. Collectively, these observations suggest that similarity may promote friendship, compatibility, and companionate love, but it is dissimilarity that sparks erotic/romantic attraction and passionate love.

This is the resolution proposed by both Tripp (1975) and Bell (1982), the senior author of the San Francisco study:

> a necessary ingredient for romantic attachment is one's perception of the loved one as essentially different from oneself in terms of gender-related attributes. According to this view it would be argued that, among homosexuals and heterosexuals alike, persons perceived as essentially *different* from ourselves become the chief candidates for our early romantic and, later, erotic investments. Only a superficial view of the matter would maintain that *heterogamy*, as it has been called, operates only among heterosexuals where anatomical differences make the principle, "opposites attract," most obvious. Among both groups we find romantic and sexual feelings aroused by others perceived to be different from ourselves, unfamiliar in manner, attitude, and interests, and whose differences offer the possibility of a relationship based upon psychological (not necessarily genital) complementarity. On the other side of the coin is the principle of *homogamy* in which perceived similarity and mutual identification and familiarity makes for friendship as opposed to the romantic . . . state. (Bell, 1982, p. 2)

But this account fails to resolve the paradox because it errs in the opposite direction, failing to account for the previously cited evidence that, except for sex itself, it is similarity and not complementarity that sustains the majority of successful heterosexual relationships. Similarly, for every gay or lesbian relationship that conforms to the "butch-femme" stereotype of the popular imagination, there appear to be many more in which the partners are strikingly similar to each other in both psychological and physical attributes—including sex. Bell's account resolves the paradox only if one is willing to accept the implausible implication that all those happy, similar partners must be devoid of erotic enthusiasm for each other.

Like the accounts of Tripp and Bell, EBE theory also proposes that dissimilarity promotes erotic/romantic attraction, but it locates the animating dissimilarity in childhood. Consider, for example, a gender-nonconforming boy whose emerging homoeroticism happens to crystallize around the muscular athlete or leather-jacketed motorcyclist. As he moves into adolescence and adulthood, he may deliberately begin to acquire the attributes and trappings of his eroticized hypermasculine ideal—working out at the gym, buying a leather jacket, getting a body tattoo, and so forth. This acquired "macho" image is not only self-satisfying but is also attractive to other gay men who have eroticized this same idealized image. Two such men will thus be erotically attracted to each other, and their striking similarities, including their shared eroticism, will have been produced by their shared childhood dissimilarities from highly masculine boys.

EBE theory thus proposes that once the dissimilarities of childhood have laid the groundwork for a sustained sexual orientation, the noncriterial attributes of one's preferred partners within the eroticized class can range from extremely similar to extremely dissimilar. More generally, the theory proposes that the protracted period of feeling different from same- or opposite-sex peers during childhood and adolescence produces a stable sexual orientation for most individuals but that within that orientation there can be wide ranging—and changing—idiosyncratic preferences for particular partners or kinds of partners.

Familiarity and unfamiliarity. Like similarity, familiarity is a major antecedent of liking. In fact, similarity probably promotes liking precisely because it increases familiarity: Social norms, situational circumstances, and mutual interests conspire to bring people together who are similar to one another, thereby increasing their mutual familiarity. When college roommates were systematically paired for similarity or dissimilarity in Newcomb's (1961) ambitious 2-year study of the acquaintance process, familiarity turned out to be a stronger facilitator of liking than similarity.

The "familiarity-breeds-liking" effect has been confirmed in so many contexts that it is now considered to be a general psychological principle. For example, rats repeatedly exposed to compositions by Mozart or Schönberg have shown an enhanced preference for the composer they heard, and humans repeatedly exposed to nonsense syllables, Chinese characters, or real people have come to prefer those they saw most often (Harrison, 1977).

But like childhood similarity, childhood familiarity does not produce erotic or romantic attraction; on the contrary, it appears to be antithetical to it. This was observed over a century ago by Westermarck (1891), who noted that two individuals who spent their childhood years together did not find each other sexually attractive even when there were strong social pressures favoring a bond between them. For example, he reported problematic sexual relations in arranged marriages in which the couple was betrothed in childhood and the girl was taken in by the future husband's family and treated like one of the siblings; similar findings have emerged from more recent studies of arranged marriages in Taiwan (cited in Bateson, 1978a).

A contemporary example is provided by children on Israeli kibbutzim, who are raised communally with age-mates in mixed-sex groups and exposed to one another constantly during their entire childhood. Sex play is not discouraged and is quite intensive during early childhood. After childhood, there is no formal or informal pressure or sanction against heterosexual activity within the peer group from educators, parents, or members of the peer group itself. Yet despite all this, there is a virtual absence of erotic attraction between peer group members in adolescence or adulthood (Bettelheim, 1969; Rabin, 1965; Shepher, 1971; Spiro, 1958; Talmon, 1964). A review of nearly 3,000 marriages contracted by second-generation adults in all Israeli kibbutzim revealed that there was not a single case of an intrapeer group marriage (Shepher, 1971).

* * *

The Sambian culture in New Guinea illustrates the phenomenon in a homosexual context. As described by Herdt in several publications (1981, 1984, 1987, 1990), Sambian males believe that boys cannot attain manhood without ingesting semen from older males. At age 7 years, Sambian boys are removed from the family household and initiated into secret male rituals, including ritualized homosexuality. For the next several years, they live in the men's clubhouse and regularly fellate older male adolescents. When they reach sexual maturity, they reverse roles and are fellated by younger initiates. During this entire time, they have no sexual contact with girls or women. And yet, when it comes time to marry and father children in their late teens or early twenties, all but a tiny minority of Sambian males become preferentially and exclusively heterosexual. Although Sambian boys enjoy their homosexual activities, the context of close familiarity in which it occurs either extinguishes or prevents the development of strongly charged homoerotic feelings.

During the years that a Sambian boy is participating in homosexual activities with his male peers, he is taught a misogynist ideology that portrays women as dangerous and exotic creatures—almost a different species. According to EBE theory, this should enhance their erotic attractiveness for him. More generally, EBE theory proposes that heterosexuality is the modal outcome across time and culture because virtually all human societies polarize the sexes to some extent, setting up a sex-based division of labor and power, emphasizing or exaggerating sex differences, and, in general, superimposing the male-female dichotomy on virtually every aspect of communal life. These gender-polarizing practices ensure that most boys and girls will grow up seeing the other sex as dissimilar, unfamiliar, and exotic—and, hence, erotic. Thus, the theory provides a culturally based alternative to the assumption that heterosexuality must necessarily be coded in the genes. I return to this point later.

Finally, the assertion that exotic becomes erotic should be amended to exotic—but not too exotic—becomes erotic (cf. Tripp, 1987). Thus, an erotic or romantic preference for partners of a different sex, race, or ethnicity is relatively common, but a preference for lying with the beasts in the field is not. This phenomenon appears to be a special case of the well-established motivational principle that there is an optimal, nonzero level of stimulus novelty and a correspondingly optimal nonzero level of internal arousal that an organism will seek to attain or maintain (Mook, 1987).

How Does Exotic Become Erotic? (D → E → F) In Plato's *Symposium*, Aristophanes explains sexual attraction by recounting the early history of human beings. Originally, we were all eight-limbed creatures with two faces and two sets of genitals. Males had two sets of male genitals, females had two sets of female genitals, and androgynes had one set of each kind. As punishment for being overly ambitious, Zeus had all humans cut in half. But because the two halves of each former individual clung to each other in such a desperate attempt to reunite, Zeus took pity on them and invented sexual intercourse so that they might at least reunite temporarily. Sexual attraction thus reflects an attempt to complete one's original self, and heterosexual attraction is what characterizes the descendents of the androgynes.

It is a durable myth. Both Bell (1982) and Tripp (1987) propose that we are erotically attracted to people who are different from us because we are embarked on a "quest for androgyny" (Bell); we seek to complete ourselves by "importing" gender-related attributes that we perceive ourselves as lacking (Tripp). As noted earlier, I do not believe this accurately characterizes the data; but even if it did, it would constitute only a description of them, not an explanation. There may not be much evidence for Aristophanes' historical account, but epistemologically at least, it is an explanation.

Because I prefer mechanism to metaphor, EBE theory is unabashedly reductionistic. As already discussed, it proposes that exotic becomes erotic because feelings of dissimilarity and unfamiliarity in childhood produce heightened nonspecific autonomic arousal (**D → E**) which is subsequently transformed into erotic/romantic attraction (**E → F**). To my knowledge, there is no direct evidence for the first step in this sequence beyond the well-documented observation that novelty and unfamiliarity produce heightened arousal (Mook, 1987); filling in this empirical gap in EBE theory must await future research. In contrast, there are at least three mechanisms that can potentially effect the second step, transforming generalized arousal into erotic/romantic attraction: the extrinsic arousal effect, the opponent process, and imprinting.[4]

The extrinsic arousal effect. In his 1st-century Roman handbook, *The Art of Love*, Ovid advised any man who was interested in sexual seduction to take the woman in whom he was interested to a gladiatorial tournament, where she would more easily be aroused to passion. He did not say why this should be so, however, and it was not until 1887 that an elaboration appeared in the literature:

> Love can only be excited by strong and vivid emotion, and it is almost immaterial whether these emotions are agreeable or disagreeable. The Cid wooed the proud heart of Donna Ximene, whose father he had slain, by shooting one after another of her pet pigeons. (Horwicz, quoted in Finck, 1887, p. 240)

A contemporary explanation of this effect was introduced by Walster (1971; Berscheid & Walster, 1974), who suggested that it constituted a special case of Schachter and Singer's (1962) two-factor theory of emotion. That theory states that the physiological arousal of our autonomic nervous system provides the cues that we are feeling emotional but that the more subtle judgment of which emotion we are feeling often depends on our cognitive appraisal of the surrounding circumstances. According to Walster, then, the experience of passionate love or erotic/romantic attraction results from the conjunction of physiological arousal and the cognitive causal attribution (or misattribution) that the arousal has been elicited by the potential lover.

---

[4]Bem's discussion of "imprinting" and the "opponent process" are not included in this excerpt.

There is now extensive experimental evidence that an individual who has been physiologically aroused will show heightened sexual responsiveness to an appropriate target stimulus. In one set of studies, male participants were physiologically aroused by running in place, by hearing an audiotape of a comedy routine, or by hearing an audiotape of a grisly killing (White, Fishbein, & Rutstein, 1981). They then viewed a taped interview with a woman who was either physically attractive or physically unattractive. Finally, they rated the woman on several dimensions, including her attractiveness, her sexiness, and the degree to which they would be interested in dating her and kissing her. The results showed that no matter how the arousal had been elicited, participants were more erotically responsive to the attractive woman and less erotically responsive to the unattractive woman than were control participants who had not been aroused. In other words, the arousal intensified both positive or negative reactions to the woman, depending on which was cognitively appropriate.

This extrinsic arousal effect (my term) is not limited to the individual's cognitive appraisal of his or her emotional state. In two studies, men or women watched a sequence of two videotapes. The first portrayed either an anxiety-inducing or non-anxiety-inducing scene; the second videotape portrayed a nude heterosexual couple engaging in sexual foreplay. Preexposure to the anxiety-inducing scene produced greater penile tumescence in men and greater vaginal blood volume increases in women in response to the erotic scene than did preexposure to the non-anxiety-inducing scene (Hoon, Wincze, & Hoon, 1977; Wolchik et al., 1980).

In addition to the misattribution explanation, several other explanations for the extrinsic arousal effect have been proposed, but experimental attempts to determine which explanation is the most valid have produced mixed results and the dispute is not yet settled (Allen, Kenrick, Linder, & McCall, 1989; Kenrick & Cialdini, 1977; McClanahan, Gold, Lenney, Ryckman, & Kulberg, 1990; White & Kight, 1984; Zillmann, 1983). For present purposes, however, it doesn't matter. It is sufficient to know that autonomic arousal, regardless of its source or affective tone, can subsequently be experienced cognitively, emotionally, and physiologically as erotic/romantic attraction. At that point, it *is* erotic/romantic attraction.

The pertinent question, then, is whether this effect can account for the link between autonomic arousal in childhood and erotic/romantic attraction later in life. In one respect, the experiments may actually underestimate the strength and reliability of the effect in real life. In the experiments, the arousal is deliberately elicited by a source extrinsic to the intended target, and there is disagreement over whether the effect even occurs when participants are aware of that fact (Allen et al., 1989; Cantor, Zillmann, & Bryant, 1975; McClanahan et al., 1990; White & Kight, 1984). But in the real-life scenario envisioned by EBE theory, the autonomic arousal is genuinely elicited by the class of individuals to which the erotic/romantic attraction develops. The exotic arousal and the erotic arousal are thus likely to be phenomenologically indistinguishable.

* * *

The Biological Connection: (A → F) Versus (A → B) In recent years, researchers, the mass media, and segments of the lesbian/gay/bisexual community have rushed to embrace the thesis that a homosexual orientation is coded in the genes or determined by prenatal hormones and brain neuroanatomy. Even the authors of the San Francisco study, whose findings disconfirm most experience-based theories of sexual orientation, seem ready to concede the ball game to biology. In contrast, EBE theory proposes that biological factors influence sexual orientation only indirectly, by intervening earlier in the chain of events to determine a child's temperaments and subsequent activity preferences. Accordingly, my persuasive task in this section is to argue that any nonartifactual correlation between a biological factor and sexual orientation is more plausibly attributed to its influence in early childhood than to a direct link with sexual orientation.

Genes. Recent studies have provided some evidence for a correlation between an individual's genotype and his or her sexual orientation. For example, in a sample of 115 gay men who had male twins, 52% of monozygotic twin brothers were also gay compared with only 22% of dizygotic twin brothers and 11% of gay men's adoptive brothers (Bailey & Pillard, 1991). In a comparable sample of 115 lesbians, 48% of monozygotic twin sisters were also lesbian compared with only 16% of dizygotic twin sisters and 6% of lesbian women's adoptive sisters (Bailey, Pillard, Neale, & Agyei, 1993). A subsequent study of nearly 5,000 twins who had been systematically drawn from a twin registry confirmed the significant heritability of sexual orientation for men but not for women (Bailey & Martin, 1995). And finally, a pedigree and linkage analysis of 114 families of gay men and a DNA linkage analysis of 40 families in which there were two gay brothers suggested a correlation between a homosexual orientation and the inheritance of genetic markers on the X chromosome (Hamer & Copeland, 1994; Hamer, Hu, Magnuson, Hu, & Pattatucci, 1993).[5]

But these same studies have also provided evidence for the link proposed by EBE theory between an individual's genotype and his or her childhood gender nonconformity, even when sexual orientation is held constant. For example, in the 1991 twin study of gay men, childhood gender nonconformity was assessed by a composite of three scales that have been shown to discriminate between gay and heterosexual men: childhood aggressiveness, interest in sports, and effeminacy. Across twin pairs in which both brothers were gay ("concordant" pairs), the correlation on gender nonconformity for monozygotic twins was as high as the reliability of the scale would permit, .76 ($p < .0001$), compared with a correlation of only .43 for concordant dizygotic twins, implying significant heritability (Bailey & Pillard, 1991). In the family pedigree study of gay men, pairs of gay brothers who were concordant for the genetic markers on the X chromosome were also more similar on gender nonconformity than were genetically discordant pairs of gay brothers (Hamer & Copeland, 1994). Finally, childhood gender nonconformity was significantly heritable for both men and women in the large twin registry study, even though sexual orientation itself was not heritable for the women (Bailey & Martin, 1995).

These studies are thus consistent with the link specified by EBE theory between the genotype and gender nonconformity (**A** → **C**). The theory further specifies that this link is composed of two parts, a link between the genotype and childhood temperaments (**A** → **B**) and a link between those temperaments and gender nonconformity (**B** → **C**). This implies that the mediating temperaments should possess three characteristics: First, they should be plausibly related to those play activities that define gender conformity and nonconformity. Second, because they manifest themselves in sex-typed preferences, they should show sex differences. And third, because they are hypothesized to derive from the genotype, they should have significant heritabilities.

One likely candidate is aggression and its benign cousin, rough-and-tumble play. As noted above, gay men score lower than heterosexual men on a measure of childhood aggression (Blanchard, McConkey, Roper, & Steiner, 1983), and parents of gender-nonconforming boys specifically rate them as having less interest in rough-and-tumble play than do parents of gender-conforming boys (Green, 1976). Second, the sex difference in aggression during childhood is about half a standard deviation, one of the largest psychological sex differences known (Hyde, 1984). Rough-and-tumble play in particular is more common in boys than in girls (DiPietro, 1981; Fry, 1990; Moller, Hymel, & Rubin, 1992). And third, individual differences in aggression have a large heritable component (Rushton, Fulker, Neale, Nias, & Eysenck, 1986).

Another likely candidate is activity level, con-

[5]This last finding is currently in dispute, and an independent attempt to replicate it has failed (Rice, Anderson, Risch, & Ebers, 1995).—Author

sidered to be one of the basic childhood temperaments (Buss & Plomin, 1975, 1984). Like aggression, differences in activity level would also seem to characterize the differences between male-typical and female-typical play activities in childhood, and gender-nonconforming boys and girls are lower and higher on activity level, respectively, than are control children of the same sex (Bates, Bentler, & Thompson, 1973, 1979; Zucker & Green, 1993). Second, the sex difference in activity level is as large as it is for aggression. A meta-analysis of 127 studies found boys to be about half a standard deviation more active than girls. Even before birth, boys in utero are about one-third of a standard deviation more active than girls (Eaton & Enns, 1986). And third, individual differences in activity level have a large heritable component (Plomin, 1986).

In sum, existing data are consistent with both a direct path between the genotype and sexual orientation and the EBE path which channels genetic influence through the child's temperaments and subsequent activity preferences. So why should one prefer the EBE account?

The missing theory for the direct path. The EBE account may be wrong, but I submit that a competing theoretical rationale for a direct path between the genotype and sexual orientation has not even been clearly articulated, let alone established. At first glance, the theoretical rationale would appear to be nothing less than the powerful and elegant theory of evolution. The belief that sexual orientation is coded in the genes would appear to be just the general case of the implicit assumption, mentioned in the introduction, that heterosexuality is the obvious, "natural" evolutionary consequence of reproductive advantage.

But if that is true, then a homosexual orientation is an evolutionary anomaly that requires further theoretical explication. How do lesbians and gay men manage to pass on their gene pool to successive generations? Several hypothetical scenarios have been offered (for a review, see Savin-Williams, 1987). One is that social institutions such as universal marriage can ensure that lesbians and gay men will have enough children to sustain a "homosexual" gene pool (Weinrich, 1987). Another is that the genes for homosexuality are linked to, or piggyback on, other genes that themselves carry reproductive advantage, such as genes for intelligence or dominance (Kirsch & Rodman, 1982; Weinrich, 1978). A third, based on kin selection, speculates that homosexual individuals may help nurture a sufficient number of their kin (e.g., nieces and nephews) to reproductive maturity to ensure that their genes get passed along to successive generations (Weinrich, 1978; Wilson, 1975, 1978).

Although these speculations have been faulted on theoretical, metatheoretical, and empirical grounds (Futuyma & Risch, 1983/84), a more basic problem with such arguments is their circularity. As Bleier has noted about similar accounts,

> this logic makes a *premise* of the genetic basis of behaviors, then cites a certain animal or human behavior, constructs a speculative story to explain how the behavior (*if* it were genetically based) could have served or could serve to maximize the reproductive success of the individual, and this *conjecture* then becomes evidence for the *premise* that the behavior was genetically determined. (1984, p. 17)

When one does attempt to deconstruct the evolutionary explanation for sexual orientation, homosexual *or* heterosexual, some problematic assumptions become explicit. For example, the belief that sexual orientation is coded in the genes embodies the unacknowledged assumption that knowledge of the distinction between male and female must also be hardwired into the human species, that sex is a natural category of human perception. After all, we cannot be erotically attracted to a class of persons unless and until we can discriminate exemplars from nonexemplars of that class.

Given what psychology has learned about human language and cognition in recent decades, the notion that humans have innate knowledge of the male-female distinction is not quite so inconceivable as it once was. An explicit version of this notion is embodied in the Jungian belief that an animus-anima archetype is part of our collective unconscious. It could also be argued that functional, if not cognitive, knowledge of the male-female distinction is embodied in innate responses to pheromones or other sensory cues, as it is for several other species.

As it happens, I find all these possibilities implausible, but that is not the point. Rather, it is that those who argue for the direct heritability of sexual orientation should be made cognizant of such assumptions and required to shoulder the burden of proof for them. More generally, any genetic argument, including a sociobiological one, must spell out the developmental pathway by which genotypes are transformed into phenotypes (Bronfenbrenner & Ceci, 1994). This is precisely what EBE theory attempts to do and what the competing claim for a direct path between genes and sexual orientation fails to do. It is not that an argument for a direct path has been made and found wanting, but that it has not yet been made.

I am certainly willing to concede that heterosexual behavior is reproductively advantageous, but it does not follow that it must therefore be sustained through genetic transmission. As noted earlier, EBE theory implies that heterosexuality is the modal outcome across time and culture because virtually every human society ensures that most boys and girls will grow up seeing the other sex as exotic and, hence, erotic.

The more general point is that as long as the environment supports or promotes a reproductively successful behavior sufficiently often, it will not necessarily get programmed into the genes. For example, it is presumably reproductively advantageous for ducks to mate with other ducks, but as long as most baby ducklings encounter other ducks before they encounter an ethologist, evolution can simply implant the imprinting process itself into the species rather than the specific content of what, reproductively speaking, needs to be imprinted. Analogously, because most cultures ensure that the two sexes will see each other as exotic, it would be sufficient for evolution to implant exotic-becomes-erotic processes into our species rather than heterosexuality per se. In fact, as noted earlier, an exotic-becomes-erotic mechanism is actually a component of sexual imprinting. If ducks, who are genetically free to mate with any moving object, have not perished from the earth, then neither shall we.

Prenatal hormones. One of the oldest hypotheses about sexual orientation is that gay men have too little testosterone and lesbians have too much. When the data failed to support this hypothesis (for reviews, see Gartrell, 1982, and Meyer-Bahlburg, 1984), attention turned from adult hormonal status to prenatal hormonal status. Reasoning from research on rats in which the experimental manipulation of prenatal androgen levels can "masculinize" or "feminize" the brain and produce sex-atypical mating postures and mounting responses, some researchers hypothesized that human males who are exposed prenatally to substantially lower than average amounts of testosterone and human females who are exposed to substantially higher than average amounts of testosterone will be predisposed toward a homosexual orientation in adult life (Ellis & Ames, 1987).

One body of data advanced in support of this hypothesis comes from interviews with women who have congenital adrenal hyperplasia (CAH), a chronic endocrine disorder that exposes them to abnormally high levels of androgen during the prenatal period, levels comparable to those received by normal male fetuses during gestation. Most of these women were born with virilized genitalia, which were surgically corrected soon after birth, and placed on cortisol medication to prevent further anatomical virilization. In three studies, CAH women have now reported more bisexual or homosexual responsiveness than control women (Dittmann et al., 1990a; Money, Schwartz, & Lewis, 1984; Zucker et al., 1992).

But a number of factors suggest that this link from prenatal hormones to sexual orientation is better explained by their effects on childhood temperaments and activity preferences. For example, both boys and girls who were exposed to high levels of androgenizing progestins during gestation have shown increased aggression later in childhood (Reinisch, 1981), and girls with CAH have shown stronger preferences for male-typical activities and male playmates in childhood than control girls (Berenbaum & Hines, 1992; Berenbaum & Snyder, 1995; Dittmann et al., 1990b; Money & Ehrhardt, 1972).

It is also possible that the correlation itself is artifactual, having nothing to do with prenatal hormonal exposure—let alone "masculinization" of the brain. The contemporaneous hormonal status of CAH girls could be producing some of these childhood effects. It is even conceivable that the cortisol medication could be increasing their activity level, thereby promoting their preference for male-typical activities (Quadagno, Briscoe, & Quadagno, 1977).

But from the perspective of EBE theory, the major reason for expecting CAH girls to be disproportionately homoerotic in adulthood is that they are overwhelmingly likely to feel different from other girls. Not only are they gender nonconforming in their play activities and peer preferences, as most lesbians are during the childhood years, but the salience of their CAH status itself aids and abets their perception of being different from other girls on gender-relevant dimensions. For example, they know about their virilized genitalia and they may be concerned that they will not be able to conceive and bear children when they grow up, one of the frequent complications of the CAH disorder. According to EBE theory, these are not girls who need masculinized brains to make them homoerotic.

A more critical test of the direct link between prenatal hormones and sexual orientation would seem to require a prenatal hormonal condition that is correlated with an adult homosexual orientation but uncorrelated with any of these childhood effects. Meyer-Bahlburg et al. (1995) have hypothesized that abnormally high levels of prenatal estrogens might produce such an outcome in women by masculinizing their brains.

Although the theoretical reasoning behind this hypothesis has been questioned (Byne & Parsons, 1993), Meyer-Bahlburg et al. (1995) cited some supporting evidence from women whose mothers had taken diethylstilbestrol (DES), a synthetic estrogen that was used to maintain high-risk pregnancies until it was banned in 1971. Three samples of such women have now been interviewed and rated on several Kinsey-like scales for heterosexual and homosexual responsiveness. According to the investigators, "more DES-exposed women than controls were rated as bisexual or homosexual . . ." (p. 12). Because DES does not produce any visible anomalies during childhood and evidence for childhood gender nonconformity among DES-exposed women was weak, this outcome would seem to favor the argument for a direct link between prenatal hormones and sexual orientation over the EBE account.

But the evidence for a bisexual or homosexual orientation among the DES-exposed women was also very weak. As Meyer-Bahlburg et al. (1995) themselves noted, "the majority of DES-exposed women in our study were exclusively or nearly exclusively heterosexual, in spite of their prenatal DES exposure" (p. 20). In fact, of 97 DES-exposed women interviewed, only 4 were rated as having a predominantly homosexual orientation, and not a single woman was rated as having an exclusively homosexual orientation. I think the jury is still out on the link between prenatal estrogens and sexual orientation.

* * *

Neuroanatomical correlates of sexual orientation. Even the general public now knows that there are neuroanatomical differences between the brains of gay men and those of heterosexual men and that some of these correspond to differences between the brains of women and men (Allen & Gorski, 1992; LeVay, 1991, 1993; Swaab & Hofman, 1990). Gay men also perform less well than heterosexual men on some cognitive, motor, and spatial tasks on which women perform less well than men (e.g., Gladue, Beatty, Larson, & Staton, 1990; McCormick & Witelson, 1991). (There are no comparable studies of lesbian women.)

But such differences are also consistent with the EBE account. Any biological factor that correlates with one or more of the intervening processes proposed by EBE theory could also emerge as a correlate of sexual orientation. For example, any neuroanatomical feature of the brain that correlates with childhood aggression or activity level could also emerge as a difference between gay men and heterosexual men, between women and men, and between heterosexual women and lesbians. Even if EBE theory turns out to be wrong, the more general point, that a mediating personality variable could account for observed correlations between biological variables and sexual orientation, still holds.

Like all well-bred scientists, biologically oriented researchers in the field of sexual orientation dutifully murmur the mandatory mantra that correlation is not cause. But the reductive temptation of biological causation is so seductive that the caveat cannot possibly compete with the excitement of discovering yet another link between the anatomy of our brains and the anatomy of our lovers' genitalia. Unfortunately, the caveat vanishes completely as word of the latest discovery moves from *Science* to *Newsweek.* The public can be forgiven for believing that research is but one government grant away from pinpointing the penis preference gene.

INDIVIDUAL VARIATIONS AND ALTERNATIVE PATHS As noted earlier, Figure 23.1 is not intended to describe an inevitable, universal path to sexual orientation but only the modal path followed by most men and women in a gender-polarizing culture like ours. Individual variations can arise in several ways. First, different individuals might enter the EBE path at different points in the sequence. For example, a child might come to feel different from same-sex peers not because of a temperamentally induced preference for gender-nonconforming activities but because of an atypical lack of contact with same-sex peers, a physical disability, or an illness (e.g., the CAH girls). Similarly, I noted earlier that the nonmasculine lesbians in the San Francisco study were not significantly gender nonconforming in childhood. But they were more likely than heterosexual women to have mostly male friends in grade school, and, consistent with the subsequent steps in the EBE path, this was the strongest predictor for these women of homosexual involvements in adolescence and a homosexual orientation in adulthood.

In general, EBE theory predicts that the effect of any childhood variable on an individual's sexual orientation depends on whether it prompts him or her to feel more similar to or more different from same-sex or opposite-sex peers. For example, it has recently been reported that a gay man is likely to have more older brothers than a heterosexual man (Blanchard & Bogaert, 1996). This could come about, in part, if having gender-conforming older brothers especially enhances a gender-nonconforming boy's sense of being different from other boys.

Individual variations can also arise from differences in how individuals interpret the "exotic" arousal emerging from the childhood years, an interpretation that is inevitably guided by social norms and expectations. For example, girls might be more socially primed to interpret the arousal as romantic attraction whereas boys might be more primed to interpret it as sexual arousal. Certainly most individuals in our culture are primed to anticipate, recognize, and interpret opposite-sex arousal as erotic or romantic attraction and to ignore, repress, or differently interpret comparable same-sex arousal. In fact, the heightened visibility of gay men and lesbians in our society is now prompting individuals who experience same-sex arousal to recognize it, label it, and act on it at earlier ages than in previous years (Fox, 1995).

In some instances, the EBE process itself may be supplemented or even superseded by processes of conditioning or social learning, both positive and negative. Such processes could also produce shifts in an individual's sexual orientation over the life course. For example, the small number of bisexual respondents in the San Francisco study appeared to have added same-sex erotic attraction to an already established heterosexual orientation after adolescence. Similar findings were reported in a more extensive study of bisexual individuals (Weinberg, Williams, & Pryor, 1994), with some respondents adding heterosexual attraction to a previously established homosexual orientation. This same study also showed that different components of an individual's sexual orientation need not coincide; for example, some of the bisexual respondents were more erotically attracted to one sex but more romantically attracted to the other.

Negative conditioning also appears to be an operative mechanism in some cases of childhood sexual abuse or other upsetting childhood sexual experiences. For example, a reanalysis of the original Kinsey data revealed that a woman was more likely to engage in sexual activity with other women as an adult if she had been pressured or coerced into preadolescent sexual activity with an older male (Van Wyk & Geist, 1984).

Finally, some women who would otherwise be predicted by the EBE model to have a heterosexual orientation might choose for social or political reasons to center their lives around other women. This could lead them to avoid seeking out men for sexual or romantic relationships, to develop affectional and erotic ties to other women, and to self-identify as lesbians or bisexuals. In general, issues of sexual orientation *identity* are beyond the formal scope of EBE theory.

Deconstructing the Concept of Sexual Orientation

As noted in the introduction, the academic discourse on sexual orientation is currently dominated by the debate between the biological essentialists, who can point to the empirical links between biology and sexual orientation, and the social constructionists, who can point to the historical and anthropological evidence that the concept of sexual orientation is itself a culture-bound notion (De Cecco & Elia, 1993). I suggest that EBE theory can accommodate both kinds of evidence. I have already shown how the theory incorporates the biological evidence. To demonstrate how EBE theory also accommodates the cultural relativism of the social constructionists, it is necessary to deconstruct the theory itself, to explicitly identify its essentialist and culture-specific elements and to see what remains when the latter are stripped away.

There are three essentialist assumptions underlying the scenario outlined in Figure 23.1. First, it is assumed that childhood temperaments are partially coded in the genes and, second, that those temperaments can influence a child's preferences for male-typical or female-typical activities. Third, and most fundamentally, it is assumed that the psychological processes that transform exotic into erotic are universal properties of the human species. That's it. Everything else is cultural overlay, including the concept of sexual orientation itself.

* * *

References

Allen, J. B., Kenrick, D. T., Linder, D. E., & McCall, M. A. (1989). Arousal and attraction: A response-facilitation alternative to misattribution and negative-reinforcement models. *Journal of Personality and Social Psychology, 57,* 261–270.

Allen, L. S., & Gorski, R. A. (1992). Sexual orientation and the size of the anterior commissure in the human brain. *Proceedings of the National Academy of Sciences, 89,* 7199–7202.

Bailey, J. M., & Martin, N. G. (1995, September). *A twin registry study of sexual orientation.* Paper presented at the annual meeting of the International Academy of Sex Research, Provincetown, MA.

Bailey, J. M., & Pillard, R. C. (1991). A genetic study of male sexual orientation. *Archives of General Psychiatry, 48,* 1089–1096.

Bailey, J. M., Pillard, R. C., Neale, M. C., & Agyei, Y. (1993). Heritable factors influence sexual orientation in women. *Archives of General Psychiatry, 50,* 217–223.

Bailey, J. M., & Zucker, K. J. (1995). Childhood sex-typed behavior and sexual orientation: A conceptual analysis and quantitative review. *Developmental Psychology, 31,* 43–55.

Bates, J. E., Bentler, P. M., & Thompson, S. K. (1973). Measurement of deviant gender development in boys. *Child Development, 44,* 591–598.

Bates, J. E., Bentler, P. M., & Thompson, S. K. (1979). Gender-deviant boys compared with normal and clinical controls boys. *Journal of Abnormal Child Psychology, 7,* 243–259.

Bateson, P. P. G. (1978a). Early experience and sexual preferences. In J. B. Hutchison (Ed.), *Biological determinants of sexual behavior* (pp. 29–53). New York: Wiley.

Bell, A. P. (1982, November). Sexual preference: A postscript. *Siecus Report, 11,* 1–3.

Bell, A. P., Weinberg, M. S., & Hammersmith, S. K. (1981a). *Sexual preference: Its development in men and women.* Bloomington: Indiana University Press.

Bell, A. P., Weinberg, M. S., & Hammersmith, S. K. (1981b). *Sexual preference: Its development in men and women. Statistical appendix.* Bloomington: Indiana University Press.

Bem, S. L. (1993). *The lenses of gender: Transforming the debate on sexual inequality.* New Haven, CT: Yale University Press.

Berenbaum, S. A., & Hines, M. (1992). Early androgens are related to childhood sex-typed toy preferences. *Psychological Science, 3,* 203–206.

Berenbaum, S. A., & Snyder, E. (1995). Early hormonal influences on childhood sex-typed activity and playmate preferences: Implications for the development of sexual orientation. *Developmental Psychology, 31,* 31–42.

Berscheid, E., & Walster, E. (1974). A little bit about love. In T. Huston (Ed.), *Foundations of interpersonal attraction* (pp. 355–381). New York: Academic Press.

Bettelheim, B. (1969). *The children of the dream.* New York: Macmillan.

Blanchard, R., & Bogaert, A. F. (1996). Homosexuality in men and number of older brothers. *American Journal of Psychiatry, 153,* 27–31.

Blanchard, R., McConkey, J. G., Roper, V., & Steiner, B. W. (1983). Measuring physical aggressiveness in heterosexual, homosexual, and transsexual males. *Archives of Sexual Behavior, 12,* 511–524.

Bleier, R. (1984). *Science and gender: A critique of biology and its theories on women.* New York: Pergamon Press.

Brehm, S. S. (1992). *Intimate relationships* (2nd ed.). New York: McGraw-Hill.

Bronfenbrenner, U., & Ceci, S. J. (1994). Nature-nurture reconceptualized in developmental perspective: A bioecological model. *Psychological Review, 101,* 568–586.

Buss, A. H., & Plomin, R. (1975). *A temperament theory of personality development.* New York: Wiley.

Buss, A. H., & Plomin, R. (1984). *Temperament: Early developing personality traits.* Hillsdale, NJ: Erlbaum.

Byne, W., & Parsons, B. (1993). Human sexual orientation: The biologic theories reappraised. *Archives of General Psychiatry, 50,* 228–239.

Cantor, J. R., Zillmann, D., & Bryant, J. (1975). Enhancement of experienced sexual arousal in response to erotic stimuli through misattribution of unrelated residual excitation. *Journal of Personality and Social Psychology, 32,* 69–75.

Caspi, A., & Herbener, E. S. (1990). Continuity and change: Assortative marriage and the consistency of personality in adulthood. *Journal of Personality and Social Psychology, 58,* 250–258.

De Cecco, J. P., & Elia, J. P. (Eds.). (1993). *If you seduce a straight person, can you make them gay? Issues in biological essentialism versus social constructionism in gay and lesbian identities.* New York: Harrington Park Press.

DiPietro, J. A. (1981). Rough and tumble play: A function of gender. *Developmental Psychology, 17,* 50–58.

Dittmann, R. W., Kappes, M. H., Kappes, M. E., Borger, D., Meyer-Bahlburg, H. F. L., Stegner, H., Willig, R. H., & Wallis, H. (1990a). Congenital adrenal hyperplasia: II. Gender-related behavior and attitudes in female salt-wasting and simple-virilizing patients. *Psychoneuroendocrinology, 15,* 421–434.

Dittmann, R. W., Kappes, M. H., Kappes, M. E., Borger, D., Stegner, H., Willig, R. H., & Wallis, H. (1990b). Congenital adrenal hyperplasia: I. Gender-related behavior and attitudes in female patients and sisters. *Psychoneuroendocrinology, 15,* 410–420.

Eaton, W. O., & Enns, L. R. (1986). Sex differences in human motor activity level. *Psychological Bulletin, 100,* 19–28.

Ellis, L., & Ames, M. A. (1987). Neurohormonal functioning and sexual orientation: A theory of homosexuality-heterosexuality. *Psychological Bulletin, 101,* 233–258.

Feingold, A. (1988). Matching for attractiveness in romantic partners and same-sex friends: A meta-analysis and theoretical critique. *Psychological Bulletin, 104,* 226–235.

Finck, H. T. (1887). *Romantic love and personal beauty: Their development, causal relations, historic and national peculiarities.* London: Macmillan.

Fox, R. C. (1995). Bisexual identities. In A. R. D'Augelli & C. J. Patterson (Eds.), *Lesbian, gay and bisexual identities over the lifespan* (pp. 48–86). New York: Oxford University Press.

Freud, S. (1962). *Three essays on the theory of sexuality.* New York: Basic Books. (Original work published 1905)

Fry, D. P. (1990). Play aggression among Zapotec children: Implications for the practice hypothesis. *Aggressive Behavior, 17,* 321–340.

Futuyma, D. J., & Risch, S. J. (1983/84). Sexual orientation, sociobiology, and evolution. *Journal of Homosexuality, 9,* 157–168.

Gartrell, N. K. (1982). Hormones and homosexuality. In W. Paul, J. D. Weinrich, J. C. Gonsiorek, & M. E. Hotvedt (Eds.), *Homosexuality: Social psychological and biological issues* (pp. 169–182). Beverly Hills, CA: Sage.

Gladue, B. A., Beatty, W. W., Larson, J., & Staton, R. D. (1990). Sexual orientation and spatial ability in men and women. *Psychobiology, 28,* 101–108.

Green, R. (1976). One-hundred ten feminine and masculine boys: Behavioral contrasts and demographic similarities. *Archives of Sexual Behavior, 5,* 425–426.

Green, R. (1987). *The "sissy boy syndrome" and the development of homosexuality.* New Haven, CT: Yale University Press.

Hamer, D., & Copeland, P. (1994). *The science of desire: The search for the gay gene and the biology of behavior.* New York: Simon & Schuster.

Hamer, D. H., Hu, S., Magnuson, V. L., Hu, N., & Patatucci, A. M. L. (1993). A linkage between DNA markers on the X chromosome and male sexual orientation. *Science, 261,* 321–327.

Harrison, A. A. (1977). Mere exposure. In L. Berkowitz (Ed.), *Advances in experimental social psychology* (Vol. 10, pp. 39–83). New York: Academic Press.

Herdt, G. (1981). *Guardians of the flutes: Idioms of masculinity.* New York: McGraw-Hill.

Herdt, G. (1987). *Sambia: Ritual and gender in New Guinea.* New York: Holt, Rinehart & Winston.

Herdt, G. (1990). Developmental discontinuities and sexual orientation across cultures. In D. P. McWhirter, S. A. Sanders, & J. M. Reinisch (Eds.), *Homosexuality/heterosexuality: Concepts of sexual orientation* (pp. 208–236). New York: Oxford University Press.

Herdt, G. (Ed.). (1984). *Ritualized homosexuality in Melanesia.* Berkeley: University of California Press.

Hill, C., Rubin, Z., & Peplau, L. A. (1976). Breakups before marriage: The end of 103 affairs. *Journal of Social Issues, 32,* 147–168.

Hoon, P. W., Wincze, J. P., & Hoon, E. F. (1977). A test of reciprocal inhibition: Are anxiety and sexual arousal in women mutually inhibitory? *Journal of Abnormal Psychology, 86,* 65–74.

Hyde, J. S. (1984). How large are gender differences in aggression? A developmental meta-analysis. *Developmental Psychology, 20,* 722–736.

Kenrick, D. T., & Cialdini, R. B. (1977). Romantic attraction: Misattribution versus reinforcement explanations. *Journal of Personality and Social Psychology, 35,* 381–391.

Kirsch, J. A. W., & Rodman, J. E. (1982). Selection and sexuality: The Darwinian view of homosexuality. In W. Paul, J. D. Weinrich, J. C. Gonsiorek, & M. E. Hotvedt (Eds.), *Homosexuality: Social psychological and biological issues* (pp. 183–195). Beverly Hills, CA: Sage.

LeVay, S. (1991). A difference in hypothalamic structure between heterosexual and homosexual men. *Science, 253,* 1034–1037.

LeVay, S. (1993). *The sexual brain.* Cambridge, MA: MIT Press.

Levinger, G., Senn, D. J., & Jorgensen, B. W. (1970). Progress toward permanence in courtship: A test of the Kerckhoff-Davis hypotheses. *Sociometry, 33,* 427–443.

McClanahan, K. K., Gold, J. A., Lenney, E., Ryckman, R. M., & Kulberg, G. E. (1990). Infatuation and attraction to a dissimilar other: Why is love blind? *Journal of Social Psychology, 130,* 433–445.

McCormick, C. M., & Witelson, S. F. (1991). A cognitive profile of homosexual men compared to heterosexual men and women. *Psychoneuroendocrinology, 16,* 459–473.

Meyer, J. P., & Pepper, S. (1977). Need compatibility and marital adjustment in young married couples. *Journal of Personality and Social Psychology, 35,* 331–342.

Meyer-Bahlburg, H. F. L. (1984). Psychoendocrine research on sexual orientation: Current status and future options. *Progress in Brain Research, 61,* 375–398.

Meyer-Bahlburg, H. F. L., Erhhardt, A. A., Rosen, L. R., Gruen, R. S., Veridiano, N. P., Vann, F. H., & Neuwalder, H. F. (1995). Prenatal estrogens and the development of homosexual orientation. *Developmental Psychology, 31,* 12–21.

Moller, L. C., Hymel, S., & Rubin, K. H. (1992). Sex typing in play and popularity in middle childhood. *Sex Roles, 26,* 331–353.

Money, J., & Ehrhardt, A. A. (1972). *Man and woman, boy and girl: The differentiation and dimorphism of gender identity from conception to maturity.* Baltimore: Johns Hopkins Press.

Money, J., Schwartz, M., & Lewis, V. G. (1984). Adult erotosexual status and fetal hormonal masculinization and demasculinization: 46, XX congenital virilizing adrenal hyperplasia and 46, XY androgen-insensitivity syndrome compared. *Psychoneuroendocrinology, 9,* 405–414.

Mook, D. B. (1987). *Motivation: The organization of action.* New York: Norton.

Murstein, B. I. (1972). Physical attractiveness and marital choice. *Journal of Personality and Social Psychology, 22,* 8–12.

Newcomb, T. M. (1961). *The acquaintance process.* New York: Holt, Rinehart & Winston.

Pitz, G. F., & Ross, R. B. (1961). Imprinting as a function of arousal. *Journal of Comparative and Physiological Psychology, 54,* 602–604.

Plomin, R. (1986). *Development, genetics, and psychology.* Hillsdale, NJ: Erlbaum.

Quadagno, D. M., Briscoe, R., & Quadagno, J. S. (1977). Effect of perinatal gonadal hormones on selected nonsexual behavior patterns: A critical assessment of the nonhuman and human literature. *Psychological Bulletin, 84,* 62–80.

Rabin, I. A. (1965). *Growing up in a kibbutz.* New York: Springer.

Reinisch, J. M. (1981). Prenatal exposure to synthetic progestins increases potential for aggression in humans. *Science, 211,* 1171–1173.

Rice, G., Anderson, C., Risch, N., & Ebers, G. (1995, September). *Male homosexuality: Absence of linkage to micro satellite markers on the X-chromosome in a Canadian study.* Paper presented at the annual meeting of the International Academy of Sex Research, Provincetown, MA.

Rubin, Z. (1973). *Liking and loving.* New York: Holt, Rinehart & Winston.

Rushton, J. P., Fulker, D. W., Neale, M. C., Nias, D. K. B., & Eysenck, H. J. (1986). Altruism and aggression: The heritability of individual differences. *Journal of Personality and Social Psychology, 50,* 1192–1198.

Savin-Williams, R. C. (1987). An ethological perspective on homosexuality during adolescence. *Journal of Adolescent Research, 2,* 283–302.

Schachter, S., & Singer, J. E. (1962). Cognitive, social, and physiological determinants of emotional state. *Psychological Review, 69,* 379–399.

Serbin, L. A. (1980). Sex-role socialization: A field in transition. In B. B. Lahey & A. E. Kazdin (Eds.), *Advances in clinical child psychology* (Vol. 3, pp. 41–96). New York: Plenum.

Shepher, J. (1971). Mate selection among second generation kibbutz adolescents and adults: Incest avoidance and negative imprinting. *Archives of Sexual Behavior, 1,* 293–307.

Silverman, I. (1971). Physical attractiveness and courtship. *Archives of Sexual Behavior, 1,* 22–25.

Spiro, M. E. (1958). *Children of the kibbutz.* Cambridge, MA: Harvard University Press.

Strong, S. R., Hills, H. I., Kilmartin, C. T., DeVries, H., Lanier, K., Nelson, B. N., Strickland, D., & Meyer, C. W., III. (1988). The dynamic relations among interpersonal behaviors: A test of complementarity and anticomplementarity. *Journal of Personality and Social Psychology, 54,* 798–810.

Swaab, D. F., & Hofman, M. A. (1990). An enlarged suprachiasmatic nucleus in homosexual men. *Brain Research, 537,* 141–148.

Talmon, Y. (1964). Mate selection in collective settlements. *American Sociological Review, 29,* 481–508.

Tripp, C. A. (1975). *The homosexual matrix.* New York: McGraw-Hill.

Tripp, C. A. (1987). *The homosexual matrix* (2nd ed.). New York: New American Library.

Van Wyk, P. H., & Geist, C. S. (1984). Psychological development of heterosexual, bisexual, and homosexual behavior. *Archives of Sexual Behavior, 13,* 505–544.

Walster, E. (1971). Passionate love. In B. I. Murstein (Ed.), *Theories of attraction and love* (pp. 85–99). New York: Springer.

Weinberg, M. S., Williams, C. J., & Pryor, D. W. (1994). *Dual attraction: Understanding bisexuality.* New York: Oxford University Press.

Weinrich, J. D. (1978). Nonreproduction, homosexuality, transsexualism, and intelligence: I. A systematic literature search. *Journal of Homosexuality, 2,* 275–289.

Weinrich, J. D. (1987). A new sociobiological theory of homosexuality applicable to societies with universal marriage. *Ethology and Sociobiology*, *8*, 37–47.

Westermarck, E. (1891). *The history of human marriage*. London: Macmillan.

White, G. L., Fishbein, S., & Rutstein, J. (1981). Passionate love and the misattribution of arousal. *Journal of Personality and Social Psychology*, *41*, 56–62.

White, G. L., & Kight, T. D. (1984). Misattribution of arousal and attraction: Effects of salience of explanations for arousal. *Journal of Experimental Social Psychology*, *20*, 55–64.

Wilson, E. O. (1975). *Sociobiology: The new synthesis*. Cambridge, MA: Harvard University Press.

Wilson, E. O. (1978). *On human nature*. Cambridge, MA: Harvard University Press.

Wolchik, S. A., Beggs, V. E., Wincze, J. P., Sakheim, D. K., Barlow, D. H., & Mavissakalian, M. (1980). The effect of emotional arousal on subsequent sexual arousal in men. *Journal of Abnormal Psychology*, *89*, 595–598.

Zillmann, D. (1983). Transfer of excitation in emotional behavior. In J. T. Cacioppo & R. E. Petty (Eds.), *Social psychophysiology: A sourcebook*. New York: Guilford Press.

Zucker, K. J. (1990). Gender identity disorders in children: Clinical descriptions and natural history. In R. Blanchard & B. W. Steiner (Eds.), *Clinical management of gender identity disorders in children and adults* (pp. 1–23). Washington, DC: American Psychiatric Press.

Zucker, K. J., Bradley, S. J., Oliver, G., Hood, J. E., Blake, J., & Fleming, S. (1992, July). *Psychosexual assessment of women with congenital adrenal hyperplasia: Preliminary analyses*. Paper presented at the 18th Annual meeting of the International Academy of Sex Research, Prague, Czechoslovakia.

Zucker, K. J., & Green, R. (1993). Psychological and familial aspects of gender identity disorder. *Child and Adolescent Psychiatric Clinics of North America*, *2*, 513–542.

PART IV

The Psychoanalytic Approach to Personality

About a century ago, the brilliant Viennese psychiatrist Sigmund Freud began to present his psycyhoanalytic theory of personality to the world. Freud continued to publish prolifically and to develop his theory right up to the time of his death, in 1939. The result of all this labor was not only a long-lasting and pervasive influence on the field of psychology, but also a fundamental influence on the way members of Western culture think about people. The "Freudian slip" is the commonplace idea most obviously identified with Freud, but his writings also continue to affect the way we talk about child-rearing, psychological conflict, sexuality, and emotion.

Freud's own contributions were impressive enough, but he also attracted a remarkable group of followers, several of whom eventually broke away from his influence. These include some of the major intellectual figures of the early 20th century, including Carl Jung, Karen Horney, and Erik Erikson. Freud's theory continues to influence modern psychological research both directly and indirectly. The readings in this section sample from the writings of Freud himself, several other important figures in psychoanalysis, and other writers who have attempted to evaluate psychoanalysis on empirical or theoretical grounds.

The two lectures by Freud that began this section concern the basic structure of the mind and the widely observed phenomenon of Freudian slips, or "parapraxes." The next selection, by Robert Sears, is the concluding chapter from a survey of empirical research relevant to psychoanalytic concepts that was published soon after Freud's death. The fourth selection, by Roy Baumeister, Karen Dale, and Kristin Sommer, is a recent survey of modern research particularly relevant to the psychoanalytic concept of the defense mechanism. The fifth selection, by Frederick Crews, summarizes some recent—and vehement—criticism of Freud and his ideas.

The following three selections are articles by Jung, Horney, and Erikson that describe key parts of the theoretical approaches of each psychologist and also address topics of interest in their own right. Jung describes the nature of extraver-

sion and introversion, Horney explains the "distrust" between the sexes, and Erikson outlines the eight stages of psychological development that occur over an individual's entire life.

Perhaps no theory in psychology has been as admired, and as reviled, as psychoanalysis. As you will see in the following articles, there are good reasons for both kinds of reaction.

Lecture XXXI: The Dissection of the Psychical Personality

Sigmund Freud

In this first selection the founder of psychoanalysis, Sigmund Freud himself, describes the core of the theory. Freud describes how the mind is divided into three parts, the now-famous id, ego, and super-ego. These roughly map onto the animalistic part, the logical part, and the moral part of the mind.

One of your editors remembers years ago having seen a Donald Duck cartoon in which the unfortunate duck was tormented by an angel who rode on one shoulder and a devil who rode on the other. The angel was always scolding him, and the devil was always egging him on to do things he knew he shouldn't do. Donald himself, in the middle, was confused and prone to obey first one of his tormentors, then the other.

Disney's animators seem to have known their Freud. The situation described near the end of this selection is nearly identical. When Freud has the poor ego cry, "Life is not easy!" he is describing the torment of having to resolve the three-way conflict between what one believes one should do, what one wants to do, and what is really possible.

This selection was written late in Freud's career and originally published in 1933, six years before his death. Freud had 15 years earlier delivered a famous set of introductory lectures on psychoanalysis, and he hit upon the idea of writing a new set of lectures to update and expand upon the earlier ones. But by this time Freud, an old man, had undergone repeated surgeries for cancer of the palate and could not speak in public. So although this and several other articles were written in the form of lectures, they were never meant to be delivered. In Freud's own words (from his preface),

> If, therefore, I once more take my place in the lecture room during the remarks that follow, it is only by an artifice of the imagination; it may help me not to forget to bear the reader in mind as I enter more deeply into my subject. . . . [this lecture is] addressed to the multitude of educated people to whom we may

perhaps attribute a benevolent, even though cautious, interest in the characteristics and discoveries of the young science. (Freud, 1965/1933, p, 5).

From *New Introductory Lectures on Psycho-analysis*, by Sigmund Freud, in *The Standard Edition of the Complete Psychological Works of Sigmund Freud*, edited and translated by James Strachey (New York: Norton, 1966), pp. 51–71.

* * *

The situation in which we find ourselves at the beginning of our enquiry may be expected itself to point the way for us. We wish to make the ego the matter of our enquiry, our very own ego.[1] But is that possible? After all, the ego is in its very essence a subject; how can it be made into an object? Well, there is no doubt that it can be. The ego can take itself as an object, can treat itself like other objects, can observe itself, criticize itself, and do Heaven knows what with itself. In this, one part of the ego is setting itself over against the rest. So the ego can be split; it splits itself during a number of its functions—temporarily at least. Its parts can come together again afterwards. That is not exactly a novelty, though it may perhaps be putting an unusual emphasis on what is generally known. On the other hand, we are familiar with the notion that pathology, by making things larger and coarser, can draw our attention to normal conditions which would otherwise have escaped us. Where it points to a breach or a rent, there may normally be an articulation present. If we throw a crystal to the floor, it breaks; but not into haphazard pieces. It comes apart along its lines of cleavage into fragments whose boundaries, though they were invisible, were predetermined by the crystal's structure. Mental patients are split and broken structures of this same kind. Even we cannot withhold from them something of the reverential awe which peoples of the past felt for the insane. They have turned away from external reality, but for that very reason they know more about internal, psychical reality and can reveal a number of things to us that would otherwise be inaccessible to us.

We describe one group of these patients as suffering from delusions of being observed. They complain to us that perpetually, and down to their most intimate actions, they are being molested by the observation of unknown powers—presumably persons—and that in hallucinations they hear these persons reporting the outcome of their observation: "now he's going to say this, now he's dressing to go out," and so on. Observation of this sort is not yet the same thing as persecution, but it is not far from it; it presupposes that people distrust them, and expect to catch them carrying out forbidden actions for which they would be punished. How would it be if these insane people were right, if in each of us there is present in his ego an agency like this which observes and threatens to punish, and which in them has merely become sharply divided from their ego and mistakenly displaced into external reality?

I cannot tell whether the same thing will happen to you as to me. Ever since, under the powerful impression of this clinical picture, I formed the idea that the separation of the observing agency from the rest of the ego might be a regular feature of the ego's structure, that idea has never left me, and I was driven to investigate the further characteristics and connections of the agency which was thus separated off. The next step is quickly taken. The content of the delusions of being observed already suggests that the observing is only a preparation for judging and punishing, and we accordingly guess that another function of this agency must be what we call our conscience. There is scarcely anything else in us that we so regularly separate from our ego and so easily set over against it as precisely our conscience. I feel an in-

---

[1]"Ego" has also been translated as "the I." Freud is referring to the self as it experiences itself—a paradoxical but common situation that leads Freud to conclude that dividing up the self is not so odd as it might seem.

clination to do something that I think will give me pleasure, but I abandon it on the ground that my conscience does not allow it. Or I have let myself be persuaded by too great an expectation of pleasure into doing something to which the voice of conscience has objected and after the deed my conscience punishes me with distressing reproaches and causes me to feel remorse for the deed. I might simply say that the special agency which I am beginning to distinguish in the ego is conscience. But it is more prudent to keep the agency as something independent and to suppose that conscience is one of its functions and that self-observation, which is an essential preliminary to the judging activity of conscience, is another of them. And since when we recognize that something has a separate existence we give it a name of its own, from this time forward I will describe this agency in the ego as the '*super-ego*.'

* * *

Hardly have we familiarized ourselves with the idea of a super-ego like this which enjoys a certain degree of autonomy, follows its own intentions and is independent of the ego for its supply of energy, than a clinical picture forces itself on our notice which throws a striking light on the severity of this agency and indeed its cruelty, and on its changing relations to the ego. I am thinking of the condition of melancholia,[2] or, more precisely, of melancholic attacks, which you too will have heard plenty about, even if you are not psychiatrists. The most striking feature of this illness, of whose causation and mechanism we know much too little, is the way in which the super-ego—"conscience," you may call it, quietly—treats the ego. While a melancholic can, like other people, show a greater or lesser degree of severity to himself in his healthy periods, during a melancholic attack his super-ego becomes over-severe, abuses the poor ego, humiliates it and ill-treats it, threatens it with the direst punishments, reproaches it for actions in the remotest past which had been taken lightly at the time—as though it had spent the whole interval in collecting accusations and had only been waiting for its present access of strength in order to bring them up and make a condemnatory judgement on their basis. The super-ego applies the strictest moral standard to the helpless ego which is at its mercy; in general it represents the claims of morality, and we realize all at once that our moral sense of guilt is the expression of the tension between the ego and the super-ego. It is a most remarkable experience to see morality, which is supposed to have been given us by God and thus deeply implanted in us, functioning [in these patients] as a periodic phenomenon. For after a certain number of months the whole moral fuss is over, the criticism of the super-ego is silent, the ego is rehabilitated and again enjoys all the rights of man till the next attack. In some forms of the disease, indeed, something of a contrary sort occurs in the intervals; the ego finds itself in a blissful state of intoxication, it celebrates a triumph, as though the super-ego had lost all its strength or had melted into the ego; and this liberated, manic ego permits itself a truly uninhibited satisfaction of all its appetites. Here are happenings rich in unsolved riddles!

No doubt you will expect me to give you more than a mere illustration when I inform you that we have found out all kinds of things about the formation of the super-ego—that is to say, about the origin of conscience. Following a well-known pronouncement of Kant's which couples the conscience within us with the starry Heavens, a pious man might well be tempted to honor these two things as the masterpieces of creation. The stars are indeed magnificent, but as regards conscience God has done an uneven and careless piece of work, for a large majority of men have brought along with them only a modest amount of it or scarcely enough to be worth mentioning. We are far from overlooking the portion of psychological truth that is contained in the assertion that conscience is of divine origin; but the thesis needs interpretation. Even if conscience is something "within us," yet it is not so from the first. In this it is a real contrast to sexual life, which is in fact there from the beginning of life and not only a

[2]"Modern terminology would probably speak of 'depression.' "—Translator

later addition. But, as is well known, young children are amoral and possess no internal inhibitions against their impulses striving for pleasure. The part which is later taken on by the super-ego is played to begin with by an external power, by parental authority. Parental influence governs the child by offering proofs of love and by threatening punishments which are signs to the child of loss of love and are bound to be feared on their own account. This realistic anxiety is the precursor of the later moral anxiety. So long as it is dominant there is no need to talk of a super-ego and of a conscience. It is only subsequently that the secondary situation develops (which we are all too ready to regard as the normal one), where the external restraint is internalized and the super-ego takes the place of the parental agency and observes, directs and threatens the ego in exactly the same way as earlier the parents did with the child.

The super-ego, which thus takes over the power, function and even the methods of the parental agency, is however not merely its successor but actually the legitimate heir of its body. It proceeds directly out of it, we shall learn presently by what process. First, however, we must dwell upon a discrepancy between the two. The super-ego seems to have made a one-sided choice and to have picked out only the parents' strictness and severity, their prohibiting and punitive function, whereas their loving care seems not to have been taken over and maintained. If the parents have really enforced their authority with severity we can easily understand the child's in turn developing a severe super-ego. But, contrary to our expectation, experience shows that the super-ego can acquire the same characteristic of relentless severity even if the upbringing had been mild and kindly and had so far as possible avoided threats and punishments. * * *

* * *

The basis of the process is what is called an 'identification'—that is to say, the assimilation of one ego to another one,[3] as a result of which the first ego behaves like the second in certain respects, imitates it and in a sense takes it up into itself. Identification has been not unsuitably compared with the oral, cannibalistic incorporation of the other person. It is a very important form of attachment to someone else, probably the very first, and not the same thing as the choice of an object. The difference between the two can be expressed in some such way as this. If a boy identifies himself with his father, he wants to *be like* his father; if he makes him the object of his choice, he wants to *have* him, to possess him. In the first case his ego is altered on the model of his father; in the second case that is not necessary. Identification and object-choice are to a large extent independent of each other; it is however possible to identify oneself with someone whom, for instance, one has taken as a sexual object, and to alter one's ego on his model. It is said that the influencing of the ego by the sexual object occurs particularly often with women and is characteristic of femininity. I must already have spoken to you in my earlier lectures of what is by far the most instructive relation between identification and object-choice. It can be observed equally easily in children and adults, in normal as in sick people. If one has lost an object or has been obliged to give it up, one often compensates oneself by identifying oneself with it and by setting it up once more in one's ego, so that here object-choice regresses, as it were, to identification.

I myself am far from satisfied with these remarks on identification; but it will be enough if you can grant me that the installation of the super-ego can be described as a successful instance of identification with the parental agency. The fact that speaks decisively for this view is that this new creation of a superior agency within the ego is most intimately linked with the destiny of the Oedipus complex[4] so that the super-ego appears

[3]"I.e., one ego coming to resemble another one."—Translator

[4]The "Oedipus complex" is the result of a complex process in which, according to Freud, a young boy falls in love with his mother, fears his father's jealous retaliation, and as a defense against that fear comes to identify with his father.

as the heir of that emotional attachment which is of such importance for childhood. With his abandonment of the Oedipus complex a child must, as we can see, renounce the intense object-cathexes[5] which he has deposited with his parents, and it is as a compensation for this loss of objects that there is such a strong intensification of the identifications with his parents which have probably long been present in his ego. Identifications of this kind as precipitates of object-cathexes that have been given up will be repeated often enough later in the child's life; but it is entirely in accordance with the emotional importance of this first instance of such a transformation that a special place in the ego should be found for its outcome. Close investigation has shown us, too, that the super-ego is stunted in its strength and growth if the surmounting of the Oedipus complex is only incompletely successful. In the course of development the super-ego also takes on the influences of those who have stepped into the place of parents—educators, teachers, people chosen as ideal models. Normally it departs more and more from the original parental figures; it becomes, so to say, more impersonal. Nor must it be forgotten that a child has a different estimate of its parents at different periods of its life. At the time at which the Oedipus complex gives place to the super-ego they are something quite magnificent; but later they lose much of this. Identifications then come about with these later parents as well, and indeed they regularly make important contributions to the formation of character; but in that case they only affect the ego, they no longer influence the super-ego, which has been determined by the earliest parental imagos.

* * *

* * * In face of the doubt whether the ego and super-ego are themselves unconscious or merely produce unconscious effects, we have, for good reasons, decided in favour of the former possibility. And it is indeed the case that large portions of the ego and super-ego can remain unconscious and are normally unconscious. That is to say, the individual knows nothing of their contents and it requires an expenditure of effort to make them conscious. It is a fact that ego and conscious, repressed and unconscious do not coincide. We feel a need to make a fundamental revision of our attitude to the problem of conscious-unconscious. At first we are inclined greatly to reduce the value of the criterion of being conscious since it has shown itself so untrustworthy. But we should be doing it an injustice. As may be said of our life, it is not worth much, but it is all we have. Without the illumination thrown by the quality of consciousness, we should be lost in the obscurity of depth-psychology; but we must attempt to find our bearings afresh.

There is no need to discuss what is to be called conscious: it is removed from all doubt. The oldest and best meaning of the word "unconscious" is the descriptive one; we call a psychical process unconscious whose existence we are obliged to assume—for some such reason as that we infer it from its effects—but of which we know nothing. In that case we have the same relation to it as we have to a psychical process in another person, except that it is in fact one of our own. If we want to be still more correct, we shall modify our assertion by saying that we call a process unconscious if we are obliged to assume that it is being activated *at the moment*, though *at the moment* we know nothing about it. This qualification makes us reflect that the majority of conscious processes are conscious only for a short time; very soon they become *latent*, but can easily become conscious again. We might also say that they had become unconscious, if it were at all certain that in the condition of latency they are still something psychical. So far we should have learnt nothing new; nor should we have acquired the right to introduce the concept of an unconscious into psychology. [But] in order to explain a slip of the tongue, for instance, we find ourselves obliged to assume that the intention to make a particular remark was present in the subject. We infer it with certainty from the interference with his remark which has occurred; but the intention did not put

[5]An "object-cathexis" is an investment of emotional energy in an important "object," usually a person.

itself through and was thus unconscious. If, when we subsequently put it before the speaker, he recognizes it as one familiar to him, then it was only temporarily unconscious to him; but if he repudiates it as something foreign to him, then it was permanently unconscious. From this experience we retrospectively obtain the right also to pronounce as something unconscious what had been described as latent. A consideration of these dynamic relations permits us now to distinguish two kinds of unconscious—one which is easily, under frequently occurring circumstances, transformed into something conscious, and another with which this transformation is difficult and takes place only subject to a considerable expenditure of effort or possibly never at all. In order to escape the ambiguity as to whether we mean the one or the other unconscious, whether we are using the word in the descriptive or in the dynamic sense, we make use of a permissible and simple way out. We call the unconscious which is only latent, and thus easily becomes conscious, the "preconscious" and retain the term "unconscious" for the other. We now have three terms, "conscious," "preconscious," and "unconscious," with which we can get along in our description of mental phenomena. Once again: the preconscious is also unconscious in the purely descriptive sense, but we do not give it that name, except in talking loosely or when we have to make a defence of the existence in mental life of unconscious processes in general.

You will admit, I hope, that so far that is not too bad and allows of convenient handling. Yes, but unluckily the work of psychoanalysis has found itself compelled to use the word "unconscious" in yet another, third, sense, and this may, to be sure, have led to confusion. Under the new and powerful impression of there being an extensive and important field of mental life which is normally withdrawn from the ego's knowledge so that the processes occurring in it have to be regarded as unconscious in the truly dynamic sense, we have come to understand the term "unconscious" in a topographical or systematic sense as well; we have come to speak of a "system" of the preconscious and a "system" of the unconscious, of a conflict between the ego and the system *Ucs.* [unconscious], and have used the word more and more to denote a mental province rather than a quality of what is mental. The discovery, actually an inconvenient one, that portions of the ego and super-ego as well are unconscious in the dynamic sense, operates at this point as a relief—it makes possible the removal of a complication. We perceive that we have no right to name the mental region that is foreign to the ego "the system *Ucs.*," since the characteristic of being unconscious is not restricted to it. Very well; we will no longer use the term "unconscious" in the systematic sense and we will give what we have hitherto so described a better name and one no longer open to misunderstanding. Following a verbal usage of Nietzsche's and taking up a suggestion by Georg Groddeck [1923],[6] we will in future call it the 'id'.[7] This impersonal pronoun seems particularly well suited for expressing the main characteristic of this province of the mind—the fact of its being alien to the ego. The super-ego, the ego and the id—these, then, are the three realms, regions, provinces, into which we divide an individual's mental apparatus, and with the mutual relations of which we shall be concerned in what follows.

* * *

You will not expect me to have much to tell you that is new about the id apart from its new name. It is the dark, inaccessible part of our personality; what little we know of it we have learnt from our study of the dream-work and of the construction of neurotic symptoms, and most of that is of a negative character and can be described only as a contrast to the ego. We approach the id with analogies: we call it a chaos, a cauldron full of seething excitations. We picture it as being open at its end to somatic influences, and as there taking up into itself instinctual needs which find their

[6]"A German physician by whose unconventional ideas Freud was much attracted."—Translator

[7]"In German, *Es*, the ordinary word for 'it.' "—Translator

psychical expression in it, but we cannot say in what substratum. It is filled with energy reaching it from the instincts, but it has no organization, produces no collective will, but only a striving to bring about the satisfaction of the instinctual needs subject to the observance of the pleasure principle. The logical laws of thought do not apply in the id, and this is true above all of the law of contradiction. Contrary impulses exist side by side, without cancelling each other out or diminishing each other: at the most they may converge to form compromises under the dominating economic pressure towards the discharge of energy. There is nothing in the id that could be compared with negation; and we perceive with surprise an exception to the philosophical theorem that space and time are necessary forms of our mental acts. There is nothing in the id that corresponds to the idea of time; there is no recognition of the passage of time, and—a thing that is most remarkable and awaits consideration in philosophical thought—no alteration in its mental processes is produced by the passage of time. Wishful impulses which have never passed beyond the id, but impressions, too, which have been sunk into the id by repression, are virtually immortal; after the passage of decades they behave as though they had just occurred. They can only be recognized as belonging to the past, can only lose their importance and be deprived of their cathexis of energy, when they have been made conscious by the work of analysis, and it is on this that the therapeutic effect of analytic treatment rests to no small extent.

Again and again I have had the impression that we have made too little theoretical use of this fact, established beyond any doubt, of the unalterability by time of the repressed. This seems to offer an approach to the most profound discoveries. Nor, unfortunately, have I myself made any progress here.

The id of course knows no judgements of value: no good and evil, no morality. The economic or, if you prefer, the quantitative factor, which is intimately linked to the pleasure principle, dominates all its processes. Instinctual cathexes seeking discharge—that, in our view, is all there is in the id.[8] It even seems that the energy of these instinctual impulses is in a state different from that in the other regions of the mind, far more mobile and capable of discharge; otherwise the displacements and condensations would not occur which are characteristic of the id and which so completely disregard the *quality* of what is cathected—what in the ego we should call an idea. We would give much to understand more about these things! You can see, incidentally, that we are in a position to attribute to the id characteristics other than that of its being unconscious, and you can recognize the possibility of portions of the ego and super-ego being unconscious without possessing the same primitive and irrational characteristics.

* * *

* * * We need scarcely look for a justification of the view that the ego is that portion of the id which was modified by the proximity and influence of the external world, which is adapted for the reception of stimuli and as a protective shield against stimuli, comparable to the cortical layer by which a small piece of living substance is surrounded. The relation to the external world has become the decisive factor for the ego; it has taken on the task of representing the external world to the id—fortunately for the id, which could not escape destruction if, in its blind efforts for the satisfaction of its instincts, it disregarded that supreme external power. In accomplishing this function, the ego must observe the external world, must lay down an accurate picture of it in the memory-traces of its perceptions, and by its exercise of the function of "reality-testing" must put aside whatever in this picture of the external world is an addition derived from internal sources of excitation. The ego controls the approaches to motility under the id's orders; but between a need and an action it has interposed a postponement in the form of the activity of thought, during

[8]In other words, the id seeks immediately to satisfy all "instinctual"—physical—desires.

which it makes use of the mnemic residues of experience. In that way it has dethroned the pleasure principle which dominates the course of events in the id without any restriction, and has replaced it by the reality principle, which promises more certainty and greater success.

* * *

* * * To adopt a popular mode of speaking, we might say that the ego stands for reason and good sense while the id stands for the untamed passions.

So far we have allowed ourselves to be impressed by the merits and capabilities of the ego; it is now time to consider the other side as well. The ego is after all only a portion of the id, a portion that has been expediently modified by the proximity of the external world with its threat of danger. From a dynamic point of view it is weak, it has borrowed its energies from the id, and we are not entirely without insight into the methods —we might call them dodges—by which it extracts further amounts of energy from the id. One such method, for instance, is by identifying itself with actual or abandoned objects. The object-cathexes spring from the instinctual demands of the id. The ego has in the first instance to take note of them. But by identifying itself with the object it recommends itself to the id in place of the object and seeks to divert the id's libido on to itself. * * * The ego must on the whole carry out the id's intentions, it fulfils its task by finding out the circumstances in which those intentions can best be achieved. The ego's relation to the id might be compared with that of a rider to his horse. The horse supplies the locomotive energy, while the rider has the privilege of deciding on the goal and of guiding the powerful animal's movement. But only too often there arises between the ego and the id the not precisely ideal situation of the rider being obliged to guide the horse along the path by which it itself wants to go.

* * *

We are warned by a proverb against serving two masters at the same time. The poor ego has things even worse: it serves three severe masters and does what it can to bring their claims and demands into harmony with one another. These claims are always divergent and often seem incompatible. No wonder that the ego so often fails in its task. Its three tyrannical masters are the external world, the super-ego and the id. When we follow the ego's efforts to satisfy them simultaneously—or rather, to obey them simultaneously—we cannot feel any regret at having personified this ego and having set it up as a separate organism. It feels hemmed in on three sides, threatened by three kinds of danger, to which, if it is hard pressed, it reacts by generating anxiety. Owing to its origin from the experiences of the perceptual system, it is earmarked for representing the demands of the external world, but it strives too to be a loyal servant of the id, to remain on good terms with it, to recommend itself to it as an object and to attract its libido to itself. In its attempts to mediate between the id and reality, it is often obliged to cloak the *Ucs.* commands of the id with its own *Pcs.* [preconscious] rationalizations, to conceal the id's conflicts with reality, to profess, with diplomatic disingenuousness, to be taking notice of reality even when the id has remained rigid and unyielding. On the other hand it is observed at every step it takes by the strict super-ego, which lays down definite standards for its conduct, without taking any account of its difficulties from the direction of the id and the external world, and which, if those standards are not obeyed, punishes it with tense feelings of inferiority and of guilt. Thus the ego, driven by the id, confined by the super-ego, repulsed by reality, struggles to master its economic task of bringing about harmony among the forces and influences working in and upon it; and we can understand how it is that so often we cannot suppress a cry: "Life is not easy!" If the ego is obliged to admit its weakness, it breaks out in anxiety—realistic anxiety regarding the external world, moral anxiety regarding the super-ego and neurotic anxiety regarding the strength of the passions in the id.

I should like to portray the structural relations

of the mental personality, as I have described them to you, in the unassuming sketch which I now present you with:

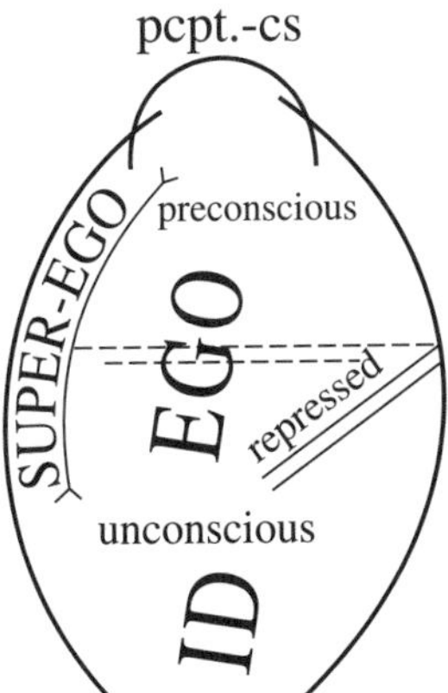

Figure 24.1 Freud's diagram of the structure of personality.

As you see here, the super-ego merges into the id; indeed, as heir to the Oedipus complex it has intimate relations with the id; it is more remote than the ego from the perceptual system. The id has intercourse with the external world only through the ego—at least, according to this diagram. It is certainly hard to say to-day how far the drawing is correct. In one respect it is undoubtedly not. The space occupied by the unconscious id ought to have been incomparably greater than that of the ego or the preconscious. I must ask you to correct it in your thoughts.

And here is another warning, to conclude these remarks, which have certainly been exacting and not, perhaps, very illuminating. In thinking of this division of the personality into an ego, a super-ego and an id, you will not, of course, have pictured sharp frontiers like the artificial ones drawn in political geography. We cannot do justice to the characteristics of the mind by linear outlines like those in a drawing or in primitive painting, but rather by areas of colour melting into one another as they are presented by modern artists. After making the separation we must allow what we have separated to merge together once more. You must not judge too harshly a first attempt at giving a pictorial representation of something so intangible as psychical processes. It is highly probable that the development of these divisions is subject to great variations in different individuals; it is possible that in the course of actual functioning they may change and go through a temporary phase of involution. Particularly in the case of what is phylogenetically the last and most delicate of these divisions—the differentiation between the ego and the super-ego—something of the sort seems to be true. There is no question but that the same thing results from psychical illness. It is easy to imagine, too, that certain mystical practices may succeed in upsetting the normal relations between the different regions of the mind, so that, for instance, perception may be able to grasp happenings in the depths of the ego and in the id which were otherwise inaccessible to it. It may safely be doubted, however, whether this road will lead us to the ultimate truths from which salvation is to be expected. Nevertheless it may be admitted that the therapeutic efforts of psychoanalysis have chosen a similar line of approach. Its intention is, indeed, to strengthen the ego, to make it more independent of the super-ego, to widen its field of perception and enlarge its organization, so that it can appropriate fresh portions of the id. Where id was, there ego shall be. It is a work of culture—not unlike the draining of the Zuider Zee.[9]

[9]The "Zuider Zee" was a landlocked arm of the North Sea in the Netherlands. Its draining was a major land-reclamation project completed in 1932, about the time this essay was written.

Lecture III: Parapraxes

Sigmund Freud

The following selection comes from one of the original series of introductory lectures that Freud delivered in Vienna in 1916, about 15 years before writing the previous lecture. In this excerpt we see Freud doing his best to sell psychoanalysis to his audience, by answering their objections as he imagines them and illustrating his points with a large number of compelling examples.

Freud contributed many ideas that have entered everyday thought and speech. One of the most influential of those was his explanation of the phenomenon now popularly called the "Freudian slip." In the following selection, you can read in his own words what Freud thought about Freudian slips.

From *Introductory Lectures on Psycho-analysis*, by Sigmund Freud, in *The Standard Edition of the Complete Psychological Works of Sigmund Freud*, translated by James Strachey (New York: W. W. Norton, 1964), pp. 48–72.

Ladies and Gentlemen,—We arrived last time at the idea of considering parapraxes[1] not in relation to the intended function which they disturbed but on their own account; and we formed an impression that in particular cases they seemed to be betraying a sense of their own. We then reflected that if confirmation could be obtained on a wider scale that parapraxes have a sense, their sense would soon become more interesting than the investigation of the circumstances in which they come about.

Let us once more reach an agreement upon what is to be understood by the "sense" of a psychical process. We mean nothing other by it than the intention it serves and its position in a psychical continuity.[2] In most of our researches we can replace "sense" by "intention" or "purpose." Was it, then, merely a deceptive illusion or a poetic exaltation of parapraxes when we thought we recognized an intention in them?

We will take slips of the tongue as our examples. If we now look through a considerable number of observations of that kind, we shall find whole categories of cases in which the intention, the sense, of the slip is plainly visible. Above all there are those in which what was intended is replaced by its contrary. The President of the Lower House said in his opening speech: "I declare the

[1]Freud used the German word "*Fehlleistungen*," which means "faulty acts" or "faulty functions." According to his translator, James Strachey, the concept did not exist before Freud and so a new word—*parapraxis*, the plural of which is *parapraxes*—was invented for use in English translations of Freud's writing (Freud, 1920/1989).

[2]By "psychical continuity" Freud means the interrelated functions of the different parts of the mind.

sitting closed."[3] That is quite unambiguous. The sense and intention of his slip was that he wanted to close the sitting. * * * We need only take him at his word. Do not interrupt me at this point by objecting that that is impossible, that we know that he did not want to close the sitting but to open it, and that he himself, whom we have just recognized as the supreme court of appeal, could confirm the fact that he wanted to open it. You are forgetting that we have come to an agreement that we will begin by regarding parapraxes on their own account; their relation to the intention which they have disturbed is not to be discussed till later. Otherwise you will be guilty of a logical error by simply evading the problem that is under discussion—by what is called in English "begging the question."

In other cases the slip of the tongue merely adds a second sense to the one intended. The sentence then sounds like a contraction, abbreviation, or condensation of several sentences. Thus, when the energetic lady said: "He can eat and drink what I want,"[4] it was just as though she had said: "He can eat and drink what he wants; but what has *he* to do with wanting? *I* will want instead of him." A slip of the tongue often gives the impression of being an abbreviation of this sort. For instance, a professor of anatomy at the end of a lecture on the nasal cavities asked whether his audience had understood what he said and, after general assent, went on: "I can hardly believe that, since even in a city with millions of inhabitants, those who understand the nasal cavities can be counted *on one finger* . . . I beg your pardon, on the fingers of one hand." The abbreviated phrase has a sense too—namely, that there is only one person who understands them.

In contrast to these groups of cases, in which the parapraxis itself brings its sense to light, there are others in which the parapraxis produces nothing that has any sense of its own, and which therefore sharply contradict our expectations. If someone twists a proper name about by a slip of the tongue or puts an abnormal series of sounds together, these very common events alone seem to give a negative reply to our question whether all parapraxes have some sort of sense. Closer examination of such instances, however, shows that these distortions are easily understood and that there is by no means so great a distinction between these more obscure cases and the earlier straightforward ones.

A man who was asked about the health of his horse replied: "Well, it *draut* [a meaningless word] . . . it *dauert* [will last] another month perhaps." When he was asked what he had really meant to say, he explained that he had thought it was a "*traurige* [sad]" story. The combination of "*dauert*" and "*traurig*" had produced "*draut*."

* * *

We seem now to have grasped the secret of a large number of slips of the tongue. If we bear this discovery in mind, we shall be able to understand other groups as well which have puzzled us hitherto. In cases of distortion of names, for instance, we cannot suppose that it is always a matter of competition between two similar but different names. It is not difficult, however, to guess the second intention. The distortion of a name occurs often enough apart from slips of the tongue; it seeks to give the name an offensive sound or to make it sound like something inferior, and it is a familiar practice (or malpractice) designed as an insult, which civilized people soon learn to abandon, but which they are *reluctant* to abandon. It is still often permitted as a "joke," though a pretty poor one. As a blatant and ugly example of this way of distorting names, I may mention that in these days [of the first World War] the name of the President of the French Republic, Poincaré, has been changed into "*Schweinskarré*."[5] It is therefore plausible to suppose that the same in-

[3]In his previous lecture, Freud had told of a politician who opened Parliament by saying, "Gentlemen, I take notice that a full quorum of members is present and herewith declare the sitting closed."

[4]The story referred to a woman who said, "My husband asked his doctor what diet he ought to follow; but the doctor told him he had no need to diet: he could eat and drink what I want."

[5]"The Viennese term for a pork chop."—Translator

sulting intention is present in these slips of the tongue and is trying to find expression in the distortion of a name. * * *

* * *

Well, it looks now as though we have solved the problem of parapraxes, and with very little trouble! They are not chance events but serious mental acts; they have a sense; they arise from the concurrent action—or perhaps rather, the mutually opposing action—of two different intentions. But now I see too that you are preparing to overwhelm me with a mass of questions and doubts which will have to be answered and dealt with before we can enjoy this first outcome of our work. I certainly have no desire to force hasty decisions upon you. Let us take them all in due order, one after the other, and give them cool consideration.

What is it you want to ask me? Do I think that this explanation applies to *all* parapraxes or only to a certain number? Can this same point of view be extended to the many other kinds of parapraxis, to misreading, slips of the pen, forgetting, bungled actions, mislaying, and so on? In view of the psychical nature of parapraxes, what significance remains for the factors of fatigue, excitement, absent-mindedness and interference with the attention? Further, it is clear that of the two competing purposes in a parapraxis one is always manifest, but the other not always. What do we do, then, in order to discover the latter? And, if we think we have discovered it, how do we prove that it is not merely a probable one but the only correct one? Is there anything else you want to ask? If not, I will go on myself. You will recall that we do not set much store by parapraxes themselves, and that all we want is to learn from studying them something that may be turned to account for psycho-analysis. I therefore put this question to you. What are these intentions or purposes which are able to disturb others in this way? And what are the relations between the disturbing purposes and the disturbed ones? Thus, no sooner is the problem solved than our work begins afresh.

First, then, is this the explanation of *all* cases of slips of the tongue? I am very much inclined to think so, and my reason is that every time one investigates an instance of a slip of the tongue an explanation of this kind is forthcoming. But it is also true that there is no way of proving that a slip of the tongue cannot occur without this mechanism. It may be so; but theoretically it is a matter of indifference to us, since the conclusions we want to draw for our introduction to psycho-analysis remain, even though—which is certainly not the case—our view holds good of only a minority of cases of slips of the tongue. The next question—whether we may extend our view to other sorts of parapraxis—I will answer in advance with a "yes." You will be able to convince yourselves of this when we come to examining instances of slips of the pen, bungled actions, and so on. * * *

A more detailed reply is called for by the question of what significance remains for the factors put forward by the authorities—disturbances of the circulation, fatigue, excitement, absent-mindedness and the theory of disturbed attention—if we accept the psychical mechanism of slips of the tongue which we have described. Observe that we are not denying these factors. It is in general not such a common thing for psycho-analysis to *deny* something asserted by other people; as a rule it merely adds something new—though no doubt it occasionally happens that this thing that has hitherto been overlooked and is now brought up as a fresh addition is in fact the essence of the matter. The influence on the production of slips of the tongue by physiological dispositions brought about by slight illness, disturbances of the circulation or states of exhaustion, must be recognized at once; daily and personal experience will convince you of it. But how little they explain! Above all, they are not necessary preconditions of parapraxes. Slips of the tongue are just as possible in perfect health and in a normal state. These somatic factors only serve therefore, to facilitate and favour the peculiar mental mechanism of slips of the tongue. I once used an analogy to describe this relation, and I will repeat it here since I can think of none better to take its place. Suppose that one dark night I went to a lonely spot and was there attacked by a rough who took away my watch and purse. Since I did not see the robber's face clearly, I laid my complaint at the nearest police station with the words: "Loneliness and darkness have just robbed me of my valuables." The police officer might then say to me: "In what you say you seem to be unjustifiably adopting an extreme mechanistic view. It would be better to represent the facts in this way: 'Under the shield of darkness and favoured by loneliness, an unknown thief robbed you of your valuables.' In your case the essential task seems to me to be that we should find the thief. Perhaps we shall then be able to recover the booty."

Such psycho-physiological factors as excitement, absent-mindedness and disturbances of attention will clearly help us very little towards an explanation. They are only empty phrases, screens behind which we must not let ourselves be prevented from having a look. The question is rather what it is that has been brought about here by the excitement, the particular distracting of attention. And again, we must recognize the importance of the influence of sounds, the similarity of words and the familiar associations aroused by words. These facilitate slips of the tongue by pointing to the paths they can take. But if I have a path open to me, does that fact automatically decide that I shall take it? I need a motive in addition before I resolve in favour of it and furthermore a force to propel me along the path. So these relations of sounds and words are also, like the somatic dispositions, only things that *favour* slips of the tongue and cannot provide the true explanation of them. Only consider: in an immense majority of cases my speech is not disturbed by the circumstance that the words I am using recall others with a similar sound, that they are intimately linked with their contraries or that familiar associations branch off from them. Perhaps we might still find a way out by following the philosopher Wundt, when he says that slips of the tongue arise if, as a result of physical exhaustion, the inclination to associate gains the upper hand over what the speaker otherwise intends to say. That would be most convincing if it were not contradicted by experience, which shows that in one set of cases the *somatic* factors favouring slips of the tongue are absent and in another set of cases the *associative* factors favouring them are equally absent.

I am particularly interested, however, in your next question: how does one discover the two mutually interfering purposes? You do not realize, probably, what a momentous question this is. One of the two, the purpose that is disturbed, is of course unmistakable: the person who makes the slip of the tongue knows it and admits to it. It is only the other, the disturbing purpose, that can give rise to doubt and hesitation. Now, we have already seen, and no doubt you have not forgotten, that in a number of cases this other purpose is equally evident. It is indicated by the *outcome* of the slip, if only we have the courage to grant that outcome a validity of its own. Take the President of the Lower House, whose slip of the tongue said the contrary of what he intended. It is clear that he wanted to open the sitting, but it is equally clear that he also wanted to close it. That is so obvious that it leaves us nothing to interpret. But in the other cases, in which the disturbing purpose only *distorts* the original one without itself achieving complete expression, how do we arrive at the disturbing purpose from the distortion?

In a first group of cases this is done quite simply and securely—in the same way, in fact, as with the *disturbed* purpose. We get the speaker to give us the information directly. After his slip of the tongue he at once produces the wording which he originally intended: "It *draut* . . . no, it *dauert* [will last] another month perhaps." [p. 257]. Well, in just the same way we get him to tell us the *disturbing* purpose. 'Why', we ask him, 'did you say "*draut*"?' He replies: 'I wanted to say "It's a *traurige* [sad] story".' * * * The speaker had to be asked why he had made the slip and what he could say about it. Otherwise he might perhaps have passed over his slip without wanting to explain it. But when he was asked he gave the explanation with the first thing that occurred to him. And now please observe that this small active step and its successful outcome are already a psycho-analysis and are a model for every psycho-analytic investigation which we shall embark upon later.

Am I too mistrustful, however, if I suspect that at the very moment at which psycho-analysis makes its appearance before your resistance to it simultaneously raises its head? Do you not feel inclined to object that the information given by the person of whom the question was asked—the person who made the slip of the tongue—is not completely conclusive? He was naturally anxious, you think, to fulfil the request to explain the slip, so he said the first thing that came into his head which seemed capable of providing such an explanation. But that is no proof that the slip did in fact take place in that way. It *may* have been so, but it may just as well have happened otherwise. And something else might have occurred to him which would have fitted in as well or perhaps even better.

It is strange how little respect you have at bottom for a psychical fact! Imagine that someone had undertaken the chemical analysis of a certain substance and had arrived at a particular weight for one component of it—so and so many milligrammes. Certain inferences could be drawn from this weight. Now do you suppose that it would ever occur to a chemist to criticize those inferences on the ground that the isolated substance might equally have had some other weight? Everyone will bow before the fact that this was the weight and none other and will confidently draw his further inferences from it. But when you are faced with the psychical fact that a particular thing occurred to the mind of the person questioned, you will not allow the fact's validity: something else might have occurred to him! You nourish the illusion of there being such a thing as psychical freedom, and you will not give it up. I am sorry to say I disagree with you categorically over this.

You will break off at that, but only to take up your resistance again at another point. You proceed: "It is the special technique of psycho-analysis, as we understand, to get people under analysis themselves to produce the solution of their problems. Now let us take another example—the one in which a speaker proposing the toast of honour on a ceremonial occasion called on his audience to hiccough [*aufzustossen*] to the health of the Chief. You say that the disturbing intention in this case was an insulting one: that was what was opposing the speaker's expression of respect. But this is pure interpretation on your part, based upon observations apart from the slip of the tongue. If in this instance you were to question the person responsible for the slip, he would not confirm your idea that he intended an insult; on the contrary, he would energetically repudiate it. Why, in view of this clear denial, do you not abandon your unprovable interpretation?"

Yes. You have lighted on a powerful argument this time. I can imagine the unknown proposer of the toast. He is probably a subordinate to the Chief of the Department who is being honoured—perhaps he himself is already an Assistant Lecturer, a young man with excellent prospects in life. I try to force him to admit that he may nevertheless have had a feeling that there was something in him opposing his toast in honour of the Chief. But this lands me in a nice mess. He gets impatient and suddenly breaks out: "Just you stop trying to cross-question me or I shall turn nasty. You're going to ruin my whole career with your suspicions. I simply said '*aufstossen* [hiccough to]' instead of '*anstossen* [drink to]' because I'd said '*auf*' twice before in the same sentence. That's what Meringer calls a perseveration and there's nothing more to be interpreted about it. D'you understand? *Basta!*"—H'm! That was a surprising reaction, a truly energetic denial. I see there's nothing more to be done with the young man. But I also reflect that he shows a strong personal interest in insisting on his parapraxis not having a sense. You may also feel that there was something wrong in his being quite so rude about a purely theoretical enquiry. But, you will think, when all is said and done he must know what he wanted to say and what he didn't.

But must he? Perhaps that may still be the question.

Now, however, you think you have me at your mercy. "So that's your technique," I hear you say. "When a person who has made a slip of the tongue says something about it that suits you, you pronounce him to be the final decisive authority on the subject. "He says so himself!" But when what he says doesn't suit your book, then all at once you say he's of no importance—there's no need to believe him."

That is quite true. But I can put a similar case to you in which the same monstrous event occurs. When someone charged with an offence confesses his deed to the judge, the judge believes his confession; but if he denies it, the judge does not believe him. If it were otherwise, there would be no administration of justice, and in spite of occasional errors we must allow that the system works.

"Are you a judge, then? And is a person who has made a slip of the tongue brought up before you on a charge? So making a slip of the tongue is an offence, is it?"

Perhaps we need not reject the comparison. But I would ask you to observe what profound differences of opinion we have reached after a little investigation of what seemed such innocent problems concerning the parapraxes—differences which at the moment we see no possible way of smoothing over. I propose a provisional compromise on the basis of the analogy with the judge and the defendant. I suggest that you shall grant me that there can be no doubt of a parapraxis having a sense if the subject himself admits it. *I* will admit in return that we cannot arrive at a direct proof of the suspected sense if the subject refuses us information, and equally, of course, if he is not at hand to give us the information. Then, as in the case of the administration of justice, we are obliged to turn to circumstantial evidence, which may make a decision more probable in some instances and less so in others. In the law courts it may be necessary for practical purposes to find a defendant guilty on circumstantial evidence. We are under no such necessity; but neither are we obliged to disregard the circumstantial evidence. It would be a mistake to suppose that a science consists entirely of strictly proved theses, and it would be unjust to require this. Only a disposition with a passion for authority will raise such a demand, someone with a craving to replace his religious catechism by another, though it is a scientific one. Science has only a few apodeictic[6] propositions in its catechism: the rest are assertions promoted by it to some particular degree of probability. It is actually a sign of a scientific mode of thought to find satisfaction in these approximations to certainty and to be able to pursue constructive work further in spite of the absence of final confirmation.

But if the subject does not himself give us the explanation of the sense of a parapraxis, where are we to find the starting-points for our interpretation—the circumstantial evidence? In various directions. In the first place from analogies with phenomena apart from parapraxes: when, for instance, we assert that distorting a name when it occurs as a slip of the tongue has the same insulting sense as a deliberate twisting of a name. Further, from the psychical situation in which the parapraxis occurs, the character of the person who makes the parapraxis, and the impressions which he has received before the parapraxis and to which the parapraxis is perhaps a reaction. What happens as a rule is that the interpretation is carried out according to general principles: To begin with there is only a suspicion, a suggestion for an interpretation, and we then find a confirmation by examining the psychical situation. Sometimes we have to wait for subsequent events as well (which have, as it were, announced themselves by the parapraxis) before our suspicion is confirmed.

I cannot easily give you illustrations of this if I limit myself to the field of slips of the tongue, though even there some good instances are to be found. * * * The lady whose husband could eat and drink what *she* wanted is known to me as one of those energetic women who wear the breeches in their home. * * *

But I can give you a large selection of circumstantial evidence of this kind if I pass over to the wide field of the other parapraxes.

If anyone forgets a proper name which is familiar to him normally or if, in spite of all his

---

[6]Indisputable.

efforts, he finds it difficult to keep it in mind, it is plausible to suppose that he has something against the person who bears the name so that he prefers not to think of him. Consider, for instance, what we learn in the following cases about the psychical situation in which the parapraxis occurred.

"A Herr Y. fell in love with a lady, but he met with no success, and shortly afterward she married a Herr X. Thereafter, Herr Y., in spite of having known Herr X. for a long time and even having business dealings with him, forgot his name over and over again, so that several times he had to enquire what it was from other people when he wanted to correspond with Herr X." Herr Y. evidently wanted to know nothing of his more fortunate rival: "never thought of shall he be."

Or: A lady enquired from her doctor for news of a common acquaintance, but called her by her maiden name. She had forgotten her friend's married name. She admitted afterwards that she had been very unhappy about the marriage and disliked her friend's husband.

* * *

The forgetting of intentions can in general be traced to an opposing current of thought, which is unwilling to carry out the intention. But this view is not only held by us psycho-analysts; it is the general opinion, accepted by everyone in their daily lives and only denied when it comes to theory. A patron who gives his protégé the excuse of having forgotten his request fails to justify himself. The protégé immediately thinks: "It means nothing to him; it's true he promised, but he doesn't really want to do it." For that reason forgetting is banned in certain circumstances of ordinary life; the distinction between the popular and the psycho-analytic view of these parapraxes seems to have disappeared. Imagine the lady of the house receiving her guest with the words: "What? have you come today? I'd quite forgotten I invited you for today." Or imagine a young man confessing to his fiancée that he had forgotten to keep their last rendezvous. He will certainly not confess it; he will prefer to invent on the spur of the moment the most improbable obstacles which prevented his appearing at the time and afterwards made it impossible for him to let her know. We all know too that in military affairs the excuse of having forgotten something is of no help and is no protection against punishment, and we must all feel that that is justified. Here all at once everyone is united in thinking that a particular parapraxis has a sense and in knowing what that sense is. Why are they not consistent enough to extend this knowledge to the other parapraxes and to admit them fully? There is of course an answer to this question too.

* * *

Cases of forgetting an intention are in general so clear that they are not of much use for our purpose of obtaining circumstantial evidence of the sense of a parapraxis from the psychical situation. Let us therefore turn to a particularly ambiguous and obscure kind of parapraxis—to losing and mislaying. You will no doubt find it incredible that we ourselves can play an intentional part in what is so often the painful accident of losing something. But there are plenty of observations like the following one. A young man lost a pencil of his of which he had been very fond. The day before, he had received a letter from his brother-in-law which ended with these words: "I have neither the inclination nor the time at present to encourage you in your frivolity and laziness." The pencil had actually been given to him by this brother-in-law. Without this coincidence we could not, of course, have asserted that a part was played in the loss by an intention to get rid of the thing. Similar cases are very common. We lose an object if we have quarreled with the person who gave it to us and do not want to be reminded of him; or if we no longer like the object itself and want to have an excuse for getting another and better one instead. The same intention directed against an object can also play a part, of course, in cases of dropping, breaking, or destroying things. Can we regard it as a matter of chance when a schoolchild immediately before his birthday loses, ruins or smashes some of his personal belongings, such as his satchel or his watch?

Nor will anyone who has sufficiently often experienced the torment of not being able to find something that he himself has put away feel inclined to believe that there is a purpose in mislaying things. Yet instances are far from rare in which the circumstances attendant on the mislaying point to an intention to get rid of the object temporarily or permanently.

Here is the best example, perhaps, of such an occasion. A youngish man told me the following story: "Some years ago there were misunderstandings between me and my wife. I found her too cold, and although I willingly recognized her excellent qualities we lived together without any tender feelings. One day, returning from a walk, she gave me a book which she had bought because she thought it would interest me. I thanked her for this mark of 'attention,' promised to read the book and put it on one side. After that I could never find it again. Months passed by, in which I occasionally remembered the lost book and made vain attempts to find it. About six months later my dear mother, who was not living with us, fell ill. My wife left home to nurse her mother-in-law. The patient's condition became serious and gave my wife an opportunity of showing the best side of herself. One evening I returned home full of enthusiasm and gratitude for what my wife had accomplished. I walked up to my desk, and without any definite intention but with a kind of somnambulistic certainty opened one of the drawers. On the very top I found the long-lost book I had mislaid." With the extinction of the motive the mislaying of the object ceased as well.

Ladies and Gentlemen, I could multiply this collection of examples indefinitely; but I will not do so here. You will in any case find a profusion of case material for the study of parapraxes in my *Psychopathology of Everyday Life* (first published in 1901). All these examples lead to the same result: they make it probable that parapraxes have a sense, and they show you how that sense is discovered or confirmed by the attendant circumstances. I will be briefer to-day, because we have adopted the limited aim of using the study of these phenomena as a help towards a preparation for psychoanalysis. There are only two groups of observations into which I need enter more fully here: accumulated and combined parapraxes and the confirmation of our interpretations by subsequent events.

Accumulated and combined parapraxes are without doubt the finest flower of their kind. If we had only been concerned to prove that parapraxes have a sense we should have confined ourselves to them from the first, for in their case the sense is unmistakable even to the dull-witted and forces itself on the most critical judgement. An accumulation of these phenomena betrays an obstinacy that is scarcely ever a characteristic of chance events but fits in well with something intentional. Finally, the mutual interchangeability between different species of parapraxes demonstrates what it is in parapraxes that is important and characteristic: not their form or the method which they employ but the purpose which they serve and which can be achieved in the most various ways. For this reason I will give you an instance of repeated forgetting. Ernest Jones[7] tells us that once, for reasons unknown to him, he left a letter lying on his desk for several days. At last he decided to send it off, but he had it returned to him by the Dead Letter Office since he had forgotten to address it. After he had addressed it he took it to the post, but this time it had no stamp. And then at last he was obliged to admit his reluctance to sending the letter off at all.

In another case a bungled action is combined with an instance of mislaying. A lady travelled to Rome with her brother-in-law, who was a famous artist. The visitor was received with great honour by the German community in Rome, and among other presents he was given an antique gold medal. The lady was vexed that her brother-in-law did not appreciate the lovely object sufficiently. When she returned home (her place in Rome having been taken by her sister) she discovered while unpacking that she had brought the medal with her—how, she did not know. She at once sent a letter with the news to her brother-in-law, and announced that she would send the article she had

[7]An English psychoanalyst.

walked off with back to Rome next day. But next day the medal had been so cleverly mislaid that it could not be found and sent off; and it was at this point, that the meaning of her "absent-mindedness" dawned on the lady: she wanted to keep the object for herself.

* * *

It would be agreeable to add further, similar examples. But I must proceed, and give you a glimpse of the cases in which our interpretation has to wait for the future for confirmation. The governing condition of these cases, it will be realized, is that the present psychical situation is unknown to us or inaccessible to our enquiries. Our interpretation is consequently no more than a suspicion to which we ourselves do not attach too much importance. Later, however, something happens which shows us how well-justified our interpretation had been. I was once the guest of a young married couple and heard the young woman laughingly describe her latest experience. The day after her return from the honeymoon she had called for her unmarried sister to go shopping with her as she used to do, while her husband went to his business. Suddenly she noticed a gentleman on the other side of the street, and nudging her sister had cried: "Look, there goes Herr L." She had forgotten that this gentleman had been her husband for some weeks. I shuddered as I heard the story, but I did not dare to draw the inference. The little incident only occurred to my mind some years later when the marriage had come to a most unhappy end.

Maeder tells of a lady who, on the eve of her wedding had forgotten to try on her wedding-dress and, to her dressmaker's despair, only remembered it late in the evening. He connects this forgetfulness with the fact that she was soon divorced from her husband. I know a lady now divorced from her husband, who in managing her money affairs frequently signed documents in her maiden name, many years before she in fact resumed it.—I know of other women who have lost their wedding-rings during the honeymoon, and I know too that the history of their marriages has given a sense to the accident.—And now here is one more glaring example, but with a happier ending. The story is told of a famous German chemist that his marriage did not take place, because he forgot the hour of his wedding and went to the laboratory instead of to the church. He was wise enough to be satisfied with a single attempt and died at a great age unmarried.

The idea may possibly have occurred to you that in these examples parapraxes have taken the place of the omens or auguries of the ancients. And indeed some omens were nothing else than parapraxes, as, for instance, when someone stumbled or fell down. Others of them, it is true, had the character of objective happenings and not of subjective acts. But you would hardly believe how difficult it sometimes is to decide whether a particular event belongs to the one group or to the other. An act so often understands how to disguise itself as a passive experience.

All those of us who can look back on a comparatively long experience of life will probably admit that we should have spared ourselves many disappointments and painful surprises if we had found the courage and determination to interpret small parapraxes experienced in our human contacts as auguries and to make use of them as indications of intentions that were still concealed. As a rule we dare not do so; it would make us feel as though, after a detour through science, we were becoming superstitious again. Nor do all auguries come true, and you will understand from our theories that they do not all need to come true.

Survey of Objective Studies of Psychoanalytic Concepts: Conclusions

Robert R. Sears

There has been a great deal of interest and controversy about Freud and his psychoanalytic theory, both when he was alive and in the many years since he died. Many psychologists of Freud's time tried to work with and test psychoanalytic concepts in the laboratory, although Freud himself never did this. Soon after Freud died, in 1939, the Social Science Research Council decided it was important to summarize the laboratory-based research done up to that time to try to test psychoanalytic concepts. They commissioned Robert Sears to do the summary, and in 1943 he published a 152-page monograph reporting all the relevant research he could find. The specific studies are not included in the excerpt here, because the subsequent selection, by Baumeister et al., provides a good summary of some much more recent research. Instead, this selection is from Sears's final chapter, where he presented his overall conclusions. One of the most important is Sears's conclusion that—contrary to Freud's most hostile critics—psychoanalysis is indeed a science, but that as practiced by Freud and his followers it is "a bad science." Interestingly, Sears also concludes that to fully *evaluate psychoanalytic theory we will need to understand* all *of human psychology, and the future research he suggests (e.g., longitudinal studies of development) are aimed at that goal. In this way, Sears shows how psychoanalytic theory provides a research agenda that continues to guide and organize all of personality psychology.*

From Survey of objective studies of psychoanalytic concepts. In *Social Science Research Council Bulletin, 51*, 133–143, 1943.

Psychoanalysis is a science of personality. By the criteria of the physical sciences it is not a *good* science, but whatever its weaknesses it deals with many things other sciences have ignored, the development of forbidden impulses, the unconscious, a whole host of fantastic mechanisms of self-deceit. These aspects of human behavior can no longer be ignored; they must be incorporated into the general body of scientific knowledge. How to do this is a puzzler.

The experiments and observations examined in this report stand testimony that few investigators feel free to accept Freud's statements at face value. The reason lies in the same factor that makes psychoanalysis a bad science—its method. Psychoanalysis relies upon techniques that do not admit of the repetition of observation, that have no self-evident or denotative validity, and that are tinctured to an unknown degree with the observer's own suggestions. These difficulties may not seriously interfere with therapy, but when the method is used for uncovering psychological facts that are required to have objective validity it simply fails.

This does not mean that all psychoanalytic findings are false, but it does mean that other methods must be sought for their critical evaluation and validation. This present report has served as a summary of such efforts to date.

So, how much of psychoanalysis is "true"? Blunt as it may sound, this question is reasonable enough if it is interpreted to mean: how similar are the descriptions of personality development and operation that are given by the psychoanalytic method and by other methods of investigation? There can be no simple quantitative answer, of course, and there are no critical comparisons of the two kinds of personality description. It is possible to say only that certain facts do or do not support the theory. When a fact is said to support the theory nothing more is meant than that if the theory is true, the facts in question would be expected to exist. Nothing is implied about the *uniqueness* of the theory as an explanation of the facts—perhaps a dozen other theories would provide as good or better explanations—but the facts do not contravene the theory.

Still another consideration must be held in mind in trying to evaluate the degree of correspondence between the two sources of data: the nature of any fact is in part a function of the method by which it is obtained. The findings of psychoanalysis relate to the ideas and verbalizations that accompany various kinds of behavior, for example, sexual development. The data are secured from the free associations of adults, usually, and depend upon recall of childhood events. Like any other verbalizations about the experienced world, these communicate to others a picture of the world that cannot accord exactly with anyone's else; in other words, there are individualized distortions in the picture created by each person's unique language habits. Since the facts of psychoanalysis are derived entirely through verbal channels, allowance must be made for discrepancies that hinge mainly on the fact that non-analytic investigations frequently represent observations of other kinds of behavior.

This matter becomes very important in connection with such notions as the Oedipus complex. Freud assumed the Oedipus relationship to exist universally, and while other investigators have found instances of it, no indications of a universal cross-sex parental preference have been discovered in either children or adults.[1] Is this discrepancy a function of the small and specialized sample of personalities in Freud's private practice, or is it a reflection of two different kinds of behavior samples, one a verbal recall by adults, the other a verbal affect judgment by children?* * *

In spite of these various difficulties and qualifications, a few conclusions relative to specific concepts and principles can be reached.

Infantile Sexuality

Freud's conception of infantile sexuality is rather well supported by other sources of information. The erotogenic[2] character of the oral and anal-urethral zones has been established; children seek stimulation of these areas, interference with such behavior induces characteristic frustration reactions, and consummatory reactions[3] appear to oc-

[1]You may recall that the "Oedipus complex," named for the ancient Greek who unknowingly killed his father and married his mother, is the label for Freud's description of how children's—especially boys'—first erotic attraction is to their opposite-sex parent. This description would seem to predict that children tend to prefer their opposite-sex parent over the same-sex parent, but Sears is noting that other investigators have not found this to be true.

[2]Productive of sexual feelings.

[3]Satisfaction.

cur as the end of the activity. But there is no information on the degree to which this erotogeneity is native, although some cross-cultural comparisons suggest that practice at the securing of gratification increases the strength of the drive. There is no evidence, however, to confirm Freud's assumptions about the interrelationship between the various erotogenic zones. Whether one zone can serve as substitute for another is still undetermined. Evidence has been discovered, however, that certain conditions which might conduce to the development of such interrelationship do exist; in infancy there is frequent simultaneous activation of behavior centering around all three erotogenic zones.

Sexual behavior in childhood has been shown to be exceedingly common, and the so-called pregenital impulses give rise to exactly the same kinds of guilt and shame reactions (because they are forbidden) as do genital impulses. To this extent children may be said to be polymorphous perverse.[4] There is no indication, however, that the castration complex[5] is common. Quite the contrary. Children whose sex information is adequate show little tendency toward fears or curious beliefs about the sexual process. It seems probable that Freud's notions about children's attitudes toward sex were based on a small sample that was far from characteristic of contemporary American children.

Oedipus: A Lesson in Cultural Relativity

It is a truism today that adult behavior is a function of the culture in which it was learned. Psychiatric thought had not gone so far at the beginning of the century, however, and Freud's notion of the universal Oedipus complex stands as a sharply etched grotesquerie against his otherwise informative description of sexual development. From the analysis of data relating to object choice, it is apparent that in this matter perhaps more than in any other the nature of the chosen object and the reactions to other similar or dissimilar objects are dependent on the early home environment of the child. So far are we in agreement with Freud. But, beyond this, Freud seeks a common or typical pattern of development. If such existed, it could come only from a common culture pattern, i.e., from a constant situation in which learning could take place in a uniform way.

But there are no universal patterns of family life. Monogamy may be the legal marriage form, income tax laws may, by a system of exemptions, strongly reinforce the role of the mother as a child raiser and of the father as an income producer, and social custom may be so organized as to make difficult the lives of people who deviate from the standard culture pattern, but still there is only partial uniformity in family structure. Fathers die, or flee from their wives, or are constantly irritated, or become successful and absorbed in their work or unsuccessful and absorbed in their families—or vice versa. Mothers can differ in as many ways as fathers, and hence no two family situations are the same. Each one is to some extent unique *as a learning situation for the children.*

With this fact in mind it does not seem surprising that Freud's description of sexual development is inaccurate and incomplete. Furthermore, sex behavior is subject to such strong social control that it has become taboo in many of its forms in our own society. This factor probably serves to increase the variability of attitudes toward sex on the part of parents, and hence to add still another factor that creates variability in the conditions under which object choices and other aspects of sex behavior are learned.

The data from non-analytic sources include descriptions of sequences like those described by Freud; in other words, Freud was able to abstract one of the not too uncommon developmental patterns. But other sequences have been observed,

---

[4]Freud labeled children as "polymorphous perverse" because of what he described as their ability to obtain quasi-sexual stimulation from almost anything.

[5]Boys' fear of being castrated, especially by their fathers, as punishment for sexual activity (including interest in their mothers) is an important part of Freud's story of the Oedipus complex.

too, and lead inescapably to the conclusion that Freud vastly underrated the importance of the child's immediate social milieu as a source for these kinds of learning, and overrated the uniformity of family patterns.

Development and Regression: The Role of Learning

The psychoanalytic emphasis on life history is reflected in the non-analytic studies as a prepossession[6] with the influence of learning. This interest applies principally in two connections—personality development and experimentally induced regression. In the case of the former there are few critical comparisons of different learning conditions that can be used to demonstrate the exact influence of rewards and punishments, although the nature of adult sexual distortions cries out for interpretation in such terms. In general it can be said that the objective data strongly reinforce the desirability of the life history approach so urgently required by psychoanalysis.[7] * * *

* * *

Mental Mechanisms

* * * The work on the mechanisms of repression and projection[8] has proved relatively unproductive. In each case there has been demonstration by non-analytic techniques that these processes exist and can be roughly measured. But in neither instance have the new methods of investigation been found to add appreciably to the available information. No new variables have been isolated and no new conditions of occurrence have been discovered. On the other hand, the fact of differential recallability for gratifying and anxiety-inducing experiences is of great importance, and the demonstrations of its existence (even with measurement by the coarse techniques of experimental psychology) lend some hope that future investigation may be more profitable. The same is true of projection, and in this case there is the additional satisfaction of knowing that Freud's suppositions about the importance of lack of insight and guilt feelings were correct.

Part of the reason for the unsatisfactory character of this research undoubtedly lies in the nature of the processes themselves. The so-called mental mechanisms are intangible processes at best. They are intimately related to both language and motivation, and in neither of these areas has experimental psychology yet developed either a sound systematic orientation or a body of technical information into which such concepts can easily be fitted. Also, the methods of experiment in these fields are less exact and less firmly embedded in theory than are the techniques for the study of the learning process.

Beyond these difficulties lies another, which is perhaps less easily overcome than these may be. Repression, projection and dreams are intimately dependent on strong emotions and motives. They are also dependent on language and verbal report. And these two dependencies taken together create difficulty in the laboratory. Strong emotion may safely be generated in animals, and nonemotional language or perceptual behavior may be studied in man. But animals are impossible reagents for the study of language, and the strong emotions cannot safely be used with man.

It appears that until some new conceptual organization of the facts from which these processes are inferred can be devised, progress in their investigation by non-analytic techniques must be slow.

The Directions of Progress

If psychoanalysis is viewed as a science of personality, there is reason to ask whether future research

[6]Almost exclusive interest.

[7]That is, to evaluate theories of development—including Freud's—psychologists need to follow samples of children all the way from early infancy into adulthood. Such studies were nonexistent in Freud's time, were rare in Sears's time, and are still uncommon today.

[8]In Freudian terms, "repression" is the pushing of unwanted thoughts out of consciousness, and "projection" is the attribution of unwanted aspects of oneself onto others.

should follow in the same framework or whether some different theoretical orientation holds more promise. Such a question requires consideration of the use to which the science is to be put, of course. Two areas appear at present to cover the matter: one is education, conceived in the broadest sense; and the other is therapy or re-education. Psychoanalysis has been more or less successful at the latter task, but although Freud's influence has pervaded the mental hygiene movement, social work, child psychology and even the more formal aspects of education, there is little indication that the details of the theory have been widely used in formulating the details of educational practice. The kind of personality science that is more widely used in such work is *behavioral* rather than *experiential*, and since the behavioral way of thinking about personality is of even more recent origin than psychoanalysis, there seems good reason for concluding that a behavioral science of personality has been found more useful in the past and may be expected to be so in the future. In any case, the educative process deals directly with behavior rather than with consciousness or the unconscious, and presumably would find behavioral principles of more value than experiential ones.

The greater efficacy with which nonpsychoanalytic techniques deal with behavioral processes has already been sufficiently emphasized. It would seem desirable, therefore, that future research by such methods should be designed to aid in the development of a science of personality that is not structured along the same lines as psychoanalysis, but has a systematic structure of its own based on the triumvirate of influences loosely defined as *growth*, *learning*, and *the social milieu*.

From a research standpoint, the data that have been surveyed in this report suggest * * * kinds of investigatory effort that give outstanding promise of contributing richly to the development of such a science of personality.

* * * There is crying need for the results of longitudinal research on personality development. Several projects have collected intimate and detailed data on the growing personalities of children, and some of these findings have been mentioned here. There are a great number of important hypotheses to be derived from psychoanalytic theory, however, that have not been tested with these data. Until such problems as the organization and interrelationships of pregenital impulses have been examined by reference to records obtained *year after year from the same child*, there are going to be serious lacunae in our knowledge of the motivational sources of adult sexuality and dependencies.

* * *

* * * Cross-cultural comparisons of personality development can assist in evaluating the significance of the social milieu as a source of motivational and trait characteristics. If the basic assumption of both psychoanalysis and behavioral personality science is correct, i.e., if the conditions of childhood learning largely determine adult characteristics, it is evident that the social milieu in which the child grows up is of pre-eminent significance in determining the nature of his secondary motives and his basic personality structure. * * *

The suggestion of these * * * types of research does not argue against pure psychoanalytic research. Such research must be evaluated on other grounds, and the present report gives no basis for estimating its desirability. The present suggestions are designed to support the development of a science of personality that is behavioral in character. They reflect the general conclusion from this survey that other social and psychological sciences must gain as many hypotheses and intuitions as possible from psychoanalysis but that the further analysis of psychoanalytic concepts by nonpsychoanalytic techniques may be relatively fruitless so long as those concepts rest in the theoretical framework of psychoanalysis.

Freudian Defense Mechanisms and Empirical Findings in Modern Social Psychology: Reaction Formation, Projection, Displacement, Undoing, Isolation, Sublimation, and Denial

Roy F. Baumeister, Karen Dale, and Kristin L. Sommer

The following selection summarizes a much more up-to-date research survey of the sort Sears, in the previous selection, had in mind. In this survey, Roy Baumeister, Karen Dale, and Kristin Sommer manage to recruit a surprising amount of contemporary research to the task of evaluating Freudian ideas. They do this by making a crucial reinterpretation of the psychoanalytic idea of the defense mechanism. Freud originally said that defense mechanisms existed to protect the ego. Baumeister and colleagues interpret the purpose of these mechanisms as the defense of self-esteem. *This narrows the focus of the defense mechanisms because a psychoanalyst would surely believe that their purpose is to defend against* anxiety, *and a threat to self-esteem is just one among many things that might cause a person anxiety. However, this narrowing of focus makes a huge amount of literature suddenly relevant; nearly everything published on the self—thousands of studies—is pertinent to psychological defense.*

From *Journal of Personality*, 66, 1081–1124, 1998.

Nearly all adults hold preferred views of themselves. In most cases, these are favorable views of self—indeed, somewhat more favorable than the objective facts would entirely warrant, as nearly all writers on the self have observed. A recurrent problem of human functioning, therefore, is how to sustain these favorable views of self. Patterns of self-deception can help create these inflated self-perceptions (for reviews, see Baumeister, 1998; Gilovich, 1991; Taylor, 1989). Yet a particular crisis in self-perception may arise when an internal or external event occurs that clearly violates the preferred view of self. In such cases, it is necessary for the self to have some mechanism or process to defend itself against the threatening implications of this event. Such processes are commonly called *defense mechanisms* (e.g., Cramer, 1991; A. Freud, 1936).

Sigmund Freud proposed a set of defense mechanisms, in a body of work that has long been influential (e.g., S. Freud, 1915/1961a, 1923/1961c, 1926/1961d). His work focused on how the ego defended itself against internal events, specifically, impulses that were regarded by the ego as unacceptable. He emphasized sexual or aggressive desires that would violate the ego's internalized standards, such as if those desires were directed toward one's parents. In his view, the efforts by the self to avoid recognizing its own sexual and aggressive desires were systematically important in shaping the personality.

Modern personality and social psychology has not generally accepted the view that personality is heavily based on efforts to disguise one's sexual and aggressive impulses. Nonetheless, the need for defense mechanisms remains quite strong. A revisionist idea, proposed by Fenichel (1945), is that defense mechanisms are actually designed to protect self-esteem. This reformulation is far more in keeping with current work in social and personality psychology than Freud's original view was. One can search long and hard through today's research journals without finding much evidence about how human behavior reflects attempts to ward off sexual and violent feelings, but evidence about efforts to protect self-esteem is abundant.

Ultimately, the view that defense mechanisms are oriented toward protecting self-esteem may not contradict Freud's views so much as it merely changes his emphasis. Acknowledging that one possessed socially unacceptable impulses of sex or violence may have constituted a self-esteem threat for the Victorian middle-class adults he studied. Today's adults are presumably less afraid of having sexual or violent feelings, and indeed the absence of sexual interest may constitute an esteem threat to some modern citizens—in which case their defense mechanisms would ironically try to increase the self-perceived frequency or power of sexual impulses, contrary to the Freudian pattern.

Most researchers in personality and social psychology today would readily acknowledge that people defend their self-concepts against esteem threats. Yet relatively few researchers have made explicit efforts to relate their findings about defensive processes to the general theory of defense mechanisms. The purpose of the present article is to review research findings from personality and social psychology that can be interpreted as reflecting the major defense mechanisms that Freud proposed. In a sense, then, this review will ask how Freud's list of insights stacks up against today's experimental work.

How much should one expect? Obviously, any accuracy at all would be impressive. Few researchers today would feel confident about having dozens of their theoretical hypotheses tested many decades into the future by empirical techniques that they today could not even imagine.

To anticipate the conclusion, we found substantial support for many (but not all) of the processes of defense Freud outlined. There are also some aspects to the causal process that Freud does not appear to have anticipated, as one would naturally expect. We shall describe a series of the major defense mechanisms and conclude that some of his ideas were correct, some require minor or major revision, and others have found little support. All in all, this amounts to a rather impressive positive testimony to Freud's seminal theorizing.

Plan and Task

* * *

We have chosen to emphasize defenses that are arguably most relevant to normal (as opposed to clinical) human functioning. The list is as follows: reaction formation, projection, displacement, * * * and denial.[1]

With each defense mechanism, we shall first ask whether research evidence shows that it actu-

---

[1]The original article also addressed three other defense mechanisms: undoing, isolation, and sublimation.

ally occurs. The strength and generality of this evidence must also be considered. If the defense mechanism is supported in some sense, then we must ask what the cognitive, affective, and behavioral processes are. A related question is whether there is evidence of defensive motivation, as opposed to evidence of some merely cognitive error or bias. To qualify as a full-fledged defense, it must do more than merely make people feel better: It must actually ward off some threat to the self.

Purely conscious maneuvers are not generally considered full-fledged defense mechanisms. Like self-deception generally, defense mechanisms must involve some motivated strategy that is not consciously recognized, resulting in a desirable conclusion or favorable view of self that is conscious.

Review of Findings

In this section, we shall examine * * * major defense mechanisms in turn. The review will try to ascertain how well each defense mechanism is supported in modern research in personality and social psychology and what theoretical adjustments may be required to make the theory fit modern findings.

* * *

Reaction Formation

Concept. The concept of reaction formation involves converting a socially unacceptable impulse into its opposite. To apply this notion to esteem protection, one may propose the following: People respond to the implication that they have some unacceptable trait by behaving in a way that would show them to have the opposite trait. Insinuations of hostility or intolerance might, for example, be countered with exaggerated efforts to prove oneself a peace-loving or tolerant person.

Evidence. The original ideas about reaction formation pertained to aggressive and sexual impulses, and these are still plausible places for finding defenses, provided that acknowledging those impulses or feelings would damage self-esteem. With sex, there are undoubtedly still cases in which people regard their own potential sexual responses as unacceptable.

One such finding was provided by Morokoff (1985), who exposed female subjects to erotic stimuli after assessing sex guilt. Women high in sex guilt would presumably regard erotica as unacceptable, and consistent with this attitude they reported lower levels of arousal in response to those stimuli. Physiological measures suggested, however, that these women actually had higher sexual arousal than other participants. The contradiction between the genital response and the self-report findings suggests that these women subjectively repudiated their physical sexual arousal and insisted that they were not aroused.

A comparable finding with male subjects was recently reported by Adams, Wright, and Lohr (1996). They assessed homophobia and then exposed participants to videotapes depicting homosexual intercourse. Homophobic men reported low levels of sexual arousal, but physiological measures indicated higher levels of sexual response than were found among other participants. Thus, again, the subjective response reported by these participants was the opposite of what their bodies actually indicated. This finding also fits the view that homophobia may itself be a reaction formation against homosexual tendencies, insofar as the men who were most aroused by homosexuality were the ones who expressed the most negative attitudes toward it.

Prejudice would provide the most relevant form of unacceptable aggressive impulse, because American society has widely endorsed strong norms condemning prejudice. If people are led to believe that they may hold unacceptably prejudiced beliefs (or even that others perceive them as being prejudiced), they may respond with exaggerated displays of not being prejudiced.

An early and convincing demonstration of reaction formation (although it was not called that) against prejudice was provided by Dutton and Lake (1973; see also Dutton, 1976). Nonprejudiced, egalitarian, White individuals were provided with false physiological feedback allegedly indicating that they held racist prejudices against Blacks. In one study, for example, they were shown slides of interracial couples, and the experimenter commented that the subject's skin response indicated severe intolerance of interracial romance, which was tantamount to racism. After the procedure was ostensibly completed, the participant left the building and was accosted by either a Black or a White panhandler. People who had been implicitly accused of racism gave significantly more money to the Black panhandler than people who had not been threatened in that way. Donations to the White panhandler were unaffected by the racism feedback. The implication was that people became generous toward the Black individual as a way of counteracting the insinuation that they were prejudiced against Blacks.

* * *

There is a related set of findings in which White subjects show preferential favorability toward Black stimulus persons without any threat. One might argue that White people often feel threatened by the possibility of seeming racist when interacting with Black people. Rogers and Prentice-Dunn (1981) found that White subjects playing the role of teacher administered fewer shocks to a Black than to a White confederate in the role of learner, although the effect was reversed if the learner had previously insulted them. Johnson, Whitestone, Jackson, and Gatto (1995) showed that White subjects as simulated jurors gave lighter sentences to Black than to White defendants, although this effect was reversed when a more severe sentence to the Black man could be defended on nonracial grounds. Shaffer and Case (1982) found that heterosexual simulated jurors gave lighter sentences to a homosexual defendant than to a heterosexual one, although this effect was found only among people who scored low in dogmatism.

Whether these effects constitute reaction formation is not entirely clear. Biernat, Manis, and Nelson (1991) provided evidence that people may use different standards when judging minority targets as opposed to judging members of the majority category. For example, a Black candidate for law school might be judged more favorably than a White candidate with identical credentials if the judges use more lenient criteria for Blacks. (Then again, the use of more lenient criteria might itself qualify as a reaction formation, insofar as it is a strategy to defend against one's own prejudice.)

* * *

Reaction formation may also be involved when self-appraisals paradoxically rise in response to negative feedback. McFarlin and Blascovich (1981) showed that people with high self-esteem made more optimistic predictions for future performance following initial failure than following initial success. Baumeister, Heatherton, and Tice (1993) showed this confidence to be irrational and unwarranted, and also showed it to be sufficiently powerful to motivate costly monetary bets. These responses do appear defensive and irrational, for there is no obvious reason that confidence should be increased by an initial failure experience.

Last, some evidence suggests a loose pattern of increasing favorable self-ratings in response to receiving bad (instead of good) personality feedback. Baumeister and Jones (1978) found enhanced self-ratings in response to bad feedback that was seen by other people, although the increased favorability was found only on items unrelated to the content of the feedback, indicating a compensatory mechanism rather than a pure reaction formation. Baumeister (1982b) provided evidence that people with high self-esteem were mainly responsible for the effect. Greenberg and Pyszczynski (1985) showed that this inflation of self-ratings occurred even on private ratings, although again mainly in response to public feedback. They pointed out that public bad feedback constitutes a stronger threat than private feedback. * * *

Conclusion Plenty of research findings conform to the broad pattern of reaction formation, defined loosely as a means of defending against esteem threat by exhibiting an exaggerated or extreme reaction in the opposite direction. Although the mechanism underlying reaction formation may not conform precisely to Freud's model, the human phenomena he characterized with that term do appear to be real. In particular, when people are publicly or implicitly accused of having socially undesirable sexual feelings, prejudiced attitudes, or failures of competence, some respond by asserting the opposite (and attempting to prove it) to an exceptionally high degree.

The consistency of these results across seemingly quite different spheres of esteem threat suggests that reaction formation deserves acceptance in social and personality psychology. Apparently it is one of the more prominent and common responses to esteem threat.

Still, the causal process underlying reaction formation remains to be elaborated. Many of the findings may be merely self-presentational strategies designed to correct another person's misperception rather than a genuinely intrapsychic defense mechanism. Moreover, if reaction formation can be firmly established as an intrapsychic response, it would be desirable to know how it operates. How, for example, does someone manage to feel sexually turned off when his or her body is exhibiting a strong positive arousal? How do people come to convince themselves that the money they give to a Black panhandler reflects a genuine attitude of racial tolerance rather than a response to the specific accusation of racism they recently received—especially when, as the researchers can show, those people would not have given nearly as much money to the same panhandler if they had not been accused of racism?

Projection

Concept. Projection is a popular concept in everyday discourse as well as in psychological thought. In its simplest form, it refers to seeing one's own traits in other people. A more rigorous understanding involves perceiving others as having traits that one inaccurately believes oneself not to have. As a broad form of influence of self-concept on person perception, projection may be regarded as more a cognitive bias than a defense mechanism. Nonetheless, projection *can* be seen as defensive if perceiving the threatening trait in others helps the individual in some way to avoid recognizing it in himself or herself, and indeed this is how Freud (e.g., 1915/1961a) conceptualized projection. Thus, there are multiple ways of understanding projection, and they vary mainly along the dimension of how effectively the undesirable trait or motive is repudiated as part of the self.

Evidence. The simpler, more loosely defined version of projection is fairly well documented. The *false consensus effect*, first described by Ross, Greene, and House (1977), is probably the best-known form of this, insofar as it is a broad tendency to assume that others are similar to oneself. The false consensus effect is defined as overestimating the percentage of other people who share one's traits, opinions, preferences, or motivations. This effect has both cognitive and motivational influences (Krueger & Clement, 1994; Marks, Graham, & Hansen, 1992; Sherman, Presson, & Chassin, 1984); is found if anything more with positive, desirable traits than with bad traits (Davis, Conklin, Smith, & Luce 1996; Halpern & Goldschmitt, 1976; Lambert & Wedell, 1991; Paulhus & Reynolds, 1995); has been especially shown with competitiveness (Kelley & Stahelski, 1970a, 1970b) and jealousy (Pines & Aronson, 1983); and is linked to higher self-esteem and lower depression (Campbell, 1986; Crocker, Alloy, & Kayne, 1988). Some contrary patterns have been found, especially insofar as people wish to regard their good traits and abilities as unusual (Dunning & Cohen, 1992; Suls & Wan, 1987). In general, these findings show that people like to see themselves as similar to others, but the evidence does not show this to be a defense mechanism that helps people avoid recognizing their own bad traits.

It could be argued that the false consensus effect achieves a kind of defensive success insofar as it reduces the distinctiveness of one's bad traits. To be the only person who cheats on taxes or breaks the speed limit would imply that one is uniquely immoral, even evil—but if everyone else is likewise breaking those laws, one's own actions can hardly be condemned with great force. Consistent with this, Sherwood (1981) concluded that attributing one's undesirable traits to targets who are perceived favorably can reduce stress. This explanation could also fit Bramel's (1962, 1963) demonstration that males who were told they had homosexual tendencies were later more likely to interpret other males' behavior as having similar tendencies. Likewise, it may explain the findings of Agostinelli, Sherman, Presson, and Chassin (1992): Receiving bogus failure feedback on a problem-solving task made people (except depressed people) more likely to predict that others would fail too.

None of these findings links seeing the trait in others to denying it in oneself, and so they fall short of the more rigorous definition of projection. Given the failure to show that projective responses can function to conceal one's own bad traits, Holmes (1968, 1978, 1981) concluded that defensive projection should be regarded as a myth. In retrospect, it was never clear how seeing another person as dishonest (for example) would enable the individual to avoid recognizing his or her own dishonesty. The notion that projection would effectively mask one's own bad traits was perhaps incoherent.

Recognizing the implausibility in the classical concept of projection, Newman, Duff, and Baumeister (1997) proposed a new model of defensive projection. In this view, people try to suppress thoughts of their undesirable traits, and these efforts make those trait categories highly accessible —so that they are then used all the more often when forming impressions of others (see Wegner, 1994; Wegner & Erber, 1992). In a series of studies, Newman et al. showed that repressors (as defined by Weinberger, Schwartz, & Davidson, 1979) were more likely than others to deny having certain bad traits, even though their acquaintances said they did have those bad traits. Repressors were then also more likely to interpret the ambiguous behaviors of others as reflecting those bad traits. Thus, they both denied their own faults and overinterpreted other people as having those faults.

The view that suppressing thoughts about one's undesirable traits leads to projection was then tested experimentally by Newman et al. (1997). Participants were given bogus feedback based on a personality test, to the effect that they had both good and bad traits. They were then instructed to avoid thinking about one dimension on which they had received (bad) feedback. Next, they observed a videotape of a stimulus person and rated that person on all the dimensions on which they had received feedback. Participants rated the stimulus person about the same on all dimensions, except that they rated her higher on the trait for which they had received bad feedback and been instructed to suppress. They did not rate the stimulus person higher on traits for which they had received bad feedback without trying to suppress it. Thus, projection results from trying to suppress thoughts about some bad trait in oneself.

Conclusion. Considerable evidence indicates that people's conceptions of themselves shape their perceptions of other people. The tendency to see others as having one's own traits has limitations and is found with good traits along with bad ones. The view that people defensively project specific bad traits of their own onto others as a means of denying that they have them is not well supported. The concept of projection thus needs to be revised in order to fit modern research findings.

The view of projection as a defense mechanism is best supported by the findings of Newman et al. (1997), but even these deviate from the classic psychodynamic theory of projection. Newman et al. found that efforts to suppress thoughts about a particular bad trait made this trait into a highly accessible category that thereafter shaped the perception of others. In this view, the projecting of the trait onto other people is a by-product of the defense, rather than being central to the defensive strategy. To put this another way: In the original Freudian view, seeing the bad trait in another person is the essential means of avoiding seeing it in oneself. In Newman et al.'s view, however, the defense is simply a matter of trying not to recognize one's bad trait, and the success of that effort is not related to whether a suitable target for projection presents himself or herself.

This mechanism could well account for the observations that might have led Freud to postulate the defense mechanism of projection in the first place. After all, the person does refuse at some level to accept some fault in himself or herself and does, as a result, end up seeing other people as having that same fault. The Freudian view implied the transfer of the schema from one's self-concept directly into the impression of the other person. It may, however, be more accurate to see the effect on impression formation as simply a consequence of heightened accessibility resulting from efforts at suppression.

DISPLACEMENT

Concept. Displacement refers to altering the target of an impulse. For example, an unacceptable violent impulse toward one's father might be transformed into a hostile attitude toward policemen or other authority figures. The targets of the actual aggression would be related by meaningful associations to the target of the original, inhibited impulse.

Evidence. Several studies have directly examined displacement of aggression. In a study by Hokanson, Burgess, and Cohen (1963), subjects were frustrated (or not) by the experimenter and then given an opportunity to aggress against the experimenter, the experimenter's assistant, a psychology student, or no one. The experiment yielded a marginal main effect for frustration, insofar as frustrated subjects were more aggressive than others, but the target made no difference. Measurements of systolic blood pressure did, however, suggest that tension levels among frustrated subjects dropped most when they aggressed against the experimenter, followed by the assistant, followed by the psychology major. Thus, the level of aggression remained the same whether it was aimed at the original target, at a relevant displaced target, or at an irrelevant target, but there was some physiological evidence suggesting that aggressing against the original target (or a closely linked one) was most satisfying.

The possibility of displaced aggression was also investigated by Fenigstein and Buss (1974). In this study, the instigator was not the experimenter, thereby removing alternative explanations based on the experimenter–subject relationship. Angered and nonangered subjects were given an opportunity to aggress either toward the instigator directly or toward a friend of his. As in the Hokanson et al. (1963) study, anger produced a main effect on aggression, but there were no differences in aggressive behavior as a function of target.

These findings can be interpreted in various ways. One might point to them as evidence for the high efficacy of displacement, given that people are equally aggressive toward other people as toward the person who has provoked them—suggesting, in other words, that the full amount of aggression can be displaced readily.

On the other hand, they could be interpreted as mere mood or arousal effects: People who are angry are more aggressive in general. Indeed, Miller (1948) showed similar effects with rats (e.g., attacking a dummy doll when the original enemy, another rat, is absent), and it is difficult to assert that rats have defense mechanisms. Meanwhile, there is ample evidence that arousal can carry over from one situation to another. Research by Zillman and his colleagues has shown *excitation transfer* effects, in which arousal from one situation can carry over into another and influence aggressive behavior. Riding a stationary bicycle boosts arousal while not being either especially pleasant or unpleasant, but people who ride a bicycle are then subsequently more aggressive in response to a provocation than people who have not just exercised (Zillman, Katcher, & Milavsky, 1972), and indeed highly aroused subjects will ignore mitigating circumstances when someone provokes them, unlike moderately aroused people who will tone down their aggressive responses when they learn of the same mitigating facts (Zillman, Bryant, Cantor, & Day, 1975). Arousal that is caused by watching exciting films can likewise increase aggressive responses to provocation, even though the arousal itself has no relation to the provocation (Cantor, Zillmann, & Einsiedel, 1978; Ramirez, Bryant, & Zillman, 1982; Zillman, 1971).

To complicate matters further, recent work has not confirmed displacement. Bushman and Baumeister (1998) studied aggressive responses to an ego threat as a function of narcissism. Narcissists became more aggressive toward someone who had insulted them, but neither narcissists nor nonnarcissists showed any increased aggression toward a third person. This study was specifically designed to examine displaced aggression and failed to find any sign of it.

Scapegoating has been regarded as one instance of displaced aggression. In this view, people may become angry or hostile toward one target but are required for whatever reasons to avoid aggressing, and so they redirect their aggression toward a safer target. A classic paper by Hovland and Sears (1940) showed that the frequency of lynchings in the American South was negatively correlated with cotton prices. When prices dropped, according to the scapegoat interpretation, farmers suffered material deprivation, frustration, and hostility, and they redirected their hostility toward relatively safe targets in the form of Black men accused of crimes. Hepworth and West (1988) reexamined those data with more modern statistical techniques and confirmed the relationship.

Such evidence of scapegoating does not, however, embody a pure instance of displacement. The original hostility may not have had a specific target; rather, the cotton farmers may have been generally distraught. Recent work by Esses and Zanna (1995) offered an alternative explanation in terms of mood-congruent stereotypes. They showed that bad moods induced by musical stimuli (hence having no esteem threat) caused negative stereotypes to become more accessible. This accessibility might explain the southern farmers' willingness to react violently to alleged misdeeds by Black citizens, without postulating that the violence was borrowed from another source or impulse.

In principle, unacceptable sexual or other impulses should also be amenable to displacement. Mann, Berkowitz, Sidman, Starr, and West (1974) exposed long-married couples to pornographic movies and found that this exposure led to an increased likelihood of marital intercourse on that same evening. This could be interpreted as displacement of sexual desire from the inaccessible movie star onto the socially acceptable target of one's mate. Unfortunately, however, this effect is likewise amenable to alternative explanations based simply on a generalized arousal response.

Conclusion. Despite the intuitive appeal of the concept of displacement, research has not provided much in the way of clear evidence for it. The handful of findings that do suggest displacement are susceptible to alternative explanations such as general tendencies for arousal or bad moods to facilitate aggression.

Some might contend that the arousal or mood effects should not be considered alternative explanations but rather can be subsumed under a looser conception of displacement. If Harry gets angry at his boss for criticizing him, and because of this anger Harry later gets into a fight with a stranger whom he normally might have ignored, should this qualify as displacement? It is, however, in no sense the same impulse that is displaced onto a new target. Whether he had inhibited his anger against his boss or expressed it might make no difference. Given that artificial mood or arousal inductions, even including the arousal from riding a bicycle, can produce the same readiness to respond aggressively to a new provocation, it seems misleading to speak of such an effect as displacement.

More to the point, there is no evidence that such arousal or mood effects serve a defensive function. Displacement would only qualify as a defense mechanism if the original, unacceptable impulse were prevented from causing some damage to self-esteem (or having some similar effect, such as stimulating anxiety). There is no evidence of any such effect.

The concept of displacement seems to be based on the now largely discredited catharsis model, according to which people have a well-defined quantity of aggressive impulses that require expression in one sphere or another. If aggression (or sexual desire, for that matter) cannot be expressed toward its original target, it must be redirected toward another, in this view. Meanwhile, of course, if it could be expressed toward the original target, there would be no displacement. Both effects seem highly implausible in light of what is now known about aggression. More likely, a person who is aggressive in one situation would be more, not less, aggressive in a subsequent one.

* * *

DENIAL

Concept. Freudian conceptions of denial embrace everything from a rare, almost psychotic refusal to perceive the physical facts of the immediate environment, to the common reluctance to accept the implications of some event (e.g., Laplanche & Pontalis, 1973). The distinction between denial and repression is sometimes blurred and difficult to articulate in a meaningful fashion (Cramer, 1991). For the present, it is sufficient to consider denial as the simple refusal to face certain facts. Insofar as these facts are highly upsetting or represent potential damage to self-esteem, denial can in principle be a very useful defense mechanism.

Denial can be understood very narrowly or quite broadly. Broad definitions encompass an assortment of other defenses. Cramer (1991) subsumes perceptual defenses, constructing personal fantasies, negation, minimizing, maximizing, ridicule, and reversal as forms of denial. Paulhus, Fridhandler, and Hayes (1997) suggested that previous theoretical works were sufficient to distinguish at least seven different kinds of denial. If such a broad view proves correct, it may be more appropriate to regard denial as a category of defense mechanisms than as a single defense.

Evidence. Personality and social psychologists have not provided much evidence that people systematically refuse to accept the physical reality of actual events, especially when confronted with palpable proof. (They are of course willing to be skeptical of rumors or other reports that lack credibility and that attest to disagreeable events.) On the other hand, there is abundant evidence that people will reject implications and interpretations that they find threatening.

Probably the most common form of denial involves dismissive responses to failure or other bad feedback. When people receive negative evaluations, they often reject the implications rather than incorporating them into their self-concepts. Making external attributions for failure, such as by pointing to bad luck or task difficulty, is one common and well-documented pattern of denying the implications of failure, because it insists that the failure does not reflect any lack of ability or of other good traits on the part of the self. Zuckerman (1979) reviewed 38 studies to confirm a general pattern that people make more external attributions for failure than for success.

A variation on the response of external attribution is to find faults or flaws in whatever method of evaluation led to one's bad feedback. Several studies have shown that students believe a test to be invalid or unfair when they perform poorly on it, whereas the same test will be regarded more favorably if their feedback is positive (Pyszczynski, Greenberg, & Holt, 1985; Schlenker, Weigold, & Hallam, 1990; Wyer & Frey, 1983; see also Kunda, 1990). Kernis, Cornell, Sun, Berry, and Harlow (1993) found this to be especially common among people with unstable high self-esteem, suggesting that it is an appealing mode of defense to people who especially need to shore up a fragile sense of personal superiority.

Another variation is to dismiss bad feedback as motivated by prejudice. Crocker, Voelkl, Testa, and Major (1991) measured self-esteem among

African American subjects who had received negative feedback from a White evaluator. Self-esteem decreased in response to the criticism if the subject believed the evaluator to be unware of his race. But if the subject thought the evaluator did know his race, then the evaluation had no effect on self-esteem. In the latter case, subjects attributed the bad evaluation to racist prejudice and therefore denied its validity, so it did not affect their self-esteem.

Researchers in health psychology have provided some findings that parallel the ones about threats to self-esteem. The notion that people use denial in response to health-related threats can be traced back at least to Kübler-Ross's (1969) listing of denial as one "stage" or type of response to learning that one's illness will be fatal. Recent work has demonstrated some mechanisms of denial with less extreme threats. Croyle and Hunt (1991) showed that people minimize risks, specifically reducing their level of personal concern over a threatening test result if a confederate made a minimizing comment ("It doesn't seem like a big deal to me"; p. 384). Ditto and Lopez (1992) showed that people selectively questioned the validity of a test when it produced an unfavorable result. Liberman and Chaiken (1992) showed that caffeine users tended to criticize (selectively) and dismiss evidence of a link between caffeine consumption and fibrocystic disease, whereas nonusers showed no such bias.

A quite different sphere in which to find evidence of denial is people's projections about their personal futures. Weinstein (1980) demonstrated that people tend to be unrealistically optimistic, and subsequent work has confirmed that pattern repeatedly (see Taylor & Brown, 1988, for a review). That is, on average people think they are less likely than the average person to suffer various misfortunes, such as career failure, debilitating illness, or accidental crippling. Perloff and Fetzer (1986) coined the term "the illusion of unique invulnerability" to refer to the average person's sense that bad things will not happen to him or her. By definition, the average person cannot be below average in the likelihood of experiencing such misfortunes, so the subjective perceptions must be based in some sense on a denial of the actual likelihood of such events.

The illusion of unique invulnerability does not remain an abstract or vague surmise. Burger and Burns (1988) linked it to sexual risk-taking, as in unprotected promiscuous sexual intercourse. It is well established that sexually transmitted diseases can be serious and even fatal and that they can be prevented by condom use, but people's sense of personal invulnerability leads them to neglect such precautions. In such cases, denying risks makes people take more extreme ones.

Potentially maladaptive consequences of denial were also shown by Carver and Scheier (1994). In a longitudinal study, they measured stress and coping responses before an exam, right after the exam, and later when grades were posted. Various forms of denial were evident at all times, but none was effective overall at reducing negative emotions. Dispositional denial, evident particularly among people who used denial prior to the exam, led to greater feelings of threat and harm. Carver et al. (1993) found that denial predicted greater distress among breast cancer patients. A review by Suls and Fletcher (1985) concluded that avoidance responses such as denial promote positive outcomes in the short run but are inferior to other coping strategies in the long run.

Although denial may undermine some potentially adaptive responses, it may be quite adaptive in other circumstances. We have already noted that denial of personal responsibility for failure tends to be associated with high self-esteem. Indeed, much of the impact of works by Alloy and Abramson (1979) and Taylor and Brown (1988) came from their conclusion that mental health and high self-esteem were associated with biased processing patterns that denied personal responsibility for bad outcomes while taking credit for good outcomes. Low self-esteem and depression were associated with the more even-handed approach of accepting responsibility equally for both positive and negative outcomes.

Such links are essentially correlational, but they could possibly mean that denial contributes (presumably as a successful defense mechanism) to mental health and high self-esteem. Recent work by Forgas (1994) suggests the opposite causal direction, however. Forgas induced sad and happy moods experimentally, by having people read passages with a strong affective tone, and then he investigated their attributions for relationship conflicts. Sad people blamed themselves more than happy people, who attributed conflict to the situation or to the partner. Apparently happy moods foster denial while sad moods undermine it. An optimal defense mechanism would presumably show the opposite pattern.

Janoff-Bulman (1992) suggested that denial may be especially adaptive following trauma, because it allows the reinterpretation process to proceed piecemeal. After suffering a serious personal trauma such as an accident or victimization, there is often little that the person can do, and so denial does not prevent adaptive responses. Meanwhile, the task of coping with the trauma involves restoring one's positive conceptions of self and world. In Janoff-Bulman's view, one starts by denying the trauma in general, and then the denial drops away piece by piece, allowing the person to begin the task of rebuilding those positive conceptions, as opposed to having to find some new interpretations all at once.

Although we have emphasized the more elaborate forms of denial, such as discrediting sources of criticism, there is some evidence for the more elementary forms as well. Lipp, Kolstoe, James, and Randall (1968) defined perceptual defense operationally in terms of the difference in minimal recognition time for nonthreatening pictures as opposed to threatening ones. The threatening ones in their study were pictures of people who were disabled. Subjects in the study included disabled and nondisabled people. The researchers found that disabled people showed greater perceptual defense: that is, they took relatively longer to recognize tachistoscopically presented slides of disabled people. The authors interpreted this as evidence of denial. To be sure, it was hardly a successful defense mechanism in this case, because all it accomplished was delaying the recognition by a fraction of second. Still, it suggests that some people do have defenses that work to minimize the recognition of threatening stimuli.

Perceptual denial may be difficult, but memory may be far more amenable to denial. Crary (1966) showed that people protected their self-esteem by not remembering failures. Kulper and Derry (1982) showed that nondepressed people recalled favorable adjectives pertaining to self better than unfavorable ones. Mischel, Ebbesen, and Zeiss (1976) found that people recalled feedback about their good traits better than feedback about their faults and shortcomings. Whether these effects reflect biased encoding, biased recall, or both is unclear. Baumeister and Cairns (1992) showed that repressors tend to minimize the encoding of bad feedback, but it is plausible that additional biases operate on recall processes. In any case, the memory processes seem quite up to the task of selectively denying disagreeable information.

The heterogeneity of findings on denial suggests that a more differentiated conceptual framework may be useful. Baumeister and Newman (1994) reviewed the ways in which people try to alter and direct their cognitive processes, and in particular they distinguished between regulating the collection of evidence versus regulating the interpretive meaning assigned to the evidence. Most of what we have reviewed here pertains to the latter (interpretation) stage, such as denying the possible implications. More evidence is needed about whether (and how) people prevent disagreeable evidence from entering into the conscious decision process.

Conclusion. The concept of denial encompasses a variety of possible defenses, and it may eventually become desirable on theoretical grounds for the concept to be replaced by several more specific and particular mechanisms. This may be particularly desirable insofar as the various mechanisms are not all equally well documented. Still, for the present, it is fair to say that denial is a genuine and efficacious defense mechanism.

The most stringent definition of denial involves the failure of sensory perception to recognize physical stimuli associated with threat. Restricted to this definition, denial is not a common or successful defense mechanism. There is some evidence of perceptual defense, but it seems to involve slight delays rather than an effective misperception of threat. It is possible that such processes occur among the mentally ill, but researchers in personality and social psychology have found little evidence of perceptual denial in the normal population.

There is, however, ample evidence of other forms of denial. People dispute or minimize information that threatens their self-esteem, and they reject its implications. They discount bad feedback about their health. They dismiss various risks and dangers and sometimes act as if they were personally invulnerable. They selectively forget material that is disagreeable or esteem-threatening. Some patterns have been linked to high self-esteem, adjustment, and happiness, which is consistent with the view that denial can be an effective defense, although some questions remain about how denial actually operates and whether it actually functions to defend self-esteem.

General Discussion

* * *

REVISING DEFENSE MECHANISM THEORY The present review has identified several key challenges for the theory of the defense mechanisms. One concerns the extremity of the response. We noted for several defense mechanisms (* * * [e.g.], denial) that pure, severe forms of the defense had not been documented in the normal population whereas weaker versions were well supported. It is plausible that the extreme forms (e.g., being physically unable to see a person who represents a threat) would occur among the mentally ill.

* * *

Another key issue is whether defense mechanisms involve intrapsychic maneuvers or interpersonal, self-presentational strategies. Freud's theories pertained mainly to the former, but many research findings used explicitly interpersonal settings. In our view, it would be justified to speak of defense mechanisms in both cases, because the logic would be similar. For example, donating money to someone of a different race may counter the accusation of racism regardless of whether the origin of that accusation is internal or external. Furthermore, it is well established that there are important links between public self and private self, so that convincing others of one's good traits may be an important step toward convincing oneself (e.g., Baumeister, 1982a, 1986; Haight, 1980; Schlenker, 1980; Tice, 1992; Wicklund & Gollwitzer, 1982). In any case, further work would benefit from attending to evidence of any systematic differences between defense mechanisms that operate at the interpersonal level and those that operate intrapsychically.

Meanwhile, the change from an energy model to a cognitive model as the basic framework for defense mechanism theory appears to be underway. It is probably no accident that the * * * least well supported defense mechanism in our survey (displacement * * *) * * * [was] also the one most tied to a model based on instinctual energy—while the more cognitive defenses, such as denial, * * * and projection, fared much better. Clearly, shifting the emphasis from unacceptable impulses to self-esteem threats has implications beyond the nature of the threat: Self-esteem threats are more easily rendered in cognitive terms, while the transformation of unacceptable impulses is inherently more closely tied to energy models. Modern theories about the self tend to be heavily cognitive and not at all energy-based, and defense mechanism theory may have to adjust similarly. Thus, the thrust of our review suggests that defense mechanism theory may need to shift its emphasis from impulse transformation to cognitive and behavioral rejection.

The nature of threat is perhaps the undesirable image of self rather than the impulse itself. The nature of defense is therefore to refute or otherwise reject an undesirable view of self. Such a characterization fits the defenses that fared best in this review (reaction formation, * * * denial). It also encompasses other defenses that were not necessarily on Freud's list. It is far beyond the scope of this article to suggest what further defense mechanisms might exist, but while doing this review we did certainly find plenty of evidence of various self-esteem maintenance strategies that did not correspond directly to our list of Freudian defense mechanisms. Future work may make a valuable contribution by listing, taxonomizing, and providing a conceptual framework for all these defenses.

CONCLUDING REMARKS It is impressive to consider how well modern findings in social psychology, mostly obtained in systematic laboratory experiments with well-adjusted American university students, have confirmed the wisdom of Freud's theories, which were mostly based on informal observations of mentally afflicted Europeans nearly a century ago. Not only were several of the defense mechanisms well supported, but in other cases the basic behavioral observations appear to have been sound and only the underlying causal process needs revision.

To be sure, social psychologists have not always given Freud full credit for his insights. Many of the findings covered in this literature review made no reference to defense mechanism theory or to Freud's work. The phenomena Freud described have in some cases been relabeled or rediscovered under the aegis of social cognition or other current theoretical frameworks. Some of these cases may be attributable to career pressures to come up with novel ideas, but others may reflect the fact that researchers working with new ideas and problems are led back to defensive patterns resembling what Freud discussed. The latter cases suggest the pervasive and fundamental importance of defense mechanisms, insofar as Freudian observations and modern socially psychological experimentation converge in producing evidence for the same phenomena.

Our review has suggested that some specific psychoanalytic concepts of defense should be tentatively discarded and some other views need serious revision. More generally, we have suggested that defense mechanism theory may need to downplay its original focus on impulse transformations and instead focus more directly on how possible images of self are protected and rejected. Regardless of these changes, our review provides a solid endorsement of the fundamental insight that human life in civilized society powerfully motivates people to cultivate a set of cognitive and behavioral strategies in order to defend their preferred views of self against threatening events.

References

Adams, H. E., Wright, L. W., & Lohr, B. A. (1996). Is homophobia associated with homosexual arousal? *Journal of Abnormal Psychology, 105*, 440–445.

Agostinelli, G., Sherman, S. J., Presson, C. C., & Chassin, L. (1992). Self-protection and self-enhancement biases in estimates of population prevalence. *Personality and Social Psychology Bulletin, 18*, 631–642.

Alloy, L. B., & Abramson, L. Y. (1979). Judgment of contingency in depressed and nondepressed students: Sadder but wiser? *Journal of Experimental Psychology: General, 108*, 441–485.

Baumeister, R. F. (1982a). A self-presentational view of social phenomena. *Psychological Bulletin, 91*, 3–26.

Baumeister, R. F. (1982b). Self-esteem, self-presentation, and future interaction: A dilemma of reputation. *Journal of Personality, 50*, 29–45.

Baumeister, R. F. (Ed.). (1986). *Public self and private self.* New York: Springer-Verlag.

Baumeister, R. F. (1998). The self. In D. T. Gilbert, S. T. Fiske, & G. Lindzey (Eds.), *Handbook of social psychology* (4th ed., pp. 680–740). New York: McGraw-Hill.

Baumeister, R. F., & Caims, K. J. (1992). Repression and self-presentation: When audiences interfere with self-deceptive strategies. *Journal of Personality and Social Psychology, 62*, 851–862.

Baumeister, R. F., Heatherton, T. F., & Tice, D. M. (1993). When ego-threats lead to self-regulation failure: The negative consequences of high self-esteem. *Journal of Personality and Social Psychology, 64*, 141–156.

Baumeister, R. F., & Jones, E. E. (1978). When self-presentation is constrained by the target's knowledge: Consistency and compensation. *Journal of Personality and Social Psychology, 36*, 608–618.

Baumeister, R. F., & Newman, L. S. (1994). Self-regulation of cognitive inference and decision processes. *Personality and Social Psychology Bulletin, 20*, 3–19.

Biemat, M., Manis, M., & Nelson, T. E. (1991). Stereotypes and standards of judgment. *Journal of Personality and Social Psychology, 60*, 485–499.

Bramel, D. (1962). A dissonance theory approach to defensive projection. *Journal of Abnormal and Social Psychology, 64,* 121–129.

Bramel, D. (1963). Selection of a target for defensive projection. *Journal of Abnormal and Social Psychology, 66,* 318–324.

Burger, J. M., & Burns, L. (1988). The illusion of unique invulnerability and the use of effective contraception. *Personality and Social Psychology Bulletin, 14,* 264–270.

Bushman, B., & Baumeister, R. F. (1998). Threatened egotism, narcissism, self-esteem, and direct and displaced aggression: Does self-love or self-hate lead to violence? *Journal of Personality and Social Psychology, 75,* 219–229.

Campbell, J. D. (1986). Similarity and uniqueness: The effects of attribute type, relevance, and individual differences in self-esteem and depression. *Journal of Personality and Social Psychology, 50,* 281–294.

Cantor, J. R., Zillman, D., & Einsiedel, E. G. (1978). Female responses to provocation after exposure to aggressive and erotic films. *Communication Research, 5,* 395–411.

Carver, C. S., Pozo, C., Harris, S. D., Noriega, V., Scheier, M. F., Robinson, D. S., Ketcham, A. S., Moffat, F. L., Jr., & Clark, K. C. (1993). How coping mediates the effect of optimism on distress: A study of women with early stage breast cancer. *Journal of Personality and Social Psychology, 65,* 375–390.

Carver, C. S., & Scheier, M. F. (1994). Situational coping and coping dispositions in a stressful transaction. *Journal of Personality and Social Psychology, 66,* 184–195.

Cramer, P. (1991). *The development of defense mechanisms.* New York: Springer-Verlag.

Crary, W. G. (1966). Reactions to incongruent self-experiences. *Journal of Consulting Psychology, 30,* 246–252.

Crocker, J., Alloy, L. B., & Kayne, N. T. (1988). Attributional style, depression, and perceptions of consensus for events. *Journal of Personality and Social Psychology, 54,* 840–846.

Crocker, J., Voelkl, K., Testa, M., & Major, B. (1991). Social stigma: The affective consequences of attributional ambiguity. *Journal of Personality and Social Psychology, 60,* 218–228.

Croyle, R. T., & Hunt, J. R. (1991). Coping with health threat: Social influence processes in reactions to medical test results. *Journal of Personality and Social Psychology, 60,* 382–389.

Davis, M. H., Conklin, L., Smith, A., & Luce, C. (1996). Effects of perspective taking on the cognitive representation of persons: A merging of self and other. *Journal of Personality and Social Psychology, 70,* 713–726.

Ditto, P. H., & Lopez, D. F. (1992). Motivated skepticism: Use of differential decision criteria for preferred and nonpreferred conclusions. *Journal of Personality and Social Psychology, 63,* 568–584.

Dunning, D., & Cohen, G. L. (1992). Egocentric definitions of traits and abilities in social judgment. *Journal of Personality and Social Psychology, 63,* 341–355.

Dutton, D. G. (1976). Tokenism, reverse discrimination, and egalitarianism in interracial behavior. *Journal of Social Issues, 32,* 93–107.

Dutton, D. G., & Lake, R. A. (1973). Threat of own prejudice and reverse discrimination in interracial situations. *Journal of Personality and Social Psychology, 28,* 94–100.

Esses, V. M., & Zanna, M. P. (1995). Mood and the expression of ethnic stereotypes. *Journal of Personality and Social Psychology, 69,* 1052–1068.

Fenichel, O. (1945). *The psychoanalytic theory of neurosis.* New York: Norton.

Fenigstein, A., & Buss, A. H. (1974). Association and affect as determinants of displaced aggression. *Journal of Research in Personality, 7,* 306–313.

Forgas, P. (1994). Sad and guilty? Affective influences on the explanation of conflict in close relationships. *Journal of Personality and Social Psychology, 66,* 56–68.

Freud, A. (1936). *The ego and the mechanisms of defense.* New York: Hogarth Press.

Freud, S. (1961a). Instincts and their vicissitudes. In J. Strachey (Ed. and Trans.), *The standard edition of the complete works of Sigmund Freud* (Vol. 14, pp. 111–142). London: Hogarth Press. (Original work published in 1915)

Freud, S. (1961c). The ego and the id. In J. Strachey (Ed. and Trans.), *The standard edition of the complete works of Sigmund Freud* (Vol. 19, pp. 12–66). London: Hogarth Press. (Original work published in 1923)

Freud, S. (1961d). Inhibitions, symptoms, and anxiety. In J. Strachey (Ed. and Trans.), *The standard edition of the complete works of Sigmund Freud* (Vol. 20, pp. 77–178). London: Hogarth Press. (Original work published in 1926)

Gilovich, T. (1991). *How we know what isn't so: The fallibility of human reason in everyday life.* New York: Free Press.

Greenberg, J., & Pyszczynski, J. (1985). Compensatory self-inflation: A response to the threat to self-regard of public failure. *Journal of Personality and Social Psychology, 49,* 273–280.

Haight, M. R. (1980). *A study of self-deception.* Atlantic Highlands, NJ: Humanities Press.

Halpern, J., & Goldschmitt, M. (1976). Attributive projection: Test of defensive hypotheses. *Perceptual and Motor Skills, 42,* 707–711.

Hepworth, J. T., & West, S. G. (1988). Lynchings and the economy: A time-series reanalysis of Hofland and Sears (1940). *Journal of Personality and Social Psychology, 55,* 239–247.

Hokanson, J. E., Burgess, M., & Cohen, M. F. (1963). Effects of displaced aggression on systolic blood pressure. *Journal of Abnormal and Social Psychology, 67,* 214–218.

Holmes, D. S. (1968). Dimensions of projection. *Psychological Bulletin, 69,* 248–268.

Holmes, D. S. (1978). Projection as a defense mechanism. *Psychological Bulletin, 85,* 677–688.

Holmes, D. S. (1981). Existence of classical projection and the stress-reducing function of attributive projection: A reply to Sherwood. *Psychological Bulletin, 90,* 460–466.

Hovland, C. I., & Sears, R. (1940). Minor studies of aggression: Correlation of lynchings with economic indices. *Journal of Psychology, 9,* 301–310.

Janoff-Bulman, R. (1992). *Shattered assumptions: Towards a new psychology of trauma.* New York: Free Press.

Johnson, J. D., Whitestone, E., Jackson, L. A., & Gatto, L. (1995). Justice is still not colorblind: Differential racial effects of exposure to inadmissible evidence. *Personality and Social Psychology Bulletin, 21,* 893–898.

Kelley, H. H., & Stahelski, A. J. (1970a). Errors in perception of intentions in a mixed motive game. *Journal of Experimental Social Psychology, 6,* 379–400.

Kelley, H. H., & Stahelski, A. J. (1970b). Social interaction basis of cooperators and competitors' beliefs about others. *Journal of Personality and Social Psychology, 16,* 66–91.

Kernis, M. H., Cornell, D. P., Sun, C-R., Berry, A., & Harlow, T. (1993). There's more to self-esteem whether it's high or low: The importance of stability of self-esteem. *Journal of Personality and Social Psychology, 65*, 1190–1204.

Krueger, J., & Clement, R. W. (1994). The truly false consensus effect: An ineradicable and egocentric bias in social perception. *Journal of Personality and Social Psychology, 67*, 596–610.

Kubler-Ross, E. (1969). *On death and dying.* New York: Macmillan.

Kuiper, N. A., & Derry, P. A. (1982). Depressed and nondepressed content self-reference in mild depression. *Journal of Personality, 50*, 67–79.

Kunda, Z. (1990). The case for motivated reasoning. *Psychological Bulletin, 108*, 480–498.

Lambert, A. J., & Weddell, D. H. (1991). The self and social judgment: Effects of affective reaction and "own position" on judgments of unambiguous and ambiguous information about others. *Journal of Personality and Social Psychology, 61*, 884–897.

Laplanche, J., & Pontalis, J.-B. (1973). *The language of psychoanalysis* (D. Nicholson-Smith, Trans.). New York: Norton.

Liberman, A., & Chaiken, S. (1992). Defensive processing of personally relevant health messages. *Personality and Social Psychology Bulletin, 18*, 669–679.

Lipp, L., Kolstoe, R., James, W., & Randall, H. (1968). Denial of disability and internal control of reinforcement: A study using a perceptual defense paradigm. *Journal of Consulting and Clinical Psychology, 32*, 72–75.

Mann, J., Berkowitz, L., Sidman, J., Starr, S., & West, S. (1974). Satiation of the transient stimulating effect of erotic films. *Journal of Personality and Social Psychology, 30*, 729–735.

Marks, G., Graham, J. W., & Hansen, W. B. (1992). Social projection and social conformity in adolescent alcohol use: A longitudinal analysis. *Personality and Social Psychology Bulletin, 18*, 96–107.

McFarlin, D. B., & Blascovich, J. (1981). Effects of self-esteem and performance feedback on future affective preferences and cognitive expectations. *Journal of Personality and Social Psychology, 40*, 521–531.

Miller, N. E. (1948). Theory and experiment relating psychoanalytic displacement to stimulus-response generalization. *Journal of Abnormal and Social Psychology, 43*, 155–178.

Mischel, W., Ebbesen, E. B., & Zeiss, A. R. (1976). Determinants of selective memory about the self. *Journal of Consulting and Clinical Psychology, 44*, 92–103.

Morokoff, P. J. (1985). Effects of sex guilt, repression, sexual "arousability," and sexual experience on female sexual arousal during erotica and fantasy. *Journal of Personality and Social Psychology, 49*, 177–187.

Newman, L. S., Duff, K., & Baumeister, R. F. (1997). A new look at defensive projection: Suppression, accessibility, and biased person perception. *Journal of Personality and Social Psychology, 72*, 980–1001.

Paulhus, D. L., Fridhandler, B., & Hayes, S. (1997). Psychological defense: Contemporary theory and research. In R. Hogan & J. Johnson (Eds.), *Handbook of personality psychology* (pp. 543–579). San Diego, CA: Academic Press.

Paulhus, D. L., & Reynolds, S. (1995). Enhancing target variance in personality impressions: Highlighting the person in person perception. *Journal of Personality and Social Psychology, 69*, 1233–1242.

Perloff, L. S., & Fetzer, B. K. (1986). Self-other judgments and perceived vulnerability to victimization. *Journal of Personality and Social Psychology, 50*, 502–510.

Pines, M., & Aronson, E. (1983). Antecedents, correlates, and consequences of sexual jealousy. *Journal of Personality, 51*, 108–135.

Pyszczynski, T., Greenberg, J., & Holt, K. (1985). Maintaining consistency between self-serving beliefs and available data: A bias in information processing. *Personality and Social Psychology Bulletin, 11*, 179–190.

Ramirez, J., Bryant, J., & Zillman, D. (1982). Effects of erotica on retaliatory behavior as a function of level of prior provocation. *Journal of Personality and Social Psychology, 43*, 971–978.

Rogers, R. W., & Prentice-Dunn, S. (1981). Deindividuation and anger-mediated interracial aggression: Unmasking regressive racism. *Journal of Personality and Social Psychology, 41*, 63–73.

Ross, L., Greene, D., & House, P. (1977). The "false consensus effect": An egocentric bias in social perception and attribution processes. *Journal of Experimental Social Psychology, 13*, 279–301.

Schlenker, B. R. (1980). *Impression management: The self-concept, social identity, and interpersonal relations.* Monterey, CA: Brooks/Cole.

Schlenker, B. R., Weigold, M. F., & Hallam, J. R. (1990). Self-serving attributions in social context: Effects of self-esteem and social pressure. *Journal of Personality and Social Psychology, 58*, 855–863.

Shaffer, D. R., & Case, T. (1982). On the decision to testify in one's own behalf: Effects of withheld evidence, defendant's sexual preferences, and juror dogmatism on juridic decisions. *Journal of Personality and Social Psychology, 42*, 335–346.

Sherman, S. J., Presson, C. C., & Chassin, L. (1984). Mechanisms underlying the false consensus effect: The special role of threats to the self. *Personality and Social Psychology Bulletin, 10*, 127–138.

Sherwood, G. G. (1981). Self-serving biases in person perception: A reexamination of projection as a mechanism of defense. *Psychological Bulletin, 90*, 445–459.

Suls, J., & Fletcher, B. (1985). The relative efficacy of avoidant and nonavoidant coping strategies: A meta-analysis. *Health Psychology, 4*, 249–288.

Suls, J., & Wan, C. K. (1987). In search of the false-uniqueness phenomenon: Fear and estimates of social consensus. *Journal of Personality and Social Psychology, 52*, 211–217.

Taylor, S. E. (1989). *Positive illusions: Creative self-deception and the healthy mind.* New York: Basic Books.

Taylor, S. E., & Brown, J. D. (1988). Illusion and well-being: A social psychological perspective on mental health. *Psychological Bulletin, 103*, 193–210.

Tice, D. M. (1992). Self-presentation and self-concept change: The looking glass self as magnifying glass. *Journal of Personality and Social Psychology, 63*, 435–451.

Wegner, D. M. (1994). Ironic processes of mental control. *Psychological Review, 101*, 34–52.

Wegner, D. M., & Erber, R. (1992). The hyperaccessibility of supressed thoughts. *Journal of Personality and Social Psychology, 63*, 903–912.

Weinberger, D. A., Schwartz, G. E., & Davidson, R. J. (1979). Low-anxious, high-anxious, and repressive coping styles: Psychometric patterns and behavioral and physiological responses to stress. *Journal of Abnormal Psychology, 88*, 369–380.

Weinstein, N. D. (1980). Unrealistic optimism about future life events. *Journal of Personality and Social Psychology, 39*, 806–820.

Wicklund, R. A., & Gollwitzer, P. M. (1982). *Symbolic self-completion.* Hillsdale, NJ: Erlbaum.

Wyer, R. S., & Frey, D. (1983). The effects of feedback about self and others on the recall and judgments of feedback-relevant information. *Journal of Experimental Social Psychology, 19*, 540–559.

Zillmann, D. (1971). Excitation transfer in communication-mediated aggressive behavior. *Journal of Experimental Social Psychology, 7*, 419–434.

Zillmann, D., Bryant, J., Cantor, J. R., & Day, K. D. (1975). Irrelevance of mitigating circumstances in retaliatory behavior at high levels of excitation. *Journal of Research in Personality, 9*, 286–306.

Zillman, D., Katcher, A. H., & Milavsky, B. (1972). Excitation transfer from physical exercise to subsequent aggressive behavior. *Journal of Experimental Social Psychology, 8*, 247–259.

Zuckerman, M. (1979). Attribution of success and failure revisited; or, The motivational bias is alive and well in attribution theory. *Journal of Personality, 47*, 245–287.

The Verdict on Freud

Frederick Crews

As Freud anticipated, psychoanalysis has inspired many bitter enemies. In the modern literature, one of Freud's most influential critics is Frederick Crews, the author of the following selection. This selection, a book review of a volume by another critic, Macolm Macmillan, is included because it provides summary of that book and several other recent critiques as well as a good deal of criticism by Crews himself.

Freud's brand of theorizing and his style of evidence—or lack thereof—certainly leave him vulnerable to criticism on many grounds, and the points raised by Crews and others are worth pondering. But notice how the zeal of some of Freud's critics, and perhaps their annoyance at Freudian devotees who give him credit for everything, prevent them from giving him credit for anything. Indeed, they are not content to attack just the theorizing or its evidentiary base. They also accuse Freud himself of plagiarism, ruthlessness, opportunism, deceptiveness, and worse. The very vehemence of their reaction to psychoanalysis is one of the most remarkable things about their critique, and is a phenomenon Freud would not have found difficult to explain.

From *Psychological Science, 7,* 63–68, 1996.

During the past 25 years, a momentous change has been overtaking the study of Sigmund Freud and his elaborate, engrossing, but ever more controversial creation, psychoanalysis. Formerly, authors who deemed Freud worth discussing at book length tended to be either Freudian loyalists or partisans of some variant doctrine that shared at least a few of Freud's depth-psychological premises. Their critiques were often selectively astute but rarely rigorous or thoroughgoing. No doubt the same can still be said of most new books in the field, produced as they are by practicing analysts on the one hand and, on the other, by academic humanists who have raised their sights above narrowly "positivistic" (alias empirical) concerns. Increasingly, however, Freud's oeuvre has been receiving sustained attention from scholars who hold no personal stake in the fortunes of psychoanalysis. As recent works by Scharnberg (1993), Esterson (1993), Wilcocks (1994), Dawes (1994), Webster (1995), and Erwin (1996) attest, independent studies have begun to converge toward a verdict that was once considered a sign of extremism or even of neurosis: that there is literally nothing to be said, scientifically or therapeutically, to the advantage of the entire

Freudian system or any of its component dogmas.

Four books stand out as paramount contributions to the emergence of this still-contested but, in my view, warranted judgment:

1. Priority in time belongs to the late Henri Ellenberger's *The Discovery of the Unconscious* (1970), whose long and learned chapter on Freud demolished the myth, carefully nurtured by Freud himself and his Boswell, Ernest Jones, of the master's utter originality, his facing up to disturbing truths unearthed in his clinical practice, and his solitary defiance of his contemporaries' prudish hypocrisy. By displaying Freud's all-too-human opportunism and disingenuousness and by bringing him down from the clouds into 19th-century intellectual history, Ellenberger tacitly invited other scholars to inquire whether the vast cultural success of psychoanalysis rested on any actual discoveries.
2. One such scholar was Frank Sulloway, whose monumental *Freud, Biologist of the Mind* (1979), went farther than its author himself initially intended, or even realized, toward dismantling Freud's claims. Sulloway's Freud is an ingenious plagiarist, a dogged and ruthless self-promoter, and a habitual devotee of crackpot ideas and premature conclusions. After Sulloway, it became harder to avoid perceiving that Freud's conveniently unexaminable case material always fit perfectly with whatever notion he had most recently pressed into service from unacknowledged and often questionable sources.
3. Adolf Grünbaum's formidable *The Foundations of Psychoanalysis* (1984) demonstrated that "clinical evidence," the purported engine of reliable psychoanalytic knowledge, could not underwrite that knowledge even in principle. The problem of contamination through therapist suggestion, Grünbaum showed, is pervasive and intractable, and even uncontaminated clinical data, if any such could be found, would necessarily lack the causal import that Freud and others have ascribed to them.
4. The fourth classic of Freud revisionism is the book now under review. To call it a classic, however, is more a prediction than a statement of settled fact. Although Malcolm Macmillan's *Freud Evaluated*[1] has been in print since 1991, and although it has been highly praised by Eagle (1993) and Spence (in press), among others, its influence thus far has been slight. I indicate later why this is the case, why I am confident of a very different future for this book, and, most important, why *Freud Evaluated* must be painstakingly studied by anyone who aspires to make pronouncements about the good, the bad, and the ugly in Freudian thought.

First, precisely because Macmillan is still largely unknown to American readers, a word of introduction is in order.

Evaluation in Historical Context

Until his recent retirement, Macmillan was senior lecturer in psychology at Monash University, Australia; he now serves as adjunct professor in the School of Psychology at Deakin University in the same country. A past president of the Australian Psychological Society, he has published widely on such diverse topics as Janet and Charcot, Freud's seduction theory, brain localization and injury, retardation, and even the kinesiology of the football kick. However, if one does not count a precursor volume printed internally by Monash's Department of Psychology (Macmillan, 1974), *Freud Evaluated* is Macmillan's only book to date.

Significantly, this work emerged from a set of lectures that "had dealt separately," as the preface informs us, "with the twin themes of psychoana-

[1]The book being reviewed is *Freud Evaluated: The Completed Arc*, by Malcom Macmillan, published in 1991 by North-Holland Publishers of Amsterdam.

lytic personality theory and the application of scientific method in psychology" (p. v). The seed of *Freud Evaluated* was planted when Macmillan realized that those themes belonged together: Freud's style of theory building was casting a useful light on basic issues of methodology. The book that eventuated is no mere compendium of lecture notes, but rather the most comprehensive, coherent, and unimpeachable assessment of Freud's concepts and tenets that has yet been mounted—or is ever likely to be.* * *

* * * Macmillan has molded his text to the shape of Freud's career, describing, contextualizing, and then evaluating each burst of theory in its chronological order. Thus, although the reader soon gathers that Freud's confusions, unsolved problems, and ill-advised expedients at one stage will probably plague his efforts at the next one, the book continues to proceed inductively, postponing what Erwin would call "a final accounting" until the full journey has been negotiated from Josef Breuer's Anna O. case and its aftermath through Freud's culminating "structural" version of metapsychology. Only then does Macmillan permit himself to sum up his findings and to look beyond Freud to the standing of psychoanalysis in general as a theory, a therapy, an investigative method, and a putative science.

* * *

Complexities Redoubled

* * * Macmillan's approach is ideally geared to dislodging a prejudice that still deters most observers from gazing on the perfect nakedness of Emperor Freud: the belief that the intricacy of Freudian theory more or less matches that of the human mind. So long as that misunderstanding prevails, a wholesale rejection of Freud will look like an unthinkable throwback to behaviorism, positivism, associationism, or a primitive psychology of faculties or humors. But no such drastic choice is required if we realize that psychoanalysis owes its complexity to a sequence of peremptory and indefensible moves. Macmillan shows, and any diligent reader can now be satisfied, that each major complication in Freud's model was added not to account for observations of conflicted behavior but to paper over a failure of coherent linkage between his prior constructs and the reputed evidence for them.

When Freud declared that the unconscious draws no distinction between real and fantasized events, for example, he was not reporting a testable finding but concocting an excuse for the collapse of his seduction theory,[2] sparing himself the embarrassment of admitting that he had secured no relation at all between supposedly repressed sexual material and the origin of psychoneuroses, and concealing the ominous tendency of his method of inquiry—the one that he kept right on using—to generate false results. Likewise, as Macmillan shows, Freud was led into the conceptual maze of infantile sexuality not by any observation of children but by this same unwillingness to face the seduction debacle forthrightly. Rather than abandon his thwarted belief in the sexual meaning of symptoms, he chose to transplant the blame for precocious eroticism from the "seducer" to the child's own constitution. The result was a veritable funhouse of zones, modes, phases, and drives, proliferating with a wildly cavalier disregard for parsimony.* * * All in all, psychoanalytic theory became ever more byzantine, and mental activity was alleged to be ever more "overdetermined," as a consequence of Freud's insistence on salvaging his far-fetched repression etiology by any means necessary.

Illusions of Determinism

But this is only part of the story. Macmillan's distinctive achievement is to have shown that Freud's

[2]At an early point in his theorizing, Freud believed that many of his female patients' neuroses originated in childhood sexual molestation by their fathers—the so-called (and badly misnamed) seduction hypothesis. Later, Freud decided that many and perhaps nearly all adult memories of childhood abuse were fantasies, but that such fantasies could become "real" in their unconscious psychological consequences.

excesses also derived from his loyalty to certain key assumptions that he could never bring into doubt. Chief among them was psychic determinism, which in Freud's apprehension meant not just that all mental events bear causes but that regularly observed phenomena must have invariable causes, rooted in physiology. In the tradition of Sulloway (1979), Macmillan shows that Freud remained faithful to the views of his early mentor Theodor Meynert, who conceived of the coupling between one association and its temporal successor as a literal matter of contact between cortical nerve cells connected to one another by nerve fibers. Thus, "following a train of associations in the way Freud did was equivalent to unravelling a chain of causes and so revealing the internal logic of hysteria" (p. 113 [in Macmillan's book]). This assumption accounts for the bewildering doubleness of Freud's explanatory manner, whereby, for example, dreaming is ascribed both to a struggle over the expression of forbidden wishes and to a regressive flow of excitation.

We would be losing Macmillan's point if we took such parallel descriptions as a mere sign that Freud felt obliged to touch base with physiology from time to time. Rather, his determinism of successive and reversible innervations shaped the very heart of psychoanalytic theory. For a relatively simple instance, consider the idea that every dream expresses a repressed infantile wish. As an inference drawn from the consulting room, it is flatly preposterous; there is no thinkable way of discerning which element of the patient's dream report is a holdover from the nursery. But if we begin from Meynert's schema and assume, simplistically, that each associative chain is a row of dominos extending into the past, the notion becomes at least conceivable. So, too, does Freud's generous array of sexualized and desexualized instincts, none of which have anything to do with clinical observation; they were called into being by a felt need to make his imagined excitations run both forward and backward on the rails of a mechanized psyche.

* * *

Marks of Pseudoscience

Let us suppose, as a mental exercise, that Freud had not been such a prisoner of his billiard-ball determinism and that we could trust him as a reporter of his own and other investigators' findings. Would his theory then have approached scientific respectability? The question is of interest because even the most orthodox contemporary Freudians acknowledge that Freud left them with a defective doctrine—though there is nothing resembling a consensus about the needed repairs. In Macmillan's view, the most serious demerits of Freud's way of gathering and evaluating data apply with equal force to the approach to psychoanalytic theory formation that prevails today. They are not specific errors of fact and emphasis but fundamental departures from the scientific ethos. For example:

1. Hypothetical entities or processes should be characterized; that is, they ought to possess attributed properties that lend themselves to confirmation outside their immediate role in the theory at issue. If they lack this quality, "their referents are the very relations they are supposed to explain" (p. 193); they are only placeholders for mechanisms that may not exist at all. This is just what we regularly find in the case of psychoanalytic postulates. A term like *repression*, Macmillan notes, points to no independently known reality but merely gives a name to the questionable survival of traumatic memory traces in an unconscious that itself remains uncharacterized. Moreover, incompatible burdens are placed upon the term, indicating that the theory behind it is fatally muddled. When repression is then invoked as an explanatory factor in new contexts, true believers may feel that fresh territory is being conquered, but the scope of Freud's circularity is simply being widened. The same flaw of empty conceptualization appears in virtually every feature of his system, from the preconscious

through the ego, introjection, the death instinct, and so forth.

2. A theory should not create its own facts. Psychoanalysis, however, does so at every turn. For example, repression is invoked to account for the delayed effect of childhood trauma in producing adult psychoneuroses, but the only reason for believing that such an effect occurs is a prior belief in repression. A dream is regarded as a disguised representation of its latent content, the dream thoughts, but such thoughts can be detected only by Freudian dream interpretation. So, too, castration threats, real or fantasized, supposedly trigger the onset of the male latency period, but the latency period is itself a pure artifact of the theory. Or again, Freud invoked penis envy to explain female submissiveness, masochism, and incapacity for cultural strivings, but in this instance the theory and the "facts" alike derived from cultural prejudice.
3. A theory should have testable consequences; "only if the facts [to be independently verified] can be deduced from the fundamental statements of the theory can we say that they are explained by it" (p. 168). Notoriously, however, Freudian tenets are scarcely challenged, much less refuted, by unexpected outcomes. The vagueness of the theory is such that it can withstand almost any number of surprises and be endlessly revised according to the theorist's whim, without reference to data. Indeed, as Macmillan emphasizes, Freud drew on the same pool of evidence in offering three incompatible etiologies for homosexuality (pp. 352–353), and he did the same in proposing three incompatible paths for overcoming narcissism (pp. 358–359). Throughout his whole career of lawgiving, the linkage between evidence and theory was established by rhetorical guile and nothing more.
4. A hypothesis should be treated as such; that is, its adequacy ought to be methodically tested. Instead, Macmillan shows, Freud habitually offered postulates that he labeled as hypotheses but treated as firm expectations or even as certainties. Understandably, premature closure about one issue left him vulnerable to the same mistake with the next one. For example, all the while that he was pretending to be alarmed at his reluctant clinical discovery of sexual factors in hysteria, he was importing the conclusions he had already erroneously reached about the sexual roots of the (nonexistent) actual neuroses.
5. Finally—though this list could be considerably extended—heed must be paid to the difference between necessary and sufficient causes. An assertion that factor x causes effect y in neurotic Group A is vacuous if one merely establishes the presence of factor x in typical members of that group. Even on the most optimistic interpretation (that x is necessary to produce neurosis), x cannot be regarded as a sufficient cause unless, at a minimum, it is shown to be absent from nonneurotic Group B. Never once in his psychoanalytic career, however, did Freud conduct such a demonstration or publicly indicate that it was called for.[3] On the contrary, he consistently maintained that all the reassurance of correctness he required was the stream of confirmations that flowed from clinical experience—in other words, from Group A alone. At his most scrupulous, he was content to find a few cases in which the positive correlation he was seek-

[3]The closest Freud came to such recognition was in an early letter to Wilhelm Fliess announcing that neurasthenia in men is caused by masturbation—a practice, he assured Fliess, completely lacking among "the circle of one's acquaintances" who have not contracted the neurosis despite having been "seduced by women at an early age" (Freud, 1985, p. 40). One strains to imagine the interviews that could have assured Freud of his correctness on this point.—Author

ing appeared, however momentarily, to obtain. A palm reader or faith healer could have done as well.

In summary, we learn from Macmillan that the founder of psychoanalysis, once he had forsaken laboratory work for the care and understanding of neurotics, neither thought nor acted like a scientist; he sincerely but obtusely mistook his loyalty to materialist reductionism for methodological rigor. In fact, it was just the opposite, an inducement to dogmatic persistence in folly. Thus, we cannot be amazed—except insofar as we may be veteran subscribers to the Freud legend—that the product of his efforts proved to be a pseudoscience.

Can a pseudoscience be reformed into a science through piecemeal interventions? Freud's successors "tamper with the structures or alter the nature and status of the drives," Macmillan observes, "but their own concepts of drive and structure are inferred from facts gathered by a defective method" (p. 506). A defective method can produce only ersatz results. Although *Freud Evaluated* shows that nearly everything that can be said against Freudian theory has been pointed out by one uneasy psychoanalyst or another, it also shows that analysis as a whole remains powerless to address the heart of the problem—and understandably so, because a thoroughgoing epistemic critique, based on commonly acknowledged standards of evidence and logic, decertifies every distinctively psychoanalytic proposition. As I indicated at the outset, Macmillan is hardly alone in reaching that conclusion. Now, however, he steps to the forefront of those who have offered a detailed rational basis for affirming it.

References

Dawes, R. M. (1994). *House of cards: Psychology and psychotherapy built on myth.* New York: Free Press.

Eagle, M. N. (1993). Freud in historical context. *Contemporary Psychology, 38,* 993–995.

Ellenberger, H. (1970). *The discovery of the unconscious: The history and evolution of dynamic psychiatry.* New York: Basic Books.

Erwin, E. (1996). *A final accounting: Philosophical and empirical issues in Freudian psychology.* Cambridge, MA: MIT Press.

Esterson, A. (1993). *Seductive mirage: An exploration of the work of Sigmund Freud.* Chicago: Open Court.

Freud, S. (1985). *The complete letters of Sigmund Freud to Wilhelm Fliess, 1887–1904* (J. M. Masson, Ed. and Trans.). Cambridge, MA: Harvard University Press.

Grünbaum, A. (1984). *The foundations of psychoanalysis: A philosophical critique.* Berkeley: University of California Press.

Macmillan, M. B. (1974). *The historical and scientific evaluation of psychoanalytic personality theory.* Melbourne, Australia: Monash University Department of Psychology.

Scharnberg, M. (1993). *The non-authentic nature of Freud's observations* (2 vols.). Uppsala, Sweden: University of Uppsala.

Spence, D. (in press). [Review of the book *Freud evaluated*]. *International Journal of Clinical and Experimental Hypnosis.*

Sulloway, F. J. (1979). *Freud, biologists of the mind: Beyond the psychoanalytic legend.* New York: Basic Books.

Webster, R. (1995). *Why Freud was wrong: Sin, science, and psychoanalysis.* New York: Basic Books.

Wilcocks, R. (1994). *Maelzel's chess player: Sigmund Freud and the rhetoric of deceit.* Lanham, MD: Rowman & Littlefield.

Psychological Types

Carl Jung

One mark of Freud's stature in intellectual history is the number of his adherents—and former adherents—who became major figures in their own right. Perhaps the best known of these is Carl Jung. Jung began his career in psychoanalysis as Freud's anointed "crown prince." Freud intended that Jung succeed him as president of the International Psychoanalytic Association. The two carried on an intense correspondence for years and also traveled to the United States together in 1909.

When it came, the split between Freud and Jung was bitter. Jung felt that Freud overemphasized the role of sexuality and underemphasized the constructive role of the unconscious. But the conflict may have been deeper than that; Jung chafed under Freud's dominating role as his intellectual father figure and felt a need to achieve more independence. For his part, Freud regarded major departures from his theory simply as error, and was particularly alarmed by a turn Jung took in midlife toward a mystical view of the human psyche. Jung formulated ideas, still famous today, about a "collective unconscious" full of mysterious images and ideas shared by all members of the human race, and an "oceanic feeling" of being at one with the universe. Such ideas were anathema to the atheistic and hardheaded Freud.

In the following selection Jung explains one of the more down-to-earth of his theoretical ideas, his conception of introversion and extraversion and four related styles of thinking. These ideas have had an obvious and lasting influence. Recall, for example, that extraversion is one of the Big Five factors of personality espoused in the second section of this reader by Costa and McCrae. But Jung's conception is somewhat different from the behavioral styles labeled as extraversion and introversion today. Jung's introvert is someone who in a fundamental way has turned into himself or herself and away from the world; his extravert is wholly dependent on others for his or her intellectual and emotional life.

A widely used personality test, the Myers-Briggs Type Indicator (Myers & McCaulley, 1985), was designed to classify people as to their style of thinking, in Jungian terms. You might be classified as dominated by sensation, thinking, feeling, or intuition. This test is often used for vocational guidance. For example, the sensation style might be appropriate for an athlete, the thinking style for a lawyer, the feeling style for a poet, and the intuitive style for a clinical psychologist.

The following selection is an excerpt from a lecture Jung delivered in Territet, Switzerland in 1923. By this time Jung had split thoroughly from Freud and was well known for his own work.

From *Psychological Types*, translated by R. Hull and H. Baynes (Princeton, NJ: Princeton University Press, 1971), pp. 510–523.

* * *

We shall discover, after a time, that in spite of the great variety of conscious motives and tendencies, certain groups of individuals can be distinguished who are characterized by a striking conformity of motivation. For example, we shall come upon individuals who in all their judgments, perceptions, feelings, affects, and actions feel external factors to be the predominant motivating force, or who at least give weight to them no matter whether causal or final motives are in question. I will give some examples of what I mean. St. Augustine: "I would not believe the Gospel if the authority of the Catholic Church did not compel it." A dutiful daughter: "I could not allow myself to think anything that would be displeasing to my father." One man finds a piece of modern music beautiful because everybody else pretends it is beautiful. Another marries in order to please his parents but very much against his own interests. There are people who contrive to make themselves ridiculous in order to amuse others; they even prefer to make butts of themselves rather than remain unnoticed. There are not a few who in everything they do or don't do have but one motive in mind: what will others think of them? "One need not be ashamed of a thing if nobody knows about it." There are some who can find happiness only when it excites the envy of others; some who make trouble for themselves in order to enjoy the sympathy of their friends.

Such examples could be multiplied indefinitely. They point to a psychological peculiarity that can be sharply distinguished from another attitude which, by contrast, is motivated chiefly by internal or subjective factors. A person of this type might say: "I know I could give my father the greatest pleasure if I did so and so, but I don't happen to think that way." Or: "I see that the weather has turned out bad, but in spite of it I shall carry out my plan." This type does not travel for pleasure but to execute a preconceived idea. Or: "My book is probably incomprehensible, but it is perfectly clear to me." Or, going to the other extreme: "Everybody thinks I could do something, but I know perfectly well I can do nothing." Such a man can be so ashamed of himself that he literally dares not meet people. There are some who feel happy only when they are quite sure nobody knows about it, and to them a thing is disagreeable just because it is pleasing to everyone else. They seek the good where no one would think of finding it. At every step the sanction of the subject must be obtained, and without it nothing can be undertaken or carried out. Such a person would have replied to St. Augustine: "I would believe the Gospel if the authority of the Catholic Church did *not* compel it." Always he has to prove that everything he does rests on his own decisions and convictions, and never because he is influenced by anyone, or desires to please or conciliate some person or opinion.

This attitude characterizes a group of individuals whose motivations are derived chiefly from the subject, from inner necessity. There is, finally, a third group, and here it is hard to say whether the motivation comes chiefly from within or without. This group is the most numerous and includes the less differentiated normal man, who is considered normal either because he allows himself no excesses or because he has no need of them. The normal man is, by definition, influenced as much from within as from without. He constitutes the extensive middle group, on one side of which are those whose motivations are determined mainly by the external object, and, on the other, those whose motivations are determined from within. I call the first group *extraverted*, and the second group *introverted*. The terms scarcely require elucidation as they explain themselves from what has already been said.

Although there are doubtless individuals whose type can be recognized at first glance, this is by no means always the case. As a rule, only careful observation and weighing of the evidence permit a sure classification. However simple and clear the fundamental principle of the two opposing attitudes may be, in actual reality they are complicated and hard to make out, because every individual is an exception to the rule. Hence one can never give a description of a type, no matter how complete, that would apply to more than one individual, despite the fact that in some ways it aptly characterizes thousands of others. Conformity is one side of a man, uniqueness is the other. Classification does not explain the individual psyche. Nevertheless, an understanding of psychological types opens the way to a better understanding of human psychology in general.

Type differentiation often begins very early, so early that in some cases one must speak of it as innate. The earliest sign of extraversion in a child is his quick adaptation to the environment, and the extraordinary attention he gives to objects and especially to the effect he has on them. Fear of objects is minimal; he lives and moves among them with confidence. His apprehension is quick but imprecise. He appears to develop more rapidly than the introverted child, since he is less reflective and usually without fear. He feels no barrier between himself and objects, and can therefore play with them freely and learn through them. He likes to carry his enterprises to the extreme and exposes himself to risks. Everything unknown is alluring.

To reverse the picture, one of the earliest signs of introversion in a child is a reflective, thoughtful manner, marked shyness and even fear of unknown objects. Very early there appears a tendency to assert himself over familiar objects, and attempts are made to master them. Everything unknown is regarded with mistrust; outside influences are usually met with violent resistance. The child wants his own way, and under no circumstances will he submit to an alien rule he cannot understand. When he asks questions, it is not from curiosity or a desire to create a sensation, but because he wants names, meanings, explanations to give him subjective protection against the object. I have seen an introverted child who made his first attempts to walk only after he had learned the names of all the objects in the room he might touch. Thus very early in an introverted child the characteristic defensive attitude can be noted which the adult introvert displays towards the object; just as in an extraverted child one can very early observe a marked assurance and initiative, a happy trustfulness in his dealings with objects. This is indeed the basic feature of the extraverted attitude: psychic life is, as it were, enacted outside the individual in objects and objective relationships. In extreme cases there is even a sort of blindness for his own individuality. The introvert, on the contrary, always acts as though the object possessed a superior power over him against which he has to defend himself. His real world is the inner one.

Sad though it is, the two types are inclined to speak very badly of one another. This fact will immediately strike anyone who investigates the problem. And the reason is that the psychic values have a diametrically opposite localization for the two types. The introvert sees everything that is in any way valuable for him in the subject; the extravert sees it in the object. This dependence on the object seems to the introvert a mark of the greatest inferiority, while to the extravert the preoccupation with the subject seems nothing but infantile autoeroticism. So it is not surprising that the two types often come into conflict. This does not, however, prevent most men from marrying women of the opposite type. Such marriages are very valuable as psychological symbioses so long as the partners do not attempt a mutual "psychological" understanding. But this phase of understanding belongs to the normal development of every marriage provided the partners have the necessary leisure or the necessary urge to development—though even if both these are present real courage is needed to risk a rupture of the marital peace. In favourable circumstances this phase enters automatically into the lives of both types, for the reason that each type is an example of one-sided development. The one develops only external relations and neglects the inner; the other develops inwardly but remains outwardly at a standstill. In time the need arises for the individual to develop what has been neglected. The development takes the form of a differentiation of certain functions, to which I must now turn in view of their importance for the type problem.

The conscious psyche is an apparatus for adaptation and orientation, and consists of a number of different psychic functions. Among these we can distinguish four basic ones: *sensation, thinking, feeling, intuition*. Under sensation I include all perceptions by means of the sense organs; by thinking I mean the function of intellectual cognition and the forming of logical conclusions; feeling is a function of subjective valuation; intuition I take as perception by way of the unconscious, or perception of unconscious contents.

So far as my experience goes, these four basic functions seem to me sufficient to express and represent the various modes of conscious orientation. For complete orientation all four functions should contribute equally: thinking should facilitate cognition and judgment, feeling should tell us how and to what extent a thing is important or unimportant for us, sensation should convey concrete reality to us through seeing, hearing, tasting, etc., and intuition should enable us to divine the hidden possibilities in the background, since these too belong to the complete picture of a given situation.

In reality, however, these basic functions are seldom or never uniformly differentiated and equally at our disposal. As a rule one or the other function occupies the foreground, while the rest remain undifferentiated in the background. Thus there are many people who restrict themselves to the simple perception of concrete reality, without thinking about it or taking feeling values into account. They bother just as little about the possibilities hidden in a situation. I describe such people as *sensation types*. Others are exclusively oriented by what they think, and simply cannot adapt to a situation which they are unable to understand intellectually. I call such people *thinking types*. Others, again, are guided in everything entirely by feeling. They merely ask themselves whether a thing is pleasant or unpleasant, and orient themselves by their feeling impressions. These are the *feeling types*. Finally, the *intuitives* concern themselves neither with ideas nor with feeling reactions, nor yet with the reality of things, but surrender themselves wholly to the lure of possibilities, and abandon every situation in which no further possibilities can be scented.

Each of these types represents a different kind of one-sidedness, but one which is linked up with and complicated in a peculiar way by the introverted or extraverted attitude. It was because of this complication that I had to mention these function-types, and this brings us back to the question of the one-sidedness of the introverted and extraverted attitudes. This one-sidedness would lead to a complete loss of psychic balance if it were not compensated by an unconscious counterposition. Investigation of the unconscious has shown, for example, that alongside or behind the introvert's conscious attitude there is an unconscious extraverted attitude which automatically compensates his conscious one-sidedness.

* * *

The alteration of the conscious attitude is no light matter, because any habitual attitude is essentially a more or less conscious ideal, sanctified by custom and historical tradition, and founded on the bedrock of one's innate temperament. The conscious attitude is always in the nature of a *Weltanschauung*, if it is not explicitly a religion. It is this that makes the type problem so important. The opposition between the types is not merely an external conflict between men, it is the source of endless inner conflicts; the cause not only of external disputes and dislikes, but of nervous ills and psychic suffering. It is this fact, too, that obliges us physicians constantly to widen our medical horizon and to include within it not only general psychological standpoints but also questions concerning one's views of life and the world.

* * *

Recapitulating, I would like to stress that each of the two general attitudes, introversion and extraversion, manifests itself in a special way in an individual through the predominance of one of the four basic functions. Strictly speaking, there are no introverts and extraverts pure and simple, but only introverted and extraverted function-types, such as thinking types, sensation types, etc. There are thus at least eight clearly distinguishable types. Obviously one could increase this number at will if each of the functions were split into three subgroups, which would not be impossible empirically. One could, for example, easily divide thinking into its three well-known forms: intuitive and speculative, logical and mathematical, empirical and positivist, the last being mainly dependent on sense perception. Similar subgroups could be made of the other functions, as in the case of intuition, which has an intellectual as well as an emotional and sensory aspect. In this way a large number of types could be established, each new division becoming increasingly subtle.

For the sake of completeness, I must add that I do not regard the classification of types according to introversion and extraversion and the four basic functions as the only possible one. Any other psychological criterion could serve just as well as a classifier, although, in my view, no other possesses so great a practical significance.

THE DISTRUST BETWEEN THE SEXES

Karen Horney

Like Jung and Adler, Karen Horney began her own psychoanalytic career as a follower and defender of Freud. But Horney was too much of an independent thinker to remain anyone's disciple for long. First practicing in Germany and then in America for most of her career, Horney invented a distinctly feminist form of psychoanalysis. The combination of a psychoanalytic style of thinking with ideas of the sort that it is difficult to imagine a male analyst propounding is well illustrated in the following selection.

The selection comes from a paper Horney delivered before the German Women's Medical Association in 1930. Like the previous selection by Adler, this paper also has a contemporary feel to it. Horney was ahead of her time, and her gentle critique of and subtle revisions to conventional psychoanalytic theory anticipated feminist objections that would be expressed over the following decades.

From *Feminine Psychology* (New York: Norton, 1967), pp. 104–116.

* * *

The relationship between men and women is quite similar to that between children and parents, in that we prefer to focus on the positive aspects of these relationships. We prefer to assume that love is the fundamentally given factor and that hostility is an accidental and avoidable occurrence. Although we are familiar with slogans such as "the battle of the sexes" and "hostility between the sexes," we must admit that they do not mean a great deal. They make us overfocus on sexual relations between men and women, which can very easily lead us to a too one-sided view. Actually, from our recollection of numerous case histories, we may conclude that love relationships are quite easily destroyed by overt or covert hostility. On the other hand we are only too ready to blame such difficulties on individual misfortune, on incompatibility of the partners, and on social or economic causes.

The individual factors, which we find causing poor relations between men and women, may be the pertinent ones. However, because of the great frequency, or better, the regular occurrence of disturbances in love relations, we have to ask ourselves whether the disturbances in the individual cases might not arise from a common background; whether there are common denominators for this easily and frequently arising suspiciousness between the sexes?

* * *

I would like to start with something very commonplace—namely, that a good deal of this atmosphere of suspiciousness is understandable and even justifiable. It apparently has nothing to do with the individual partner, but rather with the intensity of the affects and with the difficulty of taming them.

We know or may dimly sense that these affects can lead to ecstasy, to being beside oneself, to surrendering oneself, which means a leap into the unlimited and the boundless. This is perhaps why real passion is so rare. For like a good businessman, we are loath to put all our eggs in one basket. We are inclined to be reserved and ever ready to retreat. Be that as it may, because of our instinct for self-preservation, we all have a natural fear of losing ourselves in another person. That is why what happens to love, happens to education and psychoanalysis; everybody thinks he knows all about them, but few do. One is inclined to overlook how little one gives of oneself, but one feels all the more this same deficiency in the partner, the feeling of "You never really loved me." A wife who harbors suicidal thoughts because her husband does not give her all his love, time, and interest will not notice how much of her own hostility, hidden vindictiveness, and aggression are expressed through her attitude. She will feel only despair because of her abundant "love," while at the same time she will feel most intensely and see most clearly the lack of love in her partner. * * *

Here we are not dealing with pathological phenomena at all. In pathological cases we merely see a distortion and exaggeration of a general and normal occurrence. Anybody, to a certain extent, will be inclined to overlook his own hostile impulses, but under pressure of his own guilty conscience, may project them onto the partner. This process must, of necessity, cause some overt or covert distrust of the partner's love, fidelity, sincerity, or kindness. This is the reason why I prefer to speak of distrust between the sexes and not of hatred; for in keeping with our own experience we are more familiar with the feeling of distrust.

A further, almost unavoidable, source of disappointment and distrust in our normal love life derives from the fact that the very intensity of our feelings of love stirs up all of our secret expectations and longings for happiness, which slumber deep inside us. All our unconscious wishes, contradictory in their nature and expanding boundlessly on all sides, are waiting here for their fulfillment. The partner is supposed to be strong, and at the same time helpless, to dominate us and be dominated by us, to be ascetic and to be sensuous. He should rape us and be tender, have time for us exclusively and also be intensely involved in creative work. As long as we assume that he could actually fulfill all these expectations, we invest him with the glitter of sexual overestimation. We take the magnitude of such overvaluation for the measure of our love, while in reality it merely expresses the magnitude of our expectations. The very nature of our claims makes their fulfillment impossible. Herein lies the origin of the disappointments with which we may cope in a more or less effective way. Under favorable circumstances we do not even have to become aware of the great number of our disappointments, just as we have not been aware of the extent of our secret expectations. Yet there remain traces of distrust in us, as in a child who discovers that his father cannot get him the stars from the sky after all.

Thus far, our reflections certainly have been neither new nor specifically analytical and have often been better formulated in the past. The analytical approach begins with the question: What special factors in human development lead to the discrepancy between expectations and fulfillment and what causes them to be of special significance in particular cases? Let us start with a general consideration. There is a basic difference between human and animal development—namely, the long period of the infant's helplessness and dependency. The paradise of childhood is most often an illusion with which adults like to deceive themselves. For the child, however, this paradise is inhabited by too many dangerous monsters. Unpleasant experiences with the opposite sex seem to be unavoidable. We need only recall the capacity that children possess, even in their very early years, for passionate and instinctive sexual desires similar to those of adults and yet different from them. Children are different in the aims of their drives, but above all, in the pristine integrity of their demands. They find it hard to express their desires directly, and where they do, they are not taken seriously. Their seriousness sometimes is looked upon as being cute, or it may be overlooked or rejected. In short, children will undergo painful and humiliating experiences of being rebuffed, being betrayed, and being told lies. They also may have to take second place to a parent or sibling, and they are threatened and intimidated when they seek, in playing with their own bodies, those pleasures that are denied them by adults. The child is relatively powerless in the face of all this. He is not able to ventilate his fury at all, or only to a minor degree, nor can he come to grips with the experience by means of intellectual comprehension. Thus, anger and aggression are pent up within him in the form of extravagant fantasies, which hardly reach the daylight of awareness, fantasies that are criminal when viewed from the standpoint of the adult, fantasies that range from taking by force and stealing, to those about killing, burning, cutting to pieces, and choking. Since the child is vaguely aware of these destructive forces within him, he feels, according to the talion law,[1] equally threatened by the adults. Here is the origin of those infantile anxieties of which no child remains entirely free. This already enables us to understand better the fear of love of which I have spoken before. Just here, in this most irrational of all areas, the old childhood fears of a threatening father or mother are reawakened, putting us instinctively on the defensive. In other words, the fear of love will always be mixed with the fear of what we might do to the other person, or what the other person might do to us. A lover in the Aru Islands, for example, will never make a gift of a lock of hair to his beloved, because should an argument arise, the beloved might burn it, thus causing the partner to get sick.

I would like to sketch briefly how childhood conflicts may affect the relationship to the opposite sex in later life. Let us take as an example a typical situation: The little girl who was badly hurt through some great disappointment by her father will transform her innate instinctual wish to receive from the man into a vindictive one of taking from him by force. Thus the foundation is laid for a direct line of development to a later attitude, according to which she will not only deny her maternal instincts, but will have only one drive, i.e., to harm the male, to exploit him, and to suck him dry. She has become a vampire. Let us assume that there is a similar transformation from the wish to receive to the wish to take away. Let us further assume that the latter wish was repressed due to anxiety from a guilty conscience; then we have here the fundamental constellation for the formation of a certain type of woman who is unable to relate to the male because she fears that every male will suspect her of wanting something from him. This really means that she is afraid that he might guess her repressed desires. Or by completely projecting onto him her repressed wishes, she will imagine that every male merely intends to exploit her, that he wants from her only sexual satisfaction, after which he will discard her. Or let us assume that a reaction formation of excessive modesty will mask the repressed drive for power. We then have the type of woman who shies away from demanding or accepting anything from her husband. Such a woman, however, due to the return of the repressed, will react with depression to the nonfulfillment of her unexpressed, and often unformulated, wishes. She thus unwittingly jumps from the frying pan into the fire, as does her partner, because a depression will hit him much harder than direct aggression. Quite often the repression of aggression against the male drains all her vital energy. The woman then feels helpless to meet life. She will shift the entire responsibility for her helplessness onto the man, robbing him of the very breath of life. Here you have the type of woman who, under the guise of being helpless and childlike, dominates her man.

These are examples that demonstrate how the

[1]The law of retaliative justice, sometimes called "an eye for an eye."

fundamental attitude of women toward men can be disturbed by childhood conflicts. In an attempt to simplify matters, I have stressed only one point, which, however, seems crucial to me—the disturbance in the development of motherhood.

I shall now proceed to trace certain traits of male psychology. I do not wish to follow individual lines of development, though it might be very instructive to observe analytically how, for instance, even men who consciously have a very positive relationship with women and hold them in high esteem as human beings, harbor deep within themselves a secret distrust of them; and how this distrust relates back to feelings toward their mothers, which they experienced in their formative years. I shall focus rather on certain typical attitudes of men toward women and how they have appeared during various eras of history and in different cultures, not only as regards sexual relationships with women, but also, and often more so, in nonsexual situations, such as in their general evaluation of women.

I shall select some random examples, starting with Adam and Eve.[2] Jewish culture, as recorded in the Old Testament, is outspokenly patriarchal. This fact reflects itself in their religion, which has no maternal goddesses; in their morals and customs, which allow the husband the right to dissolve the marital bond simply by dismissing his wife. Only by being aware of this background can we recognize the male bias in two incidents of Adam's and Eve's history. First of all, woman's capacity to give birth is partly denied and partly devaluated: Eve was made of Adam's rib and a curse was put on her to bear children in sorrow. In the second place, by interpreting her tempting Adam to eat of the tree of knowledge as a sexual temptation, woman appears as the sexual temptress, who plunges man into misery. I believe that these two elements, one born out of resentment, the other out of anxiety, have damaged the relationship between the sexes from the earliest times to the present. Let us follow this up briefly. Man's fear of woman is deeply rooted in sex, as is shown by the simple fact that it is only the sexually attractive woman of whom he is afraid and who, although he strongly desires her, has to be kept in bondage. Old women, on the other hand, are held in high esteem, even by cultures in which the young woman is dreaded and therefore suppressed. In some primitive cultures the old woman may have the decisive voice in the affairs of the tribe; among Asian nations also she enjoys great power and prestige. On the other hand, in primitive tribes woman is surrounded by taboos during the entire period of her sexual maturity. Women of the Arunta tribe are able to magically influence the male genitals. If they sing to a blade of grass and then point it at a man or throw it at him, he becomes ill or loses his genitals altogether. Women lure him to his doom. In a certain East African tribe, husband and wife do not sleep together, because her breath might weaken him. If a woman of a South African tribe climbs over the leg of a sleeping man, he will be unable to run; hence the general rule of sexual abstinence two to five days prior to hunting, warfare, or fishing. Even greater is the fear of menstruation, pregnancy, and childbirth. Menstruating women are surrounded by extensive taboos—a man who touches a menstruating woman will die. There is one basic thought at the bottom of all this: Woman is a mysterious being who communicates with spirits and thus has magic powers that she can use to hurt the male. He must therefore protect himself against her powers by keeping her subjugated. Thus the Miri in Bengal do not permit their women to eat the flesh of the tiger, lest they become too strong. The Watawela of East Africa keep the art of making fire a secret from their women, lest women become their rulers. The Indians of California have ceremonies to keep their women in submission; a man is disguised as a devil to intimidate the women. The Arabs of Mecca exclude women from religious festivities to prevent familiarity between women and their

[2]The long paragraph that follows provides a good illustration of Horney's distinctly feminist style of psychoanalytic thinking.

overlords. We find similar customs during the Middle Ages—the Cult of the Virgin side by side with the burning of witches; the adoration of "pure" motherliness, completely divested of sexuality, next to the cruel destruction of the sexually seductive woman. Here again is the implication of underlying anxiety, for the witch is in communication with the devil. Nowadays, with our more humane forms of aggression, we burn women only figuratively, sometimes with undisguised hatred, sometimes with apparent friendliness. * * * In friendly and secret autos-da-fé, many nice things are said about women, but it is just unfortunate that in her God-given natural state, she is not the equal of the male. Moebius pointed out that the female brain weighs less than the male one, but the point need not be made in so crude a way. On the contrary, it can be stressed that woman is not at all inferior, only different, but that unfortunately she has fewer or none of those human or cultural qualities that man holds in such high esteem. She is said to be deeply rooted in the personal and emotional spheres, which is wonderful; but unfortunately, this makes her incapable of exercising justice and objectivity, therefore disqualifying her for positions in law and government and in the spiritual community. She is said to be at home only in the realm of eros. Spiritual matters are alien to her innermost being, and she is at odds with cultural trends. She therefore is, as Asians frankly state, a second-rate being. Woman may be industrious and useful but is, alas, incapable of productive and independent work. She is, indeed, prevented from real accomplishment by the deplorable, bloody tragedies of menstruation and childbirth. And so every man silently thanks his God, just as the pious Jew does in his prayers, that he was not created a woman.

Man's attitude toward motherhood is a large and complicated chapter. One is generally inclined to see no problem in this area. Even the misogynist is obviously willing to respect woman as a mother and to venerate her motherliness under certain conditions, as mentioned above regarding the Cult of the Virgin. In order to obtain a clearer picture, we have to distinguish between two attitudes: men's attitudes toward motherliness, as represented in its purest form in the Cult of the Virgin, and their attitude toward motherhood as such, as we encounter it in the symbolism of the ancient mother goddesses. Males will always be in favor of motherliness, as expressed in certain spiritual qualities of women, i.e., the nurturing, selfless, self-sacrificing mother; for she is the ideal embodiment of the woman who could fulfill all his expectations and longings. In the ancient mother goddesses, man did not venerate motherliness in the spiritual sense, but rather motherhood in its most elemental meaning. Mother goddesses are earthy goddesses, fertile like the soil. They bring forth new life and they nurture it. It was this life-creating power of woman, an elemental force, that filled man with admiration. And this is exactly the point where problems arise. For it is contrary to human nature to sustain appreciation without resentment toward capabilities that one does not possess. Thus, a man's minute share in creating new life became, for him, an immense incitement to create something new on his part.[3] He has created values of which he might well be proud. State, religion, art, and science are essentially his creations, and our entire culture bears the masculine imprint.

However, as happens elsewhere, so it does here; even the greatest satisfactions or achievements, if born out of sublimation,[4] cannot fully make up for something for which we are not endowed by nature. Thus there has remained an obvious residue of general resentment of men against women. This resentment expresses itself, also in our times, in men's distrustful defensive maneuvers against the threat of women's invasion of their domains; hence their tendency to devalue

[3]Famously, Freud thought women suffered from "penis envy." In this passage, Horney seems to claim that men suffer from womb envy.

[4]"Sublimation" is the psychoanalytic mechanism by which a motivation to do one thing is turned to another purpose.

pregnancy and childbirth and to overemphasize male genitality. This attitude does not express itself in scientific theories alone, but is also of far-reaching consequence for the entire relationship between the sexes, and for sexual morality in general. Motherhood, especially illegitimate motherhood, is very insufficiently protected by law. * * * Conversely, there is ample opportunity for the fulfillment of the male's sexual needs. Emphasis on irresponsible sexual indulgence, and devaluation of women to an object of purely physical needs, are further consequences of this masculine attitude.

* * *

I do not want to be misunderstood as having implied that all disaster results from male supremacy and that relations between the sexes would improve if women were given the ascendency. However, we must ask ourselves why there should have to be any power struggle at all between the sexes. At any given time, the more powerful side will create an ideology suitable to help maintain its position and to make this position acceptable to the weaker one. In this ideology the differentness of the weaker one will be interpreted as inferiority, and it will be proven that these differences are unchangeable, basic, or God's will.[5] It is the function of such an ideology to deny or conceal the existence of a struggle. Here is one of the answers to the question raised initially as to why we have so little awareness of the fact that there is a struggle between the sexes. It is in the interest of men to obscure this fact; and the emphasis they place on their ideologies has caused women, also, to adopt these theories. Our attempt at resolving these rationalizations and at examining these ideologies as to their fundamental driving forces, is merely a step on the road taken by Freud.

* * *

That many-faceted thing called love succeeds in building bridges from the loneliness on this shore to the loneliness on the other one. These bridges can be of great beauty, but they are rarely built for eternity and frequently they cannot tolerate too heavy a burden without collapsing. Here is the other answer to the question posed initially of why we see love between the sexes more distinctly than we see hate—because the union of the sexes offers us the greatest possibilities for happiness. We therefore are naturally inclined to overlook how powerful are the destructive forces that continually work to destroy our chances for happiness.

We might ask in conclusion, how can analytical insights contribute to diminish the distrust between the sexes? There is no uniform answer to this problem. The fear of the power of the affects and the difficulty in controlling them in a love relationship, the resulting conflict between surrender and self-preservation, between the I and the Thou, is an entirely comprehensible, unmitigatable, and as it were, normal phenomenon. The same thing applies in essence to our readiness for distrust, which stems from unresolved childhood conflicts. These childhood conflicts, however, can vary greatly in intensity, and will leave behind traces of variable depth. Analysis not only can help in individual cases to improve the relationship with the opposite sex, but it can also attempt to improve the psychological conditions of childhood and forestall excessive conflicts. This, of course, is our hope for the future. In the momentous struggle for power, analysis can fulfill an important function by uncovering the real motives of this struggle. This uncovering will not eliminate the motives, but it may help to create a better chance for fighting the struggle on its own ground instead of relegating it to peripheral issues.

[5]Some modern, feminist critiques of evolutionary personality theory (see Part III) are suspicious of its account of sex differences on exactly these grounds.

Eight Stages of Man

Erik Erikson

The last of the classic neo-Freudians to be included in these readings, Erik Erikson, was not really a contemporary of Freud. His career took place across the years following Freud's death in 1939, until Erikson's own death in 1994. But Erikson became the major figure among the neo-Freudians who never broke with the master. He considered himself a loyal disciple to the end, as many passages in the following selection demonstrate.

Despite his loyalty, Erikson's theory goes into territory far outside anything Freud ever seriously considered. The theoretical development for which he is best known, described in this selection, goes beyond Freud in a specific way. Freud viewed psychosexual development as a process that occurred in infancy and early childhood, and was essentially finished shortly after the attainment of puberty. For many years developmental psychology followed the same basic presumption.

But Erikson changed all that. Of his "eight stages of man," four take place during and after the final stage of development from a traditional Freudian perspective. Erikson viewed psychological development as something that occurs throughout life, as challenges, opportunities, and obligations change. At the very last stage, one comes to terms with one's impending death and the meaning of one's life past. The outcome of this stage is crucial for the next generation. In one of his most thought-provoking comments, Erikson writes "healthy children will not fear life if their parents have integrity enough not to fear death." So the last stage of one's own development intersects with the earlier stages in one's children, and the cycle begins again.

The entire field of developmental psychology—not just the part within psychoanalysis—was changed in a profound way as Erikson's framework became widely influential. Without ever using the term, Erikson invented what is today called "life-span developmental psychology," a psychology that studies the way people develop every step of the way from the first day of their life to the last. Erikson's most lasting contribution is the reminder that development is not aimed at an end point, but is a continuing process.

From *Childhood and Society* (New York: Norton, 1950), pp. 219–234.

1. Trust vs. Basic Mistrust

The first demonstration of social trust in the baby is the ease of his feeding, the depth of his sleep, the relaxation of his bowels. The experience of a mutual regulation of his increasingly receptive capacities with the maternal techniques of provision gradually helps him to balance the discomfort caused by the immaturity of homeostasis with which he was born. In his gradually increasing waking hours he finds that more and more adventures of the senses arouse a feeling of familiarity, of having coincided with a feeling of inner goodness. Forms of comfort, and people associated with them, become as familiar as the gnawing discomfort of the bowels. The infant's first social achievement, then, is his willingness to let the mother out of sight without undue anxiety or rage, because she has become an inner certainty as well as an outer predictability. Such consistency, continuity, and sameness of experience provide a rudimentary sense of ego identity which depends, I think, on the recognition that there is an inner population of remembered and anticipated sensations and images which are firmly correlated with the outer population of familiar and predictable things and people. Smiling crowns this development.

The constant tasting and testing of the relationship between inside and outside meets its crucial test during the rages of the biting stage, when the teeth cause pain from within and when outer friends either prove of no avail or withdraw from the only action which promises relief: biting. I would assume that this experience of an urge turning upon the self has much to do with the masochistic tendency of finding cruel and cold comfort in hurting oneself whenever an object has eluded one's grasp.

Out of this, therefore, comes that primary sense of badness, that original sense of evil and malevolence which signifies the potential loss of all that is good because we could not help destroying it inside, thus driving it away outside. This feeling persists in a universal homesickness, a nostalgia for familiar images undamaged by change. Tribes dealing with one segment of nature develop a collective magic which seems to treat the Supernatural Providers of food and fortune as if they were angry and must be appeased by prayer and self-torture. Primitive religions, the most primitive layer in all religions, and the religious layer in each individual, abound with efforts at atonement which try to make up for vague deeds against a maternal matrix and try to restore faith in the goodness of one's strivings and in the kindness of the powers of the universe.

* * * The general state of trust implies not only that one has learned to rely on the sameness and continuity of the outer providers, but also that one may trust oneself and the capacity of one's own organs to cope with urges; and that one is able to consider oneself trustworthy enough so that the providers will not need to be on guard lest they be nipped.

In psychopathology the absence of basic trust can best be studied in infantile schizophrenia, while weakness of such trust is apparent in adult personalities of schizoid and depressive character. The reestablishment of a state of trust has been found to be the basic requirement for therapy in these cases. For no matter what conditions may have caused a psychotic break, the bizarreness and withdrawal in the behavior of many very sick individuals hides an attempt to reconquer social mutuality by a testing of the borderlines between senses and physical reality, between words and social meanings.

Psychoanalysis assumes the early process of differentiation between inside and outside to be the origin of the mechanisms of projection and introjection which remain some of our deepest and most dangerous defense mechanisms. In introjection we feel and act as if an outer goodness had become an inner certainty. In projection, we experience an inner harm as an outer one: we endow significant people with the evil which actually is in us. These two mechanisms, then, projection and introjection, are assumed to be modeled after whatever goes on in infants when they would like to externalize pain and internalize pleasure, an intent which must yield to the testimony of the maturing senses and ultimately of reason. These mechanisms are, more or less normally, reinstated in acute crises of love, trust, and faith in the adult. Where they persist, they mark the "psychotic character."

The firm establishment of enduring patterns for the solution of the nuclear conflict of basic trust versus basic mistrust in mere existence is the first task of the ego, and thus first of all a task for maternal care. But let it be said here that the amount of trust derived from earliest infantile experience does not seem to depend on absolute quantities of food or demonstrations of love, but rather on the quality of the maternal relationship. Mothers, I think, create a sense of trust in their children by that kind of administration which in its quality combines sensitive care of the baby's individual needs and a firm sense of personal trustworthiness within the trusted framework of their culture's life style. This forms the basis in the child for a sense of identity which will later combine a sense of being "all right," of being oneself, and of becoming what other people trust one will become. * * *

2. Autonomy vs. Shame and Doubt

Anal-muscular maturation sets the stage for experimentation with two simultaneous sets of social modalities: holding on and letting go. As is the case with all of these modalities, their basic conflicts can lead in the end to either hostile or benign expectations and attitudes. Thus, to hold can become a destructive and cruel retaining or restraining, and it can become a pattern of care: to have and to hold. To let go, too, can turn into an inimical letting loose of destructive forces, or it can become a relaxed "to let pass" and "to let be." Culturally speaking, these attitudes are neither good nor bad; their value depends on whether their hostile implications are turned against enemy, or fellow man—or the self.

The latter danger is the one best known to us. For if denied the gradual and well-guided experience of the autonomy of free choice (or if, indeed, weakened by an initial loss of trust) the child will turn against himself all his urge to discriminate and to manipulate. He will overmanipulate himself, he will develop a precocious conscience. Instead of taking possession of things in order to test them by purposeful repetition, he will become obsessed by his own repetitiveness. By such obsessiveness, of course, he then learns to repossess the environment and to gain power by stubborn and minute control, where he could not find large-scale mutual regulation. Such hollow victory is the infantile model for a compulsion neurosis. It is also the infantile source of later attempts in adult life to govern by the letter, rather than by the spirit.

Outer control at this stage, therefore, must be firmly reassuring. The infant must come to feel that the basic faith in existence, which is the lasting treasure saved from the rages of the oral stage, will not be jeopardized by this about-face of his, this sudden violent wish to have a choice, to appropriate demandingly, and to eliminate stubbornly. Firmness must protect him against the potential anarchy of his as yet untrained sense of discrimination, his inability to hold on and to let go with discretion. As his environment encourages him to "stand on his own feet," it must protect him against meaningless and arbitrary experiences of shame and of early doubt.

Shame is an emotion insufficiently studied, because in our civilization it is so early and easily absorbed by guilt. Shame supposes that one is completely exposed and conscious of being looked at: in one word, self-conscious. One is visible and not ready to be visible; which is why we dream of shame as a situation in which we are stared at in a condition of incomplete dress, in night attire, "with one's pants down." Shame is early expressed in an impulse to bury one's face, or to sink, right then and there, into the ground. But this, I think, is essentially rage turned against the self. He who is ashamed would like to force the world not to look at him, not to notice his exposure. He would like to destroy the eyes of the world. Instead he must wish for his own invisibility. This potentiality is abundantly used in the educational method of "shaming" used so exclusively by some primitive peoples; its destructiveness is balanced in some civilizations by devices for "saving face." Visual shame precedes auditory guilt, which is a sense of badness to be had all by oneself when nobody watches and when everything is quiet—except the voice of the superego. Such shaming exploits an increasing sense of being small, which can develop only as the child stands up and as his awareness permits him to note the relative measures of size and power. * * *

Doubt is the brother of shame. Where shame is dependent on the consciousness of being upright and exposed, doubt, so clinical observation leads me to believe, has much to do with a consciousness of having a front and a back—and especially a "behind." For this reverse area of the body, with its aggressive and libidinal focus in the sphincters and in the buttocks, cannot be seen by the child, and yet it can be dominated by the will of others. The "behind" is thus the individual's dark continent, an area of the body which can be magically dominated and effectively invaded by those who would attack one's power of autonomy and who would designate as evil those products of the bowels which were felt to be all right when they were being passed. This basic sense of doubt in whatever one has left behind forms a substratum for later and more verbal forms of compulsive doubting; this finds its adult expression in paranoiac fears concerning hidden persecutors and secret persecutions threatening from behind and from within the behind.

3. Initiative vs. Guilt

The ambulatory stage and that of infantile genitality add to the inventory of basic social modalities that of "making," first in the sense of "being on the make." There is no simpler, stronger word to match the social modalities previously enumerated. The word suggests pleasure in attack and conquest. In the boy, the emphasis remains on phallic-intrusive modes; in the girl it turns to modes of "catching" in more aggressive forms of snatching and "bitchy" possessiveness, or in the milder form of making oneself attractive and endearing.

The danger of this stage is a sense of guilt over the goals contemplated and the acts initiated in one's exuberant enjoyment of new locomotor and mental power: acts of aggressive manipulation and coercion which go far beyond the executive capacity of organism and mind and therefore call for an energetic halt on one's contemplated initiative. While autonomy concentrates on keeping potential rivals out, and is therefore more an expression of jealous rage most often directed against encroachments by younger siblings, initiative brings with it anticipatory rivalry with those who have been there first and may, therefore, occupy with their superior equipment the field toward which one's initiative is directed. Jealousy and rivalry, those often embittered and yet essentially futile attempts at demarcating a sphere of unquestioned privilege, now come to a climax in a final contest for a favored position with the mother; the inevitable failure leads to resignation, guilt, and anxiety. The child indulges in fantasies of being a giant and a tiger, but in his dreams he runs in terror for dear life. This, then, is the stage of the "castration complex," the fear of losing the (now energetically eroticized) genitals as a punishment for the fantasies attached to their excitements.

Infantile sexuality and incest taboo, castration complex and superego all unite here to bring about that specifically human crisis during which the child must turn from an exclusive, pregenital attachment to his parents to the slow process of becoming a parent, a carrier of tradition. Here the most fateful split and transformation in the emotional powerhouse occurs, a split between potential human glory and potential total destruction. For here the child becomes forever divided in himself. The instinct fragments which before had enhanced the growth of his infantile body and mind now become divided into an infantile set which perpetuates the exuberance of growth potentials, and a parental set which supports and increases self-observation, self-guidance, and self-punishment.

Naturally, the parental set is at first infantile in nature: the fact that human conscience remains partially infantile throughout life is the core of human tragedy. For the superego of the child can be primitive, cruel, and uncompromising, as may be observed in instances where children overcontrol and overconstrict themselves to the point of self-obliteration; where they develop an over-obedience more literal than the one the parent has wished to exact; or where they develop deep regressions and lasting resentments because the parents themselves do not seem to live up to the new conscience which they have installed in the child. One of the deepest conflicts in life is the hate for a parent who served as the model and the executor of the superego, but who (in some form) was found trying to get away with the very transgressions which the child can no longer tolerate in himself. The suspiciousness and evasiveness which is thus mixed in with the all-or-nothing quality of the superego, this organ of tradition, makes moral (in the sense of moralistic) man a great potential danger to his own ego—and to that of his fellow men.

The problem, again, is one of mutual regulation. Where the child, now so ready to overmanipulate himself, can gradually develop a sense of paternal responsibility, where he can gain some insight into the institutions, functions, and roles which will permit his responsible participation, he will find pleasurable accomplishment in wielding tools and weapons, in manipulating meaningful toys—and in caring for younger children.

* * *

4. Industry vs. Inferiority

Before the child, psychologically already a rudimentary parent, can become a biological parent, he must begin to be a worker and potential provider. With the oncoming latency period,[1] the normally advanced child forgets, or rather sublimates, the necessity to "make" people by direct attack or to become papa and mama in a hurry: he now learns to win recognition by producing things. He has mastered the ambulatory field and the organ modes. He has experienced a sense of finality regarding the fact that there is no workable future within the womb of his family, and thus becomes ready to apply himself to given skills and tasks, which go far beyond the mere playful expression of his organ modes or the pleasure in the function of his limbs. He develops industry—i.e., he adjusts himself to the inorganic laws of the tool world. He can become an eager and absorbed unit of a productive situation. To bring a productive situation to completion is an aim which gradually supersedes the whims and wishes of his autonomous organism. His ego boundaries include his tools and skills: the work principle teaches him the pleasure of work completion by steady attention and persevering diligence.

His danger, at this stage, lies in a sense of inadequacy and inferiority. If he despairs of his tools and skills or of his status among his tool partners, his ego boundaries suffer, and he abandons hope for the ability to identify early with others who apply themselves to the same general section of the tool world. To lose the hope of such "industrial" association leads back to the more isolated, less tool-conscious "anatomical" rivalry of the Oedipal time.[2] The child despairs of his equipment in the tool world and in anatomy, and considers himself doomed to mediocrity or mutilation. It is at this point that wider society becomes significant in its ways of admitting the child to an understanding of meaningful roles in its total economy. Many a child's development is disrupted when family life may not have prepared him for school life, or when school life may fail to sustain the promises of earlier stages.

[1]At the end of the phallic period, around age 7, Freud described children as entering a "latency period" until the beginning of puberty a few years later. During this period issues of sexual development are temporarily set aside while the child learns important skills for later life.

[2]Part of the story of the Oedipal crisis told by Freud consists of the young boy comparing the size of his genitals with that of his father's, and feeling thoroughly inferior as a result.

5. Identity vs. Role Diffusion

With the establishment of a good relationship to the world of skills and tools, and with the advent of sexual maturity, childhood proper comes to an end. Youth begins. But in puberty and adolescence all samenesses and continuities relied on earlier are questioned again, because of a rapidity of body growth which equals that of early childhood and because of the entirely new addition of physical genital maturity. The growing and developing youths, faced with this physiological revolution within them, are now primarily concerned with what they appear to be in the eyes of others as compared with what they feel they are, and with the question of how to connect the roles and skills cultivated earlier with the occupational prototypes of the day. In their search for a new sense of continuity and sameness, adolescents have to refight many of the battles of earlier years, even though to do so they must artificially appoint perfectly well-meaning people to play the roles of enemies; and they are ever ready to install lasting idols and ideals as guardians of a final identity: here puberty rites "confirm" the inner design for life.

The integration now taking place in the form of ego identity is more than the sum of the childhood identifications. It is the accrued experience of the ego's ability to integrate these identifications with the vicissitudes of the libido, with the aptitudes developed out of endowment, and with the opportunities offered in social roles. The sense of ego identity, then, is the accrued confidence that the inner sameness and continuity are matched by the sameness and continuity of one's meaning for others, as evidenced in the tangible promise of a "career."

The danger of this stage is role diffusion. Where this is based on a strong previous doubt as to one's sexual identity, delinquent and outright psychotic incidents are not uncommon. If diagnosed and treated correctly, these incidents do not have the same fatal significance which they have at other ages. It is primarily the inability to settle on an occupational identity which disturbs young people. To keep themselves together they temporarily overidentify, to the point of apparent complete loss of identity, with the heroes of cliques and crowds. This initiates the stage of "falling in love," which is by no means entirely, or even primarily, a sexual matter—except where the mores demand it. To a considerable extent adolescent love is an attempt to arrive at a definition of one's identity by projecting one's diffused ego images on one another and by seeing them thus reflected and gradually clarified. This is why many a youth would rather converse, and settle matters of mutual identification, than embrace.

Puberty rites and confirmations help to integrate and to affirm the new identity. * * *

6. Intimacy vs. Isolation

It is only as young people emerge from their identity struggles that their egos can master the sixth stage, that of intimacy. What we have said about genitality now gradually comes into play. Body and ego must now be masters of the organ modes and of the nuclear conflicts, in order to be able to face the fear of ego loss in situations which call for self-abandon: in orgasms and sexual unions, in close friendships and in physical combat, in experiences of inspiration by teachers and of intuition from the recesses of the self. The avoidance of such experiences because of a fear of ego loss may lead to a deep sense of isolation and consequent self-absorption.

This, then, may be the place to complete our discussion of genitality.

For a basic orientation in the matter I shall quote what has come to me as Freud's shortest saying. It has often been claimed, and bad habits of conversation seem to sustain the claim, that psychoanalysis as a treatment attempts to convince the patient that before God and man he has only one obligation: to have good orgasms, with a fitting "object," and that regularly. This, of course, is not true. Freud was once asked what he thought a normal person should be able to do well. The questioner probably expected a complicated answer. But Freud, in the curt way of his old days, is reported to have said: "Lieben und arbeiten" (to love and to work). It pays to ponder on this simple formula; it gets deeper as you think about it. For when Freud said "love" he meant *genital* love, and genital *love*; when he said love *and* work, he meant a general work-productiveness which would not preoccupy the individual to the extent that he loses his right or capacity to be a genital and a loving being. Thus we may ponder, but we cannot improve on the formula which includes the doctor's prescription for human dignity—and for democratic living.

Genitality, then, consists in the unobstructed capacity to develop an orgastic potency so free of pregenital interferences that genital libido (not just the sex products discharged in Kinsey's "outlets"[3]) is expressed in heterosexual mutuality, with full sensitivity of both penis and vagina, and with a convulsion-like discharge of tension from the whole body. This is a rather concrete way of saying something about a process which we really do not understand. To put it more situationally: the total fact of finding, via the climactic turmoil of the orgasm, a supreme experience of the mutual regulation of two beings in some way breaks the point off the hostilities and potential rages caused by the oppositeness of male and female, of fact and fancy, of love and hate. Satisfactory sex relations thus make sex less obsessive, overcompensation less necessary, sadistic controls superfluous.

* * * The kind of mutuality in orgasm which psychoanalysis has in mind[4] is apparently easily obtained in classes and cultures which happen to make a leisurely institution of it. In more complex societies this mutuality is interfered with by so many factors of health, of tradition, of opportunity, and of temperament, that the proper formulation of sexual health would be rather this: A human being should be potentially able to accomplish mutuality of genital orgasm, but he should also be so constituted as to bear frustration in the matter without undue regression wherever considerations of reality and loyalty call for it.

* * * In order to be of lasting social significance, the utopia of genitality should include:

1. mutuality of orgasm
2. with a loved partner
3. of the other sex[5]
4. with whom one is able and willing to share a mutual trust
5. and with whom one is able and willing to regulate the cycles of
   a. work
   b. procreation
   c. recreation
6. so as to secure to the offspring, too, a satisfactory development.

It is apparent that such utopian accomplishment on a large scale cannot be an individual or, indeed, a therapeutic task. Nor is it a purely sexual matter by any means.

7. Generativity vs. Stagnation

The discussion of intimacy versus isolation has already included a further nuclear conflict which, therefore, requires only a short explicit formulation: I mean generativity versus stagnation. I apologize for creating a new and not even pleasant term. Yet neither creativity nor productivity nor any other fashionable term seems to me to convey what must be conveyed—namely, that the ability to lose oneself in the meeting of bodies and minds leads to a gradual expansion of ego interests and of libidinal cathexis over that which has been thus generated and accepted as a responsibility. Generativity is primarily the interest in establishing and guiding the next generation or whatever in a given case may become the absorbing object of a parental kind of responsibility. Where this enrichment fails, a regression from generativity to an obsessive

[3]The reference here is to Alfred Kinsey, one of the first modern sex researchers. Kinsey focused closely on the nature and meaning of literal sex acts and "outlets," a term and approach Erikson obviously found limited and even distasteful.

[4]As the ideal outcome of a sexual relationship.

[5]Although Erikson obviously here expresses a different view, current psychology generally does not regard homosexuality as a neurosis or psychological failure.

need for pseudo intimacy, punctuated by moments of mutual repulsion, takes place, often with a pervading sense (and objective evidence) of individual stagnation and interpersonal impoverishment.

8. Ego Integrity vs. Despair

Only he who in some way has taken care of things and people and has adapted himself to the triumphs and disappointments adherent to being, by necessity, the originator of others and the generator of things and ideas—only he may gradually grow the fruit of these seven stages. I know no better word for it than ego integrity. Lacking a clear definition, I shall point to a few constituents of this state of mind. It is the ego's accrued assurance of its proclivity for order and meaning. It is a post-narcissistic love of the human ego—not of the self—as an experience which conveys some world order and spiritual sense, no matter how dearly paid for. It is the acceptance of one's one and only life cycle as something that had to be and that, by necessity, permitted of no substitutions; it thus means a new, a different love of one's parents. It is a comradeship with the ordering ways of distant times and different pursuits, as expressed in the simple products and sayings of such times and pursuits. Although aware of the relativity of all the various lifestyles which have given meaning to human striving, the possessor of integrity is ready to defend the dignity of his own life style against all physical and economic threats. For he knows that an individual life is the accidental coincidence of but one life cycle with but one segment of history; and that for him all human integrity stands or falls with the one style of integrity of which he partakes. The style of integrity developed by his culture or civilization thus becomes the "patrimony of his soul," the seal of his moral paternity of himself.[6] * * * Before this final solution, death loses its sting.

The lack or loss of this accrued ego integration is signified by fear of death: the one and only life cycle is not accepted as the ultimate of life. Despair expresses the feeling that the time is short, too short for the attempt to start another life and to try out alternate roads to integrity. Disgust hides despair.

Each individual, to become a mature adult, must to a sufficient degree develop all the ego qualities mentioned, so that a wise Indian, a true gentleman, and a mature peasant share and recognize in one another the final stage of integrity. But each cultural entity, to develop the particular style of integrity suggested by its historical place, utilizes a particular combination of these conflicts, along with specific provocations and prohibitions of infantile sexuality. Infantile conflicts become creative only if sustained by the firm support of cultural institutions and of the special leader classes representing them. In order to approach or experience integrity, the individual must know how to be a follower of image bearers in religion and in politics, in the economic order and in technology, in aristocratic living and in the arts and sciences. Ego integrity, therefore, implies an emotional integration which permits participation by followership as well as acceptance of the responsibility of leadership.

Webster's dictionary is kind enough to help us complete this outline in a circular fashion. Trust (the first of our ego values) is here defined as "the assured reliance on another's integrity," the last of our values. I suspect that Webster had business in mind rather than babies, credit rather than faith. But the formulation stands. And it seems possible to further paraphrase the relation of adult integrity and infantile trust by saying that healthy children will not fear life if their parents have integrity enough not to fear death.

* * * In order to indicate the whole conceptual area which is awaiting systematic treatment, I shall conclude this chapter with a diagram.[7] In

[6]Erikson seemed to take this advice to heart. He never knew his father and in midlife abandoned his stepfather's name and took instead the name Erikson, as a way of claiming his own moral paternity of himself.

[7]The meaning of this diagram, reproduced in many textbooks, is not made entirely clear by Erikson. But Franz and White (1985) "fill in" the rows and columns

Oral Sensory	Trust vs. Mistrust							
Muscular-Anal		Autonomy vs. Shame, Doubt						
Locomotor-Genital			Initiative vs. Guilt					
Latency				Industry vs. Inferiority				
Puberty and Adolescence					Identity vs. Role Diffusion			
Young Adulthood						Intimacy vs. Isolation		
Adulthood							Generativity vs. Stagnation	
Maturity								Integrity vs. Disgust, Despair

Figure 31.1

this, as in the diagram of pregenital zones and modes, the diagonal represents the sequence of enduring solutions, each of which is based on the integration of the earlier ones. At any given stage of the life cycle the solution of one more nuclear conflict adds a new ego quality, a new criterion of increasing strength. The criteria proposed in this chart are to be treated in analogy to the criteria for health and illness in general—i.e., by ascertaining whether or not there is "a pervading subjective sense of" the criterion in question, and whether or not "objective evidence of the dominance of" the criterion can be established by indirect examination (by means of depth psychology). Above the diagonal there is space for a future elaboration of the precursors of each of these solutions, all of which begin with the beginning; below the diagonal there is space for the designation of the derivatives of these solutions in the maturing and the mature personality.

associated with identity and intimacy, showing the heuristic power of Erikson's theory even as they seek to offer their own revision of it.

PART V

Humanistic Approaches to Personality

Humanistic approaches to personality emphasize what is uniquely human about psychology's object of study. Studying people is not the same as studying rocks, trees, or animals because people are fundamentally different. The unique aspects on which humanistic approaches focus are experience, awareness, free will, dignity, and the meaning of life. None of these mean much to rocks, trees, or animals, but they are all crucial to the human condition.

Our first selection, by the philosopher Jean-Paul Sartre, describes the existential philosophy that forms the bedrock of humanistic psychology. Existential analysis begins with the concrete and specific analysis of a single human being existing in a particular moment in time and space. It leads directly to concerns with phenomenology (the study of experience), free will, and the meaning of life. All of these existential issues are important for humanistic psychologists.

Sartre seems to view free will as a burden—it leaves one "forlorn," without external guidance about the right way to live. But the humanistic psychologists who borrowed so much of existential philosophy instead view free will as an opportunity. In the second selection, Abraham Maslow briefly describes what he sees as the implications of existential philosophy for psychology, and argues that an existential viewpoint not only reclaims free will but also offers new opportunities for personal growth and fulfillment.

This message is echoed by Gordon Allport, another pioneering humanistic psychologist, in the next selection. Allport focuses on the need in psychology for a "self," by which he means a psychological construct that has purpose, identity, experience, and a will to live and to grow. Nonhumanistic areas of psychology ignore these, Allport claims, but each is essential.

The next selection is another article by Maslow. This one presents his well-known theory of motivation, often referred to as the "hierarchy of needs." What is humanistic about this theory is that motivation begins rather than ends with the basic needs for survival and safety. After those are satisfied, Maslow pro-

poses, uniquely human needs for understanding, beauty, and self-actualization become important.

The best known of the humanistic psychologists surely was Carl Rogers. In the fifth selection, Rogers argues that the "unconditional positive regard" that a humanistic psychotherapist gives his or her clients allows a clear, undistorted picture of his or her personality to emerge. He then draws on some experiences in the therapeutic context to illustrate his theory of personality dynamics, particularly what he regards as every individual's ability to reorganize his or her own personality.

The final selection is by the modern humanistic psychologist Mihaly Csikszentmihalyi. Csikszentmihalyi addresses the classic humanistic question, what is positive experience (the good life) and how does one attain it? He concludes that true happiness consists not of ecstasy but rather in choosing to enter a state of calm absorption he calls flow.

The psychologist Ernest Hilgard once warned of the example of the entomologist who found a bug he couldn't classify, so he stepped on it. The largest contribution of the humanistic psychologists is their sustained focus on issues—such as experience, free will, and the meaning of the good life—that other areas of psychology are content to ignore.

The Humanism of Existentialism

Jean-Paul Sartre

The philosophical basis of humanistic psychology is existentialism. And the leading exponent of existentialism has been Jean-Paul Sartre. Sartre was a French philosopher, dramatist, and novelist. He was a person of high principles. He was imprisoned by the Germans when they invaded France in 1940, and after his release he became active in the French Resistance. He was awarded the 1964 Nobel Prize in Literature but rejected it, saying that to accept such an award would compromise his integrity as a writer.

Existentialism is a philosophy that claims that "existence precedes essence." This means that first one exists—this is the only given—and then one must decide what such existence means. Since a person's existence occurs only a moment at a time, the experience of life in each moment is all-important. Any influence from the environment, the past, or the future can only affect one to the degree one is aware of it now. *Sartre derives from these postulates an ethical code that emphasizes the freedom of oneself and others, and an accompanying, inescapable, total responsibility for everything one thinks and does.*

We will see in later selections how humanistic psychologists integrate several key observations of existential philosophy into their theories. For now, note how Sartre argues that

- *the experience of each moment of existence is the basis for all else;*
- *each individual must interpret what reality is and what it means;*
- *people have complete freedom and total responsibility for their actions;*
- *there is no moral or ethical code beyond that which each individual must invent —with the one exception that it is essential to take responsibility for our own free choices, whatever they are; and*
- *it is in accepting freedom and taking responsibility—despite everything—that humans achieve dignity.*

From *Essays in Existentialism*, edited by W. Baskin (Secaucus, NJ: Citadel Press, 1965), pp. 31–62.

* * *

What is meant by the term *existentialism*?

* * *

It is the most austere of doctrines. It is intended strictly for specialists and philosophers. Yet it can be defined easily. * * * What [existentialists] have in common is that they think that existence precedes essence, or, if you prefer, that subjectivity must be the starting point.

* * *

Atheistic existentialism, which I represent, states that if God does not exist, there is at least one being in whom existence precedes essence, a being who exists before he can be defined by any concept, and that this being is man, or, as Heidegger[1] says, human reality. What is meant here by saying that existence precedes essence? It means that, first of all, man exists, turns up, appears on the scene, and, only afterwards, defines himself. If man, as the existentialist conceives him, is indefinable, it is because at first he is nothing. Only afterward will he be something, and he himself will have made what he will be. Thus, there is no human nature, since there is no God to conceive it. Not only is man what he conceives himself to be, but he is also only what he wills himself to be after this thrust toward existence.

Man is nothing else but what he makes of himself. Such is the first principle of existentialism. It is also what is called subjectivity. * * * [By this,] we mean that man first exists, that is, that man first of all is the being who hurls himself toward a future and who is conscious of imagining himself as being in the future. Man is at the start a plan which is aware of itself, rather than a patch of moss, a piece of garbage, or a cauliflower; nothing exists prior to this plan; there is nothing in heaven; man will be what he will have planned to be. Not what he will want to be. Because by the word "will" we generally mean a conscious decision, which is subsequent to what we have already made of ourselves. I may want to belong to a political party, write a book, get married; but all that is only a manifestation of an earlier, more spontaneous choice that is called "will." But if existence really does precede essence, man is responsible for what he is. Thus, existentialism's first move is to make every man aware of what he is and to make the full responsibility of his existence rest on him. And when we say that a man is responsible for himself, we do not only mean that he is responsible for his own individuality, but that he is responsible for all men.

* * * When we say that man chooses his own self, we mean that every one of us does likewise; but we also mean by that that in making this choice he also chooses all men. In fact, in creating the man that we want to be, there is not a single one of our acts which does not at the same time create an image of man as we think he ought to be. To choose to be this or that is to affirm at the same time the value of what we choose, because we can never choose evil. We always choose the good, and nothing can be good for us without being good for all.

If, on the other hand, existence precedes essence, and if we grant that we exist and fashion our image at one and the same time, the image is valid for everybody and for our whole age. Thus, our responsibility is much greater than we might have supposed, because it involves all mankind. * * * If I want to marry, to have children; even if this marriage depends solely on my own circumstances or passion or wish, I am involving all humanity in monogamy and not merely myself. Therefore, I am responsible for myself and for everyone else. I am creating a certain image of man of my own choosing. In choosing myself, I choose man.

This helps us understand what the actual content is of such rather grandiloquent words as anguish, forlornness, despair.[2] As you will see, it's all quite simple.

---

[1]A German existentialist philosopher whose thinking underlies much of the theory that Sartre espouses in this article.

[2]Gloomy-sounding words like these are a staple of existentialist philosophy.

First, what is meant by anguish? The existentialists say at once that man is anguish. What that means is this: the man who involves himself and who realizes that he is not only the person he chooses to be, but also a lawmaker who is, at the same time, choosing all mankind as well as himself, can not help escape the feeling of his total and deep responsibility. Of course, there are many people who are not anxious; but we claim that they are hiding their anxiety, that they are fleeing from it. Certainly, many people believe that when they do something, they themselves are the only ones involved, and when someone says to them, "What if everyone acted that way?" they shrug their shoulders and answer, "Everyone doesn't act that way." But really, one should always ask himself, "What would happen if everybody looked at things that way?" There is no escaping this disturbing thought except by a kind of double-dealing. A man who lies and makes excuses for himself by saying "Not everybody does that," is someone with an uneasy conscience, because the act of lying implies that a universal value is conferred upon the lie.

Anguish is evident even when it conceals itself. This is the anguish that Kierkegaard called the anguish of Abraham. You know the story: an angel has ordered Abraham to sacrifice his son; if it really were an angel who has come and said, "You are Abraham, you shall sacrifice your son," everything would be all right. But everyone might first wonder, "Is it really an angel, and am I really Abraham? What proof do I have?"

There was a madwoman who had hallucinations; someone used to speak to her on the telephone and give her orders. Her doctor asked her, "Who is it who talks to you?" She answered, "He says it's God." What proof did she really have that it was God? If an angel comes to me, what proof is there that it's an angel? And if I hear voices, what proof is there that they come from heaven and not from hell, or from the subconscious, or a pathological condition? What proves that they are addressed to me? What proof is there that I have been appointed to impose my choice and my conception of man on humanity? I'll never find any proof or sign to convince me of that. If a voice addresses me, it is always for me to decide that this is the angel's voice; if I consider that such an act is a good one, it is I who will choose to say that it is good rather than bad.

Now, I'm not being singled out as an Abraham, and yet at every moment I'm obliged to perform exemplary acts. For every man, everything happens as if all mankind had its eyes fixed on him and were guiding itself by what he does. And every man ought to say to himself, "Am I really the kind of man who has the right to act in such a way that humanity might guide itself by my actions?" And if he does not say that to himself, he is masking his anguish.

There is no question here of the kind of anguish which would lead to quietism, to inaction. It is a matter of a simple sort of anguish that anybody who has had responsibilities is familiar with. For example, when a military officer takes the responsibility for an attack and sends a certain number of men to death, he chooses to do so, and in the main he alone makes the choice. Doubtless, orders come from above, but they are too broad; he interprets them, and on this interpretation depend the lives of ten or fourteen or twenty men. In making a decision he can not help having a certain anguish. All leaders know this anguish. That doesn't keep them from acting; on the contrary, it is the very condition of their action. For it implies that they envisage a number of possibilities, and when they choose one, they realize that it has value only because it is chosen. We shall see that this kind of anguish, which is the kind that existentialism describes, is explained, in addition, by a direct responsibility to the other men whom it involves. It is not a curtain separating us from action, but is part of action itself.

When we speak of forlornness, a term Heidegger was fond of, we mean only that God does not exist and that we have to face all the consequences of this. The existentialist is strongly opposed to a certain kind of secular ethics which would like to abolish God with the least possible expense. About 1880, some French teachers tried to set up a secular ethics which went something like this: God is a useless and costly hypothesis; we are discarding it; but, meanwhile, in order for there to be an ethics, a society, a civilization, it is essential that certain values be taken seriously and that they be considered as having an *a priori* existence. It must be obligatory, *a priori*, to be honest, not to lie, not to beat your wife, to have children, etc., etc. So we're going to try a little device which will make it possible to show that values exist all the same, inscribed in a heaven of ideas, though otherwise God does not exist. In other words—and this, I believe, is the tendency of everything called reformism in France—nothing will be changed if God does not exist. We shall find ourselves with the same norms of honesty, progress, and humanism, and we shall have made of God an outdated hypothesis which will peacefully die off by itself.

The existentialist, on the contrary, thinks it very distressing that God does not exist, because all possibility of finding values in a heaven of ideas disappears along with Him; there can no longer be an *a priori* Good, since there is no infinite and perfect consciousness to think it. Nowhere is it written that the Good exists, that we must be honest, that we must not lie; because the fact is we are on a plane where there are only men. Dostoievsky[3] said, "If God didn't exist, everything would be possible." That is the very starting point of existentialism. Indeed, everything is permissible if God does not exist, and as a result man is forlorn, because neither within him nor without does he find anything to cling to. He can't start making excuses for himself.

If existence really does precede essence, there is no explaining things away by reference to a fixed and given human nature. In other words, there is no determinism, man is free, man is freedom. On the other hand, if God does not exist, we find no values or commands to turn to which legitimize our conduct. So, in the bright realm of values, we have no excuse behind us, nor justification before us. We are alone, with no excuses.

That is the idea I shall try to convey when I say that man is condemned to be free. Condemned, because he did not create himself, yet, in other respects is free; because, once thrown into the world, he is responsible for everything he does. The existentialist does not believe in the power of passion. He will never agree that a sweeping passion is a ravaging torrent which fatally leads a man to certain acts and is therefore an excuse. He thinks that man is responsible for his passion.

The existentialist does not think that man is going to help himself by finding in the world some omen by which to orient himself. Because he thinks that man will interpret the omen to suit himself. Therefore, he thinks that man, with no support and no aid, is condemned every moment to invent man. * * *

To give you an example which will enable you to understand forlornness better, I shall cite the case of one of my students who came to see me under the following circumstances: his father was on bad terms with his mother, and, moreover, was inclined to be a collaborationist[4]; his older brother had been killed in the German offensive of 1940, and the young man, with somewhat immature but generous feelings, wanted to avenge him. His mother lived alone with him, very much upset by the half-treason of her husband and the death of her older son; the boy was her only consolation.

The boy was faced with the choice of leaving for England and joining the Free French Forces—that is, leaving his mother behind—or remaining with his mother and helping her to carry on. He was fully aware that the woman lived only for him and that his going-off—and perhaps his death—would plunge her into despair. He was also aware that every act that he did for his mother's sake was a sure thing, in the sense that it was helping

[3]Fyodor Dostoyevsky (the more common English spelling) was a 19th-century Russian novelist.

[4]A "collaborationist" was a resident of a country occupied by Germany in World War II who cooperated with the invaders. Germany conquered France, where Sartre lived, in 1940. Sartre was imprisoned by the Germans for a year, then freed. Upon his release, Sartre became active in the French Resistance, at great personal risk.

her to carry on, whereas every effort he made toward going off and fighting was an uncertain move which might run aground and prove completely useless; for example, on his way to England he might, while passing through Spain, be detained indefinitely in a Spanish camp; he might reach England or Algiers and be stuck in an office at a desk job. As a result, he was faced with two very different kinds of action: one, concrete, immediate, but concerning only one individual; the other concerned an incomparably vaster group, a national collectivity, but for that very reason was dubious, and might be interrupted en route. And, at the same time, he was wavering between two kinds of ethics. On the one hand, an ethics of sympathy, of personal devotion; on the other, a broader ethics, but one whose efficacy was more dubious. He had to choose between the two.

Who could help him choose? Christian doctrine? No. Christian doctrine says, "Be charitable, love your neighbor, take the more rugged path, etc., etc." But which is the more rugged path? Whom should he love as a brother? The fighting man or his mother? Which does the greater good, the vague act of fighting in a group, or the concrete one of helping a particular human being to go on living? Who can decide *a priori*? Nobody. No book of ethics can tell him. The Kantian ethics says, "Never treat any person as a means, but as an end." Very well, if I stay with mother, I'll treat her as an end and not as a means; but by virtue of this very fact, I'm running the risk of treating the people around me who are fighting, as means; and, conversely, if I go to join those who are fighting, I'll be treating them as an end, and, by doing that, I run the risk of treating my mother as a means.

If values are vague, and if they are always too broad for the concrete and specific case that we are considering, the only thing left for us is to trust our instincts. That's what this young man tried to do; and when I saw him, he said, "In the end, feeling is what counts. I ought to choose whichever pushes me in one direction. If I feel that I love my mother enough to sacrifice everything else for her—my desire for vengeance, for action, for adventure—then I'll stay with her. If, on the contrary, I feel that my love for my mother isn't enough, I'll leave."

But how is the value of a feeling determined? What gives his feeling for his mother value? Precisely the fact that he remained with her. I may say that I like so-and-so well enough to sacrifice a certain amount of money for him, but I may say so only if I've done it. I may say "I love my mother well enough to remain with her" if I have remained with her. The only way to determine the value of this affection is, precisely, to perform an act which confirms and defines it. But, since I require this affection to justify my act, I find myself caught in a vicious circle.

On the other hand, a mock feeling and a true feeling are almost indistinguishable; to decide that I love my mother and will remain with her, or to remain with her by putting on an act, amount somewhat to the same thing. In other words, the feeling is formed by the acts one performs; so, I can not refer to it in order to act upon it. Which means that I can neither seek within myself the true condition which will impel me to act, nor apply to a system of ethics for concepts which will permit me to act. You will say, "At least, he did go to a teacher for advice." But if you seek advice from a priest, for example, you have chosen this priest; you already knew, more or less, just about what advice he was going to give you. In other words, choosing your adviser is involving yourself. The proof of this is that if you are a Christian, you will say, "Consult a priest." But some priests are collaborating, some are just marking time, some are resisting. Which to choose? If the young man chooses a priest who is resisting or collaborating, he has already decided on the kind of advice he's going to get. Therefore, in coming to see me he knew the answer I was going to give him, and I had only one answer to give: "You're free, choose, that is, invent." No general ethics can show you what is to be done; there are no omens in the world. The Catholics will reply, "But there are." Granted—but, in any case, I myself choose the meaning they have.

When I was a prisoner,[5] I knew a rather remarkable young man who was a Jesuit. He had entered the Jesuit order in the following way: he had had a number of very bad breaks; in childhood, his father died, leaving him in poverty, and he was a scholarship student at a religious institution where he was constantly made to feel that he was being kept out of charity; then, he failed to get any of the honors and distinctions that children like; later on, at about eighteen, he bungled a love affair; finally, at twenty-two, he failed in military training, a childish enough matter, but it was the last straw.

This young fellow might well have felt that he had botched everything. It was a sign of something, but of what? He might have taken refuge in bitterness or despair. But he very wisely looked upon all this as a sign that he was not made for secular triumphs, and that only the triumphs of religion, holiness, and faith were open to him. He saw the hand of God in all this, and so he entered the order. Who can help seeing that he alone decided what the sign meant?

Some other interpretation might have been drawn from this series of setbacks; for example, that he might have done better to turn carpenter or revolutionist. Therefore, he is fully responsible for the interpretation. Forlornness implies that we ourselves choose our being. Forlornness and anguish go together.

As for despair, the term has a very simple meaning. It means that we shall confine ourselves to reckoning only with what depends upon our will, or on the ensemble of probabilities which make our action possible. When we want something, we always have to reckon with probabilities. I may be counting on the arrival of a friend. The friend is coming by rail or street-car; this supposes that the train will arrive on schedule, or that the street-car will not jump the track. I am left in the realm of possibility; but possibilities are to be reckoned with only to the point where my action comports with the ensemble of these possibilities, and no further. The moment the possibilities I am considering are not rigorously involved by my action, I ought to disengage myself from them, because no God, no scheme, can adapt the world and its possibilities to my will. When Descartes said, "Conquer yourself rather than the world," he meant essentially the same thing.

* * *

Things will be as man will have decided they are to be. Does that mean that I should abandon myself to quietism? No. First, I should involve myself; then, act on the old saw "Nothing ventured, nothing gained." Nor does it mean that I shouldn't belong to a party, but rather that I shall have no illusions and shall do what I can. For example, suppose I ask myself, "Will socialization, as such, ever come about?" I know nothing about it. All I know is that I'm going to do everything in my power to bring it about. Beyond that, I can't count on anything. Quietism is the attitude of people who say, "Let others do what I can't do." The doctrine I am presenting is the very opposite of quietism, since it declares, "There is no reality except in action." Moreover, it goes further, since it adds, "Man is nothing else than his plan; he exists only to the extent that he fulfills himself; he is therefore nothing else than the ensemble of his acts, nothing else than his life."

According to this, we can understand why our doctrine horrifies certain people. Because often the only way they can bear their wretchedness is to think, "Circumstances have been against me. What I've been and done doesn't show my true worth. To be sure, I've had no great love, no great friendship, but that's because I haven't met a man or woman who was worthy. The books I've written haven't been very good because I haven't had the proper leisure. I haven't had children to devote myself to because I didn't find a man with whom I could have spent my life. So there remains within me, unused and quite viable, a host of propensities, inclinations, possibilities, that one wouldn't guess from the mere series of things I've done."

Now, for the existentialist there is really no love other than one which manifests itself in a person's being in love. There is no genius other than one which is expressed in works of art; the

[5]That is, a prisoner of the Germans in 1940–1941.

genius of Proust is the sum of Proust's works; the genius of Racine is his series of tragedies. Outside of that, there is nothing. Why say that Racine could have written another tragedy, when he didn't write it? A man is involved in life, leaves his impress on it, and outside of that there is nothing. To be sure, this may seem a harsh thought to someone whose life hasn't been a success. But, on the other hand, it prompts people to understand that reality alone is what counts, that dreams, expectations, and hopes warrant no more than to define a man as a disappointed dream, as miscarried hopes, as vain expectations. In other words, to define him negatively and not positively. However, when we say, "You are nothing else than your life," that does not imply that the artist will be judged solely on the basis of his works of art; a thousand other things will contribute toward summing him up. What we mean is that a man is nothing else than a series of undertakings, that he is the sum, the organization, the ensemble of the relationships which make up these undertakings.

When all is said and done, what we are accused of, at bottom, is not our pessimism, but an optimistic toughness. If people throw up to us our works of fiction[6] in which we write about people who are soft, weak, cowardly, and sometimes even downright bad, it's not because these people are soft, weak, cowardly, or bad; because if we were to say that they are that way because of heredity, the workings of environment, society, because of biological or psychological determinism, people would be reassured. They would say, "Well, that's what we're like, no one can do anything about it." But when the existentialist writes about a coward, he says that this coward is responsible for his cowardice. He's not like that because he has a cowardly heart or lung or brain; he's not like that on account of his physiological make-up; but he's like that because he has made himself a coward by his acts. There's no such thing as a cowardly constitution; there are nervous constitutions; there is poor blood, as the common people say, or there are strong constitutions. But the man whose blood is poor is not a coward on that account, for what makes cowardice is the act of renouncing or yielding. A constitution is not an act; the coward is defined on the basis of the acts he performs. People feel, in a vague sort of way, that this coward we're talking about is guilty of being a coward, and the thought frightens them. What people would like is that a coward or a hero be born that way.

* * *

[Existentialism] is the only [theory] which gives man dignity, the only one which does not reduce him to an object. The effect of all materialism is to treat every man, including the one philosophizing, as an object, that is, as an ensemble of determined reactions in no way distinguished from the ensemble of qualities and phenomena which constitute a table or a chair or a stone. We definitely wish to establish the human realm as an ensemble of values distinct from the material realm. But the subjectivity that we have thus arrived at, and which we have claimed to be truth, is not a strictly individual subjectivity, for we have demonstrated that one discovers in the *cogito*[7] not only himself, but others as well.

* * *

If it is impossible to find in every man some universal essence which would be human nature, yet there does exist a universal human condition. It's not by chance that today's thinkers speak more readily of man's condition than of his nature. By condition they mean, more or less definitely, the *a priori* limits which outline man's fundamental situation in the universe. Historical situations vary; a man may be born a slave in a pagan society or a feudal lord or a proletarian. What does not vary is the necessity for him to exist in the world, to be at work there, to be there in the midst of other people, and to be mortal there. The limits are neither subjective nor objective, or, rather,

[6]Sartre wrote novels and plays about the human condition, including the novel *Nausea* (published in 1938) and the play *No Exit* (1944).

[7]The reference here is to *cogito ergo sum*, "I think, therefore I am." This is the famous existentialist pronouncement by the philosopher Descartes.

they have an objective and a subjective side. Objective because they are to be found everywhere and are recognizable everywhere; subjective because they are *lived* and are nothing if man does not live them, that is, freely determine his existence with reference to them. And though the configurations may differ, at least none of them are completely strange to me, because they all appear as attempts either to pass beyond these limits or recede from them or deny them or adapt to them. Consequently, every configuration, however individual it may be, has a universal value.

* * *

* * * One may choose anything if it is on the grounds of free involvement.

* * *

* * * Fundamentally [humanism means] this: man is constantly outside of himself; in projecting himself, in losing himself outside of himself, he makes for man's existing; and, on the other hand, it is by pursuing transcendent goals that he is able to exist; man, being this state of passing-beyond, and seizing upon things only as they bear upon this passing-beyond, is at the heart, at the center of this passing-beyond. There is no universe other than a human universe, the universe of human subjectivity. This connection between transcendency, as a constituent element of man—not in the sense that God is transcendent, but in the sense of passing beyond—and subjectivity, in the sense that man is not closed in on himself but is always present in a human universe, is what we call existentialist humanism. Humanism, because we remind man that there is no lawmaker other than himself, and that in his forlornness he will decide by himself; because we point out that man will fulfill himself as man, not in turning toward himself, but in seeking outside of himself a goal which is just this liberation, just this particular fulfillment.

* * *

Existential Psychology—What's in It for Us?

Abraham H. Maslow

One of the founders of American humanistic psychology was Abraham Maslow. In the following brief article Maslow specifically addresses the ways in which European existentialist philosophy, of the sort described by Sartre in the previous selection, is relevant to psychology. At the very end, Maslow also demonstrates the manner in which American psychologists typically have drawn a more optimistic message from existentialism than did the existentialists themselves. Dismissing the existentialist obsession with anguish, forlornness, and despair as so much "high-IQ whimpering," Maslow claims that the loss of illusions is always, in the end, exhilarating and strengthening.

From *Existential Philosophy*, 2d ed., edited by R. May (New York: Random House, 1969), pp. 49–57.

I am not an existentialist, nor am I even a careful and thorough student of this movement. There is much in the existentialist writings that I find extremely difficult, or even impossible, to understand and that I have not made much effort to struggle with.

I must confess also that I have studied existentialism not so much for its own sake as in the spirit of, "What's in it for me as a psychologist?" trying all the time to translate it into terms I could use. Perhaps this is why I have found it to be not so much a totally new revelation as a stressing, confirming, sharpening, and rediscovering of trends already existing in American psychology (the various self psychologies, growth psychologies, self-actualization psychologies, organismic psychologies, certain neo-Freudian psychologies, the Jungian psychology, not to mention some of the psychoanalytic ego psychologists, the Gestalt therapists, and I don't know how many more).

For this and other reasons, reading the existentialists has been for me a very interesting, gratifying, and instructive experience. And I think this will also be true for many other psychologists, especially those who are interested in personality theory and in clinical psychology. It has enriched, enlarged, corrected, and strengthened my thinking about the human personality, even though it has not necessitated any fundamental reconstruction.

First of all, permit me to define existentialism in a personal way, in terms of "what's in it for me." To me it means essentially a radical stress on the concept of identity and the experience of identity as a *sine qua non* of human nature and of any philosophy or science of human nature. I choose this concept as *the* basic one partly because I understand it better than terms like essence, existence, and ontology and partly because I also feel that it can be worked with empirically, if not now, then soon.

But then a paradox results, for the Americans have *also* been impressed with the quest for identity (Allport, Rogers, Goldstein, Fromm, Wheelis, Erikson, Horney, May, *et al.*). And I must say that these writers are a lot clearer and a lot closer to raw fact, that is, more empirical than are, e.g., the Germans Heidegger and Jaspers.[1]

1. Conclusion number one is, then, that the Europeans and Americans are not so far apart as appears at first. We Americans have been "talking prose all the time and didn't know it." Partly, of course, this simultaneous development in different countries is itself an indication that the people who have independently been coming to the same conclusions are all responding to something real outside themselves.

2. This something real is, I believe, the total collapse of all sources of values outside the individual. Many European existentialists are largely reacting to Nietzsche's conclusion that God is dead and perhaps to the fact that Marx also is dead. The Americans have learned that political democracy and economic prosperity do not in themselves solve any of the basic value problems. There is no place else to turn but inward, to the self, as the locus of values.[2] Paradoxically, even some of the religious existentialists will go along with this conclusion part of the way.

3. It is extremely important for psychologists that the existentialists may supply psychology with the underlying philosophy that it now lacks. Logical positivism has been a failure, especially for clinical and personality psychologists.[3] At any rate, the basic philosophical problems will surely be opened up for discussion again, and perhaps psychologists will stop relying on pseudosolutions or on unconscious, unexamined philosophies that they picked up as children.

4. An alternative phrasing of the core (for us Americans) of European existentialism is that it deals radically with that human predicament presented by the gap between human aspirations and human limitations (between what the human being *is*, what he would *like* to be, and what he *could* be). This is not so far off from the identity problem as it might at first sound. A person is both actuality *and* potentiality.

That serious concern with this discrepancy could revolutionize psychology, there is no doubt in my mind. Various literatures already support such a conclusion, e.g., projective testing, self-actualization, the various peak experiences (in which this gap is bridged), the Jungian psychologies, various theological thinkers.

Not only this, but they raise also the problems and techniques of integration of this twofold nature of man, his lower and his higher, his creatureliness and his Godlikeness. On the whole, most philosophies and religions, Eastern as well as Western, have dichotomized them, teaching that the way to become "higher" is to renounce and master "the lower." The existentialists however, teach that *both* are simultaneously defining characteristics of human nature. Neither can be repudiated; they can only be integrated. But we already know something of these integration techniques—of insight, of intellect in the broader sense, of love, of creativeness, of humor and tragedy, of play, of art. I suspect we will focus our studies on these integrative techniques more than

[1]The psychologists listed were identified with humanistic or humanistic-psychoanalytic positions; the Germans were speculative philosophers.

[2]This was a key point in the previous selection by Sartre.

[3]In this context, Maslow is using the term "logical positivism" to refer to the position that truth can be known with certainty if correct methods are used. In psychology this leads to a superscientific outlook that emphasizes operational definitions and precise measurements over deeper meanings.

we have in the past. Another consequence for my thinking of this stress on the twofold nature of man is the realization that some problems must remain eternally insoluble.

5. From this flows naturally a concern with the ideal, authentic, or perfect, or Godlike human being, a study of human potentialities as *now* existing in a certain sense, as *current* knowable reality. This, too, may sound merely literary, but it is not. I remind you that this is just a fancy way of asking the old, unanswered questions, "What are the goals of therapy, of education, of bringing up children?"

It also implies another truth and another problem that calls urgently for attention. Practically every serious description of the "authentic person" extant implies that such a person, by virtue of what he has become, assumes a new relation to his society and, indeed, to society in general. He not only transcends himself in various ways; he also transcends his culture. He resists enculturation. He becomes more detached from his culture and from his society. He becomes a little more a member of his species and a little less a member of his local group. My feeling is that most sociologists and anthropologists will take this hard.[4] I therefore confidently expect controversy in this area.

6. From the European writers, we can and should pick up their greater emphasis on what they call "philosophical anthropology," that is, the attempt to define man, and the differences between man and any other species, between man and objects, and between man and robots. What are his unique and defining characteristics? What is as essential to man that without it he would no longer be defined as a man?

On the whole, this is a task from which American psychology has abdicated. The various behaviorisms do not generate any such definition, at least none that can be taken seriously. (What *would* an S-R man be like?)[5] Freud's picture of man was clearly unsuitable, leaving out as it did his aspirations, his realizable hopes, his Godlike qualities. * * *

7. The Europeans are stressing the self-making of the self, in a way that the Americans do not. Both the Freudians and the self-actualization and growth theorists in this country talk more about discovering the *self* (as if it were there waiting to be found) and of *uncovering* therapy (shovel away the top layers and you will see what has been always lying there, hidden). To say, however, that the self is a project and is *altogether* created by the continual choices of the person himself is almost surely an overstatement in view of what we know of, e.g., the constitutional and genetic determinants of personality. This clash of opinion is a problem that can be settled empirically.

8. A problem we psychologists have been ducking is the problem of responsibility and, necessarily tied in with it, the concepts of courage and of will in the personality. Perhaps this is close to what the psychoanalysts are now calling "ego strength."

9. American psychologists have listened to Allport's call for an idiographic psychology[6] but have not done much about it. Not even the clinical psychologists have. We now have an added push from the phenomenologists and existentialists in this direction, one that will be *very* hard to resist, indeed, I think, theoretically *impossible* to resist. If the study of the uniqueness of the individual does not fit into what we know of science, then so much the worse for the conception of science. It, too, will have to endure re-creation.

[4]Many anthropologists work from the assumption that members of different cultures are basically and even irreducibly different. But Sartre spoke of the "universal human condition," a viewpoint Maslow here seems to endorse.

[5]By "S-R man," Maslow is referring to the image of humanity implied by the behavioral approaches to psychology that were dominant when this piece was written (S-R stands for "stimulus-response").

[6]At times Gordon Allport called for an "idiographic" approach that treated each person as a unique case rather than as a point on a continuum. But neither Allport nor his successors ever seemed entirely clear about how to do this, as Maslow mentions.

10. Phenomenology[7] has a history in American psychological thinking, but on the whole I think it has languished. The European phenomenologists, with their excruciatingly careful and laborious demonstrations, can reteach us that the best way of understanding another human being, or at least *a* way necessary for some purposes, is to get into *his Weltanschauung*[8] and to be able to see *his* world through *his* eyes. Of course such a conclusion is rough on any positivistic philosophy of science.

11. The existentialist stress on the ultimate aloneness of the individual is a useful reminder for us not only to work out further the concepts of decision, of responsibility, of choice, of self-creation, of autonomy, of identity itself. It also makes more problematic and more fascinating the mystery of communication between alonenesses via, e.g., intuition and empathy, love and altruism, identification with others, and homonomy in general. We take these for granted. It would be better if we regarded them as miracles to be explained.

12. Another preoccupation of existentialist writers can be phrased very simply, I think. It is the dimension of seriousness and profundity of living (or perhaps the "tragic sense of life") contrasted with the shallow and superficial life, which is a kind of diminished living, a defense against the ultimate problems of life. This is not just a literary concept. It has real operational meaning, for instance, in psychotherapy. I (and others) have been increasingly impressed with the fact that tragedy can sometimes be therapeutic and that therapy often seems to work best when people are *driven* into it by pain. It is when the shallow life does not work that it is questioned and that there occurs a call to fundamentals. Shallowness in psychology does not work either, as the existentialists are demonstrating very clearly.

13. The existentialists, along with many other groups, are helping to teach us about the limits of verbal, analytic, conceptual rationality. They are part of the current call back to raw experience as prior to any concepts or abstractions. This amounts to what I believe to be a justified critique of the whole way of thinking of the Western world in the twentieth century, including orthodox positivistic science and philosophy, both of which badly need reexamination.

14. Possibly most important of all the changes to be wrought by phenomenologists and existentialists is an overdue revolution in the theory of science. I should not say "wrought by," but rather "helped along by," because there are many other forces helping to destroy the official philosophy of science or "scientism." It is not only the Cartesian split between subject and object that needs to be overcome. There are other radical changes made necessary by the inclusion of the psyche and of raw experience in reality, and such a change will affect not only the science of psychology but all other sciences as well. For example, parsimony, simplicity, precision, orderliness, logic, elegance, definition are all of the realm of abstraction.

15. I close with the stimulus that has most powerfully affected me in the existentialist literature, namely, the problem of future time in psychology. Not that this, like all the other problems or pushes I have mentioned up to this point, was totally unfamiliar to me, nor, I imagine, to *any* serious student of the theory of personality. * * * Growth and becoming and possibility necessarily point toward the future, as do the concepts of potentiality and hoping and of wishing and imagining; reduction to the concrete is a loss of future; threat and apprehension point to the future (no future = no neurosis); self-actualization is meaningless without reference to a currently active future; life can be a gestalt in time, etc., etc.

And yet the *basic and central* importance of this problem for the existentialists has something to teach us. * * * I think it fair to say that no theory of psychology will ever be complete that does not centrally incorporate the concept that man has his future within him, dynamically active at this present moment. * * * Also we must realize that *only* the future is *in principle* unknown

[7]"Phenomenology" is the study of experience; in psychology it treats an individual's perception of reality as the essential fact about him or her.

[8]World view.

and unknowable, which means that all habits, defenses, and coping mechanisms are doubtful and ambiguous because they are based on past experience. Only the flexibly creative person can really manage [the] future, *only* the one who can face novelty with confidence and without fear. I am convinced that much of what we now call psychology is the study of the tricks we use to avoid the anxiety of absolute novelty by making believe the future will be like the past.

* * *

It is possible that existentialism will not only enrich psychology. It may also be an additional push toward the establishment of another *branch* of psychology, the psychology of the fully evolved and authentic self and its ways of being. * * *

Certainly it seems more and more clear that what we call "normal" in psychology is really a psychopathology of the average, so undramatic and so widely spread that we do not even notice it ordinarily. The existentialist's study of the authentic person and of authentic living helps to throw this general phoniness, this living by illusions and by fear, into a harsh, clear light which reveals it clearly as sickness, even though widely shared.

I do not think we need take too seriously the European existentialists' harping on dread, on anguish, on despair, and the like, for which their only remedy seems to be to keep a stiff upper lip.[9] This high-IQ whimpering on a cosmic scale occurs whenever an external source of values fails to work. They should have learned from the psychotherapists that the loss of illusions and the discovery of identity, though painful at first, can be ultimately exhilarating and strengthening.

---

[9]This is Maslow's sarcastic construal of Sartre's call for existential courage.

Is the Concept of Self Necessary?

Gordon W. Allport

Gordon Allport is usually remembered as a trait psychologist, and we have already seen one of his important articles in the trait section of this reader (Part II). But Allport was also one of the early humanistic psychologists. He was deeply interested in the process of personal growth (a process he called "becoming") and believed that personality was much more than the collection of instincts, habits, and reflexes represented in the behaviorist psychology dominant in America in the early 20th century. Allport had the very humanistic concern that such descriptions leave out something essential. In the following essay Allport argues that the central concept for psychology should be that of the self.

Allport describes eight functions of the self that cannot easily be subsumed by other kinds of psychological concepts. For example, the self has purpose, identity, experience, and a will to live. These are not complex learned reflexes but essential aspects of human existence. Allport further points out that some things we do—such as speak English or obey traffic laws—are experienced as matters of mere fact rather than matters of importance. Other things we do, however, seem "to be vital and central in becoming." For example, for the explorer Raold Amundsen the quest to see the North and South Poles dominated his entire life. Allport observes that we feel a certain "warm" ownership of the central aspects of our selves, and so uses the term "proprium" to refer to that feeling of proprietariness.

Allport's description of the self had a wide influence on later generations of humanistic psychologists. And its roots can be seen in existential philosophy of the sort described by Sartre. Allport's "propriate striving" is a seeking after goals one has freely and consciously chosen; Sartre believed that such conscious choice is the essence of existence.

From *Becoming: Basic Consideration for a Psychology of Personality* (New Haven, CT: Yale University Press, 1955), pp. 36–65.

* * *

The first thing an adequate psychology of growth should do is to draw a distinction between what are matters of *importance* to the individual and what are merely matters of *fact* to him; that is, between what he feels to be vital and central in becoming and what belongs to the periphery of his being.

Many facets of our life-style are not ordinarily felt to have strong personal relevance. Each of us, for example, has innumerable tribal habits that mark our life-style but are nothing more than opportunistic modes of adjusting. The same holds true for many of our physiological habits. We keep to the right in traffic, obey the rules of etiquette, and make countless unconscious or semiconscious adjustments, all of which characterize our life-style but are not *propriate*, i.e., not really central to our sense of existence. Consider, for example, the English language habits that envelop our thinking and communication. Nothing could be of more pervasive influence in our lives than the store of concepts available to us in our ancestral tongue and the frames of discourse under which our social contacts proceed. And yet the use of English is ordinarily felt to be quite peripheral to the core of our existence. It would not be so if some foreign invader should forbid us to use our native language. At such a time our vocabulary and accent and our freedom to employ them would become very precious and involved with our sense of self. So it is with the myriad of social and physiological habits we have developed that are never, unless interfered with, regarded as essential to our existence as a separate being.

Personality includes these habits and skills, frames of reference, matters of fact and cultural values, that seldom or never seem warm and important. But personality includes what is warm and important also—all the regions of our life that we regard as peculiarly ours, and which for the time being I suggest we call the *proprium*. The proprium includes all aspects of personality that make for inward unity.

Psychologists who allow for the proprium use both the term "self" and "ego"—often interchangeably; and both terms are defined with varying degrees of narrowness or of comprehensiveness. Whatever name we use for it, this sense of what is "peculiarly ours" merits close scrutiny. The principal functions and properties of the proprium need to be distinguished.

To this end William James over sixty years ago proposed a simple taxonomic scheme (James, 1890). There are, he maintained, two possible orders of self: an empirical self (the *Me*) and a knowing self (the *I*). Three subsidiary types comprise the empirical Me: the material self, the social self, and the spiritual self. Within this simple framework he fits his famous and subtle description of the various states of mind that are "peculiarly ours." His scheme, however, viewed in the perspective of modern psychoanalytic and experimental research, seems scarcely adequate. In particular it lacks the full psychodynamic flavor of modern thinking. With some trepidation, therefore, I offer what I hope is an improved outline for analyzing the propriate aspects of personality. Later we shall return to the question, Is the concept of *self* necessary?

The Proprium

1. Bodily Sense The first aspect we encounter is the bodily *me*. It seems to be composed of streams of sensations that arise within the organism—from viscera, muscles, tendons, joints, vestibular canals, and other regions of the body. The technical name for the bodily sense is *coenesthesis*. Usually this sensory stream is experienced dimly; often we are totally unaware of it. At times, however, it is well configurated in consciousness in the exhilaration that accompanies physical exercise, or in moments of sensory delight or pain. The infant, apparently, does not know that such experiences are "his." But they surely form a necessary foundation for his emerging sense of self. The baby who at first cries from unlocalized discomfort will,

in the course of growth, show progressive ability to identify the distress as his own.

The bodily sense remains a lifelong anchor for our self-awareness, though it never alone accounts for the entire sense of self, probably not even in the young child who has his memories, social cues, and strivings to help in the definition. Psychologists have paid a great deal of attention, however, to this particular component of self-awareness, rather more than to other equally important ingredients. One special line of investigation has been surprisingly popular: the attempt to locate self in relation to specific bodily sensations. When asked, some people will say that they *feel* the self in their right hands, or in the viscera. Most, however, seem to agree with Claparède that a center midway between the eyes, slightly behind them within the head, is the focus. It is from this cyclopean eye that we estimate what lies before and behind ourselves, to the right or left, and above and below. Here, phenomenologically speaking, is the locus of the ego (Claparède, 1924). * * *

How very intimate (propriate) the bodily sense is can be seen by performing a little experiment in your imagination. Think first of swallowing the saliva in your mouth, or do so. Then imagine expectorating it into a tumbler and drinking it! What seemed natural and "mine" suddenly becomes disgusting and alien. Or picture yourself sucking blood from a prick in your finger; then imagine sucking blood from a bandage around your finger! What I perceive as belonging intimately to my body is warm and welcome; what I perceive as separate from my body becomes, in the twinkling of an eye, cold and foreign.

Certainly organic sensations, their localization and recognition, composing as they do the bodily *me*, are a core of becoming. But it would be a serious mistake to think, as some writers do, that they alone account for our sense of what is "peculiarly ours."

2. SELF-IDENTITY Today I remember some of my thoughts of yesterday; and tomorrow I shall remember some of my thoughts of both yesterday and today; and I am subjectively certain that they are the thoughts of the same person. In this situation, no doubt, the organic continuity of the neuromuscular system is the leading factor. Yet the process involves more than reminiscence made possible by our retentive nerves. The young infant has retentive capacity during the first months of life but in all probability no sense of self-identity. This sense seems to grow gradually, partly as a result of being clothed and named, and otherwise marked off from the surrounding environment. Social interaction is an important factor. It is the actions of the other to which he differentially adjusts that force upon a child the realization that he is not the other, but a being in his own right. The difficulty of developing self-identity in childhood is shown by the ease with which a child depersonalizes himself in play and in speech (Allport, 1937). Until the age of four or five we have good reason to believe that as perceived by the child personal identity is unstable. Beginning at about this age, however, it becomes the surest attest a human being has of his own existence.

3. EGO-ENHANCEMENT We come now to the most notorious property of the proprium, to its unabashed self-seeking. Scores of writers have featured this clamorous trait in human personality. It is tied to the need for survival, for it is easy to see that we are endowed by nature with the impulses of self-assertion and with the emotions of self-satisfaction and pride. Our language is laden with evidence. The commonest compound of self is *selfish*, and of ego *egoism*. Pride, humiliation, self-esteem, narcissism are such prominent factors that when we speak of ego or self we often have in mind only this aspect of personality. And yet, self-love may be prominent in our natures without necessarily being sovereign. The proprium, as we shall see, has other facets and functions.

4. EGO-EXTENSION The three facets we have discussed—coenesthesis, self-identity, ego-enhancement—are relatively early developments in personality, characterizing the whole of the child's proprium. Their solicitations have a heavily bio-

logical quality and seem to be contained within the organism itself. But soon the process of learning brings with it a high regard for possessions, for loved objects, and later, for ideal causes and loyalties. We are speaking here of whatever objects a person calls "mine." They must at the same time be objects of *importance*, for sometimes our sense of "having" has no affective tone and hence no place in the proprium. A child, however, who identifies with his parent is definitely extending his sense of self, as he does likewise through his love for pets, dolls, or other possessions, animate or inanimate.

As we grow older we identify with groups, neighborhood, and nation as well as with possessions, clothes, home. They become matters of importance to us in a sense that other people's families, nations, or possessions are not. Later in life the process of extension may go to great lengths, through the development of loyalties and of interests focused on abstractions and on moral and religious values. Indeed, a mark of maturity seems to be the range and extent of one's feeling of self-involvement in abstract ideals.

5. Rational Agent The ego, according to Freud, has the task of keeping the organism as a whole in touch with reality, of intermediating between unconscious impulses and the outer world. Often the rational ego can do little else than invent and employ defenses to forestall or diminish anxiety. These protective devices shape the development of personality to an extent unrealized sixty years ago. It is thanks to Freud that we understand the strategies of denial, repression, displacement, reaction formation, rationalization, and the like better than did our ancestors.

We have become so convinced of the validity of these defense mechanisms, and so impressed with their frequency of operation, that we are inclined to forget that the rational functioning of the proprium is capable also of yielding true solutions, appropriate adjustments, accurate planning, and a relatively faultless solving of the equations of life.

Many philosophers, dating as far back as Boethius in the sixth century, have seen the rational nature of personality as its most distinctive property. * * * It may seem odd to credit Freud, the supreme irrationalist of our age, with helping preserve for psychology the emphasis upon the ego as the rational agent in personality, but such is the case. For whether the ego reasons or merely rationalizes, it has the property of synthesizing inner needs and outer reality. Freud [has] not let us forget this fact, and [has] thus made it easier for modern cognitive theories to deal with this central function of the proprium.

6. Self-Image A propriate function of special interest today is the self-image, or as some writers call it, the phenomenal self. Present-day therapy is chiefly devoted to leading the patient to examine, correct, or expand this self-image. The image has two aspects: the way the patient regards his present abilities, status, and roles; and what he would like to become, his *aspirations* for himself. The latter aspect, which Karen Horney calls the "idealized self-image," (Horney, 1950) is of especial importance in therapy. On the one hand it may be compulsive, compensatory, and unrealistic, blinding its possessor to his true situation in life. On the other hand, it may be an insightful cognitive map, closely geared to reality and defining a wholesome ambition. The ideal self-image is the imaginative aspect of the proprium, and whether accurate or distorted, attainable or unattainable, it plots a course by which much propriate movement is guided and therapeutic progress achieved.

There are, of course, many forms of becoming that require no self-image, including automatic cultural learning and our whole repertoire of opportunistic adjustments to our environment. Yet there is also much growth that takes place only with the aid of, and because of, a self-image. This image helps us bring our view of the present into line with our view of the future. * * *

7. Propriate Striving We come now to the nature of motivation. Unfortunately we often fail to distinguish between propriate and peripheral motives. The reason is that at the rudimentary levels of becoming, which up to now have been the chief

levels investigated, it *is* the impulses and drives, the immediate satisfaction and tension reduction, that are the determinants of conduct. Hence a psychology of opportunistic adjustment seems basic and adequate, especially to psychologists accustomed to working with animals. At low levels of behavior the familiar formula of drives and their conditioning appears to suffice. But as soon as the personality enters the stage of ego-extension, and develops a self-image with visions of self-perfection, we are, I think, forced to postulate motives of a different order, motives that reflect propriate striving. Within experimental psychology itself there is now plenty of evidence that conduct that is "ego involved" (propriate) differs markedly from behavior that is not (Allport, 1943).

* * *

In his autobiography Raold Amundsen tells how from the age of fifteen he had one dominant passion—to become a polar explorer. The obstacles seemed insurmountable, and all through his life the temptations to reduce the tensions engendered were great. But the propriate striving persisted. While he welcomed each success, it acted to raise his level of aspiration, to maintain an over-all commitment. Having sailed the Northwest Passage, he embarked upon the painful project that led to the discovery of the South Pole. Having discovered the South Pole, he planned for years, against extreme discouragement, to fly over the North Pole, a task he finally accomplished. But his commitment never wavered until at the end he lost his life in attempting to rescue a less gifted explorer, Nobile, from death in the Arctic. Not only did he maintain one style of life, without ceasing, but this central commitment enabled him to withstand the temptation to reduce the segmental tensions continually engendered by fatigue, hunger, ridicule, and danger (Amundsen, 1928).

* * *

Propriate striving distinguishes itself from other forms of motivation in that, however beset by conflicts, it makes for unification of personality. There is evidence that the lives of mental patients are marked by the proliferation of unrelated subsystems, and by the loss of more homogeneous systems of motivation (McQuitty, 1950). When the individual is dominated by segmental drives, by compulsions, or by the winds of circumstance, he has lost the integrity that comes only from maintaining major directions of striving. The possession of long-range goals, regarded as central to one's personal existence, distinguishes the human being from the animal, the adult from the child, and in many cases the healthy personality from the sick.[1]

Striving, it is apparent, always has a future reference. As a matter of fact, a great many states of mind are adequately described only in terms of their futurity. Along with *striving*, we may mention *interest*, *tendency*, *disposition*, *expectation*, *planning*, *problem solving*, and *intention*. While not all future-directedness is phenomenally propriate, it all requires a type of psychology that transcends the prevalent tendency to explain mental states exclusively in terms of past occurrences. People, it seems, are busy leading their lives into the future, whereas psychology, for the most part, is busy tracing them into the past.

8. THE KNOWER Now that we have isolated these various propriate functions—all of which we regard as peculiarly ours—the question arises whether we are yet at an end. Do we not have in addition a cognizing self—a knower, that transcends all other functions of the proprium and holds them in view? In a famous passage, William James wrestles with this question, and concludes that we have not. There is, he thinks, no such thing as a substantive self distinguishable from the sum total, or stream, of experiences. Each moment of consciousness, he says, appropriates each previous moment, and the knower is thus somehow embedded in what is known. "The thoughts themselves are the thinker."

Opponents of James argue that no mere series of experiences can possibly turn themselves into

[1]Compare this to Sartre's prescription for authentic existence. It is the choosing of one's own goals in life that is uniquely human; thus a concern with such choices is "humanistic."

an awareness of that series as a unit. Nor can "passing thoughts" possibly regard themselves as important or interesting. To whom is the series important or interesting if not to *me*? I am the ultimate monitor. The self as *knower* emerges as a final and inescapable postulate.

* * *

We not only know *things*, but we know (i.e., are acquainted with) the empirical features of our own proprium. It is I who have bodily sensations, I who recognize my self-identity from day to day; I who note and reflect upon my self-assertion, self-extension, my own rationalizations, as well as upon my interests and strivings. When I thus think about my own propriate functions I am likely to perceive their essential togetherness, and feel them intimately bound in some way to the knowing function itself.

Since such knowing is, beyond any shadow of doubt, a state that is peculiarly ours, we admit it as the eighth clear function of the proprium. (In other words, as an eighth valid meaning of "self" or "ego.") But it is surely one of nature's perversities that so central a function should be so little understood by science, and should remain a perpetual bone of contention among philosophers. Many, like Kant, set this function (the "pure ego") aside as something qualitatively apart from other propriate functions (the latter being assigned to the "empirical me"). Others, like James, say that the ego *qua* knower is somehow contained within the ego *qua* known. Still others, personalistically inclined, find it necessary to postulate a single self as knower, thinker, feeler, and doer—all in one blended unit of a sort that guarantees the continuance of all becoming (Bertocci, 1945).

We return now to our unanswered question: Is the concept of self necessary in the psychology of personality? Our answer cannot be categorical since all depends upon the particular usage of "self" that is proposed. Certainly all legitimate phenomena that have been, and can be ascribed, to the self or ego must be admitted as data indispensable to a psychology of personal becoming. All eight functions of the "proprium" (our temporary neutral term for central interlocking operations of personality) must be admitted and included. In particular the unifying act of perceiving and knowing (of comprehending propriate states at belonging together and belonging to me) must be fully admitted.

At the same time, the danger is very real that a homunculus[2] may creep into our discussions of personality, and be expected to solve all our problems without in reality solving any. Thus, if we ask "What determines our moral conduct?" the answer may be "The self does it." Or, if we pose the problem of choice, we say "The self chooses." Such question-begging would immeasurably weaken the scientific study of personality by providing an illegitimate regressus. There are, to be sure, ultimate problems of philosophy and of theology that psychology cannot even attempt to solve, and for the solution of such problems "self" in some restricted and technical meaning may be a necessity.

But so far as psychology is concerned our position, in brief, is this: all psychological functions commonly ascribed to a self or ego must be admitted as data in the scientific study of personality. These functions are not, however, coextensive with personality as a whole. They are rather the special aspects of personality that have to do with warmth, with unity, with a sense of personal importance. In this exposition I have called them "propriate" functions. If the reader prefers, he may call them self-functions, and in this sense self may be said to be a necessary psychological concept. * * *

* * *

References

Allport, G. W. (1937). *Personality: A Psychological Interpretation.* New York: Henry Holt.

[2]A "homunculus theory" is one that posits a "little man in the head" that does all the thinking for a person. Such a theory explains nothing because the question of why the little man does what he does remains unanswered.

Allport, G. W. (1943). The ego in contemporary psychology. *Psychological Review, 50,* 451–478.

Amundsen, R. (1928). *My Life as an Explorer.* Garden City, NY: Doubleday, Doran.

Bertocci, P. A. (1945). The psychological self, the ego, and personality. *Psychological Review, 52,* 91–99.

Claparède, E. (1924). Note sur la localisation du moi. *Archives de psychologie, 19,* 172–182.

Horney, K. (1950). *Neurosis and Human Growth: The Struggle toward Self-realization.* New York: Norton.

James, W. (1890). *Principles of Psychology* (Vol. 1). New York: Henry Holt.

McQuitty, L. (1950). A measure of personality integration in relation to the concept of self. *Journal of Personality, 18,* 461–482.

A Theory of Human Motivation

Abraham H. Maslow

Maslow's best-known contribution to psychology is his proposal that human motivation is organized by a hierarchy of needs. Lower, physiological and safety needs must be satisfied before higher needs can emerge. These include the need for esteem, the need for self-actualization, the need to know and understand, and aesthetic needs. None of these latter needs are directly tied to survival; they become potent only after the survival needs are taken care of.

Maslow's theory, described in the following selection, is humanistic in two ways. First, he explicitly states that the study of human motivation does not need to be based on findings from research with animals. "It is no more necessary to study animals before one can study man than it is to study mathematics before one can study geology or psychology or biology." Second and more important, Maslow's higher needs are uniquely human. The needs to experience beauty, to understand the world, and to fulfill one's potential all stem from the quest for authentic existence at the core of existential philosophy and humanistic psychology.

Maslow's theory leads him to write a couple of prescriptions for human development. First, he observes that a child satisfied in basic needs early in life becomes relatively tolerant of deprivation in later life, and better able to focus on higher goals. Therefore, children should be raised to feel satisfied and safe. Second, "a man who is thwarted in any of his basic needs may fairly be envisaged as a sick man." Maslow concludes that a society that thwarts the basic needs of individuals is therefore itself sick. On the other hand, "the good or healthy society would then be defined as one that permitted man's highest purposes to emerge by satisfying all his basic needs."

From *Motivation and Personality*, 3d ed., by A. H. Maslow, revised by R. Frager, J. Fadiman, C. McReynolds, and R. Cox (New York: Harper & Row, 1954), pp. 80–106.

* * *

The Basic Needs

THE PHYSIOLOGICAL NEEDS The needs that are usually taken as the starting point for motivation theory are the so-called physiological drives. Two recent lines of research make it necessary to revise our customary notions about these needs: first, the development of the concept of homeostasis, and second, the finding that appetites (preferential choices among foods) are a fairly efficient indication of actual needs or lacks in the body.

Homeostasis refers to the body's automatic efforts to maintain a constant, normal state of the blood stream. * * *

* * * If the body lacks some chemical, the individual will tend (in an imperfect way) to develop a specific appetite or partial hunger for that food element.

Thus it seems impossible as well as useless to make any list of fundamental physiological needs, for they can come to almost any number one might wish, depending on the degree of specificity of description. We cannot identify all physiological needs as homeostatic. That sexual desire, sleepiness, sheer activity, and maternal behavior in animals are homeostatic has not yet been demonstrated. Furthermore, this list would not include the various sensory pleasures (tastes, smells, tickling, stroking), which are probably physiological and which may become the goals of motivated behavior.

These physiological drives or needs are to be considered unusual rather than typical because they are isolable, and because they are localizable somatically. That is to say, they are relatively independent of each other, of other motivations, and of the organism as a whole, and second, in many cases, it is possible to demonstrate a localized, underlying somatic base for the drive. This is true less generally than has been thought (exceptions are fatigue, sleepiness, maternal responses) but it is still true in the classic instances of hunger, sex, and thirst.

It should be pointed out again that any of the physiological needs and the consummatory behavior involved with them serve as channels for all sorts of other needs as well. That is to say, the person who thinks he is hungry may actually be seeking more for comfort, or dependence, than for vitamins or proteins. Conversely, it is possible to satisfy the hunger need in part by other activities such as drinking water or smoking cigarettes. In other words, relatively isolable as these physiological needs are, they are not completely so.

Undoubtedly these physiological needs are the most prepotent of all needs. What this means specifically is that in the human being who is missing everything in life in an extreme fashion, it is most likely that the major motivation would be the physiological needs rather than any others. A person who is lacking food, safety, love, and esteem would most probably hunger for food more strongly than for anything else.

If all the needs are unsatisfied, and the organism is then dominated by the physiological needs, all other needs may become simply nonexistent or be pushed into the background. It is then fair to characterize the whole organism by saying simply that it is hungry, for consciousness is almost completely preëmpted by hunger. All capacities are put into the service of hunger-satisfaction, and the organization of these capacities is almost entirely determined by the one purpose of satisfying hunger. The receptors and effectors, the intelligence, memory, habits, all may now be defined simply as hunger-gratifying tools. Capacities that are not useful for this purpose lie dormant, or are pushed into the background. The urge to write poetry, the desire to acquire an automobile, the interest in American history, the desire for a new pair of shoes are, in the extreme case, forgotten or become of secondary importance. For the man who is extremely and dangerously hungry, no other interests exist but food. He dreams food, he remembers food, he thinks about food, he emotes only about food, he perceives only food, and he wants only food. The more subtle determinants that ordinarily fuse with the physiological drives in organizing even feeding, drinking, or sexual behavior, may now be so completely overwhelmed as to allow us to speak at this time (but *only* at this time) of pure hunger drive and behavior, with the one unqualified aim of relief.

Another peculiar characteristic of the human organism when it is dominated by a certain need is that the whole philosophy of the future tends also to change. For our chronically and extremely hungry man, Utopia can be defined simply as a place where there is plenty of food. He tends to think that, if only he is guaranteed food for the rest of his life, he will be perfectly happy and will never want anything more. Life itself tends to be defined in terms of eating. Anything else will be defined as unimportant. Freedom, love, community feeling, respect, philosophy, may all be waved aside as fripperies that are useless, since they fail to fill the stomach. Such a man may fairly be said to live by bread alone.

It cannot possibly be denied that such things are true, but their *generality* can be denied. Emergency conditions are, almost by definition, rare in the normally functioning peaceful society. That this truism can be forgotten is attributable mainly to two reasons. First, rats have few motivations other than physiological ones, and since so much of the research upon motivation has been made with these animals, it is easy to carry the rat picture over to the human being. Second, it is too often not realized that culture itself is an adaptive tool, one of whose main functions is to make the physiological emergencies come less and less often. In most of the known societies, chronic extreme hunger of the emergency type is rare, rather than common. In any case, this is still true in the United States. The average American citizen is experiencing appetite rather than hunger when he says, "I am hungry." He is apt to experience sheer life-and-death hunger only by accident and then only a few times through his entire life.

Obviously a good way to obscure the higher motivations, and to get a lopsided view of human capacities and human nature, is to make the organism extremely and chronically hungry or thirsty. Anyone who attempts to make an emergency picture into a typical one, and who will measure all of man's goals and desires by his behavior during extreme physiological deprivation is certainly being blind to many things. It is quite true that man lives by bread alone—when there is no bread. But what happens to man's desires when there *is* plenty of bread and when his belly is chronically filled?

At once other (and higher) needs emerge and these, rather than physiological hungers, dominate the organism. And when these in turn are satisfied, again new (and still higher) needs emerge, and so on. This is what we mean by saying that the basic human needs are organized into a hierarchy of relative prepotency.

One main implication of this phrasing is that gratification becomes as important a concept as deprivation in motivation theory, for it releases the organism from the domination of a relatively more physiological need, permitting thereby the emergence of other more social goals. The physiological needs, along with their partial goals, when chronically gratified cease to exist as active determinants or organizers of behavior. They now exist only in a potential fashion in the sense that they may emerge again to dominate the organism if they are thwarted. But a want that is satisfied is no longer a want. The organism is dominated and its behavior organized only by unsatisfied needs. If hunger is satisfied, it becomes unimportant in the current dynamics of the individual.

This statement is somewhat qualified by a hypothesis to be discussed more fully later, namely, that it is precisely those individuals in whom a certain need has always been satisfied who are best equipped to tolerate deprivation of that need in the future, and that furthermore, those who have been deprived in the past will react differently to current satisfactions than the one who has never been deprived.

THE SAFETY NEEDS If the physiological needs are relatively well gratified, there then emerges a new set of needs, which we may categorize roughly as the safety needs. All that has been said of the physiological needs is equally true, although in less degree, of these desires. The organism may equally well be wholly dominated by them. They may serve as the almost exclusive organizers of behavior, recruiting all the capacities of the organism in their service, and we may then fairly describe the whole organism as a safety-seeking mechanism. Again we may say of the receptors, the effectors, of the intellect, and of the other capacities that they are primarily safety-seeking tools. Again, as in the hungry man, we find that the dominating goal is a strong determinant not only of his current world outlook and philosophy but also of his philosophy of the future. Practically everything looks less important than safety (even sometimes the physiological needs, which being satisfied are now underestimated). A man in this state, if it is extreme enough and chronic enough, may be characterized as living almost for safety alone.

Although in this chapter we are interested primarily in the needs of the adult, we can approach an understanding of his safety needs perhaps more efficiently by observation of infants and children, in whom these needs are much more simple and obvious. One reason for the clearer appearance of the threat or danger reaction in infants is that they do not inhibit this reaction at all, whereas adults in our society have been taught to inhibit it at all costs. Thus even when adults do feel their safety to be threatened, we may not be able to see this on the surface. Infants will react in a total fashion and as if they were endangered, if they are disturbed or dropped suddenly, startled by loud noises, flashing light, or other unusual sensory stimulation, by rough handling, by general loss of support in the mother's arms, or by inadequate support.

Another indication of the child's need for safety is his preference for some kind of undisrupted routine or rhythm. He seems to want a predictable, orderly world. For instance, injustice, unfairness, or inconsistency in the parents seems to make a child feel anxious and unsafe. This attitude may be not so much because of the injustice *per se* or any particular pains involved, but rather because this treatment threatens to make the world look unreliable, or unsafe, or unpredictable. Young children seem to thrive better under a system that has at least a skeletal outline of rigidity, in which there is a schedule of a kind, some sort of routine, something that can be counted upon, not only for the present but also far into the future. Child psychologists, teachers, and psychotherapists have found that permissiveness within limits, rather than unrestricted permissiveness is preferred as well as *needed* by children. Perhaps one could express this more accurately by saying that the child needs an organized world rather than an unorganized or unstructured one.

The central role of the parents and the normal family setup are indisputable. Quarreling, physical assault, separation, divorce, or death within the family may be particularly terrifying. Also parental outbursts of rage or threats of punishment directed to the child, calling him names, speaking to him harshly, handling him roughly, or actual physical punishment sometimes elicit such total panic and terror that we must assume more is involved than the physical pain alone. While it is true that in some children this terror may represent also a fear of loss of parental love, it can also occur in completely rejected children, who seem to cling to the hating parents more for sheer safety and protection than because of hope of love.

Confronting the average child with new, unfamiliar, strange, unmanageable stimuli or situations will too frequently elicit the danger or terror reaction, as for example, getting lost or even being separated from the parents for a short time, being confronted with new faces, new situations, or new tasks, the sight of strange, unfamiliar, or uncontrollable objects, illness, or death. Particularly at such times, the child's frantic clinging to his parents is eloquent testimony to their role as protectors (quite apart from their roles as food givers and love givers).

From these and similar observations, we may generalize and say that the average child in our society generally prefers a safe, orderly, predictable, organized world, which he can count on, and in which unexpected, unmanageable, or other dangerous things do not happen, and in which, in any case, he has all-powerful parents who protect and shield him from harm.

* * *

The healthy, normal, fortunate adult in our culture is largely satisfied in his safety needs. The peaceful, smoothly running, good society ordinarily makes its members feel safe enough from wild animals, extremes of temperature, criminal assault, murder, tyranny, etc. Therefore, in a very real sense, he no longer has any safety needs as active motivators. Just as a sated man no longer feels hungry, a safe man no longer feels endangered. If we wish to see these needs directly and clearly we must turn to neurotic or near-neurotic individuals, and to the economic and social underdogs. In between these extremes, we can perceive the expressions of safety needs only in such phenomena as, for instance, the common preference for a job with tenure and protection the desire for a savings account and for insurance of various kinds (medical, dental, unemployment, disability, old age).

Other broader aspects of the attempt to seek safety and stability in the world are seen in the very common preference for familiar rather than unfamiliar things, or for the known rather than the unknown. The tendency to have some religion or world philosophy that organizes the universe and the men in it into some sort of satisfactorily coherent, meaningful whole is also in part motivated by safety seeking. Here too we may list science and philosophy in general as partially motivated by the safety needs (we shall see later that there are also other motivations to scientific, philosophical, or religious endeavor).

Otherwise the need for safety is seen as an active and dominant mobilizer of the organism's resources only in emergencies, e.g., war, disease, natural catastrophes, crime waves, societal disorganization, neurosis, brain injury, chronically bad situations.

Some neurotic adults in our society are, in many ways, like the unsafe child in their desire for safety, although in the former it takes on a somewhat special appearance. Their reaction is often to unknown, psychological dangers in a world that is perceived to be hostile, overwhelming, and threatening. Such a person behaves as if a great catastrophe were almost always impending, i.e., he is usually responding as if to an emergency. His safety needs often find specific expression in a search for a protector, or a stronger person on whom he may depend, perhaps a fuehrer.

* * *

The neurosis in which the search for safety takes its clearest form is in the compulsive-obsessive neurosis. Compulsive-obsessives try frantically to order and stabilize the world so that no unmanageable, unexpected, or unfamiliar dangers will ever appear. They hedge themselves about with all sorts of ceremonials, rules, and formulas so that every possible contingency may be provided for and so that no new contingencies may appear. They are much like the brain-injured cases, described by Goldstein,[1] who manage to maintain their equilibrium by avoiding everything unfamiliar and strange and by ordering their restricted world in such a neat, disciplined, orderly fashion that everything in the world can be counted on. They try to arrange the world so that anything unexpected (dangers) cannot possibly occur. If, through no fault of their own, something unexpected does occur, they go into a panic reaction as if this unexpected occurrence constituted a grave danger. What we can see only as a none-too-strong preference in the healthy person, e.g., preference for the familiar, becomes a life-and-death necessity in abnormal cases. The healthy taste for the novel and unknown is missing or at a minimum in the average neurotic.

The Belongingness and Love Needs If both the physiological and the safety needs are fairly well gratified, there will emerge the love and affection and belongingness needs, and the whole cycle already described will repeat itself with this new center. Now the person will feel keenly, as never before, the absence of friends, or a sweet-

[1]Kurt Goldstein was a neurologist and psychiatrist who wrote on clinical psychology, human nature, and language.

heart, or a wife, or children. He will hunger for affectionate relations with people in general, namely, for a place in his group, and he will strive with great intensity to achieve this goal. He will want to attain such a place more than anything else in the world and may even forget that once, when he was hungry, he sneered at love as unreal or unnecessary or unimportant.

In our society the thwarting of these needs is the most commonly found core in cases of maladjustment and more severe psychopathology. Love and affection, as well as their possible expression in sexuality, are generally looked upon with ambivalence and are customarily hedged about with many restrictions and inhibitions. Practically all theorists of psychopathology have stressed thwarting of the love needs as basic in the picture of maladjustment. * * *

One thing that must be stressed at this point is that love is not synonymous with sex. Sex may be studied as a purely physiological need. Ordinarily sexual behavior is multidetermined, that is to say, determined not only by sexual but also by other needs, chief among which are the love and affection needs. Also not to be overlooked is the fact that the love needs involve both giving *and* receiving love.

THE ESTEEM NEEDS All people in our society (with a few pathological exceptions) have a need or desire for a stable, firmly based, usually high evaluation of themselves, for self-respect, or self-esteem, and for the esteem of others. These needs may therefore be classified into two subsidiary sets. These are, first, the desire for strength, for achievement, for adequacy, for mastery and competence, for confidence in the face of the world, and for independence and freedom.[2] Second, we have what we may call the desire for reputation or prestige (defining it as respect or esteem from other people), status, dominance, recognition, attention, importance, or appreciation. These needs have been relatively stressed by Alfred Adler and his followers, and have been relatively neglected by Freud. More and more today, however, there is appearing wide-spread appreciation of their central importance, among psychoanalysts as well as among clinical psychologists.

Satisfaction of the self-esteem need leads to feelings of self-confidence, worth, strength, capability, and adequacy, of being useful and necessary in the world. But thwarting of these needs produces feelings of inferiority, of weakness, and of helplessness. These feelings in turn give rise to either basic discouragement or else compensatory or neurotic trends. * * *

* * * We have been learning more and more of the dangers of basing self-esteem on the opinions of others rather than on real capacity, competence, and adequacy to the task. The most stable and therefore most healthy self-esteem is based on *deserved* respect from others rather than on external fame or celebrity and unwarranted adulation.

THE NEED FOR SELF-ACTUALIZATION Even if all these needs are satisfied, we may still often (if not always) expect that a new discontent and restlessness will soon develop, unless the individual is doing what he is fitted for. A musician must make music, an artist must paint, a poet must write, if he is to be ultimately at peace with himself. What a man *can* be, he *must* be. This need we may call self-actualization.

* * * [This term] refers to a man's desire for self-fulfillment, namely, to the tendency for him to become actualized in what he is potentially. This tendency might be phrased as the desire to

[2]Whether or not this particular desire is universal we do not know. The crucial question, especially important today, is, Will men who are enslaved and dominated inevitably feel dissatisfied and rebellious? We may assume on the basis of commonly known clinical data that a man who has known true freedom (not paid for by giving up safety and security but rather built on the basis of adequate safety and security) will not willingly or easily allow his freedom to be taken away from him. But we do not know that this is true for the person born into slavery.—Author

become more and more what one is, to become everything that one is capable of becoming.

The specific form that these needs will take will of course vary greatly from person to person. In one individual it may take the form of the desire to be an ideal mother, in another it may be expressed athletically, and in still another it may be expressed in painting pictures or in inventions.

The clear emergence of these needs usually rests upon prior satisfaction of the physiological, safety, love, and esteem needs.

* * *

The Desires to Know and to Understand

The main reason we know little about the cognitive impulses, their dynamics, or their pathology, is that they are not important in the clinic, and certainly not in the clinic dominated by the medical-therapeutic tradition, i.e., getting rid of disease. The florid, exciting, and mysterious symptoms found in the classical neuroses are lacking here. Cognitive psychopathology is pale, subtle, and easily overlooked, or defined as normal. It does not cry for help. As a consequence we find nothing on the subject in the writings of the great inventors of psychotherapy and psychodynamics, Freud, Adler, Jung, etc. Nor has anyone yet made any systematic attempts at constructing cognitive psychotherapies.

* * *

* * * There are some reasonable grounds for postulating positive *per se* impulses to satisfy curiosity, to know, to explain, and to understand.

1. Something like human curiosity can easily be observed in the higher animals. The monkey will pick things apart, will poke his finger into holes, will explore in all sorts of situations where it is improbable that hunger, fear, sex, comfort status, etc., are involved. Harlow's experiments (1950) have amply demonstrated this in an acceptably experimental way.

2. The history of mankind supplies us with a satisfactory number of instances in which man looked for facts and created explanations in the face of the greatest danger, even to life itself. There have been innumerable humbler Galileos.

3. Studies of psychologically healthy people indicate that they are, as a defining characteristic, attracted to the mysterious, to the unknown, to the chaotic, unorganized, and unexplained. This seems to be a *per se* attractiveness; these areas are in themselves and of their own right interesting. The contrasting reaction to the well known is one of boredom.

4. It may be found valid to extrapolate from the psychopathological. The compulsive-obsessive neurotic (and neurotic in general), Goldstein's brain-injured soldiers, Maier's fixated rats (1939), all show (at the clinical level of observation) a compulsive and anxious clinging to the familiar and a dread of the unfamiliar, the anarchic, the unexpected, the undomesticated. On the other hand, there are some phenomena that may turn out to nullify this possibility. Among these are forced unconventionality, a chronic rebellion against any authority whatsoever, Bohemianism, the desire to shock and to startle, all of which may be found in certain neurotic individuals, as well as in those in the process of deacculturation.

* * *

5. Probably there are true psychopathological effects when the cognitive needs are frustrated. For the moment, though, we have no really sound data available. The following clinical impressions are pertinent.

6. I have seen a few cases in which it seemed clear to me that the pathology (boredom, loss of zest in life, self-dislike, general depression of the bodily functions, steady deterioration of the intellectual life, of tastes, etc.) were produced in intelligent people leading stupid lives in stupid jobs. I have at least one case in which the appropriate cognitive therapy (resuming part-time studies, getting a position that was more intellectually demanding, insight) removed the symptoms.

I have seen *many* women, intelligent, prosperous, and unoccupied, slowly develop these same symptoms of intellectual inanition. Those who followed my recommendation to immerse themselves in something worthy of them showed improvement or cure often enough to impress me with the reality of the cognitive needs. In those countries in which access to the news, to information, and to the facts [was] cut off, and in those where official theories were profoundly contradicted by obvious facts, at least some people responded with generalized cynicism, mistrust of *all* values, suspicion even of the obvious, a profound disruption of ordinary interpersonal relationships, hopelessness, loss of morale, etc. Others seem to have responded in the more passive direction with dullness, submission, loss of capacity, coarctation, and loss of initiative.

7. The needs to know and to understand are seen in late infancy and childhood, perhaps even more strongly than in adulthood. Furthermore this seems to be a spontaneous product of maturation rather than of learning, however defined. Children do not have to be taught to be curious. But they *may* be taught, as by institutionalization, *not* to be curious.

8. Finally, the gratification of the cognitive impulses is subjectively satisfying and yields end-experience. Though this aspect of insight and understanding has been neglected in favor of achieved results, learning, etc., it nevertheless remains true that insight is usually a bright, happy, emotional spot in any person's life, perhaps even a high spot in the life span.

The overcoming of obstacles, the occurrence of pathology upon thwarting, the widespread occurrence (cross-species, cross-cultural), the never-dying (though weak) insistent pressure, the need of gratification of this need as a prerequisite for the fullest development of human potentialities, the spontaneous appearance in the early history of the individual, all these point to a basic cognitive need.

This postulation, however, is not enough. Even after we know, we are impelled to know more and more minutely and microscopically on the one hand, and on the other, more and more extensively in the direction of a world philosophy, theology, etc. The facts that we acquire, if they are isolated or atomistic, inevitably get theorized about, and either analyzed or organized or both. This process has been phrased by some as the search for meaning. We shall then postulate a desire to understand, to systematize, to organize, to analyze, to look for relations and meanings, to construct a system of values.

Once these desires are accepted for discussion, we see that they too form themselves into a small hierarchy in which the desire to know is prepotent over the desire to understand. All the characteristics of a hierarchy of prepotency that we have described above seem to hold for this one as well.

We must guard ourselves against the too easy tendency to separate these desires from the basic needs we have discussed above, i.e., to make a sharp dichotomy between cognitive and conative needs. The desire to know and to understand are themselves conative, i.e., having a striving character, and are as much personality needs as the basic needs we have already discussed. Furthermore, as we have seen, the two hierarchies are interrelated rather than sharply separated; and as we shall see below, they are synergic rather than antagonistic.

THE AESTHETIC NEEDS We know even less about these than about the others, and yet the testimony of history, of the humanities, and of aestheticians forbids us to bypass this uncomfortable (to the scientist) area. I have attempted to study this phenomenon on a clinical-personological basis with selected individuals, and have at least convinced myself that in *some* individuals there is a truly basic aesthetic need. They get sick (in special ways) from ugliness, and are cured by beautiful surroundings; they *crave* actively, and their cravings can be satisfied *only* by beauty. It is seen almost universally in healthy children. Some evidence of such an impulse is found in every culture and in every age as far back as the cavemen.

Much overlapping with conative and cognitive needs makes it impossible to separate them sharply. The needs for order, for symmetry, for closure, for completion of the act, for system, and for structure may be indiscriminately assigned to *either* cognitive, conative, or aesthetic, or even to neurotic needs. * * * What, for instance, does it mean when a man feels a strong conscious impulse to straighten the crookedly hung picture on the wall?

Further Characteristics of the Basic Needs

THE DEGREE OF FIXITY OF THE HIERARCHY OF BASIC NEEDS We have spoken so far as if this hierarchy were a fixed order, but actually it is not nearly so rigid as we may have implied. It is true that most of the people with whom we have worked have seemed to have these basic needs in about the order that has been indicated. However, there have been a number of exceptions.

1. There are some people in whom, for instance, self-esteem seems to be more important than love. This most common reversal in the hierarchy is usually due to the development of the notion that the person who is most likely to be loved is a strong or powerful person, one who inspires respect or fear, and who is self-confident or aggressive. Therefore such people who lack love and seek it may try hard to put on a front of aggressive, confident behavior. But essentially they seek high self-esteem and its behavior expressions more as a means to an end than for its own sake; they seek self-assertion for the sake of love rather than for self-esteem itself.

2. There are other apparently innately creative people in whom the drive to creativeness seems to be more important than any other counterdeterminant. Their creativeness might appear not as self-actualization released by basic satisfaction, but in spite of lack of basic satisfaction.

3. In certain people the level of aspiration may be permanently deadened or lowered. That is to say, the less prepotent goals may simply be lost, and may disappear forever, so that the person who has experienced life at a very low level, e.g., chronic unemployment, may continue to be satisfied for the rest of his life if only he can get enough food.

4. The so-called psychopathic personality is another example of permanent loss of the love needs. These are people who, according to the best data available, have been starved for love in the earliest months of their lives and have simply lost forever the desire and the ability to give and to receive affection (as animals lose sucking or pecking reflexes that are not exercised soon enough after birth).

5. Another cause of reversal of the hierarchy is that when a need has been satisfied for a long time, this need may be underevaluated. People who have never experienced chronic hunger are apt to underestimate its effects and to look upon food as a rather unimportant thing. If they are dominated by a higher need, this higher need will seem to be the most important of all. It then becomes possible, and indeed does actually happen, that they may, for the sake of this higher need, put themselves into the position of being deprived in a more basic need. We may expect that after a longtime deprivation of the more basic need there will be a tendency to reevaluate both needs so that the more prepotent need will actually become consciously prepotent for the individual who may have given it up lightly. Thus a man who has given up his job rather than lose his self-respect, and who then starves for six months or so, may be willing to take his job back even at the price of losing his self-respect.

6. Another partial explanation of *apparent* reversals is seen in the fact that we have been talking about the hierarchy of prepotency in terms of consciously felt wants or desires rather than of behavior. Looking at behavior itself may give us the wrong impression. What we have claimed is that the person will *want* the more basic of two needs when deprived in both. There is no necessary implication here that he will act upon his desires. Let us stress again that there are many determinants of behavior other than the needs and desires.

7. Perhaps more important than all these exceptions are the ones that involve ideals, high social standards, high values, and the like. With such values people become martyrs; they will give up everything for the sake of a particular ideal, or value. These people may be understood, at least

in part, by reference to one basic concept (or hypothesis), which may be called increased frustration-tolerance through early gratification. People who have been satisfied in their basic needs throughout their lives, particularly in their earlier years, seem to develop exceptional power to withstand present or future thwarting of these needs simply because they have strong, healthy character structure as a result of basic satisfaction. They are the strong people who can easily weather disagreement or opposition, who can swim against the stream of public opinion, and who can stand up for the truth at great personal cost. It is just the ones who have loved and been well loved, and who have had many deep friendships who can hold out against hatred, rejection, or persecution.

I say all this in spite of the fact that a certain amount of sheer habituation is also involved in any full discussion of frustration tolerance. For instance, it is likely that those persons who have been accustomed to relative starvation for a long time are partially enabled thereby to withstand food deprivation. What sort of balance must be made between these two tendencies, of habituation on the one hand, and of past satisfaction breeding present frustration tolerance on the other hand, remains to be worked out by further research. Meanwhile we may assume that both are operative, side by side, since they do not contradict each other. In respect to this phenomenon of increased frustration tolerance, it seems probable that the most important gratifications come in the first two years of life. That is to say, people who have been made secure and strong in the earliest years, tend to remain secure and strong thereafter in the face of whatever threatens.

DEGREES OF RELATIVE SATISFACTION So far, our theoretical discussion may have given the impression that these five sets of needs are somehow in such terms as the following: If one need is satisfied, then another emerges. This statement might give the false impression that a need must be satisfied 100 percent before the next need emerges. In actual fact, most members of our society who are normal are partially satisfied in all their basic needs and partially unsatisfied in all their basic needs at the same time. A more realistic description of the hierarchy would be in terms of decreasing percentages of satisfaction as we go up the hierarchy of prepotency. For instance, if I may assign arbitrary figures for the sake of illustration, it is as if the average citizen is satisfied perhaps 85 percent in his physiological needs, 70 percent in his safety needs, 50 percent in his love needs, 40 percent in his self-esteem needs, and 10 percent in his self-actualization needs.

As for the concept of emergence of a new need after satisfaction of the prepotent need, this emergence is not a sudden, saltatory phenomenon, but rather a gradual emergence by slow degrees from nothingness. For instance, if prepotent need A is satisfied only 10 percent, then need B may not be visible at all. However, as this need A becomes satisfied 25 percent, need B may emerge 5 percent; as need A becomes satisfied 75 percent, need B may emerge 50 percent, and so on.

* * *

ANIMAL AND HUMAN CENTERING This theory starts with the human being rather than any lower and presumably simpler animal. Too many of the findings that have been made in animals have been proved to be true for animals but not for the human being. There is no reason whatsoever why we should start with animals in order to study human motivation. The logic or rather illogic behind this general fallacy of pseudosimplicity has been exposed often enough by philosophers and logicians as well as by scientists in each of the various fields. It is no more necessary to study animals before one can study man than it is to study mathematics *before* one can study geology or psychology or biology.

* * *

THE ROLE OF GRATIFIED NEEDS It has been pointed out above several times that our needs usually emerge only when more prepotent needs have been gratified. Thus gratification has an important role in motivation theory. Apart from this, however, needs cease to play an active determining or organizing role as soon as they are gratified.

What this means is that, e.g., a basically satisfied person no longer has the needs for esteem, love, safety, etc. The only sense in which he might be said to have them is in the almost metaphysical sense that a sated man has hunger, or a filled bottle has emptiness. If we are interested in what *actually* motivates us, and not in what has, will, or might motivate us, then a satisfied need is not a motivator. It must be considered for all practical purposes simply not to exist, to have disappeared. This point should be emphasized because it has been either overlooked or contradicted in every theory of motivation I know. The perfectly healthy, normal, fortunate man has no sex needs or hunger needs, or needs for safety, or for love, or for prestige, or self-esteem, except in stray moments of quickly passing threat. * * *

It is such considerations as these that suggest the bold postulation that a man who is thwarted in any of his basic needs may fairly be envisaged simply as a sick man. This is a fair parallel to our designation as sick of the man who lacks vitamins or minerals. Who will say that a lack of love is less important than a lack of vitamins? Since we know the pathogenic effects of love starvation, who is to say that we are invoking value questions in an unscientific or illegitimate way, any more than the physician does who diagnoses and treats pellagra or scurvy? If I were permitted this usage, I should then say simply that a healthy man is primarily motivated by his needs to develop and actualize his fullest potentialities and capacities. If a man has any other basic needs in any active, chronic sense, he is simply an unhealthy man. He is as surely sick as if he had suddenly developed a strong salt hunger or calcium hunger. If we were to use the word *sick* in this way, we should then also have to face squarely the relations of man to his society. One clear implication of our definition would be that (1) since a man is to be called sick who is basically thwarted, and (2) since such basic thwarting is made possible ultimately only by forces outside the individual, then (3) sickness in the individual must come ultimately from a sickness in the society. The good or healthy society would then be defined as one that permitted man's highest purposes to emerge by satisfying all his basic needs.

* * *

References

Harlow, H. F. (1950). Learning motivated by a manipulation drive. *Journal of Experimental Psychology, 40,* 228–234.

Maier, N. R. F. (1939). *Studies of abnormal behavior in the rat.* New York: Harper.

Some Observations on the Organization of Personality

Carl R. Rogers

This selection is an article by perhaps the best known of the classic humanistic psychologists, Carl Rogers. One of the most famous and important parts of Roger's theory is that a therapist needs to give his or her client "unconditional positive regard." This frees the client to say whatever is on his or her mind, and eventually helps the client to develop unconditional self-regard. Unconditional self-regard, in turn, allows the client to see himself or herself without defenses or distortions and thereby to become a fully functioning person.

In this article, Rogers argues that the nonjudgmental attitude of the therapist allows a complete and undistorted picture of the client's personality to emerge. He draws on some clinical experiences to illustrate his point, and—perhaps not surprisingly—finds that what his clients say in therapy tends to support his theory of personality dynamics and self-organization.

After you read this article, you may wish to think back to the earlier selections by Freud and his critics, and to note that the free-wheeling use of clinical anecdotes in support of one's theoretical position is not a practice limited to psychoanalysis. Just as Freud repeatedly found "confirmation" for his theoretical ideas in his clinical cases—and was roundly criticized for the shortcomings of such evidence later—so too Rogers was able to interpret what his clients said in the light of his own preferred theory. However, Rogers has yet to receive the kind of criticism for his method that Freud receives continually, and it is interesting to ponder just why this may be.

From *American Psychologist, 2*, 358–368, 1947.

In various fields of science rapid strides have been made when direct observation of significant processes has become possible. In medicine, when circumstances have permitted the physician to peer directly into the stomach of his patient, understanding of digestive processes has increased and the influence of emotional tension upon all aspects of that process has been more accurately observed and understood. In our work with nondirective therapy we often feel that we are having a psychological opportunity comparable to this medical experience—an opportunity to observe directly a number of the effective processes of personality. Quite aside from any question regarding nondirective therapy as therapy, here is a precious vein of observational material of unusual value for the study of personality.

Characteristics of the Observational Material

There are several ways in which the raw clinical data to which we have had access is unique in its value for understanding personality. The fact that these verbal expressions of inner dynamics are preserved by electrical recording makes possible a detailed analysis of a sort not heretofore possible. Recording has given us a microscope by which we may examine at leisure, and in minute detail, almost every aspect of what was, in its occurence, a fleeting moment impossible of accurate observation.

Another scientifically fortunate characteristic of this material is the fact that the verbal productions of the client are biased to a minimal degree by the therapist. Material from client-centered interviews probably comes closer to being a "pure" expression of attitudes than has yet been achieved through other means. One can read through a complete recorded case or listen to it, without finding more than a half-dozen instances in which the therapist's views on any point are evident. One would find it impossible to form an estimate as to the therapist's views about personality dynamics. One could not determine his diagnostic views, his standards of behavior, his social class. The one value or standard held by the therapist which would exhibit itself in his tone of voice, responses, and activity, is a deep respect for the personality and attitudes of the client as a separate person. It is difficult to see how this would bias the content of the interview, except to permit deeper expression than the client would ordinarily allow himself. This almost complete lack of any distorting attitude is felt, and sometimes expressed by the client. One woman says:

> "It's almost impersonal. I like you—of course I don't know why I should like you or why I shouldn't like you. It's a peculiar thing. I've never had that relationship with anybody before and I've often thought about it. . . . A lot of times I walk out with a feeling of elation that you think highly of me, and of course at the same time I have the feeling that 'Gee, he must think I'm an awful jerk' or something like that. But it doesn't really—those feelings aren't so deep that I can form an opinion one way or the other about you."

Here it would seem that even though she would like to discover some type of evaluational attitude, she is unable to do so. Published studies and research as yet unpublished bear out this point that counselor responses which are in any way evaluational or distorting as to content are at a minimum, thus enhancing the worth of such interviews for personality study.

The counselor attitude of warmth and understanding, well described by Snyder (1946) and Rogers (1946), also helps to maximize the freedom of expression by the individual. The client experiences sufficient interest in him as a person, and sufficient acceptance, to enable him to talk openly, not only about surface attitudes, but increasingly about intimate attitudes and feelings hidden even from himself. Hence in these recorded interviews we have material of very considerable depth so far as personality dynamics is concerned, along with a freedom from distortion.

Finally the very nature of the interviews and the techniques by which they are handled give us a rare opportunity to see to some extent through the eyes of another person—to perceive the world as it appears to him, to achieve at least partially, the internal frame of reference of another person. We see his behavior through his eyes, and also the psychological meaning which it had for him. We see also changes in personality and behavior, and the meanings which those changes have for the individual. We are admitted freely into the backstage of the person's living where we can observe from within some of the dramas of internal change, which are often far more compelling and moving than the drama which is presented on the stage viewed by the public. Only a novelist or a poet could do justice to the deep struggles which we are permitted to observe from within the client's own world of reality.

This rare opportunity to observe so directly and so clearly the inner dynamics of personality is a learning experience of the deepest sort for the clinician. Most of clinical psychology and psychiatry involves judgements *about* the individual, judgements which must, of necessity, be based on some framework brought to the situation by the clinician. To try continually to see and think *with* the individual, as in client-centered therapy, is a mindstretching experience in which learning goes on apace because the clinician brings to the interview no pre-determined yardstick by which to judge the material.

I wish in this paper to try to bring you some of the clinical observations which we have made as we have repeatedly peered through these psychological windows into personality, and to raise with you some of the questions about the organization of personality which these observations have forced upon us. I shall not attempt to present these observations in logical order, but rather in the order in which they impressed themselves upon our notice. What I shall offer is not a series of research findings, but only the first step in that process of gradual approximation which we call science, a description of some observed phenomena which appear to be significant, and some highly tentative explanations of these phenomena.

The Relation of the Organized Perceptual Field to Behavior

One simple observation, which is repeated over and over again in each successful therapeutic case, seems to have rather deep theoretical implications. It is that as changes occur in the perception of self and in the perception of reality, changes occur in behavior. In therapy, these perceptual changes are more often concerned with the self than with the external world. Hence we find in therapy that as the perception of self alters, behavior alters. Perhaps an illustration will indicate the type of observation upon which this statement is based.

A young woman, a graduate student whom we shall call Miss Vib, came in for nine interviews. If we compare the first interview with the last, striking changes are evident. Perhaps some features of this change may be conveyed by taking from the first and last interviews all the major statements regarding self, and all the major statements regarding current behavior. In the first interview, for example, her perception of herself may be crudely indicated by taking all her own statements about herself, grouping those which seem similar, but otherwise doing a minimum of editing, and retaining so far as possible, her own words. We then come out with this as the conscious perception of self which was hers at the outset of counseling.

> "I feel disorganized, muddled; I've lost all direction; my personal life has disintegrated.
>
> "I sorta experience things from the forefront of my consciousness, but nothing sinks in very deep; things don't seem real to me; I feel nothing matters; I don't have any emotional response to situations; I'm worried about myself.
>
> "I haven't been acting like myself; it doesn't seem like me; I'm a different person altogether from what I used to be in the past.
>
> "I don't understand myself; I haven't known what was happening to me.
>
> "I have withdrawn from everything, and feel all right only when I'm all alone and no one can expect me to do things.
>
> "I don't care about my personal appearance.
>
> "I don't know *anything* anymore.
>
> "I feel guilty about the things I have left undone.
>
> "I don't think I could ever assume responsibility for anything."

If we attempt to evaluate this picture of self from an external frame of reference various diagnostic labels may come to mind. Trying to perceive it solely from the client's frame of reference we observe that to the young woman herself she appears disorganized, and not herself. She is perplexed and almost unacquainted with what is going on in herself. She feels unable and unwilling to function in any responsible or social way. This is at least a sampling of the way she experiences or perceives her self.

Her behavior is entirely consistent with this picture of self. If we abstract all her statements describing her behavior, in the same fashion as we abstracted her statements about self, the following pattern emerges—a pattern which in this case was corroborated by outside observation.

> "I couldn't get up nerve to come in before; I haven't availed myself of help.
>
> "Everything I should do or want to do, I don't do.
>
> "I haven't kept in touch with friends; I avoid making the effort to go with them; I stopped writing letters home; I don't answer letters or telephone calls; I avoid contacts that would be professionally helpful; I didn't go home though I said I would.
>
> "I failed to hand in my work in a course though I had it all done; I didn't even buy clothing that I needed; I haven't even kept my nails manicured.
>
> "I didn't listen to material we were studying; I waste hours reading the funny papers; I can spend the whole afternoon doing absolutely nothing."

The picture of behavior is very much in keeping with the picture of self, and is summed up in the statement that "Everything I should do or want to do, I don't do." The behavior goes on, in ways that seem to the individual beyond understanding and beyond control.

If we contrast this picture of self and behavior with the picture as it exists in the ninth interview, thirty-eight days later, we find both the perception of self and the ways of behaving deeply altered. Her statements about self are as follows:

> "I'm feeling much better; I'm taking more interest in myself.
>
> "I do have some individuality, some interests.
>
> "I seem to be getting a newer understanding of myself. I can look at myself a little better.
>
> "I realize I'm just one person, with so much ability, but I'm not worried about it; I can accept the fact that I'm not always right.
>
> "I feel more motivation, have more of a desire to go ahead.
>
> "I still occasionally regret the past, though I feel less unhappy about it; I still have a long ways to go; I don't know whether I can keep the picture of myself I'm beginning to evolve.
>
> "I can go on learning—in school or out.
>
> "I do feel more like a normal person now; I feel more I can handle my life myself; I think I'm at the point where I can go along on my own."

Outstanding in this perception of herself are three things—that she knows herself, that she can view with comfort her assets and liabilities, and finally that she has drive and control of that drive.

In this ninth interview the behavioral picture is again consistent with the perception of self. It may be abstracted in these terms.

> "I've been making plans about school and about a job; I've been working hard on a term paper; I've been going to the library to trace down a topic of special interest and finding it exciting.
>
> "I've cleaned out my closets; washed my clothes.
>
> "I finally wrote my parents; I'm going home for the holidays.
>
> "I'm getting out and mixing with people; I am reacting sensibly to a fellow who is interested in me—seeing both his good and bad points.
>
> "I will work toward my degree; I'll start looking for a job this week."

Her behavior, in contrast to the first interview, is now organized, forward-moving, effective, realistic and planful. It is in accord with the realistic and organized view she has achieved of her self.

It is this type of observation, in case after case, that leads us to say with some assurance that as perceptions of self and reality change, behavior changes. Likewise, in cases we might term failures, there appears to be no appreciable change in perceptual organization or in behavior.

What type of explanation might account for these concomitant changes in the perceptual field and the behavioral pattern? Let us examine some of the logical possibilities.

In the first place, it is possible that factors unrelated to therapy may have brought about the altered perception and behavior. There may have been physiological processes occurring which produced the change. There may have been alterations in the family relationships, or in the social forces, or in the educational picture or in some other area of cultural influence, which might account for the rather drastic shift in the concept of self and in the behavior.

There are difficulties in this type of explanation. Not only were there no known gross changes in the physical or cultural situation as far as Miss Vib was concerned, but the explanation gradually becomes inadequate when one tries to apply it to the many cases in which such change occurs. To postulate that some external factor brings the change and that only by chance does this period of change coincide with the period of therapy, becomes an untenable hypothesis.

Let us then look at another explanation, namely that the therapist exerted, during the nine hours of contact, a peculiarly potent cultural influence which brought about the change. Here again we are faced with several problems. It seems that nine hours scattered over five and one-half weeks is a very minute portion of time in which to bring about alteration of patterns which have been building for thirty years. We would have to postulate an influence so potent as to be classed as traumatic. This theory is particularly difficult to maintain when we find, on examining the recorded interviews, that not once in the nine hours did the therapist express any evaluation, positive or negative, of the client's initial or final perception of self, or her initial or final mode of behavior. There was not only no evaluation, but no standards expressed by which evaluation might be inferred.

There was, on the part of the therapist, evidence of warm interest in the individual, and thoroughgoing acceptance of the self and of the behavior as they existed initially, in the intermediate stages, and at the conclusion of therapy. It appears reasonable to say that the therapist established certain definite conditions of interpersonal relations, but since the very essence of this relationship is respect for the person as he is at that moment, the therapist can hardly be regarded as a cultural force making for change.

We find ourselves forced to a third type of explanation, a type of explanation which is not new to psychology, but which has had only partial acceptance. Briefly it may be put that the observed phenomena of change seem most adequately explained by the hypothesis that *given certain psychological conditions, the individual has the capacity to reorganize his field of perception, including the way he perceives himself, and that a concomitant or a resultant of this perceptual reorganization is an appropriate alteration of behavior.* This puts into formal and objective terminology a clinical hypothesis which experience forces upon the therapist using a client-centered approach. One is compelled through clinical observation to develop a high degree of respect for the ego-integrative forces residing within each individual. One comes to recognize that under proper conditions the self is a basic factor in the formation of personality and in the determination of behavior. Clinical experience would strongly suggest that the self is, to some extent, an architect of self, and the above hypothesis simply puts this observation into psychological terms.

In support of this hypothesis it is noted in some cases that one of the concomitants of success in therapy is the realization on the part of the client that the self has the capacity for reorganization. Thus a student says:

> "You know I spoke of the fact that a person's background retards one. Like the fact that my family life wasn't good for me, and my mother certainly didn't give me any of the kind of bringing up that I should have had. Well, I've been thinking that over. It's true up to a point. But when you get so that you can see the situation, then it's really up to you."

Following this statement of the relation of the self to experience many changes occurred in this young man's behavior. In this, as in other cases, it appears that when the person comes to see himself as the perceiving, organizing agent, then reorganization of perception and consequent change in patterns of reaction take place.

On the other side of the picture we have frequently observed that when the individual has been authoritatively told that he is governed by certain factors or conditions beyond his control, it makes therapy more difficult, and it is only when the individual discovers for himself that he can organize his perceptions that change is possible. In veterans who have been given their own psychiatric diagnosis, the effect is often that of making the individual feel that he is under an unalterable doom, that he is unable to control the organization of his life. When however the self sees itself as capable of reorganizing its own perceptual field, a marked change in basic confidence occurs. Miss Nam, a student, illustrates this phenomenon when she says, after having made progress in therapy:

> "I think I do feel better about the future, too, because it's as if I won't be acting in darkness. It's sort of, well, knowing somewhat why I act the way I do . . . and at least it isn't the feeling that you're simply out of your own control and the fates are driving you to act that way. If you realize it, I think you can do something more about it."

A veteran at the conclusion of counseling puts it more briefly and more positively: "My attitude toward myself is changed now to where I feel I *can* do something with my self and life." He has come to view himself as the instrument by which some reorganization can take place.

There is another clinical observation which may be cited in support of the general hypothesis that there is a close relationship between behavior and the way in which reality is viewed by the individual. It has been noted in many cases that behavior changes come about for the most part imperceptibly and almost automatically, once the perceptual reorganization has taken place. A young wife who has been reacting violently to her maid, and has been quite disorganized in her behavior as a result of this antipathy, says "After I . . . discovered it was nothing more than that she resembled my mother, she didn't bother me any more. Isn't that interesting? She's still the same." Here is a clear statement indicating that though the basic perceptions have not changed, they have been differently organized, have acquired a new meaning, and that behavior changes then occur. * * *

Thus we have observed that appropriate changes in behavior occur when the individual acquires a different view of his world of experience, including himself; that this changed perception does not need to be dependent upon a change in the "reality," but may be a product of internal reorganization; that in some instances the awareness of the capacity for reperceiving experience accompanies this process or reorganization; that the altered behavioral responses occur automatically and without conscious effort as soon as the perceptual reorganization has taken place, apparently as a result of this.

In view of these observations a second hypothesis may be stated, which is closely related to the first. It is that *behavior is not directly influenced or determined by organic or cultural factors, but primarily,* (and perhaps only,) *by the perception of these elements.* In other words the crucial element in the determination of behavior is the perceptual field of the individual. While this perceptual field is, to be sure, deeply influenced and largely shaped by cultural and physiological forces, it is nevertheless important that it appears to be only the field as it is *perceived*, which exercises a specific determining influence upon behavior. This is not a new idea in psychology, but its implications have not always been fully recognized.

It might mean, first of all, that if it is the perceptual field which determines behavior, then the primary object of study for psychologists would be the person and his world as *viewed by the person himself.* It could mean that the internal frame of reference of the person might well constitute the field of psychology. * * * It might mean that the laws which govern behavior would be discovered more deeply by turning our attention to the laws which govern perception.

Now if our speculations contain a measure of truth, if the *specific* determinant of behavior is the perceptual field, and if the self can reorganize that perceptual field, then what are the limits of this process? Is the reorganization of perception capricious, or does it follow certain laws? Are there limits to the degree of reorganization? If so, what are they? In this connection we have observed with some care the perception of one portion of the field of experience, the portion we call the self.

The Relation of the Perception of the Self to Adjustment

Initially we were oriented by the background of both lay and psychological thinking to regard the outcome of successful therapy as the solution of problems. If a person had a marital problem, a vocational problem, a problem of educational adjustment, the obvious purpose of counseling or therapy was to solve that problem. But as we observe and study the recorded accounts of the conclusion of therapy, it is clear that the most characteristic outcome is not necessarily solution of problems, but a freedom from tension, a different feeling about, and perception of, self. Perhaps something of this outcome may be conveyed by some illustrations.

Several statements taken from the final interview with a twenty year old young woman, Miss Mir, give indications of the characteristic attitude toward self, and the sense of freedom which appears to accompany it.

> "I've always tried to be what the others thought I should be, but now I am wondering whether I shouldn't just see that I am what I am."
>
> "Well, I've just noticed such a difference. I find that when I feel things, even when I feel hate, I don't care. I don't mind. I feel more free somehow. I don't feel guilty about things."
>
> "You know it's suddenly as though a big cloud has been lifted off. I feel so much more content."

Note in these statements the willingness to perceive herself as she is, to accept herself "realistically," to perceive and accept her "bad" attitudes as well as "good" ones. This realism seems to be accompanied by a sense of freedom and contentment.

Miss Vib, whose attitudes were quoted earlier, wrote out her own feelings about counseling some six weeks after the interviews were over, and gave the statement to her counselor. She begins:

> "The happiest outcome of therapy has been a new feeling about myself. As I think of it, it might be the only outcome. Certainly it is basic to all the changes in my behavior that have resulted." In discussing her experience in therapy she states, "I was coming to see myself as a whole. I began to realize that I am *one* person. This was an important insight to me. I saw that the former good academic achievement, job success, ease in social situations, and the present withdrawal, dejection, apathy and failure were all adaptive behavior, performed by *me.* This meant that I had to reorganize my feelings about myself, no longer holding to the unrealistic notion that the very good adjustment was the expression of the real "me" and this neurotic behavior was not. I came to feel that I am the same person, sometimes functioning maturely, and sometimes assuming a neurotic role in the face of what I had conceived as insurmountable problems. The acceptance of myself as one person gave me strength in the process of reorganization. Now I had a substratum, a core of unity on which to work." As she continues her discussion there are such statements as "I am getting more happiness in being myself." "I approve of myself more, and I have so much less anxiety."

As in the previous example, the outstanding aspects appear to be the realization that all of her behavior "belonged" to her, that she could accept both the good and bad features about herself and that doing so gave her a release from anxiety and a feeling of solid happiness. In both instances there is only incidental reference to the serious "problems" which had been initially discussed.

Since Miss Mir is undoubtedly above average intelligence and Miss Vib is a person with some psychological training, it may appear that such results are found only with the sophisticated individual. To counteract this opinion a quotation may be given from a statement written by a veteran of limited ability and education who had just completed counseling, and was asked to write whatever reactions he had to the experience. He says:

> "As for the consoleing I have had I can say this, It really makes a man strip his own mind bare, and when he does he knows then what he realy is and what he can do. Or at least thinks he knows himself

> party well. As for myself, I know that my ideas were a little too big for what I realy am, but now I realize one must try start out at his own level.
>
> "Now after four visits, I have a much clearer picture of myself and my future. It makes me feel a little depressed and disappointed, but on the other hand, it has taken me out of the dark, the load seems a lot lighter now, that is I can see my way now, I know what I want to do, I know about what I can do, so now that I can see my goal, I will be able to work a whole lot easyer, at my own level."

Although the expression is much simpler one notes again the same two elements—the acceptance of self as it is, and the feeling of easiness, of lightened burden, which accompanies it.

As we examine many individual case records and case recordings, it appears to be possible to bring together the findings in regard to successful therapy by stating another hypothesis in regard to that portion of the perceptual field which we call the self. It would appear that *when all of the ways in which the individual perceives himself—all perceptions of the qualities, abilities, impulses, and attitudes of the person, and all perceptions of himself in relation to others—are accepted into the organized conscious concept of the self, then this achievement is accompanied by feelings of comfort and freedom from tension which are experienced as psychological adjustment.*

This hypothesis would seem to account for the observed fact that the comfortable perception of self which is achieved is sometimes more positive than before, sometimes more negative. When the individual permits all his perceptions of himself to be organized into one pattern, the picture is sometimes more flattering than he has held in the past, sometimes less flattering. It is always more comfortable.

It may be pointed out also that this tentative hypothesis supplies an operational type of definition, based on the client's internal frame of reference, for such hitherto vague terms as "adjustment," "integration," and "acceptance of self." They are defined in terms of perception, in a way which it should be possible to prove or disprove. When all of the organic perceptual experiences—the experiencing of attitudes, impulses, abilities and disabilities, the experiencing of others and of "reality"—when all of these perceptions are freely assimilated into an organized and consistent system, available to consciousness, then psychological adjustment or integration might be said to exist. The definition of adjustment is thus made an internal affair, rather than dependent upon an external "reality."

Something of what is meant by this acceptance and assimilation of perceptions about the self may be illustrated from the case of Miss Nam, a student. Like many other clients she gives evidence of having experienced attitudes and feelings which are defensively denied because they are not consistent with the concept or picture she holds of herself. The way in which they are first fully admitted into consciousness, and then organized into a unified system may be shown by excerpts from the recorded interviews. She has spoken of the difficulty she has had in bringing herself to write papers for her university courses.

> "I just thought of something else which perhaps hinders me, and that is that again it's two different feelings. When I have to sit down and do (a paper), though I have a lot of ideas, underneath I think I always have the feeling that I just can't do it. . . . I have this feeling of being terrifically confident that I can do something, without being willing to put the work into it. At other times I'm practically afraid of what I have to do. . . ."

Note that the conscious self has been organized as "having a lot of ideas," being "terrifically confident" but that "underneath," in other words not freely admitted into consciousness, has been the experience of feeling "I just can't do it." She continues:

> "I'm trying to work through this funny relationship between this terrific confidence and then this almost fear of doing anything . . . and I think the kind of feeling that I can really do things is part of an illusion I have about myself of being, in my imagination, sure that it will be something good and very good and all that, but whenever I get down to the actual task of getting started, it's a terrible feeling of—well, incapacity, that I won't get it done

> either the way I want to do it, or even not being sure how I want to do it."

Again the picture of herself which is present in consciousness is that of a person who is "very good," but this picture is entirely out of line with the actual organic experience in the situation.

Later in the same interview she expresses very well the fact that her perceptions are not all organized into one consistent conscious self.

> "I'm not sure about what kind of a person I am—well, I realize that all of these are a part of me, but I'm not quite sure of how to make all of these things fall in line."

In the next interview we have an excellent opportunity to observe the organization of both of these conflicting perceptions into one pattern, with the resultant sense of freedom from tension which has been described above.

> "It's very funny, even as I sit here I realize that I have more confidence in myself, in the sense that when I used to approach new situations I would have two very funny things operating at the same time. I had a fantasy that I could do anything, which was a fantasy which covered over all these other feelings that I really couldn't do it, or couldn't do it as well as I wanted to, and it's as if now those two things have merged together, and it is more real, that a situation isn't either testing myself or proving something to myself or anyone else. It's just in terms of doing it. And I think I have done away both with that fantasy and that fear. . . . So I think I can go ahead and approach things—well, just sensibly."

No longer is it necessary for this client to "cover over" her real experiences. Instead the picture of herself as very able, and the experienced feeling of complete inability, have now been brought together into one integrated pattern of self as a person with real, but imperfect abilities. Once the self is thus accepted the inner energies making for self-actualization are released and she attacks her life problems more efficiently.

Observing this type of material frequently in counseling experience would lead to a tentative hypothesis of maladjustment, which like the other hypothesis suggested, focuses on the perception of self. It might be proposed that the tensions called psychological maladjustment exist when the organized concept of self (conscious or available to conscious awareness) is not in accord with the perceptions actually experienced.

This discrepancy between the concept of self and the actual perceptions seems to be explicable only in terms of the fact that the self concept resists assimilating into itself any percept which is inconsistent with its present organization. The feeling that she may not have the ability to do a paper is inconsistent with Miss Nam's conscious picture of herself as a very able and confident person, and hence, though fleetingly perceived, is denied organization as a part of her self, until this comes about in therapy.

The Conditions of Change of Self Perception

If the way in which the self is perceived has as close and significant a relationship to behavior as has been suggested, then the manner in which this perception may be altered becomes a question of importance. If a reorganization of self-perceptions brings a change in behavior; if adjustment and maladjustment depend on the congruence between perceptions as experienced and the self as perceived, then the factors which permit a reorganization of the perception of self are significant.

Our observations of psychotherapeutic experience would seem to indicate that absence of any threat to the self-concept is an important item in the problem. Normally the self resists incorporating into itself those experiences which are inconsistent with the functioning of self. But a point overlooked by Lecky and others[1] is that when the self is free from any threat of attack or likelihood of attack, then it is possible for the self to consider these hitherto rejected perceptions, to make new differentiations, and to reintegrate the self in such a way as to include them.

---

[1]That is, by Rogers's intellectual adversaries.

An illustration from the case of Miss Vib may serve to clarify this point. In her statement written six weeks after the conclusion of counseling Miss Vib thus describes the way in which unacceptable percepts become incorporated into the self. She writes:

> "In the earlier interviews I kept saying such things as, 'I am not acting like myself', 'I never acted this way before.' What I meant was that this withdrawn, untidy, and apathetic person was not myself. Then I began to realize that I was the same person, seriously withdrawn, etc. now, as I had been before. That did not happen until after I had talked out my self-rejection, shame, despair, and doubt, in the accepting situation of the interview. The counselor was not startled or shocked. I was telling him all these things about myself which did not fit into my picture of a graduate student, a teacher, a sound person. He responded with complete acceptance and warm interest without heavy emotional overtones. Here was a sane, intelligent person wholeheartedly accepting this behavior that seemed so shameful to me. I can remember an organic feeling of relaxation. I did not have to keep up the struggle to cover up and hide this shameful person."

Note how clearly one can see here the whole range of denied perceptions of self, and the fact that they could be considered as a part of self only in a social situation which involved no threat to the self, in which another person, the counselor, becomes almost an alternate self and looks with understanding and acceptance upon these same perceptions. She continues:

> "Retrospectively, it seems to me that what I felt as 'warm acceptance without emotional overtones' was what I needed to work through my difficulties. . . . The counselor's impersonality with interest allowed me to talk out my feelings. The clarification in the interview situation presented the attitude to me as a 'ding an sich' which I could look at, manipulate, and put in place. In organizing my attitudes, I was beginning to organize me."

Here the nature of the exploration of experience, of seeing it as experience and not as a threat to self, enables the client to reorganize her perceptions of self, which as she says was also "reorganizing me."

If we attempt to describe in more conventional psychological terms the nature of the process which culminates in an altered organization and integration of self in the process of therapy it might run as follows. The individual is continually endeavoring to meet his needs by reacting to the field of experience as he perceives it, and to do that more efficiently by differentiating elements of the field and reintegrating them into new patterns. Reorganization of the field may involve the reorganization of the self as well as of other parts of the field. The self, however, resists reorganization and change. In everyday life individual adjustment by means of reorganization of the field exclusive of the self is more common and is less threatening to the individual. Consequently, the individual's first mode of adjustment is the reorganization of that part of the field which does not include the self.

Client-centered therapy is different from other life situations inasmuch as the therapist tends to remove from the individual's immediate world all those aspects of the field which the individual can reorganize except the self. The therapist, by reacting to the client's feelings and attitudes rather than to the objects of his feelings and attitudes, assists the client in bringing from background into focus his own self, making it easier than ever before for the client to perceive and react to the self. By offering only understanding and no trace of evaluation, the therapist removes himself as an object of attitudes, becoming only an alternate expression of the client's self. The therapist by providing a consistent atmosphere of permissiveness and understanding removes whatever threat existed to prevent all perceptions of the self from emerging into figure. Hence in this situation all the ways in which the self has been experienced can be viewed openly, and organized into a complex unity.

It is then this complete absence of any factor which would attack the concept of self, and second, the assistance in focusing upon the perception of self, which seems to permit a more differentiated view of self and finally the reorganization of self.

* * *

Implications

* * * We have discovered with some surprise that our clinical observations, and the tentative hypotheses which seem to grow out of them, raise disturbing questions which appear to cast doubt on the very foundations of many of our psychological endeavors, particularly in the fields of clinical psychology and personality study. To clarify what is meant, I should like to restate in more logical order the formulations I have given, and to leave with you certain questions and problems which each one seems to raise.

If we take first the tentative proposition that the specific determinant of behavior is the perceptual field of the individual, would this not lead, if regarded as a working hypothesis, to a radically different approach in clinical psychology and personality research? It would seem to mean that instead of elaborate case histories full of information about the person as an object, we would endeavor to develop ways of seeing his situation, his past, and himself, as these objects appear to him. We would try to see with him, rather than to evaluate him. It might mean the minimizing of the elaborate psychometric procedures by which we have endeavored to measure or value the individual from our own frame of reference. It might mean the minimizing or discarding of all the vast series of labels which we have painstakingly built up over the years. Paranoid, preschizophrenic, compulsive, constricted—terms such as these might become irrelevant because they are all based in thinking which takes an external frame of reference. They are not the ways in which the individual experiences himself. If we consistently studied each individual from the internal frame of reference of that individual, from within his own perceptual field, it seems probable that we should find generalizations which could be made, and principles which were operative, but we may be very sure that they would be of a different order from these externally based judgements *about* individuals.

Let us look at another of the suggested propositions. If we took seriously the hypothesis that integration and adjustment are internal conditions related to the degree of acceptance or nonacceptance of all perceptions, and the degree of organization of these perceptions into one consistent system, this would decidedly affect our clinical procedures. It would seem to imply the abandonment of the notion that adjustment is dependent upon the pleasantness or unpleasantness of the environment, and would demand concentration upon those processes which bring about self-integration within the person. It would mean a minimizing or an abandoning of those clinical procedures which utilize the alteration of environmental forces as a method of treatment. It would rely instead upon the fact that the person who is internally unified has the greatest likelihood of meeting environmental problems constructively, either as an individual or in cooperation with others.

If we take the remaining proposition that the self, under proper conditions, is capable of reorganizing, to some extent, its own perceptual field, and of thus altering behavior, this too seems to raise disturbing questions. Following the path of this hypothesis would appear to mean a shift in emphasis in psychology from focusing upon the fixity of personality attributes and psychological abilities, to the alterability of these same characteristics. It would concentrate attention upon process rather than upon fixed status. Whereas psychology has, in personality study, been concerned primarily with the measurement of the fixed qualities of the individual, and with his past in order to explain his present, the hypothesis here suggested would seem to concern itself much more with the personal world of the present in order to understand the future, and in predicting that future would be concerned with the principles by which personality and behavior are altered, as well as the extent to which they remain fixed.

Thus we find that a clinical approach, client-centered therapy, has led us to try to adopt the client's perceptual field as the basis for genuine understanding. In trying to enter this internal world of perception, not by introspection, but by observation and direct inference, we find ourselves in a new vantage point for understanding personality dynamics, a vantage point which opens up some disturbing vistas. We find that behavior seems to be better understood as a reaction to this reality-as-perceived. We discover that the way in which the person sees himself, and the perceptions he dares not take as belonging to himself, seem to have an important relationship to the inner peace which constitutes adjustment. We discover within the person, under certain conditions, a capacity for the restructuring and the reorganization of self, and consequently the reorganization of behavior, which has profound social implications. We see these observations, and the theoretical formulations which they inspire, as a fruitful new approach for study and research in various fields of psychology.

References

Rogers, Carl R. (1946). Significant aspects of client-centered therapy. *American Psychologist, 1*, 415–422.

Snyder, W. U. (1946). 'Warmth' in nondirective counseling. *Journal of Abnormal and Social Psychology, 41*, 491–495.

If We Are So Rich, Why Aren't We Happy?

Mihaly Csikszentmihalyi

What was classically called "humanistic psychology" has faded from view in recent years, but now a successor is stepping forward in its place. The "positive psychology movement" has become suddenly quite prominent and has taken up the humanistic mission of arguing that human nature is basically good and that the proper topic of psychology is human experience—especially positive human experience, also known as "the good life." The author of the next selection, Mihaly Csikszentmihalyi (pronounced chick-sent-me-high), directly addresses the questions, what is positive experience and how does one attain it?

Csikszentmihalyi argues that positive experience—happiness—is not a matter of material goods or entertainment but rather comes from matching one's capacities to one's activities. This produces a state he calls "flow," characterized by total focus, a loss of sense of time, and mildly pleasant emotion.

Notice how the modern humanist Csikszentmihalyi draws directly on the classic theorist Carl Rogers, when he refers to the way "human consciousness uses its self-organizing ability to achieve a positive internal state through its own efforts" (see footnote 1). This is just one indication that the positive psychology movement is the modern version of humanistic psychology.

From *American Psychologist, 54*, 821–827, 1999.

Psychology is the heir to those "sciences of man" envisioned by Enlightenment thinkers such as Gianbattista Vico, David Hume, and the Baron de Montesquieu. One of their fundamental conclusions was that the pursuit of happiness constituted the basis of both individual motivation and social well-being. This insight into the human condition was condensed by John Locke (1690/1975) in his famous statement, "That we call Good which is apt to cause or increase pleasure, or diminish pain" (p. 2), whereas evil is the reverse—it is what causes or increases pain and diminishes pleasure.

The generation of utilitarian philosophers that followed Locke, including David Hartley, Joseph Priestley, and Jeremy Bentham, construed a good society as that which allows the greatest happiness for the greatest number (Bentham, 1789/1970, pp.

64–65). This focus on pleasure or happiness as the touchstone of private and public life is by no means a brainchild of post-Reformation Europe. It was already present in the writings of the Greeks—for instance, Aristotle noted that although humankind values a great many things, such as health, fame, and possessions, because we think that they will make us happy, we value happiness for itself. Thus, happiness is the only intrinsic goal that people seek for its own sake, the bottom line of all desire. The idea that furthering the pursuit of happiness should be one of the responsibilities of a just government was of course enshrined later in the Declaration of Independence of the United States.

Despite this recognition on the part of the human sciences that happiness is the fundamental goal of life, there has been slow progress in understanding what happiness itself consists of. Perhaps because the heyday of utilitarian philosophy coincided with the start of the enormous forward strides in public health and in the manufacturing and distribution of goods, the majority of those who thought about such things assumed that increases in pleasure and happiness would come from increased affluence, from greater control over the material environment. The great self-confidence of the Western technological nations, and especially of the United States, was in large part because of the belief that materialism—the prolongation of a healthy life, the acquisition of wealth, the ownership of consumer goods—would be the royal road to a happy life.

However, the virtual monopoly of materialism as the dominant ideology has come at the price of a trivialization that has robbed it of much of the truth it once contained. In current use, it amounts to little more than a thoughtless hedonism, a call to do one's thing regardless of consequences, a belief that whatever feels good at the moment must be worth doing.

This is a far cry from the original view of materialists, such as John Locke, who were aware of the futility of pursuing happiness without qualifications and who advocated the pursuit of happiness through prudence—making sure that people do not mistake imaginary happiness for real happiness.

What does it mean to pursue happiness through prudence? Locke must have derived his inspiration from the Greek philosopher Epicurus, who 2,300 years ago already saw clearly that to enjoy a happy life, one must develop self-discipline. The materialism of Epicurus was solidly based on the ability to defer gratification. He claimed that although all pain was evil, this did not mean one should always avoid pain—for instance, it made sense to put up with pain now if one was sure to avoid thereby a greater pain later. He wrote to his friend Menoeceus

> The beginning and the greatest good . . . is prudence. For this reason prudence is more valuable even than philosophy: from it derive all the other virtues. Prudence teaches us how impossible it is to live pleasantly without living wisely, virtuously, and justly . . . take thought, then, for these and kindred matters day and night. . . . You shall be disturbed neither waking nor sleeping, and you shall live as a god among men. (Epicurus of Samos, trans. 1998, p. 48)

This is not the image of epicureanism held by most people. The popular view holds that pleasure and material comforts should be grasped wherever they can, and that these alone will improve the quality of one's life. As the fruits of technology have ripened and the life span has lengthened, the hope that increased material rewards would bring about a better life seemed for a while justified.

Now, at the end of the second millennium, it is becoming clear that the solution is not that simple. Inhabitants of the wealthiest industrialized Western nations are living in a period of unprecedented riches, in conditions that previous generations would have considered luxuriously comfortable, in relative peace and security, and they are living on the average close to twice as long as their great-grandparents did. Yet, despite all these improvements in material conditions, it does not seem that people are so much more satisfied with their lives than they were before.

The Ambiguous Relationship Between Material and Subjective Well-being

The indirect evidence that those of us living in the United States today are not happier than our ancestors were comes from national statistics of social pathology—the figures that show the doubling and tripling of violent crimes, family breakdown, and psychosomatic complaints since at least the halfway mark of the century. If material well-being leads to happiness, why is it that neither capitalist nor socialist solutions seem to work? Why is it that the crew on the flagship of capitalist affluence is becoming increasingly addicted to drugs for falling asleep, for waking up, for staying slim, for escaping boredom and depression? Why are suicides and loneliness such a problem in Sweden, which has applied the best of socialist principles to provide material security to its people?

Direct evidence about the ambiguous relationship of material and subjective well-being comes from studies of happiness that psychologists and other social scientists have finally started to pursue, after a long delay in which research on happiness was considered too soft for scientists to undertake. It is true that these surveys are based on self-reports and on verbal scales that might have different meanings depending on the culture and the language in which they are written. Thus, the results of culturally and methodologically circumscribed studies need to be taken with more than the usual grain of salt. Nevertheless, at this point they represent the state of the art—an art that will inevitably become more precise with time.

Although cross-national comparisons show a reasonable correlation between the wealth of a country as measured by its gross national product and the self-reported happiness of its inhabitants (Inglehart, 1990), the relationship is far from perfect. The inhabitants of Germany and Japan, for instance, nations with more than twice the gross national product of Ireland, report much lower levels of happiness.

Comparisons within countries show an even weaker relationship between material and subjective well-being. Diener, Horwitz, and Emmons (1985), in a study of some of the wealthiest individuals in the United States, found their levels of happiness to be barely above that of individuals with average incomes. After following a group of lottery winners, Brickman, Coates, and Janoff-Bulman (1978) concluded that despite their sudden increase in wealth, their happiness was no different from that of people struck by traumas, such as blindness or paraplegia. That having more money to spend does not necessarily bring about greater subjective well-being has also been documented on a national scale by David G. Myers (1993). His calculations show that although the adjusted value of after-tax personal income in the United States has more than doubled between 1960 and 1990, the percentage of people describing themselves as "very happy" has remained unchanged at 30% (Myers, 1993, pp. 41–42).

In the *American Psychologist's* January 2000 special issue on positive psychology, David G. Myers (2000) and Ed Diener (2000) discuss in great detail the lack of relationship between material and subjective well-being, so I will not belabor the point here. Suffice it to say that in current longitudinal studies of a representative sample of almost 1,000 American adolescents conducted with the experience sampling method * * *, a consistently low negative relationship between material and subjective well-being has been found (Csikszentmihalyi & Schneider, in press). For instance, the reported happiness of teenagers (measured several times a day for a week in each of three years) shows a very significant inverse relationship to the social class of the community in which teens live, to their parents' level of education, and to their parents' occupational status. Children of the lowest socioeconomic strata generally report the highest happiness, and upper middle-class children generally report the least happiness. Does this mean that more affluent children are in fact less happy, or does it mean that the norms of their social class prescribe that they should present themselves as less happy? At this point, we are unable to make this vital distinction.

Yet despite the evidence that the relationship between material wealth and happiness is tenuous at best, most people still cling to the notion that their problems would be resolved if they only had more money. In a survey conducted at the University of Michigan, when people were asked what would improve the quality of their lives, the first and foremost answer was "more money" (Campbell, 1981).

Given these facts, it seems that one of the most important tasks psychologists face is to better understand the dynamics of happiness and to communicate these findings to the public at large. If the main justification of psychology is to help reduce psychic distress and support psychic well-being, then psychologists should try to prevent the disillusionment that comes when people find out that they have wasted their lives struggling to reach goals that cannot satisfy them. Psychologists should be able to provide alternatives that in the long run will lead to a more rewarding life.

Why Material Rewards Do Not Necessarily Make People Happy

To answer this question, I'll start by reflecting on why material rewards, which people regard so highly, do not necessarily provide the happiness expected from them. The first reason is the well-documented escalation of expectations. If people strive for a certain level of affluence thinking that it will make them happy, they find that on reaching it, they become very quickly habituated, and at that point they start hankering for the next level of income, property, or good health. In a 1987 poll conducted by the *Chicago Tribune*, people who earned less than $30,000 a year said that $50,000 would fulfill their dreams, whereas those with yearly incomes of over $100,000 said they would need $250,000 to be satisfied ("Pay Nags," 1987; "Rich Think Big," 1987; see also Myers, 1993, p. 57). Several studies have confirmed that goals keep getting pushed upward as soon as a lower level is reached. It is not the objective size of the reward but its difference from one's "adaptation level" that provides subjective value (e.g., Davis, 1959; Michalos, 1985; Parducci, 1995).

The second reason is related to the first. When resources are unevenly distributed, people evaluate their possessions not in terms of what they need to live in comfort, but in comparison with those who have the most. Thus, the relatively affluent feel poor in comparison with the very rich and are unhappy as a result. This phenomenon of "relative deprivation" (Martin, 1981; Williams, 1975) seems to be fairly universal and well-entrenched. In the United States, the disparity in incomes between the top percentage and the rest is getting wider; this does not bode well for the future happiness of the population.

The third reason is that even though being rich and famous might be rewarding, nobody has ever claimed that material rewards alone are sufficient to make us happy. Other conditions—such as a satisfying family life, having intimate friends, having time to reflect and pursue diverse interests—have been shown to be related to happiness (Myers, 1993; Myers & Diener, 1995; Veenhoven, 1988). There is no intrinsic reason why these two sets of rewards—the material and the socioemotional—should be mutually exclusive. In practice, however, it is very difficult to reconcile their conflicting demands. As many psychologists from William James (1890) to Herbert A. Simon (1969) have remarked, time is the ultimate scarce resource, and the allocation of time (or more precisely, of attention over time) presents difficult choices that eventually determine the content and quality of our lives. This is why professional and business persons find it so difficult to balance the demands of work and family, and why they so rarely feel that they have not shortchanged one of these vital aspects of their lives.

Material advantages do not readily translate into social and emotional benefits. In fact, to the extent that most of one's psychic energy becomes invested in material goals, it is typical for sensitivity to other rewards to atrophy. Friendship, art, literature, natural beauty, religion, and philosophy become less and less interesting. The Swedish economist Stephen Linder was the first to point out that as income and therefore the value of one's time increases, it becomes less and less "rational" to spend it on anything besides making money—or on spending it conspicuously (Linder, 1970). The opportunity costs of playing with one's child, reading poetry, or attending a family reunion become too high, and so one stops doing such irrational things. Eventually a person who only responds to material rewards becomes blind to any other kind and loses the ability to derive happiness from other sources (see also Benedikt, 1999; Scitovsky, 1975). As is true of addiction in general, material rewards at first enrich the quality of life. Because of this, we tend to conclude that more must be better. But life is rarely linear; in most cases, what is good in small quantities becomes commonplace and then harmful in larger doses.

Dependence on material goals is so difficult to avoid in part because our culture has progressively eliminated every alternative that in previous times used to give meaning and purpose to individual lives. Although hard comparative data are lacking, many historians (e.g., Polanyi, 1957) have claimed that past cultures provided a greater variety of attractive models for successful lives. A person could be valued and admired because he or she was a saint, a bon vivant, a wise person, a good craftsman, a brave patriot, or an upright citizen. Nowadays the logic of reducing everything to quantifiable measures has made the dollar the common metric by which to evaluate every aspect of human action. The worth of a person and of a person's accomplishments are determined by the price they fetch in the marketplace. It is useless to claim that a painting is good art unless it gets high bids at Sotheby's, nor can we claim that someone is wise unless he or she can charge five figures for a consultation. Given the hegemony of material rewards in our culture's restricted repertoire, it is not surprising that so many people feel that their only hope for a happy life is to amass all the earthly goods they can lay hands on.

To recapitulate, there are several reasons for the lack of a direct relationship between material well-being and happiness. Two of them are sociocultural: (a) The growing disparity in wealth makes even the reasonably affluent feel poor. (b) This relative deprivation is exacerbated by a cultural factor, namely, the lack of alternative values and a wide range of successful lifestyles that could compensate for a single, zero-sum hierarchy based on dollars and cents. Two of the reasons are more psychological: (a) When we evaluate success, our minds use a strategy of escalating expectations, so that few people are ever satisfied for long with what they possess or what they have achieved. (b) As more psychic energy is invested in material goals, less of it is left to pursue other goals that are also necessary for a life in which one aspires to happiness.

None of this is intended to suggest that the material rewards of wealth, health, comfort, and fame detract from happiness. Rather, after a certain minimum threshold—which is not stable but varies with the distribution of resources in the given society—they seem to be irrelevant. Of course, most people will still go on from cradle to grave believing that if they could only have had more money, or good looks, or lucky breaks, they would have achieved that elusive state.

Psychological Approaches to Happiness

If people are wrong about the relation between material conditions and how happy they are, then what *does* matter? The alternative to the materialist approach has always been something that used to be called a "spiritual" and nowadays we may call a "psychological" solution. This approach is based on the premise that if happiness is a mental state, people should be able to control it through cognitive means. Of course, it is also possible to control the mind pharmacologically. Every culture has developed drugs ranging from peyote to heroin to alcohol in an effort to improve the quality of experience by direct chemical means. In my opinion, however, chemically induced well-being lacks a vital ingredient of happiness: the knowledge that one is responsible for having achieved it. Happiness is not something that happens to people but something that they make happen.

In some cultures, drugs ingested in a ritual, ceremonial context appear to have lasting beneficial effects, but in such cases the benefits most likely result primarily from performing the ritual, rather than from the chemicals per se. Thus, in discussing psychological approaches to happiness, I focus exclusively on processes in which human consciousness uses its self-organizing ability to achieve a positive internal state through its own efforts[1] with minimal reliance on external manipulation of the nervous system.

There have been many very different ways to program the mind to increase happiness or at least to avoid being unhappy. Some religions have done it by promising an eternal life of happiness follows our earthly existence. Others, on realizing that most unhappiness is the result of frustrated goals and thwarted desires, teach people to give up desires altogether and thus avoid disappointment. Still others, such as Yoga and Zen, have developed complex techniques for controlling the stream of thoughts and feelings, thereby providing the means for shutting out negative content from consciousness. Some of the most radical and sophisticated disciplines for self-control of the mind were those developed in India, culminating in the Buddhist teachings 25 centuries ago. Regardless of its truth content, faith in a supernatural order seems to enhance subjective well-being: Surveys generally show a low but consistent correlation between religiosity and happiness (Csikszentmihalyi & Patton, 1997; Myers, 1993).

Contemporary psychology has developed several solutions that share some of the premises of these ancient traditions but differ drastically in content and detail. What is common to them is the assumption that cognitive techniques, attributions, attitudes, and perceptual styles can change the effects of material conditions on consciousness, help restructure an individual's goals, and consequently improve the quality of experience. Maslow's (1968, 1971) *self-actualization*, Block and Block's (1980) *ego-resiliency*, Diener's (1984, 2000) *positive emotionality*, Antonovsky's (1979) *salutogenic approach*, Seeman's (1996) *personality integration*, Deci and Ryan's (1985; Ryan & Deci, 2000) *autonomy*, Scheier and Carver's (1985) *dispositional optimism*, and Seligman's (1991) *learned optimism* are only a few of the theoretical concepts developed recently, many with their own preventive and therapeutic implications.

THE EXPERIENCE OF FLOW My own addition to this list is the concept of the *autotelic experience*, or *flow*, and of the autotelic personality. The concept describes a particular kind of experience that is so engrossing and enjoyable that it becomes autotelic, that is, worth doing for its own sake even though it may have no consequence outside itself. Creative activities, music, sports, games, and religious rituals are typical sources for this kind of experience. Autotelic persons are those who have such flow experiences relatively often, regardless of what they are doing.

Of course, we never do anything purely for its own sake. Our motives are always a mixture of intrinsic and extrinsic considerations. For instance, composers may write music because they hope to sell it and pay the bills, because they want to become famous, because their self-image depends on writing songs—all of these being extrinsic motives. But if the composers are motivated only by these extrinsic rewards, they are missing an essential ingredient. In addition to these rewards, they could also enjoy writing music for its own sake—in which case, the activity would become autotelic. My studies (e.g., Csikszentmihalyi, 1975, 1996, 1997) have suggested that happiness depends on whether a person is able to derive flow from whatever he or she does.

A brief selection from one of the more than 10,000 interviews collected from around the world might provide a sense of what the flow experience

[1]This "self-organizing" ability is a classic concern of humanistic psychologists such as Maslow and Rogers.

is like. Asked how it felt when writing music was going well, a composer responded.

> You are in an ecstatic state to such a point that you feel as though you almost don't exist. I have experienced this time and time again. My hand seems devoid of myself, and I have nothing to do with what is happening. I just sit there watching in a state of awe and wonderment. And the music just flows out by itself. (Csikszentmihalyi, 1975, p. 44)

This response is quite typical of most descriptions of how people feel when they are thoroughly involved in something that is enjoyable and meaningful to the person. First of all, the experience is described as "ecstatic": in other words, as being somehow separate from the routines of everyday life. This sense of having stepped into a different reality can be induced by environmental cues, such as walking into a sport event, a religious ceremony, or a musical performance, or the feeling can be produced internally, by focusing attention on a set of stimuli with their own rules, such as the composition of music.

Next, the composer claims that "you feel as though you almost don't exist." This dimension of the experience refers to involvement in the activity being so demanding that no surplus attention is left to monitor any stimuli irrelevant to the task at hand. Thus, chess players might stand up after a game and realize that they have splitting headaches and must run to the bathroom, whereas for many hours during the game they had excluded all information about their bodily states from consciousness.

The composer also refers to the felt spontaneity of the experience: "My hand seems devoid of myself . . . I have nothing to do with what is happening." Of course, this sense of effortless performance is only possible because the skills and techniques have been learned and practiced so well that they have become automatic. This brings up one of the paradoxes of flow: One has to be in control of the activity to experience it, yet one should not try to consciously control what one is doing.

As the composer stated, when the conditions are right, action "just flows out by itself." It is because so many respondents used the analogy of spontaneous, effortless flow to describe how it felt when what they were doing was going well that I used the term *flow* to describe the autotelic experience. Here is what a well-known lyricist, a former poet laureate of the United States, said about his writing:

> You lose your sense of time, you're completely enraptured, you are completely caught up in what you're doing, and you are sort of swayed by the possibilities you see in this work. If that becomes too powerful, then you get up, because the excitement is too great. . . . The idea is to be so, so saturated with it that there's no future or past, it's just an extended present in which you are . . . making meaning. And dismantling meaning, and remaking it. (Csikszentmihalyi, 1996, p. 121)

This kind of intense experience is not limited to creative endeavors. It is reported by teenagers who love studying, by workers who like their jobs, by drivers who enjoy driving. Here is what one woman said about her sources of deepest enjoyment:

> [It happens when] I am working with my daughter, when she's discovered something new. A new cookie recipe that she has accomplished, that she has made herself, an artistic work that she's done and she is proud of. Her reading is something that she is really into, and we read together. She reads to me and I read to her, and that's a time when I sort of lose touch with the rest of the world. I am totally absorbed in what I am doing. (Allison & Duncan, 1988, p. 129)

This kind of experience has a number of common characteristics. First, people report knowing very clearly what they have to do moment by moment, either because the activity requires it (as when the score of a musical composition specifies what notes to play next), or because the person sets clear goals every step of the way (as when a rock climber decides which hold to try for next). Second, they are able to get immediate feedback on what they are doing. Again, this might be because the activity provides information about the performance (as when one is playing tennis and after each shot one knows whether the ball went where it was supposed to go), or it might be because the person has an internalized standard that makes it possible to know whether one's actions meet the standard (as when a poet reads the last word or the last sentence written and judges it to be right or in need of revision).

Another universal condition for the flow experience is that the person feels his or her abilities to act match the opportunities for action. If the challenges are too great for the person's skill, anxiety is likely to ensue; if the skills are greater than the challenges, one feels bored. When challenges are in balance with skills, one becomes lost in the activity and flow is likely to result (Csikszentmihalyi, 1975, 1997).

Even this greatly compressed summary of the flow experience should make it clear that it has little to do with the widespread cultural trope of "going with the flow." To go with the flow means to abandon oneself to a situation that feels good, natural, and spontaneous. The flow experience that I have been studying is something that requires skills, concentration, and perseverance. However, the evidence suggests that it is the second form of flow that leads to subjective well-being.

The relationship between flow and happiness is not entirely self-evident. Strictly speaking, during the experience people are not necessarily happy because they are too involved in the task to have the luxury to reflect on their subjective states. Being happy would be a distraction, an interruption of the flow. But afterward, when the experience is over, people report having been in as positive a state as it is possible to feel. Autotelic persons, those who are often in flow, tend also to report more positive states overall and to feel that their lives are more purposeful and meaningful (Adlai-Gail, 1994; Hektner, 1996).

The phenomenon of flow helps explain the contradictory and confusing causes of what we usually call happiness. It explains why it is possible to achieve states of subjective well-being by so many different routes: either by achieving wealth and power or by relinquishing them; by cherishing either solitude or close relationships; through ambition or through its opposite, contentment; through the pursuit of objective science or through religious practice. *People are happy not because of what they do, but because of how they do it.* If they can experience flow working on the assembly line, chances are they will be happy, whereas if they don't have flow while lounging at a luxury resort, they are not going to be happy. The same is true of the various psychological techniques for achieving positive mental health: If the process of becoming resilient or self-efficacious is felt to be boring or an external imposition, the technique is unlikely to lead to happiness, even if it is mastered to the letter. You have to enjoy mental health to benefit from it.

MAKING FLOW POSSIBLE The prerequisite for happiness is the ability to get fully involved in life. If the material conditions are abundant, so much the better, but lack of wealth or health need not prevent one from finding flow in whatever circumstances one finds at hand. In fact, our studies suggest that children from the most affluent families find it more difficult to be in flow—compared with less well-to-do teenagers, they tend to be more bored, less involved, less enthusiastic, less excited.

At the same time, it would be a mistake to think that each person should be left to find enjoyment wherever he or she can find it or to give up efforts for improving collective conditions. There is so much that could be done to introduce more flow in schools, in family life, in the planning of communities, in jobs, in the way we commute to work and eat our meals—in short, in almost every aspect of life. This is especially important with respect to young people. Our research suggests, for instance, that more affluent teenagers experience flow less often because, although they dispose of more material possessions, they spend less time with their parents, and they do fewer interesting things with them (Hunter, 1998). Creating conditions that make flow experiences possible is one aspect of that "pursuit of happiness" for which the social and political community should be responsible.

Nevertheless, flow alone does not guarantee a happy life. It is also necessary to find flow in activities that are complex, namely, activities that provide a potential for growth over an entire life span, allow for the emergence of new opportunities for action, and stimulate the development of new skills. A person who never learns to enjoy the company of others and who finds few opportunities within a meaningful social context is unlikely to achieve inner harmony (Csikszentmihalyi, 1993; Csikszentmihalyi & Rathunde, 1998; Inghilleri, 1999), but when flow comes from active physical, mental, or emotional involvement—from work, sports, hobbies, meditation, and interpersonal relationships—then the chances for a complex life that leads to happiness improve.

The Limits of Flow

There is at least one more important issue left to consider. In reviewing the history of materialism, I have discussed John Locke's warnings about the necessity of pursuing happiness with prudence and about the importance of distinguishing real from imaginary happiness. Are similar caveats applicable to flow? Indeed, flow is necessary to happiness, but it is not sufficient. This is because people can experience flow in activities that are enjoyable at the moment but will detract from enjoyment in the long run. For instance, when a person finds few meaningful opportunities for action in the environment, he or she will often resort to finding flow in activities that are destructive, addictive, or at the very least wasteful (Csikszentmihalyi & Larson, 1978; Sato, 1988). Juvenile crime is rarely a direct consequence of deprivation but rather is caused by boredom or the frustration teenagers experience when other opportunities for flow are blocked. Vandalism, gang fights, promiscuous sex, and experimenting with psychotropic drugs might provide flow at first, but such experiences are rarely enjoyable for long.

Another limitation of flow as a path to happiness is that a person might learn to enjoy an activity so much that everything else pales by comparison, and he or she then becomes dependent on a very narrow range of opportunities for action while neglecting to develop skills that would open up a much broader arena for enjoyment later. A chess master who can enjoy only the game and a workaholic who feels alive only while on the job are in danger of stunting their full development as persons and thus of forfeiting future opportunities for happiness.

In one respect, the negative impact on the social environment of an addiction to flow is less severe than that of an addiction to material rewards. Material rewards are zero–sum: To be rich means that others must be poor; to be famous means that others must be anonymous; to be powerful means that others must be helpless. If everyone strives for such self-limiting rewards, most people will necessarily remain frustrated, resulting in personal unhappiness and social instability. By contrast, the rewards of flow are open-ended and inexhaustible: If I get my joy from cooking Mediterranean food, or from surfing, or from coaching Little League, this will not decrease anyone else's happiness.

Unfortunately, too many institutions have a vested interest in making people believe that buying the right car, the right soft drink, the right watch, the right education will vastly improve their chances of being happy, even if doing so will mortgage their lives. In fact, societies are usually structured so that the majority is led to believe that their well-being depends on being passive and contented. Whether the leadership is in the hands of a priesthood, of a warrior caste, of merchants, or of financiers, their interest is to have the rest of the population depend on whatever rewards they have to offer—be it eternal life, security, or material comfort. But if one puts one's faith in being a passive consumer—of products, ideas, or mind-altering drugs—one is likely to be disappointed. However, materialist propaganda is clever and convincing. It is not so easy, especially for young people, to tell what is truly in their interest from what will only harm them in the long run. This is why John Locke cautioned people not to mistake imaginary happiness for real happiness and why 25 centuries ago Plato wrote that the most urgent task for educators is to teach young people to find pleasure in the right things. Now this task falls partly on our shoulders. The job description for psychologists should encompass discovering what promotes happiness, and the calling of psychologists should include bringing this knowledge to public awareness.

References

Adlai-Gail, W. (1994). *Exploring the autotelic personality.* Unpublished doctoral dissertation, University of Chicago.

Allison, M. T., & Duncan. M. C. (1988). Women, work, and flow. In M. Csikszentmihalyi & I. Csikszentmihalyi (Eds.). *Optimal experience: Psychological studies of flow in consciousness* (pp. 118–137). New York: Cambridge University Press.

Antonovsky, A. (1979). *Health, stress, and coping.* San Francisco: Jossey-Bass.

Benedikt, M. (1999). *Values.* Austin: The University of Texas Press.

Bentham, J. (1970). *An introduction to the principles of morals and legislation.* Darien. CT: Hafner. (Original work published 1789)

Block, J. H., & Block, J. (1980). The role of ego-control and ego-resiliency in the organization of behavior. In W. A. Collins (Ed.). *The Minnesota Symposium on Child Psychology* (Vol. 13, pp. 39–101). Hillsdale, NJ: Erlbaum.

Brickman, P., Coates, D., & Janoff-Bulman, R. (1978). Lottery winners and accident victims: Is happiness relative? *Journal of Personality and Social Psychology, 36,* 917–927.

Campbell, A. (1981). *The sense of well-being in America.* New York: McGraw-Hill.

Csikszentmihalyi, M. (1975). *Beyond boredom and anxiety.* San Francisco: Jossey-Bass.

Csikszentmihalyi, M. (1993). *The evolving self.* New York: HarperCollins.

Csikszentmihalyi, M. (1996). *Creativity: Flow and the psychology of discovery and invention.* New York: HarperCollins.

Csikszentmihalyi, M. (1997). *Finding flow.* New York: Basic Books.

Csikszentmihalyi, M., & Larson, R. (1978). Intrinsic rewards in school crime. *Crime and Delinquency, 24,* 322–335.

Csikszentmihalyi, M., & Patton, J. D. (1997). *Le bonheur, l'experience optimale et les valeurs spirituelles: Une etude empirique aupres d'adolescents* [Happiness, the optimal experience, and spiritual values: An empirical study of adolescents]. *Revue Quebecoise de Psychologie, 18,* 167–190.

Csikszentmihalyi, M., & Rathunde, K. (1998). The development of the person: An experiential perspective on the ontogenesis of psychological complexity: In R. M. Lerner (Ed.). *Handbook of child psychology* (5th ed., Vol. 1). New York: Wiley.

Csikszentmihalyi, M., & Schneider, B. (in press). *Becoming adult: How teenagers prepare for work.* New York: Basic Books.

Davis, J. A. (1959). A formal interpretation of the theory of relative deprivation. *Sociometry, 22,* 289–296.

Deci, E., & Ryan, M. (1985). *Intrinsic motivation and self-determination in human behavior.* New York: Plenum.

Diener, E. (1984). Subjective well-being. *Psychological Bulletin, 95,* 542–575.

Diener, E. (2000). Subjective well-being: The science of happiness, and a proposal for a national index. *American Psychologist, 55,* 34–43.

Diener, E., Horwitz, J., & Emmons, R. A. (1985). Happiness of the very wealthy. *Social Indicators, 16,* 263–274.

Epicurus of Samos, (1998). Achieving the happy life. *Free Inquiry, 18,* 47–48.

Hektner, J. (1996). *Exploring optimal personality development: A longitudinal study of adolescents.* Unpublished doctoral dissertation, University of Chicago.

Hunter, J. (1998). The importance of engagement: A preliminary analysis. *North American Montessori Teacher's Association Journal, 23,* 58–75.

Inghilleri, P. (1999). *From subjective experience to cultural evolution.* New York: Cambridge-University Press.

Inglehart, R. (1990). *Culture shift in advanced industrial society.* Princeton, NJ: Princeton University Press.

James, W. (1890). *Principles of psychology* (Vol. 1). New York: Holt.

Linder, S. (1970). *The harried leisure class.* New York: Columbia University Press.

Locke, J. (1975). *Essay concerning human understanding.* Oxford, England: Clarendon Press. (Original work published 1690)

Martin, J. (1981). Relative deprivation: A theory of distributive injustice for an era of shrinking resources. *Research in Organizational Behavior, 3,* 53–107.

Maslow, A. (1968). *Towards a psychology of being.* New York: Van Nostrand.

Maslow, A. (1971). *The farthest reaches of human nature.* New York: Viking.

Michalos, A. C. (1985). Multiple discrepancy theory (MDT). *Social Indicators Research, 16,* 347–413.

Myers, D. G. (1993). *The pursuit of happiness.* New York: Avon.

Myers, D. G. (2000). The funds, friends, and faith of happy people. *American Psychologist, 55,* 56–67.

Myers, D. G., & Diener, E. (1995). Who is happy? *Psychological Science, 6,* 10–19.

Parducci, A. (1995). *Happiness, pleasure, and judgment.* Mahwah, NJ: Erlbaum.

Pay nags at workers' job views. (1987, October 18). *Chicago Tribune,* 10B.

Polanyi, K. (1957). *The great transformation.* Boston: Beacon Press.

Rich think big about living well. (1987, September 24). *Chicago Tribune,* 3.

Ryan, R. M., & Deci, E. L. (2000). Self-determination theory and the facilitation of intrinsic motivation, social development, and well-being. *American Psychologist, 55,* 68–78.

Sato, I. (1988). Bozozoku: Flow in Japanese motorcycle gangs.

In M. Csikszentmihalyi & I. Csikszentmihalyi (Eds.), *Optimal experience* (pp. 92–117). New York: Cambridge University Press.

Scheier, M. F., & Carver, C. S. (1985). Optimism, coping, and health: Assessment and implications of generalized outcome expectancies. *Health Psychology, 4*, 210–247.

Scitovsky, T. (1975). *The joyless economy.* New York: Random House.

Seeman, (1996). Social ties and health: The benefits of social integration. *Annals of Epidemiology, 6*, 442–451.

Seligman, M. E. P. (1991). *Learned optimism.* New York: Random House.

Simon, H. A. (1969). *Sciences of the artificial.* Boston: MIT Press.

Voenhoven, R. (1988). The utility of happiness. *Social Indicators Research, 20*, 333–354.

Williams, R. M., Jr. (1975). Relative deprivation. In L. A. Coser (Ed.). *The idea of social structure: Papers in honor of Robert K. Merton* (pp. 355–378). New York: Harcourt Brace Jovanovich.

PART VI

Cross-cultural Approaches to Personality

Migrations and technological advances have caused many cultures around the world to become both increasingly diverse and increasingly interconnected. This is perhaps nowhere more true than in America, where subcultures of European, African, Latin, and Asian origin coexist within the same borders. But elsewhere in the world as well, cultural diversity is becoming more the rule than the exception.

It is only natural, therefore, that recent years have seen an increasing and international interest in the way psychological processes and personality might be different in different cultures. Sometimes this interest has led to broad claims that psychology is culturally specific and that nothing can be said about people in general. But more often, psychologists interested in culture have tried to draw general lessons out of comparing the personalities of people who live in different cultural contexts.

And not just different contexts. The first selection in this section, by the anthropologist Horace Miner, shows how turning an objective (though satirical), anthropological eye on any set of behavioral practices can make even the familiar and everyday seem exotic and strange. Culture is not something that is found only in other lands, this selection illustrates; it is something that surrounds us but may be difficult to see because of its very familiarity.

The second selection, by the psychologists Kuo-shu Yang and Michael Bond, illustrates one method for comparing different cultures to each other. Yang and Bond use questionnaires and psychometric methodology to investigate whether personality descriptions in Chinese can be reduced to the same Big Five traits many psychologists believe to be useful in English.

In the third selection, Hazel Markus and Shinobu Kitayama propose that Asian and Western cultures are more different than Yang and Bond might make them seem. They argue that the idea that the self is an independent, bounded entity that can be described by personality traits of any sort is itself a cultural construction—specifically, a construction of Western culture. Asian cultures, they assert, view the self as much more interconnected with other selves and with the culture at large. The reader might find it interesting to consider whether the findings of Yang and Bond, on the one hand, and Markus and Kitayama, on the other, can ever be reconciled.

The fourth selection is by the important cross-cultural psychologist Harry Triandis. Triandis seeks a middle ground between the idea of a "one size fits all" psychology and the radical deconstructionist idea that members of different cultures simply cannot be compared. Triandis proposes a triad of traits that can be used to characterize both individuals and whole cultures. Through the use of many examples, he demonstrates how the dimensions of collectivism–individualism, tightness–looseness, and complexity can account for an important part of the ways in which the psychologies of different cultures both differ from and are similar to one another.

The final two selections bring cross-cultural psychology closer to home. In an innovative piece of research, Dov Cohen and his colleagues use the familiar methods of experimental social psychology to examine the differences between two American subcultures—the north and the south. The last selection, by Carolyn Murray and her colleagues, examines some of the reasons why African Americans and Euro-Americans had, on average, such different reactions to the verdict of the O. J. Simpson trial. Interestingly, her method is based on the facts that while most African Americans thought him innocent, some believed him guilty, and that while most Euro-Americans thought him guilty, some believed him to be innocent. The research not only illustrates the basis of this difference between groups but also serves to remind us that members of a culture—Asian, Western, southern, African American, or any other—are not all the same. Important differences between people exist within as well as across cultures.

Body Ritual Among the Nacirema

Horace Miner

A frequent activity of anthropology is to focus our attention on the unfamiliar and sometimes strange-seeming aspects of another culture. This focus on the unfamiliar can leave the impression that "culture" is something that exists only in faraway, exotic locales. Furthermore, because each of us lives everyday within our own culture, it can be difficult to see the familiar aspects of it that, from an outsider's perspective, might seem as peculiar as anything that has been found anywhere else.

This selection, by Horace Miner, describes the interesting and complex practices of the "Nacirema" people concerning the care of their bodies. These practices might seem strange at first, but if you think about it you will soon realize that you know Nacirema culture very well. Culture is not something "other peoples" have; it is under our very noses.

From *American Anthropologist, 58*, 503–507, 1956.

The anthropologist has become so familiar with the diversity of ways in which different peoples behave in similar situations that he is not apt to surprised by even the most exotic customs. In fact, if all of the logically possible combinations of behavior have not been found somewhere in the world, he is apt to suspect that they must be present in some yet undescribed tribe.* * * In this light, the magical beliefs and practices of the Nacirema present such unusual aspects that it seems desirable to describe them as an example of the extremes to which human behavior can go.

Professor Linton first brought the ritual of the Nacirema to the attention of anthropologists twenty years ago (1936, p. 326), but the culture of this people is still very poorly understood. They are a North American group living in the territory between the Canadian Cree, the Yaqui and Tarahumare of Mexico, and the Carib and Arawak of the Antilles. Little is known of their origin, although tradition states that they came from the east. According to Nacirema mythology, their nation was originated by a culture hero, Notgnihsaw, who is otherwise known for two great feats of strength—the throwing of a piece of wampum across the river Pa-To-Mac and the chopping down of a cherry tree in which the Spirit of Truth resided.

Nacirema culture is characterized by a highly developed market economy which has evolved in a rich natural habitat. While much of the people's time is devoted to economic pursuits, a large part of the fruits of these labors and a considerable portion of the day are spent in ritual activity. The focus of this activity is the human body, the appearance and health of which loom as a dominant concern in the ethos of the people. While such a concern is certainly not unusual, its ceremonial aspects and associated philosophy are unique.

The fundamental belief underlying the whole system appears to be that the human body is ugly and that its natural tendency is to debility and disease. Incarcerated in such a body, man's only hope is to avert these characteristics through the use of the powerful influences of ritual and ceremony. Every household has one or more shrines devoted to this purpose. The more powerful individuals in the society have several shrines in their houses and, in fact, the opulence of a house is often referred to in terms of the number of such ritual centers it possesses. Most houses are of wattle and daub construction, but the shrine rooms of the more wealthy are walled with stone. Poorer families imitate the rich by applying pottery plaques to their shrine walls.

While each family has at least one such shrine, the rituals associated with it are not family ceremonies but are private and secret. The rites are normally only discussed with children, and then only during the period when they are being initiated into these mysteries. I was able, however, to establish sufficient rapport with the natives to examine these shrines and to have the rituals described to me.

The focal point of the shrine is a box or chest which is built into the wall. In this chest are kept the many charms and magical potions without which no native believes he could live. These preparations are secured from a variety of specialized practitioners. The most powerful of these are the medicine men, whose assistance must be rewarded with substantial gifts. However, the medicine men do not provide the curative potions for their clients, but decide what the ingredients should be and then write them down in an ancient and secret language. This writing is understood only by the medicine men and by the herbalists who, for another gift, provide the required charm.

The charm is not disposed of after it has served its purpose, but is placed in the charm-box of the household shrine. As these magical materials are specific for certain ills, and the real or imagined maladies of the people are many, the charm-box is usually full to overflowing. The magical packets are so numerous that people forget what their purposes were and fear to use them again. While the natives are very vague on this point, we can only assume that the idea in retaining all the old magical materials is that their presence in the charm-box, before which the body rituals are conducted, will in some way protect the worshipper.

Beneath the charm-box is a small font. Each day every member of the family, in succession, enters the shrine room, bows his head before the charm-box, mingles different sorts of holy water in the font, and proceeds with a brief rite of ablution. The holy waters are secured from the Water Temple of the community, where the priests conduct elaborate ceremonies to make the liquid ritually pure.

In the hierarchy of magical practitioners, and below the medicine men in prestige, are specialists whose designation is best translated "holy-mouth-men." The Nacirema have an almost pathological horror of and fascination with the mouth, the condition of which is believed to have a supernatural influence on all social relationships. Were it not for the rituals of the mouth, they believe that their teeth would fall out, their gums bleed, their jaws shrink, their friends desert them, and their lovers reject them. They also believe that a strong relationship exists between oral and moral characteristics. For example, there is a ritual ablution of the mouth for children which is supposed to improve their moral fiber.

The daily body ritual performed by everyone includes a mouth-rite. Despite the fact that these people are so punctilious about care of the mouth, this rite involves a practice which strikes the uninitiated stranger as revolting. It was reported to me that the ritual consists of inserting a small bundle of hog hairs into the mouth, along with certain magical powders, and then moving the bundle in a highly formalized series of gestures.

In addition to the private mouth-rite, the people seek out a holy-mouth-man once or twice a year. These practitioners have an impressive set of paraphernalia, consisting of a variety of augers, awls, probes, and prods. The use of these objects in the exorcism of the evils of the mouth involves almost unbelievable ritual torture of the client. The holy-mouth-man opens the client's mouth and, using the above mentioned tools, enlarges any holes which decay may have created in the teeth. Magical materials are put into these holes. If there are no naturally occurring holes in the teeth, large sections of one or more teeth are gouged out so that the supernatural substance can be applied. In the client's view, the purpose of these ministrations is to arrest decay and to draw friends. The extremely sacred and traditional character of the rite is evident in the fact that the natives return to the holy-mouth-men year after year, despite the fact that their teeth continue to decay.

It is to be hoped that, when a thorough study of the Nacirema is made, there will be careful inquiry into the personality structure of these people. One has but to watch the gleam in the eye of a holy-mouth-man, as he jabs an awl into an exposed nerve, to suspect that a certain amount of sadism is involved. If this can be established, a very interesting pattern emerges, for most of the population shows definite masochistic tendencies. It was to these that Professor Linton referred in discussing a distinctive part of the daily body ritual which is performed only by men. This part of the rite involves scraping and lacerating the surface of the face with a sharp instrument. Special women's rites are performed only four times during each lunar month, but what they lack in frequency is made up in barbarity. As part of this ceremony, women bake their heads in small ovens for about an hour. The theoretically interesting point is that what seems to be a preponderantly masochistic people have developed sadistic specialists.

The medicine men have an imposing temple, or *lati pso*, in every community of any size. The more elaborate ceremonies required to treat very sick patients can only be performed at this temple. These ceremonies involve not only the thaumaturge[1] but a permanent group of vestal maidens who move sedately about the temple chambers in distinctive costume and headdress.

The *lati pso* ceremonies are so harsh that it is phenomenal that a fair proportion of the really sick natives who enter the temple ever recover. Small children whose indoctrination is still incomplete have been known to resist attempts to take them to the temple because "that is where you go to die." Despite this fact, sick adults are not only willing but eager to undergo the protracted ritual purification, if they can afford to do so. No matter how ill the supplicant or how grave the emergency, the guardians of many temples do not admit a client if he cannot give a rich gift to the custodian. Even after he has gained admission and survived the ceremonies, the guardians will not permit the neophyte to leave until he makes still another gift.

The supplicant entering the temple is first stripped of all his or her clothes. In every-day life the Nacirema avoids exposure of his body and its natural functions. Bathing and excretory acts are performed only in the secrecy of the household shrine, where they are ritualized as part of the body-rites. Psychological shock results from the fact that body secrecy is suddenly lost upon entry into the *lati pso*. A man, whose own wife has never seen him in an excretory act, suddenly finds himself naked and assisted by a vestal maiden while he performs his natural functions into a sacred vessel. This sort of ceremonial treatment is necessitated by the fact that the excreta are used by a diviner to ascertain the course and nature of the client's sickness. Female clients, on the other hand, find their naked bodies are subjected to the scrutiny, manipulation and prodding of the medicine men.

Few supplicants in the temple are well enough to do anything but lie on their hard beds. The

---

[1]A "thaumaturge" is a performer of miracles or magical feats.

daily ceremonies, like the rites of the holy-mouth-men, involve discomfort and torture. With ritual precision, the vestals awaken their miserable charges each dawn and roll them about on their beds of pain while performing ablutions, in the formal movements of which the maidens are highly trained. At other times they insert magic wands in the supplicant's mouth or force him to eat substances which are supposed to be healing. From time to time the medicine men come to their clients and jab magically treated needles into their flesh. The fact that these temple ceremonies may not cure, and may even kill the neophyte in no way decreases the people's faith in the medicine men.

There remains one other kind of practitioner, known as a "listener." This witch-doctor has the power to exorcise the devils that lodge in the heads of people who have been bewitched. The Nacirema believe that parents bewitch their own children. Mothers are particularly suspected of putting a curse on children while teaching them the secret body rituals. The counter-magic of the witch-doctor is unusual in its lack of ritual. The patient simply tells the "listener" all his troubles and fears, beginning with the earliest difficulties he can remember. The memory displayed by the Nacirema in these exorcism sessions is truly remarkable. It is not uncommon for the patient to bemoan the rejection he felt upon being weaned as a babe, and a few individuals even see their troubles going back to the traumatic effects of their own birth.

In conclusion, mention must be made of certain practices which have their base in native esthetics but which depend upon the pervasive aversion to the natural body and its functions. There are ritual fasts to make fat people thin and ceremonial feasts to make thin people fat. Still other rites are used to make women's breasts larger if they are small, and smaller if they are large. General dissatisfaction with breast shape is symbolized in the fact that the ideal form is virtually outside the range of human variation. A few women afflicted with almost inhuman hypermammary development are so idolized that they make a handsome living by simply going from village to village and permitting the natives to stare at them for a fee.

Reference has already been made to the fact that excretory functions are ritualized, routinized, and relegated to secrecy. Natural reproductive functions are similarly distorted. Intercourse is taboo as a topic and scheduled as an act. Efforts are made to avoid pregnancy by the use of magical materials or by limiting intercourse to certain phases of the moon. Conception is actually very infrequent. When pregnant, women dress so as to hide their condition. Parturation takes place in secret, without friends or relatives to assist, and the majority of women do not nurse their infants.[2]

Our review of the ritual life of the Nacirema has certainly shown them to be magic-ridden people. It is hard to understand how they have managed to exist so long under the burdens which they have imposed upon themselves. But even such exotic customs as these take on real meaning when they are viewed with the insight provided by Malinowski when he wrote (1948: 70):

> Looking from far and above, from our high places of safety in the developed civilization, it is easy to see all the crudity and irrelevance of magic. But without its power and guidance early man could not have mastered his practical difficulties as he has done, nor could man have advanced to the higher stages of civilization.

References Cited

Lexton, Ralph. (1936). *The study of man.* New York: D. Appleton-Century Co.

Malnowski, Bronislaw. (1948). *Magic, science, and religion.* Glencoe: Free Press.

---

[2]Several of the "Nacireman" practices described in this article have changed since the 1950s, when the article was written. Here is one example: both breast-feeding of infants and a father's presence at birth are much more common today than they were then. But most of the strange aspects of this culture remain unchanged.

Exploring Implicit Personality Theories With Indigenous or Imported Constructs: The Chinese Case

Kuo-shu Yang and Michael Harris Bond

The next selection illustrates how cross-cultural psychologists examine the terms used to describe personality in different cultures. Kuo-shu Yang, a psychologist based in Taiwan, and Michael Bond, a psychologist who has lived and worked for many years in Hong Kong, collaborate on a comparison of "indigenous" versus "imported" constructs to describe personality in a Chinese culture. To this end, they apply an arsenal of psychometric techniques.

Yang and Bond begin with the observation that some cross-cultural research has made the mistake of beginning with Western or English terms, then assessing their applicability in other cultures. This approach reminds them of colonialism, in which an outside power imposes its view on a native culture. They argue that a preferable approach is to begin one's investigation within a culture, just as investigations of the Big Five began within English.

Yang and Bond began by culling 150 personality-trait adjectives from Chinese-language books and newspapers. They then had a sample of residents of Taiwan use these adjectives to describe six persons on a scale from 0 to 3. For purposes of comparison, they also had these same subjects use translations of 20 terms used, in English, to assess the Big Five.

Yang and Bond then did a factor analysis—a statistical technique for assessing correlations among variables and reducing many down to a few—of the Chinese adjectives and came up with five factors. They then correlated the "Chinese Big Five" with the English Big Five.

Perhaps inevitably, the conclusion they reached was less than crystal clear. There seems to be some overlap between the Chinese and English five factors, and some important differences. The lesson of this research, therefore, may be that to ask "are the five factors universal?" is to ask the wrong question. A better question is, what are the important terms for understanding personality within each of the major cultures of the world? Yang and Bond provide a good start toward the answer to this question for the Chinese culture of Taiwan.

From *Journal of Personality and Social Psychology, 58,* 1087–1095, 1990.

The semantic repertoire of a language has been treated as a repository for those constructs that its community of users has found useful in parceling their natural and human world (Dixon, 1977). For this reason, psychologists have often turned to the trait lexicon of a language in their search for the fundamental dimensions used by that language community in perceiving persons. As John, Goldberg, and Angleitner (1984) have argued,

> A taxonomy of these personality descriptors can provide us with a systematic account of how people who speak that language conceive of personality, especially which kinds of individual differences they regard as most important in their daily transactions. (p. 86)

The typical procedure involves a number of steps: First, a representative selection of the descriptors for personality functioning is taken; second, this subset is further refined to eliminate synonyms, and occasionally to group similar items into clusters; third, the resulting list is presented to speakers of that language to rate the applicability of each trait or trait scale to a target person, usually peers; and fourth, these ratings are intercorrelated across targets and dimensions of person perception are then extracted, usually by factor analysis (e.g., Goldberg, 1981).

In an earlier study, Tupes and Christal (1961) isolated five orthogonal factors used by Americans to perceive one another, namely, Surgency, Agreeableness, Conscientiousness, Emotional Stability, and Culture (also, see Norman, 1963). These five dimensions have also been unearthed by Goldberg (1981), using variations in procedure and subject populations. There is still considerable debate over the number and nature of such dimensions (Peabody & Goldberg, 1989), but for our purposes, it seemed safe to conclude that these Big Five dimensions of personality variation may represent the basic ways in which persons from the United States construct their interpersonal world (Digman & Takemoto-Chock, 1981), that is, one representation of the implicit personality theory of Americans.

How strongly may one claim that these five dimensions are universal or pancultural? To date, the descriptions used by Norman (1963) have been imported into three very different cultures, namely, those of the Philippines (Guthrie & Bennett, 1971), Japan (Bond, Nakazato, & Shiraishi, 1975), and Hong Kong (Bond, 1979). Broadly, the results may be synthesized to indicate that university students in all three societies use at least the first four of these dimensions and construe them in roughly similar ways.

The shortfall of this research approach, however, is that raters outside the United States have been invited to use personality descriptors taken from the English language and then interpreted by Americans. It has not yet been determined how dimensions derived by this use of the American materials might overlap with those derived from that culture's own language system. Do users of the Chinese language, for example, blend conscientiousness and agreeableness to form a broader dimension of social morality, as Yang and Bond (1985) asserted? Nor is it certain how successfully the imported American materials allow researchers to detect the full range of dimensions for perception available in the host culture's legacy of personality language. So, does the failure to detect a separable dimension of Culture in the Philippines (Guthrie & Bennett, 1971) reflect its absence in Tagalog or merely the insensitivity of the American descriptors for this language community?

A small but growing number of studies have begun appearing that examine the dimensions of personality perception available to users of languages other than English (e.g., Brokken, 1978; Nakazato, Bond, & Shiraishi, 1976; Yang & Bond, 1985). In many cases the dimensions so elicited bear a striking resemblance to those originally found in the United States. So, for example, Brokken's Agreeableness appears to correspond with the American. In other cases, some interpretive leap to assert equivalence is made by psychologists fluent in both linguistic and cultural systems. So, for example, Yang and Bond maintained that their Extraversion corresponds with Norman's (1963) Extraversion. In yet other cases, dimensions emerge for which no clear parallel with the Big Five appears obvious. So, for example, Nakazato et al.'s Volition is difficult to relate to any of the American dimensions.

A more objective solution to this equivalence issue could be achieved by including the 20 bipolar descriptors[1] used by Norman (1963) along with the pool of descriptors gleaned from the indigenous language. The resulting pattern of intercorrelations would then indicate how the items defining the American Big Five align themselves with respect to native dimensions. One could determine, for example, whether the American clusters are divided or combined when associating with local factors, whether the American groupings define unique dimensions of perceptual space, and whether the indigenous language isolates novel factors immune to the American probes. Any of these results would have important implications for cross-cultural person perception, and hence interaction (Bond & Forgas, 1984).

The issue of importing measuring tools versus developing indigenous materials enjoys a classic status in cross-cultural psychology, where it is related to the emic-etic issue (Berry, 1969).[2] The law of least effort combined with psychology's origin in the West has meant that many cultures elsewhere have been studied through a foreign looking glass. Psychologists interested in a particular construct, say locus of control (Hui, 1982), translate the relevant test into the local language, administer it to comparable groups, and then make comparative statements about psychological process. Because this approach assumes the universal or etic status of the underlying construct and applies it in cultures where its status is uncertain, this approach to research has been labeled *imposed etic*.

This ubiquitous procedure has obvious parallels in the colonial experience that many of these now liberated countries have struggled to put behind them, and understandably draws considerable fire (see e.g., Yang, 1986). In the midst of these political and social debates, however, the scientific issue is easy to overlook, namely, are the imposed etics in fact tapping culture-general processes, as hoped, or pasting one culture's emic or particular processes over another's checkerboard of constructs, as feared? In the area of intelligence, for example, there is evidence of considerable construct equivalence from culture to culture (Vandenberg, 1959, 1967). With one or two exceptions, however, there is much less research on this problem in the area of social processes (Bond, 1988b; Triandis & Marin, 1983). This study enables the examination of this volatile issue in the area of person perception, because its design involves the rating of common target persons with both imported and indigenous constructs, using their attendant measurement scales.

In this case, we are examining the rich legacy of the Chinese language, as used by inhabitants of Taiwan. This would appear to be a useful group to compare with the American for a number of reasons. There is a substantial body of empirical knowledge about the Chinese (Bond, 1986) to which the findings may be linked, and growing evidence that the Chinese will modernize in ways different from cultures in the West (Bond & King, 1985; Chinese Culture Connection, 1987; Yang, 1988). Furthermore, the Chinese are activated by collectivist concerns (Hsu, 1953). This cultural di-

[1]This refers to pairs of opposite traits used in earlier research by Norman to measure the Big Five traits of personality. These included "talkative-silent," "adventurous-cautious," and others.

[2]The emic-etic issue refers to the distinction between aspects of thought that are universal, or "etic," versus those that are local, or "emic."

mension of collectivism-individualism is receiving considerable theoretical (Triandis, 1978) and empirical (Triandis et al., 1986) attention these days, and may provide a fulcrum for prying the psychological mainstream loose from its Western center of gravity (Bond, 1988a). Results of the research linking Chinese and American dimensions of personality perception should thus command more than local interest.

Method

INSTRUMENTS In the present study, two major assessment instruments were used for data collection. The first had six versions specifically designed to use the same set of 150 personality-trait adjectives in the Chinese language to describe six different target persons significant in one's life. The 150 personality-trait adjectives used in each questionnaire were drawn from a pool of 557 Chinese personality-trait adjectives that had earlier been collected by Yang and Lee (1971) to form a compendium representative of the most widely used personality-descriptive predicates of the Chinese language. This breadth was ensured by selecting trait descriptors from a variety of printed media, including books and newspapers.

To choose the best adjectives for use in the present study, Yang and Lee's (1971) 557 entries were first classified into three groups:

1. Other-oriented adjectives, which describe personality traits that concern mainly behavior involving some other person or group; examples are *considerate, gregarious, obedient*, and *patriotic*.
2. Thing-oriented adjectives, which describe personality traits that concern mainly behavior involving some external thing or things; examples are *greedy, punctual, superstitious*, and *thrifty*.
3. Self-oriented adjectives, which describe personality traits that concern behavior that involves neither other persons nor groups, nor an external thing or things; examples are *changeable, clever, moody*, and *self-respectful*.

Adjectives in each of these three groups were further divided into three subgroups in terms of their average ratings on social desirability (SD) provided in Yang and Lee's list. Adjectives with an SD average greater than 5.28 (on a 7-step rating scale that ranged from 1 to 7) were considered positive, those with an SD value smaller than 2.87 were considered negative, and those with an SD value between these were considered neutral.

The semantic meanings of the adjectives in each of nine subgroups were carefully examined and compared, and those whose meanings were vague, ambiguous, or similar to some other adjective in the same subgroup were discarded. From the remaining pool, about one third of all adjectives were randomly chosen in proportion to the percentages of adjectives in the nine subgroups. The 150 adjectives so obtained were considered an unbiased sample representative of the most frequently used trait adjectives in the Chinese language. It is in this sense that such adjectives may be said to be emic or indigenous in nature.

Given that the adjectives were culled from newspapers, they represent Chinese written talk about personality. This written talk is identical to that used in other Chinese communities, however, as virtually the same written script is used in China and in Hong Kong, Singapore, and elsewhere.

The same 150 adjectives with a fixed randomized order were used to construct six separate versions for the assessment of the emic dimensions of Chinese person perception with respect to the six most familiar persons in one's life. Specifically, the same adjectives were used to describe the following six target persons in six different questionnaires: (a) your own father, (b) your own mother, (c) your best known teacher, (d) your most familiar neighbor, (e) your best friend of the same sex, and (f) yourself.

In each questionnaire the subject was supposed to use the adjectives to describe the specific target person on a four-step rating scale ranging from 0 to 3. He or she was required to indicate how much the target person possessed the personality trait described by each adjective: *definitely not at all* (0), *just a little* (1), *substantially* (2), or *very much* (3). To raise the validity of the subject's responses, the instructions in the questionnaire reminded the subject that he or she should describe the personality of the rated target person as objectively as possible without being influenced by his or her affect, no matter how strong it was toward that person, that he or she should do each rating as independently as possible without letting the rating of one trait be affected by that of the others, and that data collected from all subjects would be statistically analyzed on a group basis, rather than on an individual basis.

Another major assessment tool in this study was composed of the 20 bipolar rating scales drawn from Cattell's (1947) reduced personality sphere set on the basis of the results of several analyses presented by Tupes and Christal (1958). The four scales with the highest median factor loadings for each of the following five factors identified in these earlier analyses were chosen: Extraversion (or Surgency), Agreeableness, Conscientiousness, Emotional Stability, and Culture (see Norman, 1963).[3] The bipolar descriptions of the 20 personality traits were first translated into Chinese and then checked using the back-translation procedure (Brislin, 1970).[4] The 20 anchored rating scales in the final Chinese version were converted into a seven-step format with a labeled neutral point, rather than the original peer-nomination, forced-choice format used in the studies by Tupes and Christal (1958) and Norman (1961, 1963). All 20 scales were printed in the same randomized order in the six different questionnaires for those six target persons. When applied to Chinese subjects, these translated scales would provide empirical measures of person perception that are obviously imposed etic in Berry's (1969) sense.

The inventory of adjectives and of bipolar descriptions for the same target person were put together in that order to form a questionnaire for that person. The six questionnaires so constructed were labeled Questionnaire A (*father*), B (*mother*), C (*teacher*), D (*neighbor*), E (*friend*), and F (*self*).

Subjects Adequate comprehension of the exact meanings of the instructions, adjectives, and descriptions in each questionnaire requires a rather high level of Chinese literacy. For this reason, only university and college students were used as subjects. In total, more than 2,000 Chinese students were drawn from 60 different departments of seven universities and four colleges in northern Taiwan (mostly in Taipei). Each subject had to complete two of the six questionnaires as a set, and different students in each class received different sets of questionnaires according to a prearranged systematic order to ensure that the obtained samples would be sufficiently equivalent or comparable in their composition.

After eliminating those few subjects who were unable to complete their questionnaires, the following sizes of the samples for the various target persons were obtained, that is. Questionnaire A (*father*), 718; B (*mother*), 692; C (*teacher*), 636; D (*neighbor*), 633; E (*friend*), 670; and F (*self*), 668. In each of the six samples, approximately half of the subjects were male and half were female. Each sample was composed of more first- and second-year students than third- and fourth-year students.

Procedure The six questionnaires were divided into three sets of two each, namely, *AD*, *BE*, and *CF*. About 800 copies of each set were printed and thoroughly mixed with copies of the other two sets. More than 2,000 copies of questionnaire sets were administered to the subjects on a group basis in their classrooms. Care was taken to make the final sample for each target person consist of students with approximately equal proportions by sex, from all four years, and from such major colleges as agriculture, engineering, law, liberal arts, medicine, science, and social sciences.

Each time the questionnaires were given to the subjects by one of the research assistants experienced in test administration, without the teacher's being present. Each subject was allowed to take as

[3]Yang and Bond have just described how they chose the 20 trait terms to serve, in translation, as measures of the Big Five for comparison purposes.

[4]"Back-translation" is a procedure for ensuring the accuracy of translation from one language to another. A translated word or phrase is translated back to its original language, and a native speaker of the original language compares the translation with the original.

TABLE 39.1

MOST SALIENT VARIABLES AND THEIR AVERAGE VARIMAX LOADINGS ON THE FIVE FACTORS

Salient variable	Average loading	Salient variable	Average loading	Salient variable	Average loading	Salient variable	Average loading
Social Orientation–Self-Centeredness				Expressiveness–Conservatism (continued)			
Honest	.61	Untruthful	−.53	Straightforward	.43	Rigid	−.45
Good and gentle	.57	Selfish	−.50	Humorous	.43	Solemn	−.43
Loyal	.55	Opportunistic	−.49	Talkative	.43	Awkward	−.41
Cordial	.55	Sly	−.49	Mischievous	.41	Introverted	−.41
Kind	.54	Greedy	−.47	Optimistic	.39	Stubborn	−.35
Friendly	.48	Naughty	−.47	Broad-minded	.38	Indifferent	−.35
Frank	.48	Ruthless	−.45	Gracious	.37		
Morally clean	.47	Merciless	−.44	Generous	.36		
Responsible	.45	Hostile	−.44	Self-Control–Impulsiveness			
Gracious	.43	Harsh	−.44	Quiet and refined	.42	Impulsive	−.55
Competence–Impotence				Cultured	.41	Irritable	−.53
Determined	.46	Dependent	−.49	Modest	.40	Frivolous	−.42
Resolute and firm	.46	Fearful	−.48	Upright and correct	.38	Bad-tempered	−.42
Capable	.46	Timid	−.48	Self-possessed	.37	Headstrong	−.39
Tactful	.46	Childish	−.43	Steady	.36	Stubborn	−.38
Brave	.44	Foolish	−.41	Objective	.35	Opinionated	−.37
Smart	.43	Dull	−.40			Extreme	−.37
Rational	.43	Shallow	−.39	Optimism–Neuroticism			
Independent	.42	Vulgar	−.36	Optimistic	.47	Moody	−.67
Wise	.42	Shy	−.35	Pleasant	.38	Worrying	−.64
Quick and sharp	.41	Self-disdainful	−.34	Self-confident	.34	Pessimistic	−.55
Expressiveness–Conservatism						Anxious	−.50
Vivacious	.56	Old-fashioned	−.46			Sensitive	−.42
Passionate	.47	Conservative	−.46			Self-pitying	−.38

Note. Data is derived from the 150 adjective scales for the six target persons (i.e., father, mother, teacher, neighbor, friend, and self).

much time as he or she needed to complete the anonymous questionnaire.

The final samples for the six target persons were composed of about four times as many respondents as the total number of variables (150 + 20 = 170). The dimensions of Chinese person perception were identified by separately factor analyzing the data collected by the adjective inventory and those collected by the bipolar descriptions, one pair of such analyses for each of the six target persons. The emic dimensions were then related to the imposed etic dimensions for the same target person by correlational analysis.

Results

EMIC DIMENSIONS

* * *

* * * [For each of the six target persons,] a transformation procedure was adopted to standardize each subject's raw scores on the 150 adjective scales into *z* scores with the mean of the

150 raw scores as the origin and the standard deviation as the unit. We then carried out separate factor analyses for the six target persons, starting with correlational matrices computed from standardized scores. The principal-axis and varimax procedures were used as the methods for factoring and rotation, respectively, and the number of extracted factors was determined simultaneously by the scree test and the examination of the salient variables and their loadings obtained in several trial factor analyses.[5]

THE CHINESE BIG FIVE For each target person, five–six bipolar[6] factors were finally identified to represent the emic dimensions of Chinese person perception. * * * Although the number of factors extracted varied slightly, five were common to all the targets. The most salient variables, and their average loadings, for each of these five common factors are given in Table 39.1.[7] The semantic meanings of the salient adjectives for the various factors justify the use of the following verbal titles for factor labeling: *Social Orientation–Self-Centeredness, Competence–Impotence, Expressiveness–Conservatism, Self-Control–Impulsiveness,* and *Optimism–Neuroticism.* These five bipolar factors may be regarded as the basic emic dimensions of Chinese person perception.

* * *

OVERLAP OF INDIGENOUS AND IMPORTED FACTORS Five-factor solutions have been proposed for both the indigenous and the imported descriptors of personality. In terms of the relation between these two sets of factors, a number of questions can be asked.

First, are there any indigenous factors that are not represented in the perceptual space defined by the imported factors? The answer to this question addresses the issue of whether imported instruments overlook dimensions that are used and tapped by local descriptors.

Second, for those indigenous factors that can be so defined, is there a one-to-one correspondence between an imported factor and an indigenous factor? The answer to this question addresses the issue of whether the imported instrument cuts the perceptual pie into the same segments as does the indigenous instrument.

Third, what is the overall degree of overlap between the indigenous set of personality trait dimensions and the imported set? This global question summarizes the preceding, more specific questions.

To address these three questions we computed approximate factor scores for each subject's rating of the six target persons, using the five indigenous and five imported dimensions. For the indigenous items, we calculated a factor score by summing the scores of the salient variables defining the factors as listed in Table 39.1; for the imported items, we calculated it by summing scores on bipolar descriptions with loadings greater than .50.

We computed an intercorrelation matrix of the indigenous and imported factor scores for each of the six targets. An average of these correlations was then taken, based on their Z score transformations (see Table 39.2).[8]

* * *

Discussion

The purpose of this study was to examine the relation between indigenous and imported descriptors of personality. We argued that a fair examination of both emics and imposed etics

[5]This is a description of the standard technical procedure for deciding how many factors serve as an adequate summary of a longer list of adjectives.

[6]Factors each labeled by a pair of opposite terms.

[7]The numbers [varimax loadings] in Table 39.1 can be interpreted as correlations between each term and the factor with which it is associated.

[8]Yang and Bond reported several other, more technical analyses that have been omitted from this excerpt. Their results are presented most clearly in Table 39.2. This table shows the correlations between the English Big Five, down the rows, and the Chinese Big Five, across the columns. The two schemes clearly overlap, and equally clearly are not perfectly equivalent.

TABLE 39.2

AVERAGE CORRELATIONS BETWEEN THE EMIC AND IMPOSED ETIC FACTORS

Imposed etic factor	Emic factors S-S	C-I	E-C	S-I	O-N
Extraversion	.21	.09	.51	.01	.16
Agreeableness	.66	.29	.30	.56	.14
Conscientiousness	.28	.31	−.09	.43	.01
Emotional Stability	.35	.55	.36	.43	.44
Culture	.29	.50	.37	.28	.11

Note. Data derived from the six target persons (i.e., father, mother, teacher, neighbor, friend, and self).
S-S = Social Orientation–Self-Centeredness, C-I = Competence–Importance,
E-C = Expressiveness–Conservatism, S-I = Self-Control–Impulsiveness,
O-N = Optimism–Neurotism, respectively.

would help address the tempestuous issue of cultural imperialism in psychology (Bond, 1988a, 1988b; Enriquez, 1988; Sampson, 1985; Yang, 1986). There are, of course, important personal, social, and political dimensions underlying this concern. The intellectual component of the concern, however, is that the importation of foreign instrumentation and theorizing results in an incomplete and distorted science. This study was conducted to provide some empirical ballast that is in short supply.

For the area of person perception, this debate can be focused on the concern about whether salient constructs in the local culture will be overlooked by the foreign scales, and how close the degree of overlap is, both overall and for specific dimensions.

To address these questions, Chinese personality descriptors were gathered in a manner that ensured that the resulting sample would be both comprehensive and representative of terms in use. Although a culling was not made from the dictionary, it is extremely unlikely that any personality dimension of importance has been neglected by sampling from newspapers. Indeed, the five factors extracted from the Chinese terms have a breadth and validity that [are] readily apparent to any Chinese psychologist. They constitute obvious starting points for anyone exploring the functional relations between these dimensions of personality perception and social behavior (e.g., Bond & Forgas, 1984) or personality itself (e.g., McCrae & Costa, 1987).

If only these indigenous materials had been used, many cross-culturalists would probably have detected some apparent universals. Optimism–Neuroticism would have been tied to Emotional Stability, Expressiveness to Extraversion, and so forth. Indeed, in our earlier report (Yang & Bond, 1985), we asserted that Social Orientation was a blend of Agreeableness and Conscientiousness. By actually including the original markers for these American dimensions, however, a more reliable and sobering pattern emerges.

So, Optimism does indeed relate to Emotional Stability, but Emotional Stability is in fact correlated more highly with Competence. Expressiveness does indeed relate to Extraversion, but it is also significantly related to Culture and Emotional Stability and is negatively related to Conscientiousness. Social Orientation does indeed relate strongly to Agreeableness, but its connection to Conscientiousness is dramatically smaller. In fact, the addition of the other four imported factors to Agreeableness only increased the variance explained in Social Orientation by 3.4%, from 43.6% to 47.0%.

Overall, the imported dimensions do a reasonable job of identifying four of the five indigenous factors. There is, however, a one-to-one correspondence for only one of these four factors. Even there, only 43.6% of the variance was shared. Of course, reliability issues may lower the estimate of overlap, but one could well ask if construct identity has been established; even in this one case it is unlikely that Social Orientation and Agreeableness ratings would bear the same relation to other criterion variables (as, for example, in Bond & Forgas, 1984). McCrae and Costa (1987) have argued the case that Norman's Big Five represent fundamental dimensions of personality and are perceived because they map a reality inherent in other people. As such, these dimensions are in the targets and hence need to be assessed with some degree of accuracy for effective social functioning. This assessment will then be tied to various dimensions of interpersonal behavior. Consistent with this reasoning is Bond's (1983) study, animated by Gibson's (1979) dictum that "Perception is for doing" (p. 143).[9] Bond argued that each dimension of personality perception functioned to guide the perceiver's responses toward the target across the fundamental dimensions of interpersonal behavior (Triandis, 1978), reasoning that has been confirmed cross-culturally (Bond & Forgas, 1984). We hope that more research energy will be directed to this interpersonal aspect of the perception issue (Tagiuri, 1969).

Returning to this study, we must acknowledge an inevitable arbitrariness in our conclusions about overlap in the indigenous and imported measures. There is no scientific rule to help us answer the question of how much similarity is enough. The bottom line is variance explained and how much slippage one is willing to tolerate. Although we believe that indigenous instruments will evidence more powerful relation to criterion variables than will imports, this empirical issue has not been addressed in the present study. We hope that future research will grasp this fascinating nettle (e.g., Triandis & Marin, 1983).

Even if our confidence in local instruments is vindicated, they will only be relatively better than imports. There will always be an obvious trade-off, as considerable time and energy can be saved by importing instruments as compared with developing them locally. Many social scientists will sacrifice and have sacrificed the putative power of indigenous instruments for the convenience of using ready-made imports.

As we have discovered, however, the pattern of interrelations between imported and indigenous factors is complex. The construct validation of the imported and indigenous instruments is likely to yield somewhat different theories about the local reality (often construed as reality) even if they are both true (i.e., useful). And it is this broader area of indigenous theory development that the use of imported instruments may especially compromise.

[9]This is an oft-quoted maxim of the psychologist J. J. Gibson, who studied visual perception.

References

Berry, J. W. (1969). On cross-cultural comparability. *International Journal of Psychology, 4,* 119–128.

Bond, M. H. (1979). Dimensions of personality used in perceiving peers: Cross-cultural comparisons of Hong Kong, Japanese, American, and Filipino university students. *International Journal of Psychology, 14,* 47–56.

Bond, M. H. (1983). Linking person perception dimensions to behavioral intention dimensions: The Chinese connection. *Journal of Cross-Cultural Psychology, 14,* 41–63.

Bond, M. H. (Ed.). (1986). *The psychology of the Chinese people.* Hong Kong: Oxford University Press.

Bond, M. H. (Ed.). (1988a). *The cross-cultural challenge to social psychology.* Newbury Park, CA: Sage.

Bond, M. H. (1988b). Finding universal dimensions of individual variation in multicultural studies of values: The Rokeach and Chinese value surveys. *Journal of Personality and Social Psychology, 55,* 1009–1015.

Bond, M. H., & Forgas, J. P. (1984). Linking person perception to behavioral intention across cultures. The role of cultural collectivism. *Journal of Cross-Cultural Psychology, 15,* 337–352.

Bond, M. H., & King, A. Y. C. (1985). Coping with the threat of Westernization in Hong Kong. *International Journal of Intercultural Relations, 9,* 351–364.

Bond, M. H., Nakazato, H., & Shiraishi, D. (1975). Universality and distinctiveness in dimensions of Japanese person perception. *Journal of Cross-Cultural Psychology, 6,* 346–57.

Brislin, R. W. (1970). Back-translation for cross-cultural research. *Journal of Cross-Cultural Psychology, 1,* 185–216.

Brokken, F. B. (1978). *The language of personality.* Unpublished doctoral dissertation, University of Groningen, The Netherlands.

Cattell, R. B. (1947). Confirmation and clarification of primary personality traits. *Psychometrica, 42,* 402–421.

Chinese Culture Connection. (1987). Chinese values and the search for culture-free dimensions of culture. *Journal of Cross-Cultural Psychology, 18,* 143–164.

Digman, J. M., & Takemoto-Chock, N. K. (1981). Factors in the natural language of personality: Reanalysis, comparison and interpretation of six major studies. *Multivariate Behavioral Research, 16,* 149–170.

Dixon, R. M. W. (1977). Where have all the adjectives gone? *Studies in Language, 1,* 19–80.

Enriquez, V. (1988). The structure of Philippine social values: Towards integrating indigenous values and appropriate technology. In D. Sinha & H. S. R. Kao (Eds.), *Social values and development: Asian perspectives* (pp. 124–148). New Delhi, India: Sage.

Gibson, J. J. (1979). *The ecological approach to visual perception.* Boston: Houghton Mifflin.

Goldberg, L. R. (1981). Language and individual differences: The search for universals in personality lexicons. In L. Wheeler (Ed.), *Review of personality and social psychology* (Vol. 2, pp. 141–165). Beverly Hills, CA: Sage.

Guthrie, G. M., & Bennett, A. B. (1971). Cultural differences in implicit personality theory. *International Journal of Psychology, 6,* 305–312.

Hsu, F. L. K. (1953). *Americans and Chinese: Two ways of life.* New York: Abelard-Schuman.

Hui, C. C. H. (1982). Locus of control: A review of cross-cultural research. *International Journal of Intercultural Relations, 6,* 301–323.

John, O. P., Goldberg, L. R., & Angleitner, A. (1984). Better than the alphabet: Taxonomics of personality descriptive terms in English, Dutch, and German. In H. Bonarius, G. van Heck, & N. Smid (Eds.), *Personality psychology in Europe: Theoretical and empirical developments* (pp. 83–100). Lisse, The Netherlands: Swets & Zeitlinger.

McCrae, R. R., & Costa, P. T., Jr. (1987). Validation of the five-factor model of personality across instruments and observers. *Journal of Personality and Social Psychology, 52,* 81–90.

Nakazato, H., Bond, M. H., & Shiraishi, D. (1976). Dimensions of personality perception: An examination of Norman's hypothesis. *Japanese Journal of Psychology, 47,* 139–148. (In Japanese)

Norman, W. T. (1961). Development of self-report tests to measure personality factors identified from peer nominations (USAF ASD *Technical Note* No. 61-44).

Norman, W. T. (1963). Toward an adequate taxonomy of personality attributes: Replicated factor structure in peer nomination personality ratings. *Journal of Abnormal and Social Psychology, 66,* 574–583.

Peabody, D., & Goldberg, L. R. (1989). Some determinants of factor structures from personality-trait descriptors. *Journal of Personality and Social Psychology, 57,* 552–567.

Sampson, E. E. (1985). The decentralization of identity: Toward a revised concept of personal and social order. *American Psychologist, 40,* 1203–1211.

Tagiuri, R. (1969). Person perception. In G. Lindzey & E. Aronson (Eds.), *The handbook of social psychology* (2nd ed., Vol. 3, pp. 395–449). Reading, MA: Addison-Wesley.

Triandis, H. C. (1978). Some universals of social behavior. *Personality and Social Psychology Bulletin, 4,* 1–16.

Triandis, H. C., Bontempo, R., Betancourt, H., Bond, M. H., Leung, K., Brenes, A., Georgas, J., Hui, H. C., Marin, G., Setiadi, B., Sinha, J. B. P., Verma, J., Spangenberg, J., Touzard, H., & de Montmollin, G. (1986). The measurement of the etic aspects of individualism and collectivism across cultures. *Australian Journal of Psychology, 38,* 257–267.

Triandis, H. C., & Marin, G. (1983). Etic plus emic versus pseudo etic: A test of a basic assumption of contemporary cross-cultural psychology. *Journal of Cross-Cultural Psychology, 14,* 489–499.

Tupes, E. C., & Christal, R. E. (1958). Stability of personality trait rating factors obtained under diverse conditions (USAF WADC *Technical Note* No. 58-61).

Tupes, E. C., & Christal, R. E. (1961). Recurrent personality factors based on trait ratings. (USAF ASD *Technical Report* No. 61-97).

Vandenberg, S. G. (1959). The primary mental abilities of Chinese students: A comparative study of the stability of a factor structure. *Annals of the New York Academy of Sciences, 79,* 257–304.

Vandenberg, S. G. (1967). The primary mental abilities of South American students: A second comparative study of the generality of a cognitive factor structure. *Multivariate Behavioral Research, 2,* 175–198.

Yang, K. S. (1986). Chinese personality and its change. In M. H. Bond (Ed.), *The psychology of the Chinese people* (pp. 106–170). Hong Kong: Oxford University Press.

Yang, K. S. (1988). Will societal modernization eventually eliminate cross-cultural psychological differences? In M. H. Bond (Ed.), *The cross-cultural challenge to social psychology* (pp. 67–85). Newbury Park, CA: Sage.

Yang, K. S., & Bond, M. H. (1985). Dimensions of Chinese person perception: An emic approach. In C. Chiao (Ed.), *Proceedings of the conference on modernization and Chinese culture* (pp. 309–325). Hong Kong: Institute of Social Studies, Chinese University of Hong Kong. (In Chinese)

Yang, K. S., & Lee, P. H. (1971). Likeability, meaningfulness, and familiarity of 557 Chinese adjectives for personality trait description. *Acta Psychologica Taiwanica, 13,* 36–37. (In Chinese)

A Collective Fear of the Collective: Implications for Selves and Theories of Selves

Hazel Rose Markus and Shinobu Kitayama

The preceding selection by Yang and Bond, although it acknowledges important differences among cultures, takes one universal fact for granted: human beings are individuals who can be meaningfully characterized, one at a time, using personality traits. This assumption, "that people are independent, bounded, autonomous entities," is precisely what the authors of the next selection bring into question. The well-known American social psychologist Hazel Markus and her Japanese colleague Shinobu Kitayama describe the idea of the autonomous individual as a notion that is peculiar to Western, Euro-American culture. Japanese and other Asian cultures, they claim, have a very different view of what a person is all about.

Cultures outside Europe and North American emphasize the interdependence of the person with the larger culture, which Markus and Kitayama call "the collective." Habitual Western modes of thought as well as political ideology combine to see people as essentially separate from each other and emphasize independence, autonomy, and individual differences. However, this seemingly obvious idea may be a cultural artifact. In the East, individuals are seen as part of a greater whole, and it is not so important for one person to compete with or dominate another.

Perhaps because they are arguing against what they see as the conventional wisdom, Markus and Kitayama somewhat romanticize the Eastern view of the self. For example, they write that Asian child-rearing "places a continual emphasis on understanding and relating to others," and that the collective view is characterized by caring, responsibility, and love. But of course there is a trade-off of advantages and disadvantages between the Eastern and Western way of life. For example, in collectivist cultures one's spouse is commonly chosen by others on the basis of a negotiation between families. Perhaps as a result of cultural conditioning, most Europeans and Americans would rather choose their own spouses! As Markus and Kitayama point out, individual rights of all sorts are not given a high priority in collectivist cultures.

Two aspects of the following article are of particular value. First, the article urges us to reexamine an assumption about human psychology held so deeply that few people in our culture are probably even aware of holding it. Second, Markus and Kitayama present, in Figure 40.1, a comprehensive model of the relationship between a culture's collective reality, social processes, individual reality, habitual psychological tendencies, and action. This model has the potential to be useful for the analysis of psychological differences among cultures on many different dimensions, not just collectivism vs. individualism.

From *Personality and Social Psychology Bulletin, 20,* 568–579, 1994.

Our cultural nightmare is that the individual throb of growth will be sucked dry in slavish social conformity. All life long, our central struggle is to defend the individual from the collective.

—Plath, 1980, p. 216

Selves, as well as theories of selves, that have been constructed within a European-American cultural frame show the influence of one powerful notion—the idea that people are independent, bounded, autonomous entities who must strive to remain unshackled by their ties to various groups and collectives (Bellah, Madsen, Sullivan, Swidler, & Tipton, 1985; Farr, 1991; Sampson, 1985; Shweder & Bourne, 1984). This culturally shared idea of the self is a pervasive, taken-for-granted assumption that is held in place by language, by the mundane rituals and social practices of daily life, by the law, the media, the foundational texts like the Declaration of Independence and the Bill of Rights, and by virtually all social institutions. The individualist ideal as sketched in its extreme form in the opening quotation might not be explicitly endorsed by many Americans and Europeans. Some version of this view is, however, the basis of social science's persistent belief in the person as a rational, self-interested actor, and it occasions a desire not to be defined by others and a deep-seated wariness, in some instances even a fear, of the influence of the generalized other, of the social, and of the collective.

* * *

Recent analyses of the self in cultures other than the European-American (e.g., Daniels, 1984; Derné, 1992; Markus & Kitayama, 1991; Triandis, 1990; White & Kirkpatrick, 1985) reveal some very different perspectives on the relation between the self and the collective. Japanese culture, for example, emphasizes the *inter*dependence of the individual with the collective rather than independence from it. The analysis of non–European-American views of self has two notable benefits. First, such an analysis can illuminate some central characteristics of these non-Western cultures themselves. Second, and more important for our purposes, it can help uncover some aspects of European-American social behavior that are not well captured in the current social psychological theories.

Culture and Self

Independence of Self From the Collective—A Cultural Frame The model that underlies virtually all current social science views the self as an entity that (a) comprises a unique, bounded configuration of internal attributes (e.g., preferences, traits, abilities, motives, values, and rights) and (b) behaves primarily as a consequence of these internal attributes. It is the individual level of reality—the thoughts and feelings of the single individual—that is highlighted and privileged in the explanation and analysis of behavior; the collective level of reality recedes and remains secondary. The major normative task is to maintain the independence of the individual as a self-contained entity or, more specifically, to be true to one's own internal structures of preferences, rights, convictions, and goals and, further, to be confident and to be efficacious. According to this *independent* view of the self, there is an enduring concern with expressing one's internal attributes both in public and in private. Other people are crucial in maintaining this construal of the self, but they are primarily crucial for their role in evaluating and appraising the self or as standards of comparison (see Markus & Kitayama, 1991; Triandis, 1990, for a discussion of the independent or individualist self). Others do not, however, *participate* in the individual's own subjectivity.

* * *

INTERDEPENDENCE OF THE SELF AND THE COLLECTIVE—AN ALTERNATIVE FRAME The pervasive influence of the individualist ideal in many aspects of European-American social behavior has appeared in high relief as we have carried out a set of studies on the self and its functioning in a variety of Asian countries, including Japan, Thailand, and Korea (Kitayama & Markus, 1993; Kitayama, Markus, & Kurokawa, 1991; Markus & Kitayama, 1991, 1992). What has become apparent is that the European-American view of the self and its relation to the collective is only *one* view. There are other, equally powerful but strikingly different, collective notions about the self and its relation to the collective.

From one such alternative view, the self is viewed not as an independent entity separate from the collective but instead as a priori fundamentally interdependent with others. Individuals do not stand in opposition to the confines and constraints of the external collective, nor do they voluntarily choose to become parts of this external collective. Instead, the self *is* inherently social—an integral part of the collective. This interdependent view grants primacy to the *relationship* between self and others. The self derives only from the individual's relationships with specific others in the collective. There is no self without the collective; the self is a part that becomes whole only in interaction with others (e.g., Kondo, 1990; Kumagai & Kumagai, 1985; Lebra, 1992). It is defined and experienced as inherently connected with others. In contrast to the European-American orientation, there is an abiding fear of being on one's own, of being separated or disconnected from the collective. A desire for independence is cast as unnatural and immature.

The major normative task of such a self is not to maintain the independence of the individual as a self-contained entity but instead to maintain *inter*dependence with others. Rather than as an independent decision maker, the self is cast as "a single thread in a richly textured fabric of relationships" (Kondo, 1990, p. 33). This view of the self and of the collective requires adjusting and fitting to important relationships, occupying one's proper place in the group, engaging in collectively appropriate actions, and promoting the goals of others. One's thoughts, feelings, and actions are made meaningful only in reference to the thoughts, feelings, and actions of others in the relationship, and consequently others are crucially important in the very definition of the self. (For more detailed descriptions of the interdependent self, see Hsu, 1953; Kondo, 1990; Markus & Kitayama, 1991.)

Interdependence in this sense is theoretically distinct from social identity (e.g., Tajfel & Turner, 1985; Turner & Oakes, 1989), which refers to social categorizations that define a person as a member of particular social categories (e.g., American, male, Protestant, engineer). Social identity, in the framework of Turner and colleagues, is always defined in counterpoint to personal identity, which is all the ways a person is *different* from his or her in-groups. The key feature of interdependence is not distinctiveness or uniqueness but a heightened awareness of the other, and of the nature of one's relation to the other, and an expectation of some mutuality in this regard across all behavioral domains, even those that can be designated as private or personal.

DIFFERENCES IN THE ENCULTURATION OF THE "BASIC" TASKS Although both European-

American and Asian cultural groups recognize that independence from others and interdependence with others are essential human tendencies or tasks, these two tasks are weighted and organized quite differently in the two groups. The notion of the autonomous individual in continuous tension with the external collective is "natural" only from a particular cultural perspective. From an alternative perspective, such an arrangement appears somewhat unnatural and contrived. In Japan, for example, the culture in its dominant ideology, patterns of social customs, practices, and institutions emphasizes and foregrounds not independence from others but interdependence with others. Interdependence is the first goal to be taken care of; it is crafted and nurtured in the social episodes and scripted actions of everyday social life, so that it becomes spontaneous, automatic, and taken for granted. Although independence is also essential for social functioning, it remains a tacit and less culturally elaborated pursuit. It is left to the intentions and initiatives of each individual member, and so its pursuit is relatively optional and is the focus of personal and unofficial discourse because it is not strongly constrained or widely supported by socially sanctioned cultural practices.

THE CULTURAL SHAPING OF PSYCHOLOGICAL PROCESSES In Figure 40.1, we have illustrated how the "reality" of independence is created and maintained in selves, as well as in theories of selves. According to this view, a cultural group's way of self-understanding is simultaneously related to a set of macrolevel phenomena, such as cultural views of personhood and their supporting collective practices, and to a set of microlevel phenomena, like individual lives and their constituent cognitive, emotional, and motivational processes.

Collective reality. Under the heading "collective reality" we have included cultural values and their related ecological, historical, economic, and sociopolitical factors. For example, the United States is a nation with a rich tradition of moral imperatives, but the most well elaborated is the need to protect the "natural rights" of each individual. This core cultural ideal is rooted most directly in the Declaration of Independence and the Bill of Rights, which protect certain inalienable rights, including life, liberty, and the pursuit of happiness. This high-lighting of individuals and their rights is objectified and reified in a variety of democratic political institutions and free-market capitalism. In Japan, as throughout Asia, the prevalent ideological and moral discourses are not tied to individual rights but to the inevitability of a strict hierarchical order and to the achievement of virtue through cultivation of the individual into a "social man" (Yu, 1992). This core cultural ideal is anchored in the works of Confucius and Mencius and finds expression in an array of economic, political, and social institutions.

Sociopsychological products and processes—transmitting the core ideas. The cultural ideals and moral imperatives of a given cultural group are given life by a diverse set of customs, norms, scripts, practices, and institutions that carry out the transformation of the collective reality into the largely personal or psychological reality. These sociopsychological products and processes objectify and make "real" the core ideas of the society (Bourdieu, 1972; D'Andrade, 1984; Durkheim, 1898/1953; Farr & Moscovici, 1984; Geertz, 1973; Oyserman & Markus, in press). For example, in the United States, the idea of human rights (including liberty from the thrall of the collective) as inherent and God-given gains its force from a large array of legal statutes protecting individual rights. In this way the individual gains superiority to the collective.

Child-rearing practices in the United States, rooted in Freudian theory and filtered through Dr. Spock and most recently the self-esteem movement, also work to develop the constituent elements of the self and to reinforce the importance of having a distinct self that the individual can feel good about. A recent study (Chao, 1993), for example, found that 64% of European-American mothers, in comparison with 8% of Chinese mothers, stressed building children's "sense of

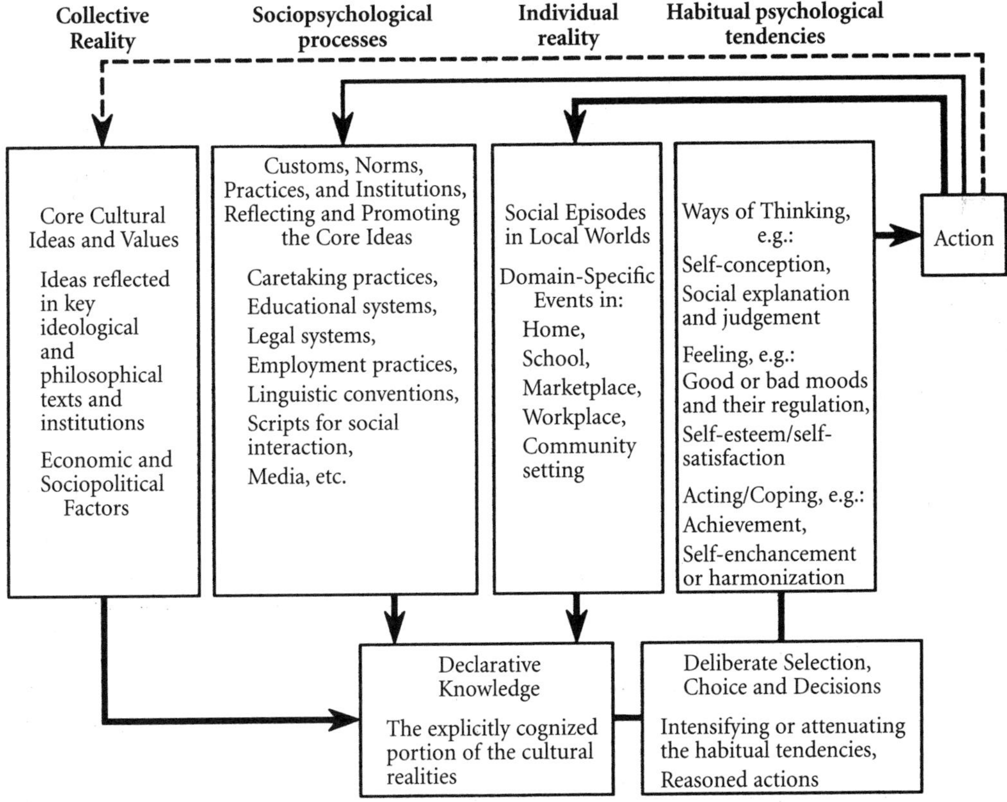

Figure 40.1 Cultural shaping of psychological reality.

themselves" as an important goal of child rearing. Many American mothers take every opportunity to praise children and to help them realize the ways in which they are positively unique or different from their peers. Training in autonomy and the development of the appreciation of being alone also comes early. Day-old children sleep alone in their cribs, often in separate rooms from their parents (Shweder, Jensen, & Goldstein, 1995). On the playground, children are taught to stand up for themselves and fight back if necessary (Kashiwagi, 1989).

Another important quality of personhood, from the independent perspective, is the capacity to make one's own choice. In much of Western culture, but especially in North America, there are numerous examples of everyday scripts that presuppose the actor's right to make a choice. It is common for American hosts to instruct their guests, "Help yourself." With this suggestion, the host invites the guest to affirm the self by expressing some of those preferences that are thought to constitute the "real self." American children, then, are socialized to have distinct preferences. Long before the child is old enough to answer, caretakers pose questions like "Do you want the red cup or the blue cup?" With such questions, mothers signal to children that the capacity for independent choice is an important and desirable attribute. And the availability of choice gives rise to the need for preferences by which to make choices.

The practices of the media further create and foster the objectivity of the autonomous, independent self. Advertising in the United States makes appeals to nonconformity, originality, and uniqueness. A hard-sell approach is common in which the product is presented as the best or the leader of its kind, and purchasing it is claimed to reveal that the consumer has the "right" preferences or attitudes (Mueller, 1987; Zandpour, Chang, & Catalano, 1992). For example, Chanel recently marketed, in both the United States and Europe, a men's cologne with the strikingly unsubtle name of *Egoïste* and the slogan "For the man who walks on the right side of the fine line between arrogance and awareness of self-worth."

Perhaps the most powerful practice of all for the purpose of creating a shared concern with independence is that of advancing, promoting, and compensating people according to their "merit." This practice places a lifelong emphasis on inner attributes, capacities, and abilities as the "real" measure of the self and encourages people to define and develop these attributes.

In many Asian cultures, there is an equally diverse and powerful set of sociopsychological processes in each of these corresponding domains, but these practices are rooted in a view of the self as an interdependent entity. For example, in place of (or, to a certain extent, in addition to) the emphasis on human rights, there exist dense systems of rules and norms that highlight the duties of each individual to the pertinent collective, whether it is the company, school, or nation. Moreover, there are many fewer statutes protecting individual rights, and the Japanese resort to court suits to secure their rights far less readily than European-Americans (Hideo, 1988).

In the course of interpersonal interaction, the Japanese are encouraged to try to read the partner's mind and to satisfy what is taken as the partner's expectations or desires. A Japanese mother does not ask for a child's preference but instead tries to determine what is best for the child and to arrange it. Rather than asking a guest to make a choice, Japanese hosts do their best to prepare and offer what they infer to be the best possible meal for the guest, saying, for example, "Here's a turkey sandwich for you. I thought you said you like turkey better than beef last time we met."

Child rearing in many Asian cultures places a continual emphasis on understanding and relating to others, first to the mother and then to a wide range of others. The rules of interdependence are explicitly modeled, and the goal is to maintain harmonious relationships (Hsu, 1953). Interdependence can be found in all domains. In stark opposition to American practices and Freudian wisdom, cosleeping and cobathing are common in Japanese families. The emphasis is not on developing a good, private sense of self but on tuning in to and being sensitive to others. Punishing or reprimanding Japanese children often involves not the withholding of rights and privileges but a threat to the relationship. Mothers will say, "I don't like children like you" or "People will laugh at you" (Okimoto & Rohlen, 1988).

With respect to media practices, Japanese advertising often uses soft-sell appeals that focus on harmony or connection with nature or with others (Mueller, 1987). In classified ads, employers explicitly seek individuals with good interpersonal relations, as opposed to self-starters or innovators (Caproni, Rafaeli, & Carlile, 1993). A focus on relationships is also evident in all types of business practices. Japan stands out from all countries in the West because of its emphasis on durable and pervasive ties between government and industry, between banks and businesses, and among corporations. Okimoto and Rohlen (1988) contend that the emphasis on organizational networks and human relationships is so strong that Japanese capitalism can be labeled *relational capitalism.* In the pursuit of long-term relationships and mutual trust, Japanese corporations operate quite differently, often, for example, forgoing the maximization of short-term profits with the hope of gaining a long-term market share. And in contrast to the European-American emphasis on merit for promotion and compensation, wages and advancement in the majority of Japanese companies and institutions are tied to seniority in the system. In addition, employment in large corporations is typically permanent, and there is little lateral entry from the outside—all publicly scripted collective practices that foster and promote a view of the self as inherently relational and interdependent.

Beyond the caretaking, legal, business, and

media practices we have alluded to are a host of others, including educational and linguistic practices, and all the scripts and institutions that structure everyday social interactions. An important element in understanding which practices will become socially established is how the practices reflect and carry the group's underlying cultural values. Americans, for example, will be particularly susceptible to ideas and practices that directly follow from individualism (Sperber, 1985). Other practices—welfare and universal health care programs are good examples—will have a more difficult time taking hold in the United States.

Local worlds—living the core ideas. The third segment of Figure 40.1 represents the specific settings, circumstances, and situations of everyday life that make up an individual's immediate social environment and in which particular customs, norms, and practices become lived experience. The local worlds—home, school, the workplace, the community center, the church, the restaurant, bar, or café, the marketplace—and the specific activities or episodes they support—helping a child with homework, shopping for a gift, drinking with friends, discussing politics, playing baseball, working with others to meet a deadline—demand specific, culturally appropriate responses if a person is to become a valued member of the family, school, workplace, or community.

It is within the demands and expectations of these domain-specific, recurrent social episodes that people, often quite unknowingly, live out the core cultural values. So Americans are likely to create and live within settings that elicit and promote the sense that one is a positively unique individual who is separate and independent from others. For example, in many American schools, each child in the class has the opportunity to be a "star" or a "Very Special Person" for a week during the school year. Likewise, Japanese will create and live with situations that promote the sense of self as interdependent with others. In Japanese schools, children routinely produce group pictures or story boards, and no child leaves to go to the playground or lunch until all members of the group are ready to leave.

Habitual psychological tendencies reflecting the core ideas. As a result of efforts to respond or adjust to the set of specific episodes that constitute the individual's life space, episodes that have themselves been shaped by norms, practices, and institutions supporting the cultural group's core ideas, a set of habitual psychological tendencies is likely to develop. The final segment of Figure 40.1 represents the individual's "authentic" subjective experience —particular, proceduralized ways of thinking, feeling, striving, knowing, understanding, deciding, managing, adjusting, adapting, which are, in some large part, structured, reinforced, and maintained by the constraints and affordances of the particular social episodes of the individual's local worlds. In this way, people who live within a society whose daily practices and formal institutions all promote independence will come not just to believe that they are, but to experience themselves as, autonomous, bounded selves who are distinct from other members of the collective. This will be evident in many ways of thinking, feeling, and acting, but it is particularly evident when people are asked to characterize themselves.

For example, by the time they are young adults, many Americans will seek an optimal distinctiveness from others (Brewer, 1990) and will "naturally" experience an ambivalence about their collective nature and a deep concern with being categorically perceived or socially determined. The journalist Barbara Ehrenreich (1992) describes an interchange with an acquaintance who has just rediscovered her own ethnic and religious heritage and now feels in contact with her 2000-year ancestral traditions. The acquaintance asks about Ehrenreich's ethnic background. The first word to come out of Ehrenreich's mouth in answer to the question is "None." She is surprised at how natural and right her answer seems, yet slightly embarrassed. She reflects and decides that her response when asked the nature of her ethnicity was quite correct. Her identity, she claims, comes from the realization that "we are the kind of people that whatever our distant ancestors' religions —we do not believe, we do not carry on traditions, we do not do things just because someone has done them before." Her ethnicity, she contends, is rooted not in a given group but in the ideas "Think for yourself" and "Try new things." In conclusion, Ehrenreich tells of asking her own children whether they ever had any stirring of "ethnic or religious identity." "None," they all conclude, and she reports, "My chest swelled with pride as would my mother's to know that the race of 'None' marches on."

A tendency to define one's "real" self as distinct from one's social groups and obligations is characteristic of both younger and older cohorts of Americans as well. In a series of studies with young children, Hart and his colleagues (Hart, 1988; Hart & Edelstein, 1992) asked American children to imagine a "person machine" that makes the original person disappear but at the same time manufactures other people, copies of the original, which receive some but not all of the original person's characteristics. The respondent's task is to judge which new manufactured person —the one with the same physical attributes (looks like you), the one with the same social attributes (has the same friends and family), or the one with the same psychological attributes (same thoughts and feelings)—will be most like the original person. By ninth grade, Hart et al. (Hart, Fegley, Hung Chan, Mulvey, & Fischer, 1993) finds that most respondents believe it is the copy with the original's psychological characteristics that is the most similar to the original.

These findings are consistent with those of several other studies of cultural variation in self-categorization (Cousins, 1989; Triandis, 1990) and suggest that, for American students, it is the internal features of the self—the traits, attributes, and attitudes—that are privileged and regarded as critical to self-definition. From this perspective, the significant aspects of the self are those that are the inside, the private property—one's characteristic ways of behaving, one's habitual thoughts, feelings, and beliefs (e.g., think for yourself, try new things)—the elements that do not explicitly reference others or the social world. Such internal attributes are also mentioned by the Japanese, but they appear to be understood as relatively situation specific and therefore elusive and unreliable (Cousins, 1989) as defining features of self. For the Japanese, the critical features are those attributes—social roles, duties, obligations—that connect one to the larger world of social relationships. (For other detailed examples of the cultural shaping of judgment, self, and emotion, see Kitayama & Markus, 1993, 1995; Markus & Kitayama, 1994.) In a study examining response time for self-description,[1] Kitayama et al. (1991) find that Japanese respondents are decidedly slower to characterize themselves than American respondents and that this is particularly true for positive attributes.

The top level of Figure 40.1 indicates feedback loops from each individual's action. The most immediate and frequent feedback occurs at the micro level. Most obviously, what an individual does influences the very nature of the situation in which he or she has acted. There are, however, people who at times contribute, through their actions, not just to the micro level but also to the more macro level. The bottom level of Figure 40.1 represents a more cognitive influence. Some portion of the social realities—both macro and micro—can be represented cognitively. This cognized portion of culture is shaded in each segment of the figure. The articulated, declarative knowledge of cultural values, practices, and conventions may be recruited in modulating social action, either facilitating or inhibiting the automatized psychological tendencies. Importantly, however, psychological tendencies can develop independently of this second, articulated route of cultural influence. In this way, cultural values and beliefs can cause differences in psychological processes even when these

[1]In such a study personality adjectives are presented on a screen, and subjects must respond "me" or "not me" by pressing a key. The time taken to respond is measured in milliseconds. A slower response implies that a particular attribute is a less central aspect of the self-concept.

beliefs (e.g., a fear of influence by the collective) are not cognitively encoded and overtly articulated. Of course, the values and beliefs often are encoded cognitively, but this current analysis implies that cognitive representations need not be central in the cultural shaping of psychological processes. Instead, we suggest that psychological processes and behavior can be best understood as an important, but only partial, element of the dynamic cultural and historical process that involves the systematic (though by no means error-free or "faxlike") transmission of cultural imperatives to shape and define the nature of the specific, immediate life space—the microlevel reality—for each individual.

Implications of a Collective Fear of the Collective for Psychological Theorizing

Using Asian cultures, particularly Japan, as a point of reference and standard, we have sketched how the European-American fear of the collective may arise and how it is naturalized, enacted, and embodied so that people rarely see or feel the collective nature or source of their behavior and instead experience themselves as separate and self-contained entities. A large set of mutually reinforcing everyday rituals, social practices, and institutions work together to elaborate and objectify the culture's view of what the self is and what it should be. Independence and autonomy are thus the "natural" mode of being—in Geertz's (1975) terms, they become "experience near" phenomena. The subjective authenticity or "naturalness" of this mode, however, is a function of the degree of fit between habitual psychological tendencies and the cultural and social systems that are grounded in these cultural imperatives.

Theorists of European-American behavior have also been extremely influenced by the prevailing ideology of individualism. They have often viewed the self as in tension, or even as in opposition, to the "ruck of society" (Plath, 1980) or the "thrall of society" (Hewitt, 1989). The source of all important behavior is typically "found" in the unique configuration of internal attributes—thoughts, feelings, motives, abilities—that form the bounded, autonomous whole. As a consequence, the ways in which the self is, in fact, quite interdependent with the collective have been underanalyzed and undertheorized. It is our view that there are a number of important reasons for theorists to go beyond theories that are directly shaped by the cultural ideal of individualism and to consider a broader view of the self.

First, and most obviously, although current descriptions of the largely independent and autonomous self could be argued to be reasonably adequate for European-American selves, a growing body of evidence suggests that they are simply not valid for many other cultural groups (see extended discussions of this point in Markus & Kitayama, 1991; Triandis, 1990; Triandis, Bontempo, & Villareal, 1988). Second, although the cultural ideal of independence is very influential in the nature and functioning of the European-American self, it does not determine it completely. For example, with respect to the bounded or fixed nature of the self, there are a variety of studies that reveal the self as decidedly malleable and its content and functioning as dependent on the social context. Typically these studies are not integrated with the literature that suggests stability of the self (e.g., Fazio, Effrein, & Falender, 1981; James, 1993; Jones & Pittman, 1982; Markus & Kunda, 1986; McGuire & McGuire, 1982; Schlenker, 1980).

Third, at least in the United States, the analysis of the selves of those groups in society that are somewhat marginalized—women, members of nondominant ethnic groups, the poor, the unschooled, and the elderly—reveals a more obvious interdependence between the self and the collective. For example, women describe themselves in relational terms (Gilligan, 1982; Jordan, Kaplan, Miller, Stivey, & Surrey, 1991), and they do not reveal the "typical" preference for being positively unique or different from others (Josephs, Markus, & Tafarodi, 1992). Other studies reveal that those groups that are in the minority with respect to language, skin color, or religion are decidedly more likely to define themselves in collective terms (Allen, Dawson, & Brown, 1989; Bowman, 1987; Husain, 1992). Further, Americans with less schooling are more likely to describe themselves in terms of habitual actions and roles, and less likely to characterize themselves in terms of psychological attributes, than those with more schooling (Markus, Herzog, Holmberg, & Dielman, 1992). And those with low self-esteem show a marked tendency to describe themselves as similar to others (Josephs et al., 1992). These findings suggest that those with power and privilege are those most likely to internalize the prevailing European-American cultural frame to achieve Ehrenreich's "ethnicity of none" and to "naturally" experience themselves as autonomous individuals.

Fourth, a number of recent studies show many Americans to be extremely concerned about others and the public good (Bellah et al., 1985; Bellah, Madsen, Sullivan, Swidler, & Tipton, 1991; Hewitt, 1989; Withnow, 1992) and to characterize themselves in interdependent terms. For example, a recent representative sample of 1,500 adults, aged 30 or over, found that although Americans indeed characterized themselves in terms of trait attributes and not social roles or obligations, the most frequently used attributes were *caring, responsible, loved*—all terms that imply some concern with a connection to the collective (Markus et al., 1992). Even if, as we have suggested, this connection is clearly voluntary and done on one's own terms, the prevailing model of the self could be modified.

And finally, increasingly throughout social psychology, there are indications that the individualist model of the self is too narrow and fails to take account of some important aspects of psychological reality. For example, within social psychology specifically, there is a great deal of evidence that people are exquisitely sensitive to others and to social pressure. People conform, obey, diffuse responsibility in a group, allow themselves to be easily persuaded about all manner of things, and become powerfully committed to others on the basis of minimal action (Myers, 1993). Despite the powerful cultural sanctions against allowing the collective to influence one's thoughts and actions, most people are still much less self-reliant, self-contained, or self-sufficient than the ideology of individualism suggests they should be. It appears in these cases that the European-American model of self is somewhat at odds with observed individual behavior and that it might be reformulated to reflect the substantial interdependence that characterizes even Western individualists.

Alternative Views of the Self and the Collective

In trying to formulate the collective sources of the self among Europeans or Americans, models of the self and the collective "Asian style" may be particularly informative.[2] If we assume, as does Shweder (1991), that every group can be considered an expert on some features of human experience and that different cultural groups "light up" different aspects of this experience, then Asian cultures may be an important source of conceptual resources in the form of concepts, frameworks, theories, or methods that can be employed to "see" interdependence. Even though interdependence American style will doubtlessly look quite different from interdependence Japanese style, an analysis of divergent cultural groups may further any theorist's understanding of the possibilities,

[2]Some of the most important work suggesting the need for alternative models of the self comes from feminist theorists who have argued in the last 15 years that relations have a power and significance in women's lives that has gone unrecognized (Belenky, Clinchy, Goldberger, & Tarule, 1986; Gilligan, 1982; Jordan et al., 1991). The development of a psychology of women has shown that the "Lone Ranger" model of the self simply does not fit many women's experience because women's sense of self seems to involve connection and engagement with relationships and collective. In this work, being dependent does not invariably mean being helpless, powerless, or without control. It often means being interdependent—having a sense that one is able to have an effect on others and is willing to be responsive to others and become engaged with them (Jordan, 1991).—Author

potential, and consequences, both positive and negative, for socialness, for engagement, for interdependence, and for the ties that bind.

* * *

We have argued here that the cultural frame of individualism has put a very strong stamp on how social psychologists view the individual and his or her relation to the collective. Although this individualist view has provided a powerful framework for the analysis of social behavior, it has also, necessarily, constrained theories, methods, and dominant interpretations of social behavior. Because individualism is not just a matter of belief or value but also one of everyday practice, including scientific practice, it is not easy for theorists to view social behavior from another cultural frame, and it is probably harder still to reflect a different frame in empirical work. But the comparative approach that is characteristic of the developing cultural psychology (e.g., Cole, 1990; Stigler, Shweder, & Herdt, 1990) may eventually open new and productive possibilities for the understanding and analysis of behavior.

For example, just as social influence, from the perspective of an interdependent cultural frame, can be seen as the mutual negotiation of social reality, helping can be seen as a result of obligation, duty, or morality, rather than as voluntary or intentional (e.g., Miller, Bersoff, & Harwood, 1990). Similarly, emotion can be viewed as an enacted interpersonal process (Rosaldo, 1984) or as an interpersonal atmosphere, as it is characterized in some non-Western theories (White, 1990). Further, cognition can be seen as an internalized aspect of communication (Zajonc, 1992), and the early idea of the social and interactive nature of the mind (e.g., Asch, 1952; Bruner, 1990; Vygotsky, 1978) can be taken much more seriously than it has been. In general, viewing the self and social behavior from alternative perspectives may enable theorists to see and elaborate at least one important and powerful universal that might otherwise be quite invisible—the ways in which psychological functioning (in this case, the nature of the self), as well as theories about psychological functioning (here, theories of the nature of the self), are in many ways culture specific and conditioned by particular, but tacit and taken-for-granted, meaning systems, values, and ideals.

References

Allen, R. L., Dawson, M. C., & Brown, R. E. (1989). A schema based approach to modeling an African American racial belief system. *American Political Science Review, 83,* 421–442.

Asch, S. E. (1952). *Social psychology.* Englewood Cliffs, NJ: Prentice-Hall.

Belenky, M. F., Clinchy, B. M., Goldberger, N. R., & Tarule, J. M. (1986). *Women's ways of knowing: The development of self, voice, and mind.* New York: Basic Books.

Bellah, R. N., Madsen, R., Sullivan, W. M., Swidler, A., & Tipton, S. M. (1985). *Habits of the heart: Individualism and commitment in American life.* Berkeley: University of California Press.

Bellah, R. N., Madsen, R., Sullivan, W. M., Swidler, A., & Tipton, S. M. (1991). *The good society.* New York: Knopf.

Bourdieu, P. (1972). *Outline of a theory of practice.* Cambridge: Cambridge University Press.

Bowman, P. J. (1987). Post-industrial displacement and family role strains: Challenges to the Black family. In P. Voydanoff & L. C. Majka (Eds.), *Families and economic distress.* Newbury Park, CA: Sage.

Brewer, M. B. (1990, August). *The social self: On being the same and different at the same time.* Presidential address to the Society for Personality and Social Psychology presented at the annual meeting of the American Psychological Association, Boston.

Bruner, J. (1990). *Acts of meaning.* Cambridge, MA: Harvard University Press.

Caproni, P., Rafaeli, A., & Carlile, P. (1993, July). *The social construction of organized work: The role of newspaper employment advertising.* Paper presented at the European Group on Organization Studies conference, Paris, France.

Chao, R. K. (1993). *East and West: Concepts of the self reflected in mothers' reports of their child-rearing.* Unpublished manuscript, University of California, Los Angeles.

Cole, M. (1990). Cultural psychology: A once and future discipline? In J. J. Berman (Ed.), *Nebraska Symposium on Motivation, 1989* (Vol. 37, pp. 279–336). Lincoln: University of Nebraska Press.

Cousins, S. (1989). Culture and selfhood in Japan and the U.S. *Journal of Personality and Social Psychology, 56,* 124–131.

D'Andrade, R. (1984). Cultural meaning systems. In R. A. Shweder & R. A. LeVine (Eds.), *Cultural theories: Essays on mind, self, and emotion* (pp. 88–119). New York: Cambridge University Press.

Daniels, E. V. (1984). *Fluid signs; Being a person the Tamil way.* Berkeley: University of California Press.

Derné, S. (1992). Beyond institutional and impulsive conceptions of self: Family structure and the socially anchored real self. *Ethos, 20,* 259–288.

Durkheim, E. (1953). Individual representations and collective representations. In E. Durkheim (Ed.), *Sociology and philosophy* (D. F. Pocok, Trans.) (pp. 1–38). New York: Free Press. (Original work published 1898)

Ehrenreich, B. (1992, March). The race of none. *Sunday New York Times Magazine*, pp. 5–6.

Farr, R. M. (1991). Individualism as a collective representation. In V. Aebischer, J. P. Deconchy, & M. Lipiansky (Eds.), *Idéologies et représentations sociales* (pp. 129–143). Cousset (Fribourg), Switzerland: Delval.

Farr, R. M., & Moscovici, S. (Eds.). (1984). *Social representations*. Cambridge: Cambridge University Press.

Fazio, R. H., Effrein, E. A., & Falender, Y. J. (1981). Self-perceptions following social interactions. *Journal of Personality and Social Psychology, 41*, 232–242.

Geertz, C. (1973). *The interpretation of cultures*. New York: Basic Books.

Geertz, C. (1975). On the nature of anthropological understanding. *American Scientist, 63*, 47–53.

Gilligan, C. (1982). *In a different voice: Psychological theory and women's development*. Cambridge, MA: Harvard University Press.

Hart, D. (1988). The adolescent self-concept in social context. In D. Lapsley & F. Power (Eds.), *Self, ego, and identity: Integrative approaches* (pp. 71–90). New York: Springer-Verlag.

Hart, D., & Edelstein, W. (1992). Self understanding development in cultural context. In T. M. Brinthaupt & R. P. Lipka (Eds.), *The self: Definitional and methodological issues*. Albany: State University of New York Press.

Hart, D., Fegley, S., Hung Chan, Y., Mulvey, D., & Fischer, L. (1993). *Judgment about personal identity in childhood and adolescence*. Unpublished manuscript.

Hewitt, J. P. (1989). *Dilemmas of the American self*. Philadelphia: Temple University Press.

Hideo, T. (1988). The role of law and lawyers in Japanese society. In D. I. Okimoto & T. P. Rohlen (Eds.), *Inside the Japanese system: Readings on contemporary society and political economy* (pp. 194–196). Stanford, CA: Stanford University Press.

Hsu, F. L. K. (1953). *Americans and Chinese: Two ways of life*. New York: H. Schuman.

Husain, M. G. (1992, July). *Ethnic uprising and identity*. Paper presented at the 11th Congress of the International Association for Cross-Cultural Psychology, Liege, Belgium.

James, K. (1993). Conceptualizing self with in-group stereotypes: Context and esteem precursors. *Personality and Social Psychology Bulletin, 19*, 117–121.

Jones, E. E., & Pittman, T. S. (1982). Towards a general theory of strategic self-preservation. In J. Suls (Ed.), *Psychological perspectives on the self* (Vol. 1, pp. 231–262). Hillsdale, NJ: Lawrence Erlbaum.

Jordan, J. V. (1991). Empathy and self boundaries. In J. V. Jordan, A. G. Kaplan, J. B. Miller, I. P. Stivey, & J. L. Surrey (Eds.), *Women's growth in connection* (pp. 67–80). New York: Guilford.

Jordan, J. V., Kaplan, A. G., Miller, J. B., Stivey, I. P., & Surrey, J. L. (Eds.). (1991). *Women's growth in connection*. New York: Guilford.

Josephs, R. A., Markus, H., & Tafarodi, R. W. (1992). Gender differences in the source of self-esteem. *Journal of Personality and Social Psychology, 63*, 391–402.

Kashiwagi, K. (1989, July). *Development of self-regulation in Japanese children*. Paper presented at the tenth annual meeting of the International Society for the Study of Behavioral Development, Jyväskylā, Finland.

Kitayama, S., & Markus, H. (1993). Construal of the self as a cultural frame: Implications for internationalizing psychology. In J. D'Arms, R. G. Hastie, S. E. Hoelscher, & H. K. Jacobson (Eds.), *Becoming more international and global: Challenges for American higher education*. Manuscript submitted for publication.

Kitayama, S., & Markus, H. (1995). A cultural perspective on self-conscious emotions. In J. P. Tangney & K. W. Fisher (Eds.), *Shame, guilt, embarrassment and pride: Empirical studies of self-conscious emotions*. New York: Guilford.

Kitayama, S., Markus, H., & Kurokawa, M. (1991, October). *Culture, self, and emotion: The structure and frequency of emotional experience*. Paper presented at the biannual meeting of the Society for Psychological Anthropology, Chicago.

Kondo, D. (1990). *Crafting selves: Power, gender, and discourses of identity in a Japanese work place*. Chicago: University of Chicago Press.

Kumagai, H. A., & Kumagai, A. K. (1985). The hidden "I" in *amae*: "Passive love" and Japanese social perception. *Ethos, 14*, 305–321.

Lebra, T. S. (1992, June). *Culture, self, and communication*. Paper presented at the University of Michigan, Ann Arbor.

Markus, H., Herzog, A. R., Holmberg, D. E., & Dielman, L. (1992). *Constructing the self across the life span*. Unpublished manuscript, University of Michigan, Ann Arbor.

Markus, H., & Kitayama, S. (1991). Culture and the self: Implications for cognition, emotion, and motivation. *Psychological Review, 98*, 224–253.

Markus, H., & Kitayama, S. (1992). The what, why and how of cultural psychology: A review of R. Shweder's *Thinking through cultures*. *Psychological Inquiry, 3*, 357–364.

Markus, H., & Kitayama, S. (1994). The cultural construction of self and emotion: Implications for social behavior. In S. Kitayama & H. R. Markus (Eds.), *Emotion and culture: Empirical studies of mutual influence* (pp. 89–130). Washington, DC: American Psychological Association.

Markus, H., & Kunda, Z. (1986). Stability and malleability in the self-concept in the perception of others. *Journal of Personality and Social Psychology, 51*, 1–9.

McGuire, W. J., & McGuire, C. V. (1982). Significant others in self space: Sex differences and developmental trends in social self. In J. Suls (Ed.), *Psychological perspectives on the self* (Vol. 1, pp. 71–96). Hillsdale, NJ: Lawrence Erlbaum.

Miller, J. G., Bersoff, D. M., & Harwood, R. L. (1990). Perceptions of social responsibilities in India and in the United States: Moral imperatives or personal decisions? *Journal of Personality and Social Psychology, 58*, 33–46.

Mueller, B. (1987, June/July). Reflections of culture: An analysis of Japanese and American advertising appeals. *Journal of Advertising Research*, pp. 51–59.

Myers, D. (1993). *Social psychology* (4th ed.). New York: McGraw-Hill.

Okimoto, D. I., & Rohlen, T. P. (Eds.). (1988). *Inside the Japanese system: Readings on contemporary society and political economy*. Stanford, CA: Stanford University Press.

Oyserman, D., & Markus, H. R. (in press). Self as social representation. In S. Moscovici and U. Flick (Eds.), *Psychology of the social*. Berlin: Rowohlt Taschenbuch Verlag Gmbh.

Plath, D. W. (1980). *Long engagements: Maturity in modern Japan*. Stanford, CA: Stanford University Press.

Rosaldo, M. (1984). Toward an anthropology of self and feeling. In R. A. Shweder & R. A. LeVine (Eds.), *Culture theory: Essays on mind, self, and emotion* (pp. 137–157). Cambridge: Cambridge University Press.

Sampson, E. E. (1985). The decentralization of identity: Toward a revised concept of personal and social order. *American Psychologist, 40,* 1203–1211.

Schlenker, B. R. (1980). *Impression management.* Pacific Grove, CA: Brooks/Cole.

Shweder, R. A. (1991). *Thinking through cultures: Expeditions in cultural psychology.* Cambridge, MA: Harvard University Press.

Shweder, R. A., & Bourne, E. (1984). Does the concept of the person vary cross-culturally? In R. A. Shweder & R. A. LeVine (Eds.), *Culture theory: Essays on mind, self, and emotion* (pp. 158–199). Cambridge: Cambridge University Press.

Shweder, R. A., Jensen, L. A., & Goldstein, W. M. (1995). Who sleeps by whom revisted: A method for extracting the moral goods implicit in practice. In J. Goodnow, P. Miller, & F. Kessel (Eds.), *Cultural practices as contexts for development.* San Francisco: Jossey-Bass.

Sperber, D. (1985). Anthropology and psychology: Towards an epidemiology of representations. *MAN, 20,* 73–89.

Stigler, J. W., Shweder, R. A., & Herdt, G. (Eds.). (1990). *Cultural psychology: Essays on comparative human development.* London: Cambridge University Press.

Tajfel, H., & Turner, J. C. (1985). The social identity theory of intergroup behavior. In S. Worchel & W. G. Austin (Eds.), *Psychology of intergroup relations* (pp. 7–24). Chicago: Nelson-Hall.

Triandis, H. C. (1990). Cross-cultural studies of individualism and collectivism. In J. J. Berman (Ed.), *Nebraska Symposium on Motivation, 1989* (Vol. 37, pp. 41–143).

Triandis, H. C., Bontempo, R., & Villareal, M. (1988). Individualism and collectivism: Cross-cultural perspectives on self-ingroup relationships. *Journal of Personality and Social Psychology, 54,* 323–338.

Turner, J. C., & Oakes, P. J. (1989). Self-categorization theory and social influence. In P. B. Paulus (Ed.), *The psychology of group influence* (2nd ed.). Hillsdale, NJ: Lawrence Erlbaum.

Vygotsky, L. S. (1978). *Mind in society: The development of higher psychological processes* (M. Cole, V. John-Steiner, S. Scribner, & E. Souberman, Eds.). Cambridge, MA: Harvard University Press.

White, G. M. (1990). Moral discourse and the rhetoric of emotion. In C. Lutz & L. Abu-Lughod (Eds.), *Language and the politics of emotion.* Cambridge: Cambridge University Press.

White, G. M., & Kirkpatrick, J. (Eds.). (1985). *Person, self, and experience: Exploring Pacific ethnopsychologies.* Berkeley and Los Angeles: University of California Press.

Withnow, R. (1992). *Acts of compassion.* Princeton, NJ: Princeton University Press.

Yu, A. B. (1992, July). *The self and life goals of traditional Chinese: A philosophical and cultural analysis.* Paper presented at the 11th Congress of the International Association for Cross-Cultural Psychology, Liege, Belgium.

Zajonc, R. B. (1992, April). *Cognition, communication, consciousness: A social psychological perspective.* Invited address at the 20th Katz-Newcomb Lecture at the University of Michigan, Ann Arbor.

Zandpour, F., Chang, C., & Catalano, J. (1992, January/February). Stories, symbols, and straight talk: A comparative analysis of French, Taiwanese, and U.S. TV commercials. *Journal of Advertising Research,* pp. 25–38.

The Self and Social Behavior in Differing Cultural Contexts

Harry C. Triandis

We have seen that some cultural psychologists are fond of citing the phenomenological idea that it is one's experience of reality—not reality itself—that is all-important. This is sometimes taken to imply that it is not meaningful to compare one culture's view of reality with that of another, because no common frame of reference is possible. But recall that in Part V Jean-Paul Sartre argued not only that each individual's view of reality is distinct, but also that there is a universal human condition. This idea implies that the ultimate goal of cultural psychology should be to reconcile cultural variety with common humanity.

Few psychologists have achieved this goal so well as Harry Triandis. Born in Greece, for the past several decades Triandis has had a steady influence on the development of cross-cultural psychology from his base at the University of Illinois. In his research Triandis has consistently tried to describe the ways in which different cultures are both the same and different, and to formulate a set of dimensions along which all cultures can be characterized.

In the following selection, an excerpt from one of his major theoretical papers, Triandis proposes that cultures vary along three dimensions that are psychologically important. Some cultures are collectivist while others are relatively individualist; this is the dimension that was discussed in detail in the earlier selection by Markus and Kitayama. In addition, cultures vary in the degree to which they do or do not tolerate deviations from social norms (a dimension called looseness vs. tightness) and in their complexity. Triandis describes the relations between these variables and the development of the self. For example, North American culture is individualist, loose, and complex, which may produce a uniquely American kind of personality. He also describes how these dimensions are related to aspects of the environment, child-rearing patterns, and social behavior.

Notice how Triandis manages to sidestep a couple of common pitfalls of cultural psychology. First, he avoids the trap of being painted into one or another extreme corner on the question of whether human nature is universal or variable. He consistently expresses the view that all cultures have aspects they share with each other (called etics) and *aspects that are locally unique (called emics). Second, he never implies—as do other writers such as Markus and Kitayama—that some positions on the dimensions of cultural variation are better than others. It is neither good nor bad to be collectivist, individualist, tight, loose, complex or simple. It is always a matter of trade-offs; the disadvantages of one position are compensated for by advantages of the other. For example, members of collectivist cultures gain in group support what they lose in individual freedom; the reverse could be said about members of individualistic cultures.*

In the end, what Triandis describes could be called a "Big Three" for cultures. The traits of collectivism-individualism, tightness-looseness, and complexity are a group of psychologically relevant attributes that, Triandis demonstrates, can provide a sort of personality profile for an entire culture.

From *Psychological Review, 96*, 506–520, 1989.

The study of the self has a long tradition in psychology (e.g., Allport, 1943, 1955; Baumeister, 1987; Gordon & Gergen, 1968; James, 1890/1950; Murphy, 1947; Schlenker, 1985; Smith, 1980; Ziller, 1973), anthropology (e.g., Shweder & LeVine, 1984), and sociology (e.g., Cooley, 1902; Mead, 1934; Rosenberg, 1979). There is a recognition in most of these discussions that the self is shaped, in part, through interaction with groups. However, although there is evidence about variations of the self across cultures (Marsella, DeVos, & Hsu, 1985; Shweder & LeVine, 1984), the specification of the way the self determines aspects of social behavior in different cultures is undeveloped.

This article will examine first, aspects of the self; second, dimensions of variation of cultural contexts that have direct relevance to the way the self is defined; and third, the link between culture and self.

Definitions

THE SELF For purposes of this article, the self consists of all statements made by a person, overtly or covertly, that include the words "I," "me," "mine," and "myself" (Cooley, 1902). This broad definition indicates that all aspects of social motivation are linked to the self. Attitudes (e.g., *I* like X), beliefs (e.g., *I* think that X results in Y), intentions (e.g., *I* plan to do X), norms (e.g., in *my* group, people should act this way), roles (e.g., in *my* family, fathers act this way), and values (e.g., *I* think equality is very important) are aspects of the self.

The statements that people make that constitute the self have implications for the way people sample information (sampling information that is self-relevant more frequently than information that is not self-relevant), the way they process information (sampling more quickly information that is self-relevant than information that is not self-relevant), and the way they assess information (assessing more positively information that supports their current self-structure than information that challenges their self-structure). Thus, for instance, a self-instruction such as "I must do X" is more likely to be evaluated positively, and therefore accepted, if it maintains the current self-structure than if it changes this structure. This has implications for behavior because such self-instructions are among the several processes that lead to behavior (Triandis, 1977, 1980).

In other words, the self is an active agent that promotes differential sampling, processing, and evaluation of information from the environment, and thus leads to differences in social behavior. Empirical evidence about the link of measures of the self to behavior is too abundant to review here. A sample will suffice: People whose self-concept was manipulated so that they thought of themselves (a) as "charitable" gave more to charity (Kraut, 1973), (b) as "neat and tidy" threw less garbage on the floor (Miller, Brickman, & Bolen, 1975), and (c) as "honest" were more likely to return a pencil (Shotland & Berger, 1970). Self-definition results in behaviors consistent with that definition (Wicklund & Gollwitzer, 1982). People who defined themselves as doers of a particular behavior were more likely to do that behavior (Greenwald, Carnot, Beach, & Young, 1987). Identity salience leads to behaviors consistent with that identity (Stryker & Serpe (1982). Self-monitoring (Snyder, 1974) has been linked to numerous behaviors (e.g., Snyder, 1987; Snyder, Simpson, & Gangestad, 1986). The more an attitude (an aspect of the self) is accessible to memory, the more likely it is to determine behavior (Fazio & Williams, 1986). Those with high self-esteem were found to be more likely to behave independently of group norms (Ziller, 1973).

* * *

To the extent such aspects are *shared* by people who speak a common language and who are able to interact because they live in adjacent locations during the same historical period, we can refer to all of these elements as a cultural group's *subjective culture* (Triandis, 1972). This implies that people who speak different languages (e.g., English and Chinese) or live in nonadjacent locations (e.g., England and Australia) or who have lived in different time periods (e.g., 19th and 20th centuries) may have different subjective cultures.

Some aspects of the self may be universal. "I am hungry" may well be an element with much the same meaning worldwide and across time. Other elements are extremely culture-specific. For instance, they depend on the particular mythology-religion-worldview and language of a culture. "My soul will be reincarnated" is culture-specific. Some elements of the self imply action. For example, "I should be a high achiever" implies specific actions under conditions in which standards of excellence are present. Other elements do not imply action (e.g., I am tall).

* * *

One major distinction among aspects of the self is between the private, public, and collective self (Baumeister, 1986b; Greenwald & Pratkanis, 1984). Thus, we have the following: *the private self*—cognitions that involve traits, states, or behaviors of the person (e.g., "I am introverted," "I am honest," "I will buy X"); *the public self*—cognitions concerning the *generalized other*'s view of the self, such as "People think I am introverted" or "People think I will buy X"; and *the collective self*—cognitions concerning a view of the self that is found in some collective (e.g., family, coworkers, tribe, scientific society); for instance, "My family thinks I am introverted" or "My coworkers believe I travel too much."

The argument of this article is that people sample these three kinds of selves with different probabilities, in different cultures, and that has specific consequences for social behavior.

The private self is an assessment of the self by the self. The public self corresponds to an assessment of the self by the generalized other. The collective self corresponds to an assessment of the self by a specific reference group. Tajfel's (1978) notion of a *social identity*, "that part of the individual's self-concept which derives from his (or her) knowledge of his (her) membership in a social group (or groups) together with the values and emotional significance attached to that membership," (p. 63) is part of the collective self. Tajfel's theory is that people choose ingroups that maximize their positive social identity. However, that notion reflects an individualistic emphasis, because in many collectivist cultures people do not have a choice of ingroups. For instance, even though the Indian constitution has banned castes, caste is still an important aspect of social identity in that culture. Historical factors shape different identities (Baumeister, 1986a).

The notion of sampling has two elements: a *universe* of units to be sampled and a *probability* of choice of a unit from that universe. The universe can be more or less complex. By complexity is meant that the number of distinguishable elements might be few versus many, the differentiation within the elements may be small or large, and the integration of the elements may be small or large. The number of nonoverlapping elements (e.g., I am bold; I am sensitive) is clearly relevant to complexity. The differentiation of the elements refers to the number of distinctions made within the element. For example, in the case of the social class element, a person may have a simple conception with little differentiation (e.g., people who are unemployed vs. working vs. leading the society) or a complex conception with much differentiation (e.g., rich, with new money, well educated vs. rich with new money, poorly educated). *Integration* refers to the extent a change in one element changes few versus many elements. Self-structures in which changes in one element result in changes in many elements are more complex than self-structures in which such changes result in changes of only a few elements (Rokeach, 1960).

In families in which children are urged to be themselves, in which "finding yourself" is valued, or in which self-actualization is emphasized, the private self is likely to be complex. In cultures in which families emphasize "what other people will think about you," the public self is likely to be complex. In cultures in which specific groups are emphasized during socialization (e.g., "remember you are a member of this family," ". . . you are a Christian"), the collective self is likely to be complex, and the norms, roles, and values of that group acquire especially great emotional significance.

* * *

One of many methods that are available to study the self requires writing 20 sentence completions that begin with "I am . . ." (Kuhn & McPartland, 1954). The answers can be content-analyzed to determine whether they correspond to the private, public, or collective self. If a social group is part of the answer (e.g., I am a son = family; I am a student = educational institution; I am Roman Catholic = religion), one can classify the response as part of the collective self. If the generalized other is mentioned (e.g., I am liked by most people), it is part of the public self. If there is no reference to an entity outside the person (e.g., I am bold), it can be considered a part of the private self. Experience with this scoring method shows that coders can reach interrater reliabilities in the .9+ range. The percentage of the collective responses varies from 0 to 100, with sample means in Asian cultures in the 20% to 52% range and in European and North American samples between 15% and 19%. Public-self responses are relatively rare, so sample means of private-self responses (with student samples) are commonly in the 81% to 85% range. In addition to such content analyses, one can examine the availability (how frequently a particular group, e.g., the family, is mentioned) and the accessibility (when is a particular group mentioned for the first time in the rank-order) of responses (Higgins & King, 1981).

This method is useful because it provides an operational definition of the three kinds of selves under discussion. Also, salience is reflected directly in the measure of accessibility, and the complexity of particular self is suggested by the availability measure.

Although this method has many advantages, a multimethod strategy for the study of the self is highly recommended, because every method has some limitations and convergence across methods increases the validity of our measurements. Furthermore, when methods are used in different cultures in which people have different expectations about what can be observed, asked, or analyzed, there is an interaction between culture and method. But when methods converge similarly in different cultures and when the antecedents and consequences of the self-construct in each culture are similar, one can have greater confidence that the construct has similar or equivalent meanings across cultures.

Other methods that can tap aspects of the self have included interviews (e.g., Lobel, 1984),

Q-sorts of potentially self-descriptive attributes (e.g., Block, 1986), the Multistage Social Identity Inquirer (Zavalloni, 1975; Zavalloni & Louis-Guerin, 1984), and reaction times when responding to whether a specific attribute is self-descriptive (Rogers, 1981).

* * *

I have defined the self as one element of subjective culture (when it is shared by members of a culture) and distinguished the private, public, and collective selves, and indicated that the complexity of these selves will depend on cultural variables. The more complex a particular self, the more probable it is that it will be sampled. Sampling of a particular self will increase the probability that behaviors implicated in this aspect of the self will occur, when situations favor such occurrence. For example, data suggest that people from East Asia sample their collective self more frequently than do Europeans or North Americans. This means that elements of their reference groups, such as group norms or group goals, will be more salient among Asians than among Europeans or North Americans. In the next section I will describe cultural variation along certain theoretical dimensions that are useful for organizing the information about the sampling of different selves, and hence can account for differences in social behavior across cultures.

CULTURAL PATTERNS There is evidence of different selves across cultures (Marsella et al., 1985). However, the evidence has not been linked systematically to particular dimensions of cultural variation. This section will define three of these dimensions.

Cultural complexity. A major difference across cultures is in cultural complexity. Consider the contrast between the human bands that existed on earth up to about 15,000 years ago and the life of a major metropolitan city today. According to archaeological evidence, the bands rarely included more than 30 individuals. The number of relationships among 30 individuals is relatively small; the number of relationships in a major metropolitan area is potentially almost infinite. The number of potential relationships is one measure of cultural complexity. Students of this construct have used many others. One can get reliable rank orders by using information about whether cultures have writing and records, fixity of residence, agriculture, urban settlements, technical specialization, land transport other than walking, money, high population densities, many levels of political integration, and many levels of social stratification. Cultures that have all of these attributes (e.g., the Romans, the Chinese of the 5th century B.C., modern industrial cultures) are quite complex. As one or more of the aforementioned attributes are missing, the cultures are more simple, the simplest including the contemporary food gathering cultures (e.g., the nomads of the Kalahari desert).

Additional measures of complexity can be obtained by examining various domains of culture. Culture includes language, technology, economic, political, and educational systems, religious and aesthetic patterns, social structures, and so on. One can analyze each of these domains by considering the number of distinct elements that can be identified in it. For example, (a) language can be examined by noting the number of terms that are available (e.g., 600 camel-related terms in Arabic; many terms about automobiles in English), (b) economics by noting the number of occupations (the U.S. Employment and Training Administration's *Dictionary of Occupational Titles* contains more than 250,000), and (c) religion by noting the number of different functions (e.g., 6,000 priests in one temple in Orissa, India, each having a different function).

One of the consequences of increased complexity is that individuals have more and more potential ingroups toward whom they may or may not be loyal. As the number of potential ingroups increases, the loyalty of individuals to any one ingroup decreases. Individuals have the option of giving priority to their personal goals rather than to the goals of an ingroup. Also, the greater the affluence of a society, the more financial independence can be turned into social and emotional independence, with the individual giving priority to personal rather than ingroup goals. Thus, as societies become more complex and affluent, they also can become more individualistic. However, there are some moderator variables that modify this simple picture, that will be discussed later, after I examine more closely the dimension of individualism-collectivism.

Individualism-collectivism. Individualists give priority to personal goals over the goals of collectives; collectivists either make no distinctions between personal and collective goals, or if they do make such distinctions, they subordinate their personal goals to the collective goals (Triandis, Bontempo, Villareal, Asai, & Lucca, 1988). Closely related to this dimension, in the work of Hofstede (1980), is *power distance* (the tendency to see a large difference between those with power and those without power). Collectivists tend to be high in power distance.

Although the terms *individualism* and *collectivism* should be used to characterize cultures and societies, the terms *idiocentric* and *allocentric* should be used to characterize individuals. Triandis, Leung, Villareal, and Clack (1985) have shown that within culture (Illinois) there are individuals who differ on this dimension, and the idiocentrics report that they are concerned with achievement, but are lonely, whereas the allocentrics report low alienation and receiving much social support. These findings were replicated in Puerto Rico (Triandis et al., 1988). The distinction of terms at the cultural and individual levels of analysis is useful because it is convenient when discussing the behavior of allocentrics in individualist cultures and idiocentrics in collectivist cultures (e.g., Bontempo, Lobel, & Triandis, 1989).

In addition to subordinating personal to collective goals, collectivists tend to be concerned about the results of their actions on members of their ingroups, tend to share resources with ingroup members, feel interdependent with ingroup members, and feel involved in the lives of ingroup members (Hui & Triandis, 1986). They emphasize the integrity of ingroups over time and deemphasize their independence from ingroups (Triandis et al., 1986).

Shweder's data (see Shweder & LeVine, 1984) suggest that collectivists perceive ingroup norms as universally valid (a form of ethnocentrism). A considerable literature suggests that collectivists automatically obey ingroup authorities and are willing to fight and die to maintain the integrity of the ingroup, whereas they distrust and are unwilling to cooperate with members of outgroups (Triandis, 1972). However, the definition of the ingroup keeps shifting with the situation. Common fate, common outside threat, and proximity (which is often linked to common fate) appear to be important determinants of the ingroup/outgroup boundary. Although the family is usually the most important ingroup, tribe, coworkers, coreligionists, and members of the same political or social collective or the same aesthetic or scientific persuasion can also function as important ingroups. When the state is under threat, it becomes the ingroup.

Ingroups can also be defined on the basis of similarity (in demographic attributes, activities, preferences, or institutions) and do influence social behavior to a greater extent when they are stable and impermeable (difficult to gain membership or difficult to leave). Social behavior is a function of ingroup norms to a greater extent in collectivist than individualist cultures (Davidson, Jaccard, Triandis, Morales, and Diaz-Guerrero, 1976).

In collectivist cultures, ingroups influence a wide range of social situations (e.g., during the cultural revolution in China, the state had what was perceived as "legitimate influence" on every collective). In some cases, the influence is extreme (e.g., the Rev. Jones's People's Temple influenced 911 members of that collective to commit suicide in 1978).

* * *

As discussed earlier, over the course of cultural evolution there has been a shift toward individualism. Content analyses of social behaviors recorded in written texts (Adamopoulos & Bontempo, 1986) across historical periods show a shift from communal to exchange relationships. Behaviors related to trading are characteristic of individualistic cultures, and contracts emancipated individuals from the bonds of tribalism (Pearson, 1977).

The distribution of collectivism-individualism, according to Hofstede's (1980) data, contrasts most of the Latin American, Asian, and African cultures with most of the North American and Northern and Western European cultures. However, many cultures are close to the middle of the dimension, and other variables are also relevant. Urban samples tend to be individualistic, and traditional-rural samples tend toward collectivism within the same culture (e.g., Greece in the work of Doumanis, 1983; Georgas, 1989; and Katakis, 1984). Within the United States one can find a good deal of range on this variable, with Hispanic samples much more collectivist than samples of Northern and Western European backgrounds (G. Marin & Triandis, 1985).

The major antecedents of individualism appear to be cultural complexity and affluence. The more complex the culture, the greater the number of ingroups that one may have, so that a person has the option of joining ingroups or even forming new ingroups. Affluence means that the individual can be independent of ingroups. If the ingroup makes excessive demands, the individual can leave it. Mobility is also important. As individuals move (migration, changes in social class) they join new ingroups, and they have the opportunity to join ingroups whose goals they find compatible with their own. Furthermore, the more costly it is in a particular ecology for an ingroup to reject ingroup members who behave according to their own goals rather than according to ingroup goals, the more likely are people to act in accordance with their personal goals, and thus the more individualistic is the culture. Such costs are high when the ecology is thinly populated. One can scarcely afford to reject a neighbor if one has only one neighbor. Conversely, densely populated ecologies are characterized by collectivism, not only because those who behave inappropriately can be excluded, but also because it is necessary to regulate behavior more strictly to overcome problems of crowding.

As rewards from ingroup membership increase, the more likely it is that a person will use ingroup goals as guides for behavior. Thus, when ingroups provide many rewards (e.g., emotional security, status, income, information, services, willingness to spend time with the person) they tend to increase the person's commitment to the ingroup and to the culture's collectivism.

The size of ingroups tends to be different in the two kinds of cultures. In collectivist cultures, ingroups tend to be small (e.g., family), whereas in individualist cultures they can be large (e.g., people who agree with me on important attitudes).

Child-rearing patterns are different in collectivist and individualist cultures. The primary concern of parents in collectivist cultures is obedience, reliability, and proper behavior. The primary concern of parents in individualistic cultures is self-reliance, independence, and creativity. Thus, we find that in simple, agricultural societies, socialization is severe and conformity is demanded and obtained (Berry, 1967, 1979). Similarly, in working-class families in industrial societies, the socialization pattern leads to conformity (Kohn, 1969, 1987). In more individualist cultures such as food gatherers (Berry, 1979) and very individualistic cultures such as the United States, the child-rearing pattern emphasizes self-reliance and independence; children are allowed a good deal of autonomy and are encouraged to explore their environment. Similarly, creativity and self-actualization are more important traits and are emphasized in child-rearing in the professional social classes (Kohn, 1987).

It is clear that conformity is functional in simple, agricultural cultures (if one is to make an irrigation system, each person should do part of the job in a well-coordinated plan) and in working-class jobs (the boss does not want subordinates who do their own thing). Conversely, it is dysfunctional in hunting cultures, in which one must be ingenious, and in professional jobs, in which one must be creative. The greater the cultural complexity, the more is conformity to one ingroup dysfunctional, inasmuch as one cannot take advantage of new opportunities available in other parts of the society.

The smaller the family size, the more the child is allowed to do his or her own thing. In large families, rules must be imposed, otherwise chaos will occur. As societies become more affluent (individualistic), they also reduce the size of the family, which increases the opportunity to raise children to be individualists. Autonomy in childrearing also leads to individualism. Exposure to other cultures (e.g., through travel or because of societal heterogeneity) also increases individualism, inasmuch as the child becomes aware of different norms and has to choose his or her own standards of behavior.

* * *

Tight versus loose cultures. In collectivist cultures, ingroups demand that individuals conform to ingroup norms, role definitions, and values. When a society is relatively homogeneous, the norms and values of ingroups are similar. But heterogeneous societies have groups with dissimilar norms. If an ingroup member deviates from ingroup norms, ingroup members may have to make the painful decision of excluding that individual from the ingroup. Because rejection of ingroup members is emotionally draining, cultures develop tolerance for deviation from group norms. As a result, homogeneous cultures are often rigid in requiring that ingroup members behave according to the ingroup norms. Such cultures are *tight.* Heterogeneous cultures and cultures in marginal positions between two major cultural patterns are flexible in dealing with ingroup members who deviate from ingroup norms. For example, Japan is considered tight, and it is relatively homogeneous. Thailand is considered loose, and it is in a marginal position between the major cultures of India and China; people are pulled in different directions by sometimes contrasting norms, and hence they must be more flexible in imposing their norms. In short, tight cultures (Pelto, 1968) have clear norms that are reliably imposed. Little deviation from normative behavior is tolerated, and severe sanctions are administered to those who deviate. *Loose* cultures either have unclear norms about most social situations or tolerate deviance from the norms. For example, it is widely reported in the press that Japanese children who return to Japan after a period of residence in the West, are criticized most severely by teachers because their behavior is not "proper." Japan is a tight culture in which deviations that would be considered trivial in the West (such as bringing Western food rather than Japanese food for lunch) are noted and criticized. In loose cultures, deviations from "proper" behavior are tolerated, and in many cases there are no standards of "proper" behavior. Theocracies[1] are prototypical of tight cultures, but some contemporary relatively homogeneous cultures (e.g., the Greeks, the Japanese) are also relatively tight. In a heterogeneous culture, such as the United States, it is more difficult for people to agree on specific norms, and even more difficult to impose severe sanctions. Geographic mobility allows people to leave the offended communities in ways that are not available in more stable cultures. Urban environments are more loose than rural environments, in which norms are clearer and sanctions can be imposed more easily. Prototypical of loose cultures are the Lapps and the Thais. In very tight cultures, according to Pelto, one finds corporate control of property, corporate ownership of stored food and production power, religious figures as leaders, hereditary recruitment into priesthood, and high levels of taxation.

* * *

The intolerance of inappropriate behavior characteristic of tight cultures does not extend to all situations. In fact, tight cultures are quite tolerant of foreigners (they do not know better), and of drunk, and mentally ill persons. They may even have rituals in which inappropriate behavior is expected. For example, in a tight culture such as Japan one finds the office beer party as a ritual institution, where one is expected to get drunk and to tell the boss what one "really" thinks of him (it is rarely her). Similarly, in loose cultures,

[1]Nations run by religious rule.

there are specific situations in which deviance is not tolerated. For example, in Orissa (India), a son who cuts his hair the day after his father dies is bound to be severely criticized, although the culture is generally loose.

* * *

Culture and Self

Culture is to society what memory is to the person. It specifies designs for living that have proven effective in the past, ways of dealing with social situations, and ways to think about the self and social behavior that have been reinforced in the past. It includes systems of symbols that facilitate interaction (Geertz, 1973), rules of the game of life that have been shown to "work" in the past. When a person is socialized in a given culture, the person can use custom as a substitute for thought, and save time.

The three dimensions of cultural variation just described reflect variations in culture that have emerged because of different ecologies, such as ways of surviving. Specifically, in cultures that survive through hunting or food gathering, in which people are more likely to survive if they work alone or in small groups because game is dispersed, individualism emerges as a good design for living. In agricultural cultures, in which cooperation in the building of irrigation systems and food storage and distribution facilities is reinforced, collectivist designs for living emerge. In complex, industrial cultures, in which loosely linked ingroups produce the thousands of parts of modern machines (e.g., a 747 airplane), individuals often find themselves in situations in which they have to choose ingroups or even form their own ingroups (e.g., new corporation). Again, individualistic designs for living become more functional. In homogeneous cultures, one can insist on tight norm enforcement; in heterogeneous, or fast changing, or marginal (e.g., confluence of two major cultural traditions) cultures, the imposition of tight norms is difficult because it is unclear whose norms are to be used. A loose culture is more likely in such ecologies.

Over time, cultures become more complex, as new differentiations prove effective. However, once complexity reaches very high levels, moves toward simplification emerge as reactions to too much complexity. For example, in art styles, the pendulum has been swinging between the "less is more" view of Oriental art and the "more is better" view of the rococo period in Europe. Similarly, excessive individualism may create a reaction toward collectivism, and excessive collectivism, a reaction toward individualism; or tightness may result from too much looseness, and looseness from too much tightness. Thus, culture is dynamic, ever changing.

* * *

The three dimensions of cultural variation described earlier are systematically linked to different kinds of self. In this section I provide hypotheses linking culture and self.

INDIVIDUALISM-COLLECTIVISM Child-rearing patterns in individualistic cultures tend to emphasize self-reliance, independence, finding yourself, and self-actualization. As discussed earlier, such child-rearing increases the complexity of the private self, and because there are more elements of the private self to be sampled, more are sampled. Thus, the probability that the private rather than the other selves will be sampled increases with individualism. Conversely, in collectivist cultures, child-rearing emphasizes the importance of the collective; the collective self is more complex and more likely to be sampled.

* * *

Such patterns are usually associated with rewards for conformity to ingroup goals, which leads to internalization of the ingroup goals. Thus, people do what is expected of them, even if that is not enjoyable. Bontempo et al. (1989) randomly assigned subjects from a collectivist (Brazil) and an individualist (U.S.) culture to two conditions of questionnaire administration: public and private. The questionnaire contained questions about how the subject was likely to act when the ingroup expected a behavior that was costly to the individual (e.g., visit a friend in the hospital, when this was time consuming). Both of the questions How should the person act? and How enjoyable would it be to act? were measured. It was found that Brazilians gave the same answers under both the anonymous and public conditions. Under both conditions they indicated that they would do what was expected of them. The U.S. sample indicated they would do what was expected of them in the public but not in the private condition. The U.S. group's private answers indicated that the subjects thought that doing the costly behaviors was unlikely, and certainly not enjoyable. Under the very same conditions the Brazilians indicated that they thought the costly prosocial behaviors were likely and enjoyable. In short, the Brazilians had internalized[2] the ingroup norms so that conformity to the ingroup appeared enjoyable to them.

* * *

Observations indicate that the extent to which an ingroup makes demands on individuals in few or in many areas shows considerable variance. For example, in the United States, states make very few demands (e.g., pay your income tax), whereas in China during the cultural revolution, the Communist Party made demands in many areas (artistic expression, family life, political behavior, civic action, education, athletics, work groups, even location, such as where to live). It seems plausible that the more areas of one's life that are affected by an ingroup, the more likely the individual is to sample the collective self.

* * *

TIGHT-LOOSE CULTURES Homogeneous, relatively isolated cultures tend to be tight, and they will sample the collective self more than will heterogeneous, centrally located cultures. The more homogeneous the culture, the more the norms will be clear and deviation from normative behavior can be punished. Cultural heterogeneity increases the confusion regarding what is correct and proper behavior. Also, cultural marginality[3] tends to result in norm and role conflict and pressures individuals toward adopting different norms. Because rejection of the ingroup members who have adopted norms of a different culture can be costly, individuals moderate their need to make their ingroup members conform to their ideas of proper behavior. So, the culture becomes loose (i.e., tolerant of deviations from norms).

The looser the culture, the more the individual can choose what self to sample. If several kinds of collective self are available, one may choose to avoid norm and role conflict by rejecting all of them and developing individual conceptions of proper behavior. Thus, sampling of the private self is more likely in loose cultures and sampling of the collective self is more likely in tight cultures. Also, tight cultures tend to socialize their children by emphasizing the expectations of the generalized other. Hence, the public self will be complex and will be more likely to be sampled. In other words, tight cultures tend to sample the public and collective self, whereas loose cultures tend to sample the private self.

When the culture is both collectivist and tight, then the public self is extremely likely to be sampled. That means people act "properly," as that is defined by society, and are extremely anxious [about not acting] correctly. Their private self does not matter. As a result, the private and public selves are often different. Doi (1986) discussed this point extensively, comparing the Japanese public self (*tatemae*) with the private self (*honne*). He suggested that in the United States there is virtue in keeping public and private consistent (not being a hypocrite). In Japan, proper action matters. What you feel about such action is irrelevant. Thus, the Japanese do not like to state their personal opinions, but rather seek consensus.

Consistently with Doi's (1986) arguments is Iwao's (1988) research. She presented scenarios to Japanese and Americans and asked them to judge various actions that could be appropriate responses to these situations. For example, one scenario (daughter brings home person from another race) included as a possible response "thought that he would never allow them to marry but told

---

[2]Made a part of themselves.

[3]Not being part of the mainstream of a culture and feeling that one or one's group is at the "margins."

them he was in favor of their marriage." This response was endorsed as the *best* by 44% of the Japanese sample but by only 2% of the Americans; it was the *worst* in the opinion of 48% of the Americans and 7% of the Japanese.

Although the private self may be complex, this does not mean that it will be communicated to others if one can avoid such communication. In fact, in tight cultures people avoid disclosing much of the self, because by disclosing they may reveal some aspect of the self that others might criticize. In other words, they may be aware of the demands of the generalized other and avoid being vulnerable to criticism by presenting little of this complex self to others. Barlund (1975) reported studies of the self-disclosure to same-sex friend, opposite-sex friend, mother, father, stranger, and untrusted acquaintance in Japan and in the United States. The pattern of self-disclosure was the same—that is, more to same-sex friend, and progressively less to opposite-sex friend, mother, father, stranger, and least to the untrusted acquaintance. However, the amount disclosed in each relationship was about 50% more in the United States than in Japan.

Cultural Complexity The more complex the culture, the more confused is likely to be the individual's identity. Dragonas (1983) sampled the self-concepts of 11- and 12-year-olds in Greek small villages (simple), traditional cities (medium), and large cities (complex) cultures. She found that the more complex the culture, the more confusing was the identity. Similarly, Katakis (1976, 1978, 1984) found that the children of farmers and fishermen, when asked what they would be when they are old, unhesitatingly said "farmer" or "fisherman," whereas in the large cities the responses frequently were of the "I will find myself" variety. Given the large number of ingroups that are available in a complex environment and following the logic presented here, individuals may well opt for sampling their private self and neglect the public or collective selves.

Content of Self in Different Cultures The specific content of the self in particular cultures will reflect the language and availability of mythological constructs of that culture. Myths often provide ideal types that are incorporated in the self forged in a given culture (Roland, 1984a). For example, peace of mind and being free of worries have been emphasized as aspects of the self in India (Roland, 1984b) and reflect Indian values that are early recognizable in Hinduism and Buddhism (which emerged in India). Mythological, culture-specific constructs become incorporated in the self (Sinha, 1982, 1987). Roland (1984b) claimed that the private self is more "organized around 'we', 'our' and 'us' . . ." (p. 178) in India than in the West. But particular life events may be linked to more than one kind of self. For example, Sinha (1987) found that the important goals of Indian managers are their own good health and the good health of their family (i.e., have both private and collective self-elements).

Sinha (personal communication, November 1985) believes the public self is different in collectivist and individualist cultures. In individualistic cultures it is assumed that the generalized other will value autonomy, independence, and self-reliance, and thus individuals will attempt to act in ways that will impress others (i.e., indicate that they have these attributes). To be distinct and different are highly valued, and people find innumerable ways to show themselves to others as different (in dress, possessions, speech patterns). By contrast, in collectivist cultures, conformity to the other in public settings is valued. Thus, in a restaurant, everyone orders the same food (in traditional restaurants, only the visible leader gets a menu and orders for all). The small inconvenience of eating nonoptimal food is more than compensated by the sense of solidarity that such actions generate. In collectivist cultures, being "nice" to ingroup others is a high value, so that one expects in most situations extreme politeness and a display of harmony (Triandis, Marin, Lisansky, & Betancourt, 1984). Thus, in collectivist cultures, the public self is an extension of the collective self.

One must make a good impression by means of prosocial behaviors toward ingroup members, acquaintances, and others who may become ingroup members. At the same time, one can be quite rude to outgroup members, and there is no concern about displaying hostility, exploitation, or avoidance of outgroup members.

* * *

The collective self in collectivist cultures includes elements such as "I am philotimos" (traditional Greece, meaning "I must act as is expected of me by my family and friends"; see Triandis, 1972), "I must sacrifice myself for my ingroup," "I feel good when I display affection toward my ingroup," and "I must maintain harmony with my ingroup even when that is very disagreeable." The person is less self-contained in collectivist than in individualistic cultures (Roland, 1984b, p. 176).

Identity is defined on the basis of different elements in individualistic and collectivist cultures. Individualistic cultures tend to emphasize elements of identity that reflect possessions—what do I own, what experiences have I had, what are my accomplishments (for scientists, what is my list of publications). In collectivist cultures, identity is defined more in terms of relationships—I am the mother of X, I am a member of family Y, and I am a resident of Z. Furthermore, the qualities that are most important in forming an identity can be quite different. In Europe and North America, being logical, rational, balanced, and fair are important attributes; in Africa, personal style, ways of moving, the unique spontaneous self, sincere self-expression, unpredictability, and emotional expression are most valued. The contrast between classical music (e.g., Bach or Mozart) and jazz reflects this difference musically.

Consequences of Sampling the Private and Collective Self In the previous section I examined the relationship between the three dimensions of cultural variation and the probabilities of differential sampling of the private, public, and collective selves. In this section I review some of the empirical literature that is relevant to the theoretical ideas just presented.

An important consequence of sampling the collective self is that many of the elements of the collective become salient. Norms, roles, and values (i.e., proper ways of acting as defined by the collective) become the "obviously" correct ways to act. Behavioral intentions reflect such processes. Thus, the status of the other person in the social interaction—for example, is the other an ingroup or an outgroup member—becomes quite salient. Consequently, in collectivist cultures, individuals pay more attention to ingroups and outgroups and moderate their behavior accordingly, than is the case in individualistic cultures (Triandis, 1972).

* * *

Who is placed in the ingroup is culture specific. For example, ratings of the "intimacy" of relationships on a 9-point scale suggest that in Japan there is more intimacy with acquaintances, co-workers, colleagues, best friends, and close friends than in the United States (Gudykunst & Nishida, 1986).

Atsumi (1980) argued that understanding Japanese social behavior requires distinguishing relationships with benefactors, true friends, co-workers, acquaintances, and outsiders (strangers). The determinants of social behavior shift depending on this classification. Behavior toward benefactors requires that the person go out of his way to benefit them. Behavior toward true friends is largely determined by the extent the behavior is enjoyable in itself, and the presence of these friends makes it enjoyable. Behavior toward co-workers is determined by both norms and cost/benefit considerations. Finally, behavior toward outsiders is totally determined by cost/benefit ratios.

* * *

The behavioral intentions of persons in collectivist cultures appear to be determined by cognitions that are related to the survival and benefit of their collective. In individualist cultures, the concerns are personal. An example comes from a study of smoking. A collectivist sample (Hispanics in the U.S.) showed significantly more concern than an individualist sample (non-Hispanics) about smoking affecting the health of others, giving a bad example to children, harming children, and bothering others with the bad smell of cigarettes, bad breath, and bad smell on clothes and belongings, whereas the individualist sample was more concerned about the physiological symptoms they might experience during withdrawal from cigarette smoking (G. V. Marin, Marin, Otero-Sabogal, Sabogal, & Perez-Stable, 1987).

The emphasis on harmony within the ingroup, found more strongly in collectivist than in individualist cultures, results in the more positive evaluation of group-serving partners (Bond, Chiu, & Wan, 1984), the choice of conflict resolution techniques that minimize animosity (Leung, 1985, 1987), the greater giving of social support (Triandis et al., 1985), and the greater support of ingroup goals (Nadler, 1986). The emphasis on harmony may be, in part, the explanation of the lower heart-attack rates among unacculturated than among acculturated Japanese-Americans (Marmot & Syme, 1976). Clearly, a society in which confrontation is common is more likely to increase the blood pressure of those in such situations, and hence the probability of heart attacks; avoiding conflict and saving face must be linked to lower probabilities that blood pressure will become elevated. The probability of receiving social support in collectivist cultures may be another factor reducing the levels of stress produced by unpleasant life events and hence the probabilities of heart attacks (Triandis et al., 1988).

Although ideal ingroup relationships are expected to be smoother, more intimate, and easier in collectivist cultures, outgroup relationships can be quite difficult. Because the ideal social behaviors often cannot be attained, one finds many splits of the ingroup in collectivist cultures. Avoidance relationships are frequent and, in some cases, required by norms (e.g., mother-in-law avoidance in some cultures). Fights over property are common and result in redefinitions of the ingroup. However, once the ingroup is defined, relationships tend to be very supportive and intimate within the ingroup, whereas there is little trust and often hostility toward outgroup members. Gabrenya and Barba (1987) found that collectivists are not as effective in meeting strangers as are individualists. Triandis (1967) found unusually poor communication among members of the same corporation who were not ingroup members (close friends) in a collectivist culture. Bureaucracies in collectivist cultures function especially badly because people hoard information (Kaiser, 1984). Manipulation and exploitation of outgroups is common (Pandey, 1986) in collectivist cultures. When competing with outgroups, collectivists are more competitive than individualists (Espinoza & Garza, 1985) even under conditions when competitiveness is counterproductive.

In individualistic cultures, people exchange compliments more frequently than in collectivist cultures (Barlund & Araki, 1985). They meet people easily and are able to cooperate with them even if they do not know them well (Gabrenya & Barba, 1987). Because individualists have more of a choice concerning ingroup memberships, they stay in those groups with whom they can have relatively good relationships and leave groups with whom they disagree too frequently (Verma, 1985).

Competition tends to be interpersonal in individualistic and intergroup in collectivist cultures (Hsu, 1983; Triandis et al., 1988). Conflict is frequently found in family relationships in individualistic cultures and between families in collectivist cultures (Katakis, 1978).

There is a substantial literature (e.g., Berman, Murphy-Berman, & Singh, 1985; Berman, Murphy-Berman, Singh, & Kumar, 1984; Hui, 1984; G. Marin, 1985; Triandis et al., 1985) indicating that individualists are more likely to use equity, and collectivists to use equality or need, as the norms for the distribution of resources (Yang, 1981). This is consistent with the emphasis on trading discussed earlier. By contrast, the emphasis on communal relationships (Mills & Clark, 1982) found in collectivist cultures leads to emphases on equality and need. The parallel with gender differences, where men emphasize exchange and women emphasize communal relationships (i.e., equity and need; Major & Adams, 1983; Brockner & Adsit, 1986), respectively, is quite striking. * * *

* * *

Conclusions

Aspects of the self (private, public, and collective) are differentially sampled in different cultures, depending on the complexity, level of individualism, and looseness of the culture. The more complex, individualistic, and loose the culture, the more likely it is that people will sample the private self and the less likely it is that they will sample the collective self. When people sample the collective self, they are more likely to be influenced by the norms, role definitions, and values of the particular collective, than when they do not sample the collective self. When they are so influenced by a collective, they are likely to behave in ways considered appropriate by members of that collective. The more they sample the private self, the more their behavior can be accounted for by exchange theory and can be described as an exchange relationship. The more they sample the collective self, the less their behavior can be accounted for by exchange theory; it can be described as a communal relationship. However, social behavior is more likely to be communal when the target of that behavior is an ingroup member than when the target is an outgroup member. Ingroups are defined by common goals, common fate, the presence of an external threat, and/or the need to distribute resources to all ingroup members for the optimal survival of the ingroup. Outgroups consist of people with whom one is in competition or whom one does not trust. The ingroup-outgroup distinction determines social behavior more strongly in collectivist than in individualist cultures. When the culture is both collectivist and tight, the public self is particularly likely to be sampled. In short, a major determinant of social behavior is the kind of self that operates in the particular culture.

References

Adamopoulos, J., & Bontempo, R. N. (1986). Diachronic universals in interpersonal structures. *Journal of Cross-Cultural Psychology, 17*, 169–189.

Allport, G. W. (1943). The ego in contemporary psychology. *Psychological Review, 50*, 451–478.

Allport, G. W. (1955). *Becoming*. New Haven, CT: Yale University Press.

Atsumi, R. (1980). Patterns of personal relationships: A key to understanding Japanese thought and behavior. *Social Analysis, 6*, 63–78.

Barlund, D. C. (1975). *Public and private self in Japan and the United States*. Tokyo: Simul Press.

Barlund, D. C., & Araki, S. (1985). Intercultural encounters: The management of compliments by Japanese and Americans. *Journal of Cross-Cultural Psychology, 16*, 9–26.

Baumeister, R. F. (1986a). *Identity: Cultural change and the struggle for self*. New York: Oxford University Press.

Baumeister, R. F. (1986b). *Public self and private self*. New York: Springer.

Baumeister, R. F. (1987). How the self became a problem: A psychological review of historical research. *Journal of Personality and Social Psychology, 52*, 163–176.

Berman, J. J., Murphy-Berman, V., & Singh, P. (1985). Cross-cultural similarities and differences in perceptions of fairness. *Journal of Cross-Cultural Psychology, 16*, 55–67.

Berman, J. J., Murphy-Berman, V., Singh, P., & Kumar, P. (1984, September). *Cross-cultural similarities and differences in perceptions of fairness*. Paper presented at the International Congress of Psychology, in Acapulco, Mexico.

Berry, J. W. (1967). Independence and conformity in subsistence level societies. *Journal of Personality and Social Psychology, 7*, 415–418.

Berry, J. W. (1979). A cultural ecology of social behavior. In L. Berkowitz (Ed.), *Advances in experimental social psychology* (Vol. 12, pp. 177–207). New York: Academic Press.

Block, J. (1986, March). *Longitudinal studies of personality*. Colloquium given at the University of Illinois, Psychology Department.

Bond, M. H., Chiu, C., & Wan, K. (1984). When modesty fails: The social impact of group effacing attributions following success or failure. *European Journal of Social Psychology, 16*, 111–127.

Bontempo, R., Lobel, S. A., & Triandis, H. C. (1989). *Compliance and value internalization among Brazilian and U.S. students*. Manuscript submitted for publication.

Brockner, J., & Adsit, L. (1986). The moderating impact of sex on the equity satisfaction relationship: A field study. *Journal of Applied Psychology, 71*, 585–590.

Cooley, C. H. (1902). *Human nature and the social order*. New York: Scribner.

Davidson, A. R., Jaccard, J. J., Triandis, H. C., Morales, M. L., & Diaz-Guerrero, R. (1976). Cross-cultural model testing:

Toward a solution of the etic-emic dilemma. *International Journal of Psychology, 11*, 1–13.

Doumanis, M. (1983). *Mothering in Greece: From collectivism to individualism.* New York: Academic Press.

Doi, T. (1986). *The anatomy of conformity: The individual versus society.* Tokyo: Kodansha.

Dragonas, T. (1983). *The self-concept of preadolescents in the Hellenic context.* Unpublished doctoral dissertation, University of Ashton, Birmingham, England.

Espinoza, J. A., & Garza, R. T. (1985). Social group salience and interethnic cooperation. *Journal of Experimental Social Psychology, 231*, 380–392.

Fazio, R. H., & Williams, C. J. (1986). Attitude accessibility as a moderator of the attitude-perception and attitude-behavior relations: An investigation of the 1984 presidential election. *Journal of Personality and Social Psychology, 51*, 505–514.

Gabrenya, W. K., & Barba, L. (1987, March). *Cultural differences in social interaction during group problem solving.* Paper presented at the meetings of the Southeastern Psychological Association, Atlanta.

Geertz, C. (1973). *The interpretation of cultures.* New York: Basic Books.

Georgas, J. (1989). Changing family values in Greece: From collectivist to individualist. *Journal of Cross-Cultural Psychology, 20*, 80–91.

Gordon, C., & Gergen, K. J. (Eds.). (1968). *The self in social interaction.* New York: Wiley.

Greenwald, A. G., Carnot, C. G., Beach, R., & Young, B. (1987). Increasing voting behavior by asking people if they expect to vote. *Journal of Applied Psychology, 71*, 315–318.

Greenwald, A. G., & Pratkanis, A. R. (1984). The self. In R. S. Wyer & T. K. Srull (Eds.), *Handbook of social cognition* (Vol. 3, pp. 129–178). Hillsdale, NJ: Erlbaum.

Gudykunst, W. B., & Nishida. T. (1986). The influence of cultural variability on perceptions of communication behavior associated with relationship terms. *Human Communication Research, 13*, 147–166.

Higgins, E. T., & King, G. (1981). Accessibility of social constructs: Information-processing consequences of individual and contextual variability. In N. Cantor & J. F. Kihlstrom (Eds.), *Personality, cognition and social interaction* (pp. 69–121). Hillsdale, NJ: Erlbaum.

Hofstede, G. (1980). *Culture's consequences.* Beverly Hills, CA: Sage.

Hsu, F. L. K. (1983). *Rugged individualism reconsidered.* Knoxville: University of Tennessee Press.

Hui, C. H. (1984). *Individualism-collectivism: Theory, measurement and its relationship to reward allocation.* Unpublished doctoral dissertation, Department of Psychology, University of Illinois at Champaign-Urbana.

Hui, C. H., & Triandis, H. C. (1986). Individualism-collectivism: A study of cross-cultural researchers. *Journal of Cross Cultural Psychology, 17*, 225–248.

Iwao, S. (1988, August). *Social psychology's models of man: Isn't it time for East to meet West?* Invited address to the International Congress of Scientific Psychology, Sydney, Australia.

James, W. (1950). *The principles of psychology.* New York: Dover. (Original work published 1890)

Kaiser, R. G. (1984). *Russia: The people and the power.* New York: Washington Square Press.

Katakis, C. D. (1976). An exploratory multilevel attempt to investigate interpersonal and intrapersonal patterns of 20 Athenian families. *Mental Health and Society, 3*, 1–9.

Katakis, C. D. (1978). On the transaction of social change processes and the perception of self in relation to others. *Mental Health and Society, 5*, 275–283.

Katakis, C. D. (1984). Oi tris tautotites tis Ellinikis oikogenoias [The three identities of the Greek family]. Athens, Greece: Kedros.

Kohn, M. L. (1969). *Class and conformity.* Homewood, IL: Dorsey.

Kohn, M. L. (1987). Cross-national research as an analytic strategy. *American Sociological Review, 52*, 713–731.

Kraut, R. E. (1973). Effects of social labeling on giving to charity. *Journal of Experimental Social Psychology, 9*, 551–562.

Kuhn, M. H., & McPartland, T. (1954). An empirical investigation of self-attitudes. *American Sociological Review, 19*, 68–76.

Leung, K. (1985). *Cross-cultural study of procedural fairness and disputing behavior.* Unpublished doctoral dissertation, Department of Psychology, University of Illinois, Champaign-Urbana.

Leung, K. (1987). Some determinants of reactions to procedural models for conflict resolution: A cross-national study. *Journal of Personality and Social Psychology, 53*, 898–908.

Lobel, S. A. (1984). *Effects of sojourn to the United States. A SYMLOG content analysis of in-depth interviews.* Unpublished doctoral dissertation, Harvard University.

Major, B., & Adams, J. B. (1983). Role of gender, interpersonal orientation, and self-presentation in distributive justice behavior. *Journal of Personality and Social Psychology, 45*, 598–608.

Marin, G. (1985). Validez transcultural del principio de equidad: El colectivismo-individualismo como una variable moderatora [Transcultural validity of the principle of equity: Collectivism–individualism as a moderating variable]. *Revista Interamericana de Psichologia Occupational, 4*, 7–20.

Marin, G., & Triandis, H. C. (1985). Allocentrism as an important characteristic of the behavior of Latin Americans and Hispanics. In R. Diaz-Guerrero (Ed.), *Cross-cultural and national studies in social psychology* (69–80). Amsterdam, The Netherlands: North Holland.

Marin, G. V., Marin, G., Otero-Sabogal, R., Sabogal, F., & Perez-Stable, E. (1987). *Cultural differences in attitudes toward smoking: Developing messages using the theory of reasoned action* (Tech. Rep.). (Available from Box 0320, 400 Parnassus Ave., San Francisco, CA 94117)

Marmot, M. G., & Syme, S. L. (1976). Acculturation and coronary heart disease in Japanese Americans. *American Journal of Epidemiology, 104*, 225–247.

Marsella, A. J., DeVos, G., & Hsu, F. L. K. (1985). *Culture and self.* New York: Tavistock.

Mead, G. H. (1934). *Mind, self, and society.* Chicago: University of Chicago Press.

Miller, R. L., Brickman, P., & Bolen, D. (1975). Attribution versus persuasion as a means of modifying behavior. *Journal of Personality and Social Psychology, 31*, 430–441.

Mills, J., & Clark, E. S. (1982). Exchange and communal relationships. In L. Wheeler (Ed.), *Review of personality and social psychology* (Vol. 3, pp. 121–144). Beverly Hills, CA: Sage.

Murphy, G. (1947). *Personality.* New York: Harper.

Nadler, A. (1986). Help seeking as a cultural phenomenon: Differences between city and kibbutz dwellers. *Journal of Personality and Social Psychology, 51*, 976–982.

Pandey, J. (1986). Sociocultural perspectives on ingratiation. *Progress in Experimental Personality Research, 14*, 205–229.

Pearson, H. W. (Ed.). (1977). *The livelihood of man: Karl Polanyi.* New York: Academic Press.

Pelto, P. J. (1968, April). The difference between "tight" and "loose" societies. *Transaction*, 37–40.

Rogers, T. B. (1981). A model of the self as an aspect of the human information processing system. In N. Cantor & J. F. Kihlstrom (Eds.), *Personality, cognition and social interaction* (pp. 193–214). Hillsdale, NJ: Erlbaum.

Rokeach, M. (1960). *The open and closed mind.* New York: Basic Books.

Roland, A. (1984a). Psychoanalysis in civilization perspective. *Psychoanalytic Review, 7*, 569–590.

Roland, A. (1984b). The self in India and America: Toward a psychoanalysis of social and cultural contexts. In V. Kovolis (Ed.), *Designs of selfhood* (pp. 123–130). New Jersey: Associated University Press.

Rosenberg, M. (1979). *Conceiving the self.* New York: Basic Books.

Schlenker, B. R. (1985). Introduction. In B. R. Schlenker (Ed.). *Foundations of the self in social life* (pp. 1–28). New York: McGraw-Hill.

Shotland, R. L., & Berger, W. G. (1970). Behavioral validation of several values from the Rokeach value scale as an index of honesty. *Journal of Applied Psychology, 54*, 433–435.

Shweder, R. A., & LeVine, R. A. (1984). *Cultural theory: Essays on mind, self and emotion.* New York: Cambridge University Press.

Sinha, J. B. P. (1982). The Hindu (Indian) identity. *Dynamische Psychiatrie, 15*, 148–160.

Sinha, J. B. P. (1987). *Work cultures in Indian Organizations* (ICSSR Report). New Delhi, India: Concept Publications House.

Smith, M. B. (1980). Attitudes, values and selfhood. In H. E. Howe & M. M. Page (Eds.), *Nebraska Symposium on Motivation*, 1979 (pp. 305–358). Lincoln: University of Nebraska Press.

Snyder, M. (1974). Self-monitoring and expressive behavior. *Journal of Personality and Social Psychology, 30*, 526–537.

Snyder, M. (1987). *Public appearances as private realities: The psychology of self-monitoring.* New York: Freeman.

Snyder, M., Simpson, J. A., & Gangestad, S. (1986). Personality and sexual relations. *Journal of Personality and Social Psychology, 51*, 181–190.

Stryker, S., & Serpe, R. T. (1982). Commitment, identity salience, and role behavior: Theory and research example. In W. Ickes & E. S. Knowles (Eds.), *Personality, roles and social behavior* (pp. 199–218). New York: Springer.

Tajfel, H. (1978). *Differentiation between social groups.* London: Academic Press.

Triandis, H. C. (1967). Interpersonal relations in international organizations. *Journal of Organizational Behavior and Human Performance, 2*, 26–55.

Triandis, H. C. (1972). *The analysis of subjective culture.* New York: Wiley.

Triandis, H. C. (1977). *Interpersonal behavior.* Monterey, CA: Brooks/Cole.

Triandis, H. C. (1980). Values, attitudes, and interpersonal behavior. In H. Howe & M. Page (Eds.), *Nebraska Symposium on Motivation*, 1979 (pp. 195–260). Lincoln: University of Nebraska Press.

Triandis, H. C., Bontempo, R., Betancourt, H., Bond, M., Leung, K., Brenes, A., Georgas, J., Hui, C. H., Marin, G., Setiadi, B., Sinha, J. B. P., Verma, J., Spangenberg, J., Touzard, H., & de Montmollin, G. (1986). The measurement of etic aspects of individualism and collectivism across cultures. *Australian Journal of Psychology* (Special issue on cross-cultural psychology), *38*, 257–267.

Triandis, H. C., Bontempo, R., Villareal, M. J., Asai, M., & Lucca, N. (1988). Individualism and collectivism: Cross-cultural perspectives on self-ingroup relationships. *Journal of Personality and Social Psychology, 54*, 323–338.

Triandis, H. C., Leung, K., Villareal, M. J., & Clack, F. L. (1985). Allocentric versus idiocentric tendencies: Convergent and discriminant validation. *Journal of Research in Personality, 19*, 395–415.

Triandis, H. C., Marin, G., Lisansky, J., & Betancourt, H. (1984). *Simpatia* as a cultural script of Hispanics. *Journal of Personality and Social Psychology, 47*, 1363–1375.

United States Employment and Training Administration. *Dictionary of occupational titles.* Washington, DC: Government Printing Office.

Verma, J. (1985). The ingroup and its relevance to individual behaviour: A study of collectivism and individualism. *Psychologia, 28*, 173–181.

Wicklund, R. A., & Gollwitzer, P. M. (1982). *Symbolic self-completion.* Hillsdale, NJ: Erlbaum.

Yang, K. S. (1981). Social orientation and individual modernity among Chinese students in Taiwan. *Journal of Social Psychology, 113*, 159–170.

Zavalloni, M. (1975). Social identity and the recoding of reality. *International Journal of Psychology, 10*, 197–217.

Zavalloni, M., & Louis-Guerin, C. (1984). *Identité sociale et conscience: Introduction á l'égo-écologie* [Social identity and conscience: Introduction to the ego ecology]. Montréal, Canada: Les presses de l'université de Montreal.

Ziller, R. C. (1973). *The social self.* New York: Pergamon.

Insult, Aggression, and the Southern Culture of Honor: An "Experimental Ethnography"

Dov Cohen, Richard E. Nisbett, Brian F. Bowdle, and Norbert Schwarz

Anthropologists typically examine psychological attributes of a culture through field work. A researcher visits the culture, consults native informants, and writes a report based on what he or she has seen and heard. The following selection, by the social psychologists Dov Cohen, Richard Nisbett, Brian Bowdle, and Norbert Schwarz, introduces a very different method for this purpose: the social psychological experiment. The authors investigated the distinctive culture of the southern United States by directly observing and then contrasting the responses of northerners and southerners to experimentally controlled challenges of various sorts, including insults. The results support the authors' idea that the southern United States is a "culture of honor," in which insults and attacks call for an immediate, aggressive response.

For cultural psychology, the methods of this research are innovative and the results are important. The research also raises a further question: how many cultures does each of us belong to? Cohen and colleagues compared northerners and southerners but also could have contrasted college students vs. nonstudents, Americans vs. Canadians, members of upper-class vs. lower-class families, and so on. The implication is that each of us belongs to many different cultures at the same time, each of which may have a distinctive and important influence on our behavior and outlook on life.

From *Journal of Personality and Social Psychology, 70*, 945–960, 1996.

Approximately 20,000–25,000 Americans will die in homicides this year, and tens of thousands more will be injured in stabbings or gunfights that could have ended in death. In about half of the homicides for which police can find a cause, the triggering incident seems argument- or conflict-related (Fox & Pierce, 1987); and, in many of these cases, this triggering incident might be classified as "trivial" in origin, arising from a dispute over a small amount of money, an offensive comment, or a petty argument.

Such incidents, however, are not trivial to the participants in them. Rather, the participants behave as if something important is at stake (Daly & Wilson, 1988). They act as if they were members of what anthropologists call a *culture of honor*, in which even small disputes become contests for reputation and social status. The United States is home to several subcultures holding such norms (Anderson, 1994; Fischer, 1989; Gilmore, 1990; Guerra, in press; McCall, 1994; McWhiney, 1988; Peristiany, 1965; Pitt-Rivers, 1968; Wolfgang & Ferracuti, 1967). The research presented here is a first attempt at what might be called an *experimental ethnography* of one such subculture within the United States—that of the southern White male.

Historical Background

For centuries, the American South has been regarded as more violent than the North (Fischer, 1989). Over the years, historians, social scientists, and other observers have developed a number of explanations for this, drawing on such facts about the South as its higher temperature, its poverty, and its history of slavery. There is evidence to support all these explanations, and they have been dealt with more fully elsewhere (Cohen, 1996; Cohen & Nisbett, 1994; Nisbett, 1993; Nisbett & Cohen, 1996; Reaves & Nisbett, 1994). We think the best single explanation has to do with the South being home to a version of the culture of honor, in which affronts are met with violent retribution.

Historians and other observers have often noted that, in the South, men have had to take action against insults or else lose status before their family and peers (McWhiney, 1988; Wyatt-Brown, 1982). As Fischer (1989) noted,

> From an early age, small boys were taught to think much of their own honor and to be active in its defense. Honor in this society meant a pride of manhood in masculine courage, physical strength, and warrior virtue. Male children were trained to defend their honor without a moment's hesitation —lashing out against their challengers with savage violence. (p. 690)

Originally, there were good historic and economic reasons for such norms to take hold in the South. For one, the economy of the South was initially based to a large extent on herding (McWhiney, 1988), and cultural anthropologists have observed that herding cultures the world over tend to be more approving of certain forms of violence (J. K. Campbell, 1965; Edgerton, 1971; Peristiany, 1965). Herdsmen must be willing to use force to protect themselves and their property when law enforcement is inadequate and when one's wealth can be rustled away. The settlers of the South came primarily from herding economies on the fringes of Britain, where lawlessness, instability, political upheaval, and clan rule had been present for centuries (Fischer, 1989; McWhiney, 1988). The people from the border country of Britain were forced to be self-reliant in their pursuit of justice, and they brought with them this tradition as they settled the lawless frontier South. As Fischer (1989) wrote,

> In the absence of any strong sense of order as unity, hierarchy, or social peace, backsettlers shared an idea of order as a system of retributive justice. The prevailing principle was lax talionis, the rule of retaliation. It held that a good man must seek to do right in the world, but when wrong was done to him, he must punish the wrongdoer himself by an act of retribution that restored order and justice in the world. (p. 765)

If the ethic of self-protection had been adaptive in Britain, the frontier conditions of the South and the vulnerability of southerners to the theft of their herds and other lawlessness probably reinforced the self-reliant stance. Law enforcement in the frontier South was either inadequate, corrupt, or just too far away (Brown, 1969; Gastil, 1971; Ireland, 1979; McWhiney, 1988). So, as a North Carolina proverb put it, every man "should be sheriff on his own hearth" (Fischer, 1989, p. 765).

Such conditions perpetuated the culture of honor in the South, as it became important to establish one's reputation for toughness—even on matters that might seem small on the surface. If one had been crossed, trifled with, or affronted, retribution had to follow as a warning to the community. Defense of honor can be an important part of defense of self, as Daly and Wilson (1988) observed:

> A seemingly minor affront is not merely a "stimulus" to action, isolated in time and space. It must be understood within a larger social context of reputations, face, relative social status, and enduring relationships. Men are known by their fellows as "the sort who can be pushed around" or "the sort who won't take any shit," as people whose word means action and people who are full of hot air, as guys whose girlfriends you can chat up with impunity or guys you don't want to mess with. (p. 128)

In the Old South, allowing oneself to be pushed around or affronted without retaliation amounted to admitting that one was an easy mark and could be taken advantage of. As Pitt-Rivers (1968) noted, "Whenever the authority of law is questioned or ignored, the code of honor re-emerges to allocate the right to precedence and dictate the principles of conduct" (cited in Ayers, 1984, p. 275).

Persistence of the Culture of Honor

Though frontier conditions in the South disappeared and the herding economy has become less and less important, culture-of-honor norms appear to have persisted into this century. Brearley (1934), for example, argued that in much of the South of his day it was impossible to convict someone of murder if (a) the killer had been insulted and (b) he had warned the victim of his intent to kill if the insult were not retracted or compensated.

Nisbett and colleagues recently have shown that violence stemming from culture-of-honor norms is still part of the southern legacy today (Nisbett, 1993; Nisbett & Cohen, 1996; Nisbett, Polly, & Lang, 1994; Reaves & Nisbett, 1994). White male homicide rates of the South are higher than those of the North, and the South exceeds the North *only* in homicides that are argument- or conflict-related, not in homicides that are committed while another felony, such as robbery or burglary, is being performed. Such findings are consistent with a stronger emphasis on honor and protection in the South.

Cohen and Nisbett (1994) came to similar conclusions about a southern culture of honor in analyzing data from major national surveys. They showed that the South was more approving of particular types of violence and not of others. The South's approval of violence seemed limited to violence used for self-protection, to respond to an insult, or to socialize children. Thus, although southern white males were not more likely to endorse statements about violence in general ("Many people only learn through violence"), they were more willing to endorse violence when it was used to protect ("A man has the right to kill to defend his house") or to answer an affront (approving of a man punching a stranger who "was drunk and bumped into the man and his wife on the street"). Southern white males were also more likely to stigmatize men, described in brief scenarios, who did *not* respond with violence, criticizing them for being "not much of a man" if they failed to fight or shoot the person who challenged or affronted them. Such results suggest that southern white male approval of violence is produced by culture-of-honor norms.

The culture seems to be perpetuated as well by the institutions of the South. Cohen (1996) argued that culture-of-honor norms are embodied in the laws and social policies of southern states—as reflected in looser gun control laws, less restrictive self-defense statutes, and more hawkish voting by federal legislators on foreign policy issues, for example. In two field experiments, Cohen and Nisbett (1995) showed that southern institutions, such as employers and the media, may perpetuate culture-of-honor norms by being less likely to stigmatize violence in defense of honor and more likely to see it as justifiable or sympathetic.

In the work presented here, we supplement the attitude, homicide rate, law and social policy, and field experimental evidence with experimental evidence from the laboratory. In these laboratory experiments, we examined whether even college students who are from the South subscribe to culture-of-honor norms, and we explored how these norms might manifest themselves in the cognitions, emotions, behaviors, and physiological reactions of our participants. The overarching theme of these experiments was the importance of an affront to southern white males and their need to respond to it. If southerners subscribe to a culture of honor and northerners do not, the reactions of northern and southern participants to an insult should differ in predictable ways. Compared with northerners, southerners should be (a) more likely to view an insult as damaging to their status and reputation, (b) more upset (emotionally and physiologically) by the insult, and (c) more prepared (cognitively, physiologically, and behaviorally) for aggressive and dominant behavior after being insulted. The present studies were designed to test these hypotheses.

When we refer to *southerners* and *northerners*, we refer only to the particular populations we have studied to date, namely nonHispanic white males from the North and from the South of the United States. It is these populations for which extensive anthropological and historical literature indicates there are substantial differences with respect to culture-of-honor norms. When we refer to northerners and southerners participating in the experiments described below, we are using this as a short-hand way of referring to students at the University of Michigan meeting these restricted definitions.

Because our sample is limited to students at the University of Michigan, it is also certainly not representative of all white male northerners and southerners. The students—both northern and southern—come from families that are well off financially. (In Experiment 3, the median income for northerners was between $80,000 and $90,000; for southerners it was between $90,000 and $100,000.) The southerners may be unusual in that they have chosen to leave the South at least temporarily and come to school in the North. We suspect both of these factors work against us and that regional differences would be bigger if representative samples of northerners and southerners were examined. Thus, our sample probably provides for a rather conservative test of our hypotheses.

The three experiments we report all included the same basic manipulation: A confederate of the experimenter bumps into the unsuspecting participant as he walks down a hallway and calls the participant an "asshole." The three experiments focused on the different behavioral, cognitive, emotional, and physiological effects of the insult.

Experiment 1

In Experiment 1 we examined the effect of the insult on the immediate emotional reaction of the participant and on subsequently expressed hostility during the rest of the experiment. Subsequent hostility was assessed with a word-completion task, a face-rating task, and a neutral scenario-completion task to see if the participant would project his anger onto these stimuli. We also assessed hostility by having the participant complete the ending of a scenario that involved affront and sexual challenge. These procedures allowed us to examine whether (a) relatively neutral stimuli would bring out aggression after priming by the insult or (b) only subsequent stimuli that also involve affront or challenge would bring out aggression. In either case, a positive result calls for an interaction effect of regional origin and insult, with southerners reacting with more aggression after an insult than northerners.

Our theory led us to predict that this interaction would definitely be obtained when subsequent stimuli involve issues of insult or challenge. However, it was an open question whether the interaction would also be obtained for ambiguous or neutral stimuli. We did not make predictions regarding whether the interaction would occur on the face rating, word completion, or neutral scenario task. We believed, however, that it would be informative to examine these variables in an exploratory way to see how specific or general the effect of the insult was.

METHOD The experiment involved a 2 × 2 design with participant's region of origin (North vs. South) as one variable and condition (insulted vs. not insulted) as the other variable.

Participants Participants were 83 University of Michigan white male undergraduates (42 northern, 41 southern) who were recruited by telephone and paid $5 for their time. Students who had lived in the South for a period of at least 6 years were considered southern. The South was defined as census divisions 5, 6, and 7. This includes the states of Delaware, Maryland. West Virginia, Virginia, North Carolina, South Carolina, Georgia, Florida, Kentucky, Tennessee, Alabama, Mississippi, Arkansas, Oklahoma, Louisiana, and Texas. In this experiment—as in Experiments 2 and 3—students from Washington, DC and from towns we could identify as its immediate suburbs were excluded, because DC is probably not representative of either northern or southern culture. All other students were considered northern.

So that all students would be equated at least with respect to whether they had self-selected to attend school in another state, all participants were non-Michigan residents. On average, southern students had spent 87% of their lives in the South, whereas northern students had spent only 4% of their lives in the South, Jewish students were excluded because we hypothesized that Jewish culture might dilute regional differences. We are aware, however, that some researchers might have different intuitions on this matter (see Fischer, 1989, p. 874).

Procedure Students came to the laboratory of the Institute for Social Research, where they were informed that the experiment concerned the effects of "limited response time conditions on certain facets of human judgment." After an initial introduction to the experiment, participants were told to fill out a short demographic questionnaire and were asked to take it to a table at the end of a long, narrow hallway.

As the participant walked down the hall, a confederate of the experimenter walked out of a door marked "Photo Lab" and began working at a file cabinet in the hall. The confederate had to push the file drawer in to allow the participant to pass by him and drop his paper off at the table. As the participant returned seconds later and walked back down the hall toward the experimental room, the confederate (who had reopened the file drawer) slammed it shut on seeing the participant approach and bumped into the participant with his shoulder, calling the participant an "asshole." The confederate then walked back into the "Photo Lab." Two observers were stationed in the hall. They appeared to be working on homework, paying no attention to the goings-on in the hall. One (male) observer was seated on the floor in a location where he could glance up and see the participant's face at the moment he was bumped. The other (female) observer was sitting at the table at the end of the hall where she could glance at the participant's face if he turned around (which occurred about 86% of the time across Experiments 1 and 3). Both observers could hear everything the participant said and could read his body language (though from different perspectives). Immediately after the bumping incident, the observers rated the participant's emotional reactions on 7-point scales. The reactions of anger and amusement were the ones of greatest interest, but observers also rated how aroused, flustered, resigned, or wary participants seemed. The correlation for the two observers' judgments was .52 for amusement ($p < .001$) and .57 for anger ($p < .001$). Observers also rated the effectiveness of the bump. There was no North–South difference on this rating, $t(41) < 1$.[1] (Observers, of course, did not know the re-

[1]The p of these correlations refers to the probability that they would be this large if the correlation in the population was actually 0; t is a statistic commonly used to compare means of different groups, and the number in parentheses following the t is its degrees of freedom (related to the number of participants in the sample).

gional origin of the participant.) Participants who were assigned to the control condition completed the same procedures without being bumped. (Obviously, there were no observers and hence no ratings of emotional reaction in the control condition.)

After the participant returned to the room, the judgment tasks began. The first task was a word completion task, in which the participant was given a string of letters (e.g.,__ight or gu__) that he could complete either in a hostile way (e.g., *fight* or *gun*) or a nonhostile way (e.g., *light* or *gum*). The second task was a face rating task, in which the participant tried to guess which emotion was being expressed in a series of photographs of faces: anger, fear, disgust, sadness, or happiness. The third task was a scenario completion task, in which the participant needed to fill in the beginning or ending of a story. In one scenario, a man was rescued by an ambulance, and the participant was asked to fill in the beginning of the story. The other scenario involved issues of affront and challenge. The scenario began:

> It had only been about twenty minutes since they had arrived at the party when Jill pulled Steve aside, obviously bothered about something.
>
> "What's wrong?" asked Steve.
>
> "It's Larry, I mean, he knows that you and I are engaged, but he's already made two passes at me tonight."
>
> Jill walked back into the crowd, and Steve decided to keep his eye on Larry. Sure enough, within five minutes Larry was reaching over and trying to kiss Jill.

Participants were asked to complete the ending to this story.

After all tasks were completed, participants were thoroughly debriefed and reconciled with the bumper. The debriefer explained why the research was important and why the deception and insult were used. The bumper met the participants and talked with them to make sure they were not upset or angered by the experience. Informal conversations made it clear that participants were not unhappy with the treatment accorded them and understood the reasons for it. To establish this in a more formal way, we asked several questions of participants at the end of the debriefing in Experiment 2. We asked participants how interested they were by the experiment on a scale that ranged from 0 (*not at all*) to 7 (*extremely*). The modal answer was 7, and the mean was 5.8. We asked how glad participants were that they had been in the experiment. The mode again was 7, with 96% of participants at or above the midpoint on the scale. Participants also were asked how angry they were at having been in the experiment. Eighty-nine percent of participants answered 0, and no participant answered as high as the midpoint on the scale. In fact, on every measure, insulted participants were more favorable toward the experiment than controls.

Results and Discussion

Emotional Reactions Northerners and southerners differed in how angry or amused they appeared to be after the bump. Observers rated northern participants as significantly more amused by the bump than southern participants (northern $M = 2.77$, southern $M = 1.74$),[2] $t(41) = 2.85$, $p < .01$, and southern participants tended to be more angry than northern participants (northern $M = 2.34$, southern $M = 3.05$), $t(41) = 1.61$, $.10 < p < .15$. * * *

We subtracted the amusement rating from the anger rating for each participant to show the very different reaction patterns of northerners and southerners. As may be seen in Table 42.1, the most common emotional reaction for northerners was to show more amusement than anger. The overwhelmingly dominant reaction for southerners was to show as much or more anger than amusement. There were no significant differences on how aroused, flustered, resigned, or wary participants seemed (all *ts* < 1.1, all *ps* > .25).

[2] *M* is the mean score of the participants in the group (in this case the northerners' group or the southerners' group).

TABLE 42.1

OBSERVERS' RATINGS OF NORTHERN VERSUS SOUTHERN PARTICIPANTS' REACTIONS TO INSULT

Participants	Percentage anger ratings as high or higher than amusement ratings	Percentage amusement ratings higher than anger ratings
Northern	35	65
Southern	85	15

Projective Hostility We examined whether the insult would make southerners more hostile while leaving northerners unaffected.

Word completion. The insult did not significantly affect either southerners, $t(39) < 1.2$, $p > .25$, or northerners, $t(40) < 1.2$, $p > .25$. There was also no main effect for either region or insult (both $Fs < 1$).[3]

Face ratings: Southerners were not more likely to project anger, disgust, fear, happiness, or sadness onto the faces shown to them after the insult than were northerners (all interaction $Fs < 1$). There was again no main effect of either region or insult for any of the ratings (all $ps > .25$), except for happiness. Both control and insulted southerners were less likely to project happiness onto the faces than northerners were, $F(1, 76) = 5.19$, $p < .05$.

Scenario completions. There were no region, insult, or interaction effects on how likely participants were to begin the "ambulance" scenario with interpersonal violence (all $ps > .15$). In sum, none of the projective measures showed a differential impact of the insult as a function of the participant's regional origin. This was not true, however, for the insult scenario.

Insult Prime Scenario For the scenario describing the attempted pass at the fianceé, there was a significant interaction between region and insult. If southerners were insulted, they were much more likely to end the scenario with violence, whereas northerners were unaffected by the insult. Seventy-five percent of insulted southerners completed this scenario with events in which the man injured or threatened to injure his challenger, whereas only 20% of control southerners did so, χ_2 (1, $N = 40$) = 12.13, $p < .001$.[4] Northerners were unaffected by the manipulation, being somewhat less likely to conclude this scenario with violence if they had been insulted (41% vs. 55%); χ_2 (1, $N = 42$) = 0.83, $p > .25$. To examine the interaction between region and insult, we performed an analysis of variance (ANOVA) on a three-level variable (no violence, violence suggested, actual violence). Higher numbers indicated greater violence, and means were: southern insult = 2.30, southern control = 1.40, northern insult = 1.73, and northern control = 2.05, interaction $F(1, 78) = 7.65$, $p < .005$).

Experiment 1 indicated that southerners were likely to see the insult as a cause for anger rather than amusement, whereas northerners were not much affected by the insult, taking it as a cause more for amusement than for anger. In addition, southerners (but not northerners) were much more likely to complete the "affront" script with

[3]The F statistic, from the analysis of variance, is another method for comparing group means in more complex research designs.

[4]The χ_2 statistic (chi-square) is used to compare frequencies with which participants can be sorted into categories. The "1" refers to the degrees of freedom in the design (related, but not equivalent to the number of categories), N is the number of participants, the p level refers to the probability that participants would have sorted themselves into the categories in the proportions observed if chance were the only determinant.

violence if they had been insulted than if they had not. This greater hostility on the part of insulted southerners was manifested only in response to the affront prime, however. Insulted southerners were no more likely to project hostility onto neutral stimuli than were other participants. These findings indicate that an insult may make a southern male angry and may lower his threshold for anger in response to subsequent affronts, without necessarily producing hostility in response to innocuous stimuli.

Experiment 2

In Experiment 2 we explored whether, for southerners, responses to insult go beyond annoyance and mere cognitive priming for aggression and are accompanied by physiological changes of a sort that might mediate genuine behavioral aggression.* * *

PHYSIOLOGICAL MEASURE OF STRESS To measure how upset or stressed the participant became, we examined the cortisol level of the participant before and after the bump. Cortisol is a hormone associated with high levels of stress, anxiety, and arousal in humans and in animals (Booth, Shelley, Mazur, Tharp, & Kittok, 1989; Dabbs & Hooper, 1990; Kirschbaum, Bartussek, & Strasburger, 1992; Leshner, 1983; Popp & Baum, 1989; Thompson, 1988). If southerners are more upset by the acute stress of the insult, they should show a rise in cortisol levels compared with control participants. If northerners are relatively unaffected by the insult, as they seemed to be in Experiment 1, they should show little or no rise in cortisol levels compared with control participants.

PHYSIOLOGICAL MEASURE OF PREPAREDNESS FOR FUTURE AGGRESSION To measure how prepared for future challenges the participants became, we examined their testosterone levels before and after the bump. Testosterone is a hormone associated with aggression and dominance behavior in animals and both male and female humans. The causations seems to go both ways: High levels of testosterone facilitate dominance or aggressive behaviors, and successful dominance encounters lead to increases in testosterone (Booth et al., 1989; Dabbs, 1992; Elias, 1981; Gladue, 1991; Gladue, Boechler, & McCaul, 1989; Kemper, 1990; Mazur, 1985; Mazur & Lamb, 1980; Olweus, 1986; Popp & Baum, 1989). Research has suggested that testosterone plays a role in preparing participants for competitions or dominance contests (Booth et al., 1989; B. Campbell, O'Rourke, & Rabow, 1988, cited in Mazur, Booth, & Dabbs, 1992; Dabbs, 1992; Mazur et al., 1992; see also Gladue et al., 1989, p. 416; but see Salvador, Simon, Suay, & Llorens, 1987). Higher testosterone levels may facilitate the aggressive behaviors and display of dominance cues that make one act and even look tougher (Dabbs, 1992, pp. 311–313; Mazur, 1985). In addition, testosterone may raise fear thresholds. In male rats, injections of testosterone act as an anxiolytic agent, reducing the rat's fear of novel environments (Osborne, Niekrasz, & Seale, 1993). It would obviously be useful in challenge or competition situations if this fear-reducing effect were to occur in humans.

If southerners respond to the insult as a challenge and prepare themselves for future aggression or dominance contests, we might expect a testosterone increase after the bump. If northerners are relatively unaffected, we would not expect their testosterone levels to rise very much.

* * *

INTERPRETATION OF AMBIGUOUS STIMULI In Experiment 1, insulted southerners did not project more hostility onto neutral stimuli, but they did project more hostility onto the scenario in which a clear affront was offered. In Experiment 2 we examined whether insulted southerners would project more hostility onto *ambiguous* scenarios in which there is only the *possibility* that an affront or challenge is being offered. Again, we included these ambiguous stimuli as exploratory variables to see how general or how specific the effect of the insult would be.

In Experiment 2 we also examined the importance of the public versus private nature of the insult, predicting that all insult effects would be greater if the insult were carried out publicly.

Method

Participants Participants were 173 white male undergraduates (111 northern, 62 southern) at the University of Michigan who were recruited by telephone and paid $10. Again, students were considered southern if they had spent at least 6 years in the South. All other students were considered northern. On average, southern participants had spent 81% of their lives in the South, compared with northern participants, who had spent only 3% of their lives in the South. Again, Black, Jewish, Hispanic, and Michigan-resident students were excluded.

Procedure Participants were met in the laboratory by an experimenter who explained that the experiment concerned people's performance on tasks under various conditions. The experimenter said that she would be measuring the participant's blood sugar levels throughout the experiment by taking saliva samples. To get a baseline measurement, the participant was given a piece of sugarless gum to generate saliva, a test tube to fill to the 5-mL level, and a brief questionnaire to fill out as he provided the first saliva sample.

After the saliva sample was given, the participant was sent down the hall to drop off his questionnaire and was bumped and insulted as described in Experiment 1. The participant was either bumped publicly, bumped privately, or not at all. In the public condition, there were two witnesses to the insult. Both witnesses were confederates who were identified as fellow participants by the experimenter before the participant began his walk down the hall. Both observers made eye contact with the participant so that he knew they had witnessed the incident. In the private condition, there were no observers in the hallway. In the control condition, the participant was not bumped or insulted.

As the participant walked down the hall, he continued to chew the sugarless gum and was told not to talk while he had the gum in his mouth. This was to keep the participant from talking to observers after the insult in the public condition. As witnesses to the insult, the public observers rated the participant's emotional reaction to the bump. No private observation could be made because there were no observers in the hall for the private bump in this experiment. (In all conditions, observers and confederates were, of course, aware of the condition but did not know whether the participant was a southerner or a northerner.)

* * *

* * * The participant was then asked to give another saliva sample. On average, this second sample was given 13 min after the first.

* * *

After the participant [completed some other procedures], the experimenter asked him to fill out an "opinions test." This questionnaire had a number of scenarios that were ambiguous with respect to whether an insult had been delivered. In one scenario, for example, one character cuts another off as they are driving down the road. For each situation, the participant was asked to guess the likelihood of either a physical fight or a verbal argument occurring. After the participant finished the questionnaire, he was asked to give another saliva sample. On average, this third sample was given 25 min after the first. (We timed the second and third samples at these intervals after consulting with experts who believed that testosterone changes could be detected in saliva between 10 and 30 min after the bump.)

Participants were extensively debriefed and reconciled with the bumper as in Experiment 1. No participants were actually shocked during the experiment.

Assays Saliva samples were frozen at –20°F so they could be assayed later for testosterone and cortisol by the University of Michigan Reproductive Sciences Program. Median variance ratios for the assays ranged from .01 to .04. Split-half reliabilities for these assays were above .85.

RESULTS

* * *

Cortisol Levels We averaged the two postbump measurements and then computed a change score: (average postbump cortisol level − prebump cortisol level) ÷ (prebump cortisol level). As may be seen in Figure 42.1, cortisol levels rose 79% for insulted southerners and 42% for control southerners. They rose 33% for insulted northerners and 39% for control northerners. We had predicted that insulted southerners would show large increases in cortisol levels, whereas control southerners and both insulted and control northerners would show smaller changes. This was because, in the absence of provocation, there was no reason to assume the cortisol levels of southerners would rise more than the cortisol levels of northerners. * * * This contrast—indicating that the effect of the insult was seen only for southerners, not for northerners—described the data well and was significant, $t(165) = 2.14$, $p < .03$. * * *

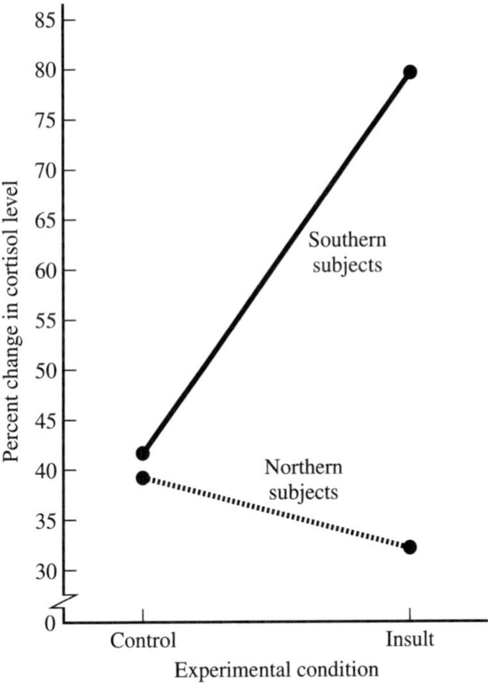

Figure 42.1 Changes in cortisol level for insulted and noninsulted southerners and northerners.

Testosterone Levels As with cortisol, we averaged the two postbump measurements and then computed a change score: (average postbump testosterone level − prebump testosterone level) ÷ (prebump testosterone level). As may be seen in Figure 42.2, testosterone levels rose 12% for insulted southerners and 4% for control southerners. * * *

* * *

Ambiguous Insult Scenarios There was no effect for region, insult, or the interaction on whether participants expected the ambiguous scenarios to end with either physical or verbal aggression (all $Fs < 1$).

DISCUSSION Experiment 1 indicated that although northerners were able to brush off the insult and remain unaffected by it, southerners were not able to do so and became primed for aggression if given the right stimulus. Experiment 2 showed that southerners became upset and prepared for aggression on the physiological level. Southerners were more stressed by the insult, as shown by the rise in their cortisol levels, and more primed for future aggression, as indicated by the rise in their testosterone levels. Cortisol and testosterone levels of northerners were hardly affected by the insult.

* * *

The results for the ambiguous insult scenarios are consistent with the results for the ambiguous materials in Experiment 1. There is no evidence that insulted southerners were more likely than other participants to see malevolent intent in the protagonists' actions or to regard violence as an appropriate response to their actions. There are two plausible interpretations for this. The first is that it takes a clear-cut challenge or affront to bring out southerners' increased hostility and aggressiveness. The second is that our ambiguous measures were too uninvolving to pick up the effects: Perhaps we might have seen increased hostility on the part of insulted southerners if we had

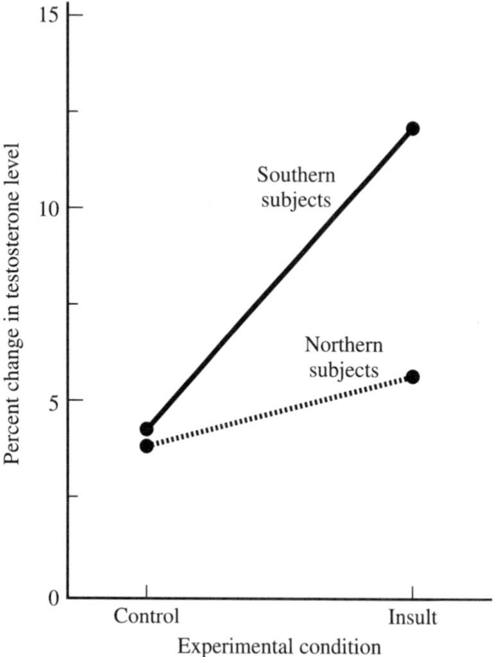

Figure 42.2 Changes in testosterone level for insulted and noninsulted southerners and northerners.

examined real behavior after putting participants in an ambiguously insulting (yet emotionally involving) live situation. We do not know which explanation is correct, but in any case the conclusion seems to be that measures that are unthreatening (either because they are uninvolving or because they are ambiguous with regard to issues of affront) will not elicit increased hostility from insulted southern participants.

Experiment 3

In Experiment 3 we tried to extend the results of Experiments 1 and 2 by exploring whether southerners would perceive an insult as damaging to their status and reputation (consistent with a culture-of-honor worldview) and would actually behave in more aggressive and domineering ways after an insult. We examined three major sets of variables.

Perceived Effect of the Insult on One's Masculine Status In a public-insult condition, participants were bumped in front of an observer, whom they later met. The participant's task was to guess what that observer really thought of him. We expected southerners to think that the observer would see them as less masculine or tough after witnessing the insult. Northerners, however, should not feel that their status had been changed by the insult.

Aggressive Behavior in a Challenge Situation After the Insult After the participant was bumped or not bumped, he continued walking down the long hallway. Another confederate—who was 6 ft 3 in. (1.91 m) and 250 lbs (114 kg)—appeared around the corner and began walking toward the participant at a good pace. The hall was lined with tables, so there was room for only one person to pass without the other person giving way. The new confederate walked down the center of the hall on a collision course with the participant and did not move (except at the last second to avoid another bumping).

In essence, we set up a "chicken" game similar to that played by American teenagers who drive at each other in their cars. In its many forms, "chicken" games are important in cultures of honor and situations in which participants try to establish their toughness for status or strategic advantage (Kahn, 1968; Schelling, 1963). The main dependent variable in this "chicken" game was the distance at which the participant decided to "chicken out" or give way to our confederate. We expected insulted southern participants to respond aggressively to the challenge and go farthest in this "game."

Dominance Behavior in Subsequent Encounters After the Insult After the participant was bumped or not and had returned to the experimental room, he had a brief meeting with another confederate. This confederate, the "evaluator," was always the same person and was 5 ft 6 in. (1.67 m) and 140 lbs (64 kg). The confederate rated the firmness of the participant's handshake and the degree of eye contact, and he made summary ratings of how domineering or submissive the participant was during the encounter, all on 7-point scales. We expected insulted southern participants to be more domineering and less submissive after the insult and northerners to be little affected by the insult.

After all other dependent measures were collected, we gave the participant two questionnaires asking about traditional "macho" behaviors. For example, the inventories asked the participant about how many pushups he could do, how much alcohol he had ever drunk in one night, and how fast he had ever driven a car. One of the questionnaires was "private," but the other was "public," as the participant believed he would have to discuss his answers with other experiment participants. We predicted that southerners would answer the questions in a more macho way after the insult, whether it had been public or private, and that the effect would be stronger on the public questionnaire.

Finally, participants were asked to fill out an extensive questionnaire about personal history and demographic status so we could examine the comparability of southern and northern participants on a variety of dimensions.

Method

Participants Participants were 148 white male undergraduates (88 northern, 60 southern) at the University of Michigan who were recruited by telephone and paid $15. Southerners were defined as anyone who had lived at least 6 years in the South; all other participants were considered northerners. On average, southern participants had spent 80% of their life in the South, compared with northerners, who had spent 5% of their life in the South. Black, Jewish, and Hispanic students were excluded.

Procedure The experimenter told the participants that the experiment concerned people's personality and the contributions of nature versus nurture to personality. She explained that the participants would fill out a few personality inventories, answer some demographic questions, and provide a saliva sample that could be assayed for biological properties. She gave participants a demographic questionnaire as well as another filler questionnaire and had them provide a saliva sample as in Experiment 2. (Saliva samples were in fact not assayed later. They were collected to give credibility to the nature-versus-nurture cover story and to provide a pretext for the participant to chew gum so that he could be prohibited from talking after being bumped, as was the case in Experiment 2.)

After the participant provided the saliva sample, the experimenter sent him down the hall to be bumped publicly, privately, or not at all. When the participant reached a specified point in the hall, he was either bumped or not; a few seconds later, a confederate covertly signaled the "chicken" confederate to appear. The "chicken" confederate walked toward the participant and estimated the distance in inches at which the participant gave way to him. * * * (In trial runs, the "chicken's" estimate of distance correlated more than .90 with actual distance. The chicken, the observers, and the evaluator were, of course, aware of the condition but did not know whether participants were southern or northern.)

When the participant returned to the room, the experimenter said that the experiment concerned "who you are" and that "one big part of who we are is who other people think we are." She explained the importance of first impressions for this and said that sometimes people are aware of the first impressions they make and sometimes they are not. She explained that the participant would have a brief meeting with another participant (actually the "evaluator" confederate). She added that the participant's task would be to guess what this other person really thought of him. The participant and his counterpart would be allowed to shake hands, but that was all. She said that no talking was allowed.

The experimenter explained that pairs of people would be meeting like this all semester. She added that to encourage as much accuracy and honesty as possible, the participant in the experiment who came closest to guessing what the other person thought of him would win $100.

The experimenter then brought in the "evaluator" confederate, who shook hands with the participant. In the public bump condition, the evaluator was one of the witnesses to the bump. In the private bump condition, there had been no witnesses at all. In the control condition, there was, of course, no bump to observe.

After the brief handshake between the participant and the evaluator, the experimenter sent the evaluator out into the hall to record his impressions. Back in the experimental room, the experimenter explained that the participant would now have to guess what the evaluator thought of him. On a 1-to-5 scale, the participant guessed what the other person thought of him on dimensions such as *cowardly–courageous, strong–weak,* and *manly–not manly,* as well as filler dimensions such as *introverted–extroverted, attractive–unattractive,* and so on.

* * *

After the participant completed * * * [other procedures], he was debriefed and reconciled with the bumper.

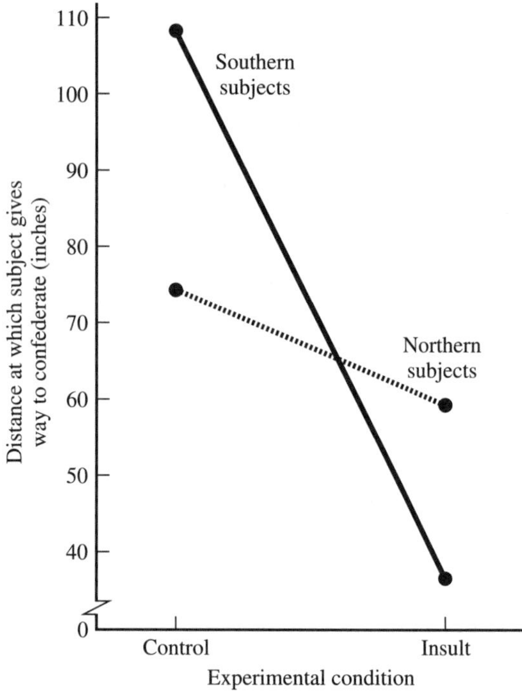

Figure 42.3 Distance at which the participant gave way to the confederate in the "chicken" game for insulted and noninsulted southerners and northerners.

RESULTS Once again, the public versus private nature of the insult was not an important factor in participants' responses to the insult (all *ps* > .15 for the interaction between region and public vs. private condition) with the exception of participants' beliefs about how the "evaluator" confederate rated their personalities (interaction $p < .06$). Except for that variable, we collapsed over the public–private variable for purposes of analysis.

"Chicken" Game As may be seen in Figure 42.3, the insult dramatically changed the behavior of southerners in the "chicken" game. Insulted southerners went much farther before "chickening out" and deferring to the confederate (37 in. [0.94 m]), compared with control southerners (108 in. [2.74 m]). The insult did not much affect the behavior of northerners. * * *

* * *

Encounter With the Evaluator The evaluator's ratings for the firmness of the handshake and the degree to which eye contact was domineering were made on a 1-to-7 scale. As can be seen in Figure 42.4, southern participants gave firmer handshakes if they had been insulted than if they had not. Northerners were unaffected by the insult. The standard contrast was significant at $p = .06$, $t(144) = 1.89$. * * *

The rating for how domineering versus submissive the participant was during the encounter in general was computed by reversing the rating of how submissive the evaluator rated the participant to be and adding it to how domineering the evaluator rated him to be. As can be seen in Figure 42.5, insulted southerners were much more domineering than control southerners (mean for insulted southerners = 3.90, mean for control southerners = 2.95). Northerners were little affected by the insult (mean for insulted northerners = 3.61, mean for control northerners = 3.35.) The * * * interaction contrast was significant at $p < .01$, $t(144) = 2.52$. * * *

Although dominance-related ratings showed the predicted effects, northerners and southerners were not differentially affected by the insult for ratings that did not concern dominance or submission. There was no differential effect of the insult on ratings for how friendly, uneasy, or embarrassed the participant was. There was also no differential effect of the insult on ratings of specific participant behaviors such as smiling, standing up, or verbally greeting the evaluator.

Damage to Reputation To create a masculine or macho reputation scale, we combined the participant's guesses of what the other person thought of him on the dimensions *manly–not manly, courageous–cowardly, assertive–timid, tough–wimpy, strong–weak, aggressive–passive, risk seeking–risk avoiding*, and *leader–follower*. The dimensions were on 1-to-5 scales with higher numbers indicating more masculinity. The appropriate contrast here is the *publicly* insulted group (of southerners) with all other conditions. This is because the public insult condition is the only condition in which the confederate saw the participant get insulted. In the private insult condition the evaluator confederate did *not* witness the bump (even as a covert observer), and in the control condition there was no bump to observe.

As can be seen in Figure 42.6, control and privately insulted southerners and northerners believed they had equal status in the eyes of the evaluator on these dimensions. However, publicly bumped southerners were more likely to believe that their status was hurt in the eyes of the person who saw the insult, whereas northerners were hardly affected. The standard contrast was significant at $p < .01$, $t(144) = 2.53$. * * *

Moreover, damage to the participant's perceived reputation was limited to character traits associated with masculinity or machismo. We coded the 13 filler dimensions so that all were positively valenced and summed them to produce a positive impression scale that included none of the macho items. The public insult did not differentially affect how northerners and southerners thought the other person saw them on these nonmasculine dimensions ($p > .75$).

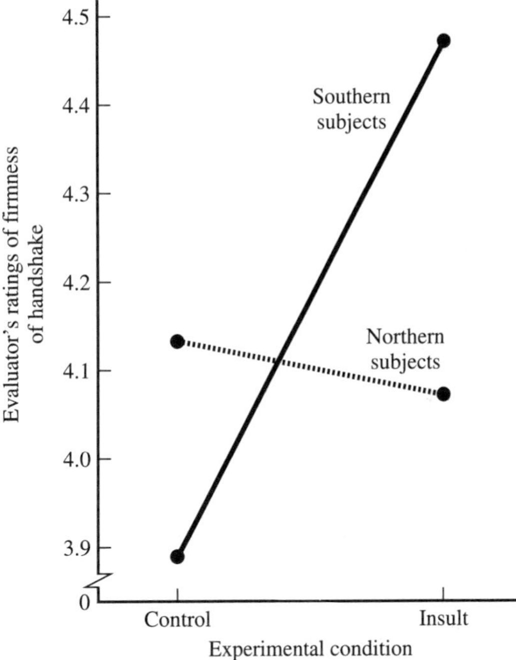

Figure 42.4 Firmness of handshake given by insulted and noninsulted southerners and northerners. Higher numbers indicate a firmer handshake.

The participant also rated himself on how he really was on all dimensions. Unlike the ratings of how the other person saw him, the participants' self-ratings for the macho items were not affected by the public insult for either northerners or southerners ($p > .75$).

* * *

DISCUSSION The results of Experiment 3 indicate that southerners who were insulted in front of others saw themselves as diminished in masculine reputation and status. Perhaps partly as a result, the insult produced more aggressive or domineer-

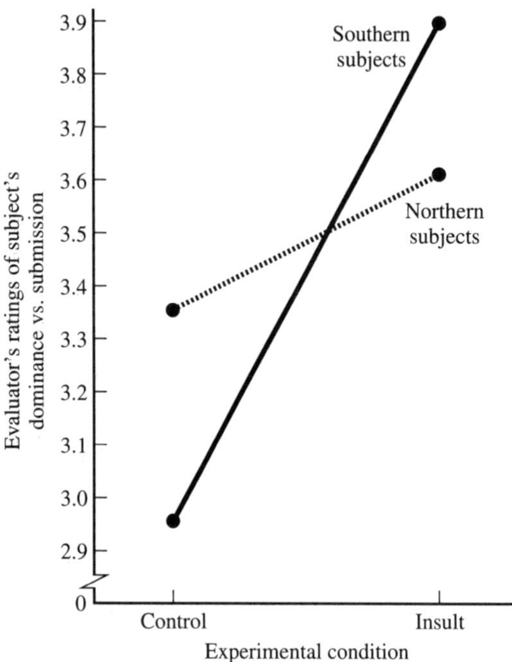

Figure 42.5 General domineering versus submissive impression given by insulted and noninsulted southerners and northerners. Higher numbers indicate more dominance.

ing behavior. Although uninsulted southerners were, if anything, more polite than northerners, insulted southerners were much more aggressive than any other group.

The increased aggressiveness and the desire of insulted southern participants to reestablish themselves was demonstrated in the direct challenge situation of the "chicken" game with the 6-ft-3-in. (1.91 m) confederate. Insulted southerners went much farther in the "chicken" game than did control southerners, whereas northerners were unaffected by the insult. Furthermore, the effect of the insult on southerners was demonstrated more subtly in the interpersonal encounter with the evaluator. Insulted southerners were much more domineering toward the evaluator than were control southerners, whereas northerners were again unaffected. The increased aggressive and dominance behavior of insulted southerners in Experiment 3 is consistent with the cognitive and physiological preparation for aggression and competition found in Experiments 1 and 2.

General Discussion

The findings of the present experiments are consistent with survey and archival data showing that the South possesses a version of the culture of honor. Southerners and northerners who were not insulted were indistinguishable on most measures, with the exception that control southerners appeared somewhat more polite and deferential on behavioral measures than did control northerners. However, insult dramatically changed this picture. After the affront, southern participants differed from northern participants in several important cognitive, emotional, physiological, and behavioral respects.

(a) Southerners were made more upset by the insult, as indicated by their rise in cortisol levels and the pattern of emotional responses they displayed as rated by observers (though the finding about emotional reactions must be considered tentative because of the failure to replicate it in Experiments 2 and 3, in which emotional expression may have been inhibited); (b) southerners were more likely to believe the insult damaged their masculine reputation or status in front of others; (c) southerners were more likely to be cognitively primed for future aggression in insult situations, as indicated by their violent completions of the "attempted kiss script" in Experiment 1; (d) southerners were more likely to show physiological preparedness for dominance or aggressive behaviors, as indicated by their rise in testosterone levels; (e) southerners were more likely to actually behave in aggressive ways during subsequent challenge situations, as indicated by their behavior in the "chicken" game; and (f) southerners were more likely to actually behave in domineering ways during interpersonal encounters, as shown in the meeting with the evaluator.

It also is important to note that there were several measures—[e.g.,] the neutral projective hostility tasks of Experiment 1, * * * —on

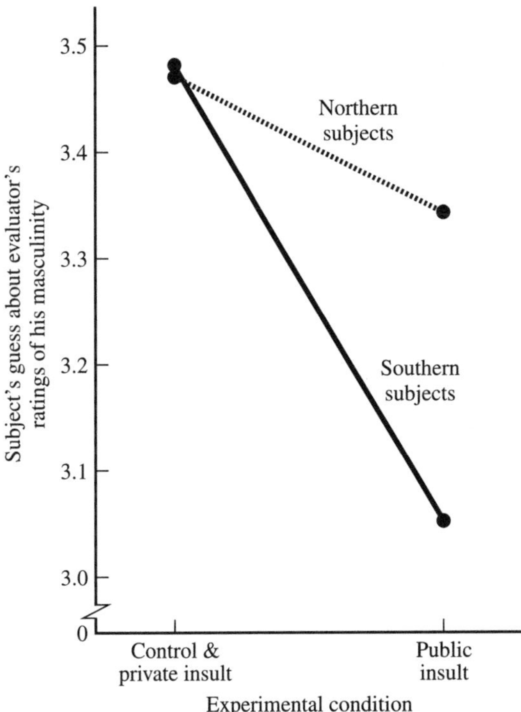

Figure 42.6 Perceived masculine status of insulted and noninsulted southerners and northerners. Higher numbers indicate higher perceived masculine status.

which northerners and southerners were *not* differentially affected by the insult. These null results suggest that the insult did not create a generalized hostility or perceived threat to self that colored everything southern participants did or thought. Measures that were irrelevant or ambiguous with respect to issues of affront and status, that were uninvolving because they were paper-and-pencil, and that were ecologically unnatural did not show an effect of the insult. Instead, the effect of the affront was limited to situations that concerned issues of honor, were emotionally involving, and had actual consequences for the participant's masculine status and reputation.

There are at least two explanations for why the insult produced a greater response from southerners. First, it could be that our bump and "asshole" insult were a greater affront to southerners, who are less accustomed to such rudeness than northerners are. Second, it could be that southerners have different "rules" for what to do once they are insulted. We believe both hypotheses to be true. Numerous observers have argued that southern culture is indeed more polite than northern culture (perhaps as a way of avoiding conflict), and some data from Experiment 3 support this assertion. We also believe, on the basis of survey data (Cohen & Nisbett, 1994) and in-depth interview data collected with F. Lennox and J. Riad (Lennox et al., 1996), that southerners have different rules for how to respond to an affront. The expectations for what one should do when one's honor, self, or property is threatened are different in the South than in the North. For example, we found that southerners are more likely to believe that the appropriate response for a child who is being bullied is to fight back, and southerners are more likely to think it is right for a man to hit someone who insults him (Cohen & Nisbett, 1994). Such responses seem better described as rules about what to do when provoked then as beliefs about what constitutes an insult.

However, data from the present experiments cannot untangle the two explanations—both of which are probably true in any case. Whatever the relative contributions of the two factors, we think the results help us understand something about the etiology of violence in the South and in similar cultures of honor. The results provide strong additional evidence that the insult is crucially important in such cultures. A male who is insulted but does not retaliate risks having his masculine reputation diminished, or at any rate believes that to be the case. When a challenging or highly status-relevant situation is encountered (usually but not necessarily in the ongoing insult situation itself), the person may lash out with violent or aggressive behavior to reassert him- or herself.

* * *

Our laboratory experiments did not produce any truly violent behavior in our participants, so using these experiments as a direct analogy to homicide-producing processes in the South is inappropriate. Nevertheless, we believe the experiments might represent a microcosm of the insult–

aggression cycle that is responsible for a good deal of violence in the South and in similar cultures of honor in the United States and elsewhere. A male who is affronted may be expected to respond with violence because he will be seen as "not much of a man" if he does not (Carter, 1950; Cohen & Nisbett, 1994).

It is not hard to see how insult–aggression cycles lead to violence and death in real-life situations. Arguments that start over petty matters can quickly escalate into deadly conflicts once a challenge or insult has been issued. At that point, backing down marks one as a "wimp," and standing up for oneself becomes a matter of honor.

In the words of one Dallas homicide detective,

> Murders result from little ol' arguments over nothing at all. Tempers flare. A fight starts, and somebody gets stabbed or shot. I've worked on cases where the principals had been arguing over a 10 cent record on a juke box, or over a one dollar gambling debt from a dice game." (Mulvihill, Tumin, & Curtis, 1969, cited in Daly & Wilson, 1988, p. 127)

As Daly and Wilson (1988) noted, however, these homicides are not really about petty slights: The "participants in these 'trivial altercations' behave as if a great deal more is at issue than small change or access to a pool table" (p. 127). These contests escalate and become quite serious for participants because their status, reputation, and masculinity are on the line. Once the challenge or insult is offered, it is up to the affronted party to redeem himself by a display of toughness, dominance, or aggression.

Such concerns might appear outdated for southern participants now that the South is no longer a lawless frontier based on a herding economy. However, we believe these experiments may also hint at how the culture of honor has sustained itself in the South. It is possible that the culture-of-honor stance has become "functionally autonomous" from the material circumstances that created it (cf. Allport, 1937; Evans, 1970). Culture-of-honor norms are now socially enforced and perpetuated because they have become embedded in social roles, expectations, and shared definitions of manhood.

Experiment 3 provides a suggestion about how culture-of-honor norms might be enforced by one's peers. Insulted southerners saw themselves as shamed before people who witnessed their diminishment. Participants were realistic in their fears if it is indeed the case that southern observers would regard the episode as a serious put-down requiring a response. Perhaps our southern participants were thus being rational in their subsequent aggressive and domineering behavior, if they wanted to avoid the stigma of the insult before their peers.

The dynamics and specific mechanisms of the social enforcement of the culture of honor are important topics for future study. Until then, the present data, added to the homicide rate data and attitude data, offer support for three important points: (a) a version of the culture of honor persists in the South, and (b) the insult plays a central role in the culture of honor and the aggression that it produces, because (c) the affronted person feels diminished and may use aggressive or domineering behavior to reestablish his masculine status.

References

Allport, G. W. (1937). *Personality: A psychological interpretation.* London: Constable and Company.

Anderson, E. (1994). The code of the streets. *The Atlantic Monthly, 5,* 81–94.

Ayers, E. L. (1984). *Vengeance and justice.* New York: Oxford University Press.

Booth, A., Shelley, G., Mazur, A., Tharp, G., & Kittok, R. (1989). Testosterone and winning and losing in human competition. *Hormones and Behavior, 23,* 556–571.

Brearley, H. C. (1934). The pattern of violence. In W. T. Couch (Ed.), *Culture in the South* (pp. 678–692). Chapel Hill: University of North Carolina Press.

Brown, R. M. (1969). The American vigilante tradition. In H. Graham & T. Gurr (Eds.), *The history of violence in America* (pp. 154–226). New York: Bantam.

Campbell, B., O'Rourke, M., & Rabow, M. (1988). *Pulsatile response of salivary testosterone and cortisol to aggressive competition in young males.* Paper presented at the annual meeting of the American Association of Physical Anthropologists, Kansas City, MO.

Campbell, J. K. (1965). Honour and the devil. In J. G. Peristiany (Ed.), *Honour and shame: The values of Mediterranean society* (pp. 112–175). London: Weidenfeld & Nicolson.

Carter, H. (1950). *Southern legacy.* Baton Rouge: Louisiana State University Press.

Cohen, D. (1996). Law, social policy, and violence: The impact of regional cultures. *Journal of Personality and Social Psychology, 70,* 961–978.

Cohen, D., & Nisbett, R. E. (1994). Self-protection and the culture of honor: Explaining southern violence. *Personality and Social Psychology Bulletin, 20,* 551–567.

Cohen, D., & Nisbett, R. E. (1995). *Field experiments examining the culture of honor: The role of institutions in perpetuating norms.* Manuscript submitted for publication.

Dabbs, J. M. (1992). Testosterone measurements in social and clinical psychology. *Journal of Social and Clinical Psychology, 11,* 302–321.

Dabbs, J. M., & Hooper, C. H. (1990). Cortisol, arousal, and personality in two groups of normal men. *Personality and Individual Differences, 11,* 931–935.

Daly, M., & Wilson, M. (1988). *Homicide.* Hawthorne, New York: Aldine de Gruyter.

Edgerton, R. (1971). *The individual in cultural adaptation.* Berkeley: University of California Press.

Elias, M. (1981). Serum cortisol, testosterone, and testosterone-binding globulin responses to competitive fighting in human males. *Aggressive Behavior, 7,* 215–224.

Evans, R. I. (1970). *Gordon Allport.* New York: E. P. Dutton.

Fischer, D. H. (1989). *Albion's seed: Four British folkways in America.* New York: Oxford University Press.

Fox, J. A., & Pierce, G. L. (1987). *Uniform crime reports (United States): Supplementary homicide reports, 1976–1983* [machine-readable data file]. Ann Arbor, MI: Inter-University Consortium for Political and Social Research.

Gastil, R. D. (1971). Homicide and a regional culture of violence. *American Sociological Review, 36,* 416–427.

Gilmore, D. D. (1990). *Manhood in the making: Cultural concepts of masculinity.* New Haven, CT: Yale University Press.

Gladue, B. A. (1991). Aggressive behavioral characteristics, hormones, and sexual orientation in men and women. *Aggressive Behavior, 17,* 313–326.

Gladue, B. A., Boechler, M., & McCaul, K. D. (1989). Hormonal response to competition in human males. *Aggressive Behavior, 15,* 409–422.

Guerra, N. (in press). Intervening to prevent childhood aggression in the inner city. In J. McCord (Ed.), *Growing up violent.* New York: Cambridge University Press.

Ireland, R. M. (1979). Law and disorder in nineteenth-century Kentucky. *Vanderbilt Law Review, 32,* 281–299.

Kahn, H. (1968). *On escalation: Metaphors and scenarios.* Baltimore: Penguin Books.

Kemper, T. D. (1990). *Social structure and testosterone.* New Brunswick, NJ: Rutgers University Press.

Kirschbaum, C., Bartussek, D., & Strasburger, C. J. (1992). Cortisol responses to psychological stress and correlations with personality traits. *Personality and Individual Differences, 13,* 1353–1357.

Lennox, F., Riad, J., Cohen, D., Dabbs, J., & Nisbett, R. E. (1996). [Culture, aggression, and masculinity]. Unpublished raw data.

Leshner, A. I. (1983). Pituitary–adrenocortical effects on intermale agonistic behavior. In B. Svare (Ed.), *Hormones and aggressive behavior* (pp. 27–38). New York: Plenum.

Mazur, A. (1985). A biosocial model of status in face-to-face primate groups. *Social Forces, 64,* 377–402.

Mazur, A., Booth, A., & Dabbs, J. M. (1992). Testosterone and chess competition. *Social Psychology Quarterly, 55,* 70–77.

Mazur, A., & Lamb, T. A. (1980). Testosterone, status, and mood in human males. *Hormones and Behavior, 14,* 236–246.

McCall, N. (1994). *Makes me wanna holler.* New York: Random House.

McWhiney, G. (1988). *Cracker culture: Celtic ways in the Old South.* Tuscaloosa: University of Alabama Press.

Mulvihill, D. J., Tumin, M. M., & Curtis, L. A. (1969). *Crimes of violence* (Vol. 11). Washington, DC: U.S. Government Printing Office.

Nisbett, R. E. (1993). Violence and U.S. regional culture. *American Psychologist, 48,* 441–449.

Nisbett, R. E., & Cohen, D. (1996). *Culture of honor: The psychology of violence in the South.* Boulder, CO: Westview Press.

Nisbett, R. E., Polly, G., & Lang, S. (1994). *Homicide and regional U.S. culture.* Unpublished manuscript, University of Michigan.

Olweus, D. (1986). Aggression and hormones: Behavioral relationship with testosterone and adrenaline. In D. Olweus, J. Block, & M. Radke-Yarrow (Eds.), *Development of antisocial and prosocial behavior* (pp. 51–72). Orlando, FL: Academic Press.

Osborne, R. E., Niekrasz, I., & Seale, T. W. (1993). *Testosterone induces rapid onset of anxiolytic-like behaviors in mice.* Paper presented at the Evolution and Human Behavior Meeting, Buffalo, NY.

Peristiany, J. G. (Ed.). (1965). *Honour and shame: The values of Mediterranean society.* London: Weidenfeld & Nicolson.

Pitt-Rivers, J. (1968). Honor. In D. Sills (Ed.), *International encyclopedia of the social sciences* (pp. 509–510). New York: Macmillan.

Popp, K., & Baum, A. (1989). Hormones and emotions: Affective correlates of endocrine activity. In H. Wagner & A. Manstead (Eds.), *Handbook of social psychophysiology* (pp. 99–120). Chichester, England: Wiley.

Reaves, A. L., & Nisbett, R. E. (1994). *The cultural ecology of rural White homicide in the southern United States.* Unpublished manuscript, University of Michigan.

Salvador, A., Simon, V., Suay, F., & Llorens, L. (1987). Testosterone and cortisol responses to competitive fighting in human males: A pilot study. *Aggressive Behavior, 13,* 9–13.

Schelling, T. C. (1963). The threat of violence in international affairs. *Proceedings of the American Society of International Law* (pp. 103–115). Washington, DC: American Society of International Law.

Thompson, J. G. (1988). *The psychobiology of emotions.* New York: Plenum.

Wolfgang, M. E., & Ferracuti, F. (1967). *The subculture of violence.* London: Tavistock.

Wyatt-Brown, B. (1982). *Southern honor: Ethics and behavior in the Old South.* New York: Oxford University Press.

The O. J. Simpson Verdict: Predictors of Beliefs About Innocence or Guilt

Carolyn B. Murray, Robert Kaiser, and Shelby Taylor

Few incidents in recent years revealed so graphically the differences in outlook between African Americans and Euro-Americans as their differing reactions to the verdict of the O. J. Simpson trial. The popular television announcer and former football star was accused of murdering his wife and one of her friends, and the televised trial lasted for months. The eventual verdict—not guilty—delighted many African Americans and horrified many Euro-Americans. The final selection in this section, by Carolyn Murray, Robert Kaiser, and Shelby Taylor, examines the roots of this difference.

The strategy employed takes advantage of an interesting and often-overlooked fact: Not all *African Americans thought O. J. was innocent and not all Euro-Americans thought he was guilty. By examining the differences among members of each group who felt differently about the verdict, Murray and her colleagues illuminate the nature of the differences between groups. Furthermore, they use a moment where the disunity of American society became starkly apparent, to help understand the points of view of each societal subgroup and thereby promote mutual understanding, the ultimate goal of all of psychology.*

From *Journal of Social Issues, 53*, 455–475, 1997.

The not guilty verdict in the O. J. Simpson murder trial was largely condemned by the White community and supported by the Black community (Streisand, 1995; Whitaker, 1995). Clearly, in general Blacks and Whites do not share the same social reality because of differential treatment of the two groups by the society at large. However, within-group variations occur in treatment received, and thus within-group variations in cognitive schemata exist. * * * Two interesting groups whose views have yet to be addressed are Blacks who believed Mr. Simpson guilty and Whites who believed him innocent (at least one in four of each group). Who are these people and what sets them apart from other racial group members?

This study investigated the roles of ethnic identity, intergroup attitudes, degree of out-group contact, and authoritarianism in responses to the verdict. We also investigated the extent to which beliefs concerning Simpson's image (including whether he abused his spouse), trial publicity, and perceived police competence influenced beliefs in his guilt or innocence.

ETHNIC IDENTITY One plausible antecedent to perceived guilt or innocence is ethnic identity. Individuals with a secure and confident sense of their own culture or ethnicity may hold positive attitudes toward other groups (Berry, 1984). This assumption is consistent with models of minority identity development (e.g., Atkinson, Morten, & Sue, 1993; Cross, 1995). In contrast, the ethnocentrism hypothesis argues that in-group and out-group attitudes are negatively related at either the individual or group level (Masson & Verkuyten, 1993). According to the ethnocentrism hypothesis, those high in ethnocentrism hold positive in-group attitudes and negative attitudes towards out-groups. These attitudes occur because these individuals view their own group as "the center of everything, and all others are scaled and rated with reference to it" (Summer, cited in Feagin & Feagin, 1996, p. 15). The empirical evidence, however, is inconsistent on whether there exists a positive * * * or a negative (Masson & Verkuyten, 1993; Heaven, 1985) relationship between in-group identity and attitudes toward out-groups.

The Simpson verdict provided an opportunity to investigate this contradiction in the literature. The contradictory nature of the empirical evidence on ethnic identity and out-group attitudes raises several questions. Specifically, does a person's degree of ethnic identity predict beliefs in innocence or guilt? Does identity have an indirect or a direct relationship beliefs in innocence or guilt? In addition, does the relationship between ethnic identity and belief in innocence or guilt vary across racial groups?

INTERGROUP CONTACT In terms of the public response to the verdict, we investigated the degree to which the quantity and quality of intergroup contact mediated beliefs about the trial's outcome. An assumption of contact theory is that prejudice and discrimination are emotion-based outgrowths of ignorance that accompany the physical separation of two groups—for instance, Blacks and Whites. Contact theory argues that prejudice can be reduced through cross-group contacts (Brown & Ross, 1982). Initially, research investigating the contact hypothesis assumed that contact with another group would, under certain conditions (e.g., equal status, common goals, etc.) lead to more positive attitudes towards members of the out-group (Hewstone & Brown, 1986; Miller & Brewer, 1984). Empirical evidence indicates that contact among members of different groups can have positive outcomes (Stephan & Stephan, 1989), make no difference (Jackman & Crane, 1986), or have negative outcomes (Armor, 1972). Thus, the contact hypothesis remains debatable given that the number and nature of qualifying conditions (e.g., equal status, common goals, etc.) necessary for contact to be beneficial remain unclear. Some research (Jackman & Crane, 1986) also suggests that affective and social dispositions (e.g., of Whites) towards a group (e.g., Blacks) change with greater ease than beliefs about that group.

The extreme emotional valence of the Simpson trial and the contradictions in the literature raised several questions surrounding the role of contact and beliefs in innocence or guilt. First, is there a relationship between intergroup contact and beliefs in innocence or guilt? Second, what is the relationship between contact and beliefs in innocence or guilt? Third, does contact have a direct or indirect relationship with these beliefs? And fourth, are there racial or ethnic differences in degree of contact and beliefs in innocence or guilt?

INTERGROUP ATTITUDES Racial attitudes were the third set of predictors investigated relative to beliefs in innocence or guilt. The impetus for examining the role of racial attitudes was two-fold. First, attitudes affect the processing of social information—what is noticed, entered into memory, and later remembered (Wyer & Srull, 1994). For instance, two people who hold different attitudes about Blacks (one positive and the other negative) and hear the same evidence presented in the Simpson trial may arrive at very different conclusions.

Both attitudes and situational factors codetermine intergroup behavior (Duckitt, 1992–93). The link between attitudes and behavior, however, is more complex than was originally assumed. Factors that influence the behavioral expression of attitudes include situational constraints (e.g., the law) (Fazio & Roskos-Ewoldsen, 1994), attitudes formed on the basis of direct versus indirect experience (Regan & Fazio, 1977), and the attitude's degree of importance to the person (Kraus, 1995). For instance, empirical studies indicated that prejudiced Whites behaved positively or negatively toward Blacks depending on the situation, whereas less-prejudiced Whites behaved more consistently across contexts (McConahay, 1983).

The present study investigated pro- and anti-Black attitudes, along with other personal characteristics, as predictors of specific attitudes about the Simpson case. The specific attitudes investigated were (1) images—positive or negative—of Simpson; (2) assumptions concerning the competence of the police investigation; (3) perceptions of the publicity; and (4) beliefs about Simpson's alleged abuse of his ex-wife. It was predicted that people who were pro-Black would be more likely to possess a positive image of Simpson, perceive the police investigation as incompetent, and/or believe that the publicity in the case was due to Simpson's race, and thus believe him innocent. Those who held anti-Black attitudes, in contrast, were predicted more likely to assume that Simpson physically abused his ex-wife and therefore perceive him as guilty.

AUTHORITARIAN PERSONALITY The authoritarian personality is characterized by racial prejudice, a pseudo-conservative world view, submission to authority, and stereotypical beliefs (Adorno, Frenkel-Brunswik, Levinson, & Sanford, 1950). We examined authoritarianism as it related to the strength of reactions to the Simpson case.

The literature investigating the authoritarian personality has exhibited inconsistent findings (Ray, 1990), but continues to predict racism (Ray, 1988). Persons who score low on the authoritarian scale demonstrate less in-group/out-group evaluative biases, whereas high scores tend to enhance the in-group and disparage the out-group. Intergroup contact increases this bias for those high in authoritarianism (Downing & Monaco, 1986). Given the research's paradoxical nature, an exploratory investigation was conducted of the authoritarian personality construct's role in predicting beliefs in innocence or guilt. First, what is the relationship between authoritarianism and beliefs in innocence or guilt? Second, is this a direct or indirect relationship? Third, are there racial differences in authoritarianism and its relationship to beliefs in Simpson's innocence or guilt?

PREDICTIONS AND EXPLORATORY QUESTIONS In examining perceptions about the Simpson trial, three questions were of primary interest: (1) How do ethnic groups differ in trial perceptions and relevant psychological variables? (2) What characteristics and attitudes influence beliefs in innocence or guilt? and (3) How do proximal attitudes related to the trial mediate the relationships between personality and attitudinal variables and beliefs in innocence or guilt?

The present study investigated four ethnic groups (African Americans, Whites, Latinos, and Asians) in terms of trial perceptions and relevant psychological variables. It was predicted that African Americans would be the least likely to perceive Simpson as guilty, both before and after the trial, with Whites and Asians being more likely to assume him guilty before and after the trial. Latinos were predicted to fall between African Americans and Whites and Asians in their beliefs in his innocence or guilt. It was also predicted that African Americans, in comparison to the other three groups, would be more likely to possess a positive image of Simpson, assume an incompetent investigation, and assume the publicity surrounding the case was due to Simpson's race. In regard to pro- and anti-Black attitudes, it was predicted that African Americans and Latinos would hold more pro-Black attitudes, in comparison to Whites and Asians. No specific predictions were made for the remaining perceptions and relevant psychological variables.

* * *

Method

RESEARCH PARTICIPANTS Surveys were completed by 441 undergraduate college students attending two Southern California universities. The subjects were ethnically diverse (113 Whites, 120 Asians, 71 African Americans, 88 Latinos, and 49 others) and gender diverse (65.3% female and 34.7% male). By year in college, 194 freshmen, 71 sophomores, 77 juniors, 63 seniors, and 36 others participated in the study as one means of partially fulfilling an introductory psychology course requirement.

PROCEDURES The participants completed a questionnaire that examined their beliefs about Simpson's guilt or innocence before and after the trial and elicited other related information (e.g., faith in the criminal justice system, attitudes about domestic violence, etc.). Data collection began within the month following the Simpson criminal trial verdict and lasted for two months. It took students approximately one hour to complete the packet of instruments.

INSTRUMENTS Phinney (1992) developed The Multigroup Ethnic Identity Measure to measure elements of identity common to all ethnic groups. The instrument consists of 24 items to which subjects indicate agreement along a continuum numbered 4 (strongly agree) to 1 (strongly disagree). The scale consists of two factors, one for ethnic identity, and the other for orientation toward other groups. * * * Reliability (assessed by Cronbach's alpha) was .81 for a high school sample and .90 for a college sample (Phinney, 1992).[1]

Adorno et al. (1950) originally developed the California *F* Scales to measure ethnic prejudice and "prefascist tendencies" simultaneously, without mentioning minority groups by name or having a specific reference to explicit fascist ideology. There are numerous forms of the F Scale. The present study employed Form 60, a 30-item measure of ethnocentrism and political-economic conservatism. The reliability (split half) of Form 60 ranges from .81 to .91 with a mean of .87 (Christie, 1991).

For the purpose of the present study, only 16 items were administered, and the response formal was "true" or "false." A sample item is, "Obedience and respect for authority are the most important virtues children should learn."

Katz and Hass (1988) developed both the Pro-Black Scale and the Anti-Black Scale to measure conflicting sets of beliefs that turned up repeatedly in opinion surveys over a twenty-year period. Specifically, "Blacks are perceived as deserving help yet as not doing enough to help themselves; and both attitudes may exist side by side within an individual" (Katz & Hass, 1988, p. 894). Each scale has ten items, with two being keyed in reverse, and a six-point response format ("strongly agree" to "strongly disagree," with no neutral point), scored from 1 to 6. The Anti-Black Scale includes items such as, "The root cause of most of the social and economic ills of Blacks is the weakness and instability of the Black family." An example of a Pro-Black Scale item is, "It's surprising that Black people do as well as they do, considering all the obstacles they face." Cronbach's alpha for the Anti-Black Scale was .80 and for the Pro-Black Scale was .73 (Katz & Hass, 1988).

The Racial Identity Attitudes Scale (RIAS) is the most widely referenced measure of the stages of ethnic identity (Cross, Parham, & Helms, in press). The present study employed two forms of the RIAS-long form: One measured ethnic identity in Blacks, the other measured ethnic identity in all others (e.g., Whites, Latinos, and Asians). The present investigation analyzed only items that related to the quality, quantity, and desire for contact with Blacks (by non-Blacks) and Whites (by Blacks). An example of an item is, "I feel as comfortable around Blacks as I do around Whites." These items were the same for Blacks except

[1]Cronbach's alpha is a widely used measure of the degree to which participants' test scores would be expected to remain the same over repeated administrations of a test. It depends on the intercorrelations of the test items and the number of items on the test.

"White" replaced "Black" in the question wording. Twelve items were combined to form this variable.

Mediating Variables. The mediating variables were (1) images—positive or negative—of Simpson; (2) assumptions concerning the competence of the police investigation; (3) perceptions of the publicity as due to Simpson's race; and (4) beliefs about Simpson's alleged abuse of his ex-wife. Each of the four proximal variables consisted of three sentences taken from a survey instrument developed to gather information concerning the beliefs held concerning the Simpson case. The response format ranged from 1 = *Strongly Disagree* to 7 = *Strongly Agree* (with 4 = *Neutral*). The first proximal variable, Simpson's image, consisted of, "O. J. Simpson has served as a positive role model in society because of his personal qualities," "O. J. Simpson has contributed positively to society because of his excellence in football," and "O. J. Simpson is a very attractive man." The next proximal variable, competence of the police investigation, included "O. J. Simpson's rights were violated by the L.A. Police Department," "The police were incompetent in investigating this case," and "Some of the prosecution's forensic experts were incompetent in this case." A third proximal variable, publicity due to Simpson's race, was a combination of, "The treatment of O. J. Simpson in this case was related to the fact that he was a Black man married to a White woman," "If O. J. Simpson had been accused of killing a Black woman, it would not have been newsworthy," and "The public attention given to the O. J. Simpson case is due to the fact that he is African American." The last proximal variable, alleged abuse, was composed of "O. J. Simpson was physically abusive to Nicole Simpson," "O. J. Simpson had a history of stalking Nicole Simpson," and "The criminal justice system failed to protect Nicole Simpson by not putting O. J. Simpson in an effective program for batterers." The authors developed all these items for this investigation.

Outcome Variables. Three outcome variables were also specifically developed to examine beliefs about the trial: (1) pretrial beliefs in innocence or guilt; (2) post-trial beliefs in innocence or guilt; and (3) change in faith in the criminal justice system. In terms of pretrial beliefs, subjects responded, by checking the appropriate blank, to the question, "Before the trial of O. J. Simpson began, did you believe he was guilty or innocent?" Regarding posttrial beliefs, subjects completed the statement, "Regarding the murder of Nicole Simpson and Ron Goldman, O. J. Simpson is . . ." with choices from 1 (*Definitely Innocent*) to 7 (*Definitely Guilty*), with 4 neutral. The final outcome variable, faith in the criminal justice system, was solicited by having subjects respond "yes" or "no" to, "Has the O. J. Simpson verdict changed your faith in the American justice system?" and answer a follow-on question, if their response was "yes": "How has your faith in the American justice system changed?" The response format to the latter question ranged from 1 (*I now have much less faith in the American justice system*) to 5 (*I now have much more faith in the American justice system*).

Results

ETHNIC GROUP DIFFERENCES The first question addressed was whether there were any ethnic group differences in terms of trial beliefs, proximal beliefs, and distal psychological variables. * * *

To identify specific differences, univariate ANOVAs predicting each variable from ethnic group membership were conducted. F tests were highly significant for all variables examined, with effect sizes ranging from $\eta = .21$ to $.59$.[2] Table 43.1 presents results from these procedures. For distal psychological variables, African Americans were significantly less authoritarian than the other three groups, had more pro-Black attitudes and fewer anti-Black attitudes than Whites and Asians,

[2]Analysis of variance (ANOVA) yields a statistic, called F, that can be evaluated to assess the probability (p) that the obtained difference between groups would have occurred if, in fact, no difference existed. The η is a measure of the strength of the difference, or its effect size.

and had the lowest contact with other ethnic groups. Latinos were intermediately authoritarian, pro-Black, significantly less anti-Black than Asians, and, along with Asians, had the greatest amount of contact with other ethnic groups. Whites were the most authoritarian of the four groups, intermediate on pro- and anti-Black attitudes, and exhibited little contact with people of other ethnic groups. Asians were intermediately authoritarian, had the lowest scores on pro-Black attitudes, the highest scores on anti-Black attitudes, showed greater than average levels of ethnic contact, and had the lowest scores on ethnic identity achievement. (The other three groups did not significantly differ in this latter regard.)

For proximal beliefs and outcome variables, African Americans reported the greatest belief in Simpson's innocence both pre- and posttrial, showed little or no decreased faith in the system, had the lowest belief that the system is fair, had a relatively positive image of Simpson (second to Asians), were most likely to believe that the police were incompetent and that trial publicity was due to race, and were least likely to believe that Simpson abused his ex-wife. Latinos, Whites, and Asians did not differ much on the trial-related variables. They were more likely to see Simpson as guilty pretrial, showed relatively the same decreased faith in the justice system, had the same moderately positive view of the system, believed the police more competent (though still incompetent) than did African Americans, and believed that Simpson abused his ex-wife. In spite of this general pattern of similarity, these three groups showed some differences: Asians were more likely to see Simpson as guilty after the trial than Latinos; Asians had a more positive image of Simpson than either Latinos or Whites; and Asians were the least likely to believe that publicity surrounding the trial was due to Simpson's race.

Psychological Distal Predictors

* * *

* * * Only pro-Black attitudes predicted pretrial guilt beliefs, with those holding pro-Black attitudes believing Simpson to be innocent. Similarly, only authoritarian personality type and posttrial guilt beliefs predicted changes in faith in the justice system. Those who thought Simpson was guilty disagreed with the jury's verdict, and those with authoritarian personalities reported a decreased faith in the justice system. In contrast, all five of the distal psychological variables predicted posttrial guilt beliefs. Results showed that individuals with pro-Black attitudes, high ethnic identity, and high authoritarianism reported agreement with the jury's verdict (of innocence). Individuals who had contact with other ethnic groups, and individuals with anti-Black attitudes, believed Simpson guilty after the trial.

Proximal Attitude Predictors

* * *

* * * Proximal beliefs and attitudes account for all but one of the direct paths between the distal psychological variables. Essentially, distal psychological variables influence specific beliefs about Simpson's guilt and change in beliefs about the criminal justice system through their effect on more closely related attitudes. The single exception to this conclusion is that authoritarian individuals still report decreased faith in the justice system. In terms of the posttrial-specific relations, individuals who held a positive image of Simpson believed the police had been incompetent in the investigation, and those who believed that the publicity surrounding the case resulted from Simpson being Black reported a tendency to believe Simpson innocent, whereas those who believed that Simpson had abused his former wife tended to believe he was guilty. Pretrial beliefs about guilt demonstrated substantial effect on posttrial beliefs, exhibiting a significant degree of consistency. Beliefs about police incompetence and that the publicity surrounding the trial were due to Simpson's ethnicity predicted posttrial belief in his innocence, whereas belief that Simpson abused his ex-wife predicted beliefs in his guilt. Increased faith in the justice system was predicted

TABLE 43.1

MEANS FOR TRIAL OUTCOME BELIEFS, PROXIMAL ATTITUDES, AND DISTAL PSYCHOLOGICAL CONSTRUCTS FOR FOUR MAJOR ETHNIC GROUPS

Variable	Range	African Americans	Latinos	Caucasians	Asians	σ	η
Pretrial guilt beliefs (N = 413)	0–1	.32[a]	.50[a,b]	.64[b]	.59[b]	.49	.23
Posttrial guilt beliefs (N = 419)	1–7	2.97	4.62[a]	5.20[a,b]	5.43[b]	2.63	.49
Increased vs. decreased faith in justice system (N = 417)	1–5	3.03	2.40[a]	2.27[a]	2.26[a]	.81	.33
Belief that system is fair (N = 423)	1–6	2.64	3.51[a]	3.75[a]	3.76[a]	.81	.46
Positive image of Simpson (N = 422)	1–7	4.16[a,b]	3.82[b]	3.87[b]	4.46[a]	1.28	.20
Incompetent investigation (N = 422)	1–7	5.83	4.43[a]	4.45[a]	4.16[a]	1.29	.42
Simpson abused Nicole Brown Simpson (N = 422)	1–7	4.85	5.48[a]	5.29[a]	5.56[a]	1.14	.21
Publicity due to Simpson's race (N = 422)	1–7	5.41	3.17[a]	3.40[a]	2.42	1.41	.59
Social contact with other ethnicities (N = 422)	1–5	3.67[a]	4.11[b]	3.86[a]	4.12[b]	.52	.32
Authoritarian personality (N = 422)	0–1	.38	.51[b]	.62[a]	.55[a,b]	.19	.44
Ethnic identity achievement (N = 406)	1–4	3.12[a]	3.02[a]	3.03[a]	2.77[b]	.40	.32
Pro-Black attitudes (N = 420)	1–6	4.73[a]	4.02[a]	3.87[a,b]	3.68[b]	.74	.44
Anti-Black attitudes (N = 417)	1–6	2.63[a]	2.93[a,b]	3.21[b,c]	3.41[c]	.85	.32

Note. Mean values within any given row that share the same superscript letter are not different using Tukey's *HSD*. *N*'s differ due to missing values. Overall effects for every variable are significantly different at $p < .05$.[3]

by beliefs that the police investigation had been incompetent, while decreased faith was predicted from belief in Simpson's guilt, belief that Simpson abused his ex-wife, and authoritarian personality.

Whereas proximal attitudes mediated the relations between distal psychological variables and outcome variables, distal variables differentially predicted proximal beliefs. A positive image of Simpson was predicted by pro-Black attitudes and contact with people of other ethnic groups. Belief that the police investigation was incompetent was predicted by pro-Black attitudes and ethnic identity achievement and inversely by anti-Black attitudes. Pro-Black attitudes, ethnic identity achievement, and authoritarian personality pre-

[3]Tukey's HSD (Honestly Significant Difference) is a statistical procedure comparing all possible pairs of means in a set of means to determine which pairs involve a difference that is unlikely by chance.

dicted a belief that the publicity surrounding the case was due to Simpson's race, whereas anti-Black attitudes and, surprisingly, contact with other ethnic groups inversely predicted this belief. Finally, those who described themselves as ethnically identified and as authoritarian did not believe that Simpson abused his ex-wife.

* * *

Discussion

The first of three primary questions raised was whether there were any mean differences across ethnic groups in perceptions of the trial and relevant psychological variables. Mean differences were evident for all of the variables investigated. As predicted, African Americans were, by a significant margin, least likely to perceive Simpson as guilty, both before and after the trial, with Whites and Asians most likely to perceive him as guilty. Latinos, as predicted, fell between African Americans and both Whites and Asians and did not significantly differ from African Americans or Whites and Asians in pretrial beliefs. In terms of the other variables concerning the trial's outcome, African Americans were least likely to believe that Simpson was guilty and least likely to believe that the system is fair.

The finding that African Americans differed significantly from all three ethnic groups in their beliefs concerning Simpson's innocence or guilt may indicate schema differences (i.e., differences in how African Americans view their world) in comparison to the other three groups (Inman & Baron, 1996). Mental structures known as schemata are built up through experience or, in some cases, actively constructed on the spot in response to new information. Information is organized, interpreted, and later remembered in accordance with these cognitive structures. Clearly African Americans do not share the same schemata as Whites and Asians. These groups differ in how they are treated by the society's major institutions (Murray & Smith, 1995), and, in particular, the criminal justice system (Johnson, Whitestone, Jackson, & Gatto, 1995). The race of the perpetuator and/or victim often determines the treatment African Americans receive, which puts Blacks at a disadvantage (Keil & Vito, 1992; Stewart, 1980). Thus, it is not surprising that African Americans held different beliefs about the criminal justice system, and thus different beliefs about Simpson's innocence or guilt, than did Whites and Asians.

Less clear, however, is the finding that Latino beliefs about Simpson's innocence or guilt are more similar to those of Whites and Asians than to those of African Americans, especially since their experiences with the criminal justice system are more similar to those of African Americans. One plausible explanation is that Latino college students may identify more closely with the mainstream population and thus hold more mainstream attitudes than noncollege Latinos. Another plausible interpretation is that Latinos in general may not have similar attitudes to African Americans because of cultural differences and/or conflicts and competition with Blacks. A third plausible explanation is that Latinos are a heterogeneous population in terms of physical characteristics (e.g., ranging from light skin to dark skin), nationalities, and so on, which results in their receiving more variation in treatment, and therefore they possess more diverse within-group schemata. The extent to which any or all of these interpretations play a role in African American versus Latino differences in beliefs about innocence or guilt is a question for further research.

Beliefs surrounding the relevant trial variables were as predicted, with one exception. African Americans differed significantly from the other three groups in that they were more likely to believe the police investigation was incompetent and that the publicity was racially motivated. They were also less likely to believe that Simpson abused his wife. The one exception was the finding that Asian Americans perceived Simpson's pretrial image more positively than the other three groups (though not significantly differently than African Americans).

The second major question the present study addressed was, "What are the psychological characteristics and attitudes influencing beliefs of innocence or guilt?" In line with the literature, those with pro-Black attitudes thought Simpson innocent before the trial and agreed with the verdict. In terms of ethnic identity, those with positive feelings about their own group were in agreement with the verdict. These results suggest that a more positive acceptance of one's own group predicts acceptance of unpopular yet legally sanctioned actions of out-group members, which contradicts the ethnocentric thesis.

Interestingly, those who scored high in authoritarianism agreed with the verdict, even though they indicated that their faith in the criminal justice system had decreased. A plausible interpretation is that because those high in authoritarianism are obedient and respect authority, after the court had rendered its verdict, they accepted the decision. Indirect support for this position is reported by Chapdelaine and Griffin (1997). They found that traditional authoritarian scores were not related to beliefs in Simpson's guilt or innocence, but if Simpson was found guilty, authoritarian scores were positively correlated with severity of recommended sentence. Similar to our findings, people high on the traditional authoritarian scale seemingly accepted the jury's verdict. Specifically, when the hypothetical verdict was guilty, as was the case in the Chapdelaine and Griffin study, the higher the authoritarian score the more likely such persons thought Simpson should receive the maximum penalty allowed by law. However, when the actual verdict was not guilty, as in the present study, persons who score high in authoritarianism were more likely to perceive him as innocent. This raises an interesting question for future research, of whether obedience to authority overrides prejudicial attitudes for persons high in authoritarianism?

The finding that anti-Black attitudes predicted disagreement with the verdict is not surprising given the disdain many people expressed toward the predominantly Black jury. What was surprising is that more contact with Blacks predicted disagreement with the verdict. It may be that when a group experiences a high degree of personal contact with a subordinate group, feelings of personal animosity and social distance erode but not beliefs about the subordinate group. In addition, social cognition theorists indicate that people are willing to change their beliefs about an individual member of a group but not the group as a whole (Murray & Jackson, 1989). Therefore, even positive contact with members of a subordinate group does not necessarily result in more positive attitudes towards the group. Moreover, this study did not control for the nature of the contact in terms of equal status, shared goals, and the like. Thus, more contact with African Americans may relate to negative attitudes toward the group.

The third question investigated was, "Do proximal attitudes which are directly relevant to the trial mediate the relationships between the distal personality and attitudinal variables and the beliefs in innocence or guilt?" The answer is yes! The more closely related attitudes mediated the distal psychological variables' influence on the belief in innocence or guilt (for further support, see Peacock, Cowan, Bommersbach, Smith, & Stahly, 1997). The single exception was the finding indicating a direct relationship between authoritarian personality and a decreased faith in the criminal justice system. Clearly all the psychological variables and the relevant proximal beliefs about the trial all appeared to follow more or less a common set of underlying values. For instance, in terms of the pre- and posttrial relationships, individuals who held a positive image of Simpson believed the police had been incompetent in the investigation, and those who believed that the publicity surrounding the case resulted from Simpson's being Black reported a tendency to believe Simpson innocent, whereas those who believed that Simpson had abused his former wife tended to believe that he was guilty.

Whereas proximal attitudes mediated the relations between distal psychological variables and outcome variables, distal variables differentially predicted proximal beliefs. For example, a positive image of Simpson was predicted by pro-Black attitudes and contact with people of other ethnicities. Therefore, attitudes help us make sense of the world by affecting our processing, storage, and memory of information about other people. For instance, during the trial, commentary on the same evidence was interpreted as either in support of or against the defense depending on the commentator's beliefs as well as the listener's cognitive schema. Interestingly, when information is obviously discrepant with our beliefs, we either pay closer attention or ignore it (see Murray & Jackson, 1989). Though seemingly contradictory, unfortunately both outcomes are found to reinforce the original schema or expectancy, because people spend additional time reviewing evidence that supports the schema (O'Sullivan & Durso, 1984; Stern, Marrs, Millar, & Cole, 1984). This may be one reason that schemata such as stereotypes are so resistant to change: Evidence that contradicts them ironically makes them stronger, because people mentally review the stereotype and past evidence for it. Therefore it should not come as a surprise that African Americans, in contrast to the other groups, are more likely to believe Simpson is innocent.

* * *

In conclusion, the present study illuminates some of the predictors of differences within and between racial groups in beliefs concerning O. J. Simpson's innocence or guilt. For overall within-group differences, individuals who are pro-Black, ethnically identified, or authoritarian were less likely to believe Simpson was guilty. In contrast, persons within groups who hold anti-Black values or who have more contact with Blacks were more likely to believe that he was guilty. Interestingly, these patterns were also true for Blacks, with one qualification: those who had more contact with Whites were more likely to believe that Simpson was guilty.

In the aftermath of the Simpson case, we are trying to understand how people across and within different ethnic groups could see the evidence in this case so differently. The present study sheds some light on this phenomenon by examining how attitudes affect our beliefs about the case. Specifically, variations in cognitive schemata due to group membership contain specific information that helps us interpret new situations. Given that African Americans occupy a unique subordinate position in society, it is predictable that their schemata will also be different from those of the groups around them. Moreover, other groups who are also subordinate should share a similar prototype of African Americans, because they observe African Americans through lenses (e.g., news media, educational institutions, and so on) the dominant culture provides. Therefore, within- and between-group differences may reflect schematic differences due to differential experiences with societal institutions, identification with (rejection of) mainstream values, and race relations in American society.

This study raises as many questions as it answers. However, if we are to live together, it is necessary to understand our differences and to identify our similarities. Because of the extreme emotions the Simpson trial elicited, the trial provided an opportunity to learn more about these similarities and differences.

References

Adorno, T. W., Frenkel-Brunswick, E., Levinson, D. J., & Sanford, R. N. (1950). *The authoritarian personality.* New York: Harper & Row.

Armor, D. J. (1972). The evidence on busing. *Public Interest, 28,* 90–125.

Atkinson, D., Morten, G., & Sue, D. (1993). *Counseling American minorities* (4th ed.). Dubuque, IA: Brown & Benchmark.

Berry, J. (1984). Cultural relations in plural societies: Alternatives to segregation and their sociopsychological implications. In N. Miller & M. Brewer (Eds.), *Groups in contact: The psychology of desegregation* (pp. 11–29). Orlando, FL: Academic.

Brown, R., & Ross, G. (1982). The battle for acceptance: An investigation into the dynamics of intergroup behaviors. In H. Tajfel (Ed.), *Social identity and intergroup relations* (pp. 155–178). Cambridge: Cambridge University Press.

Chapdelain, A., & Griffin, S. F. (1997). Beliefs of guilt and recommended sentence as a function of juror bias in the O.J. Simpson trial. *Journal of Social Issues, 53,* 477–485.

Christie, R. (1991). Authoritarianism and related constructs. In J. P. Robinson, P. R. Shaver, & L. S. Wrightsman (Eds.), *Measures of personality and social psychological attitudes* (pp. 501–571). San Diego, CA: Academic Press.

Cross, W. E., Jr. (1995). The psychology of Nigrescence: Revising the Cross model. In *Handbook of multicultural counseling* (pp. 93–122). Thousand Oaks, CA: Sage.

Cross, W. E., Jr., Parham, T. A., & Helms, J. E. (In press). Nigrescence revisited: Theory and research. In R. L. Jones (Ed.), *African American identity development: Theory, research, and intervention.* Hampton, VA: Cobb & Henry.

Downing, L. L., & Monaco, N. R. (1986, August). In-group/out-group bias as a function of differential contact and authoritarian personality. *Journal of Social Psychology, 126*(4), 445–452.

Duckitt, John. (1992–93, Winter). Prejudice and behavior: A review. *Current Psychology: Research and Reviews, 11*(4), 291–307.

Fazio, R. H., & Roskos-Ewoldsen, R. (1994). Acting as we feel: When and how attitudes guide behavior. In S. Shavitt & T. C. Brock (Eds.), *Persuasion* (pp. 71–93). Boston: Allyn & Bacon.

Feagin, J. R., & Feagin, C. B. (1996). *Racial and ethnic relations* (5th ed.). Englewood Cliffs, NJ: Prentice-Hall.

Heaven, P. (1985). Patriotism, racism, and the disutility of the ethnocentrism concept. *Journal of Social Psychology, 125,* 181–185.

Hewstone, M., & Brown, R. (1986). Contact is not enough: An intergroup perspective on the "contact hypothesis." In M. Hewstone & R. Brown (Eds.), *Contact and conflict in intergroup encounters* (pp. 1–44). Oxford: Blackwell.

Inman, M. L., & Baron, R. S. (1996). Influence of prototypes on perceptions of prejudice. *Journal of Personality and Social Psychology, 70,* 727–739.

Jackman, M. R., & Crane, M. (1986). "Some of my best friends are black. . .": Interracial friendship and whites' racial attitudes. *Public Opinion Quarterly, 50,* 459–486.

Johnson, J. D., Whitestone, E., Jackson, L. A., & Gatto, L. (1995, September). Justice is still not colorblind: Differential racial effects of exposure to inadmissible evidence. *Personality and Social Psychology Bulletin,* 21.

Katz, I., & Hass, R. G. (1988). Racial ambivalence and American value conflict: Correlational and priming studies of dual cognitive structures. *Journal of Personality and Social Psychology, 55*(6), 893–905.

Keil, T. J., & Vito, G. F. (1992, May–June). The effects of the Furman and Gregg decisions on Black-White execution ratio in the South. *Journal of Criminal Justice, 50,* 217–226.

Kraus, S. J. (1995). Attitudes and the prediction of behavior: A meta-analysis of the empirical literature. *Personality and Social Psychology Bulletin, 21,* 58–75.

Masson, C., & Verkuyten, M. (1993). Prejudice, ethnic identity, contact, and ethnic group preferences among Dutch young adolescents. *Journal of Applied Social Psychology, 23,* 156–168.

McConahay, J. B. (1983, December). Modern racism and modern discrimination: The effects of race, racial attitudes, and context on simulated hiring decisions. *Personality and Social Psychology Bulletin, 9*(4), 551–558.

Miller, N., & Brewer, M. (1984). *Groups in contact: The psychology of desegregation.* Orlando, FL: Academic Press.

Murray, C. B., & Jackson, J. S. (1989). The conditioned failure model revisited. In J. O. Smith & Carl E. Jackson (Eds.), *Race and ethnicity: A study of intracultural socialization patterns* (pp. 319–355). Dubuque, IA: Kendall/Hunt.

Murray, C. B., & Smith, J. O. (1995). White privilege: The rhetoric and the facts. In D. A. Harris (Ed.), *Multiculturalism from the margins: Non-dominant voices on difference and diversity.* Westport, CT: Bergin & Garvey.

O'Sullivan, C. S., & Durso, F. T. (1984). Effects of schema-incongruent information on memory for stereotypical attitudes. *Journal of Personality and Social Psychology, 47,* 55–70.

Peacock, M. J., Cowan, G., Bommersbach, M., Smith, S. Y., & Stahly, G. (1997). Pretrial predictors of judgments in the O.J. Simpson case. *Journal of Social Issues, 53,* 441–454.

Phinney, J. S. (1992). The multigroup ethnic identity measure: A new scale for use with diverse groups, *Journal of Adolescent Research, 7*(2), 156–176.

Ray, J. J. (1988, December). Why the *F* scale predicts racism: A critical review. *Political Psychology, 9*(4), 671–679.

Ray, J. J. (1990, October). The old-fashioned personality. *Human Relations, 43*(10), 997–1013.

Regan, D. T., & Fazio, R. H. (1977). On the consistency between attitudes and behavior: Look to the method of attitude formation. *Journal of Experimental Social Psychology, 13,* 38–45.

Stephan, W., & Stephan, C. (1989). Antecedents of intergroup anxiety in Asian-Americans and Hispanic Americans. *International Journal of Intercultural Relations, 13,* 203–219.

Stern, L. D., Marrs, S., Millar, M. G., & Cole, E. (1984). Processing time and the recall of inconsistent and consistent behaviors of individuals and groups. *Journal of Personality and Social Psychology, 47,* 253–262.

Stewart, J. E. (1980). Defendant's attractiveness as a factor in the outcome of criminal trials: An observational study. *Journal of Applied Social Psychology, 10,* 348–361.

Streisand, B. (1995, Oct. 16). The verdict's aftermath. (O.J. Simpson case) (Black & White in America). *U.S. News & World Report, 119,* 15:34.

Whitaker, M. (1995, Oct. 16). Whites v. Blacks. (Race relations; O.J. Simpson murder trial) (Special report: The verdict). *Newsweek, 126,* 16:28.

Wyer, R. S., Jr., & Srull, T. K. (1994). *Handbook of social cognition* (2nd ed.). Hillsdale, NJ: Erlbaum.

PART VII

Behavioral and Social Learning Approaches to Personality

Behavioristic psychology treats behavior as something that is produced by the immediate environment and the individual's history of rewards and punishments. In its original version, behaviorism avoided assuming the existence of any "inner," mental states or traits at all. For a functional analysis of behavior, it was sufficient to connect visible rewards and punishments with visible behaviors.

This point of view has evolved in an interesting way over the years. Social learning theory added to behaviorism one more assumption: That one's beliefs about or "representations" of the rewards and punishments in the environment are more important than what the environment actually contains. For example, if you believe a behavior will be rewarded, you will probably do it, even if in fact the behavior will be punished. But your representation of a belief like this is a nonvisible, internal state. Social learning theory incorporated this new assumption into a variant of behaviorism that was highly influential for several decades. Researchers who continued to follow the implications of the importance of mental beliefs and processes for behavior eventually developed a new paradigm that superseded both behaviorism and social learning theory, the cognitive approach presented in the next section of this book.

The first selection in this section is by the key figure in modern behaviorism and one of the most important social scientists of the century. In "Why Organisms Behave," Skinner introduces the idea of functional analysis and dismisses neural causes, psychic causes, and everything else that orthodox behaviorists find irrelevant to a sufficient understanding of behavior. Instead, he proposes that the answer to why organisms behave is always to be found in the external variables —rewards and punishments—of which behavior is always a function, and expresses optimism that this approach will solve all of the basic issues of psychology. In the second selection, published almost 35 years later, Skinner takes a more pessimistic tack as he laments the failure of behaviorism to take over all of psychology. He blames humanistic psychology, cognitive psychology, and the sloppy habits of everyday speech and warns that a psychology that neglects func-

tional analysis will find itself dealing in myth or—just as bad—discover that it has been rendered obsolete by biology.

Despite Skinner's urgent and consistent pleading over the years, many psychologists with behaviorist sympathies nonetheless found the strict limits of classic behaviorism to be too confining. Several different psychologists developed social learning theories that attempted to combine behaviorism's empirical rigor with a renewed concern with defense mechanisms, social interaction, mental life, and other phenomena that behaviorism neglected. One of the most important of these psychologists is Julian Rotter, whose primer on the key elements of social learning theory is the third selection.

Another important social learning theorist is Albert Bandura, the author (with two colleagues) of the fourth and final selection. This article is one of the most widely cited of any in the history of psychology. It presents an influential demonstration of how learning can occur without reinforcement—thus undermining a critical assumption of behaviorism—and implies some dangers of televised violence. This article also provides an early hint of the future development of the cognitive approach, through its direct—though unstated—implication that a cognitive representation of an event that was merely depicted on film can be enough to affect an individual's future behavior.

Why Organisms Behave

B. F. Skinner

The major historical figure in behaviorism, and one of the best-known social scientists of the 20th century, is B. F. Skinner. Over a career that spanned more than 60 years (he died in 1990), Skinner argued strenuously and consistently that behavior was a scientific topic no different, in principle, from any other. That is, behavior is best studied through experimental methods, and the best way to demonstrate that you understand a behavior is to show that you can control it. Skinner always expressed annoyance with theories that located causes of behavior in the mind or even in the physical brain. He felt this practice merely postponed understanding, because the mind cannot be observed and the brain is poorly understood. Instead, Skinner argued, psychology should address the powerful causes of behavior that can be both seen and experimentally manipulated: the rewards and punishments in the environment of the "organism."

The first selection in this section, an excerpt from a basic text on behaviorism Skinner published at the height of his career in 1953, clearly sets forth the behaviorist manifesto. Skinner argues that locating causes of behavior in the stars, the physique, genetics, or even the nervous system offers nothing to psychological understanding. Each only misleads or—at best—distracts analysis away from the causes of behavior that ought to be the real business of psychologists.

Skinner's model for a science of psychology is "functional analysis." Such an analysis entails identifying—and, in many cases, controlling—the environmental causes of which behavior is a "function." Skinner further urges that these causes be conceptualized in concrete, physical terms. Rather than abstract social forces, for example, Skinner urges us to pay attention to the specific, immediate, concrete rewards and punishments in the social environment that affect what a person does. This focus on specifics, he believed, could enable people to design environments that would elicit behaviors leading to better outcomes for all.

From *Science and Human Behavior*, by B. F. Skinner (Upper Saddle River, NJ: Prentice-Hall, 1953), pp. 23–42.

We are concerned with the causes of human behavior. We want to know why men behave as they do. Any condition or event which can be shown to have an effect upon behavior must be taken into account. By discovering and analyzing these causes we can predict behavior; to the extent that we can manipulate them, we can control behavior.

There is a curious inconsistency in the zeal with which the doctrine of personal freedom has been defended,[1] because men have always been fascinated by the search for causes. The spontaneity of human behavior is apparently no more challenging than its "why and wherefore." So strong is the urge to explain behavior that men have been led to anticipate legitimate scientific inquiry and to construct highly implausible theories of causation. This practice is not unusual in the history of science. The study of any subject begins in the realm of superstition. The fanciful explanation precedes the valid. Astronomy began as astrology; chemistry as alchemy. The field of behavior has had, and still has, its astrologers and alchemists. A long history of prescientific explanation furnishes us with a fantastic array of causes which have no function other than to supply spurious answers to questions which must otherwise go unanswered in the early stages of a science.

Some Popular "Causes" of Behavior

Any conspicuous event which coincides with human behavior is likely to be seized upon as a cause. The position of the planets at the birth of the individual is an example. Usually astrologers do not try to predict specific actions from such causes, but when they tell us that a man will be impetuous, careless, or thoughtful, we must suppose that specific actions are assumed to be affected. Numerology finds a different set of causes —for example, in the numbers which compose the street address of the individual or in the number of letters in his name. Millions of people turn to these spurious causes every year in their desperate need to understand human behavior and to deal with it effectively.

The predictions of astrologers, numerologists, and the like are usually so vague that they cannot be confirmed or disproved properly. Failures are easily overlooked, while an occasional chance hit is dramatic enough to maintain the behavior of the devotee in considerable strength. * * *

Another common practice is to explain behavior in terms of the structure of the individual. The proportions of the body, the shape of the head, the color of the eyes, skin, or hair, the marks on the palms of the hands, and the features of the face have all been said to determine what a man will do.[2] The "jovial fat man," Cassius with his "lean and hungry look," and thousands of other characters or types thoroughly embedded in our language affect our practices in dealing with human behavior. A specific act may never be predicted from physique, but different types of personality imply predispositions to behave in different ways, so that specific acts are presumed to be affected. This practice resembles the mistake we all make when we expect someone who looks like an old acquaintance to behave like him also. When a "type" is once established, it survives in everyday use because the predictions which are made with it, like those of astrology, are vague, and occasional hits may be startling.

* * *

When we find, or think we have found, that conspicuous physical features explain part of a man's behavior, it is tempting to suppose that inconspicuous features explain other parts. This is implied in the assertion that a man shows certain behavior because he was "born that way." To object to this is not to argue that behavior is never determined by hereditary factors. Behavior requires a behaving organism which is the product of a genetic process. Gross differences in the behavior of different species show that the genetic constitution, whether observed in the body structure of the individual or inferred from a genetic

[1]For example, by the humanists in Part V.

[2]Recall the selection by Wells in Part III.

history, is important. But the doctrine of "being born that way" has little to do with demonstrated facts. It is usually an appeal to ignorance. "Heredity," as the layman uses the term, is a fictional explanation of the behavior attributed to it.

Even when it can be shown that some aspect of behavior is due to season of birth, gross body type, or genetic constitution, the fact is of limited use. It may help us in predicting behavior, but it is of little value in an experimental analysis or in practical control because such a condition cannot be manipulated after the individual has been conceived. The most that can be said is that the knowledge of the genetic factor may enable us to make better use of other causes. If we know that an individual has certain inherent limitations, we may use our techniques of control more intelligently, but we cannot alter the genetic factor.[3]

The practical deficiencies of programs involving causes of this sort may explain some of the vehemence with which they are commonly debated. Many people study human behavior because they want to do something about it—they want to make men happier, more efficient and productive, less aggressive, and so on. To these people, inherited determiners—as epitomized in various "racial types"—appear to be insurmountable barriers, since they leave no course of action but the slow and doubtful program of eugenics.[4] The evidence for genetic traits is therefore closely scrutinized, and any indication that it is weak or inconsistent is received with enthusiasm. But the practical issue must not be allowed to interfere in determining the extent to which behavioral dispositions are inherited. The matter is not so crucial as is often supposed, for we shall see that there are other types of causes available for those who want quicker results.

Inner "Causes"

Every science has at some time or other looked for causes of action inside the things it has studied. Sometimes the practice has proved useful, sometimes it has not. There is nothing wrong with an inner explanation as such, but events which are located inside a system are likely to be difficult to observe. For this reason we are encouraged to assign properties to them without justification. Worse still, we can invent causes of this sort without fear of contradiction. The motion of a rolling stone was once attributed to its *vis viva*. The chemical properties of bodies were thought to be derived from the *principles* or *essences* of which they were composed. Combustion was explained by the *phlogiston* inside the combustible object. Wounds healed and bodies grew well because of a *vis medicatrix*. It has been especially tempting to attribute the behavior of a living organism to the behavior of an inner agent, as the following examples may suggest.

NEURAL CAUSES The layman uses the nervous system as a ready explanation of behavior. The English language contains hundreds of expressions which imply such a causal relationship. At the end of a long trial we read that the *nerves* of the accused are *on edge*, that the wife of the accused is on the verge of a *nervous breakdown*, and that his lawyer is generally thought to have lacked the *brains* needed to stand up to the prosecution. Obviously, no direct observations have been made of the nervous systems of any of these people. Their "brains" and "nerves" have been invented on the spur of the moment to lend substance to what might otherwise seem a superficial account of their behavior.

The sciences of neurology and physiology have not divested themselves entirely of a similar prac-

[3]It is unclear why Skinner here portrays the inability to alter the genotype as an important limitation. In terms of Skinner's own analysis alteration of the phenotype (overt behavior) should be a sufficient goal.

[4]Skinner is referring to writings early in the 20th century that identified "national" or "racial" characters. For example, southern Europeans were held to be emotional and northern Europeans to be cold and analytical. Skinner expresses (well-taken) doubts that such descriptions are accurate, and further argues that even if they were accurate the only prescription they offer is to "improve" the human species through selective breeding (eugenics). Skinner calls such a eugenic strategy "doubtful," surely an understatement.

tice. Since techniques for observing the electrical and chemical processes in nervous tissue had not yet been developed, early information about the nervous system was limited to its gross anatomy. Neural processes could only be inferred from the behavior which was said to result from them. Such inferences were legitimate enough as scientific theories, but they could not justifiably be used to explain the very behavior upon which they were based. The hypotheses of the early physiologist may have been sounder than those of the layman, but until independent evidence could be obtained, they were no more satisfactory as explanations of behavior. Direct information about many of the chemical and electrical processes in the nervous system is now available. Statements about the nervous system are no longer necessarily inferential or fictional. But there is still a measure of circularity in much physiological explanation, even in the writings of specialists. In World War I a familiar disorder was called "shell shock." Disturbances in behavior were explained by arguing that violent explosions had damaged the structure of the nervous system, though no direct evidence of such damage was available. In World War II the same disorder was classified as "neuropsychiatric." The prefix seems to show a continuing unwillingness to abandon explanations in terms of hypothetical neural damage.[5]

Eventually a science of the nervous system based upon direct observation rather than inference will describe the neural states and events which immediately precede instances of behavior. We shall know the precise neurological conditions which immediately precede, say, the response, "No, thank you." These events in turn will be found to be preceded by other neurological events, and these in turn by others. This series will lead us back to events outside the nervous system and, eventually, outside the organism. * * * We do not have and may never have this sort of neurological information at the moment it is needed in order to predict a specific instance of behavior. It is even more unlikely that we shall be able to alter the nervous system directly in order to set up the antecedent conditions of a particular instance. The causes to be sought in the nervous system are, therefore, of limited usefulness in the prediction and control of specific behavior.

PSYCHIC INNER CAUSES An even more common practice is to explain behavior in terms of an inner agent which lacks physical dimensions and is called "mental" or "psychic." The purest form of the psychic explanation is seen in the animism of primitive peoples. From the immobility of the body after death it is inferred that a spirit responsible for movement has departed. The *enthusiastic* person is, as the etymology of the word implies, energized by a "god within." It is only a modest refinement to attribute every feature of the behavior of the physical organism to a corresponding feature of the "mind" or of some inner "personality." The inner man is regarded as driving the body very much as the man at the steering wheel drives a car. The inner man wills an action, the outer executes it. The inner loses his appetite, the outer stops eating. The inner man wants and the outer gets. The inner has the impulse which the outer obeys.

It is not the layman alone who resorts to these practices, for many reputable psychologists use a similar dualistic system of explanation. The inner man[6] is sometimes personified clearly, as when delinquent behavior is attributed to a "disordered personality," or he may be dealt with in fragments, as when behavior is attributed to mental processes, faculties, and traits. Since the inner man does not occupy space, he may be multiplied at will. It has been argued that a single physical organism is controlled by several psychic agents and that its behavior is the resultant of their several wills. The Freudian concepts of the ego, superego, and id are often used in this way. They are frequently regarded as nonsubstantial creatures, often in violent conflict, whose defeats or victories lead to the

[5]The current label for this syndrome, post-traumatic stress disorder, is more in line with Skinner's descriptive preference without attributing cause.

[6]Sometimes called the "homunculus."

adjusted or maladjusted behavior of the physical organism in which they reside.

Direct observation of the mind comparable with the observation of the nervous system has not proved feasible. It is true that many people believe that they observe their "mental states" just as the physiologist observes neural events, but another interpretation of what they observe is possible. Introspective psychology[7] no longer pretends to supply direct information about events which are the causal antecedents, rather than the mere accompaniments, of behavior. It defines its "subjective" events in ways which strip them of any usefulness in a causal analysis. The events appealed to in early mentalistic explanations of behavior have remained beyond the reach of observation. Freud insisted upon this by emphasizing the role of the unconscious—a frank recognition that important mental processes are not directly observable. The Freudian literature supplies many examples of behavior from which unconscious wishes, impulses, instincts, and emotions are inferred. Unconscious thought-processes have also been used to explain intellectual achievements. Though the mathematician may feel that he knows "how he thinks," he is often unable to give a coherent account of the mental processes leading to the solution of a specific problem. But any mental event which is unconscious is necessarily inferential, and the explanation is therefore not based upon independent observations of a valid cause.

The fictional nature of this form of inner cause is shown by the ease with which the mental process is discovered to have just the properties needed to account for the behavior. When a professor turns up in the wrong classroom or gives the wrong lecture, it is because his *mind* is, at least for the moment, *absent*. If he forgets to give a reading assignment, it is because it has slipped his *mind* (a hint from the class may re*mind* him of it). He begins to tell an old joke but pauses for a moment, and it is evident to everyone that he is trying to make up his *mind* whether or not he has already used the joke that term. His lectures grow more tedious with the years, and questions from the class confuse him more and more, because his *mind* is failing. What he says is often disorganized because his *ideas* are confused. He is occasionally unnecessarily emphatic because of the force of his *ideas*. When he repeats himself, it is because he has an *idée fixe*; and when he repeats what others have said, it is because he borrows his *ideas*. Upon occasion there is nothing in what he says because he lacks *ideas*. In all this it is obvious that the mind and the ideas, together with their special characteristics, are being invented on the spot to provide spurious explanations. A science of behavior can hope to gain very little from so cavalier a practice. Since mental or psychic events are asserted to lack the dimensions of physical science, we have an additional reason for rejecting them.

[7]A kind of psychology, prominent in the field's early days, in which trained "introspectionists" tried to observe their own mental processes.

CONCEPTUAL INNER CAUSES The commonest inner causes have no specific dimensions at all, either neurological or psychic. When we say that a man eats *because* he is hungry, smokes a great deal *because* he has the tobacco habit, fights *because* of the instinct of pugnacity, behaves brilliantly *because* of his intelligence, or plays the piano well *because* of his musical ability, we seem to be referring to causes. But on analysis these phrases prove to be merely redundant descriptions. A single set of facts is described by the two statements: "He eats" and "He is hungry." A single set of facts is described by the two statements: "He smokes a great deal" and "He has the smoking habit." A single set of facts is described by the two statements: "He plays well" and "He has musical ability." The practice of explaining one statement in terms of the other is dangerous because it suggests that we have found the cause and therefore need search no further. Moreover, such terms as "hunger," "habit," and "intelligence" convert what are essentially the properties of a process or relation into what appear to be things. Thus we are unprepared for the properties eventually to be discovered in the behavior itself and continue to look for something which may not exist.

The Variables of Which Behavior Is a Function

The practice of looking inside the organism for an explanation of behavior has tended to obscure the variables which are immediately available for a scientific analysis. These variables lie outside the organism, in its immediate environment and in its environmental history. They have a physical status to which the usual techniques of science are adapted, and they make it possible to explain behavior as other subjects are explained in science. These independent variables are of many sorts and their relations to behavior are often subtle and complex, but we cannot hope to give an adequate account of behavior without analyzing them.

Consider the act of drinking a glass of water. This is not likely to be an important bit of behavior in anyone's life, but it supplies a convenient example. We may describe the topography of the behavior in such a way that a given instance may be identified quite accurately by any qualified observer. Suppose now we bring someone into a room and place a glass of water before him. Will he drink? There appear to be only two possibilities: either he will or he will not. But we speak of the *chances* that he will drink, and this notion may be refined for scientific use. What we want to evaluate is the *probability* that he will drink. This may range from virtual certainty that drinking will occur to virtual certainty that it will not. The very considerable problem of how to measure such a probability will be discussed later. For the moment, we are interested in how the probability may be increased or decreased.

Everyday experience suggests several possibilities, and laboratory and clinical observations have added others. It is decidedly not true that a horse may be led to water but cannot be made to drink. By arranging a history of severe deprivation we could be "absolutely sure" that drinking would occur. In the same way we may be sure that the glass of water in our experiment will be drunk. Although we are not likely to arrange them experimentally, deprivations of the necessary magnitude sometimes occur outside the laboratory. We may obtain an effect similar to that of deprivation by speeding up the excretion of water. For example, we may induce sweating by raising the temperature of the room or by forcing heavy exercise, or we may increase the excretion of urine by mixing salt or urea in food taken prior to the experiment. It is also well known that loss of blood, as on a battlefield, sharply increases the probability of drinking. On the other hand, we may set the probability at virtually zero by inducing or forcing our subject to drink a large quantity of water before the experiment.

If we are to predict whether or not our subject will drink, we must know as much as possible about these variables. If we are to induce him to drink, we must be able to manipulate them. In both cases, moreover, either for accurate prediction or control, we must investigate the effect of each variable quantitatively with the methods and techniques of a laboratory science.

Other variables may, of course, affect the result. Our subject may be "afraid" that something has been added to the water as a practical joke or for experimental purposes. He may even "suspect" that the water has been poisoned. He may have grown up in a culture in which water is drunk only when no one is watching. He may refuse to drink simply to prove that we cannot predict or control his behavior. These possibilities do not disprove the relations between drinking and the variables listed in the preceding paragraphs; they simply remind us that other variables may have to be taken into account. We must know the history of our subject with respect to the behavior of drinking water, and if we cannot eliminate social factors from the situation, then we must know the history of his personal relations to people resembling the experimenter. Adequate prediction in any science requires information about all relevant variables, and the control of a subject matter for practical purposes makes the same demands.

Other types of "explanation" do not permit us to dispense with these requirements or to fulfill them in any easier way. It is of no help to be told that our subject will drink provided he was born under a particular sign of the zodiac which shows a preoccupation with water or provided he is the lean and thirsty type or was, in short, "born thirsty." Explanations in terms of inner states or agents, however, may require some further comment. To what extent is it helpful to be told, "He drinks because he is thirsty"? If to be thirsty means nothing more than to have a tendency to drink, this is mere redundancy. If it means that he drinks because of a state of thirst, an inner causal event is invoked. If this state is purely inferential—if no dimensions are assigned to it which would make direct observation possible—it cannot serve as an explanation. But if it has physiological or psychic properties, what role can it play in a science of behavior?

The physiologist may point out that several ways of raising the probability of drinking have a common effect: they increase the concentration of solutions in the body. Through some mechanism not yet well understood, this may bring about a corresponding change in the nervous system which in turn makes drinking more probable. In the same way, it may be argued that all these operations make the organism "feel thirsty" or "want a drink" and that such a psychic state also acts upon the nervous system in some unexplained way to induce drinking. In each case we have a causal chain consisting of three links: (1) an operation performed upon the organism from without—for example, water deprivation; (2) an inner condition—for example, physiological or psychic thirst; and (3) a kind of behavior—for example, drinking. Independent information about the second link would obviously permit us to predict the third without recourse to the first. It would be a preferred type of variable because it would be nonhistoric; the first link may lie in the past history of the organism, but the second is a current condition. Direct information about the second link is, however, seldom, if ever, available. Sometimes we infer the second link from the third: an animal is judged to be thirsty if it drinks. In that case, the explanation is spurious. Sometimes we infer the second link from the first: an animal is said to be thirsty if it has not drunk for a long time. In that case, we obviously cannot dispense with the prior history.

The second link is useless in the *control* of behavior unless we can manipulate it. At the moment, we have no way of directly altering neural processes at appropriate moments in the life of a behaving organism, nor has any way been discovered to alter a psychic process. We usually set up the second link through the first: we make an animal thirsty, in either the physiological or the psychic sense, by depriving it of water, feeding it salt, and so on. In that case, the second link obviously does not permit us to dispense with the first. Even if some new technical discovery were to enable us to set up or change the second link directly, we should still have to deal with those enormous areas in which human behavior is controlled through manipulation of the first link. A technique of operating upon the second link would increase our control of behavior, but the techniques which have already been developed would still remain to be analyzed.

The most objectionable practice is to follow the causal sequence back only as far as a hypothetical second link. This is a serious handicap both in a theoretical science and in the practical control of behavior. It is no help to be told that to get an organism to drink we are simply to "make it thirsty" unless we are also told how this is to be done. When we have obtained the necessary prescription for thirst, the whole proposal is more complex than it need be. Similarly, when an example of maladjusted behavior is explained by saying that the individual is "suffering from anxiety," we have still to be told the cause of the anxiety. But the external conditions which are then invoked could have been directly related to the maladjusted behavior. Again, when we are told that a man stole a loaf of bread because "he was hungry," we have still to learn of the external conditions responsible for the "hunger." These conditions would have sufficed to explain the theft.

The objection to inner states is not that they do not exist, but that they are not relevant in a functional analysis.[8] We cannot account for the behavior of any system while staying wholly inside it; eventually we must turn to forces operating upon the organism from without. Unless there is a weak spot in our causal chain so that the second link is not lawfully determined by the first, or the third by the second, then the first and third links must be lawfully related. If we must always go back beyond the second link for prediction and control, we may avoid many tiresome and exhausting digressions by examining the third link as a function of the first. Valid information about the second link may throw light upon this relationship but can in no way alter it.

A Functional Analysis

The external variables of which behavior is a function provide for what may be called a causal or functional analysis. We undertake to predict and control the behavior of the individual organism. This is our "dependent variable"—the effect for which we are to find the cause. Our "independent variables"—the causes of behavior—are the external conditions of which behavior is a function. Relations between the two—the "cause-and-effect relationships" in behavior—are the laws of a science. A synthesis of these laws expressed in quantitative terms yields a comprehensive picture of the organism as a behaving system.

This must be done within the bounds of a natural science. We cannot assume that behavior has any peculiar properties which require unique methods or special kinds of knowledge. It is often argued[9] that an act is not so important as the "intent" which lies behind it, or that it can be described only in terms of what it "means" to the behaving individual or to others whom it may affect. If statements of this sort are useful for scientific purposes, they must be based upon observable events, and we may confine ourselves to such events exclusively in a functional analysis. Although such terms as "meaning" and "intent" appear to refer to properties of behavior, they usually conceal references to independent variables. This is also true of "aggressive," "friendly," "disorganized," "intelligent," and other terms which appear to describe properties of behavior but in reality refer to its controlling relations.

The independent variables must also be described in physical terms. An effort is often made to avoid the labor of analyzing a physical situation by guessing what it "means" to an organism or by distinguishing between the physical world and a psychological world of "experience." This practice also reflects a confusion between dependent and independent variables. The events affecting an organism must be capable of description in the language of physical science. It is sometimes argued that certain "social forces" or the "influences" of culture or tradition are exceptions. But we cannot appeal to entities of this sort without explaining how they can affect both the scientist and the individual under observation. The physical events which must then be appealed to in such an explanation will supply us with alternative material suitable for a physical analysis.

By confining ourselves to these observable events, we gain a considerable advantage, not only in theory, but in practice. A "social force" is no more useful in manipulating behavior than an inner state of hunger, anxiety, or skepticism. Just as we must trace these inner events to the manipulable variables of which they are said to be functions before we may put them to practical use, so we must identify the physical events through which a "social force" is said to affect the organism before we can manipulate it for purposes of control. In dealing with the directly observable data we need not refer to either the inner state or the outer force.

* * *

[8]This important clarification and qualification of Skinner's position has often been neglected by his critics over the years.

[9]For example, by humanistic, phenomenological, and cognitive psychologists.

WHATEVER HAPPENED TO PSYCHOLOGY AS THE SCIENCE OF BEHAVIOR?

B. F. Skinner

By the time the following selection was first published, in 1987, Skinner was near the end of his very long career. Behaviorism had established itself as one of the major paradigms of psychology, and Skinner himself was world-famous. Yet in this article you will see both the same general ideas and a very different tone from the unbounded optimism in the previous selection. Skinner expresses a surprising amount of disappointment and even bitterness. The heyday of behaviorism had come and gone, and the "cognitive revolution" and psychology's rediscovery of the mind had become a dominant theme of the field. So although behaviorism had been dominant for a time and remains an important paradigm, Skinner asks why it did not become *psychology.*

Skinner identifies three villains. One is humanistic psychology, a longtime foe of behaviorism, and its insistence that people have the capacity for free choice. The second he labels "psychotherapy," but he really seems to have in mind the various and to Skinner, sloppy habits of speech that obscure functional analysis. For example, we just referred to something Skinner seemed to "have in mind," a phrase Skinner would have regarded as a potentially misleading verbal shorthand for what Skinner was really doing. It turned out to be difficult, even for behaviorists, to expunge from the language terms such as mind, intention, knowledge, and desire. The third culprit is cognitive psychology, which Skinner regards as no more scientific than humanistic psychology. Cognitive psychology's emphasis on the mind and its description of unobservable mental processes has distracted psychologists from their real business, which is the prediction and control of behavior. Skinner makes the further interesting point that when cognitive psychologists describe mental processes that they expect ultimately to be explained in neurological terms, they are entering risky terrain. "Once you tell the world that another science will explain what your key terms really mean," he warns, "you must forgive the world if it decides the other science is doing the important work."

In our view, the reason behaviorism did not completely and permanently take over psychology was that—despite Skinner's cogent critique—psychologists became convinced that mentalistic terms do refer to something important. Most psychologists came to believe (as do nearly all nonpsychologists) that thoughts and feelings (the inner states Skinner omitted from functional analysis) are interesting and consequential. Even as Skinner penned the words of this, one of his final essays, the social learning theorists had already bent and stretched behaviorism to include nonbehavioral phenomena, and the cognitive social learning theorists were taking those developments even further, as we shall see later in this section.

From *American Psychologist, 42*, 780–786, 1987.

There can scarcely be anything more familiar than human behavior. We are always in the presence of at least one behaving person. Nor can there be anything more important, whether it is our own behavior or that of those whom we see every day or who are responsible for what is happening in the world at large. Nevertheless it is certainly not the thing we understand best. Granted that it is possibly the most difficult subject ever submitted to scientific analysis, it is still puzzling that so little has been done with the instruments and methods that have been so productive in the other sciences. * * *

* * *

For more than half a century the experimental analysis of behavior as a function of environmental variables and the use of that analysis in the interpretation and modification of behavior in the world at large have reached into every field of traditional psychology. Yet they have not *become* psychology, and the question is, Why not? Perhaps answers can be found in looking at three formidable obstacles that have stood in the path of an experimental analysis of behavior.

Obstacle 1: Humanistic Psychology

Many people find the implications of a behavioral analysis disturbing. The traditional direction of action of organism and environment seems to be reversed. Instead of saying that the organism sees, attends to, perceives, "processes," or otherwise acts upon stimuli, an operant analysis holds that stimuli acquire control of behavior through the part they play in contingencies of reinforcement. Instead of saying that an organism stores copies of the contingencies to which it is exposed and later retrieves and responds to them again, it says that the organism is changed by the contingencies and later responds as a changed organism, the contingencies having passed into history. The environment takes over the control formerly assigned to an internal, originating agent.

Some long-admired features of human behavior are then threatened. Following the lead of evolutionary theory, an operant analysis replaces creation with variation and selection.[1] There is no longer any need for a creative mind or plan, or for purpose or goal direction. Just as we say that species-specific behavior did not evolve *in order that* a species could adapt to the environment but rather evolved *when* it adapted, so we say that operant behavior is not strengthened by reinforcement *in order that* the individual can adjust to the environment but is strengthened *when* the individual adjusts (where "adapt" and "adjust" mean "behave effectively with respect to").

The disenthronement of a creator seems to

[1]Evolutionary theory assumes that random variation creates a variety of organisms in each generation, of which some survive and reproduce more successfully than others. Similarly, Skinner's operant behavior theory assumes that organisms begin by behaving more or less randomly, but processes of reinforcement cause some behaviors to "survive" and others to drop out of the repertoire.

threaten personal freedom (Can we be free if the environment is in control?) and personal worth (Can we take credit for our achievements if they are nothing more than the effects of circumstances?). It also seems to threaten ethical, religious, and governmental systems that hold people responsible for their conduct. Who or what is responsible if unethical, immoral, or illegal behavior is due to heredity or personal history? Humanistic psychologists have attacked behavioral science along these lines. Like creationists in their attack on secular humanists (with the humanists on the other side), they often challenge the content or selection of textbooks, the appointment of teachers and administrators, the design of curricula, and the allocation of funds.

Obstacle 2: Psychotherapy

Certain exigencies of the helping professions are another obstacle in the path of a scientific analysis of behavior. Psychotherapists must talk with their clients and, with rare exceptions, do so in everyday English, which is heavy laden with references to internal causes—"I ate because I was *hungry*," "I could do it because I *knew* how to do it," and so on. All fields of science tend to have two languages, of course. Scientists speak one with casual acquaintances and the other with colleagues. In a relatively young science, such as psychology, the use of the vernacular may be challenged. How often have behaviorists heard, "You just said 'It crossed my mind!' I thought there wasn't supposed to be any mind." It has been a long time since anyone challenged a physicist who said, "That desk is made of solid oak," by protesting, "But I thought you said that matter was mostly empty space."

The two languages of psychology raise a special problem. What we feel when we are hungry or when we know how to do something are states of our bodies. We do not have very good ways of observing them, and those who teach us to observe them usually have no way at all. We were taught to say "I'm hungry," for example, by persons who knew perhaps only that we had not eaten for some time ("You missed your lunch; you must be *hungry*") or had observed something about our behavior ("You are eating ravenously. You must be *hungry*"). Similarly, we were taught to say "I know" by persons who had perhaps only seen us doing something ("Oh, you *know* how to do that!") or had told us how to do something and then said "Now you *know*." The trouble is that private states are almost always poorly correlated with the public evidence.

References to private events are, nevertheless, often accurate enough to be useful. If we are preparing a meal for a friend, we are not likely to ask, "How long has it been since you last ate?" or "Will you probably eat a great deal?" We simply ask, "How *hungry* are you?" If a friend is driving us to an appointment, we are not likely to ask, "Have you driven there before?" or "Has anyone told you where it is?" Instead we ask, "Do you *know* where it is?" Being hungry and knowing where something is are states of the body resulting from personal histories, and what is said about them may be the only available evidence of those histories. Nevertheless, how much a person eats does depend upon a history of deprivation, not upon how a deprived body feels, and whether a person reaches a given destination does depend upon whether he or she has driven there before or has been told how to get there, not upon introspective evidence of the effects.

Psychotherapists must ask people what has happened to them and how they feel because the confidential relationship of therapist and client prevents direct inquiry. (It is sometimes argued that what a person remembers may be more important than what actually happened, but that is true only if something else has happened, of which it would also be better to have independent evidence.[2]) But although the use of reports of feelings and states of mind can be justified on practical grounds, there is no justification for their use in theory making. The temptation, however, is great. Psychoanalysts, for example, specialize in feelings.

---

[2]This is a succinct rebuttal to the phenomenological position.

Instead of investigating the early lives of their patients or watching them with their families, friends, or business associates, they ask them what has happened and how they feel about it. It is not surprising that they should then construct theories in terms of memories, feelings, and states of mind or that they should say that an analysis of behavior in terms of environmental events lacks "depth."

Obstacle 3: Cognitive Psychology

A curve showing the appearance of the word *cognitive* in the psychological literature would be interesting. A first rise could probably be seen around 1960; the subsequent acceleration would be exponential. Is there any field of psychology today in which something does not seem to be gained by adding that charming adjective to the occasional noun? The popularity may not be hard to explain. When we became psychologists, we learned new ways of talking about human behavior. If they were "behavioristic," they were not very much like the old ways. The old terms were taboo, and eyebrows were raised when we used them. But when certain developments seemed to show that the old ways might be right after all, everyone could relax. Mind was back.

Information theory was one of those developments, computer technology another. Troublesome problems seemed to vanish like magic. A detailed study of sensation and perception was no longer needed; one could simply speak of processing information. It was no longer necessary to construct settings in which to observe behavior; one could simply describe them. Rather than observe what people actually did, one could simply ask them what they would probably do.

That mentalistic psychologists are uneasy about these uses of introspection is clear from the desperation with which they are turning to brain science, asking it to tell them what perceptions, feelings, ideas, and intentions "really are." And brain scientists are happy to accept the assignment. To complete the account of an episode of behavior (for example, to explain what happens when a reinforcement brings an organism under the control of a given stimulus) is not only beyond the present range of brain science, it would lack the glamour of a revelation about the nature of mind. But psychology may find it dangerous to turn to neurology for help. Once you tell the world that another science will explain what your key terms really mean, you must forgive the world if it decides that the other science is doing the important work.

Cognitive psychologists like to say that "the mind is what the brain does," but surely the rest of the body plays a part. The mind is what the *body* does. It is what the *person* does. In other words, it is behavior, and that is what behaviorists have been saying for more than half a century. * * *

* * *

Damage and Repair

By their very nature, the antiscience stance of humanistic psychology, the practical exigencies of the helping professions, and the cognitive restoration of the royal House of Mind have worked against the definition of psychology as the science of behavior. Perhaps that could be justified if something more valuable had been achieved, but has that happened? Is there a better conception of psychology? To judge from the psychological literature, there are either many conceptions, largely incompatible, or no clear conception at all. Introductory textbooks do not help because, with an eye on their books' being adopted, the authors call their subject the "science of behavior *and* mental life" and make sure that every field of interest is covered. What the public learns from the media is equally confusing.

Is there a rapidly expanding body of facts and principles? Of our three obstacles, only cognitive psychology offers itself as an experimental science. It usually does so with a certain éclat, but have its promises been kept? When the journal *Psychology Today* celebrated its 15th anniversary, it asked 10 psychologists to name the most important discoveries made during that period of time. As Nicolas Wade (1982) has pointed out, no 2 of the 10 agreed on a single achievement that could properly be called psychology. For more than two years *Science* has not published a single article on psychology, except one on memory citing work on brain-operated and brain-damaged people and one on the neurological basis of memory retrieval. Apparently the editors of *Science* no longer regard psychology itself as a member of the scientific community.

Nor has psychology developed a strong technology. Internal determiners get in the way of effective action. An article on "Energy Conservation Behavior" in the *American Psychologist* (Costanzo, Archer, Aronson, & Pettigrew, 1986) carries the significant subtitle, "The Difficult Path From Information to Action." If you take the "rational economic" path and tell people about the consequences of what they are doing or of what they might do instead, they are not likely to change. (And for good reason: Information is not enough; people seldom take advice unless taking other advice has been reinforced.) If, on the other hand, you adopt the "attitude-change" approach, people are also not likely to change. Attitudes are inferences from the behavior that is said to show their presence and are not directly accessible. If I turn off unnecessary lights and appliances in my home, it is not because I have a "positive attitude" toward conservation, but because doing so has had some kind of reinforcing consequence. To induce people to conserve energy, one must change contingencies of reinforcement, not attitudes. No one should try to beat a "path from information to action," because action is the problem and contingencies the solution. * * *

* * *

Beyond the current reach of all of the sciences lies an issue that cannot be safely neglected by any of them—the future of the world. For a variety of reasons all three of our "obstacles" have had special reasons for neglecting it. Humanistic psychologists are unwilling to sacrifice feelings of freedom and worth for the sake of a future, and when cognitive psychologists turn to feelings and states of mind for theoretical purposes and psychotherapists for practical ones, they emphasize the here and now. Behavior modification, in contrast, is more often preventive than remedial. In both instruction and therapy, current reinforcers (often contrived) are arranged to strengthen behavior that student and client will find useful *in the future.*

When Gandhi was asked, "What are we to do?" he is said to have replied, "Think of the poorest man you have ever met and then ask if what you are doing is of any benefit to him." But he must have meant "of any benefit to the many people who, without your help, will be like him." To feed the hungry and clothe the naked are remedial acts. We can easily see what is wrong and what needs to be done. It is much harder to see and do something about the fact that world agriculture must feed and clothe billions of people, most of them yet unborn. It is not enough to *advise* people how to behave in ways that will make a future possible; they must be given effective reasons for behaving in those ways, and that means effective contingencies of reinforcement now.

Unfortunately, references to feelings and states of mind have an emotional appeal that behavioral alternatives usually lack. Here is an example: "If the world is to be saved, people must learn to be noble without being cruel, to be filled with faith, yet open to truth, to be inspired by great purposes without hating those who thwart them." That is an "inspiring" sentence. We like nobility, faith, truth, and great purposes and dislike cruelty and hatred. But what does it inspire us to *do*? What must be changed if people are to behave in noble rather than cruel ways, to accept the word of others but never without questioning it, to do things that have consequences too remote to serve as reinforcers, and to refrain from attacking those who oppose them? The fault, dear Brutus, is not in our stars *nor in ourselves* that we are underlings. The fault is in the world. It is a world that we have made and one that we must change if the species is to survive.

For at least 2,500 years philosophers and psychologists have proceeded on the assumption that because they were themselves behaving organisms, they had privileged access to the causes of their behavior. But has any introspectively observed feeling or state of mind yet been unambiguously identified in either mental or physical terms? Has any ability or trait of character been statistically established to the satisfaction of everyone? Do we know how anxiety changes intention, how memories alter decisions, how intelligence changes emotion, and so on? And, of course, has anyone ever explained how the mind works on the body or the body on the mind?

Questions of that sort should never have been asked. Psychology should confine itself to its accessible subject matter and leave the rest of the story of human behavior to physiology.

References

Costanzo, M., Archer, D., Aronson, E., & Pettigrew, T. (1986). Energy conservation behavior: The difficult path from information to action. *American Psychologist, 41*, 521–528.

Wade, N. (1982, April 30). Smart apes or dumb? *New York Times*, p. 28.

An Introduction to Social Learning Theory

Julian Rotter

Although many psychologists were attracted to the precision and empirical rigor of Skinner's empirical analysis of behavior, some also found classic behaviorism to be overly limiting of what could be studied. So they tried to find a way to keep behaviorism's scientific virtues while addressing new and complex topics such as cognition (thought), individual differences, and even defense mechanisms. These efforts to extend behaviorism were called the social learning theories.

One of the important and early developers of a social learning theory was Julian Rotter. In the next selection, published in 1972, after Rotter and his theory had attained a considerable amount of prominence, Rotter describes some of the basic tenets of his theory. While his focus remains on observable behavior and variables in the environment (which he calls the "situation") that control it, Rotter reveals he is no behaviorist with his discussion of "implicit behaviors" such as rationalizing, repressing, considering alternatives, planning, and reclassifying. Rotter seems to be trying simultaneously to move behaviorism onto the turf of both psychoanalytic theory and its consideration of defense mechanisms, and also cognitive psychology and its consideration of strategies and mental categories. Later on, Rotter also tries to account for individual differences in personality, particularly along a construct he calls "locus of control"—still a widely used construct today.

The later social learning theorists, such as Albert Bandura, turned their attention away from defense mechanisms and individual differences and focused on the relation between cognition and behavior. So Rotter's approach is not as influential today as it once was. But his concept of locus of control continues in wide use. And his theory stands as the high-water mark of attempts to extend behavioristic analysis to as many psychological phenomena as possible.

From *Applications of a Social Learning Theory of Personality*, edited by J. B. Rotter, J. E. Chance, and E. J. Phares (New York: Holt, Rinehart & Winston, 1972), pp. 1–46.

* * *

Basic Concepts

In SLT[1], four basic concepts are utilized in the prediction of behavior. These concepts are *behavior potential, expectancy, reinforcement value,* and the *psychological situation.* * * *

BEHAVIOR POTENTIAL Behavior potential may be defined as the potentiality of any behavior's occurring in any given situation or situations as calculated in relation to any single reinforcement or set of reinforcements.

Behavior potential is a relative concept. That is, one calculates the potentiality of any behavior's occurring in relation to the other alternatives open to the individual. Thus, it is possible to say only that in a specific situation the potentiality for occurrence of behavior *x* is greater than that for behavior *z*.

The SLT concept of behavior is quite broad. Indeed, behavior may be that which is directly observed but also that which is indirect or implicit. This notion includes a broad spectrum of possibilities—swearing, running, crying, fighting, smiling, choosing, and so on, are all included. These are all observable behaviors, but implicit behaviors that can only be measured indirectly, such as rationalizing, repressing, considering alternatives, planning, and reclassifying, would also be included. The objective study of cognitive activity is a difficult but important aspect of social learning theory. Principles governing the occurrence of such cognitive activities are not considered different from those that might apply to any observable behavior.

EXPECTANCY Expectancy may be defined as the probability held by the individual that a particular reinforcement will occur as a function of a specific behavior on his part in a specific situation or situations. Expectancy is systematically independent of the value or importance of the reinforcement.

In SLT the concept of expectancy is defined as a subjective probability, but this definition does not imply inaccessibility to objective measurement. People's probability statements, and other behaviors relating to the probability of occurrence of an event, often differ systematically from their actuarial experience with the event in the past. A variety of other factors operate in specific instances to influence one's probability estimates. Such factors may include the nature or the categorization of a situation, patterning and sequential considerations, uniqueness of events, generalization, and the perception of causality.

REINFORCEMENT VALUE The reinforcement value of any one of a group of potential external reinforcements may be ideally defined as the degree of the person's preference for that reinforcement to occur if the possibilities of occurrence of all alternatives were equal.

Again, reinforcement value is a relative term. Measurement of reinforcement value occurs in a choice situation. That is, reinforcement value refers to a preference, and preference indicates that one favors something over something else. Such preferences show consistency and reliability within our culture and also, generally speaking, can be shown to be systematically independent of expectancy. * * *

THE PSYCHOLOGICAL SITUATION Behavior does not occur in a vacuum. A person is continuously reacting to aspects of his external and internal environment. Since he reacts selectively to many kinds of stimulation, internal and external simultaneously, in a way consistent with his unique experience and because the different aspects of his environment mutually affect each other, we choose to speak of the psychological situation rather than the stimulus. * * *

Several writers have pointed out the difficulty of identifying situations independently of behavior. That is, how can one describe a situation, as one might a physical stimulus, independently of

[1]Social learning theory.

the particular S's[2] response? However, the problem is not really so different from that of describing stimuli along dimensions of color, although it is perhaps vastly more complicated in social situations. In the case of color stimuli, ultimately the criterion is a response made by an observer, sometimes aided by an intermediate instrument. The response is one that is at the level of sensory discrimination and thus leads to high observer agreement. In the case of social situations, the level of discrimination is common sense based on an understanding of a culture rather than a reading from an instrument. As such, reliability of discrimination may be limited but still be sufficiently high to make practical predictions possible. Specific situations can be identified as school situations, employment situations, girl friend situations, and so on. For the purpose of generality, various kinds of psychological constructs can be devised to arrive at broader classes of situations having similar meaning to S. The utility of such classes would have to be empirically determined, depending on the S's response. The objective referents for these situations, which provide the basis for prediction, however, can be independent of the specific S. That is, they can be reliably identified by cultural, common sense terms.

Basic Formulas The preceding variables and their relations may be conveniently stated in the formulas that follow. It should be remembered, however, that these formulas do not at this time imply any precise mathematical relations. Indeed, although the relation between expectancy and reinforcement value is probably a multiplicative one, there is little systematic data at this point that would allow one to evolve any precise mathematical statement.

The basic formula is stated thus:

$$BP_{x,s_1,R_a} = f(E_{x,R_a,s_1} \ \& \ RV_{a,s_1}) \qquad (1)$$

Formula (1) says, The potential for behavior x to occur, in situation 1 in relation to reinforcement a, is a function of the expectancy of the occurrence of reinforcement a, following behavior x in situation 1, and the value of reinforcement a in situation 1.

Formula (1) is obviously limited, inasmuch as it deals only with the potential for a given behavior to occur in relation to a single reinforcement. As noted earlier, description at the level of personality constructs usually demands a broader, more generalized concept of behavior, reflected in the following formula:

$$BP_{(x-n),s_{(1-n)},R_{(a-n)}} = f(E_{(x-n),s_{(1-n)},R_{(a-n)}} \ \& \ RV_{(a-n),s_{(1-n)}}) \qquad (2)$$

Formula (2) says, The potentiality of functionally related behaviors x to n to occur, in specified situations 1 to n in relation to potential reinforcements a to n, is a function of the expectancies of these behaviors leading to these reinforcements in these situations and the values of these reinforcements in these situations. To enhance communication by reducing verbal complexity, three terms—*need potential, freedom of movement*, and *need value*—have been introduced. A formula incorporating these latter terms is:

$$NP = f(FM \ \& \ NV) \qquad (3)$$

Thus, need potential is a function of freedom of movement and need value. In broader predictive or clinical situations, formula (3) would more likely be used, while formula (2) would be more appropriate in testing more specific, experimental hypotheses.

The fourth variable, *situation*, is left implicit in formula (3). SLT is highly committed to the importance of the psychological situation. It is emphasized that behavior varies as the situation does. But obviously, there is also transituational generality in behavior. If there were not, there would be no point in discussing personality as a construct or as a field of study. However, along with generality there is also situational specificity. While it may be true that person A is generally more aggressive than person B, nonetheless there

[2]Subject's.

can arise many occasions on which person B behaves more aggressively than does person A. Predictions based solely on internal characteristics of the individual are not sufficient to account for the complexities of human behavior.

* * *

Need Potential

The concept *need potential* is the broader analogue of behavior potential. The difference is that need potential refers to groups of functionally related behaviors rather than single behaviors. Functional relatedness of behaviors exists when several behaviors all lead to, or are directed toward, obtaining the same or similar reinforcements. The process of generalization occurring among functionally related behaviors allows for better than chance prediction from one specific referent of the category to another. (Similarity of reinforcement is not the only basis for functional relatedness of behaviors.) Need potential, then, describes the mean potentiality of a group of functionally related behaviors, directed at obtaining the same or a set of similar reinforcements, occurring in any segment of the individual's life.

The kinds of behaviors that can be grouped into functional categories may range from very molecular physical or objectively defined acts to implicit behaviors such as identifying with authority figures. Such categories may be progressively more inclusive depending upon one's predictive goal and the level of predictive accuracy required. For example, *need potential for recognition is more inclusive than need potential for recognition in psychology.*[3]

In practice, estimates of need potential are made utilizing some sampling procedure. Perhaps, observations are made of how *S* behaves in selected or specified situations. Normally, the determination of the relation between behaviors and reinforcements is made on a cultural basis. That is, on a cultural basis we know that studying is related to a group of reinforcements called academic recognition. At this point a brief discussion of some need concepts used in social learning theory will be helpful in understanding the sections to follow.

It is crucial to the development of a theory of personality that a descriptive language be established which deals with the content of personality. One difficulty with many learning theories is their almost exclusive emphasis on the processes of acquisition of behavior and of performance and their almost total neglect of the content of personality.[4] In contrast, many personality theories suffer from the reverse situation, emphasizing content (needs, traits, and so on) while neglecting process.

In developing content terms, SLT began by attempting to profit from the experience of clinicians, psychotherapists, and students of the culture generally. Development of a reliable, communicable, and valid language of description is an ever-evolving process. Furthermore, it is an empirical process, wherein the final test is predictive utility of the terms and not armchair rumination.

Based on the foregoing considerations, six need descriptions were developed at a fairly broad level of abstraction. From these relatively broad categories, more specific abstractions can be developed. Some of these can be included almost entirely within one of the broad categories, while some others might be related as well to one category as to another. The six broad categories arrived at and their definitions are the following:

Recognition-Status: Need to be considered competent or good in a professional, social, occupational, or play activity. Need to gain social or vocational position—that is, to be more skilled or better than others.

Protection-Dependency: Need to have another

[3]That is, the need to be famous is more general than the need to be a famous psychologist.

[4]Here is an explicit statement of Rotter's disagreement with Skinner.

person or group of people prevent frustration or punishment, or to provide for the satisfaction of other needs.

Dominance: Need to direct or to control the actions of other people, including members of family and friends. To have any action taken be that which he suggests.

Independence: Need to make own decisions, to rely on oneself, together with the need to develop skills for obtaining satisfactions directly without the mediation of other people.

Love and Affection: Need for acceptance and indication of liking by other individuals. In contrast to recognition-status, *not* concerned with social or professional positions, but seeks persons' warm regard.

Physical Comfort: Learned need for physical satisfaction that has become associated with gaining security.

All of these categories were presumed to be at about the same general level of inclusiveness.

The general term *need* used in this context refers to the entire complex of *need potential, freedom of movement*, and *need value*. The term refers to a set of constructs describing directionality of behavior, *not* to a state of deprivation or arousal in the organism. Used in this way the concept *need* is neither the equivalent of need value (or preference for certain kinds of goals) only nor the equivalent of *need potential* only.

To return to the discussion of need potential, it should be apparent that relying exclusively on cultural definitions of terms can lead to problems in individual prediction. For example, even though many people may study in order to achieve academic reinforcements, it may be true that a few people study in order to attain affectional responses from their girl friends. Therefore, the latter kind of individual would not be demonstrating a high need potential for academic recognition, but rather, for love and affection from opposite sex peers.

* * *

Need Value

Need value is defined as mean preference value of a set of functionally related reinforcements. Where reinforcement value indicates preference for one reinforcement over others, need value indicates preference for one set of functionally related reinforcements over another set (always assuming that expectancy for occurrence is held constant). Recall that functionality of reinforcements comes about either through stimulus generalization or through an extension of the principle of mediated stimulus generalization. Occurrence of functionality among reinforcements has been demonstrated empirically on a substitution basis, as well as in terms of generalization of expectancies among functionally related behaviors. Demonstration of functionality by substitution involves a situation where behavior toward a goal is blocked, and it is then noted which behavior is adopted as a substitute.

Earlier, when need potential was discussed, it was emphasized that descriptions of need categories based on functionally related behaviors must ultimately be arrived at on an empirical basis. Likewise, given a workable culture-based definition, one is cautioned about generalizing beyond the confines of one's own culture. Similarly, one must be cognizant of individual development of idiosyncratic need structures which may not follow those of the larger culture.

* * *

Freedom of Movement

Freedom of movement is defined as mean expectancy of obtaining positive satisfactions as a result of a set of related behaviors directed toward obtaining a group of functionally related reinforcements. Thus, when an individual has a high expectancy of attaining reinforcements that define a given need area for him, he is said to have high freedom of movement in that need area. In short, he feels that his behavioral techniques will be successful for his goals. When freedom of movement is low, particularly in relation to a need area of high value, the individual may anticipate punishment or failure. Thus, the concept of freedom of movement bears a relation to the concept of anxiety as described by other theories. * * *

* * *

* * * When freedom of movement is low while need value is high, we have a situation of conflict. To escape punishment and failure in an area of great importance to him, the individual adopts various avoidant behaviors. He may also try to reach his goals in irreal or symbolic ways, such as fantasy, which do not run the risk of incurring failure or punishment. Most behavior regarded as psychopathological is avoidant or irreal behavior. * * *

In summary, defensive behaviors provide an indirect measure of freedom of movement because such behaviors suggest the degree to which the individual expects negative reinforcement in a given need area. It is crucial in using this method that it first be established that the individual places a high value on the need in question. Otherwise, what seems avoidant may turn out to be an uncomplicated lack of interest.

Minimal Goal Level

Related to the concept of low freedom of movement is another SLT concept—*minimal goal level.* Specifically defined, minimal goal level refers to the lowest goal in a continuum of potential reinforcements for some life situation which will be perceived by the person as satisfactory to him. This definition suggests that reinforcements may be ordered from highly positive to highly negative. The point along this dimension at which reinforcements change from positive to negative in value for the person is his minimal goal level. Internalized minimal goals are responsible for the often observed instance where a person attains many goals that appear highly desirable to others and yet he, nonetheless, experiences a sense of failure or low freedom of movement. From his point of view, he is failing. When someone has extremely high minimal goals, whether in achievement, dominance, or love and affection, and is not obtaining reinforcements at or above this level, then by definition he has low freedom of movement.

The same analysis, in reverse, supplies the reason that a person may be contented, even though observers perceive his level of goal achievement to be exceedingly low. To the extent that problems in living often derive from a too high minimal goal level (or, more infrequently, from a very low minimal goal level), psychotherapy may concentrate on changing minimal goals by changing the value of reinforcements. As discussed in the preceding section on reinforcement values, value changes are accomplished by pairing the reinforcements in question with others of either a higher or lower value. For example, the individual is led to develop the expectancy that a previously negatively valued reinforcement—such as a grade of B—can lead to the positive reinforcements of praise and acceptance. * * *

* * *

The Situation

Implicit in all the preceding discussions has been the idea that the *psychological situation* is an extremely important determinant of behavior. This view is in sharp contrast to those positions that adopt a "core" approach to personality and assert that once the basic elements of personality are identified, reliable prediction follows. Core views are inherent in both psychoanalytic theories of dynamics and in trait and typological descriptive schemes. In short, many theories are so preoccupied with identifying highly stable aspects of personality that they fail to make systematic use of the psychological situation in the prediction of behavior.[5] The SLT approach contends that such a posture severely limits prediction by permitting only global statements about future behavior which are limited to a very low level of accuracy in prediction.

[5]Notice that this complaint is very similar to that voiced by Skinner, and on this point social learning theory is allied with behaviorism.

From the SLT view, each situation is composed of cues serving to arouse in the individual certain expectancies for reinforcement of specific behaviors. For example, even though an individual may be described as possessing an extremely strong predisposition to aggressive behavior, he will not behave aggressively in a given situation if the latter contains cues suggesting to him that aggressive behavior is very likely to result in strong punishment. Meanings that cues acquire for the individual are based on prior learning history and can be determined in advance in order to help us predictively. Again, some of these meanings can be assumed on a cultural basis, but the possibilities raised by idiosyncratic life experiences must be recognized also.

Recognition that behavior is not determined solely by personal characteristics but also by situational considerations specifies the necessity for descriptive categories for different situations. Psychology can be accurately said to have made less progress in devising classifications for situations than in almost any other area. * * *

* * *

Generalized Expectancies: Problem-Solving Skills

Man is a categorizing animal. He continuously forms concepts, changes concepts, and discovers new dimensions of similarity. While similarity of reinforcements is an extremely important basis for his conceptualizations, there are also other dimensions along which he perceives similarity. Within SLT any part of the environment to which the individual responds, or its totality, is referred to as a situational determinant. When an individual perceives that a number of people are alike because they are of the same sex, color, occupation, or age, he develops expectations about these people. Experience with one of them generalizes to others of the same class. When generalization takes place, we have the basis for believing that functional relations exist. That is, prediction of one referent from another referent of the same class can be made at a better than chance level. Generalized expectancies about people, and the behaviors and reinforcements connected with them, are part of the basis for what has been traditionally called social attitudes in psychology. * * *

Situations, both social and nonsocial, may also be perceived as similar in that they present similar problems. For example, all of us are faced continuously with the problem of deciding whether what happens to us is contingent on our own behavior and can be controlled by our own actions, or whether it depends upon luck, the intervention of powerful others, or influences we cannot understand. We develop a generalized expectancy across situations which may differ in needs satisfied or reinforcements expected, but which are similar with respect to perception of control that we can exercise to change or maintain these situations. As with social attitudes, when generalization occurs from one situation to another, individual differences may develop in how the situations themselves are perceived or categorized. In such a case, generalized expectancies may deal with properties of situational stimuli. That is, the basis for similarity does not lie, in this instance, in the nature of reinforcements but in the nature of the situation. Behaviors relevant to these situationally mediated expectancies are also functionally related because of similarity of the problems to be solved.

When a behavior directed toward a goal is blocked, or fails to achieve the goal, the failure itself may be regarded as a property of a new situation involving a problem to be solved. A generalized expectancy that problems can be solved by a technique of looking for alternatives may also be developed regardless of the specific need or reinforcement involved. The degree to which a generalized problem-solving expectancy is developed may be an important source of individual differences in behavior.

Another common human experience is that of being provided with information from other people—either promises of reinforcements to come or merely statements of presumed fact. Implicit in all these situations is the problem of whether to believe or not to believe the other person. A generalized expectancy of trust or distrust can be an important determinant of behavior.

The mature human can probably perceive an extremely large number of dimensions of similarities in problem characteristics in complex social situations. Some dimensions, however, are broader than others and some, undoubtedly, are far more relevant for particular kinds of psychological predictions than others. In recent years, many SLT investigations have concerned some of these dimensions. Two of these are the dimension of internal versus external control of reinforcement[6] and the dimension of interpersonal trust. * * *

* * *

Positive and Negative Reinforcements as Situational Cues

Reinforcements, whether words, acts, or tangible objects, are also parts of the psychological situation, as are cues closely associated with occurrence of reinforcements. Content categories based on perceived similarities of reinforcement (needs), perceived similarities of social cues (social attitudes), and perceived similarities of the nature of the problems to be solved (generalized expectancies) have been discussed. There may also be similarities in situations based on the sign (whether positive or negative) or intensity of reinforcements, or combinations of these along with the circumstances in which they occur.

Occurrence of a negative reinforcement,[7] or its anticipation, as already indicated, may lead to defensive or avoidant behaviors; and such behaviors can be understood as having a potential for a particular class of reinforcements. It may be characteristic of some people, however, that they respond with aggression, repression, withdrawal, projection, depression, and so on, somewhat independently of the kind (need category) of reinforcement. These responses may be a function of the sign or strength of the reinforcement rather than its particular form. In other words, we can talk not only about a behavior potential to repress competitive failures but a behavior potential to repress all strong negative reinforcements. How functional or general such potentials are across need areas is an empirical matter. Mild failure in an achievement-related task may increase the potential for some individuals to narrow their attention, increase concentration, and so on. However, mild failure might not have the same effect should it occur in initiating a social relationship.

* * *

Part 1: Summary

This chapter describes a molar learning theory of complex behavior with special reference to behavior in which the reinforcements depend on the behavior of other people. The purpose of the theory is prediction of behavior and the internal or cognitive processes related to behavior. While the same principles may also be important in early acquisition of more simple behaviors, the theory is not primarily concerned with more molecular principles which explain why one thing in a complex situation is associated with another, nor how very simple responses are built up into complex patterns of response. It is not that such principles are unimportant; they simply are not the focus of this theory. Once the basic patterns of behavior have been developed, the problem is to determine when one is chosen over another in a specific situation. This is the focus of this theory.

In addition to the principles governing the processes of choice behavior, social learning theory attempts to describe various ways in which generality of behavior may be described. In other

[6]This concept, also called "locus of control," is a dimension of personality that distinguishes between people who believe their actions control the important outcomes in their life (internal locus of control) and those who believe these outcomes are controlled by other forces such as luck and powerful others (external locus of control). Of all of Rotter's ideas the concept of locus of control is probably the most influential today.

[7]Here by "negative reinforcement" Rotter means punishment.

words, bases for a content theory of individual differences are developed. The most important of these bases is the similarity of reinforcements. Other categories of content are based upon the similarity of social objects (social attitudes) and similarities in the type of problem to be solved in a particular situation (generalized expectancies). A fourth category of behaviors may be based upon similarities in the sign and strength of reinforcements. Finally, the need for functional categories of situations characterized in common sense social terms is described. Such categories are prerequisite to prediction of behavior in a manner that attends to both its generality and its situational specificity.

* * *

Imitation of Film-Mediated Aggressive Models

Albert Bandura, Dorothea Ross, and Sheila A. Ross

The next selection is perhaps the most widely cited article by one of the most widely cited of all American psychologists, Albert Bandura. This article, originally published in 1963, is important for several reasons. First, its demonstration of imitative learning—in which a person watches and then performs a behavior, without ever having been rewarded or reinforced *for doing so—seemed revolutionary in contrast to the orthodox behaviorism that was still a dominant force in American psychology. Classical behavior theory maintained that a response becomes more likely after it has been reinforced; Bandura and his colleagues showed that such reinforcement is in fact not necessary.*

A second reason the article is important is that it has some obvious practical implications concerning the probable effect of televised violence—an issue that is probably even more important today (as that violence continues to escalate) than it was in 1963. It implies that such programming is dangerous because it can lead watchers—perhaps especially, young watchers—to imitate what it portrays.

A third reason to pay attention to this article is that it raises a theoretical issue that became important for the future development of personality psychology. The fact that watching a film can affect the watcher's later behavior implies that the watcher's mind must hold some sort of cognitive representation *of the action depicted in the film. In other words, the study not only suggests that behaviorism's insistence on the importance of reinforcement is incorrect but also implies that behaviorism's deliberate neglect of unobservable mental processes is similarly misguided. The present article does not make much of this implication, but it led directly to the development of the most recent paradigm in personality, the cognitive approach. Several examples of more recent research focusing directly on the implications of cognitive representations for behavior are presented in the next and final section of this book.*

From *Journal of Abnormal and Social Psychology*, 66, 3–11, 1963.

* * *

A recent incident (San Francisco Chronicle, 1961) in which a boy was seriously knifed during a re-enactment of a switchblade knife fight the boys had seen the previous evening on a televised rerun of the James Dean movie, *Rebel Without a Cause*, is a dramatic illustration of the possible imitative influence of film stimulation. * * *

In an earlier experiment (Bandura & Huston, 1961), it was shown that children readily imitated aggressive behavior exhibited by a model in the presence of the model. A succeeding investigation (Bandura, Ross, & Ross, 1961) demonstrated that children exposed to aggressive models generalized aggressive responses to a new setting in which the model was absent. The present study sought to determine the extent to which film-mediated aggressive models may serve as an important source of imitative behavior.

Aggressive models can be ordered on a reality-fictional stimulus dimension with real-life models located at the reality end of the continuum, nonhuman cartoon characters at the fictional end, and films portraying human models occupying an intermediate position. It was predicted, on the basis of saliency and similarity of cues, that the more remote the model was from reality, the weaker would be the tendency for subjects to imitate the behavior of the model.

Of the various interpretations of imitative learning, the sensory feedback theory of imitation recently proposed by Mowrer (1960) is elaborated in greatest detail. According to this theory, if certain responses have been repeatedly positively reinforced, proprioceptive stimuli[1] associated with these responses acquire secondary reinforcing properties[2] and thus the individual is predisposed to perform the behavior for the positive feedback. Similarly, if responses have been negatively reinforced[3], response correlated stimuli acquire the capacity to arouse anxiety which in turn, inhibits the occurrence of the negatively valenced behavior. On the basis of these considerations, it was predicted subjects who manifest high aggression anxiety would perform significantly less imitative and nonimitative aggression than subjects who display little anxiety over aggression. Since aggression is generally considered female inappropriate behavior, and therefore likely to be negatively reinforced[4] in girls (Sears, Maccoby, & Levin, 1957), it was also predicted that male subjects would be more imitative of aggression than females.

To the extent that observation of adults displaying aggression conveys a certain degree of permissiveness for aggressive behavior, it may be assumed that such exposure not only facilitates the learning of new aggressive responses but also weakens competing inhibitory responses in subjects and thereby increases the probability of occurrence of previously learned patterns of aggression. It was predicted, therefore, that subjects who observed aggressive models would display significantly more aggression when subsequently frustrated than subjects who were equally frustrated but who had no prior exposure to models exhibiting aggression.

Method

SUBJECTS The subjects were 48 boys and 48 girls enrolled in the Stanford University Nursery School. They ranged in age from 35 to 69 months, with a mean age of 52 months.

Two adults, a male and a female, served in the role of models both in the real-life and the human film-aggression condition, and one female experimenter conducted the study for all 96 children.

GENERAL PROCEDURE Subjects were divided into three experimental groups and one control group of 24 subjects each. One group of experimental subjects observed real-life aggressive models, a second group observed these same models portraying aggression on film, while a third group viewed a

[1]These are sensations associated with a response that have stimulus qualities of their own.

[2]Become rewarding in themselves.

[3]Punished (note this use of "negatively reinforced" to refer to punishment is at variance with usual practice).

[4]Again, the authors here mean "punished."

film depicting an aggressive cartoon character. The experimental groups were further subdivided into male and female subjects so that half the subjects in the two conditions involving human models were exposed to same-sex models, while the remaining subjects viewed models of the opposite sex.

Following the exposure experience, subjects were tested for the amount of imitative and nonimitative aggression in a different experimental setting in the absence of the models.

The control group subjects had no exposure to the aggressive models and were tested only in the generalization situation.

Subjects in the experimental and control groups were matched individually on the basis of ratings of their aggressive behavior in social interactions in the nursery school. The experimenter and a nursery school teacher rated the subjects on four five-point rating scales which measured the extent to which subjects displayed physical aggression, verbal aggression, aggression toward inanimate objects, and aggression inhibition. The latter scale, which dealt with the subjects' tendency to inhibit aggressive reactions in the face of high instigation, provided the measure of aggression anxiety. Seventy-one percent of the subjects were rated independently by both judges so as to permit an assessment of interrater agreement. The reliability of the composite aggression score estimated by means of the Pearson product-moment correlation, was .80.[5]

Data for subjects in the real-life aggression condition and in the control group were collected as part of a previous experiment (Bandura et al., 1961). Since the procedure is described in detail in the earlier report, only a brief description of it will be presented here.

EXPERIMENTAL CONDITIONS Subjects in the Real-Life Aggressive condition were brought individually by the experimenter to the experimental room and the model, who was in the hallway outside the room, was invited by the experimenter to come and join in the game. The subject was then escorted to one corner of the room and seated at a small table which contained potato prints, multicolor picture stickers, and colored paper. After demonstrating how the subject could design pictures with the materials provided, the experimenter escorted the model to the opposite corner of the room which contained a small table and chair, a tinker toy set, a mallet, and a 5-foot inflated Bobo doll. The experimenter explained that this was the model's play area and after the model was seated, the experimenter left the experimental room.

The model began the session by assembling the tinker toys but after approximately a minute had elapsed, the model turned to the Bobo doll and spent the remainder of the period aggressing toward it with highly novel responses which are unlikely to be performed by children independently of the observation of the model's behavior. Thus, in addition to punching the Bobo doll, the model exhibited the following distinctive aggressive acts which were to be scored as imitative responses:

> The model sat on the Bobo doll and punched it repeatedly in the nose.
>
> The model then raised the Bobo doll and pommeled it on the head with a mallet.
>
> Following the mallet aggression, the model tossed the doll up in the air aggressively and kicked it about the room. This sequence of physically aggressive acts was repeated approximately three times interspersed with verbally aggressive responses such as, "Sock him in the nose . . . ," "Hit him down . . . ," "Throw him in the air . . . ," "Kick him . . . ," and "Pow."

Subjects in the Human Film-Aggression condition were brought by the experimenter to the semi-darkened experimental room, introduced to the picture materials, and informed that while the subjects worked on potato prints, a movie would be shown on a screen, positioned approximately 6 feet from the subject's table. The movie projector was located in a distant corner of the room

[5]The raters tended to agree in their ratings of aggressiveness.

and was screened from the subject's view by large wooden panels.

The color movie and a tape recording of the sound track was begun by a male projectionist as soon as the experimenter left the experimental room and was shown for a duration of 10 minutes. The models in the film presentations were the same adult males and females who participated in the Real-Life condition of the experiment. Similarly, the aggressive behavior they portrayed in the film was identical with their real-life performances.

For subjects in the Cartoon Film-Aggression condition, after seating the subject at the table with the picture construction material, the experimenter walked over to a television console approximately 3 feet in front of the subject's table, remarked, "I guess I'll turn on the color TV," and ostensibly tuned in a cartoon program. The experimenter then left the experimental room. The cartoon was shown on a glass lens screen in the television set by means of a rear projection arrangement screened from the subject's view by large panels.

The sequence of aggressive acts in the cartoon was performed by the female model costumed as a black cat similar to the many cartoon cats. In order to heighten the level of irreality of the cartoon, the floor area was covered with artificial grass and the walls forming the backdrop were adorned with brightly colored trees, birds, and butterflies creating a fantasyland setting. The cartoon began with a close-up of a stage on which the curtains were slowly drawn revealing a picture of a cartoon cat along with the title, *Herman the Cat*. The remainder of the film showed the cat pommeling the Bobo doll on the head with a mallet, sitting on the doll and punching it in the nose, tossing the doll in the air, and kicking it about the room in a manner identical with the performance in the other experimental conditions except that the cat's movements were characteristically feline. To induce further a cartoon set, the program was introduced and concluded with appropriate cartoon music, and the cat's verbal aggression was repeated in a high-pitched, animated voice.

In both film conditions, at the conclusion of the movie the experimenter entered the room and then escorted the subject to the test room.

Aggression Instigation In order to differentiate clearly the exposure and test situations subjects were tested for the amount of imitative learning in a different experimental room which was set off from the main nursery school building.

The degree to which a child has learned aggressive patterns of behavior through imitation becomes most evident when the child is instigated to aggression on later occasions. Thus, for example, the effects of viewing the movie, *Rebel Without a Cause*, were not evident until the boys were instigated to aggression the following day, at which time they re-enacted the televised switchblade knife fight in considerable detail. For this reason, the children in the experiment, both those in the control group, and those who were exposed to the aggressive models, were mildly frustrated before they were brought to the test room.

Following the exposure experience, the experimenter brought the subject to an anteroom which contained a varied array of highly attractive toys. The experimenter explained that the toys were for the subject to play with, but, as soon as the subject became sufficiently involved with the play material, the experimenter remarked that these were her very best toys, that she did not let just anyone play with them, and that she had decided to reserve these toys for some other children. However, the subject could play with any of the toys in the next room. The experimenter and the subject then entered the adjoining experimental room.

* * *

Test for Delayed Imitation The experimental room contained a variety of toys, some of which could be used in imitative or nonimitative aggression, and others which tended to elicit predominantly nonaggressive forms of behavior. The aggressive toys included a 3-foot Bobo doll, a mallet and peg board, two dart guns, and a tether ball with a face painted on it which hung from the ceiling. The nonaggressive toys, on the other hand, included a tea set, crayons and coloring paper, a ball, two dolls, three bears, cars and trucks and plastic farm animals.

* * *

The subject spent 20 minutes in the experimental room during which time his behavior was rated in terms of predetermined response categories by judges who observed the session through a one-way mirror in an adjoining observation room. The 20-minute session was divided in 5-second intervals by means of an electric interval timer, thus yielding a total number of 240 response units for each subject.

The male model scored the experimental sessions for all subjects. In order to provide an estimate of interjudge agreement, the performances of 40% of the subjects were scored independently by a second observer. The responses scored involved highly specific concrete classes of behavior, and yielded high interscorer reliabilities, the product-moment coefficients being in the .90s.

RESPONSE MEASURES The following response measures were obtained:

Imitative aggression. This category included acts of striking the Bobo doll with the mallet, sitting on the doll and punching it in the nose, kicking the doll, tossing it in the air, and the verbally aggressive responses, "Sock him," "Hit him down," "Kick him," "Throw him in the air," and "Pow."

Partially imitative responses. A number of subjects imitated the essential components of the model's behavior but did not perform the complete act, or they directed the imitative aggressive response to some object other than the Bobo doll. Two responses of this type were scored and were interpreted as partially imitative behavior:

Mallet aggression. The subject strikes objects other than the Bobo doll aggressively with the mallet.

Sits on Bobo doll. The subject lays the Bobo doll on its side and sits on it, but does not aggress toward it.

Nonimitative aggression. This category included acts of punching, slapping, or pushing the doll, physically aggressive acts directed toward objects other than the Bobo doll, and any hostile remarks except for those in the verbal imitation category; for example, "Shoot the Bobo," "Cut him," "Stupid ball," "Knock over people," "Horses fighting, biting."

Aggressive gun play. The subject shoots darts or aims the guns and fires imaginary shots at objects in the room.

Ratings were also made of the number of behavior units in which subjects played nonaggressively or sat quietly and did not play with any of the material at all.

Results

The mean imitative and nonimitative aggression scores for subjects in the various experimental and control groups are presented in Table 47.1.

* * *

TOTAL AGGRESSION The mean total aggression scores for subjects in the real-life, human film, cartoon film, and the control groups are 83, 92, 99, and 54, respectively. The results of the analysis of variance performed on these scores reveal that the main effect of treatment conditions is significant ($\chi_r^2 = 9.06$, $p < .05$),[6] confirming the prediction that exposure of subjects to aggressive models increases the probability that subjects will respond aggressively when instigated on later occasions. Further analyses * * * show that subjects who viewed the real-life models and the film-mediated

[6]The analysis of variance used here is known as a Friedman analysis of variance for ranks. The inferential statistic that is calculated, χ_r^2, is different from the F statistic that arises from the analysis of variance as it is now usually applied, but the two methods are conceptually equivalent. There is a low probability (p) that such differences among the aggression scores across conditions would occur by chance if there really was no condition effect.

TABLE 47.1

MEAN AGGRESSION SCORES FOR SUBGROUPS OF EXPERIMENTAL AND CONTROL SUBJECTS

Response category	Experimental groups					Control group
	Real-life aggressive		Human film-aggressive		Cartoon film-aggressive	
	F Model	M Model	F Model	M Model		
Total aggression						
Girls	65.8	57.3	87.0	79.5	80.9	36.4
Boys	76.8	131.8	114.5	85.0	117.2	72.2
Imitative aggression						
Girls	19.2	9.2	10.0	8.0	7.8	1.8
Boys	18.4	38.4	34.3	13.3	16.2	3.9
Mallet aggression						
Girls	17.2	18.7	49.2	19.5	36.8	13.1
Boys	15.5	28.8	20.5	16.3	12.5	13.5
Sits on Bobo Doll[a]						
Girls	10.4	5.6	10.3	4.5	15.3	3.3
Boys	1.3	0.7	7.7	0.0	5.6	0.6
Nonimitative aggression						
Girls	27.6	24.9	24.0	34.3	27.5	17.8
Boys	35.5	48.6	46.8	31.8	71.8	40.4
Aggressive gun play						
Girls	1.8	4.5	3.8	17.6	8.8	3.7
Boys	7.3	15.9	12.8	23.7	16.6	14.3

[a]This response category was not included in the total aggression score.

models do not differ from each other in total aggressiveness but all three experimental groups expressed significantly more aggressive behavior than the control subjects.

IMITATIVE AGGRESSIVE RESPONSES

* * *

Illustrations of the extent to which some of the subjects became virtually "carbon copies" of their models in aggressive behavior are presented in Figure 47.1. The top frame shows the female model performing the four novel aggressive responses; the lower frames depict a male and a female subject reproducing the behavior of the female model they had observed earlier on film.

The prediction that imitation is positively related to the reality cues of the model was only partially supported. While subjects who observed the real-life aggressive models exhibited significantly more imitative aggression than subjects who viewed the cartoon model, no significant differences were found between the live and film, and the film and cartoon conditions, nor did the three experimental groups differ significantly in total aggression or in the performances of partially imitative behavior. Indeed, the available data suggest that, of the three experimental conditions, exposure to humans on film portraying aggression was the most influential in eliciting and shaping aggressive behavior. Subjects in this condition, in relation to the control subjects, exhibited more total aggression, more imitative aggression, more partially imitative behavior, such as sitting on the

Figure 47.1 Photographs from the film, *Social Learning of Aggression through Imitation of Aggressive Models.*

Bobo doll and mallet aggression, and they engaged in significantly more aggressive gun play. In addition, they performed significantly more aggressive gun play than did subjects who were exposed to the real-life aggressive models.

INFLUENCE OF SEX OF MODEL AND SEX OF CHILD In order to determine the influence of sex of model and sex of child on the expression of imitative and nonimitative aggression, the data from the experimental groups were combined and the significance of the differences between groups was assessed by *t* tests for uncorrelated means. * * *

Sex of subjects had a highly significant effect on both the learning and the performmance of aggression. Boys, in relation to girls, exhibited significantly more total aggression ($t = 2.69, p < .01$), more imitative aggression ($t = 2.82, p < .005$), more aggressive gun play ($z = 3.38, p < .001$), and more nonimitative aggressive behavior ($t = 2.98, p < .005$). Girls, on the other hand, were more inclined than boys to sit on the Bobo doll but refrained from punching it ($z = 3.47, p < .001$).[7]

* * *

Discussion

The results of the present study provide strong evidence that exposure to filmed aggression heightens aggressive reactions in children. Subjects who viewed the aggressive human and cartoon models on film exhibited nearly twice as much aggression than did subjects in the control group who were not exposed to the aggressive film content.

In the experimental design typically employed * * * , subjects are first frustrated, then provided with an opportunity to view an aggres-

[7]Both the *t* and *z* statistics here are used to compare group means; the *p* level derived from these statistics evaluates the probability that a difference of the size obtained would occur if no difference actually existed.

sive film following which their overt or fantasy aggression is measured. While this procedure yields some information on the immediate influence of film-mediated aggression, the full effects of such exposure may not be revealed until subjects are instigated to aggression on a later occasion. Thus, the present study, and one recently reported by Lövaas (1961), both utilizing a design in which subjects first observed filmed aggression and then were frustrated, clearly reveal that observation of models portraying aggression on film substantially increases rather than decreases the probability of aggressive reactions to subsequent frustrations.

Filmed aggression not only facilitated the expression of aggression, but also effectively shaped the form of the subjects' aggressive behavior. The finding that children modeled their behavior to some extent after the film characters suggests that pictorial mass media, particularly television, may serve as an important source of social behavior. In fact, a possible generalization of responses originally learned in the television situation to the experimental film may account for the significantly greater amount of aggressive gun play displayed by subjects in the film condition as compared to subjects in the real-life and control groups. It is unfortunate that the qualitative features of the gun behavior were not scored since subjects in the film condition, unlike those in the other two groups, developed interesting elaborations in gun play (for example, stalking the imaginary opponent; quick drawing, and rapid firing), characteristic of the Western gun fighter.

* * * Although the results of the present experiment demonstrate that the vast majority of children *learn* patterns of social behavior through pictorial stimulation, nevertheless, informal observation suggests that children do not, as a rule, *perform* indiscriminately the behavior of televised characters, even those they regard as highly attractive models. The replies of parents whose children participated in the present study to an open-end questionnaire item concerning their handling of imitative behavior suggest that this may be in part a function of negative reinforcement,[8] as most parents were quick to discourage their children's overt imitation of television characters by prohibiting certain programs or by labeling the imitative behavior in a disapproving manner. From our knowledge of the effects of punishment on behavior, the responses in question would be expected to retain their original strength and could reappear on later occasions in the presence of appropriate eliciting stimuli, particularly if instigation is high, the instruments for aggression are available, and the threat of noxious consequences is reduced.

* * *

A question may be raised as to whether the aggressive acts studied in the present experiment constitute "genuine" aggressive responses. Aggression is typically defined as behavior, the goal or intent of which is injury to a person, or destruction of an object (Bandura & Walters, 1959; Dollard, Doob, Miller, Mowrer, & Sears, 1939; Sears, Maccoby, & Levin, 1957). Since intentionality is not a property of behavior but primarily an inference concerning antecedent events, the categorization of an act as "aggressive" involves a consideration of both stimulus and mediating or terminal response events.

According to a social learning theory of aggression recently proposed by Bandura and Walters (1963), most of the responses utilized to hurt or to injure others (for example, striking, kicking, and other responses of high magnitude), are probably learned for prosocial purposes under nonfrustration conditions. Since frustration generally elicits responses of high magnitude, the latter classes of responses, once acquired, may be called out in social interactions for the purpose of injuring others. On the basis of this theory it would be predicted that the aggressive responses acquired imitatively, while not necessarily mediating aggressive goals in the experimental situation, would be utilized to serve such purposes in other social settings, with higher frequency by children in the experimental conditions than by children in the control group.

The present study involved primarily vicarious

---

[8]Punishment.

or empathic learning (Mowrer, 1960) in that subjects acquired a relatively complex repertoire of aggressive responses by the mere sight of a model's behavior. It has been generally assumed that the necessary conditions for the occurrence of such learning is that the model perform certain responses followed by positive reinforcement to the model (Hill, 1960; Mowrer, 1960). According to this theory, to the extent that the observer experiences the model's reinforcement vicariously, the observer will be prone to reproduce the model's behavior. While there is some evidence from experiments involving both human (Lewis & Duncan, 1958; McBrearty, Marston, & Kanfer, 1961; Sechrest, 1961) and animal subjects (Darby & Riopelle, 1959; Warden, Fjeld, & Koch, 1940), that vicarious reinforcement may in fact increase the probability of the behavior in question, it is apparent from the results of the experiment reported in this paper that a good deal of human imitative learning can occur without any reinforcers delivered either to the model or to the observer. * * *

References

Bandura, A., & Huston, Aletha C. (1961). Identification as a process of incidental learning. *Journal of Abnormal and Social Psychology, 63*, 311–318.

Bandura, A., Ross, Dorothea, & Ross, Sheila A. (1961). Transmission of aggression through imitation of aggressive models. *Journal of Abnormal and Social Psychology, 63*, 575–582.

Bandura, A., & Walters, R. H. (1959). *Adolescent aggression.* New York: Ronald.

Bandura, A., & Walters, R. H. (1963). *Social learning and personality development.* New York: Holt, Rinehart, & Winston.

Darby, C. L., & Riopelle, A. J. Observational learning in the Rhesus monkey. (1959). *Journal of Comparative Physiology and Psychology, 52*, 94–98.

Dollard, J., Doob, L. W., Miller, N. E., Mowrer, O. H., & Sears, R. R. (1939). *Frustration and aggression.* New Haven: Yale University Press.

Hill, W. F. (1960). Learning theory and the acquisition of values. *Psychological Review, 67*, 317–331.

Lewis, D. J., & Duncan, C. P. (1958). Vicarious experience and partial reinforcement. *Journal of Abnormal and Social Psychology, 57*, 321–326.

Lövaas, O. J. (1961). Effect of exposure to symbolic aggression on aggressive behavior. *Child Development, 32*, 37–44.

McBrearty, J. F., Marston, A. R., & Kanfer, F. H. (1961). Conditioning a verbal operant in a group setting: Direct vs. vicarious reinforcement. *American Psychologist, 16*, 425. (Abstract)

Mowrer, O. H. (1960). *Learning theory and the symbolic processes.* New York: Wiley.

San Francisco Chronicle. (1961). "James Dean" knifing in South City. *San Francisco Chronicle*, March 1, p. 6.

Sears, R. R., Maccoby, Eleanor E., & Levin, H. (1957). *Patterns of child rearing.* Evanston: Row, Peterson.

Sechrest, L. (1961). Vicarious reinforcement of responses. *American Psychologist, 16*, 356. (Abstract)

Warden, C. J., Field, H. A., & Koch, A. M. (1940). Imitative behavior in cebus and Rhesus monkeys. *Journal of Genetic Psychology, 56*, 311–322.

PART VIII

The Cognitive Approach to Personality

How does the way a person thinks affect who he or she is, and what he or she does? This is the basic question and topic of the cognitive approach to personality. In recent years the social learning approach became less and less about the simpler forms of learning, and more and more about the way people acquire, represent, store, and use information about the world and about themselves. The result was the development of a new basic approach to personality that is generating a large amount of research and now, in this second edition, deserves its own section in this book.

The first two selections are by two psychologists, Albert Bandura and Walter Mischel, who are well known for their work as social learning theorists. Both became increasingly concerned with issues relevant to mental functioning—cognitive issues—and thus helped lead the evolution of social learning theory into what Bandura calls social cognitive *theory. The first article, by Bandura, predates the development of the cognitive approach but helped to lay important groundwork by describing the workings of the "self system." Through a process Bandura calls "reciprocal determinism," an individual's self system develops as a result of experience but also determines future behavior and the future environment. Thus, the environment may determine the person, as behaviorists would maintain, but the person also determines the environment, and the interaction between the two is essentially a cognitive process.*

The second selection, by Mischel, describes an early and extremely influential approach toward accounting for personality in cognitive terms. In Mischel's "cognitive social learning reconceptualization of personality," a person's beliefs about and representations of the environment become more important than the environment itself (in this we see an echo of the phenomenological ideas of Mischel's teacher, George Kelly). Mischel also describes five "cognitive social learning person variables" that present a reconceptualization of individual differences in personality that goes beyond trait theory.

One of Mischel's cognitive social learning person variables is the strategy. In the third selection, Julie Norem describes the differences between students who employ an optimistic vs. a pessimistic strategy in motivating themselves to do academic work. Interestingly, both strategies are effective, though optimists seem to lead a more pleasant life. Norem's point is that different people can and often do use different strategies in pursuit of the very same goal.

The fourth selection, by Seymour Epstein, is different from the others in this section in that its roots lie not in behaviorism and social learning theory but in psychoanalysis. It addresses a question which long concerned Freud, which is how can the human mind have both rational and irrational aspects? Epstein's answer is that the mind includes two cognitive subsystems, each of which is specialized to deal with certain kinds of decisions and life situations.

The next selection, by Sonja Lyubomirsky and colleagues, is an example of how experimental and correlational methods can be used in tandem to help explain why people are different from each other. In this case she contrasts "dysphorics"—unhappy people—with those who do not suffer from chronic unhappiness, and shows how part of the difference between them is due to differences in how they think and what they think about.

The final selection in this section and this book brings together several strands of personality research. Stan Klein and his colleagues use the intensive study of a single case, a young woman they call "W. J.," to explore the neurological and psychological underpinnings of personal identity. In particular, they examine the degree to which a person's self-knowledge depends on memory. In the first selection in this book, McAdams asked what we know when we know a person; in the last, Klein asks what we must know to know ourselves.

Behaviorism has evolved a long way from the classical behaviorists to the social learning theorists to the cognitive theorists. The most recent developments offer a promise for the reintegration of personality psychology. The modern cognitive theorists of personality are renewing their attention to individual differences and describing patterns of thought, motivation, and behavior of the sort that have long been of interest to some trait theorists. This development opens the possibility for cognitive and trait theorists to begin again to take one another's work seriously and develop a personality psychology that draws on the strengths of both approaches.

The Self System in Reciprocal Determinism

Albert Bandura

The most prominent of the social learning theorists, Albert Bandura, helped lead the way as social learning theory evolved into the cognitive approach of personality. Indeed, in some of his most recent writings, Bandura calls his approach social cognitive *theory.*

The following selection, published at the height of Bandura's career, could be considered one of the first important entries in this new approach. It is an ambitious effort; Bandura tackles the heavy philosophical issues that surround "basic conceptions of human nature." He points out that the behaviorists and the humanists, seemingly opposite in viewpoint, share one basic idea: the unidirectional causation of behavior. That is, behaviorists see behavior as a function of reinforcements in the environment or the situation. At the opposite end, humanists see behavior as a function of the person, of his or her characteristics and most important, his or her free choice. In the following selection, Bandura seeks a middle ground between these seemingly irreconcilable viewpoints.

Bandura does this by proposing the existence of a "self system." This cognitive system, consisting of thoughts and feelings about the self, arises as a result of experience but, once constructed, has important effects on behavior. For example, the self system sets goals and evaluates one's own progress toward those goals. Just as importantly, the self system affects one's environment by (1) administering rewards and punishments to the self (such as promising oneself an ice cream as soon as one finishes reading Bandura's chapter) and by (2) selecting the environments that one enters. For example, once a student enrolls at college he or she is buffeted by all sorts of environmental pressures—rewards and punishments—that coerce the student to study for exams, write term papers, camp out in the library, and so on. But whether to enroll in college in the first place is a choice made by the self system. Similarly, activities and self-evaluations are critically influenced by the people one is surrounded by. To an important degree, a person chooses his or her companions and so chooses who to be influenced by.

If you pushed Bandura into a corner, he would probably have to admit to being a behaviorist at heart, despite his advocacy for the self system. This is because he views the self system as being, in the final analysis, a result of the environment. But by viewing the self system as something that, once constructed, can shape behavior and even shape the environment (through a process Bandura calls "reciprocal determinism"), Bandura opens up possibilities for the analysis and prediction of behavior that go beyond anything envisaged by classical behaviorism. Furthermore, he paves the way for further research to examine implications of cognitive structures and processes for behavior.

From *American Psychologist, 33*, 344–358, 1978.

Recent years have witnessed a heightened interest in the basic conceptions of human nature underlying different psychological theories. This interest stems in part from growing recognition of how such conceptions delimit research to selected processes and are in turn shaped by findings of paradigms embodying the particular view. As psychological knowledge is converted to behavioral technologies, the models of human behavior on which research is premised have important social as well as theoretical implications (Bandura, 1974).

Explanations of human behavior have generally been couched in terms of a limited set of determinants, usually portrayed as operating in a unidirectional manner. Exponents of environmental determinism study and theorize about how behavior is controlled by situational influences. Those favoring personal determinism seek the causes of human behavior in dispositional sources in the form of instincts, drives, traits, and other motivational forces within the individual. * * *

* * * The present article analyzes the various causal models and the role of self influences in behavior from the perspective of reciprocal determinism.

Unidirectional environmental determinism is carried to its extreme in the more radical forms of behaviorism. * * * ([For example] "A person does not act upon the world, the world acts upon him," Skinner, 1971, p. 211.) The environment thus becomes an autonomous force that automatically shapes, orchestrates, and controls behavior. * * *

* * *

There exists no shortage of advocates of alternative theories emphasizing the personal determination of environments. Humanists and existentialists,[1] who stress the human capacity for conscious judgment and intentional action, contend that individuals determine what they become by their own free choices. Most psychologists find conceptions of human behavior in terms of unidirectional personal determinism as unsatisfying as those espousing unidirectional environmental determinism. To contend that mind creates reality fails to acknowledge that environmental influences partly determine what people attend to, perceive, and think. To contend further that the methods of natural science are incapable of dealing with personal determinants of behavior does not enlist many supporters from the ranks of those who are moved more by empirical evidence than by philosophic discourse.

Social learning theory (Bandura, 1974, 1977b) analyzes behavior in terms of reciprocal determinism. The term *determinism* is used here to signify the production of effects by events, rather than in the doctrinal sense that actions are completely determined by a prior sequence of causes independent of the individual. Because of the complexity of interacting factors, events produce effects proba-

---

[1]Such as represented in Part V.

bilistically rather than inevitably. In their transactions with the environment, people are not simply reactors to external stimulation. Most external influences affect behavior through intermediary cognitive processes. Cognitive factors partly determine which external events will be observed, how they will be perceived, whether they have any lasting effects, what valence and efficacy they have, and how the information they convey will be organized for future use. The extraordinary capacity of humans to use symbols enables them to engage in reflective thought, to create, and to plan foresightful courses of action in thought rather than having to perform possible options and suffer the consequences of thoughtless action. By altering their immediate environment, by creating cognitive self-inducements, and by arranging conditional incentives for themselves, people can exercise some influence over their own behavior. An act therefore includes among its determinants self-produced influences.

It is true that behavior is influenced by the environment, but the environment is partly of a person's own making. By their actions, people play a role in creating the social milieu and other circumstances that arise in their daily transactions. Thus, from the social learning perspective, psychological functioning involves a continuous reciprocal interaction between behavioral, cognitive, and environmental influences.

Reciprocal Determinism and Interactionism

* * *

Interaction processes have been conceptualized in three fundamentally different ways. These alternative formulations are summarized schematically in Figure 48.1. In the unidirectional notion of interaction, persons and situations are treated as independent entities that combine to produce behavior. This commonly held view can be called into question on both conceptual and empirical grounds. Personal and environmental factors do not function as independent determinants; rather, they determine each other. Nor can "persons" be considered causes independent of their behavior. It is largely through their actions that people produce the environmental conditions that affect their behavior in a reciprocal fashion. The experiences generated by behavior also partly determine what individuals think, expect, and can do, which in turn, affect their subsequent behavior.

A second conception of interaction acknowledges that personal and environmental influences are bidirectional, but it retains a unidirectional view of behavior. In this analysis, persons and situations are considered to be interdependent causes of behavior, but behavior is treated as though it were only a by-product that does not figure at all in the causal process. * * *

* * *

In the social learning view of interaction, which is analyzed as a process of reciprocal determinism (Bandura, 1977b), behavior, internal personal factors, and environmental influences all operate as interlocking determinants of each other. As shown in Figure 48.1, the process involves a triadic reciprocal interaction rather than a dyadic conjoint or a dyadic bidirectional one. We have already noted that behavior and environmental conditions function as reciprocally interacting determinants. Internal personal factors (e.g., conceptions, beliefs, self-perceptions) and behavior also operate as reciprocal determinants of each other. For example, people's efficacy and outcome expectations influence how they behave, and the environmental effects created by their actions in turn alter their expectations. People activate different environmental reactions, apart from their behavior, by their physical characteristics (e.g., size, physiognomy, race, sex, attractiveness) and socially conferred attributes, roles, and status. The differential social treatment affects recipients' self-conceptions and actions in ways that either maintain or alter the environmental biases.

The relative influence exerted by these three sets of interlocking factors will vary in different individuals and under different circumstances. In

Unidirectional

$$B = f(P, E)$$

Partially Bidirectional

$$B = f(P \rightleftarrows E)$$

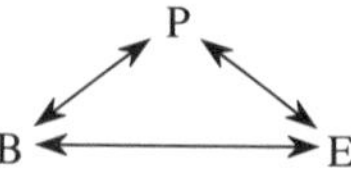

Figure 48.1 Schematic representation of three alternative conceptions of interaction: *B* signifies behavior, *P* the cognitive and other internal events that can affect perceptions and actions, and *E* the external environment.

some cases, environmental conditions exercise such powerful constraints on behavior that they emerge as the overriding determinants. If, for example, people are dropped in deep water they will all promptly engage in swimming activities, however uniquely varied they might be in their cognitive and behavioral repertoires. There are times when behavior is the central factor in the interlocking system. One example of this is persons who play familiar piano selections for themselves that create a pleasing sensory environment. The behavior is self-regulated over a long period by the sensory effects it produces, whereas cognitive activities and contextual environmental events are not much involved in the process.

In other instances, cognitive factors serve as the predominant influence in the regulatory system. The activation and maintenance of defensive behavior is a good case in point. False beliefs activate avoidance responses that keep individuals out of touch with prevailing environmental conditions, thus creating a strong reciprocal interaction between beliefs and action that is protected from corrective environmental influence. In extreme cases, behavior is so powerfully controlled by bizarre internal contingencies that neither the beliefs nor the accompanying actions are much affected even by extremely punishing environmental consequences (Bateson, 1961).

In still other instances, the development and activation of the three interlocking factors are all highly interdependent. Television-viewing behavior provides an everyday example. Personal preferences influence when and which programs, from among the available alternatives, individuals choose to watch on television. Although the potential televised environment is identical for all viewers, the actual televised environment that impinges on given individuals depends on what they select to watch. Through their viewing behavior, they partly shape the nature of the future televised environment. Because production costs and commercial requirements also determine what people are shown, the options provided in the televised environment partly shape the viewers' preferences. Here, all three factors—viewer preferences, viewing behavior, and televised offerings—reciprocally affect each other.

The methodology for elucidating psychological processes requires analysis of sequential interactions between the triadic, interdependent factors within the interlocking system. Investigations of reciprocal processes have thus far rarely, if ever, examined more than two of the interacting factors simultaneously. Some studies analyze how cognitions and behavior affect each other in a reciprocal fashion (Bandura, 1977a; Bandura & Adams, 1977). More often, however, the sequential analysis centers on how social behavior and environment determine each other. In these studies of dyadic exchanges, behavior creates certain conditions and is, in turn, altered by the very conditions it creates (Bandura, Lipsher, & Miller, 1960; Patterson, 1975; Raush, Barry, Hertel, & Swain, 1974; Thomas & Martin, 1976).

From the perspective of reciprocal determinism, the common practice of searching for the ultimate environmental cause of behavior is an idle exercise because, in an interactional process, one and the same event can be a stimulus, a response, or an environmental reinforcer, depending on where in the sequence the analysis arbitrarily begins.

* * *

* * * Regulatory processes are not governed solely by the reciprocal influence of antecedent and consequent acts. While behaving, people are also cognitively appraising the progression of

events. Their thoughts about the probable effects of prospective actions partly determine how acts are affected by their immediate environmental consequences. Consider, for example, investigations of reciprocal coercive behavior in an ongoing dyadic interaction. In discordant families, coercive behavior by one member tends to elicit coercive counteractions from recipients in a mutual escalation of aggression (Patterson, 1975). However, coercion often does not produce coercive counteractions. To increase the predictive power of a theory of behavior, it is necessary to broaden the analysis to include cognitive factors that operate in the interlocking system. Counterresponses to antecedent acts are influenced not only by their immediate effects but also by judgments of later consequences for a given course of action. Thus, aggressive children will continue, or even escalate, coercive behavior in the face of immediate punishment when they expect persistence eventually to gain them what they seek. But the same momentary punishment will serve as an inhibitor rather than as an enhancer of coercion when they expect continuance of the aversive conduct to be ineffective. * * *

Cognitions do not arise in a vacuum, nor do they function as autonomous determinants of behavior. In the social learning analysis of cognitive development, conceptions about oneself and the nature of the environment are developed and verified through four different processes (Bandura, 1977b). People derive much of their knowledge from direct experience of the effects produced by their actions. Indeed, most theories of cognitive development, whether they favor behavioristic, information-processing, or Piagetian[2] orientations, focus almost exclusively on cognitive change through feedback from direct experimentation. However, results of one's own actions are not the sole source of knowledge. Information about the nature of things is frequently extracted from vicarious experience. In this mode of verification, observation of the effects produced by somebody else's actions serves as the source and authentication of thoughts.

There are many things we cannot come to know by direct or vicarious experience because of limited accessibility or because the matters involve metaphysical ideas that are not subject to objective confirmation. When experiential verification is either difficult or impossible, people develop and evaluate their conceptions of things in terms of the judgments voiced by others. In addition to enactive, vicarious, and social sources of thought verification, all of which rely on external influences, logical verification also enters into the process, especially in later phases of development. After people acquire some rules of inference, they can evaluate the soundness of their reasoning and derive from what they already know new knowledge about things that extend beyond their experiences.

External influences play a role not only in the development of cognitions but in their activation as well. Different sights, smells, and sounds will elicit quite different trains of thought. Thus, while it is true that conceptions govern behavior, the conceptions themselves are partly fashioned from direct or mediated transactions with the environment. A complete analysis of reciprocal determinism therefore requires investigation of how all three sets of factors—cognitive, behavioral, and environmental—interact reciprocally among themselves. Contrary to common misconception, social learning theory does not disregard personal determinants of behavior. Within this perspective, such determinants are treated as integral, dynamic factors in causal processes rather than as static trait dimensions.

Self-Regulatory Functions of the Self System

The differences between unidirectional and reciprocal analyses of behavior have been drawn most sharply in the area of self-regulatory phenomena.

[2]Jean Piaget was a Swiss psychologist whose ideas have had an important influence on developmental psychology. The idea referred to here concerns Piaget's description of how the mind develops through an interaction between knowledge and experience.

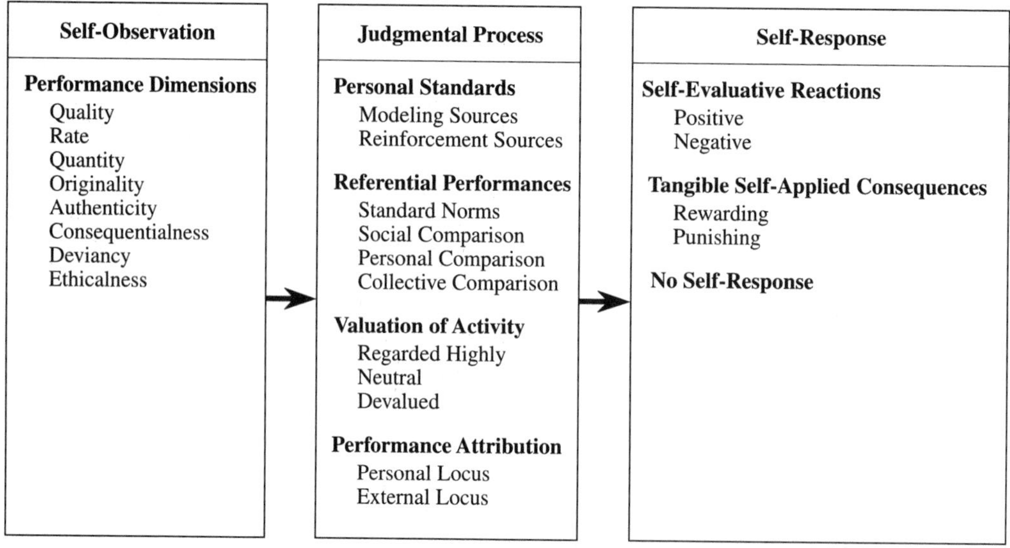

Figure 48.2 Component processes in the self-regulation of behavior by self-prescribed contingencies.

Exponents of radical behaviorism have always disavowed any construct of self for fear that it would usher in psychic agents and divert attention from physical to experiential reality.[3] While this approach encompasses a large set of environmental factors, it assumes that self-generated influences either do not exist or, if they do, that they have no effect upon behavior. Internal events are treated simply as an intermediate link in a causal chain. Since environmental conditions presumably create the intermediate link, one can explain behavior in terms of external factors without recourse to any internal determinants. Through a conceptual bypass, cognitive determinants are thus excised from the analysis of causal processes.

In contrast to the latter view, internal determinants of behavior are gaining increasing attention in contemporary theorizing and research. Indeed, self-referent processes occupy a central position in social learning theory (Bandura, 1977b). As will be shown later, self-generated events cannot be relegated to a redundant explanatory link. In the triadic reciprocal system, they not only operate as reciprocal determinants of behavior but they play a role in the perception and formation of the environmental influences themselves.

* * *

In social learning theory, a self system is not a psychic agent that controls behavior. Rather, it refers to cognitive structures that provide reference mechanisms and to a set of subfunctions for the perception, evaluation, and regulation of behavior. Before proceeding to a reciprocal analysis of self influences, the processes by which people exercise some control over their own behavior will be reviewed briefly.

Component Processes in Self-Regulation

Figure 48.2 summarizes the different component processes in the self-regulation of behavior through self-prescribed contingencies. Behavior typically varies on a number of dimensions, some of which are listed in the self-observation component. Depending on value orientations and the functional significance of given activities, people attend selectively to certain aspects of their behavior and ignore variations on nonrelevant dimensions.

Simply observing variations in one's perfor-

[3]We saw Skinner raise exactly this worry in the selections earlier in this section.

mances yields some relevant information, but such data, in themselves, do not provide any basis for personal reactions. Behavior produces self-reactions through a judgmental function that includes several subsidiary processes. Whether a given performance will be regarded as commendable or dissatisfying depends upon the personal standards against which it is evaluated. Actions that measure up to internal standards are appraised favorably; those that fall short are judged unsatisfactory.

For most activities, there are no absolute measures of adequacy. The time in which a given distance is run, the number of points obtained on an achievement test, or the size of charitable contributions often do not convey sufficient information for self-appraisal even when compared with an internal standard. When adequacy is defined relationally, performances are evaluated by comparing them with those of others. The referential comparisons may involve standard norms, the performances of particular individuals, or the accomplishments of reference groups.

One's previous behavior is continuously used as the reference against which ongoing performance is judged. In this referential process, it is self-comparison that supplies the measure of adequacy. Past attainments influence performance appraisals mainly through their effects on standard setting. After a given level of performance is attained, it is no longer challenging, and new self-satisfactions are often sought through progressive improvement.

Another important factor in the judgmental component of self-regulation concerns the evaluation of the activities. People do not much care how they perform on tasks that have little or no significance for them. And little effort is expended on devalued activities. It is mainly in areas affecting one's welfare and self-esteem that favorable performance appraisals activate personal consequences (Simon, 1978).

Self-reactions also vary depending on how people perceive the determinants of their behavior. They take pride in their accomplishments when they ascribe their successes to their own abilities and efforts. They do not derive much self-satisfaction, however, when they view their performances as heavily dependent on external factors. The same is true for judgments of failure and blameworthy conduct. People respond self-critically to inadequate performances for which they hold themselves responsible but not to those which they perceive are due to unusual circumstances or to insufficient capabilities. Performance appraisals set the occasion for self-produced consequences. Favorable judgments give rise to rewarding self-reactions, whereas unfavorable appraisals activate negative self-reactions. Performances that are judged to have no personal significance do not generate any reactions one way or another.

In the social learning view, self-regulated incentives alter performance mainly through their motivational function (Bandura, 1976). Contingent self-reward improves performance not because it strengthens preceding responses. When people make self-satisfaction or tangible gratifications conditional upon certain accomplishments, they motivate themselves to expend the effort needed to attain the desired performances. Both the anticipated satisfactions of desired accomplishments and the dissatisfactions with insufficient ones provide incentives for actions that increase the likelihood of performance attainments.

Much human behavior is regulated through self-evaluative consequences in the form of self-satisfaction, self-pride, self-dissatisfaction, and self-criticism. The act of writing is a familiar example of a behavior that is continuously self-regulated through evaluative self-reactions. Writers adopt a standard of what constitutes an acceptable piece of work. Ideas are generated and rephrased in thought before they are committed to paper. Provisional contructions are successively revised until authors are satisfied with what they have written. The more exacting the personal standards, the more extensive are the corrective improvements.

People also get themselves to do things they would otherwise put off by making tangible outcomes conditional upon completing a specified level of performance. In programs of self-directed change, individuals improve and maintain behavior on their own over long periods by arranging incentives for themselves (Bandura, 1976; Goldfried & Merbaum, 1973; Mahoney & Thoresen, 1974). In many instances, activities are regulated through self-prescribed contingencies involving both evaluative and tangible self-rewards. Authors influence how much they write by making breaks, recreational activities, and other tangible rewards contingent on completing a certain amount of work (Wallace, 1977), but they revise and improve what they write by their self-evaluative reactions.

* * *

Reciprocal Influence of External Factors on Self-Regulatory Functions

Social learning theory regards self-generated influences not as autonomous regulators of behavior but as contributory influences in a reciprocally interacting system. A variety of external factors serve as reciprocal influences on the operation of a self system. They can affect self-regulatory processes in at least three major ways: They are involved in the development of the component functions in self-regulatory systems; they provide partial support for adherence to self-prescribed contingencies; and they facilitate selective activation and disengagement of internal contingencies governing conduct.

DEVELOPMENT OF SELF-REGULATORY FUNCTIONS The development of capabilities for self-reaction requires adoption of standards against which performances can be evaluated. These internal criteria do not emerge in a vacuum. Behavioral standards are established by precept, evaluative consequences accompanying different performances, and exposure to the self-evaluative standards modeled by others (Bandura, 1976, 1977b; Masters & Mokros, 1974). People do not passively absorb behavioral standards from the environmental stimuli that happen to impinge upon them. They extract generic standards from the multiplicity of evaluative reactions that are exemplified and taught by different individuals or by the same individuals on different activities and in different settings (Bandura, 1976; Lepper, Sagotsky, & Mailer, 1975). People must therefore process the divergent information and eventually arrive at personal standards against which to measure their own behavior.

Associational preferences add another reciprocal element to the acquisition process. The people with whom one regularly associates partly influence the standards of behavior that are adopted. Value orientations, in turn, exercise selective influence on choices of activities and associates (Bandura & Walters, 1959; Krauss, 1964).

EXTERNAL SUPPORTS FOR SELF-REGULATORY SYSTEMS In analyzing regulation of behavior through self-produced consequences, one must distinguish between two different sources of incentives that operate in the system. First, there is the arrangement of self-reward contingent upon designated performances to create proximal incentives for oneself to engage in the activities. Second, there are the more distal incentives for adhering to the self-prescribed contingencies.

Adherence to performance requirements for self-reward is partly sustained by periodic environmental influences that take a variety of forms (Bandura, 1977b). First, there are the negative sanctions for unmerited self-reward. When standards are being acquired or when they are later applied inconsistently, rewarding oneself for undeserving performances is more likely than not to evoke critical reactions from others. Occasional sanctions for unmerited self-reward influence the likelihood that people will withhold rewards from themselves until their behavior matches their standards (Bandura, Mahoney, & Dirks, 1976). Personal sanctions operate as well in fostering such adherence. After people adopt codes of conduct, when they perform inadequately or violate their standards they tend to engage in self-critical and other distressing trains of thought. Anticipated, thought-produced distress over faulty behavior provides an internal incentive to abide by personal standards of performance (Bandura, 1977b).

Negative inducements, whether personal or social, are not the most reliable basis upon which to rest a system of self-regulation. Fortunately, there are more advantageous reasons for exercising some influence over one's own behavior through self-arranged incentives. Some of these personal benefits are extrinsic to the behavior; others derive from the behavior itself.

People are motivated to institute performance contingencies for themselves when the behavior they seek to change is aversive. To overweight persons, the discomforts, maladies, and social costs of obesity create inducements to control their overeating. Similarly, students are prompted to improve their study behavior when failures in course work make academic life sufficiently distressing. By making self-reward conditional upon performance attainments, individuals can reduce aversive behavior, thereby creating natural benefits for their efforts.

The benefits of self-regulated change may provide natural incentives for adherence to personal prescriptions for valued activities as well as for unpleasant ones. People often motivate themselves by conditional incentives to enhance their skills in activities they aspire to master. Here the personal benefits derived from improved proficiency support self-prescription of contingencies. Self-generated inducements are especially important in ensuring continual progress in creative endeavors, because people have to develop their own work schedules for themselves. There are no clocks to punch or supervisors to issue directives. In analyzing the writing habits and self-discipline of novelists, Wallace (1977) documents how famous novelists regulate their writing output by making self-reward contingent upon completion of a certain amount of writing each day whether the spirit moves them or not.

If societies relied solely on inherent benefits to sustain personal contingencies, many activities that are tiresome and uninteresting until proficiency in them is acquired would never be mastered. Upholding standards is therefore socially promoted by a vast system of rewards including praise, social recognition, and honors. Few accolades are bestowed on people for self-rewarding their mediocre performances. Direct praise or seeing others publicly recognized for upholding excellence fosters adherence to high performance standards (Bandura, Grusec, & Menlove, 1967).

* * *

Because personal and environmental determinants affect each other in a reciprocal fashion, attempts to assign causal priority to these two sources of influence reduce to the "chicken-or-egg" debate. The quest for the ultimate environmental determinant of activities regulated by self-influence becomes a regressive exercise that can yield no victors in explanatory contests, because for every ultimate environmental cause that is invoked, one can find prior actions that helped to produce it.

Selective Activation and Disengagement of Self-Reactive Influences The third area of research on the role of external factors in self-regulation centers on the selective activation and disengagement of self-reactive influences (Bandura, 1977b). Theories of internalization that portray incorporated entities (e.g., the conscience or superego, moral codes) as continuous internal overseers of conduct are usually at a loss to explain the variable operation of internal control and the perpetration of inhumanities by otherwise humane people.

In the social learning analysis, considerate people perform culpable acts because of the reciprocal dynamics between personal and situational determinants of behavior rather than because of defects in their moral structures. Development of self-regulatory capabilities does not create an invariant control mechanism within a person. Self-evaluative influences do not operate unless activated, and many situational dynamics influence their selective activation.

After ethical and moral standards of conduct are adopted, anticipatory self-censuring reactions for violating personal standards ordinarily serve as self-deterrents against reprehensible acts (Bandura & Walters, 1959).[4] Self-deterring consequences are likely to be activated most strongly when the causal connection between conduct and the detrimental effects it produces is unambiguous. There are various means, however, by which self-evaluative consequences can be dissociated from reprehensible behavior. * * *

One set of disengagement practices operates at the level of the behavior. What is culpable can be made honorable through moral justifications and palliative characterizations (Gambino, 1973; Kelman, 1973). In this process, reprehensible conduct is made personally and socially acceptable by portraying it in the service of beneficial or moral ends. Such cognitive restructuring of behavior is an especially effective disinhibitor because it not only eliminates self-generated deterrents but engages self-reward in the service of the behavior.

Another set of dissociative practices operates by obscuring or distorting the relationship between actions and the effects they cause. By displacing and diffusing responsibility, people do not see themselves as personally accountable for their actions and are thus spared self-prohibiting reactions (Bandura, Underwood, & Fromson, 1975; Milgram, 1974). Additional ways of weakening self-deterring reactions operate by disregarding or obscuring the consequences of actions. When people embark on a self-disapproved course of action for personal gain, or because of other inducements, they avoid facing the harm they cause. Self-censuring reactions are unlikely to be activated as long as the detrimental effects of conduct are disregarded.

The final set of disengagement practices operates at the level of the recipients of injurious effects. The strength of self-evaluative reactions partly depends on how the people toward whom actions are directed are viewed. Maltreatment of individuals who are regarded as subhuman or debased is less apt to arouse self-reproof than if they are seen as human beings with dignifying qualities (Zimbardo, 1969). Detrimental interactions usually involve a series of reciprocally escalative actions in which the victims are rarely faultless. One can always select from the chain of events an instance of defensive behavior by the adversary as the original instigation. By blaming victims, one's own actions are excusable. The disengagement of internal control, whatever the means, is not achieved solely through personal deliberation. People are socially aided in this process by indoctrination, scapegoating, and pejorative stereotyping of people held in disfavor.

As is evident from preceding discussion, the development of self-regulatory functions does not create an automatic control system, nor do situational influences exercise mechanical control. Personal judgments operating at each subfunction preclude the automaticity of the process. There is leeway in judging whether a given behavioral standard is applicable. Because of the complexity and inherent ambiguity of most events, there is even greater leeway in the judgment of behavior and its effects. To add further to the variability of the control process, most activities are performed under collective arrangements that obscure responsibility, thus permitting leeway in judging the degree of personal agency in the effects that are socially produced. In short, there exists considerable latitude for personal judgmental factors to affect whether or not self-regulatory influences will be activated in any given activity.

Reciprocal Influence of Personal Factors on Reinforcement Effects

Reinforcement has commonly been viewed as a mechanistic process in which responses are shaped automatically and unconsciously by their immediate consequences. The assumption of automaticity of reinforcement is crucial to the argument of unidirectional environmental control of behavior. One can dispense with the so-called internal link in causal chains only if persons are conceived of as mechanical respondents to external stimuli. The empirical evidence does not support such a

[4] That is, you know you will feel guilty if you do it.

view (Bandura, 1977b; Bower, 1975; Mischel, 1973; Neisser, 1976). External influences operate largely through cognitive processes.

During ongoing reinforcement, respondents are doing more than simply emitting responses. They develop expectations from observed regularities about the outcomes likely to result from their actions under given situational circumstances. Contrary to claims that behavior is controlled by its immediate consequences, behavior is related to its outcomes at the level of aggregate consequences rather than momentary effects (Baum, 1973). People process and synthesize contextual and outcome information from sequences of events over long intervals about the action patterns that are necessary to produce given outcomes.

The notion that behavior is governed by its consequences fares better for anticipated than for actual consequences (Bandura, 1977b). We have already reviewed research demonstrating how the same environmental consequences have markedly different effects on behavior depending on respondents' beliefs about the nature of the relationships between actions and outcomes and the meaning of the outcomes. When belief differs from actuality, which is not uncommon, behavior is weakly influenced by its actual consequences until more realistic expectations are developed through repeated experience. But it is not always expectations that change in the direction of social reality. Acting on erroneous expectations can alter how others behave, thus shaping the social reality in the direction of the expectations.

While undergoing reinforcing experiences, people are doing more than learning the probabilistic contingencies between actions and outcomes. They observe the progress they are making and tend to set themselves goals of progressive improvement. Investigators who have measured personal goal setting as well as changes in performance find that external incentives influence behavior partly through their effects on goal setting (Locke, Bryan, & Kendall, 1968). When variations in personal goals are partialed out, the effects of incentives on performance are reduced. Performance attainments also provide an important source of efficacy information for judging one's personal capabilities. Changes in perceived self-efficacy, in turn, affect people's choices of activities, how much effort they expend, and how long they will persist in the face of obstacles and aversive experiences (Bandura, 1977a; Brown & Inouye, 1978).

Because of the personal determinants of reinforcement effects, to trace behavior back to environmental "reinforcers" by no means completes the explanatory regress. To predict how outcomes will affect behavior, one must know how they are cognitively processed. To understand fully the mechanisms through which consequences change behavior, one must analyze the reciprocally contributory influences of cognitive factors.

Reciprocal Determinism as a Generic Analytic Principle

The discussion thus far has primarily addressed issues regarding the reciprocal interactions between behavior, thought, and environmental events as they occur at the individual level. Social learning theory treats reciprocal determinism as a basic principle for analyzing psychosocial phenomena at varying levels of complexity, ranging from intrapersonal development, to interpersonal behavior, to the interactive functioning of organizational and societal systems. At the intrapersonal level, people's conceptions influence what they perceive and do, and their conceptions are in turn altered by the effects of their actions and the observed consequences accruing to others (Bandura, 1977a; Bower, 1975). Information-processing models are concerned mainly with internal mental operations. A comprehensive theory must also analyze how conceptions are converted to actions, which furnish some of the data for conceptions. In social learning theory, people play an active role in creating information-generating experiences as well as in processing and transforming informative stimuli that happen to impinge upon them. This involves reciprocal transactions between thought, behavior, and environmental events which are not fully encompassed by a computer metaphor. People are not only perceivers, knowers, and actors. They are also self-reactors with capacities for reflective self-awareness that are generally neglected in information-processing theories based on computer models of human functioning.

At the level of interpersonal behavior, we have previously examined how people reciprocally determine each others' actions (Bandura et al., 1960; Patterson, 1975; Raush et al., 1974). Although the mutuality of behavior may be the focus of study, the reciprocal processes involve cognition as well as action. At the broader societal level, reciprocal processes are reflected in the interdependence of organizational elements, social subsystems, and transnational relations (Bandura, 1973; Keohane & Nye, 1977). Here the matters of interest are the patterns of interdependence between systems, the criteria and means used for gauging systemic performances, the mechanisms that exist for exercising reciprocal influence, and the conditions that alter the degree and type of reciprocal control that one system can exert on another.

It is within the framework of reciprocal determinism that the concept of freedom assumes meaning (Bandura, 1977b). Because people's conceptions, their behavior, and their environments are reciprocal determinants of each other, individuals are neither powerless objects controlled by environmental forces nor entirely free agents who can do whatever they choose. People can be considered partially free insofar as they shape future conditions by influencing their courses of action. By creating structural mechanisms for reciprocal influence, such as organizational systems of checks and balances, legal systems, and due process and elective procedures, people can bring their influence to bear on each other. Institutional reciprocal mechanisms thus provide not only safeguards against unilateral social control but the means for changing institutions and the conditions of life. Within the process of reciprocal determinism lies the opportunity for people to shape their destinies as well as the limits of self-direction.

References

Bandura, A. (1973). *Aggression: A social learning analysis.* Englewood Cliffs, NJ: Prentice-Hall.

Bandura, A. (1974). Behavior theory and the models of man. *American Psychologist, 29,* 859–869.

Bandura, A. (1976). Self-reinforcement: Theoretical and methodological considerations. *Behaviorism, 4,* 135–155.

Bandura, A. (1977a). Self-efficacy: Toward a unifying theory of behavioral change. *Psychological Review, 84,* 191–215.

Bandura, A. (1977b). *Social learning theory.* Englewood Cliffs, NJ: Prentice-Hall.

Bandura, A., & Adams, N. E. (1977). Analysis of self-efficacy theory of behavioral change. *Cognitive Therapy and Research, 1,* 287–308.

Bandura, A., Grusec, J. E., & Menlove, F. L. (1967). Some social determinants of self-monitoring reinforcement systems. *Journal of Personality and Social Psychology, 5,* 449–455.

Bandura, A., Lipsher, D. H., & Miller, P. E. (1960). Psychotherapists' approach-avoidance reactions to patients' expression of hostility. *Journal of Consulting Psychology,* 1960, 1–8.

Bandura, A., Mahoney, M. J., & Dirks, S. J. (1976). Discriminative activation and maintenance of contingent self-reinforcement. *Behaviour Research and Therapy, 14,* 1–6.

Bandura, A., Underwood, B., & Fromson, M. E. (1975). Disinhibition of aggression through diffusion of responsibility and dehumanization of victims. *Journal of Research in Personality, 9,* 253–269.

Bandura, A., & Walters, R. H. (1959). *Adolescent aggression.* New York: Ronald.

Bateson, G. (Ed.). (1961). *Perceval's narrative: A patient's account of his psychosis, 1830–1832.* Stanford, CA: Stanford University Press.

Baum, W. M. (1973). The correlation-based law of effect. *Journal of the Experimental Analysis of Behavior, 20,* 137–153.

Bower, G. H. (1975). Cognitive psychology: An introduction. In W. K. Estes (Ed.), *Handbook of learning and cognition.* Hillsdale, NJ: Erlbaum.

Brown, I., Jr., & Inouye, D. K. (1978). Learned helplessness through modeling: The role of perceived similarity in competence. *Journal of Personality and Social Psychology, 36,* 900–908.

Gambino, R. (1973). Watergate lingo: A language of non-responsibility. *Freedom at Issue,* No. 22.

Goldfried, M. R., & Merbaum, M. (Eds.). (1973). *Behavior change through self-control.* New York: Holt, Rinehart & Winston.

Kelman, H. C. (1973). Violence without moral restraint: Reflections on the dehumanization of victims and victimizers. *Journal of Social Issues, 29,* 25–61.

Keohane, R. O., & Nye, J. S. (1977). *Power and interdependence: World politics in transition.* Boston: Little, Brown.

Krauss, I. (1964). Sources of educational aspirations among working-class youth. *American Sociological Review, 29,* 867–879.

Lepper, M. R., Sagotsky, J., & Mailer, J. (1975). Generalization and persistence of effects of exposure to self-reinforcement models. *Child Development, 46,* 618–630.

Locke, E. A., Bryan, J. F., & Kendall, L. M. (1968). Goals and intentions as mediators of the effects of monetary incentives

on behavior. *Journal of Applied Psychology, 52*(2), 104–121.
Mahoney, M. J., & Thoresen, C. E. (1974). *Self-control: Power to the person.* Monterey, CA: Brooks/Cole.
Masters, J. C., & Mokros, J. R. (1974). Self-reinforcement processes in children. In H. W. Reese (Ed.), *Advances in child development and behavior* (Vol. 9). New York: Academic Press.
Milgram, S. (1974). *Obedience to authority: An experimental view.* New York: Harper & Row.
Mischel, W. (1973). Toward a cognitive social learning reconceptualization of personality. *Psychological Review, 80,* 252–283.
Neisser, U. (1976). *Cognition and reality: Principles and implications of cognitive psychology.* San Francisco: W. H. Freeman.
Patterson, G. R. (1975). The aggressive child: Victim and architect of a coercive system. In L. A. Hamerlynck, E. J. Mash, & L. C. Handy (Eds.), *Behavior modification and families.* New York: Brunner/Mazel.
Raush, H. L., Barry, W. A., Hertel, R. K., & Swain, M. A. (1974). *Communication conflict and marriage.* San Francisco: Jossey-Bass.
Simon, K. M. (1978). *Self-evaluative reactions to one's own performances: The role of personal significance of performance attainments.* Unpublished manuscript, Stanford University.
Skinner, B. F. (1971). *Beyond freedom and dignity.* New York: Knopf.
Thomas, E. A. C., & Martin, J. A. (1976). Analyses of parent-child interaction. *Psychological Review, 83,* 141–156.
Wallace, I. (1977). Self-control techniques of famous novelists. *Journal of Applied Behavior Analysis, 10,* 515–525.
Zimbardo, P. G. (1969). The human choice: Individuation, reason, and order versus deindividuation, impulse, and chaos. In W. J. Arnold & D. Levine (Eds.), *Nebraska Symposium on Motivation* (Vol. 17). Lincoln: University of Nebraska Press.

Toward a Cognitive Social Learning Reconceptualization of Personality

Walter Mischel

Another one-time social learning theorist who helped develop the cognitive approach to personality is Walter Mischel, whose critique of personality traits we saw in Part II. Mischel is centrally concerned with the cognitive processes by which people interpret their worlds, and so labels his theory a "cognitive social learning reconceptualization of personality." The "reconceptualization" part of this label refers to his rejection of the psychology of personality traits and his desire to formulate an alternative way of thinking about people.

The following selection is Mischel's most influential theoretical article, published in 1973. In it, Mischel presents a conceptualization of the self that overlaps in many ways with the one described by Bandura in the preceding selection. Mischel breaks the self system into five components, which he labels "cognitive social learning person variables." These variables, meant to replace personality traits as ways of thinking about individual differences, are cognitive and behavioral construction competencies, encoding strategies and personal constructs, expectancies, subjective stimulus values, and self-regulatory systems and plans.

We have already seen that self-regulatory systems are an important part of Bandura's social cognitive theory, that subjective stimulus values are an important part of Rotter's social learning, and that expectancies play a prominent role in both. Mischel's unique contribution—influenced by his teacher, the phenomenologist George Kelly—is a close focus on the cognitive processes by which people interpret their worlds and act accordingly.

From *Psychological Review, 80*, 252–283, 1973.

* * *

Cognitive Social Learning Person Variables

* * *

A set of person variables is proposed, based on theoretical developments in the fields of social learning and cognition.

Given the overall findings on the discriminativeness of behavior[1] and on the complexity of the interactions between the individual and the situation, it seems reasonable in the search for person variables to look more specifically at what the person *constructs* in particular conditions, rather than trying to infer what broad traits he generally *has*, and to incorporate in descriptions of what he does the specific psychological conditions in which the behavior will and will not be expected to occur. What people do, of course, includes much more than motor acts and requires us to consider what they do cognitively and affectively as well as motorically.

The proposed cognitive social learning approach to personality shifts the unit of study from global traits inferred from behavioral signs to the individual's cognitive activities and behavior patterns, studied in relation to the specific conditions that evoke, maintain, and modify them and which they, in turn, change (Mischel, 1968). The focus shifts from attempting to compare and generalize about what different individuals "are like" to an assessment of what they *do*—behaviorally and cognitively—in relation to the psychological conditions in which they do it. The focus shifts from describing situation-free people with broad trait adjectives to analyzing the specific interactions between conditions and the cognitions and behaviors of interest.

Personality research on social behavior and cognition in recent years has focused mainly on the processes through which behaviors are acquired, evoked, maintained, and modified (e.g., Bandura, 1969; Mischel, 1968). Much less attention has been given to the psychological products within the individual of cognitive development and social learning experiences. Yet a viable psychology of personality demands attention to person variables that are the products of the individual's total history and that in turn mediate the manner in which new experiences affect him.

The proposed person variables are a synthesis of seemingly promising constructs in the areas of cognition and social learning. The selections should be seen as suggestive and open to progressive revision rather than as final. These tentative person variables are not expected to provide ways to accurately predict broadly cross-situational behavioral differences between persons: the discriminativeness and idiosyncratic organization of behavior are facts of nature, not limitations unique to trait theories. But these variables should serve to demonstrate that a social behavior approach to persons does not imply an empty organism. They should suggest useful ways of conceptualizing and studying specifically how persons mediate the impact of stimuli and generate distinctive complex molar behavior patterns. And they should help to conceptualize person-situation interactions in a theoretical framework based on contributions from both cognitive and behavioral psychology.

The proposed cognitive social learning person variables deal first with the individual's *competencies* to construct (generate) diverse behaviors under appropriate conditions. Next, one must consider the individual's *encoding* and *categorization* of events. Furthermore, a comprehensive analysis of the behaviors a person performs in particular situations requires attention to his *expectancies* about outcomes, the *subjective values* of such outcomes, and his *self-regulatory systems and plans*. The following five sections discuss each of these proposed person variables. While these variables obviously overlap and interact, each may provide distinctive information about the individ-

[1]The variability of an individual's behavior from one situation to another.

ual and each may be measured objectively and varied systematically.

Cognitive and Behavioral Construction Competencies Through direct and observational learning the individual acquires information about the world and his relationship to it. As a result of observing events and attending to the behavior of live and symbolic models (through direct and film-mediated observation, reading, and instruction) in the course of cognitive development the perceiver acquires the potential to generate vast repertoires of organized behavior. While the pervasive occurrence and important consequences of such observational learning have been convincingly demonstrated (e.g., Bandura, 1969; Campbell, 1961), it is less clear how to conceptualize just what gets learned. The phenomena to be encompassed must include such diverse learnings as the nature of sexual gender identity (e.g., Kohlberg, 1966), the structure (or construction) of the physical world (e.g., Piaget, 1954), the social rules and conventions that guide conduct (e.g., Aronfreed, 1968), the personal constructs generated about self and others (e.g., Kelly, 1955), the rehearsal strategies of the observer (Bandura, 1971a). Some theorists have discussed these acquisitions in terms of the products of information processing and of information integration (e.g., Anderson, 1972; Bandura, 1971a; Rumelhart, Lindsey, & Norman, 1971), others in terms of schemata and cognitive templates (e.g., Aronfreed, 1968).

The concept of *cognitive and behavioral construction competencies* seems sufficiently broad to include the vast array of psychological acquisitions of organized information that must be encompassed. The term "constructions" also emphasizes the constructive manner in which information seems to be retrieved (e.g., Neisser, 1967) and the active organization through which it is categorized and transformed (Bower, 1970; Mandler, 1967, 1968). It has become plain that rather than mimicking observed responses or returning memory traces from undisturbed storage vaults, the observer selectively *constructs* (generates) his renditions of "reality." Indeed, research on modeling effects has long recognized that the products of observational learning involve a novel, highly organized synthesis of information rather than a photocopy of specific observed responses (e.g., Bandura, 1971b; Mischel & Grusec, 1966). The present concept of construction competencies should call attention to the person's cognitive activities—the operations and transformations that he performs on information—rather than to a store of finite cognitions and responses that he "has."

Although the exact cognitive processes are far from clear, it is apparent that each individual acquires the capacity to construct a great range of potential behaviors, and different individuals acquire different behavior construction capabilities. The enormous differences between persons in the range and quality of the cognitive and behavioral patterns that they can generate are evident from even casual comparison of the construction potentials of any given individual with those, for example, of an Olympic athlete, a Nobel Prize winner, a retardate, an experienced forger, or a successful actor.

* * *

For many purposes, it is valuable to assess the quality and range of the cognitive constructions and behavioral enactments of which the individual is capable. In this vein, rather than assess "typical" behavior, one assesses *potential* behaviors or achievements. One tests what the person *can* do (e.g., Wallace, 1966) rather than what he "usually" does. Indeed one of the most recurrent and promising dimensions of individual differences in research seems to involve the person's *cognitive and behavioral (social) competencies* (e.g., White, 1959; Zigler & Phillips, 1961, 1962). These competencies presumably reflect the degree to which the person can generate adaptive, skillful behaviors that will have beneficial consequences for him. Personality psychology can profit from much greater attention to cognitive and intellectual competencies since these "mental abilities" seem to have much better temporal and cross-situational stability and influence than most of the social traits and motivations traditionally favored in personality research (e.g., Mischel, 1968, 1969).

* * *

The relative stability of the person's construction capacities may be one of the important contributors to the impression of consistency in personality. The fact that cognitive skills and behavior-generating capacities tend to be relatively enduring is reflected in the relatively high stability found in performances closely related to cognitive and intellectual variables, as has been stressed before (Mischel, 1968, 1969). The individual who knows how to be assertive with waiters, for example, or who knows how to solve certain kinds of interpersonal problems competently, or who excels in singing, is *capable* of such performances enduringly.

ENCODING STRATEGIES AND PERSONAL CONSTRUCTS From the perspective of personality psychology, an especially important component of information processing concerns the perceiver's ways of encoding and grouping information from stimulus inputs. People can readily perform *cognitive transformations* on stimuli (Mischel & Moore, 1973b), focusing on selected aspects of the objective stimulus (e.g., the taste versus the shape of a food object): such selective attention, interpretation, and categorization substantially alter the impact the stimulus exerts on behavior (see also Geer, Davison, & Gatchel, 1970; Schachter, 1964). Likewise, the manner in which perceivers encode and selectively attend to observed behavioral sequences greatly influences what they learn and subsequently can do (Bandura, 1971a, 1971b). Clearly, different persons may group and encode the same events and behaviors in different ways. At a molar level, such individual differences are especially evident in the personal constructs individuals employ (e.g., Argyle & Little, 1972; Kelly, 1955) and in the kinds of information to which they selectively attend (Mischel, Ebbesen, & Zeiss, 1973).

The behaviorally oriented psychologist eschews inferences about global dispositions and focuses instead on the particular stimuli and behaviors of interest. But what are "the stimuli and behaviors of interest?" Early versions of behaviorism attempted to circumvent this question by simplistic definitions in terms of clearly delineated motor "acts" (such as bar press) in response to clicks and lights. As long as the behaviors studied were those of lower animals in experimenter-arranged laboratory situations, the units of "behavior" and "stimuli" remained manageable with fairly simple operational definitions. More recent versions of behavior theory, moving from cat, rat, and pigeon confined in the experimenter's apparatus to people in exceedingly complex social situations, have extended the domain of studied behavior much beyond motor acts and muscle twitches; they seek to encompass what people do cognitively, emotionally, and interpersonally, not merely their arm, leg, and mouth movements. Now the term "behavior" has been expanded to include virtually anything that an organism does, overtly or covertly, in relation to extremely complex social and interpersonal events. Consider, for example, "aggression," "anxiety," "defense," "dependency," "self-concepts," "self-control," "self-reinforcement." Such categories go considerably beyond self-evident behavior descriptions. A category like aggression involves inferences about the subject's intentions (e.g., harming another versus accidental injury) and abstractions about behavior, rather than mere physical description of actions and utterances.

* * *

There is considerable evidence that people categorize their own personal qualities in relatively stable trait terms (e.g., on self-ratings and self-report questionnaires). These self-categorizations, while often only complexly and tenuously related to nonverbal behavior, may be relatively durable and generalized (Mischel, 1968, 1969). * * * While traditional personality research has focused primarily on exploring the correlates of such self-categorizations, in the present view they comprise merely one kind of person variable.

EXPECTANCIES So far the person variables considered deal with what the individual is capable of doing and how he categorizes events. To move from potential behaviors to actual performance, from construction capacity and constructs to the construction of behavior in specific situations, requires attention to the determinants of performance. For this purpose, the person variables of greatest interest are the subject's expectancies. While it is often informative to know what an individual *can* do and how he construes events and himself, for purposes of specific prediction of behavior in a particular situation it is essential to consider his specific expectancies about the consequences of different behavioral possibilities in that situation. For many years personality research has searched for individual differences on the psychologist's hypothesized dimensions while neglecting the subject's own expectancies (hypotheses). More recently, it seems increasingly clear that the expectancies of the subject are central units for psychology (e.g., Bolles, 1972; Estes, 1972; Irwin, 1971; Rotter, 1954). These hypotheses guide the person's selection (choice) of behaviors from among the enormous number which he is capable of constructing within any situation.

On the basis of direct experience, instructions, and observational learning, people develop expectancies about environmental contingencies (e.g., Bandura, 1969). Since the expectancies that are learned within a given situation presumably reflect the objective contingencies in that situation, an expectancy construct may seem superfluous. The need for the expectancy construct as a person variable becomes evident, however, when one considers individual differences in response to the same situational contingencies due to the different expectancies that each person brings to the situation. An expectancy construct is justified by the fact that the person's expectancies (inferred from statements) may not be in agreement with the objective contingencies in the situation. Yet behavior may be generated in light of such expectancies, as seen, for example, in any verbal conditioning study when a subject says plural nouns on the erroneous hypothesis that the experimenter is reinforcing them.[2]

* * *

One type of expectancy concerns *behavior-outcome relations* under particular conditions. These *behavior-outcome expectancies* (hypotheses, contingency rules) represent the "if____, then____" relations between behavioral alternatives and probable outcomes anticipated with regard to particular behavioral possibilities in particular situations. In any given situation, the person will generate the response pattern which he expects is most likely to lead to the most subjectively valuable outcomes (consequences) in that situation (e.g., Mischel, 1966; Rotter, 1954). In the absence of new information about the behavior-outcome expectancies in any situation the individual's performance will depend on his previous behavior-outcome expectancies in similar situations. This point is illustrated in a study (Mischel & Staub, 1965) which showed that presituational expectancies significantly affect choice behavior in the absence of situational information concerning probable performance-outcome relationships. But the Mischel and Staub study also showed that new information about behavior-outcome relations in the particular situation may quickly overcome the effects of presituational expectancies, so that highly specific situational expectancies become the dominant influences on performance.

When the expected consequences for performance change, so does behavior, as seen in the discriminative nature of responding which was elaborated in earlier sections and documented

[2]In a verbal conditioning study, a subject talks while an experimenter reinforces certain verbalizations by saying "good." If the subject believes that he or she is being rewarded for saying plural nouns, the subject will say more of them, even if in fact the experimenter is reinforcing something else. This is a simple demonstration that it is the subject's beliefs about reinforcement, not the reinforcment itself, that controls behavior.

elsewhere (Mischel, 1968). But in order for changes in behavior-outcome relations to affect behavior substantially, the person must recognize them. In the context of operant conditioning,[3] it has become evident that the subject's awareness of the behavior-outcome relationship crucially affects the ability of response consequences (reinforcements) to modify his complex performances (e.g., Spielberger & DeNike, 1966). The essence of adaptive performance is the recognition and appreciation of new contingencies. To cope with the environment effectively, the individual must recognize new contingencies as quickly as possible and reorganize his behavior in the light of the new expectancies. Strongly established behavior-outcome expectancies with respect to a response pattern may constrain an individual's ability to adapt to changes in contingencies. Indeed, "defensive reactions" may be seen in part as a failure to adapt to new contingencies because the individual is still behaving in response to old contingencies that are no longer valid. The "maladaptive" individual is behaving in accord with expectancies that do not adequately represent the actual behavior-outcome rules in his current life situation.

In the present view, the effectiveness of response-contingent reinforcements (i.e., operant conditioning) rests on their ability to modify behavior-outcome expectancies. When information about the response pattern required for reinforcement is conveyed to the subject by instructions, "conditioning" tends to occur much more readily than when the subject must experience directly the reinforcing contingencies actually present in the operant training situation. For example, accurate instructions about the required response and the reinforcement schedule to which subjects would be exposed exerted far more powerful effects on performance than did the reinforcing contingencies (Kaufman, Baron, & Kopp, 1966). Presumably, such instructions exert their effects by altering response-outcome expectancies. To the extent that information about new response-reinforcement contingencies can be conveyed to motivated human beings more parsimoniously through instructions or observational experiences than through operant conditioning procedures (e.g., Kaufman et al., 1966), an insistence upon direct "shaping" may reflect an unfortunate (and wasteful) failure to discriminate between the animal laboratory and the human condition.

A closely related second type of expectancy concerns *stimulus-outcome relations*. As noted previously in the discussion of generalization and discrimination, the outcomes expected for any behavior hinge on a multitude of stimulus conditions that moderate the probable consequences of any pattern of behavior. These stimuli ("signs") essentially "predict" for the person other events that are likely to occur. More precisely, the individual learns (through direct and observational experiences) that certain events (cues, stimuli) predict certain other events. * * *

Stimulus-outcome expectancies seem especially important person variables for understanding the phenomena of classical conditioning. For example, through the contiguous association of a light and painful electric shock in aversive classical conditioning the subject learns that the light predicts shock. If the product of classical conditioning is construed as a stimulus-outcome expectancy, it follows that any information which negates that expectancy will eliminate the conditioned response. In fact, when subjects are informed that the "conditioned stimuli" will no longer be followed by pain-producing events, their conditioned emotional reactions are quickly eliminated (e.g., Grings & Lockhart, 1963). Conversely, when subjects were told that a particular word would be followed by shock, they promptly developed conditioned heart-rate responses (Chatterjee & Eriksen, 1962). In the same vein, but beyond the conditioning paradigm, if subjects learn to generate "happy thoughts" when faced by stimuli that otherwise would frustrate them beyond endurance, they can manage to tolerate the "aversive" situation with equanimity (Mischel, Ebbesen, & Zeiss, 1972). Outside the artificial confines of the

[3] Skinner's explanation of behavior change.

laboratory in the human interactions of life, the "stimuli" that predict outcomes often are the social behaviors of others in particular contexts. The meanings attributed to those stimuli hinge on a multitude of learned correlations between behavioral signs and outcomes.

* * *

In the present view, the person's expectancies mediate the degree to which his behavior shows cross-situational consistency or discriminativeness. When the expected consequences for the performance of responses across situations are not highly correlated, the responses themselves should not covary strongly[4] (Mischel, 1968). Since most social behaviors lead to positive consequences in some situations but not in other contexts, highly discriminative specific expectancies tend to be developed and the relatively low correlations typically found among a person's response patterns across situations become understandable (Mischel, 1968). Expectancies also will not become generalized across response modes[5] when the consequences for similar content expressed in different response modes are sharply different, as they are in most life circumstances (Mischel, 1968). Hence expectancies tend to become relatively specific, rather than broadly generalized. Although a person's expectancies (and hence performances) tend to be highly discriminative, there certainly is some generalization of expectancies, but their patterning in the individual tends to be idiosyncratically organized to the extent that the individual's history is unique. * * *

While behavior-outcome and stimulus-outcome expectancies seem viable person variables, it would be both tempting and hazardous to transform them into generalized trait-like dispositions by endowing them with broad cross-situational consistency or removing them from the context of the specific stimulus conditions on which they depend. At the empirical level, "generalized expectancies" tend to be generalized only within relatively narrow, restricted limits (e.g., Mischel & Staub, 1965; Mischel, Ebbesen, & Zeiss, 1973). For example, the generality of "locus of control" is in fact limited, with distinct, unrelated expectancies found for positive and negative outcomes and with highly specific behavioral correlates for each (Mischel, Zeiss, & Zeiss, 1974). If expectancies are converted into global trait-like dispositions and extracted from their close interaction with situational conditions, they are likely to become just as useless as their many theoretical predecessors. On the other hand, if they are construed as relatively specific (and modifiable) "if ____, then ____" hypotheses about contingencies, it becomes evident that they exert important effects on behavior (e.g., Mischel & Staub, 1965).

SUBJECTIVE STIMULUS VALUES Even if individuals have similar expectancies, they may select to perform different behaviors because of differences in the *subjective values* of the outcomes which they expect. For example, given that all persons expect that approval from a therapist depends on verbalizing particular kinds of self-references, there may be differences in the frequency of such verbalizations due to differences in the perceived value of obtaining the therapist's approval. Such differences reflect the degree to which different individuals value the response-contingent outcome. Therefore it is necessary to consider still another person variable: the subjective (perceived) value for the individual of particular classes of events, that is, his stimulus preferences and aversions. This unit refers to stimuli that have acquired the power to induce positive or negative emotional states in the person and to function as incentives or reinforcers for his behavior. The subjective value of any stimulus pattern may be acquired and modified through instructions and observational experiences as well as through direct experiences (Bandura, 1969).

[4]That is, when a person expects that a given behavior will have different consequences in two different situations, what he or she does in one of those situations will have little relation to what he or she does in the other.

[5]That is, an expectancy about the result of one behavior will not necessarily influence another behavior.

* * *

Self-Regulatory Systems and Plans While behavior is controlled to a considerable extent by externally administered consequences for actions, the individual also regulates his own behavior by self-imposed goals (standards) and self-produced consequences. Even in the absence of external constraints and social monitors, persons set performance goals for themselves and react with self-criticism or self-satisfaction to their behavior depending on how well it matches their expectations and criteria. The concept of self-imposed achievement standards is seen in Rotter's (1954) "minimal goal" construct and in more recent formulations of self-reinforcing functions (e.g., Bandura, 1971c; Kanfer, 1971; Kanfer & Marston, 1963; Mischel, 1968, 1973).

The essence of self-regulatory systems is the subject's adoption of *contingency rules* that guide his behavior in the absence of, and sometimes in spite of, immediate external situational pressures. Such rules specify the kinds of behavior appropriate (expected) under particular conditions, the performance levels (standards, goals) which the behavior must achieve, and the consequences (positive and negative) of attaining or failing to reach those standards. Each of these components of self-regulation may be different for different individuals, depending on their unique earlier histories or on more recently varied instructions or other situational information.

Some of the components in self-regulation have been demonstrated in studies of goal setting and self-reinforcement (e.g., Bandura & Whalen, 1966; Bandura & Perloff, 1967; Mischel & Liebert, 1966). Perhaps the most dramatic finding from these studies is that even young children will not indulge themselves with freely available immediate gratifications but, instead, follow rules that regulate conditions under which they may reinforce themselves. Thus, children, like adults, far from being simply hedonistic, make substantial demands of themselves and impose complex contingencies upon their own behavior. The stringency or severity of self-imposed criteria is rooted in the observed standards displayed by salient models as well as in the individual's direct socialization history (e.g., Mischel & Liebert, 1966), although after they have been adopted, the standards may be retained with considerable persistence.

After the standards (terminal goals) for conduct in a particular situation have been selected, the often long and difficult route to self-reinforcement and external reinforcement with material rewards is probably mediated extensively by covert symbolic activities, such as praise and self-instructions, as the individual reaches subgoals. When individuals imagine reinforcing and noxious stimuli, their behavior appears to be influenced in the same manner as when such stimuli are externally presented (e.g., Cautela, 1971). These covert activities serve to maintain goal-directed work until the performance matches or exceeds the person's terminal standards (e.g., Meichenbaum, 1971). Progress along the route to a goal is also mediated by self-generated distractions and cognitive operations through which the person can transform the aversive "self-control" situation into one which he can master effectively (e.g., Mischel et al., 1972; Mischel & Moore, 1973a, 1973b). While achievement of important goals leads to positive self-appraisal and self-reinforcement, failure to reach significant self-imposed standards may lead the individual to indulge in psychological self-lacerations (e.g., self-condemnation). The anticipation of such failure probably leads to extensive anxiety, while the anticipation of success may help to sustain performance, although the exact mechanisms of self-regulation still require much empirical study.

* * *

Overview of Person Variables In sum, individual differences in behavior may reflect differences in each of the foregoing person variables and in their interactions, summarized in Table 49.1.

First, people differ in their *construction competencies*. Even if people have similar expectancies about the most appropriate response pattern in a particular situation and are uniformly motivated to make it, they may differ in whether or not (and

TABLE 49.1

SUMMARY OF COGNITIVE SOCIAL LEARNING PERSON VARIABLES

1. Construction competencies: ability to construct (generate) particular cognitions and behaviors. Related to measures of IQ, social and cognitive (mental) maturity and competence, ego development, social-intellectual achievements and skills. Refers to what the subject knows and *can* do.
2. Encoding strategies and personal constructs: units for categorizing events and for self-descriptions.
3. Behavior-outcome and stimulus-outcome expectancies in particular situations.
4. Subjective stimulus values: motivating and arousing stimuli, incentives, and aversions.
5. Self-regulatory systems and plans: rules and self-reactions for performance and for the organization of complex behavior sequences.

how well) they *can* do it, that is, in their ability to construct the preferred response. For example, due to differences in skill and prior learning, individual differences may arise in interpersonal problem solving, empathy and role taking, or cognitive-intellective achievements. Response differences also may reflect differences in how individuals *categorize* a particular situation (i.e., in how they encode, group, and label the events that comprise it) and in how they construe themselves and others. Differences between persons in their performance in any situation depend on their behavior-outcome and stimulus-outcome *expectancies*, that is, differences in the expected outcomes associated with particular responses or stimuli in particular situations. Performance differences also may be due to differences in the subjective *values* of the outcomes expected in the situation. Finally, individual differences may be due to differences in the *self-regulatory systems* and plans that each person brings to the situation.

* * *

THREE PERSPECTIVES IN PERSONALITY STUDY

The study of persons may be construed alternatively from three complementary perspectives. Construed from the viewpoint of the psychologist seeking procedures or operations necessary to produce changes in performance, it may be most useful to focus on the environmental *conditions* necessary to modify the subject's behavior and therefore to speak of "stimulus control," "operant conditioning," "classical conditioning," "reinforcement control," "modeling" and so on. Construed from the viewpoint of the theorist concerned with how these operations produce their effects in the subject who undergoes them, it may be more useful to speak of alterations in processed information and specifically in constructs, expectancies, subjective values, rules, and other theoretical *person variables* that mediate the effects of conditions upon behavior. Construed from the viewpoint of the experiencing subject, it may be more useful to speak of the same events in terms of their *phenomenological impact* as thoughts, feelings, wishes, and other subjective (but communicable) internal states of experience. Confusion arises when one fails to recognize that the same events (e.g., the "operant conditioning" of a child's behavior at nursery school) may be alternatively construed from each of these perspectives and that the choice of constructions (or their combinations) depends on the construer's purpose. Ultimately, conceptualizations of the field of personality will have to be large enough to encompass the phenomena seen from all three perspectives. The present cognitive social learning approach to persons hopefully is a step in that direction.

References

Anderson, N. H. (1972). Information integration theory: A brief survey (Tech. Rep. No. 24). La Jolla: University of California at San Diego, Center for Human Information Processing.

Argyle, M., & Little, B. R. (1972). Do personality traits apply to social behavior? *Journal of Theory of Social Behavior, 2,* 1–35.

Aronfreed, J. (1968). *Conduct and conscience: The socialization of internalized control over behavior.* New York: Academic Press.

Bandura, A. (1969). *Principles of behavior modification.* New York: Holt, Rinehart & Winston.

Bandura, A. (1971a). Analysis of modeling processes. In A. Bandura (Ed.), *Psychological modeling: Conflicting theories.* Chicago: Aldine-Atherton.

Bandura, A. (1971b). *Social learning theory.* New York: General Learning Press.

Bandura, A. (1971c). Vicarious and self-reinforcement processes. In R. Glaser (Ed.), *The nature of reinforcement.* New York: Academic Press.

Bandura, A., & Perloff, B. (1967). Relative efficacy of self-monitored and externally imposed reinforcement systems. *Journal of Personality and Social Psychology, 7,* 111–116.

Bandura, A., & Whalen, C. K. (1966). The influence of antecedent reinforcement and divergent modeling cues on patterns of self-reward. *Journal of Personality and Social Psychology, 3,* 373–382.

Bolles, R. C. (1972). Reinforcement, expectancy, and learning. *Psychological Review, 79,* 394–409.

Bower, G. H. (1970). Organizational factors in memory. *Cognitive Psychology, 1,* 18–46.

Campbell, D. T. (1961). Conformity in psychology's theories of acquired behavioral dispositions. In I. A. Berg & B. M. Bass (Eds.), *Conformity and deviation.* New York: Harper.

Cautela, J. R. (1971). Covert conditioning. In A. Jacobs & L. B. Sachs (Eds.), *The psychology of private events.* New York: Academic Press.

Chatterjee, B. B., & Eriksen, C. W. (1962). Cognitive factors in heart rate conditioning. *Journal of Experimental Psychology, 64,* 272–279.

Estes, W. K. (1972). Reinforcement in human behavior. *American Scientist, 60,* 723–729.

Geer, J. H., Davison, G. C., & Gatchel, R. K. (1970). Reduction of stress in humans through nonveridical perceived control of aversive stimulation. *Journal of Personality and Social Psychology, 16,* 731–738.

Grings, W. W., & Lockhart, R. A. (1963). Effects of anxiety-lessening instructions and differential set development on the extinction of GSR. *Journal of Experimental Psychology,* 66, 292–299.

Irwin, F. W. (1971). *Intentional behavior and motivation.* New York: Lippincott.

Kanfer, F. H. (1971). The maintenance of behavior by self-generated stimuli and reinforcement. In A. Jacobs & L. B. Sachs (Eds.), *The psychology of private events.* New York: Academic Press.

Kanfer, F. H., & Marston, A. R. (1963). Determinants of self-reinforcement in human learning. *Journal of Experimental Psychology, 66,* 245–254.

Kaufman, A., Baron, A., & Kopp, R. E. (1966). Some effects of instructions on human operant behavior. *Psychonomic Monograph Supplements, 1,* 243–250.

Kelly, G. (1955). *The psychology of personal constructs.* New York: Basic Books.

Kohlberg, A. (1966). A cognitive-developmental analysis of children's sex-role concepts and attitudes. In E. E. Maccoby (Ed.), *The development of sex differences.* Stanford: Stanford University Press.

Mandler, G. (1967). Organization and memory. In K. W. Spence & J. T. Spence (Eds.), *The psychology of learning and motivation: Advances in research and theory.* New York: Academic Press.

Mandler, G. (1968). Association and organization: Facts, fancies and theories. In T. R. Dixon & D. L. Horton (Eds.), *Verbal behavior and general behavior theory.* Englewood Cliffs, NJ: Prentice-Hall.

Meichenbaum, D. H. (1971). *Cognitive factors in behavior modification: Modifying what clients say to themselves* (Research Report No. 25). Waterloo: University of Waterloo.

Mischel, W. (1966). Theory and research on the antecedents of self-imposed delay of reward. In B. A. Maher (Ed.), *Progress in experimental personality research* (Vol. 3). New York: Academic Press.

Mischel, W. (1968). *Personality and assessment.* New York: Wiley.

Mischel, W. (1969) Continuity and change in personality. *American Psychologist, 24,* 1012–1018.

Mischel, W. (1973). Processes in delay of gratification. In L. Berkowitz (Ed.), *Advances in social psychology* (Vol. 7). New York: Academic Press.

Mischel, W., Ebbesen, E. B., & Zeiss, A. R. (1972). Cognitive and attentional mechanisms in delay of gratification. *Journal of Personality and Social Psychology, 21,* 204–218.

Mischel, W., Ebbesen, E. B., & Zeiss, A. R. (1973). Selective attention to the self: Situational and dispositional determinants. *Journal of Personality and Social Psychology, 27,* 129–142.

Mischel, W., & Grusec, J. (1966). Determinants of the rehearsal and transmission of neutral and aversive behaviors. *Journal of Personality and Social Psychology, 3,* 197–205.

Mischel, W., & Liebert, R. M. (1966). Effects of discrepancies between observed and imposed reward criteria on their acquisition and transmission. *Journal of Personality and Social Psychology, 3,* 45–53.

Mischel, W., & Moore, B. (1973a). Effects of attention to symbolically presented rewards upon self-control. *Journal of Personality and Social Psychology,* in press.

Mischel, W., & Moore, B. (1973b). Cognitive transformations of the stimulus in delay of gratification. Unpublished manuscript, Stanford University.

Mischel, W., & Staub, E. (1965). Effects of expectancy on working and waiting for larger rewards. *Journal of Personality and Social Psychology, 2,* 625–633.

Mischel, W., Zeiss, R., & Zeiss, A. (1974). Internal-external control and persistence: Validation and implications of the Stanford Preschool Internal-External Scale. *Journal of Personality and Social Psychology, 29,* 265–278.

Neisser, U. (1967). *Cognitive psychology.* New York: Appleton-Century-Crofts.

Piaget, J. (1954). *The construction of reality in the child.* New York: Basic Books.

Rotter, J. B. (1954). *Social learning and clinical psychology.* Englewood Cliffs, NJ: Prentice-Hall.

Rumelhart, D. E., Lindsey, P. H., & Norman, D. A. (1971). A process model for long-term memory (Tech. Rep. No. 17). La Jolla: University of California at San Diego, Center for Human Information Processing.

Schachter, S. (1964). The interaction of cognitive and physiological determinants of emotional state. In L. Berkowitz (Ed.), *Advances in experimental social psychology* (Vol. 1). New York: Academic Press.

Spielberger, D. C., & DeNike, L. D. (1966). Descriptive behaviorism versus cognitive theory in verbal operant conditioning. *Psychological Review, 73*, 306–326.

Wallace, J. (1966). An abilities conception of personality: Some implications for personality measurement. *American Psychologist, 21*, 132–138.

White, R. W. (1959). Motivation reconsidered: The concept of competence. *Psychological Review, 66*, 297–333.

Zigler, E., & Phillips, L. (1961). Social competence and outcome in psychiatric disorder. *Journal of Abnormal and Social Psychology, 63*, 264–271.

Zigler, E., & Phillips, L. (1962). Social competence and the process-reactive distinction in psychopathology. *Journal of Abnormal and Social Psychology, 65*, 215–222.

Cognitive Strategies as Personality: Effectiveness, Specificity, Flexibility, and Change

Julie K. Norem

In the previous selection, Walter Mischel made the point that personality is not just something one "has," but also something one "does." One thing a person does, he proposed, is to formulate strategies by which to live life and fulfill goals. The following selection is by Julie Norem (who was a student of Mischel's student Nancy Cantor). Norem describes research that examines two particular strategies, which she calls defensive pessimism and "illusory glow" optimism.

In a study of college students, Norem found that optimists, who motivate themselves by expecting the best, and pessimists, who motivate themselves by fearing the worst, seemed to do about equally well in college. And Norem claims both groups did better than subjects with no strategy at all.

A couple of fundamental principles are demonstrated by this research. First, different people often use different routes to the same goal. Although the pessimists and optimists followed very different strategies, they both pursued academic success and seemed to achieve that goal about equally often. Second, a strategy that works in one domain may not work in another. Students who were pessimists about their schoolwork were not necessarily pessimists about their social life; those who were seemed to have difficulty. Pessimism seems to be a strategy that can help you get work done, but does not make you popular.

The purpose of the research in the next selection is to bring one of Mischel's cognitive social learning variables to life by showing how people develop and implement strategies for attaining their important goals in life.

From *Personality Psychology: Recent Trends and Emerging Directions*, edited by D. M. Buss and N. Cantor (New York: Springer-Verlag, 1989), pp. 45–60.

As units of personality, *cognitive strategies* describe how individuals use self-knowledge and knowledge about the social world to translate their goals into behavior. The concept of a strategy captures coherent patterns of appraisal, planning, retrospection, and effort (Bruner, Goodnow, & Austin, 1956; Cantor & Kihlstrom, 1987; Norem, 1987; Showers & Cantor, 1985). Strategies focus on *process*: the ways people direct their attention, construct expectations and goals, allocate their time and effort, protect their self-esteem, and react emotionally. Thus, strategies elaborate on the *instantiation* of traits and motives. Analysis of personality and individual differences in terms of strategies shifts emphasis away from general dispositions towards the cognitive links between motives and actions.

This perspective on personality assumes that a general trait, disposition, or motive has many potential manifestations. * * * Need for achievement, for example, may be expressed in cutthroat competition among brokers on Wall Street, or through dedication to improving on a "personal best" in a marathon. Similarly, specific behaviors may represent a number of diverse general characteristics when performed by different individuals in different situations. Organizing departmental colloquia could be an expression of affiliative motives for one person and an expression of power motives for another (Winter, 1988). The contention here is that *personality* is embodied at least as much in the different ways nAch[1] (or introversion or aggression) might be expressed by different individuals, as in differences in those characteristics themselves. Individual differences are expressed in the interpretations of situations and pursuit of specific goals: e.g., beating others vs. improving one's self, or promoting collegial discourse vs. controlling people and resources.

These assumptions, then, locate personality in the specific goals individuals construct for themselves, in the form of "life tasks" (Cantor & Kihlstrom, 1987), "personal projects" (Palys & Little, 1983), "personal strivings" (Emmons, 1986), or even situationally specific expectations; and in the strategies individuals develop to pursue these goals (e.g. Buss, 1987; Cantor, Norem, Niedenthal, Langston, & Brower, 1987). There are several important implications of personality conceived of in this way. In this chapter, I plan to discuss these implications, review some recent data that support hypotheses derived from this perspective, and conclude with a consideration of future directions in personality research that build on current data and theory.

Examples of Strategies: Defensive Pessimism and "Illusory Glow" Optimism

Throughout this discussion, research on two particular strategies will serve to illustrate the central tenets of this approach. These strategies are "illusory glow" optimism and defensive pessimism (Norem & Cantor, 1986a). The defensive pessimism strategy involves individuals with acknowledged positive performance histories in a particular domain, who, nevertheless, set unrealistically low expectations when anticipating new situations within that domain. Individuals using the strategy feel anxious and out of control, and play through a "worst-case" analysis—dwelling on possible negative outcomes—even when those outcomes seem improbable.

Data from experimental and field research on defensive pessimism in the achievement domain indicate that these negative expectations do not become self-fulfilling prophecies, or lead to effort withdrawal. Nor do they necessarily have the emotional consequences associated with more generalized pessimistic or depressive attributional style (Peterson & Seligman, 1984; Showers & Ruben, 1988). Instead, individuals using the defensive pessimist strategy invest considerable effort in tasks they see as important (Norem & Cantor, 1986b).

[1]Need for achievement.

Moreover, in the short-run at least, individuals using the strategy perform as well as subjects using an optimistic strategy, and feel just as satisfied with their performance. Unlike optimistic subjects, defensive pessimists do not seem to "revise" their understanding of a performance after the fact in order to protect their self-esteem. For example, in an experimental setting, they did not deny having control when given failure feedback relative to when given success feedback (Norem & Cantor, 1986a).

In contrast, individuals using "illusory glow" optimism do not anticipate negative outcomes; nor do they typically feel anxious or out of control prior to performance situations. Optimists set realistically high expectations, based on their past successes. They then protect or enhance their positive self-image using the battery of positive illusions and biases documented by researchers investigating the differences between depressive and non-depressive cognition (see Taylor & Brown, 1988, for a review). In the study cited in the paragraph above, optimistic subjects showed a typical "illusion of control" for success, while denying control for failure.

It is important to note that individuals using these two different strategies have constructed somewhat different goals for themselves, which follow from their appraisal of relevant situations. Research comparing these groups has focused on situations that both optimists and defensive pessimists see as important, rewarding, and absorbing. The defensive pessimists, however, also see these same situations as more stressful and less within their control than the optimists (Cantor et al., 1987). For the defensive pessimist group, therefore, there is an additional crucial dimension to the "problem" presented by these situations: dealing with anxiety and "taking control" of a situation in order to perform well.

For the optimist group, remaining in control and staying "up" is part of the challenge. Indeed, there is some evidence from the studies cited above that their performance may suffer if they confront negative information or do experience anxiety (Cantor et al., 1987). This suggests that their goal may include avoiding negative information and contemplation of the possibility of failure (Miller, 1987).

Another way of understanding the different goals of the two groups is to consider combinations of motives. Both groups resemble, in background, aspiration and cumulative performance, high need for achievement subjects (Atkinson, 1957). Both groups come from families that emphasize achievement-related activities (Norem & Cantor, 1990). The high anxiety and low expectations among defensive pessimists, however, resemble that found among high fear of failure subjects in traditional achievement research (Atkinson & Litwin, 1960). There is some reason to think that individuals using defensive pessimism might be high in nAch and high fear of failure: a motive constellation that Atkinson and his colleagues predict should cause immobilization. Indeed, Self (1988) finds that academic optimists and defensive pessimists do not differ in the satisfaction they expect to derive from success, but that pessimists expect significantly greater unhappiness from failure than the optimists. This fits with the emphasis on "working through" the implications of bad outcomes found in the defensive pessimist group, who, apparently, actively attempt to fight immobilization in order to take control of or "harness" their anxiety so that they may concentrate on the task at hand (Norem & Cantor, 1986b).

The emphasis on these two strategies throughout this chapter is, of course, not meant to suggest that they in any way exhaust the category of strategies individuals may use, even within the context of performance situations. Various emotional and behavioral self-handicapping strategies come quickly to mind as alternative ways, for example, to approach performance situations, based on somewhat differently constructed goals. There are numerous other strategies individuals may use, especially when one considers different domains of human activity (Folkman & Lazarus, 1985; Frese, Stewart, & Hannover, 1987; Kuhl, 1985; Langston

& Cantor, 1989; Miller, 1987; Paulhus & Martin, 1987; Pyszczynski & Greenberg, 1987; Snyder & Smith, 1986; Zirkel & Cantor, 1988). Aside from the author's convenience, however, there are two reasons why these particular strategies are especially useful examples for the purposes of this chapter. First, research on these strategies includes experimental work, questionnaire studies, and a longitudinal project. There are data from contrived laboratory contexts, and from "messier" real-life situations. There are self-report data, objective-performance data, experience-sampling data, and observer ratings. Although the subjects in these studies have all been college students, they are students drawn from quite different populations, demographically and otherwise. The research reviewed below has been conducted using subjects from the general undergraduate population at the University of Michigan and from a somewhat more select sample of Honors College students. In addition, there are data from undergraduate subjects at Northeastern University, who represent different demographic characteristics, who encounter a different academic environment while attending an urban school known for its cooperative education program, and who arrive at college with a much greater diversity in preparation and aptitude than students at Michigan. The convergence of these different data sources lends substantial support to the argument that strategies provide a powerful tool for exploring personality function.

Second, optimism and defensive pessimism are strategies used by individuals who *do not* appear to differ in other ways, which might suggest that differences in strategy are merely epiphenomena.[2] Among college students, there are no significant demographic or SES[3] differences between those using optimism and those using defensive pessimism. Nor do they differ significantly in high school rank, high school grade point average, SAT scores, or number of family members in college. There is no reason to suspect that the difference in strategies among these individuals is a simple function of intelligence, past performance, scholastic aptitude, preparation for college, or some readily identifiable influence from their social structure. Therefore, they provide a clear opportunity to contrast the expression of personality via different strategies with relatively less "noise" from other variables.

[2]Phenomena that play no causal role.

[3]Social-economic status, or social class.

Theoretical Implications of a Strategy-Based Approach to Personality

STRATEGY EFFECTIVENESS One implication of considering personality in terms of strategies is an emphasis on the *effectiveness* of different strategies. Adaptation and coping are thus seen as a function of individual goals, the manner in which individuals pursue their goals, and the probable consequences of various goal-strategy combinations. Strategy effectiveness involves: (a) the extent to which a strategy leads to successful outcomes; (b) the "costs" of using the strategy, in terms of emotional wear and tear, the response of others, and/or lost opportunities; (c) the potential costs of *not* using the strategy (or being without a coherent strategy for pursuing a particular goal). Effectiveness may also be a function of the indirect consequences that using a strategy in one domain has for other domains.

Research on the effectiveness of defensive pessimism and optimism within the academic domain highlights the importance of considering all of the above points when attempting to evaluate the effectiveness of a strategy. Norem and Cantor (1986a, b) found that, when left to use their habitual strategy on anagram and puzzle tasks (presented as tests of "different kinds of abilities"), subjects prescreened for self-reported use of defensive pessimism or optimism performed equivalently well.[4] They were also equivalently satisfied

[4]Prescreening for individuals using defensive pessimism and optimism is done using a nine-item, face valid questionnaire. Subjects indicate the extent to which each item is characteristic of them. The items include questions such as "I generally go into academic situa-

with their performances after the fact. This was so even though the defensive pessimism group reported feeling significantly more anxious and out of control prior to the test. When, however, the experimenter interfered with the defensive pessimists' strategy by encouraging them, their performance suffered, relative to optimists in the same condition (whose performance improved) and defensive pessimists in the control condition.

Cantor et al., (1987), as part of an ongoing longitudinal study[5] of the transition to college life, studied academic optimism and defensive pessimism among freshmen in the Honors College at the University of Michigan. Their results converged with the experimental data in that the students using defensive pessimism appraised their academic tasks significantly more negatively than the students using optimism: they felt less in control, more stressed, found academic tasks more difficult, more important, and more time consuming. They also expected to do more poorly than the optimists expected to do.

A similar pattern of emotions and appraisal appeared in data from an experience-sampling study in which a subsample of the Honors students carried electronic pagers that "beeped" on a random schedule several times a day for ten days. At each "beep," the students filled out a report of what they were doing and how they were feeling (Cantor & Norem, 1989; Norem, 1987). In these data, defensive pessimist subjects reported feeling significantly less control, less enjoyment, less progress, and more stress than optimists during academic situations, especially in "anticipatory" situations, such as when they were studying for a test. Their reports from other situations, however, were just as positive as the optimists'. As a consequence, their reported feelings of control are significantly more variable across situations than the optimists'.

Just as in the laboratory studies, the negative appraisal and lack of control reported by the defensive pessimists did not impair their performance over the short-run (although there are suggestions of relatively greater "costs" over the long-run; see below). Defensive pessimists and optimists both performed quite well academically during their first and second years in college (GPAs above 3.30), and there were no differences in average GPA between the two groups. There were also no differences between the two groups in social satisfaction or in an overall measure of perceived stress during their first two years in college.

From these studies, it seems reasonable to conclude that the defensive pessimist and optimist strategies are both *effective* insofar as the individuals using them perform well on academic tasks. It is also important to understand that the characteristic ways in which information about tasks and the self is used by the two strategy groups is not incidental to their performance. Playing through contingency plans is significantly negatively related to GPA for the optimists in the Honors College sample. In contrast, it is significantly positively related for the defensive pessimists, for whom it is an integral part of "dealing with" the problems presented by academic tasks. Negativity about the academic domain and negative beliefs about the self are negatively related to performance for the optimists—a pattern that contrasts markedly with relationships found for the defensive pessimist. Negativity of academic plans is not related to GPA for the latter group (whose plans

tions expecting the worst, even though things usually turn out OK," and "I usually go into academic situations with positive expectations." There are four questions describing aspects of the defensive pessimist strategy and four describing aspects of the optimistic strategy. There is also a question that asks subjects to indicate the extent to which they believe they have done well in the past. The sum of the pessimistic items is subtracted from the sum of the optimistic items. Subjects in the bottom and top thirds of the distribution of answers are selected for use of defensive pessimism and optimism respectively, *providing* that they strongly endorse the item about positive past experience (6 or higher on a 9-point scale). This is done to select for *defensively* pessimistic subjects, as opposed to those whose pessimism is realistic, or based on distortion of past experience.—Author

[5]A longitudinal study is one that follows a single group of subjects for an extended period of time, sometimes years.

progress from very negative possible outcomes to successful resolution of those outcomes), and negative beliefs about the academic self are strongly positively related to GPA.

Another way of assessing the effectiveness of optimism and defensive pessimism is to compare the outcomes of those using these strategies with the outcomes of other individuals. Norem and Cantor (1990) looked at the performance of a group of individuals, labelled "aschematics," who, initially, did not seem to have a coherent strategy for the academic domain. These are individuals who are in the middle third of the academic optimism-pessimism prescreening distribution,[6] and who sometimes resemble optimists, sometimes resemble pessimists, but are, characteristically, neither.

The aschematics in the Honors College sample were less absorbed in and anxious about academic tasks than the pessimists, but also felt less in control than the optimists. They were somewhat less reflective than the other two groups, and had significantly fewer mismatches between their actual and ideal self-concepts in the academic domain (Higgins, Klein, & Strauman, 1985). Data from the experience-sampling study show that a subgroup of the aschematics spend 29% of their time on academic tasks (relative to 38% and 35% for optimists and defensive pessimists), felt significantly less in control across situations than optimists, and were more lonely, angry, and more in conflict in virtually every situation sampled than the other two strategy groups. For the aschematics, *unlike* the defensive pessimists who seem able to "take control" by using their strategy, feeling out of control is negatively related to GPA performance and academic satisfaction. Finally, the aschematics achieve marginally lower GPAs than the other two groups during their first year in college, and significantly lower GPAs during their second year.

These data show the aschematic group "floundering" in their approach to academic tasks—results interpreted by Norem and Cantor as a consequence of poorly articulated goals within the achievement domain and a resultant lack of a coherent strategy for that domain. * * *

As will be seen below, the aschematics were eventually able to develop effective approaches to dealing with their academic tasks, once their goals within that domain crystallized. Initially, however, it seems clear that both the defensive pessimist strategy and the optimistic strategy were considerably more effective than no strategy at all.

The data reviewed so far strongly support the contention that defensive pessimism and optimism can be effective strategies, at least within the academic domain and with respect to performance outcomes. Consideration of strategy effectiveness should, however, also include assessment of the relative "costs" of a strategy to the individual using it. There are no current data showing significant short-term costs to the use of either optimism or defensive pessimism in the academic domain —especially when the use of those strategies is contrasted with the absence of a strategy. Looking in depth at how the strategies of optimism and defensive pessimism unfold over time, however, reveals important differences between the strategies apt to be related to differences in the longer term costs of each. The experience-sampling data reveal much greater variance in emotions—especially in feelings of control—for the pessimists than for the other two groups. Over the course of a few years, the emotional ups and downs of academic defensive pessimism may accumulate and take a heavy toll on well-being. In addition, the pessimists seem to rely heavily on a small group of close friends: they spend more time with a relatively small group of "best friends," while the optimists spend more time with a larger group of "friends." It may be that the pessimists' best friends find themselves wearying of the pessimists' worry and anxiety.

In fact, the costs or "side effects" of defensive pessimism show up strongly in data from the Honors College sample during their third year in college (Cantor & Norem, 1989). A telephone sur-

[6]That is, individuals who scored in the middle on the optimist-pessimist questionnaire.

vey assessed reports of physical and psychological symptoms, satisfaction with academic and social performance, and junior year GPA among this sample. Results indicate that the defensive pessimists, although not doing badly in any absolute sense, were suffering somewhat relative to the optimists. They reported experiencing greater frequencies of psychological and physical symptoms, felt less satisfied with their academic and social performances, and had lower GPAs than the optimists. (Again, it is important to note that, although below the optimists' GPA, the pessimists were still performing quite well: mean GPA = 3.35.) In this case, the indirect consequences of using a strategy repeatedly over time are clearly important to assessment of the effectiveness of the strategy. Of course, we do not know from these data what would have happened to the defensive pessimists if they had not been using their strategy. Recall from previous research that defensive pessimists who were "deprived" of their strategy in a performance situation were relatively debilitated (Norem & Cantor, 1986b). The pessimists' appraisal of academic situations focuses on their anxiety and feelings of being out of control. Although it may be stressful to recognize and continually experience those feelings, the pessimists are at least able to "work through" them to some extent by using their strategy. Even though defensive pessimism is apparently not "cost-free" over time, it may be preferable to feeling anxious and out of control, and to having no way of coping with those feelings.

These data about the short- and long-term consequences of different strategies within the academic domain highlight the complexity of the process by which individuals pursue their goals. So far, we have only considered these strategies within one domain—that of academic achievement activities. Another aspect of the effectiveness of strategies, however, concerns the relative fit between strategy and domain. Simply put, some strategies may be better suited to some domains than to others. This raises the question of how domain-specific an individual's strategies are and the extent to which people can adjust the strategies they use to fit particular contexts.

Domain Specificity, Flexibility, and Strategy Change

Strategies stem from appraising a situation and activating relevant goals. One of the reasons that a strategy may not be equally effective in all situations is that all situations do not provide the same opportunities to realize a given goal. Nor, in the absence of monomania, are individuals likely to interpret all situations in the same way. Therefore, there is no a priori reason to assume that individuals will use the same kind of strategy in different kinds of situations.

Moreover, there is no assumption that strategies that characterize an individual at one period in his/her life will continue to do so throughout the passing years. The concept of a strategy explicitly recognizes the potential—indeed, the probability—of change as an individual's goals change. As goals are successfully realized, as cumulative feedback indicates a strategy is unsuccessful or exacts too high a cost, or as tasks in a domain are abandoned or transformed and new goals formulated, one would expect to find corresponding strategy change.

In research to date, the academic and social versions of the defensive pessimism prescreening questionnaire show average correlations of .30 across several samples of University of Michigan students (Norem & Cantor, 1986b, Norem, 1987; Showers, 1986), and .23 for two samples of Northeastern students (Norem, 1988). Both correlations are significant, but modest: it is clear that once categorization into strategy group is made for both domains, not everyone who uses defensive pessimism academically also uses it socially, and that not all academic optimists are social optimists. There is some potential, then, for domain specificity in the application of defensive pessimism. This is also reflected in the academic defensive pessimists' appraisal of the social domain: they do not generalize their negative perspective from the academic to the social domain. Academic pessimists feel just as much control over and have just as high expectations for the social domain as academic optimists, *and* as social optimists (Cantor et al., 1987). Similarly, social defensive pessimists neither set low expectations for their academic performance nor appraise academic tasks negatively (Norem & Illingworth, 1989).

Furthermore, when the self-knowledge of social and academic defensive pessimists and optimists is compared within and across each domain, clear domain specificity appears. Academic defensive pessimists have more negative academic selves than academic optimists, but have equivalently positive social selves. The comparable pattern of domain-specific self-knowledge is found among social optimists and defensive pessimists: the latter have more negative beliefs about their social selves, but not about their academic selves (Cantor et al., 1987; Norem, 1987; Norem & Illingworth, 1989).

In addition to providing support for the idea that use of a given strategy is potentially domain-specific, social defensive pessimism provides an informative look at issues of strategy-situation fit. Recall that defensive pessimism involves setting low expectations, focusing on anxiety, reflecting extensively on negative outcomes, and working very hard on a task. Although academic defensive pessimists experience reasonable success using these procedures, the strategy might be less effective in the social domain.

First, academic situations such as those studied in the research above may differ from many social situations in that, for the most part, there are externally provided, explicit evaluations of performance. Typically, students receive grades, scores, and/or other feedback about their scholastic performance. Even if not entirely "objective," this feedback comes from outside sources and provides easy comparison to past performance and the performance of others. Rarely, in social interactions, are performance outcomes so unequivocal. It may be that in situations where there is relatively less objective positive information about past performance, the defensive pessimist strategy flounders, since it depends on contrasting defensively low expectations with realistically high past performance.

Second, the correlation between the amount of time and effort spent in preparation and eventual performance is probably quite strong and positive within academic situations. In other words, despite what students might say, there is some positive relationship between the amount of time spent studying and final exam grades in most classrooms. The same contingencies, however, may not operate as clearly in the social domain. One can hardly help but think of the prototypical adolescent repeating his/her carefully thought out greeting while waiting for a prospective date to answer the phone—only to find that every word gets jumbled on the way out, and the result is an embarrassing squeak or mumble. It is easy to come up with examples of when "trying too hard" (or being seen that way) can lead to social failure. Indeed, one might even speculate that extensive planning reflection, and effort prior to a social occasion increases the risk of bumbling, stilted interactions, emotional anticlimax, and disappointment.

Data from the Honors College sample do show that social pessimism is less effective than academic pessimism: social pessimists are less satisfied and feel significantly more stressed than social optimists during their first and third years in college (Norem, 1987). Observers of interviews with social pessimists and optimists rate them as less satisfied with their social performance, less interested in trying new things, less apt to try to make new affiliations, more reluctant to think about good social outcomes, more stressed by social tasks, and more apt to ruminate obsessively about problems than are social optimists (see Norem, 1987, for details).

The picture that emerges from these data is not one of individuals *using* defensive pessimism to work through anxiety and motivate themselves; rather, it resembles a picture of unmotivated, mildly depressed subjects, stuck in a repetitive cy-

Nearly 100 years ago, Freud introduced a dual theory of information processing that placed deviant behavior squarely in the realm of the natural sciences and, more particularly, in psychology. This was a defining moment in the development of psychology, because, up to then, grossly deviant behavior had been explained by inhabitation of spirits and organic disease. It was now possible to understand the pervasive irrationality of human beings, despite their capacity for rational thinking, as a natural outcome of the properties of the unconscious mind. This realization was as distressing as it was liberating, for, as Freud, with no lack of temerity, pointed out, it was one of three great scientific discoveries that dethroned humankind from its exalted view of itself (Jones, 1955). The first was Copernicus's discovery that our planet is not the center of the universe, the second was Darwin's discovery that humankind is not unique among the creatures of the earth, and the third was his own discovery that we are not even in control of our own minds.

Freud considered his most important work to be his book on the interpretation of dreams (Jones, 1955), because it was there that he proposed the principles by which the unconscious operated, which he referred to as the *primary process*, distinguishing it from a more logical, realistic mode of reasoning that he attributed to a *secondary process*. He identified the principles of the primary process as wish fulfillment, displacement, condensation, symbolic representation, and association. Not only did he believe these principles could account for dreams, but he also believed they could account for psychopathological symptoms and aberrant behavior of all kinds. Moreover, he assumed that they continuously undermined people's attempts at conscious, rational thinking. The only hope for thinking rationally, he believed, was to make the unconscious conscious, which was the aim of psychoanalysis. He regarded rational, conscious thinking as only the tip of the iceberg. The foundation of all mental activity consisted, he held, of the submerged part, the unconscious that operated by the primary process.

A critical weakness in Freud's conceptualization of the unconscious is that it makes little sense from an evolutionary perspective. It is essentially a maladaptive system, capable, perhaps, of generating dreams and psychotic aberrations but not up to the task, for either human or nonhuman animals, of promoting adaptive behavior in the real world. Operating under the direction of the primary process alone, individuals would starve to death amidst wish-fulfillment hallucinations of unlimited gratification. That they do not, Freud attributed to the secondary process. This ad hoc solution leaves unexplained the questions of how the maladaptive system evolved in the first place and how nonhuman animals are able to adapt to their environments at all without a secondary process (which is intimately tied to language).

This raises the interesting question of how a theory of the unconscious with such a critical flaw could have endured for so long. A not unreasonable suspicion is that it has virtues that are sufficient in the minds of many to compensate for its limitations. Hall and Lindzey (1978) described what psychoanalysis has to offer as follows:

> It tries to envisage full-bodied individuals living partly in a world of reality and partly in a world of make-believe, beset by conflicts and inner contradictions, yet capable of rational thought and action, moved by forces of which they have little knowledge and by aspirations that are beyond their reach, by turn confused and clear-headed, frustrated and satisfied, hopeful and despairing, selfish and altruistic; in short, a complex human being. For many people, this picture of the individual has an essential validity. (p. 70)

Recently, theorists outside of the psychoanalytic tradition have begun to formulate a new view of the unconscious. This new unconscious, sometimes referred to as the *cognitive unconscious*, is a fundamentally adaptive system that automatically, effortlessly, and intuitively organizes experience and directs behavior. Unlike the thinking of Freud, who assumed that all information (other than that acquired during a preverbal period) would be conscious in the absence of repression, the new concept holds that most information processing occurs automatically and effortlessly outside of awareness because that is its natural mode of operation, a mode that is far more efficient than conscious, deliberative thinking.

If most human information processing occurs out of awareness and is governed by a different set of principles from both those of conscious, rational thinking and the primary-process principles of the Freudian unconscious, surely this must have important implications for theories of personality. At the very least, a major area of unconscious processing that is outside the domain of the Freudian unconscious remains to be accounted for. It also raises questions such as how, if at all, the cognitive unconscious relates to the Freudian unconscious. Is it completely independent of it or does it overlap with it, and in either event, what functions should be assigned to each? An obvious limitation of the cognitive unconscious is that it is a bland, and, as Kihlstrom (1990) described it, "kinder, gentler" unconscious. Can it be reconceptualized in a more dynamic way that could account for the behavior of full-blooded, emotionally driven, and conflicted people? If there is a dynamic, basically adaptive unconscious, what place remains for Freud's conceptualization of the unconscious? In the present article, I examine these issues in the context of a global theory of personality—cognitive—experiential self-theory (CEST)—that emphasizes two interactive modes of information processing, rational and experiential.

* * *

Evidence in Everyday Life of Two Basic Modes of Processing Information

There is no dearth of evidence in everyday life that people apprehend reality in two fundamentally different ways, one variously labeled intuitive, automatic, natural, nonverbal, narrative, and experiential, and the other analytical, deliberative, verbal, and rational.

INFLUENCE OF EMOTIONS ON THINKING The transformation that occurs in people's thinking when they are emotionally aroused provides a dramatic illustration of a very different way of thinking from the way people think when they are unemotional. People, when they are highly emotional, characteristically think in a manner that is categorical, personal, concretive, unreflective, and action oriented, and the stronger the emotion, the more they think that way and the more their thinking appears to them to be self-evidently valid. All of these identify fundamental attributes of the experiential system (see Table 51.1).

That most people are intuitively aware of two modes of processing corresponding to the experiential and rational system is indicated by the advice they typically give others who are emotionally overwrought, such as, "Get a grip on yourself. You're too emotional to think straight. Once you calm down, you will see things differently."

INFLUENCE OF THINKING ON EMOTIONS Emotions in everyday life are almost invariably produced by the preconscious[1] interpretation of events. People are angry, sad, or frightened, not as a direct result of what objectively occurs but because of how they interpret what happens. If a person interprets an action directed at him or her as unwarranted and deserving of punishment, the person will most likely feel angry, whereas if the same action is interpreted as a serious threat to life or limb from which escape is desired, the person will more likely feel frightened. * * * The automatic, preconscious construals that are the effective instigators of such emotions are made so automatically and rapidly as to preclude the deliberative, sequential, analytical thinking that is characteristic of the rational system. Such automatic, preconscious thinking, therefore, suggests a mode of informa-

[1]Immediate and unthinking.

TABLE 51.1

Comparison of the Experiential and Rational System

Experiential system	Rational system
1. Holistic	1. Analytic
2. Affective: Pleasure–pain oriented (what feels good)	2. Logical: Reason oriented (what is sensible)
3. Associationistic connections	3. Logical connections
4. Behavior mediated by "vibes" from past experiences	4. Behavior mediated by conscious appraisal of events
5. Encodes reality in concrete images, metaphors, and narratives	5. Encodes reality in abstract symbols, words, and numbers
6. More rapid processing: Oriented toward immediate action	6. Slower processing: Oriented toward delayed action
7. Slower to change: Changes with repetitive or intense experience	7. Changes more rapidly: Changes with speed of thought
8. More crudely differentiated: Broad generalization gradient; stereotypical thinking	8. More highly differentiated
9. More crudely integrated: Dissociative, emotional complexes: context-specific processing	9. More highly integrated: Cross-context processing
10. Experienced passively and preconsciously: We are seized by our emotions	10. Experienced actively and consciously: We are in control of our thoughts
11. Self-evidently valid: "Experiencing is believing"	11. Requires justification via logic and evidence

Note. From "Cognitive–Experiential Self-Theory: An Integrative Theory of Personality" by S. Epstein, in R. C. Curtis, *The Relational Self: Theoretical Convergences in Psychoanalysis and Social Psychology*, New York: Guilford Press. Copyright 1991 by Guilford Press. Adopted by permission.

tion processing that operates by different principles from a more deliberative, analytical type of thinking.

Two Ways of Knowing Embedded in common language is evidence that people are intuitively aware of two fundamentally different ways of knowing, one associated with feelings and experience and the other with intellect. For instance, when a young woman cannot decide between two suitors, one who is more trustworthy and the other who is a greater source of pleasure, we say that she has a conflict between the head and the heart. The heart, of course, is a metaphor for emotions. But emotions have no more capacity than the heart for making judgments. As assessments are the product of cognitions, conflicts between the heart and the head are necessarily between two cognitive processes, one associated with emotions and the other not. From the perspective of CEST, the former corresponds to processing in the mode of the experiential system, which is assumed to be intimately associated with affect, and the latter corresponds to processing in the mode of the rational system, which is assumed to be relatively affect free.

It is also widely recognized that there is a difference between intellectual knowledge and insight. Information obtained from textbooks and lectures is of a different quality from information acquired from experience. Experientially derived knowledge is often more compelling and more likely to influence behavior than is abstract knowledge. * * * Psychotherapists have long recognized the importance of this distinction. They widely regard information gained through personally meaningful experience as more effective in changing feelings and behavior than impersonal information acquired from textbooks and lectures. The observation that there are two fundamentally different kinds of knowledge, intellectual and insightful, is consistent with the view that there are two kinds of information processing, analytic–rational and intuitive–experiential.

APPEAL AND INFLUENCE OF NARRATIVES Narratives are assumed in CEST to appeal to the experiential system because they are emotionally engaging and represent events in a manner similar to how they are experienced in real life, involving location in place and time, goal directed characters, and sequential unfolding (Bruner, 1986). The result is that narratives are intrinsically appealing in a way that lectures on abstract subjects and technical documents are not. This may explain why including anecdotes increases the persuasiveness of messages (Kahneman & Tversky, 1973). It is no accident that the Bible, probably the most influential Western book of all time, teaches through parables and stories and not through philosophical discourse. * * * Relatedly, good literature is valued beyond its entertainment function because it is a vicarious source of significant experience.

IRRATIONAL FEARS Irrational fears provide evidence of a nonrational way of processing information. People often maintain their unrealistic distressing beliefs at great personal cost, despite recognizing that they are irrational. Those who are afraid of flying in aircraft know full well that their fear is irrational. Nevertheless, many are willing to drive great distances in order to avoid air travel. Paradoxically, they feel safer in the situation they intellectually know is more dangerous.

An interesting example of an irrational fear was reported in a newscast in the fall of 1991. A commercial airliner had to turn back because people ran screaming into the aisles when a mouse appeared on board, thereby endangering the aircraft. The degree of objective danger produced by their behavior as calculated by their rational system was apparently no match for the threat posed by the mouse as assessed by their experiential system.

NATURAL APPEAL OF PICTURES Advertisers have learned through trial and error, focus groups, and intuition, that people's behavior and attitudes are governed by a cognitive system that is more responsive to pictures than to words. * * * Cigarette advertising agencies and their clients are willing to bet millions of dollars in advertising costs that the visual appeal of their messages to the experiential system will prevail over the verbal message of the surgeon general that smoking can endanger one's life, an appeal directed at the rational system. One wonders if the ads would be continued if the playing field were leveled by presenting the surgeon general's message in graphic pictorial form.

SUPERSTITIOUS THINKING The widespread prevalence of superstitious thinking provides compelling evidence that the human mind does not process information by reason alone. In a recent Gallup poll ("Behavior," 1991), 1,236 U.S. adults were interviewed about their superstitions. One in 4 reported that he or she believed in ghosts, one in 6 that she or he had communicated with someone deceased, one in 4 that he or she had telepathically communicated with someone, one in 10 that she or he had been in the presence of a ghost, one in 7 that he or she had seen a UFO, one in 4 that they believed in astrology, and about one half said they believed in extrasensory perception. It is evident from such data that even extreme forms of nonrational thinking are common.

UBIQUITY OF RELIGION Religion provides perhaps the most impressive evidence of all that there are two fundamentally different modes of processing information. There are few societies, if any, throughout recorded history that have not developed some form of religion. For many individuals, rational, analytical thinking fails to provide as satisfactory a way of understanding the world and of directing their behavior in it as does religious teaching. Why is this so? The answer, I believe, is that religion is better suited than analytical thinking for communicating with the experiential system.

CONCLUSIONS FROM EXAMPLES OF EVERYDAY THINKING AND BEHAVIOR It is evident from the examples above that nonrational thinking is highly prevalent and that even when people know their thinking is irrational, they often find it more compelling than their rational reasoning.

* * *

Cognitive–Experiential Self-Theory

Cognitive–experiential self-theory was introduced * * * (S. Epstein, 1973) as a global theory of personality. * * * It has undergone considerable development and has investigated in an extensive research program.

BASIC PRINCIPLES According to CEST, people automatically construct an implicit model of the world, or "theory of reality," that has two major divisions—a world theory and a self-theory—and connecting propositions. (Nonhuman animals also construct a model of the world, but it does not include a self-theory.) A theory of reality is not developed for its own sake, but in order to make life as livable, meaning as emotionally satisfying, as possible. Thus, a fundamental assumption in CEST is that the experiential system is emotionally driven.

It is assumed that there are two major systems by which people adapt to the world: rational and experiential. People have constructs about the self and the world in both systems. Those in the rational system are referred to as *beliefs* and those in the experiential system as *implicit beliefs* or, alternatively, as *schemata*. The schemata, which are the building blocks of the implicit theory of reality in the experiential system, consist primarily of generalizations derived from emotionally significant past experience. It is important to recognize that these schemata are assumed to be organized into an overall adaptive system and are not simply isolated, detached constructs. They thus affect and are affected by other constructs in the system. Evidence attesting to an overall organized experiential system is provided by the coherent, complexly integrated behavior of animals lacking a rational system and by the susceptibility of the experiential system in both human and nonhuman animals to total collapse (disorganization) following unassimilable emotionally significant experiences. Such reactions are observed in experimental neurosis in animals (Pavlov, 1941) and in acute schizophrenic disorganization in humans (S. Epstein, 1979; Perry, 1976). Reactions to threats of such disorganization are observed in paranoid schizophrenia (S. Epstein, 1987) and in posttraumatic stress disorder (S. Epstein, 1991a; Horowitz, 1976; Janoff-Bulman, 1992; McCann & Pearlman, 1990). Disorganization of a system necessarily implies, of course, a prior state of organization.

ATTRIBUTES OF THE EXPERIENTIAL SYSTEM Table 51.1 provides a summary of the comparative features of the experiential and rational systems. The experiential system is assumed to have a very long evolutionary history and to operate in nonhuman as well as in human animals. Because of their more highly developed brains, it is assumed to operate in far more complex ways in humans. At its lower levels of operation, it is a crude system that automatically, rapidly, effortlessly, and efficiently processes information. At its higher reaches, and particularly in interaction with the rational system, it is a source of intuitive wisdom and creativity. Although it represents events primarily concretely and imagistically, it is capable of generalization and abstraction through the use of prototypes, metaphors, scripts, and narratives.

The rational system, in contrast, is a deliberative, effortful, abstract system that operates primarily in the medium of language and has a very brief evolutionary history. It is capable of very high levels of abstraction and long-term delay of gratification. However, it is a very inefficient system for responding to everyday events, and its long term adaptability remains to be tested. (It may yet lead to the destruction of all life on our planet.)

PSYCHODYNAMICS All behavior is assumed, in CEST, to be the product of the joint operation of two systems. Their relative dominance is determined by various parameters, including individual differences in style of thinking and situational variables, such as the degree to which a situation is identified as one that requires formal analysis. Emotional arousal and relevant experience are considered to shift the balance of influence in the direction of the experiential system.

Most theories of personality posit a single fundamental need. For Freud (1920/1959) it was the pleasure principle (i.e., the need to maximize pleasure and minimize pain); for Rogers (1959), Lecky (1961), and other phenomenologists, it was the need to maintain a relatively stable, coherent conceptual system: for Bowlby (1988), Fairbairn (1954), and other object-relations theorists, it was the need for relatedness; and for Adler (1954), Allport (1961), and Kohut (1971), it was the need to overcome feelings of inferiority and enhance self-esteem. According to CEST, these motives are equally important, and behavior is determined by their joint influence.

Like psychoanalysis, CEST is a psychodynamic theory that posits two levels of information processing, each functioning according to its own principles. Also, like psychoanalysis, CEST assumes that the unaware level continuously influences processing at the conscious level. * * *

There are several interesting consequences that follow from assuming the interaction of four basic needs. One, as already noted, is that behavior is viewed as a compromise among the four needs. A second, not unrelated consequence, is that the needs serve as checks and balances against each other. When one need is fulfilled at the expense of the others, the need to fulfill the others increases, which normally moderates the influence of the first need, keeping it within adaptive limits. An important source of maladaptive behavior is when a particular need becomes so compelling that fulfillment of the other needs is sacrificed. A third, related principle is that good adjustment is fostered by fulfillment of the four basic needs in a synergistic, harmonious manner, and poor adjustment by attempting to fulfill the needs in a competitive, conflictual manner.

The four needs provide a useful framework for understanding some otherwise anomalous findings. For example, it has recently been concluded by some psychologists that the widespread view that realistic thinking is an important criterion of adjustment is incorrect, because research has demonstrated that well-adjusted individuals characteristically maintain positive illusions (see review in Taylor & Brown, 1988). According to CEST, this paradox is readily resolved once it is recognized that self-evaluation is influenced by both the need to maintain a realistic, coherent conceptual system and the need for self-enhancement. The interaction of these two needs fosters a modest degree of self-enhancement. Thus, the observation that well-adjusted people have moderate positive illusions does not indicate that reality awareness is an inadequate criterion of adjustment, but only that it is not the sole criterion.

* * *

The experiential system is assumed to be intimately associated with the experience of affect, including vibes, which refer to subtle feelings of which people are often unaware. When a person responds to an emotionally significant event, the sequence of reactions is assumed to be as follows: The experiential system automatically searches its memory banks for related events, including their emotional accompaniments. The recalled feelings influence the course of further processing and reactions, which in subhuman animals are actions and in humans are conscious and unconscious thoughts as well as actions. If the activated feelings are pleasant, they motivate actions and thoughts anticipated to reproduce the feelings. If the feelings are unpleasant, they motivate actions and thoughts anticipated to avoid the feelings.

As in psychoanalysis, CEST assumes there is a

ubiquitous influence of automatic thinking outside of awareness on conscious thinking and behavior. In most situations, the automatic processing of the experiential system is dominant over the rational system because it is less effortful and more efficient, and, accordingly, is the default option. Moreover, because it is generally associated with affect, it is apt to be experienced as more compelling than is dispassionate logical thinking. Finally, because the influence is usually outside of awareness, the rational system fails to control it because the person does not know there is anything to control. The advantage of insight, in such situations, is that it permits control, at least within limits. Thus, CEST does not diminish the importance of the unconscious in human behavior, relative to psychoanalysis, but emphasizes a different source of unconscious influence.

* * *

Research Support

As already noted, most of the multimodal processing theories that have been cited are supported by extensive research findings that are consistent with principles proposed by CEST. It is beyond the scope of the present article to review this vast literature. Instead, the focus is on examples of research explicitly designed to test hypotheses derived from CEST.

Research on Heuristic Processing Heuristic processing refers to the use of cognitive shortcuts for arriving at decisions. In a highly influential series of studies on decisional processes. Tversky and Kahneman and their associates demonstrated that people typically think in nonrational, heuristic ways that are efficient but error prone in certain kinds of situations (reported in Kahneman, Slovic, & Tversky, 1982). Most impressive is the degree to which the principles of heuristic processing, inductively derived by Tversky, Kahneman, Nisbett, and other social–cognitive psychologists, are consistent with the principles of operation of the experiential system as deductively proposed by CEST (e.g., S. Epstein, 1983; S. Epstein et al., 1992). My associates and I were so impressed with this confluence that we embarked on an extensive research program to more thoroughly test the validity of the principles of the experiential system by using experimental paradigms that are modifications of those used by Tversky, Kahneman, and their associates. Examples of this research follow.

Arbitrary-outcome-oriented processing. Imagine a situation in which two individuals arrive at an airport 30 minutes after the scheduled departure of their flights. One learns that her flight left on time. The other learns that, due to a delay, her flight just left. Who is more upset? Tversky and Kahneman (1983) and their associates have found that in this and in a variety of similar vignettes they introduced—despite the fact that from a logical perspective the differences in the two versions should not matter—people reported they and others would be more upset in one of the versions.

When we had people respond to similar vignettes from two perspectives, how people actually behave (which was assumed to be primarily under the jurisdiction of the experiential system) and how a rational person would behave, the phenomenon was replicated in the first condition and all but disappeared in the second (S. Epstein et al., 1992). We also demonstrated that responding in the mode of the experiential system occurs to a greater extent in response to highly emotion-arousing stimuli than in response to less emotional stimuli. Moreover, once responding in the mode of the experiential system was activated, it influenced responding in the rational mode (i.e., people believed their nonrational, experientially determined judgments were rational).

The results of this study are consistent with the following assumptions in CEST: There are two interactive processing systems, experiential and rational; the experiential system is intimately associated with the experience of affect. The experiential system is an associationistic system. Processing in the mode of the experiential system and its influence on rational thinking can lead people to judge events that are only arbitrarily related as causally related.

The ratio–bias phenomenon. Because the experiential system is a concretive system, it is less able to comprehend abstract than concrete representations. I therefore hypothesized that it would be more responsive to absolute numbers than to ratios in probability figures, whereas processing in the rational mode would exhibit the reverse pattern. To test this hypothesis, Kirkpatrick and Epstein (1992) gave participants an opportunity to win money by drawing a red jelly bean from one of two bowls, a "small bowl" that contained 1 in 10 red jelly beans and a "large bowl" that contained 10 in 100 red jelly beans. On every trial in which they wished to ensure their choice of bowls, they had to pay a dime; otherwise the selection of bowls was determined randomly. Most participants expressed a preference for the large bowl, and, of these, a considerable proportion paid dimes for the privilege of doing so. Several spontaneously commented that they felt foolish paying for a choice between equal probabilities, but, although they knew better, they felt they had a better chance of drawing a red bean when there were more of them. When, in another study in the same series, the problem was presented in the form of a vignette without an opportunity to win money, the vast majority said they had no preference and would not pay one cent for the privilege of picking from one bowl rather than from the other. However, when asked to guess how most people would respond, they said that most people would prefer to draw from the large bowl. It was concluded that people have a need to present themselves as rational, and therefore, in order to demonstrate what we have labeled the "ratio–bias phenomenon," it is necessary to either bypass the rational system by using indirect techniques (such as by having subjects estimate the behavior of others) or to strongly engage the experiential system by providing significant rewards.

The ratio–bias phenomenon has since been replicated in a more extreme version, in which unequal probabilities are offered in the small (10 jelly beans) and large (100 jelly beans) bowls. In two experiments (Denes-Raj & Epstein, 1994), most subjects made nonoptimal choices, preferring a 9% chance of winning in the large bowl to a 10% chance of winning in the small bowl. A substantial minority (20%–30%) even chose to draw from the large bowl when it offered only a 5% chance of winning, in preference to the small bowl, which always offered a 10% chance of winning. On interviewing the participants who made nonoptimal choices, many reported a conflict between what they objectively knew were the better odds and the bowl that offered more winners. Among those who made optimal choices, some said that they could not imagine why anyone would make nonoptimal choices. In contrast, others said they had to override the temptation to draw from the large bowl.

The jelly-bean experiments in their various versions provide support for the following hypotheses: There are two fundamentally different modes of processing information, rational and experiential, which can conflict with each other. The experiential system can override the rational system even when subjects know the appropriate rational response. The experiential system is more responsive to concrete than to abstract representations.

* * *

Implications

According to CEST, the experiential system processes information over a wide range of complexity. In its lower and moderate reaches, its operation is manifested in conditioning and in the rapid and crude processing identified as heuristics. It is important to recognize that even at simple levels, the experiential system under many circumstances is more effective in solving problems than the rational system (e.g., S. Epstein et al., in press; Lewicki, Hill, & Czyzewska, 1992). It has also been demonstrated that people often have intuitive knowledge that they can effectively apply without being aware of the principles that are involved (e.g., S. Epstein et al., in press; Nisbett & Ross,

1980). Moreover, rational analysis can interfere with the efficient functioning of the experiential system, resulting in poorer judgments than when people rely on their unanalyzed, intuitive impressions (Wilson & Schooler, 1991).

The experiential system also has the capacity to operate at a higher level of complexity (e.g., Fisk & Schneider, 1983; Lewicki et al., 1992) and to contribute to intuitive wisdom (e.g., Bucci, 1985). This is an important area for research about which relatively little is currently known, very likely because there has been an absence of theory for encouraging such research. * * *

Another important implication follows from the intimate association of the experiential system with emotions. As a result, the content and organization of the schemata in the experiential system are associated with physical as well as with mental well-being. Such a relation has been well demonstrated in a series of studies on emotional and minor physical disorders (e.g., S. Epstein, 1987, 1990, 1991a, 1992a, 1992b, 1993a; S. Epstein & Katz, 1992; S. Epstein & Meier, 1989; Katz & Epstein, 1991). That the processing in the experiential system has the potential for influencing the course of more serious diseases is suggested by unusual cures that have been attributed to faith healing, shamanism, and placebo effects. An important challenge for future research is to learn how to harness the power of the experiential system for alleviating illness and promoting well-being. Integration within and between systems will very likely be found to be important in this respect. A remarkable case history (A. Epstein, 1989) revealed the potential of such an approach in the treatment of a case of cancer from which the likelihood of remission was negligible. Following the use of fantasy procedures designed to communicate with the experiential system, there was a rapid reorganization of personality followed by complete recovery from the disease.

* * *

As already noted, CEST, through its assumption of an experiential system, can account for important behavioral phenomena, such as the ubiquity of superstitions and religion and the nature of appeals in politics and in advertising, about which other global personality theories have had little to say. The experiential system also has important implications for various disciplines in psychology, particularly personality, social, developmental, and clinical psychology. It is beyond the scope of this article to consider these in detail. However, a few major implications can be briefly discussed.

For personality psychology, the introduction of an experiential system that operates according to principles of processing information that differ from those of a primary process and a rational system can produce a theory with powerful integrative capacity. By introducing an adaptive, dynamic unconscious that automatically organizes experience and directs behavior, CEST is able to fill the very large void in psychoanalytic theory between rational thinking, on the one hand, and the primary process on the other. As a result (and in combination with other aspects of the theory), CEST is able to integrate significant aspects of a wide variety of personality theories, including psychoanalytic theories, learning theories, Kelly's (1955) theory of constructive alternativism, Rogers's (1959) and others' phenomenological theories, and modern cognitive theories, within a single framework (for elaboration of this position, see S. Epstein, 1980, 1983, 1985, 1991b, 1993b, 1993c).

* * *

For social psychology, CEST provides a theoretical perspective for interpreting findings on heuristic and automatic processing. There are a number of domain-specific theories in social psychology, including dual-processing theories of impression formation and stereotyping (e.g., Brewer, 1988; Chaiken, 1980; Fazio, 1990; Fiske, 1981; Petty & Cacioppo, 1986) and theories of judgment under uncertainly (see review in Fiske & Taylor, 1991, and studies in Kahneman et al., 1982), both of which refer to heuristics, but have not been related to each other. CEST may provide a basis for moving this field toward a greater integration.

* * *

The principles of operation of the experiential system have implications for the nature of prejudice. As the experiential system operates in a manner that is categorical, holistic, concrete, associationistic, and action oriented, it can be expected that people will tend to automatically seek personalized targets for their frustrations. Moreover, as people, according to CEST, organize reality largely in terms of their implicit theories of self, and as they have a vested interest in enhancing their conceptions of self, they will have a tendency to attribute what they view as bad or distressing to those outside of their identification group. Thus, it can be deduced from the nature of the experiential system that prejudice comes all too naturally to people. It follows that people do not have to be taught to be prejudiced; they have to be taught to not be prejudiced.

With respect to developmental psychology, CEST draws attention to the importance of studying the separate development of the experiential and rational systems, rather than assuming that they progress sequentially, with the latter displacing the former (S. Epstein & Erskine, 1983; Werner & Kaplan, 1963).

As for clinical psychology, CEST has important implications for diagnosis and therapy (S. Epstein, 1983, 1984, 1985, 1987, 1991a, 1991b, 1992a, 1993a, 1993c; S. Epstein & Brodsky, 1993). According to CEST, the objective of therapy is to produce changes in the experiential system. There are three basic procedures for accomplishing this: (a) using the rational system to influence the experiential system (e.g., disputing irrational thoughts, as in cognitive therapy), (b) learning directly from emotionally significant experiences (e.g., through "working through" in real life, and through constructive relationships with significant others, including therapists), and (c) communicating with the experiential system in its own medium, namely fantasy. This latter approach is particularly promising because not only can the rational system use directed fantasy to influence the experiential system but it can learn from the intuitive wisdom of the experiential system through knowledge of how that system operates. These three fundamental approaches provide a unifying framework for integrating various approaches to therapy, including insight approaches, cognitive–behavioral approaches, and experiential approaches, such as Gestalt therapy and psychosynthesis (S. Epstein, 1993c; S. Epstein & Brodsky, 1993).

Finally, and most important, the assumption that we think in two fundamentally different modes has implications for human survival. Einstein said that unless we learn to think differently, we are doomed to self-extinction. He was, of course, referring to the atom bomb. Today, there are other equally significant threats, including pollution of the environment, global warming, depletion of the ozone layer, overpopulation, the failure of our social institutions, and widespread ethnic strife. Considering that we have made this mess for ourselves, if we ever had to learn to think differently, it is now. As a first step, it is important that we learn how we do think. How we do think, I believe, is with two minds, experiential and rational. Our hope lies in learning to understand both of our minds and how to use them in a harmonious manner. Failing to understand the operation of the experiential mind and its influence on the rational mind, try as we may to be rational, our rationality will be undermined by our inherently experiential nature. Cultivating them both, we may be able to achieve greater wisdom than would seem likely from our past history.

References

Adler, A. (1954). *Understanding human nature.* New York: Fawcett.

Allport, G. W. (1961). *Pattern and growth in personality.* New York: Holt, Rinehart & Winston.

Behavior. (1991, March 9). *Science News,* p. 159.

Bowlby, J. (1988). *A secure base.* New York: Basic Books.

Brewer, M. B. (1988). A dual process model of impression formation. In T. K. Srull & R. S. Wyer, Jr. (Eds.). *Advances in social cognition* (Vol. 1, pp. 1–36). Hillsdale, NJ: Erlbaum.

Bruner, J. S. (1986). *Actual minds, possible worlds.* Cambridge, MA: Harvard University Press.

Bucci, W. (1985). Dual coding: A cognitive model for psychoanalytic research. *Journal of the American Psychoanalytic Association, 33,* 571–607.

Chaiken, S. (1980). Heuristic versus systematic information processing and the use of source versus message cues in persuasion. *Journal of Personality and Social Psychology, 39,* 752–766.

Denes-Raj, V., & Epstein, S. (1994). Conflict between experiential and rational processing: When people behave against their better judgment. *Journal of Personality and Social Psychology, 66,* 819–827.

Epstein, A. (1989). *Mind, fantasy, and healing.* New York: Delacorte.

Epstein, S. (1973). The self-concept revisited, or a theory of a theory. *American Psychologist, 28,* 404–416.

Epstein, S. (1979). Natural healing processes of the mind: I. Acute schizophrenic disorganization. *Schizophrenia Bulletin, 5,* 313–320.

Epstein, S. (1980). The self-concept: A review and the proposal of an integrated theory of personality. In E. Staub (Ed.), *Personality: Basic issues and current research* (pp. 82–132). Englewood Cliffs, NJ: Prentice Hall.

Epstein, S. (1983). The unconscious, the preconscious and the self-concept. In J. Suls & A. Greenwald (Eds.), *Psychological perspectives on the self* (Vol. 2, pp. 219–247). Hillsdale, NJ: Erlbaum.

Epstein, S. (1984). Controversial issues in emotion theory. In P. Shaver (Ed.), *Annual review of research in personality and social psychology* (pp. 64–87). Beverly Hills, CA: Sage.

Epstein, S. (1985). The implications of cognitive–experiential self-theory for research in social psychology and personality. *Journal for the Theory of Social Behaviour, 15,* 283–310.

Epstein, S. (1987). Implications of cognitive self-theory for psychopathology and psychotherapy. In N. Cheshire & H. Thomae (Eds.), *Self, symptoms and psychotherapy* (pp. 43–58). New York: Wiley.

Epstein, S. (1990). Cognitive–experiential self-theory. In L. Pervin (Ed.), *Handbook of personality: Theory and research* (pp. 165–192). New York: Guilford Press.

Epstein, S. (1991a). The self-concept, the traumatic neurosis, and the structure of personality. In D. Ozer, J. M. Healy, Jr., & A. J. Stewart (Eds.), *Perspectives in personality* (Vol. 3A, pp. 63–98). London: Jessica Kingsley.

Epstein, S. (1991b). Cognitive–experiential self-theory: An integrative theory of personality. In R. Curtis (Ed.), *The relational self: Convergences in psychoanalysis and social psychology* (pp. 111–137). New York: Guilford Press.

Epstein, S. (1992a). Constructive thinking and mental and physical well-being. In L. Montada, S. H. Filipp, & M. J. Lerner (Eds.), *Life crises & experiences of loss in adulthood* (pp. 385–409). Hillsdale, NJ: Erlbaum.

Epstein, S. (1992b). Coping ability, negative self-evaluation, and overgeneralization: Experiment and theory. *Journal of Personality and Social Psychology, 62,* 826–836.

Epstein, S. (1993a). Bereavement from the perspective of cognitive–experiential self-theory. In M. S. Stroebe, W. Stroebe, & R. O. Hansson (Eds.), *Handbook of bereavement: Theory, research, and intervention* (pp. 112–125). New York: Cambridge University Press.

Epstein, S. (1993b). Emotion and self-theory. In M. Lewis & J. Haviland (Eds.), *Handbook of emotions* (pp. 313–326). New York: Guilford Press.

Epstein, S. (1993c). Implications of cognitive–experiential self-theory for personality and developmental psychology. In D. Funder, R. Parke, C. Tomlinson-Keasey, & K. Widamen (Eds.), *Studying lives through time: Personality and development* (pp. 399–438). Washington, DC: American Psychological Association.

Epstein, S., & Brodsky, A. (1993). *You're smarter than you think.* New York: Simon & Schuster.

Epstein, S., Denes-Raj, V., & Pacini, R. (in press). The Linda problem revisited from the perspective of cognitive-experiential self-theory. *Journal of the Society for Personality and Social Psychology.*

Epstein, S., & Erskine, N. (1983). The development of personal theories of reality. In D. Magnusson & V. Allen (Eds.), *Human development: An Interactional perspective* (pp. 133–147). New York: Academic Press.

Epstein, S., & Katz, L. (1992). Coping ability, stress, productive load, and symptoms. *Journal of Personality and Social Psychology, 62,* 813–825.

Epstein, S., Lipson, A., Holstein, C., & Huh, E. (1992). Irrational reactions to negative outcomes: Evidence for two conceptual systems. *Journal of Personality and Social Psychology, 62,* 328–339.

Epstein, S., & Meier, P. (1989). Constructive thinking: A broad coping variable with specific components. *Journal of Personality and Social Psychology, 57,* 332–350.

Fairbairn, W. R. D. (1954). *An object relations theory of the personality.* New York: Basic Books.

Fazio, R. H. (1990). Multiple processes by which attitudes guide behavior. The mode model as an integrative framework. *Advances in Experimental Social Psychology, 23,* 75–109.

Fisk, A. D., & Schneider, W. (1983). Category and word search: Generalizing search principles to complex processing. *Journal of Experimental Psychology: Learning, Memory, and Cognition, 9,* 177–195.

Fiske, S. T. (1981). Social cognition and affect. In J. Harvey (Ed.), *Cognition, social behavior, and the environment* (pp. 227–264). Hillsdale, NJ: Erlbaum.

Fiske, S. T., & Taylor, S. E. (1991). *Social cognition* (2nd ed.). New York: McGraw Hill.

Freud, S. (1959). *Beyond the pleasure principle.* New York: Norton, (Original work published 1920)

Hall, C. S., & Lindzey, G. (1978). *Theories of personality* (3rd ed.). New York: Wiley.

Horowitz, M. J. (1976). *Stress response syndromes.* Northvale, NJ: Jason Aronson.

Janoff-Bulman, R. (1992). *Shattered assumptions.* New York: Free Press.

Jones, E. (1955). *The life and work of Sigmund Freud* (Vol. 2). New York: Basic Books.

Kahneman, D., Slovic, P., & Tversky, A. (1982). *Judgment under uncertainty: Heuristics and biases.* New York: Cambridge University Press.

Kahneman, D., & Tversky, A. (1973). On the psychology of prediction. *Psychological Review, 80,* 237–251.

Katz, L., & Epstein, S. (1991). Constructive thinking and coping with laboratory-induced stress. *Journal of Personality and Social Psychology, 61,* 789–800.

Kelly, G. A. (1955). *The psychology of personal constructs* (2 vols.). New York: Norton.

Kihlstrom, J. F. (1990). The psychological unconscious. In L. Pervin (Ed.), *Handbook of personality: Theory and research* (pp. 445–464). New York: Guilford Press.

Kirkpatrick, L. A., & Epstein, S. (1992). Cognitive–experiential self-theory and subjective probability: Further evidence for two conceptual systems. *Journal of Personality and Social Psychology, 63*, 534–544.

Kohut, H. (1971). *The analysis of the self.* New York: International Universities Press.

Lecky, P. (1961). *Self-consistency: A theory of personality.* Hamden, CT: Shoe String Press.

Lewicki, P., Hill, T., & Czyzewska, M. (1992). Nonconscious acquisition of information. *American Psychologist, 47*, 796–801.

McCann, I. L., & Pearlman, L. A. (1990). *Psychological trauma and the adult survivor: Theory, therapy, and transformation.* New York: Brunner/Mazel.

Nisbett, R., & Ross, L. (1980). *Human inference: Strategies and shortcomings of social judgment.* Englewood Cliffs, NJ: Prentice Hall.

Pavlov, I. P. (1941). *Conditioned reflexes and psychiatry* (W. H. Gantt, Trans.). New York: International Universities Press.

Perry, J. W. (1976). *Roots of renewal in myth and madness.* San Francisco: Jossey-Bass.

Petty, R. E., & Cacioppo, J. T. (1986). *Communication and persuasion: Central and peripheral routes to attitude change.* New York: Springer-Verlag.

Rogers, C. R. (1959). A theory of therapy, personality, and interpersonal relationships, as developed in the client-centered framework. In S. Koch (Ed.), *Psychology: A study of a science* (Vol. 3, pp. 184–256). New York: McGraw-Hill.

Taylor, S. E., & Brown, J. D. (1988). Illusion and well-being: A social psychological perspective on mental health. *Psychological Bulletin, 103*, 193–210.

Tversky, A., & Kahneman, D. (1983). Extensional versus intuitive reasoning. The conjunction fallacy in probability judgment. *Psychological Review, 90*, 293–315.

Werner, H., & Kaplan, B. (1963). *Symbol formation.* Hillsdale, NJ: Erlbaum.

Wilson, T. D., & Schooler, J. W. (1991). Thinking too much: Introspection can reduce the quality of preferences and decisions. *Journal of Personality and Social Psychology, 60*, 181–192.

Effects of Ruminative and Distracting Responses to Depressed Mood on Retrieval of Autobiographical Memories

Sonja Lyubomirsky, Nicole D. Caldwell, and Susan Nolen-Hoeksema

The next selection is an example of what the best research in the cognitive approach to personality looks like. In this article, Sonja Lyubomirsky and her colleagues explain the difference between "dysphorics"—unhappy people who are not clinically depressed—and people who do not suffer from chronic unhappiness. They do so in terms of what both kinds of people think about—specifically, the way they do (or do not) ruminate about their own feelings.

Dysphorics disproportionately attend to and recall negative stimuli, which helps to create and to perpetuate their generally negative mood. Nondysphorics are more able to direct their attention elsewhere and to cease ruminating about things that only serve to make them more upset. In a series of clever experiments, Lyubomirsky demonstrates how individual differences of this sort can be explained in terms of different styles of cognition.

Personality psychology usually is not viewed as an experimental science, because—it is thought—individual differences can be studied only correlationally. The present article shows that this view is wrong. Through experimental manipulation of the kind of thinking that correlational methods have revealed to be characteristic of certain types of people, it is possible to build a strong case that styles of thinking actually cause, and are not just correlated with, personality-relevant outcomes.

From *Journal of Personality and Social Psychology, 75*, 166–177, 1998.

Most, if not all, psychotherapies require clients to explore their autobiographical memories—in the form of either describing problems and experiences from the very recent past (e.g., yesterday) or contemplating events from long ago (e.g., one's childhood). However, if the client suffers from depressed mood, the most common complaint of individuals seeking therapy (Strickland, 1992), and shows a ruminative style of responding to that mood (Nolen-Hoeksema,

1991), he or she may generate a negatively biased set of memories. For example, a woman who engages in self-focused rumination (i.e, repetitively focusing on the meanings and implications of her negative feelings) may identify her presenting problems to the therapist as impending divorce and unemployment, recalling escalating arguments with her husband and reprimands by her boss, when in reality the arguments and the reprimands have been few and far between. This article reports four studies[1] that examined this phenomenon, all of which tested the general hypothesis that rumination in the presence of a depressed mood leads to the retrieval of negatively biased autobiographical memories.

Ruminative responses to depressed mood involve thinking about how sad, apathetic, and tired one feels (e.g., "I just can't get going"), wondering about the causes of one's depressive symptoms (e.g., "What's wrong with me that I feel this way?"), and worrying about their implications (e.g., "What if I can't muster the energy to go to work tomorrow?"), without doing anything constructive to relieve the symptoms or improve one's mood (Nolen-Hoeksema, 1991). Thus, unlike those who have recently reconceptualized rumination as instrumental (Martin & Tesser, 1996; see also Wyer, 1996), we view ruminative responses to dysphoria as a type of thinking that is generally *not* adaptive. An instrumental and adaptive alternative, by contrast, is using pleasant or neutral distractions to lift one's mood and relieve one's depressive symptoms before engaging in problem solving (Nolen-Hoeksema, 1991). Distracting responses are activities and thoughts that help divert one's attention away from one's depressed mood and its consequences—for example, going for a run, seeing a movie with friends, or concentrating on a hobby or one's work.

Many people believe that when they become depressed or dysphoric, they should try to focus inward and analyze their feelings and their problems to gain self-insight and find solutions. The tendency to engage in rumination in response to a depressed mood appears to be both a relatively common (Rippere, 1977) and stable coping style (Nolen-Hoeksema, Morrow, & Fredrickson, 1993; Nolen-Hoeksema, Parker & Larson, 1994). An increasing number of studies, however, suggest that rather than serving as an antidote to depression, self-focusing and rumination actually exacerbate and prolong depressed mood (for reviews, see Carver & Scheier, 1990; Ingram, 1990; Nolen-Hoeksema, 1991; Pyszczynski & Greenberg, 1987). Distraction from one's mood, by contrast, appears to lift dysphoria. In laboratory studies, manipulations of rumination or self-focus increase or maintain depressed mood in dysphoric or clinically depressed participants, whereas manipulations of distraction or external focus significantly relieve depressed mood (Barden, Garber, Leiman, Ford, & Masters, 1985; Fennell & Teasdale, 1984; Gibbons et al., 1985; Lyubomirsky & Nolen-Hoeksema, 1993, 1995; Morrow & Nolen-Hoeksema, 1990; Nolen-Hoeksema & Morrow, 1993). Longitudinal studies reveal that people who respond to naturally occurring dysphoria (e.g., due to negative or traumatic life events) with a ruminative style report longer and more severe periods of depressed mood than people who use pleasant distractions to manage their moods (Nolen-Hoeksema & Morrow, 1991; Nolen-Hoeksema et al., 1993; Nolen-Hoeksema. McBride, & Larson, 1997; Nolen-Hoeksema et al., 1994; Wood, Saltzberg, Neale, Stone, & Rachmiel, 1990; see also Saltzberg, 1992). For example, recently bereaved individuals with a ruminative coping style were more depressed both shortly after their loss and over the next 6 months than people without a ruminative coping style, even after their initial levels of dysphoria were controlled (Nolen-Hoeksema et al., 1994).

Previously, we have argued that dysphoric rumination exacerbates and prolongs depressed mood in part through its effects on negative thinking and poor problem solving (Lyubomirsky & Nolen-Hoeksema, 1995). A number of studies provide evidence that ruminative responses to depressed mood, relative to distracting ones, lead to

[1]The original article included four studies; only two are included here.

pessimistic attributions for hypothetical problems and upsetting experiences (e.g., "I don't seem to succeed in anything I do"); negatively biased and distorted interpretations of hypothetical life events (e.g., "I must be a loser to stay home alone on a Saturday night"); and pessimistic predictions about one's future after college (Lyubomirsky & Nolen-Hoeksema, 1995; see also Pyszczynski, Holt, & Greenberg, 1987), the likelihood of solving one's problems (Lyubomirsky, Caldwell, & Berg, 1997), and the likelihood of engaging in fun activities (Lyubomirsky & Nolen-Hoeksema, 1993). A recent study also suggested that people who respond to depressed mood by ruminating about themselves and their feelings show impaired problem-solving skills (Lyubomirsky & Nolen-Hoeksema, 1995). Dysphoric individuals induced to ruminate generated less effective solutions to hypothetical interpersonal or achievement problems than dysphoric individuals induced to distract (see also Brockner, 1979; Brockner & Hulton, 1978; Strack, Blaney, Ganellen, & Coyne, 1985). In all of these studies, dysphoric participants instructed to distract their attention away from their moods for 8 min were no more pessimistic or impaired in their problem solving than nondysphorics.

Naturalistic, correlational studies further bolster the laboratory evidence. People who are prone to ruminate when dysphoric show more dispositional pessimism and less of a tendency to engage in active problem solving in stressful times (Nolen-Hoeksema & Jackson, 1996; Nolen-Hoeksema et al., 1994). In turn, dispositional pessimism and lack of problem solving partially mediate the relationship between the tendency to ruminate and elevated levels of depressed mood.

How do ruminative responses to depressed mood promote negative thinking and poor problem solving? One critical way may be by enhancing dysphoric individuals' memories of negative events in the past. Indeed, autobiographical memories may be the most essential and basic elements of thinking and problem solving. For example, to reach a pessimistic conclusion (e.g., "My marriage is in trouble") or make a pessimistic attribution (e.g., ". . . and I'm to blame"), a man might recall recent (if trivial) spats with his spouse and his role in starting them. Or, when pondering what will happen if she says depressed, a woman might selectively remember occasions on which her symptoms have hampered her work or social life and conclude. "I'm a failure." Likewise, negatively biased memories may interfere with every stage of the problem-solving process (D'Zurilla & Goldfried, 1971). For example, an individual might perceive a problem (e.g., finding a new job) as overwhelming and uncontrollable, failing to select and implement effective job search strategies (e.g., obtaining a "headhunter," calling contacts), after recalling mediocre job interviews in college or instances of negative feedback received from colleagues. Negatively biased autobiographical memories may thus play an important role in a number of depression-enhancing cognitive processes, including pessimistic predictions and attributions; depressive and distorted interpretations, inferences, and conclusions; and ineffective problem-solving strategies (cf. Beck, Rush, Shaw, & Emery, 1979).

It is important at this point to note the intimate, if dangerous, relationship between rumination, mood, and memory. People typically engage in rumination—that is, try to answer questions about why they are depressed and what will be the consequences—by generating relevant memories from the recent past. However, ruminative responses to depressed mood are likely to draw one's attention to the network of negative memories associated with that mood, making such memories more accessible and likely to be easily retrieved (e.g., Blaney, 1986; Bower, 1981, 1991; Forgas, 1991). Ruminative responses are also self-focused, increasing the availability of negative thoughts and memories about the self (e.g., Duval & Wicklund, 1972; Pyszczynski et al., 1987; Pyszczynski, Hamilton, Herring, & Greenberg, 1989). Numerous studies have provided evidence for the link between negative moods and negative memories. Individuals who are mildly or clinically depressed or in whom a sad mood has been induced have been found to recall a greater number of unhappy life events (Clark & Teasdale, 1982; Natale & Hantas, 1982; Snyder & White, 1982), to recall experiences that are more negative (Clark & Teasdale, 1982; Lewinsohn & Rosenbaum, 1987; Madigan & Bollenbach, 1982), and to recall negative events faster (Lloyd & Lishman, 1975; Rholes, Riskind, & Lane, 1987; Teasdale & Fogarty, 1979; Williams & Scott, 1988) than nondepressed individuals or those in whom a happy or neutral mood has been induced. People who ruminate while in a depressed mood may be especially likely to retrieve or pay attention to these negative memories and to use them in interpreting their current situation. In turn, these negative memories may further exacerbate depressed mood through their effects on negative thinking and poor problem solving (as described above), thus feeding a vicious cycle between rumination, mood, and negative thinking (Teasdale, 1983).

The Present Studies

The primary hypothesis explored in our * * * studies is that instructions inducing dysphoric individuals to ruminate would lead them to retrieve more negatively biased memories from their past than instructions encouraging distraction. By contrast, rumination and distraction were not expected to influence the valence of memories in the absence of a depressed mood. Consequently, nondysphoric individuals were predicted to generate the least negative memories of all our participants because their mood would not prompt negative memories, because they are likely to have experienced fewer negative events than dysphoric individuals, and because rumination and distraction do not appear to have differential effects on negative thinking in the absence of depressed mood (Lyubomirsky & Nolen-Hoeksema, 1993, 1995).

Autobiographical memories were elicited through four different paradigms. In Study 1, participants were given 5 min to recall as many events and experiences from their lives as they could. In Study 2, participants were prompted by a computer to recall two specific positive experiences and two negative ones. * * *

Study 1

METHOD

Overview Dysphoric and nondysphoric students engaged in either a ruminative or distracting task, then spent 5 min recalling personal memories from their lives. Subsequently, participants rated the memories that they had generated for their hedonic tone. Depressed mood was assessed before and after the response manipulation task.

Participants Seventy-two introductory psychology students (48 women and 24 men) received course credit for their participation in this study. Potential participants completed the Beck Depression Inventory (BDI; Beck, 1967) as part of a larger packet of unrelated questionnaires administered at the beginning of the quarter. We recruited students with BDI scores above 16 for the moderately dysphoric group and students with BDI scores below 5 for the nondysphoric group. Because the BDI has demonstrated high test–retest stability within 2 weeks among college undergraduates (Pearson's r = .90; Lightfoot & Oliver, 1985), we conducted this study within 2 weeks after the 38 dysphoric (24 women and 14 men) and 34 nondysphoric (24 women and 10 men) participants had completed the BDI.

Materials

Mood questionnaires. Following previous recommendations (Kendall, Hollon, Beck, Hammen, & Ingram, 1987), we administered mood questionnaires at the beginning of the experiment as well as immediately following the response task manipulation (i.e., induction of rumination or distraction). Each packet contained a questionnaire that asked participants to rate their present state, including levels of sadness and depression, on Likert-type scales (1 = *not at all*, 9 = *extremely*). Ratings of sadness and depression were averaged to arrive at a single measure of depressed mood at each assessment. * * * Our Likert-type scale measures of mood at the beginning of the experimental hour were found to be highly correlated with participants' preexperimental BDI scores (Pearson's *rs* ranged from .76 to .86). To further obscure the intent of the study, we included several filler tasks, such as paper-and-pencil inventories about imagining colors and recalling one's dreams, in the packets of mood scales.

Response manipulation tasks. The response manipulation tasks were designed to influence the content of participants' thoughts by requiring them to focus their attention and "think about" a series of 45 items (adapted from Lyubomirsky & Nolen-Hoeksema, 1993, 1995; Nolen-Hoeksema & Morrow, 1993; Morrow & Nolen-Hoeksema, 1990). Following Nolen-Hoeksema's (1991) definition of ruminative responses, the rumination condition instructed students to focus their attention on thoughts that were emotion focused, symptom focused, and self-focused, although they were not told specifically to think about negative emotions or negative personal attributes. For example, participants were asked to think about "your current level of energy," "why your body feels this way," "trying to understand your feelings," "your character and who you strive to be," and "why you turned out this way." In contrast, participants in the distraction condition focused their attention on thoughts that were focused externally and not related to symptoms, emotions, or the self. For example, they were asked to think about "clouds forming in the sky," "the expression on the face of the *Mona Lisa*," and "the shiny surface of a trumpet." The items in the rumination and distraction conditions were rated as equally neutral by nondysphoric judges. In each condition, participants spent exactly 8 min focusing on the items.

Free recall task. Participants were given 5 min to recall and list autobiographical memories from their lives. They were instructed that all events and experiences were acceptable as long as they were definite and specific experiences from memory (either in the recent or distant past) and not merely current thought associations, images, dreams, or plans. No limit was placed on the number of memories recalled.

Memory rating task. After the 5-min period, students were asked to review all of the personal memories that they had previously listed and rate each event or experience on four dimensions; (a) "How positive is this event or experience?" (1 = *not at all positive*, 7 = *very positive*), (b) "How happy do you feel about this event or experience looking back on it now?" (1 = *not at all happy*, 7 = *very happy*), (c) "How negative is this event or experience?" (1 = *not at all negative*, 7 = *very negative*), and (d) "How unhappy do you feel about this event or experience looking back on it now?" (1 = *not at all unhappy*, 7 = *very unhappy*). We averaged the first two ratings to yield an overall index of positivity and averaged the second two ratings to yield an overall index of negativity. Finally, we computed a single composite positivity index by subtracting the negative ratings from the positive ones.

Procedure All participants were run individually, with the experimenter unaware of participants' dysphoria status and response manipulation condition. We used an elaborate cover story to minimize possible demand characteristics. At the beginning of the experiment, students were told that they would be participating in a series of short, independent studies put together by a number of different researchers investigating "processes of imagination, dreaming, levels of consciousness, and cognition in general." This cover story was supported by a number of neutral filler tasks, which were included in the questionnaire packets that participants completed throughout the experiment. Half of these filler tasks were distracting (e.g., imagining colors) and half were self-focused (e.g., recalling one's dreams). Participants' responses on a debriefing questionnaire and their comments during oral debriefing indicated that the cover story was successful. No participant guessed the purpose of the study or the link between the response manipulations and the memory tasks.

After describing the cover story, the experimenter gave participants the first packet of questionnaires, which contained baseline measures of depressed mood, and left the laboratory room. After participants were done with the first packet, the experimenter reentered the laboratory room and introduced the response manipulation task. This task was described as an imagination task requiring participants "to focus [their] mind on a series of ideas and thoughts" and to "use [their] ability to visualize and concentrate." Participants were instructed to spend exactly 8 min on this task. * * * After the allotted time, the experimenter returned and asked participants to complete the next packet of questionnaires, which contained the second set of mood measures as well as several filler tasks.

During the next phase, the experimenter administered the timed free recall task. Participants were told, "We are interested in the process by which people recall events and experiences from their lives." After the allotted 5-min period, the experimenter returned and instructed students to rate each of their listed memories on hedonic tone.

After completing the memory tasks, participants filled out a final packet of questionnaires, which included several filler measures and a debriefing questionnaire. The experimenter then returned and thoroughly debriefed each participant. The entire study lasted approximately 1 hr.

RESULTS AND DISCUSSION We predicted that relative to the dysphoric participants who distracted themselves or either of the nondysphoric groups, the dysphoric participants who ruminated would recall more negatively biased memories. However, because students in the dysphoric–distracting group were induced to distract for only 8 min, and because they are likely to have had more negative events in their past than the nondysphoric groups, our primary hypothesis led us to expect not that dysphoric distractors' ratings would necessarily be identical to those of the students in the two nondysphoric groups but rather that they would fall somewhere in between those of the dysphoric–ruminative students and the nondysphoric students. Rosenthal and Rosnow (1985; see also Rosnow & Rosenthal, 1989, 1995) argued that the appropriate way to test such focused predictions is by planned contrasts rather than by two-way analyses of variance. Thus, analyses using planned contrasts comparing the dysphoric–ruminative group with the other three groups were performed on all the dependent measures of interest. In addition, separate linear planned contrasts were conducted, testing whether dysphoric ruminators exhibited the most extreme responses, followed by dysphoric distractors, and, finally, by the two nondysphoric groups (contrast weights 2, 1, −1.5, and −1.5, respectively). For similar procedures, see Lyubomirsky and Nolen-Hoeksema (1993, 1995); Lyubomirsky et al. (1997).

Because there were no main effects or interactions with sex, all analyses were conducted by collapsing across sex of students. There were 18 students in the dysphoric–ruminative group, 20 in the dysphoric–distracting group, 17 in the nondysphoric–ruminative group, and 17 in the nondysphoric–distracting group.

Mood Changes At the beginning of the study, students in the dysphoric group reported greater dysphoria ($M = 3.89$, $SD = 2.02$) than students in the nondysphoric group ($M = 2.39$, $SD = 1.77$), $t(66) = 3.28$, $p < .002$.[2] The results of a pairwise comparison on changes in depressed mood between dysphoric participants in the rumination and the distraction conditions revealed a significant difference between the two groups, showing that dysphorics who were instructed to ruminate became more depressed ($M = 0.86$, $SD = 2.47$)

[2] *M* is the mean, *SD* is the standard deviation, *t* is a standard test for the difference between groups, and *p* refers to the probability that a difference between the groups of this size would be found if, in fact, no difference existed. The abbreviation *ns* stands for "not significant."

and dysphorics who were instructed to distract became less depressed (M = 0.95, SD = 1.72), $F(1, 65)=10.82$, $p < .002$.[3] In contrast, no significant difference was found in changes in depressed mood between nondysphorics who ruminated (M = 0.44, SD = 0.90) or distracted (M = –0.44, SD = 1.20), $F < 3$, *ns*. The results of a planned contrast further showed that after the response task manipulation, dysphoric participants who ruminated displayed significantly higher levels of depressed mood than the remaining three groups, $F(1, 68) = 30.93$, $p < .0001$. Mean levels of depressed mood following the response task manipulation were as follows: dysphoric–ruminative, M = 5.12, SD = 1.75; dysphoric–distracting, M = 2.52, SD = 1.66; nondysphoric–ruminative, M = 2.62, SD = 2.35; and nondysphoric–distracting, M = 2.00, SD = 1.53.

Autobiographical Memories All participants recalled at least eight autobiographical memories, with the numbers of participants recalling more than eight dropping off dramatically for each additional memory. To preserve the highest possible sample size, we analyzed our data using the average of ratings for the first eight memories only. It should be noted, however, that analyses using more than eight memories (e.g., 10, 12, and 14) yielded results very similar to those reported. There was no significant difference in the numbers of memories recalled by our four groups ($F < 1$, *ns*).

Our primary hypothesis, that dysphoric rumination would lead to the retrieval of negative autobiographical memories, was confirmed. The results of planned contrasts analyzing the positivity and negativity rating composites showed that dysphoric participants who ruminated about themselves and their moods rated their own autobiographical memories as less positive and happy, $F(1, 68) = 12.41$, $p < .0008$, and more negative and unhappy, $F(1, 68) = 9.91$. $p < .003$, than did the other three groups. Linear contrasts further revealed that dysphoric ruminators showed the most extreme ratings, followed by dysphoric distractors, and then by the nondysphoric controls, both for positive assessments, $F(1, 68) = 14.76$, $p < .0003$, and for negative ones, $F(1, 68) = 19.42$, $p < .0001$. * * *

Similar results were obtained with the overall positivity composite (i.e., positive minus negative ratings). Dysphoric participants in the rumination condition recalled less positive memories overall than did the other three groups, $F(1, 68) = 12.58$, $p < .0007$ * * * . A linear contrast testing whether dysphoric ruminators recalled the least positive memories, followed by dysphoric distractors, and, finally, the two nondysphoric groups, was also significant, $F(1, 68) = 19.22$, $p < .0001$. * * * It is notable that the spontaneous autobiographical memories generated by dysphoric participants who ruminated were rated almost equally positive and negative, whereas the memories generated by the remaining three groups received much higher positive ratings than negative ones.

Study 2 further explored our primary hypothesis, with two important differences. First, evidence for negatively biased memories in Study 1 was derived from ratings of memories by the participants themselves. This was necessary because the descriptions of these memories were typically brief and ambiguous as to whether they were positive or negative to their author (e.g., "bumped into ex-boyfriend at party"). However, as a result, it is unclear whether self-focused rumination led dysphoric participants to recall more negative events or whether it simply led them to perceive neutral events more negatively as they looked back on them. Perceiving relatively neutral events negatively should still contribute to depressed mood in the dysphoric ruminators. Yet to evaluate further whether dysphoric ruminators actually recall more negative memories, Study 2 used a method that elicited descriptions of memories that were rich enough to permit independent assessment of

[3]The F's are statistics derived from the analysis of variance, which is a flexible technique for assessing differences between groups.

hedonic tone. In addition, unlike in Study 1, in Study 2 specific types of memories were elicited: two positive or happy ones and two negative or unhappy ones. We expected that even when specifically asked to retrieve happy and unhappy memories, dysphoric individuals induced to ruminate would recall the most negative (or least positive) experiences and events.

Study 2

METHOD

Overview Dysphoric and nondysphoric students were induced to either ruminate about themselves and their feelings or distract themselves by focusing externally. Subsequently, they were prompted to recall two unhappy memories and two happy memories from their lives. Depressed mood was measured before and after the response manipulation task. All tasks were performed on the computer.

Participants Forty-nine introductory psychology students (34 women and 15 men) participated in this study in exchange for course credit. As in Study 1, potential participants completed the BDI at the beginning of the quarter. Students with BDI scores above 16 were recruited for the moderately dysphoric group, and students with BDI scores below 5 were recruited for the nondysphoric group. Twenty-five dysphoric (18 women and 7 men) and 24 nondysphoric (16 women and 8 men) students participated, all within 2 weeks after completing the BDI.

Cued Memory Task This task was introduced in the same way as the free recall task (Study 1), except that students were instructed to recall only four memories, one specific memory at a time. Four memory cues were presented in a counterbalanced order, two to recall a "positive or happy event or experience from memory" and two to recall a "negative or unhappy" one. Participants were instructed to click on "begin" as soon as they retrieved the relevant cued memory and then type a description of this memory on the next screen. (Unlimited screen space was provided.) Subsequently, two independent judges, who were unaware of participants' dysphoria status and response manipulation condition, coded the memories on how positive and how negative they were (1 = *not at all*, 4 = *neutral*, 7 = *extremely*). Agreement between judges was adequate: The intraclass correlation coefficients ranged from .78 to .86 for positivity ratings and from .81 to .88 for negativity ratings.[4] We computed a composite negativity score by averaging the negativity rating and the positivity rating (reverse coded) for the two unhappy memories. Similarly, we computed a composite negativity score for the two happy memories.

Procedure The procedure was identical to that used in Study 1, except that the two mood assessments and the response manipulation task were presented and performed on an Apple computer. In addition, autobiographical memories were elicited by way of a cued memory task rather than a free recall task. At the beginning of the study, participants were instructed in how to use a mouse to move from screen to screen, as well as how to respond to questions by either clicking on the appropriate response (e.g., a number on a Likert-type scale) or typing directly into the computer (e.g., to describe a memory). The instruction for all tasks were given orally as well as via the computer. As in the previous study, participants completed filler paper-and-pencil questionnaires at the beginning and end of the study. A debriefing questionnaire was administered after participants were finished with all tasks.

RESULTS AND DISCUSSION Because there were no main effects or interactions with sex or memory order, we conducted all analyses by collapsing

---

[4]The intraclass correlation is a particular kind of correlation that can be used, among other purposes, to assess the degree of agreement between different judges of a common stimulus. These correlations are impressively high.

across these two variables. There were 12 participants in the dysphoric–ruminative group, 12 in the dysphoric–distracting group, 12 in the nondysphoric–ruminative group, and 13 in the nondysphoric–distracting group. Statistical analyses followed the procedures used in Study 1.

Mood Changes As in Study 1, dysphoric participants reported greater depressed mood at the outset of the experiment ($M = 4.18$, $SD = 1.46$) than did nondysphoric participants ($M = 2.04$, $SD = 1.23$), $t(46) = 5.55$, $p < .0001$. The results of a pairwise comparison on changes in depressed mood between dysphoric participants in the rumination and distraction conditions revealed a significant difference between the two groups, indicating that dysphorics who were induced to ruminate became more depressed ($M = 0.42$, $SD = 1.30$), and dysphorics who were induced to distract became less depressed ($M = -0.54$, $SD = 1.20$), $F(1, 45) = 5.47$, $p < .03$. In contrast, no significant difference was found in changes in depressed mood between nondysphorics who ruminated ($M = -0.08$, $SD = 0.73$) or distracted ($M = -0.25$, $SD = 0.72$), $F < 1$, *ns*. Furthermore, the results of a planned contrast showed that after the response task manipulation, dysphoric participants who ruminated reported significantly higher levels of depressed mood than the remaining three groups, $F(1, 45) = 54.12$, $p < .0001$. Mean levels of depressed mood following the response task manipulation were as follows: dysphoric–ruminative. $M = 4.69$, $SD = 1.22$; dysphoric–distracting, $M = 3.54$, $SD = 0.81$; nondysphoric–ruminative. $M = 2.37$, $SD = 1.00$; and nondysphoric–distracting, $M = 1.38$, $SD = 0.64$.

Autobiographical Memories We hypothesized that dysphoric students who ruminated about their feelings and personal characteristics would recall the most negative memories in response to both negative (unhappy) and positive (happy) memory prompts. Our findings confirmed this hypothesis, replicating and extending the results of Study 1. A planned contrast revealed that dysphoric ruminators generated unhappy memories that were rated as more negative than those of the other three groups, $F(1, 43) = 8.57$, $p < .006$, and even generated happy memories that were rated as more negative (or less positive) than those of the other three groups, $F(1, 40) = 8.52$, $p < .006$. A linear contrast testing whether dysphoric ruminators recalled the most negative unhappy memories, followed by dysphoric distractors, and, finally, the two nondysphoric groups, was also significant, $F(1, 43) = 4.94$, $p < .04$. A linear contrast testing whether dysphoric ruminators recalled the most negative (or least positive) happy memories, followed by dysphoric distractors, and, finally, the two nondysphoric groups, was also significant, $F(1, 40) = 6.42$, $p < .02$. * * *

The results of Studies 1 and 2 together provide evidence for the proposition that self-focused, dysphoric rumination can enhance the negatively biasing effects of depressed mood on the retrieval of autobiographical memories. * * *

* * *

General Discussion

The results * * * strongly support our primary hypothesis that relative to short-term distraction, ruminative responses to depressed mood enhance the retrieval of negative life events from memory. Whether the autobiographical memories were prompted [or] recalled freely, or * * * whether the hedonic tone of memories was determined by objective judges or the participants themselves * * * did not alter this basic finding. * * * These results provide further support to a growing body of theory and research, which suggests that self-focused rumination in the context of dysphoric mood is associated with more negative thinking than externally focused distraction (Carver & Scheier, 1990; Ingram, 1990: Lyubomirsky et al., 1997; Lyubomirsky & Nolen-Hoeksema, 1993, 1995; Nolen-Hoeksema, 1991; Pyszczynski & Greenberg, 1987; Smith & Greenberg, 1981).

Depressed or dysphoric mood generally increases the accessibility of negative cognitions (Blaney, 1986; Bower, 1981, 1991; Schwarz & Bohner, 1996). Self-focused rumination among people in a depressed mood may enhance negative memories simply by drawing attention to the memories made accessible and salient by the depressed mood. In contrast, distraction temporarily relieves a dysphoric mood and may thereby reduce the accessibility of negative thoughts (see also Lyubomirsky et al., 1997; Lyubomirsky & Nolen-Hoeksema, 1993, 1995; Morrow & Nolen-Hoeksema, 1990; Nolen-Hoeksema & Morrow, 1993). Thus, newly generated memories of dysphoric individuals who have distracted will be less likely to be primed by accessible negative thoughts and, therefore, less likely also to be negative.

Rumination alone, in the absence of dysphoria, was not associated with remembering negative life events. In addition, rumination did not lead to changes in the moods of nondysphoric participants. These results suggest that rumination has adverse consequences only in the context of a depressed mood and bolster the argument that rumination affects cognition by enhancing the effects of negative mood on the accessibility of negative memories (Nolen-Hoeksema, 1991).

* * *

Similarly, rumination in the context of dysphoria might contribute to the generation of more negative memories by setting the "starting point" or anchor from which dysphoric ruminators recall additional memories. That is, dysphoric ruminators may use the fairly negative thoughts they are currently thinking as their anchor or starting point when they try to generate additional memories in the process of evaluating their lives. Thus, many of the additional memories they generate may be equally, or even more, negative than the memories currently on their minds. And even if they try to generate positive memories or thoughts, they may begin at such a negative point on the hedonic continuum that the positive memories they produce are not very positive. Wenzlaff, Wegner, and Roper (1988) showed that when depressed people are left on their own to generate distracting thoughts, they "know" that they should come up with positive thoughts to lift their mood, but they still tend to generate quite negative thoughts. This may be because their current thoughts, particularly if they are ruminating, may be so negative that most other thoughts appear positive in comparison.

Finally, another way that rumination in the context of a depressed mood may contribute to negative thinking is by increasing the attention paid to the highly elaborated negative self-schemas that dysphoric people often have (see, Nolen-Hoeksema, 1991). These self-schemas may include well-rehearsed instances of negative events from the past and negative global evaluation of the self (e.g., "I'm a terrible student"), which can be used to interpret relatively neutral events called from memory. In contrast, dysphoric people made to distract for a time may be less likely to use these negative self-schemas in generating or evaluating memories from the past. Alloy and Abramson (1997) recently found that students who had both negative self-schemas and the tendency to engage in rumination were more likely to experience onsets of major depression during their college years than students who had only negative self-schemas or only a ruminative tendency. This suggests that the tendency to ruminate interacts with and enhances the effects of negative self-schemas.

LIMITATIONS The participants in our studies were probably only moderately dysphoric or depressed: therefore, we do not know if our results generalize to a clinically depressed population. However, previous studies using clinical populations have shown that self-focusing manipulations maintain or enhance depressed mood among clinically depressed patients, whereas externally focusing manipulations lift it (Fennell & Teasdale, 1984; Gibbons et al., 1985). Furthermore, many studies have established the link between depressed mood and negative memories in depressives (e.g., Clark & Teasdale, 1982; DeMonbreun & Craighead, 1977; Fogarty & Hemsley, 1983; Gotlib, 1981, 1983; Lewinsohn & Rosenbaum, 1987; Lloyd & Lishman, 1975; MacLeod & Matthews, 1991). Still, the effects of focusing or rumination manipulations on the autobiographical memories of clinically depressed individuals are largely unknown (see Pyszczynski et al., 1989, for an exception). This is an important area of investigation for the future (see Gotlib, Roberts, & Gilboa, 1996).

* * *

IMPLICATIONS FOR PSYCHOTHERAPY Whether a therapist's approach is cognitive–behavioral, humanistic, psychodynamic, insight oriented, or eclectic, he or she is likely to encourage clients to discuss their experiences, emotions, and intimate concerns. Thus, it can be argued that all psychotherapies invite clients to remember relevant events from their very recent or their very distant past. Identifying a client's problem (all therapies), pinpointing specific situations in which a particular problem occurs (behavioral therapy), understanding how a childhood relationship continues to influence the present (psychodynamic therapy), or exploring the significance of recent life events (humanistic therapy) all require the retrieval of autobiographical memories (Beckham & Leber, 1995; see also Loftus, 1993). Although most therapists probably do not regard their clients' reports of past events as absolutely accurate, they may sometimes fail to take into account individual differences among clients in the veridicality of these reports. The evidence from our * * * studies suggests that depressed or dysphoric clients who are prone to rumination are inclined to retrieve events or experiences from memory that are negatively biased. Assessing clients' tendencies to ruminate, and taking these tendencies into account in interpreting clients' reports of past events in their lives, may be an important goal for psychotherapists.

References

Alloy, L. B., & Abramson, L. Y. (1997, May). *The Temple-Wisconsin cognitive vulnerability to depression project.* Paper presented at the annual meeting of the Midwestern Psychological Association, Chicago.

Barden, R. C., Garber, J., Leiman, B., Ford, M. E., & Masters, J. C. (1985). Factors governing the effective remediation of negative affect and its cognitive and behavioral consequences. *Journal of Personality and Social Psychology, 49,* 1040–1053.

Beck, A. T. (1967). *Depression: Clinical, experimental, and theoretical aspects.* New York: Harper & Row.

Beck, A. T., Rush, A. J., Shaw, B. F., & Emery, G. (1979). *Cognitive therapy of depression.* New York: Guilford Press.

Beckham, E. E., & Leber, W. R. (1995). *Handbook of depression* (2nd ed.). New York: Guilford Press.

Blaney, P. H. (1986). Affect and memory: A review. *Psychological Bulletin, 99,* 229–246.

Bower, G. H. (1981). Mood and memory. *American Psychologist, 36,* 129–148.

Bower, G. H. (1991). Mood congruity of social judgments. In J. P. Forgas (Ed.), *Emotion and social judgments* (pp. 31–53). Oxford, England: Pergamon Press.

Brockner, J. (1979). The effects of self-esteem, success, failure, and self-consciousness on task performance. *Journal of Personality and Social Psychology, 37,* 1732–1741.

Brockner, J., & Hulton, A. J. B. (1978). How to reverse the vicious cycle of low self-esteem: The importance of attentional focus. *Journal of Experimental Social Psychology, 14,* 564–578.

Carver, C. S., & Scheier, M. F. (1990). Origins and functions of positive and negative affect: A control-process view. *Psychological Review, 97,* 19–35.

Clark, D. M., & Teasdale, J. D. (1982). Diurnal variation in clinical depression and accessibility of memories of positive and negative experiences. *Journal of Abnormal Psychology, 91,* 87–95.

DeMonbreun, B. G., & Craighead, W. E. (1977). Distortion of perception and recall of positive and neutral feedback in depression. *Cognitive Therapy and Research, 1,* 311–329.

Duval, S., & Wicklund, R. A. (1972). *A theory of objective self-awareness.* New York: Academic Press.

D'Zurilla, T. J., & Goldfried, M. R. (1971). Problem solving and behavior modification. *Journal of Abnormal Psychology, 78,* 107–126.

Fennell, M. J. V., & Teasdale, J. D. (1984). Effects of distraction on thinking and affect in depressed patients. *British Journal of Clinical Psychology, 23,* 65–66.

Fogarty, S. J., & Hemsley, D. R. (1983). Depression and the accessibility of memories: A longitudinal study. *British Journal of Psychiatry, 142,* 232–237.

Forgas, J. (1991). *Emotion and social judgments.* Elmsford, NY: Pergamon Press.

Gibbons, F. X., Smith, T. W., Ingram, R. E., Pearce, K., Brehm, S. S., & Schroeder, D. (1985). Self-awareness and self-confrontation: Effects of self-focused attention on members of a clinical population. *Journal of Personality and Social Psychology, 48,* 662–675.

Gotlib, I. H. (1981). Self-reinforcement and recall: Differential deficits in depressed and nondepressed psychiatric inpatients. *Journal of Abnormal Psychology, 90,* 521–530.

Gotlib, I. H. (1983). Perception and recall of interpersonal feedback: Negative bias in depression. *Cognitive Therapy and Research, 7,* 399–412.

Gotlib, I. H., Roberts, J. E., & Gilboa, E. (1996). Cognitive interference in depression. In I. G. Sarason, G. R. Pierce, & B. R. Sarason (Eds.), *Cognitive interference: Theories, methods, and findings* (pp. 347–377). Mahwah, NJ: Erlbaum.

Ingram, R. E. (1990). Self-focused attention in clinical disorders: Review and a conceptual model. *Psychological Bulletin, 109,* 156–176.

Kendall, P. C., Hollon, S. D., Beck, A. T., Hammen, C. L., & Ingram, R. (1987). Issues and recommendations regarding use of the Beck Depression Inventory. *Cognitive Therapy and Research, 11,* 289–299.

Lewinsohn, P. M., & Rosenbaum, M. (1987). Recall of parental behavior by acute depressives, remitted depressives, and nondepressives. *Journal of Personality and Social Psychology, 52,* 611–619.

Lightfoot, S., & Oliver, J. M. (1985). The Beck Inventory: Psychometric properties in university students, *Journal of Personality Assessment, 49,* 434–436.

Lloyd, G. G., & Lishman, W. A. (1975). Effect of depression on the speed of recall of pleasant and unpleasant experiences. *Psychological Medicine, 5,* 173–180.

Loftus, E. F. (1993). The reality of repressed memories. *American Psychologist, 48,* 518–537.

Lyubomirsky, S., Caldwell, N. D., & Berg, K. (1997). *Why ruminators are poor problem solvers: Clues from the phenomenology of dysphoric rumination.* Manuscript submitted for publication.

Lyubomirsky, S., & Nolen-Hoeksema, S. (1993). Self-perpetuating properties of dysphoric rumination. *Journal of Personality and Social Psychology, 65,* 339–349.

Lyubomirsky, S., & Nolen-Hoeksema, S. (1995). Effects of self-focused rumination on negative thinking and interpersonal problem solving. *Journal of Personality and Social Psychology, 69,* 176–190.

MacLeod, C., & Matthews, A. (1991). Cognitive experimental approaches to the emotional disorders. In P. R. Martin (Ed.), *Handbook of behavior therapy and psychological science: An integrative approach* (pp. 116–150). New York: Pergamon Press.

Madigan, R. J., & Bollenbach A. K. (1982). Effects of induced mood on retrieval of personal episodic and semantic memories. *Psychological Reports, 50,* 147–157.

Martin, L. L., & Tesser, A. (1996). Some ruminative thoughts. In R. S. Wyer, Jr. (Ed.), *Ruminative thoughts* (pp. 1–47). Mahwah, NJ: Erlbaum.

Morrow, J., & Nolen-Hoeksema, S. (1990). Effects of responses to depression on the remediation of depressive affect. *Journal of Personality and Social Psychology, 58,* 519–527.

Natale, M., & Hantas, M. (1982). Effect of temporary mood states on selective memory about the self. *Journal of Personality and Social Psychology, 42,* 927–934.

Nolen-Hoeksema, S. (1991). Responses to depression and their effects on the duration of depressive episodes. *Journal of Abnormal Psychology, 100,* 569–582.

Nolen-Hoeksema, S., & Jackson, B. (1996, August). *Ruminative coping and gender differences in depression.* Paper presented at the 104th Annual Convention of the American Psychological Association, Toronto, Ontario, Canada.

Nolen-Hoeksema, S., McBride, A., & Larson, J. (1997). Rumination and psychological distress among bereaved partners. *Journal of Personality and Social Psychology, 72,* 855–862.

Nolen-Hoeksema, S., & Morrow, J. (1991). A prospective study of depression and posttraumatic stress symptoms after a natural disaster: The 1989 Loma Prieta earthquake. *Journal of Personality and Social Psychology, 61,* 115–121.

Nolen-Hoeksema, S., & Morrow, J. (1993). Effects of rumination and distraction on naturally occurring depressed mood. *Cognition and Emotion, 7,* 561–570.

Nolen-Hoeksema, S., Morrow, J., & Fredrickson, B. L. (1993). Response styles and the duration of episodes of depressed mood. *Journal of Abnormal Psychology, 102,* 20–28.

Nolen-Hoeksema, S., Parker, L., & Larson, J. (1994). Ruminative coping with depressed mood following loss. *Journal of Personality and Social Psychology, 67,* 92–104.

Pyszczynski, T., & Greenberg, J. (1987). Self-regulatory perseveration and the depressive self-focusing style: A self-awareness theory of reactive depression. *Psychological Bulletin, 102,* 122–138.

Pyszczynski, T., Hamilton, J. H., Herring, F., & Greenberg, J. (1989). Depression, self-focused attention, and the negative memory bias. *Journal of Personality and Social Psychology, 57,* 351–357.

Pyszczynski, T., Holt, K., & Greenberg, J. (1987). Depression, self-focused attention, and expectations for future positive and negative events for self and others. *Journal of Personality and Social Psychology, 52,* 994–1001.

Rholes, W. S., Riskind, J. H., & Lane, J. W. (1987). Emotional states and memory biases: Effects of cognitive priming and mood. *Journal of Personality and Social Psychology, 52,* 91–99.

Rippere, V. (1977). "What's the thing to do when you're feeling depressed?"—A pilot study. *Behavior Research and Therapy, 15,* 185–191.

Rosenthal, R., & Rosnow, R. L. (1985). *Contrast analysis.* Cambridge, England: Cambridge University Press.

Rosnow, R. L., & Rosenthal, R. (1989). Definition and interpretation of interaction effects. *Psychological Bulletin, 105,* 143–146.

Rosnow, R. L., & Rosenthal, R. (1995). "Some things you learn aren't so": Cohen's paradox. Asch's paradigm, and the interpretation of interaction. *Psychological Science, 6,* 3–9.

Saltzberg, J. A. (1992). Positive thinking, rumination, and adjustment to breast cancer. *Dissertation Abstracts International, 52,* 4985.

Schwarz, N., & Bohner, G. (1996). Feelings and their motivational implications: Moods and the action sequence. In P. M. Gollwitzer & J. A. Bargh (Eds.). *The psychology of action: Linking cognition and motivation to behavior* (pp. 119–145). New York: Guilford Press.

Smith, T. W., & Greenberg, J. (1981). Depression and self-focused attention. *Motivation and Emotion, 5,* 323–331.

Snyder, M., & White, P. (1982). Moods and memories: Elation, depression, and the remembering of the events of one's life. *Journal of Personality, 50,* 149–167.

Strack, F., Blaney, P. H. Ganellen, R. J., & Coyne, J. C. (1985). Pessimistic self-preoccupation, performance deficits, and depression. *Journal of Personality and Social Psychology, 49,* 1076–1085.

Strickland, B. R. (1992). Women and depression. *Current Directions in Psychological Science, 1,* 132–135.

Teasdale, J. D. (1983). Negative thinking in depression: Cause, effect, or reciprocal relationship? *Advances in Behavior Research and Therapy, 5,* 3–26.

Teasdale, J. D., & Fogarty, S. J. (1979). Differential effects of induced mood on retrieval of pleasant and unpleasant events from episodic memory. *Journal of Abnormal Psychology, 88,* 248–257.

Wenzlaff, R. M., Wegner, D. M., & Roper, D. W. (1988). Depression and mental control: The resurgence of unwanted negative thoughts. *Journal of Personality and Social Psychology, 55*, 882–892.

Williams, J. M., & Scott, J. (1988). Autobiographical memory in depression. *Psychological Medicine, 18*, 689–695.

Wood, J. V., Saltzberg, J. A., Neale, J. M., Stone, A. A., & Rachmiel, T. B. (1990). Self-focused attention, coping responses, and distressed mood in everyday life. *Journal of Personality and Social Psychology, 58*, 1027–1036.

Wyer, R. S., Jr. (Ed.). (1996). *Ruminative thoughts.* Mahwah, NJ: Erlbaum.

Self-Knowledge of an Amnesic Patient: Toward a Neuropsychology of Personality and Social Psychology

Stanley B. Klein, Judith Loftus, and John F. Kihlstrom

The final selection in this section and this book brings together nearly every tradition in personality psychology. For example, Freud's original intention was to develop a neuropsychological understanding of personality by closely studying individual cases. That is also the intention of the following article, but it goes much farther than that. The thorough assessment of "W.J." conducted by Stanley Klein and his colleagues also includes tests of cognitive ability akin to those used in trait assessment, along with self-report personality tests and personality descriptions rendered by people who know her well. The goal is to better understand the basis of self-knowledge. For example, if you forgot everything you ever did and that ever happened to you, would you still know something about who you are?

In the first selection in this book, Dan McAdams asked, "What do we know when we know a person?" In this selection, Klein and colleagues ask, "What do you really know when you know yourself—and how do you know it?"

From *Journal of Experimental Psychology: General, 125*, 250–260, 1996.

* * *

* * * In this article we offer the case of W.J., who suffered profound retrograde amnesia following a head injury, as a demonstration of the way in which questions of interest to social personality psychologists can be addressed with neurological data. Specifically, our tests of W.J. have provided us with data, unobtainable from individuals with no memory loss, that is pertinent to the debate over the relation between knowledge of traits and memory for specific personal events relevant to those traits.

The Role of Episodic and Semantic Memory in Trait Self-Knowledge

Does a person's knowledge of his or her own traits depend on an ability to recall his or her own past behavior? Is it possible for a person who cannot recall any personal experiences—and therefore cannot know how he or she behaved—to know what he or she is like? Questions such as these have stimulated debate among philosophers (e.g., Grice, 1941; Hume, 1739/1817; Locke, 1690/1731;

Shoemaker, 1963) and psychologists (e.g., Buss & Craik, 1983; James, 1980; Klein & Loftus, 1993; Locksley & Lenauer, 1981) for more than 300 years. Unfortunately, as evidenced by the number of years that debate on this topic has persisted, the question of whether trait knowledge is inseparable from memory for past behavior has proven difficult to answer. In this article we make a modest contribution to this debate by demonstrating that an individual can have detailed and accurate knowledge of her traits despite having little if any conscious access to behavioral memories from which she could infer that knowledge.

Knowledge of personality traits and recollections of specific personal events involving those traits can be considered examples of two types of knowledge about the self: semantic personal knowledge and episodic personal knowledge. * * * Semantic personal knowledge is information that has been abstracted from memories of the self in specific events. * * * Thus, semantic personal knowledge of traits might include the facts that a person is kind, outgoing, and lazy. Episodic personal knowledge, by contrast, consists of memories of specific events involving the self. * * * Thus, episodic personal knowledge of traits could include memories of instances in which behavior was kind, outgoing, or lazy.

Our previous research with individuals with no memory loss used a number of techniques to examine the relation between these two types of trait knowledge about the self. Our data consistently have supported the view that in the realm of trait knowledge, semantic personal memory and episodic personal memory are functionally independent, by which we mean that the operations of semantic personal memory do not require the operations of episodic personal memory (for reviews, see Kihlstrom & Klein, 1994, 1997; Klein & Loftus, 1993).

In our initial investigations of the relation between semantic and episodic memory for traits, we used a priming paradigm. In a series of studies, we found that participants who made self-descriptiveness judgments about trait words were no faster than participants who performed a control task to then perform a second task that required them to retrieve personal episodic memories about the same traits. * * * We concluded from this that the semantic personal knowledge required for a self-descriptiveness judgment was accessed without activating episodic personal memories. If episodic memories had been activated during the self-descriptiveness judgments, then participants who made those judgments should have had an advantage over participants who performed the control task in the speed with which they subsequently retrieved episodic memories.

We have conducted several other studies of trait self-knowledge that also support the independence of semantic and episodic personal memory. Klein, Loftus, and Plog (1992), for example, made use of the phenomenon of transfer-appropriate processing (e.g., Roediger & Blaxton, 1987; Roediger, Weldon, & Challis, 1988) in a study of recognition memory for traits to show that different processes are involved in accessing the two types of memory. In addition, Klein et al. (1989, Experiment 4) applied the principle of encoding variability (e.g., Bower, 1972; Martin, 1971, 1972) in a study of recall for traits and found that the type of information made available by accessing semantic personal memory was different from that made available by accessing episodic personal memory.

However, although this research converges in support of the functional independence of semantic and episodic trait knowledge of self, a number of theorists have noted a problem inherent in trying to infer the functional independence of semantic and episodic memory from the performance of individuals with no memory loss (e.g., Parkin, 1993; Tulving, Hayman, & Macdonald, 1991). Specifically, experiments that attempt to demonstrate such independence must be able to show that each of these memory systems can operate without the other—that participants can perform a task involving one memory system without activating the other. However, when participants have access to both episodic and semantic memory, it is difficult to rule out interplay between the two systems in the performance of experimental tasks and therefore difficult to compellingly demonstrate that the two systems are independent. For example, although Klein et al. (1989, Experiment 2; see also Klein et al., 1992, Experiments 2, 3, & 4) found that participants appeared to make self-descriptiveness judgments without retrieving episodic memories, it is possible that episodes were retrieved but that the tests used to detect retrieval were not sufficiently sensitive. * * *

However, amnesic memory impairment offers an opportunity to overcome this problem. Amnesic patients provide a particularly effective method for testing the independence of semantic and episodic personal memory, because these patients typically display intact semantic memory with impaired access to episodic memory. * * * Therefore, it is possible with amnestic patients to test semantic self-knowledge of traits with assurance that episodic memory for traits is not involved. If the two systems are indeed functionally independent, then amnesic patients should be able to make trait self-descriptiveness judgments despite their inability to recall personal events.

This hypothesis has been tested by Tulving (1993). Tulving found that the patient K.C., whose entire fund of episodic memory was permanently lost following a motorcycle accident, was able to describe his personality with considerable accuracy. Tulving asked K.C. on two occasions to rate a list of trait adjectives for self-descriptiveness. Tulving also asked K.C.'s mother to rate K.C. on the same traits. Tulving's findings revealed that K.C.'s ratings were both reliable (K.C.'s trait self-ratings showed 78% agreement across sessions) and consistent with the way he is perceived by others (there was 73% agreement between K.C.'s and his mother's ratings of K.C.'s traits). K.C. thus appears to have accurate and detailed knowledge about his personality despite the fact that he has no conscious access to any behavioral episodes from which he could infer this knowledge.

The fact that K.C., without access to episodic self-knowledge, can access semantic self-knowledge to make trait self-descriptiveness judgments confirms that semantic personal memory is functionally independent of episodic personal memory in the realm of trait knowledge. Having established this, however, a question still remains. Although K.C.'s case shows that semantic personal memory can function without episodic personal memory, does this mean that under ordinary circumstances the two types of memory do not interact? K.C. can make trait judgments: but perhaps his judgments would be different if his episodic memory were intact. * * *

To this question we bring the case of W.J., who, as a result of a head injury, suffered temporary retrograde amnesia. Retrograde amnesia is the inability to recall events that precede the onset of the amnesia. Typically, it entails loss of episodic memory with sparing of semantic memory. * * * When it occurs following a closed-head injury, retrograde amnesia typically has the additional feature of being temporary, resolving in the days or weeks following the injury. * * *

Because W.J.'s amnesia was temporary, it was possible to test her semantic personal memory both without and with access to episodic personal memory. We asked W.J. to make trait judgments about herself during the time when she was amnesic for events pertaining to those judgments and again when her episodic memory had returned. In this way, we were able to look for differences in her semantic memory performance as a function of the accessibility of episodic memory. Performance differences would tell us that semantic and episodic personal memory, although functionally independent, do interact in some way. However, consistent performance without and with episodic memory would point toward a stronger form of independence between the two memory types.

Method

PARTICIPANTS

Patient W.J. The patient, W.J., is an 18-year-old female undergraduate. During the first week of her second quarter at college she sustained a concussional head injury as a result of a fall. After complaining of a headache and difficulty in concentration and memory, she was taken to a hospital emergency room where a computerized tomography brain scan was performed. No signs of neurological abnormality were observed.

W.J. was interviewed by Stanley B. Klein on several occasions. In a meeting 5 days after her head injury, she complained of great difficulty remembering events that occurred before the accident. Questioned informally, she was unable to bring to mind a single personal event or experience from the last 6–7 months of her life—a period of time covering approximately her first quarter at college. Her memory for more remote personal events was patchy, with amnesic gaps dating back to about 4 years before her injury.

Despite her dense retrograde amnesia for events from the preceding 6–7 months, W.J.'s memory for general facts about her personal life during that period seemed largely intact. She knew, for example, which classes she attended during her first quarter at college, although she could not remember a specific occasion when she attended class or a specific event that happened during a class; she knew the names of teachers and friends from college, although she could not remember particular experiences shared with them.

W.J. also showed a moderate degree of anterograde memory impairment, which seemed limited to the period of approximately 45 min following her fall. Although her boyfriend reported that she was conscious and coherent, W.J. had no recollection of events that occurred during that time.

Eleven days after the accident, W.J.'s retrograde amnesia had cleared considerably. Her memory impairment appeared limited to events from the last 6 months, and within that period she was able to clearly recollect a number of incidents. For example, she could describe in great detail a visit to the home of her boyfriend's parents 3 months earlier. Her anterograde amnesia, on the other hand, remained unchanged.

When interviewed 3 weeks later, W.J. appeared to have completely recovered her memory for events preceding her fall. She still, however, was unable to recall events that occurred immediately afterward.

Control Participants With No Memory Loss

Control group for memory testing. Three female undergraduates, whose mean age (19 years, 4 months) was closely matched to W.J.'s age (18 years, 3 months), were tested on the same battery of memory tests that was administered to W.J.

Control group for personality testing. Two opposite-sex couples, whose arrival at college coincided with W.J.'s (6 months prior to testing) and whose mean time as a couple (4.2 years) closely matched that of W.J. and her boyfriend (3.5 years), completed the same personality trait questionnaire that was completed by W.J. and her boyfriend.

Procedure

Memory Testing Memory performance following closed-head injury follows a fairly consistent pattern of preserved and impaired function. * * * Immediate memory span and access to semantic knowledge typically are intact, whereas episodic memories of events preceding and following the injury are likely to be impaired. In most cases, the retrograde component of the amnesia shrinks in the days following the injury, with memories returning in a roughly chronological order from the most distant to the most recent events.

To evaluate W.J.'s memory function, we administered the following battery of memory tests to her and to three female control participants. Except where indicated, all testing was conducted 5 days after W.J. had sustained her head injury. Participants were tested individually.

Digit span. W.J.'s immediate memory was assessed using a digit-span technique. * * * An experimenter read aloud to the participant a list of digits, at a rate of one digit every 2 s, beginning with a list of two digits. The participants then was to immediately repeat the digits back to the experimenter in correct order. If the list was repeated correctly, the experimenter read another list of digits, increasing the length of the list by one digit. Testing continued until the participant failed to repeat a list correctly. The procedure then was repeated with new lists and a change in instructions so that participants repeated the digits in reverse order, rather than in presentation order.

Free recall. W.J.'s ability to retain information beyond the span of immediate memory was examined using a free-recall paradigm. Participants were presented with five lists of 16 unrelated nouns. Each list was read aloud by the experimenter at the rate of 1 noun every 2 s. Immediately after presentation of the last item in a list, participants were given 1 min to write as many of the items from that list as possible, in any order. Each participant's recall performance was plotted as a serial-position curve, which shows the probability of an item being correctly recalled as a function of its serial position in the input list. * * *

Semantic memory. To investigate W.J.'s access to semantic knowledge, we selected two tasks—verbal fluency and category judgment—from the battery of semantic memory tests used by Wilson & Baddeley (1988).

In the verbal fluency task, participants were required to generate as many items as possible from each of six semantic categories: animals, fruits, furniture, girls' names, birds, and metals. Participants were allowed 1 min per category in which to write responses.

In the category judgment task, participants were shown 24 pairs of words and, for each pair, were asked to decide whether the words belonged to the same semantic category (e.g., fruits, animals). Half of the pairs contained words from the same semantic category (e.g., *grape–apple*), and half contained words from different categories (e.g., *tiger–boat*). Participants were asked to state their decisions as quickly as possible, and their decision latencies were recorded.

Episodic memory. We used the autobiographical memory-cueing task originated by Galton (1879) and later modified by Crovitz and Schiffman (1974) and Robinson (1976) to test memory for personal episodes. In this task, participants were presented with cue words. For each cue, they were asked to recall a specific personal event and to provide as precise a date as possible for that event. For example, a participant might respond to the cue *dog* by recalling that she walked her dog that morning or that she received a dog as a gift for her 10th birthday.

Our study examined episodic memory under two cueing conditions: unconstrained and constrained (e.g., Schacter, Kihlstrom, Kihlstrom, & Berren, 1989; Schacter, Wang, Tulving, & Freedman, 1982). In the unconstrained condition, participants were read a list of 24 cue words, 1 word at a time. They were instructed to recall for each cue a specific personal event related to the cue from any time in their past. The 24 cues were common English words, randomly selected from the set of 48 cue words presented by Robinson (1976). The cues included 8 affect words (e.g., *lonely, surprised*), 8 object words (e.g., *car, river*) and 8 activity words (e.g., *run, visit*). All participants received the same set of 24 cue words in a fixed-random order.

At the beginning of the session, participants were told that we were interested in studying memory for personal events. They were informed that a series of words would be read to them and that they should try to think of a specific personal event that was related to each word. They were instructed to provide a brief verbal description of each memory and to date the memory as accurately as possible. If on any trial a participant was unable to retrieve a memory within 60 s, the trial was terminated and the participant was read the next cue.

After a short rest break, the constrained-cueing task was administered. This task was identical to the unconstrained task, except that participants were instructed to restrict their recall to events that had occurred within the last 6 months. The same cues were used in the constrained and unconstrained conditions.

In a second session, conducted 4 weeks after the first session, participants were tested again using only the unconstrained-cueing condition.

Personality Testing A list of 80 trait adjectives was selected from Kirby & Gardner's (1972) norms to create a personality questionnaire. The adjectives selected were close to the norm means on the dimensions of familiarity, imagery, and behavioral specificity and spanned the range of social desirability. The questionnaire consisted of four sheets of paper with 20 traits per sheet. Beside each trait were four choices: *not at all, somewhat, quite a bit,* and *definitely*.

Personality testing was conducted in two sessions. The first session took place 5 days after W.J.'s accident. W.J. was provided with a personality questionnaire and was instructed to indicate, by circling the appropriate choice, the extent to which each trait described her since her arrival at college. Her boyfriend also completed the questionnaire, indicating for each trait how well it described W.J. since her arrival at college. After a brief break, W.J. filled out the questionnaire a second time, this time indicating for each trait the extent to which it described her during high school.

Two control couples also completed the questionnaire. For each couple, the woman indicated how well each of the 80 trait adjectives on the questionnaire described her since her arrival at college, and the man indicated the extent to which the traits described his partner since her arrival at college.

A second session was conducted 4 weeks later. W.J. and the two women of the control couples again were given the personality questionnaire and asked, for each trait, to indicate how well it described them since their arrival at college.

Results

Memory Testing

Digit Span Immediate memory, as measured by the digit span, typically is normal in patients who have suffered closed-head injuries. * * * W.J.'s digit-span performance (5 digits forward and 5 digits backward) was comparable to that of the control participants (*M*s = 5.3 digits forward and 5.7 digits backward).[1] This suggests that W.J. can hold as much information in immediate memory as can control participants with no memory loss.

Free Recall Figure 53.1 shows two serial-position curves: one for W.J. and one representing the mean performance of the control participants. As can be seen, there is little difference between the curves. For both, items from the beginning and end of the list were better recalled than were items in the middle, resulting in the U-shaped curve characteristic of normal free-recall performance. * * *

Semantic Memory Amnestic patients usually perform normally or near normally on tasks requiring access to knowledge contained in semantic memory. * * * W.J.'s performance * * * was within the range established by the control participants, indicating that the speed and accuracy with which she could access material from semantic memory was unimpaired.

Episodic Memory Retrograde amnesia for personal episodes commonly is observed in cases of closed-head injury. * * * Figure 53.2 presents the proportion of episodic memories produced from four different time periods: from within the previous 12 months, from more than a year but less than 5 years ago, from more than 5 but less than 10 years ago, and from more than 10 years ago.

The temporal distributions of memories produced during the first unconstrained-cueing session are shown in Figure 53.2A. As can be seen, there is a marked difference between the performance of W.J. and that of the controls. Paralleling previous studies of participants with no memory loss (e.g., * * * Rubin, Wetzler, & Nebes, 1986), control participants showed a pronounced recency bias in their recall: The majority of memories came from the most recent 12-month period (65%), with increasingly smaller proportions recalled from each of the more distant past periods.

By contrast, W.J.'s recall was characterized by

[1]*M* is the mean.

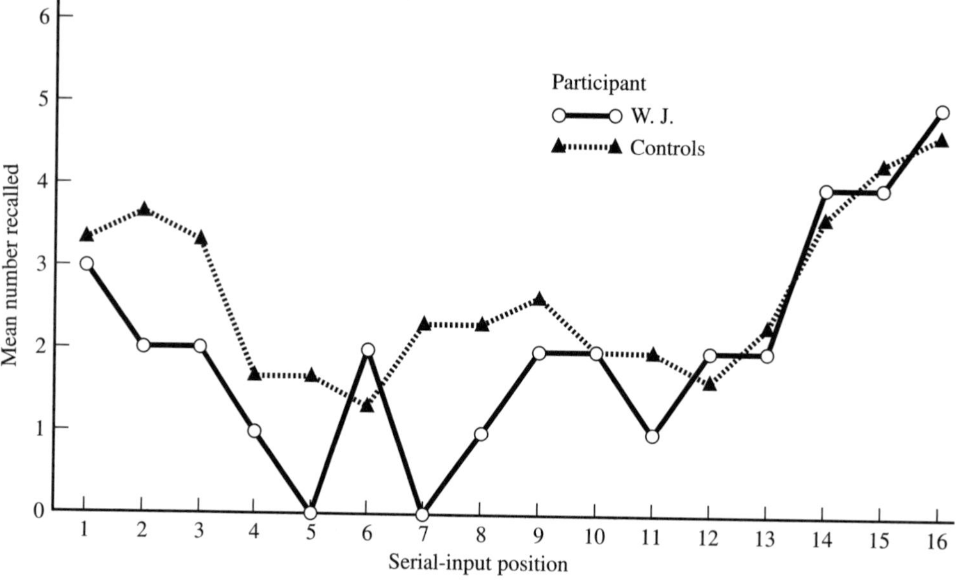

Figure 53.1 Serial-position curve, showing mean number of nouns recalled by W. J. and control participants with no memory loss as a function of serial-input position.

a strong primacy bias: She had considerable difficulty retrieving memories from the previous 12 months (she could recall only a single episode from the last year and none from the last 6 months) and progressively less difficulty retrieving memories from earlier periods. The temporal gradient found in W.J.'s recall fits nicely with a growing body of evidence showing that following closed-head injury, disruption of memory retrieval is more likely to be seen for recently acquired memories than for older memories (e.g., * * * Lucchelli et al., 1995; MacKinnon & Squire, 1989). * * *

Although W.J.'s performance on the first unconstrained autobiographical cueing task indicates that she was densely amnesic for recent personal episodes, several investigators have noted that caution must be exercised when interpreting results from this task (e.g., Evans et al., 1993; Kopelman, 1994 * * *). Because W.J. was not required to produce memories from specified time periods, it is difficult to know whether her failure to retrieve personal memories from the last 6 months reflects an inability to do so or, rather, a bias to sample from more remote time periods.

The constrained autobiographical cueing task allowed us to distinguish between these alternatives by requiring participants to restrict their recall to memories of events occuring in the previous 6 months. In this condition, W.J. was unable to retrieve a single memory. By contrast, control participants produced memories in response to 96% of the cues. These data clearly suggest that W.J.'s failure to produce recent episodic memories in the unconstrained-cueing task represents a retrieval impairment rather than a bias in sampling.

Figure 53.2B presents the results from the second unconstrained-cueing session, conducted 4 weeks after the first. As noted previously, informal questioning indicated that W.J.'s retrograde amnesia largely had cleared at this point. Consistent with this observation, W.J. and control participants produced virtually identical temporal distributions of memories, characterized by pronounced recency biases (83% and 77% of the

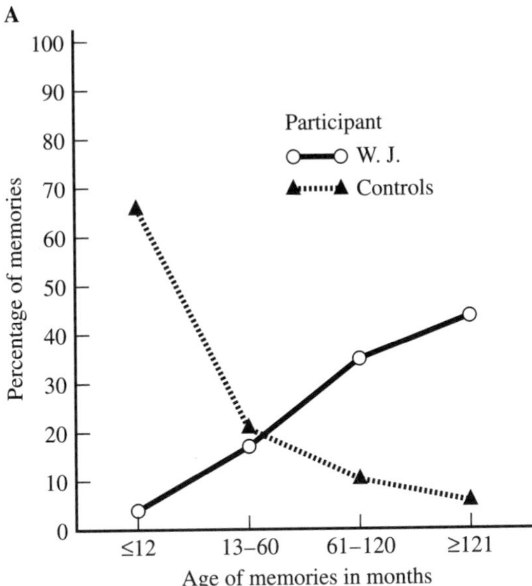

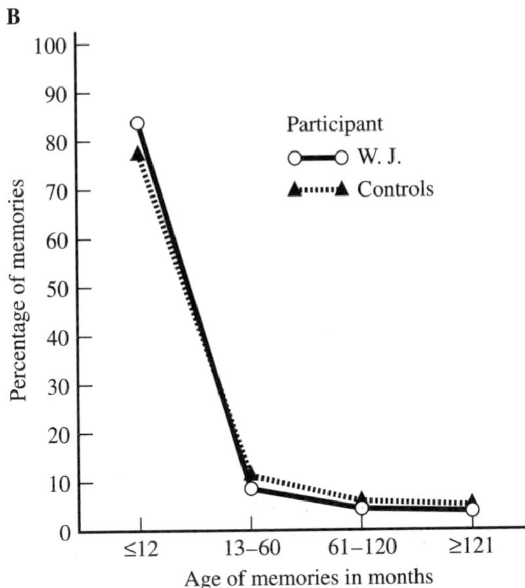

Figure 53.2 Percentage of episodic memories in four age periods produced by W. J. and control participants with no nemory loss with unconstrained cueing during Session 1 (A) and Session 2 (B).

memories retrieved by W.J. and the controls, respectively, came from the 12 months preceding the test). It should be noted that W.J.'s recency bias was not due to recall of events occurring during the 4-week period following initial testing: Only 2 of the 20 memories she dated as having occured during the last year were drawn from that period. These data, then, demonstrate a substantial recovery of W.J.'s episodic memory by the second testing session.

PERSONALITY TESTING The central question for the present research is whether semantic self-knowledge is independent of episodic self-knowledge. To examine this question, we had W.J. make trait ratings of herself at college both during her amnesia and following its resolution. We reasoned that if semantic knowledge of one's traits is not dependent on access to trait-related episodic memories, then W.J.'s trait self-ratings should be unaffected by changes in the accessibility of her episodic memories.

We asked W.J. on two occasions to provide ratings of herself at college. The first rating session took place while she was densely amnesic for personal events that had occurred during college; the second session occurred after her memory for her experiences at college had fully recovered. Two female controls provided trait ratings of themselves at college during the same two sessions.

W.J.'s ratings of herself at college showed considerable consistency across testings: The Pearson product–moment correlation coefficient between ratings produced in the first and second session was significant ($r = .74$, $p < .05$) and virtually identical to that for the control participants ($r = .78$, $p < .05$)[2] Thus, despite a dramatic change in the accessibility of her episodic memories of herself at college across testings. W.J.'s test–retest reliability was comparable to that of participants who had access to episodic memories at both

[2]The r is the correlation coefficient, and p is the probability that a correlation as large as reported would have been found if its real value were 0.

testings. It appears that W.J.'s loss of episodic memory did not affect access to her trait self-knowledge.

It is, of course, possible that W.J.'s ratings agreed over sessions because she simply endorsed positive traits and rejected negative traits on both trials. * * * To address this concern, we compared W.J.'s self-ratings from the first session with ratings of her made by her boyfriend. Research has shown that the social desirability of traits is far less likely to influence ratings made by an external assessor who knows the person well (e.g., McCrae, 1982; Wiggins, 1973). Therefore, if W.J. were basing her ratings on social desirability, we would not expect a strong correlation between her ratings and ratings of her provided by her boyfriend. However, the correlation between W.J.'s self-ratings and those made by her boyfriend was significant ($r = .65$, $p < .05$) and did not differ from that obtained from control couples ($r = .65$, $p < .05$). Thus, we conclude that W.J.'s self-ratings could not be based purely on social desirability.

* * *

Another concern is whether W.J.'s ratings of herself at college were, in fact, based on knowledge of herself during her 6 months at college. It is conceivable, for example, that during initial testing W.J. was unable to access any self-knowledge from the last 6–7 months. Under these circumstances, she may have adopted a strategy of retrieving memories from the most recent period for which she had accessible self-knowledge (i.e., high school) to make reasonable guesses about what she was like at college. Since trait self-descriptions tend to be relatively stable by adolescence (e.g., Engel, 1959; Mortimer & Lorence, 1981; O'Malley & Bachman, 1983), some agreement between ratings based on knowledge of the self in the high-school and college contexts would not be surprising.

To address this concern, we asked W.J. during the first test session to rate how she saw herself during high school. We then computed the correlation between her ratings of herself at high school and her postamnesia ratings of herself at college. We compared this correlation with the correlation between her ratings of herself at college across sessions.

We predicted that if W.J. had access to knowledge of herself at college during her amnesia, then the correlation between her ratings of herself at high school and her postamnesia ratings of herself at college would be lower than the correlation between her ratings of herself at college across testings. By contrast, if, during her amnesia, W.J. actually based her trait ratings of herself at college on knowledge of what she was like in high school, then the correlation between her ratings of herself at high school and her postamnesia ratings of herself at college should be comparable to that obtained between her ratings of herself at college across sessions.

Statistical analyses revealed that the correlation between her ratings of herself at high school and her postamnesia ratings of herself at college was significant ($r = .53$, $p < .05$), meaning that some degree of reliability in W.J.'s ratings of her college self could have been achieved by reliance on her memories of her precollege behavior and experiences. However, this figure was significantly lower than the correlation obtained between W.J.'s ratings of herself at college across sessions ($r = .74$), $t(158) = 1.71$, $p < .05$, one-tailed.[3] So, there is reliable variability in her college self that is not accounted for by her high-school self. Put another way, while she was amnesic. W.J. knew something about what she had been like at college, which was different from what she was like in high school; but she knew this despite the fact that she could not recall anything from her time in college.

Discussion

This experimental case study illustrates some of the ways in which theoretical issues of concern to personality and social psychologists, especially

[3]The *t* is a statistic used to evaluate the difference between means.

those surrounding the self, can be addressed with neurological data.

W.J., a college freshman, suffered a concussive blow to the head in the winter quarter of 1995. As a result of this injury, she showed a profound retrograde amnesia for events that had transpired over the 6 months immediately prior to the accident. Over the next month, this amnesia remitted completely. W.J.'s amnesic deficit in episodic personal memory was documented by the Crovitz–Robinson technique of cued autobiographical recall. When tested 5 days after the accident, under both free and constrained conditions. W.J.'s performance was clearly impaired compared with that of a group of participants with no memory loss. Four weeks later, W.J.'s performance had improved considerably and was indistinguishable from that of controls.

In contrast to the impairment and recovery of episodic memory, W.J.'s self-ratings of personality did not change at all over the same period of time: Her self-ratings made during the amnesic period agreed with those she made afterward.

The fact that W.J.'s episodic personal memories were affected by the concussion, but her semantic personal memories were not, is evidence that these two types of self-knowledge are represented independently and perhaps mediated by separate cognitive systems. Admittedly, it remains possible that W.J.'s ratings of her personality were based on episodic memories from high school (or earlier) that were not covered by the amnesia or on knowledge of what her personality was like before she entered college. Additionally, it is possible that the trait cues used for personality testing may have retrieved some episodic memories that were not retrieved by means of the affect, object, and activity cue words from the autobiographical memory-cueing task. One problem with neuropsychological evidence, from the investigator's point of view, is that the deficits in question rarely are complete. Still, the evidence obtained in this case is consistent with the results from K.C., the amnesic patient studied by Tulving (1993) and with evidence from intact participants derived from several different paradigms (for reviews, see Kihlstrom & Klein, 1994; Klein & Loftus, 1993). Moreover, this evidence about the self is consistent with conclusions derived from studies of person memory (* * * for a recent review, see Kihlstrom & Hastie, 1997). We believe that when considered as a whole, the evidence we have presented compels one to seriously entertain the possibility that semantic personal knowledge is represented in a manner that is independent of episodic personal knowledge.

* * *

A Neuropsychological Approach to Issues in Social and Personality Psychology Over and above this specific theoretical question, we hope that this case study will stimulate other personality and social psychologists to consider the theoretical promise of patients with neuropsychological impairments. Consider, as an example, the classic case of Phineas Gage, the 19th-century railway worker who underwent profound personality changes following traumatic injury to the anterior portion of his cerebral cortex. * * * For more than a century, this case has served as the source of speculations about the role of the frontal lobes in emotion, personality, and social relations (e.g., Damasio & Anderson, 1993), and it may be that data from frontal-lobe patients will help resolve the vexing question of the relations between cognition and emotion (e.g., Lazarus, 1984; Zajonc, 1980, 1984).

* * *

Neuropsychological evidence also is relevant to questions of the self. For example, the patient H.M., who received a bilateral resection of his temporal lobes, has suffered a gross anterograde amnesia since the day of his operation in 1953 (Milner, Corkin, & Teuber, 1968; Scoville & Milner, 1957). Despite the physical changes wrought by 40 years of aging and the fact that he remembers nothing of what he has done or experienced in all that time, H.M. has preserved a continuity of identity. Studies of amnesic patients' interpersonal, emotional, and motivational lives promise to provide new perspectives on the relations of these functions with memory.

* * *

CONCLUSIONS In the past, cognitive psychologists have made good use of neuropsychological case material in developing theories about mental function (Gazzaniga, 1995; Heilman & Valenstein, 1993; Kolb & Whishaw, 1990). With rare exceptions, however (e.g., K. Goldstein, 1934/1995; Luria, 1966; Sacks, 1974, 1985, 1995), neuropsychologists have seldom inquired into their patients personal and social lives. And, whether for lack of interest or lack of access, personality and social psychologists have rarely studied the victims of brain damage. We hope that this situation changes, for it would seem that neurological patients have much to teach us about the psychological processes involved in forming, maintaining, and using mental representations of ourselves and other people.

References

Bower, G. H. (1972). Stimulus-sampling theory of encoding variability. In A. W. Melton & E. Martin (Eds.), *Coding processes in human memory* (pp. 85–123). Washington, DC: Winston.

Buss, D. M., & Craik, K. H. (1983). The act frequency approach to personality. *Psychological Review, 90,* 105–126.

Crovitz, H. F., & Schiffman, H. (1974). Frequency of episodic memories as a function of their age. *Bulletin of the Psychonomic Society, 4(5B),* 517–518.

Damasio, A. R., & Anderson, S. W. (1993). The frontal lobes. In K. M. Heilman & E. Valenstein (Eds.), *Clinical neuropsychology* (pp. 409–560). New York: Oxford University Press.

Engel, M. (1959). The stability of the self-concept in adolescence. *Journal of Abnormal and Social Psychology, 58,* 211–215.

Evans, J., Wilson, B., Wraight, E. P., & Hodges, J. R. (1993). Neuropsychological and SPECT scan findings during and after transient global amnesia: Evidence for the differential impairment of remote episodic memory. *Journal of Neurology, Neurosurgery, and Psychiatry, 56,* 1227–1230.

Galton, F. (1879). Psychometric experiments. *Brain, 2,* 149–162.

Gazzaniga, M. S. (Ed.), (1995). *The cognitive neurosciences.* Cambridge, MA: MIT Press.

Goldstein, K. (1995). *The organism.* New York: Zone Books. (Original work published 1934)

Grice, H. P. (1941). Personal identity. *Mind, 50,* 330–350.

Heilman, K. M., & Valenstein, E. (1993). *Clinical neuropsychology* (3rd ed.). New York: Oxford University Press.

Hume, D. A. (1817). *A treatise of human nature.* London: Thomas & Joseph Allman. (Original work published 1739)

James, W. (1890). *The principles of psychology* (Vol. 1). New York: Holt.

Kihlstrom, J. F., & Hastie, R. (1997). Mental representations of self and others. In S. R. Briggs, R. Hogan, & W. H. Jones (Eds.), *Handbook of personality psychology.* San Diego, CA: Academic Press.

Kihlstrom, J. F., & Klein, S. B. (1994). The self as a knowledge structure. In R. S. Wyer & T. K. Srull (Eds.), *Handbook of social cognition: Vol. 1. Basic processes* (pp. 153–208). Hillsdale, NJ: Erlbaum.

Kihlstrom, J. F., & Klein, S. B. (1997). Self-knowledge and self-awareness. In J. G. Snodgrass & R. L. Thompson (Eds.), *Annals of the New York Academy of Sciences. The self across psychology: Self-recognition, self-awareness, and the self concept.* New York: New York Academy of Sciences.

Kirby, D. M., & Gardner, R. C. (1972). Ethnic stereotypes: Norms on 208 words typically used in their assessment. *Canadian Journal of Psychology, 26,* 140–154.

Klein, S. B., & Loftus, J. (1993). The mental representation of trait and autobiographical knowledge about the self. In T. K. Srull & R. S. Wyer (Eds.), *Advances in social cognition* (Vol. 5, pp. 1–49). Hillsdale, NJ: Erlbaum.

Klein, S. B., Loftus, J., & Burton, H. (1989). Two self-reference effects: The importance of distinguishing between self-descriptiveness judgments and autobiographical retrieval in self-referent encoding. *Journal of Personality and Social Psychology, 56,* 853–865.

Klein, S. B., Loftus, J., & Plog, A. E. (1992). Trait judgments about the self: Evidence from the encoding specificity paradigm. *Personality and Social Psychology Bulletin, 18,* 730–735.

Kolb, B., & Whishaw, I. Q. (1990). *Fundamentals of human neuropsychology* (3rd ed.). San Francisco: Freeman.

Kopelman, M. D. (1994). The autobiographical memory interview (AMI) in organic and psychogenic amnesia. *Memory, 2,* 211–235.

Lazarus, R. S. (1984). On the primacy of cognition. *American Psychologist, 39,* 124–129.

Locke, J. (1731). *An essay concerning human understanding.* London: Edmund Parker. (Original work published 1690)

Locksley, A., & Lenauer, M. (1981). Considerations for a theory of self-inference processes. In N. Cantor & J. F. Kihlstrom (Eds.), *Personality, cognition, and social interaction* (pp. 263–277). Hillsdale, NJ: Erlbaum.

Lucchelli, F., Muggia, S., & Spinnler, H. (1995). The "Petites Madeleines" phenomenon in two amnesic patients: Sudden recovery of forgotten memories. *Brain, 118,* 167–183.

Luria, A. R. (1966). *Human brain and psychological processes.* New York: McGraw-Hill.

MacKinnon, D. F., & Squire, L. R. (1989). Autobiographical memory and amnesia. *Psychobiology, 17,* 247–256.

Martin, E. (1971). Verbal learning theory and independent retrieval phenomena. *Psychological Review, 78,* 314–332.

Martin, E. (1972). Stimulus encoding in learning and transfer. In A. W. Melton & E. Martin (Eds.), *Coding process in human memory* (pp. 59–84). New York: Wiley.

McCrae, R. R. (1982). Consensual validation of personality traits: Evidence from self-reports and ratings. *Journal of Personality and Social Psychology, 43,* 293–303.

Milner, B., Corkin, S., & Teuber, H. L. (1968). Further analysis of the hippocampal amnesic syndrome: 14-year follow up study of H. M. *Neuropsychologia, 6*, 215–234.

Mortimer, J. T., & Lorence, J. (1981). Self-concept stability and change from late adolescence to early childhood. *Research in Community and Mental Health, 2*, 5–42.

O'Malley, P., & Bachman, J. (1983). Self-esteem: Change and stability between the ages 13 and 23. *Developmental Psychology, 19*, 257–268.

Parkin, A. J. (1993). *Memory.* Cambridge, MA: Blackwell.

Robinson, J. A. (1976). Sampling autobiographical memory. *Cognitive Psychology, 8*, 578–595.

Roediger, H. L., & Blaxton, T. A. (1987). Retrieval modes produce dissociations in memory for surface information. In D. Gorfein & R. R. Hoffman (Eds.), *Memory and cognitive processes: The Ebbinghaus centennial conference* (pp. 349–379). Hillsdale, NJ: Erlbaum.

Roediger, H. L., Weldon, M. S., & Challis, B. H. (1988). Explaining dissociations between implicit and explicit measures of retention: A processing account. In H. L. Roediger & F. I. M. Craik (Eds.), *Varieties of memory and consciousness: Essays in honor of Endel Tulving* (pp. 3–41). Hillsdale, NJ: Erlbaum.

Rubin, D. C., Wetzler, S. E., & Nebes, R. D. (1986). Autobiographical memory across the life span. In D. C. Rubin (Ed.), *Autobiographical memory* (pp. 202–221). New York: Cambridge University Press.

Sacks, O. (1974). *Awakenings.* Garden City, NY: Doubleday.

Sacks, O. (1985). *The man who mistook his wife for a hat.* New York: Doubleday.

Sacks, O. (1995). *An anthropologist on Mars: Seven paradoxical tales.* New York: Knopf.

Schacter, D. L., Kihlstrom, J. F., Kihlstrom, L. C., & Berren, M. B. (1989). Autobiographical memory in a case of multiple personality disorder. *Journal of Abnormal Psychology, 98*, 508–514.

Schacter, D. L., Wang, P. L., Tulving, E., & Freedman, M. (1982). Functional retrograde amnesia: A quantitative case study. *Neuropsychologia, 20*, 523–532.

Scoville, W. B., & Milner, B. (1957). Loss of recent memory after bilateral hippocampal lesions. *Journal of Neurology, Neurosurgery, and Psychiatry, 20*, 11–21.

Shoemaker, S. (1963). *Self-knowledge and self-identity.* Ithaca, NY: Cornell University Press.

Tulving, E. (1993). Self-knowledge of an amnesic is represented abstractly. In T. K. Srull & R. S. Wyer (Eds.), *Advances in social cognition* (Vol. 5, pp. 147–156). Hillsdale, NJ: Erlbaum.

Tulving, E., Hayman, C. A. G., & Macdonald, C. A. (1991). Long-lasting perceptual priming and semantic learning in amnesia: A case experiment. *Journal of Experimental Psychology: Learning, Memory, and Cognition, 17*, 595–617.

Wiggins, J. S. (1973). *Personality and prediction: Principles of personality assessment.* Reading, MA: Addison-Wesley.

Wilson, B., & Baddeley, A. D. (1988). Semantic, episodic, and autobiographical memory in a postmeningitic amnesic patient. *Brain and Cognition, 8*, 31–46.

Zajonc, R. B. (1980). Feeling and thinking: Preferences need no inferences. *American Psychologist, 35*, 151–175.

Zajonc, R. B. (1984). On the primacy of affect. *American Psychologist, 39*, 117–123.

REFERENCES FOR EDITORS' NOTES

Allport, G. W., & Odbert, H. S. (1936). Trait-names: A psycho-lexical study. *Psychological Monographs: General and Applied, 47,* 171. (1, Whole No. 211).

American Psychological Association. *Publication Manual of the American Psychological Association* (4th ed.). Washington, DC: American Psychological Association.

Barocas, R., Seifer, R., & Sameroff, A. J. (1985). Defining environmental risk: Multiple dimensions of psychological vulnerability. *American Journal of Community Psychology, 13,* 443–447.

Bem, D. J., & Allen, A. (1974). On predicting some of the people some of the time: The search for cross-situational consistencies in behavior. *Psychological Review, 81,* 506–520.

Bem, D. J., & Funder, D. C. (1978). Predicting more of the people more of the time: Assessing the personality of situations. *Psychological Review, 85,* 485–501.

Block, J. (1995). A contrarian view of the five-factor approach to personality description. *Psychological Bulletin, 117,* 187–215.

Booth-Kewley, S., & Friedman, H. S. (1987). Psychological predictors of heart disease: A quantitative review. *Psychological Bulletin, 101,* 343–362.

Briggs, S. R., & Cheek, J. M. (1986). The role of factor analysis in the development and evaluation of personality scales. *Journal of Personality, 54,* 106–148.

Briggs, S. R., & Cheek, J. M. (1988). On the nature of self-monitoring: Problems with assessment, problems with validity. *Journal of Personality and Social Psychology, 54,* 663–678.

Franz, C. E., & White, K. M. (1985). Individuation and attachment in personality development: Extending Erikson's theory. *Journal of Personality, 53,* 224–256.

Freud, S. (1965). *New introductory lectures on psychoanalysis.* (J. Strachey, Ed. & Transl.) New York: Norton. (Original work published 1933.)

Freud, S. (1989). *The psychopathology of everyday life.* (J. Strachey, Ed. & Transl.) New York: Norton. (Original work published 1920.)

Funder, D. C. (2001). *The personality puzzle* (2nd ed.). New York: Norton.

Kenny, D. A., & Kasby, D. A. (1992). Analysis of the multitrait-multimethod matrix by confirmatory factor analysis. *Psychological Bulletin, 112,* 165–172.

Mischel, W. (1968). *Personality and assessment.* New York: Wiley.

Mischel, W., & Peake, P. K. (1982). Beyond *déjà vu* in the search for cross-situational consistency. *Psychological Review, 90,* 730–755.

Myers, I. B., & McCaulley, M. H. (1985). *Manual: A guide to the development and use of the Myers-Briggs Type Indicator.* Palo Alto, CA: Consulting Psychologists Press.

Ozer, D. J. (1989). Construct validity in personality assessment. In D. M. Buss & N. Cantor (Eds.), *Personality psychology: Recent trends and emerging directions* (pp. 224–234). New York: Springer-Verlag.

Ozer, D. J., & Reise, S. P. (1994). Personality assessment. *Annual Review of Psychology, 45,* 357–388.

Ross, L. (1977). The intuitive psychologist and his shortcomings. In L. Berkowitz (Ed.), *Advances in experimental social psychology* (Vol. 10, pp. 174–214). New York: Academic Press.

Sameroff, A. J., & Seifer, R. (1995). Accumulation of environmental risk and child mental health. In H. E. Fitzgerald, B. M. Lester, & B. S. Zuckerman (Eds.), *Children of poverty: Research, health, and policy issues.* New York: Garland.

Snyder, M., & Gangestad, S. (1986). On the nature of self-monitoring: Matters of assessment, matters of validity. *Journal of Personality and Social Psychology, 51,* 125–139.

Credits

Figures

Figure 14.1: From "A Five-Factor Theory of Personality," by R. R. McCrae and P. T. Costa Jr. In *Handbook of Personality: Theory and Research*, edited by L. A. Pervin & O. P. John, pp. 139–153. Copyright © 1999 by Guilford Press. Reprinted by permission.

Figure 17.1: Linda Huff / *American Scientist*

Figure 17.2: Linda Huff / *American Scientist*

Figure 47.1: Used by permission of Albert Bandura.

Figure 53.1: From "Self-Knowledge of an Amnesic Patient: Toward a Neuropsychology of Personality and Social Psychology," by S. B. Klein, J. Loftus, and J. F. Kihlstrom. In *Journal of Experimental Psychology: General, 125*, 250–260. Copyright © 1996 by the American Psychological Association. Adapted with permission.

Figure 53.2: From "Self-Knowledge of an Amnesic Patient: Toward a Neuropsychology of Personality and Social Psychology," by S. B. Klein, J. Loftus, and J. F. Kihlstrom. In *Journal of Experimental Psychology: General, 125*, 250–260. Copyright © 1996 by the American Psychological Association. Adapted with permission.

Text

Page 3: From "What Do We Know When We Know a Person?" by D. P. McAdams (1995). In *Journal of Personality, 63*, 365–396. Copyright © by Blackwell Publishers. Reprinted with permission.

Page 15: From "Studying Personality the Long Way," by J. Block. In *Studying Lives Through Time: Personality and Development*, edited by D. C. Funder, R. D. Parke, C. Tomlinson-Keasey, and K. Widaman, pp. 9–41. Washington, DC: American Psychological Association. Copyright © 1993 by the American Psychological Association. Adapted with permission.

Page 23: From "A Simple, General-Purpose Display of Magnitude of Experimental Effect," by R. Rosenthal and D. B. Rubin. In *Journal of Educational Psychology, 74*, 166–169. Copyright © 1982 by the American Psychological Association. Adapted with permission.

Page 27: From "Construct Validity in Psychological Tests," by L. J. Cronbach and P. E. Meehl (1955). In *Psychological Bulletin, 52*, 281–301.

Page 36: From "Convergent and Discriminant Validation by the Multitrait-Multimethod Matrix," by D. T. Campbell and D. W. Fiske (1959). In *Psychological Bulletin, 56*, 81–105.

Page 45: From "Conceptual Analysis of Psychological Test Scores and Other Diagnostic Variables," by H. G. Gough. In *Journal of Abnormal Psychology, 70*, 294–302. Copyright © 1965 by the American Psychological Association. Adapted with permission.

Page 54: From "Do People Know How They Behave? Self-Reported Act Frequencies Compared with On-line Codings by Observers," by S. D. Gosling, O. P. John, K. H. Kraik, and R. W. Robins. In *Journal of Personality and Social Psychology, 74*, 1397–1349. Copyright © 1998 by the American Psychological Association. Adapted with permission.

Page 71: From *The Last Hurrah*, by E. O'Connor, pp. 17–19. Copyright © 1956 by Edwin O'Connor.

Page 73: From "What Is a Trait of Personality?" by G. W. Allport. *Journal of Abnormal and Social Psychology, 25*, 368–371. Copyright © 1931 by the American Psychological Association. Adapted with permission.

Page 77: From *Personality and Assessment*, by W. Mischel (1968), pp. 13–39. New York: Wiley.

Page 91: From "Some Reasons for the Apparent Inconsistency of Personality," by J. Block. In *Psychological Bulletin, 70*, 210–212. Copyright © 1968 by the American Psychological Association. Adapted with permission.

Page 94: From "Profiting from Controversy: Lessons from the Person-Situation Debate," by D. T. Kenrick and D. C. Funder. In *American Psychologist, 43*, 23–34. Copyright © 1988 by the American Psychological Association. Adapted with permission.

Page 111: From "Self-Monitoring of Expressive Behavior," by M. Snyder. In *Journal of Personality and Social Psychology, 30*, 526–537. Copyright © 1974 by the American Psychological Association. Adapted with permission.

Page 120: From "A Five-Factor Theory of Personality," by R. R. McCrae and P. T. Costa Jr. In *Handbook of Personality: Theory and Research*, edited by L. A. Pervin and O. P. John, pp. 139–153. Copyright © 1999 by Guilford Press. Reprinted by permission.

Page 135: From *New Physiognomy, or, Signs of Character, as Manifested Through Temperament and External Forms, and Especially in 'the Human Face Divine,'* by S. R. Wells (1873), pp. 94–109. New York: Samuel R. Wells, Publisher.

Page 142: From "Testosterone Differences Among College Fraternities: Well-Behaved vs. Rambunctious," by J. M. Dabbs Jr., M. F. Hargrove, and C. Heusel. In *Personality and Individual Differences, 20,* 157–161.

Page 149: From "Reward Deficiency Syndrome," by K. Blum, J. G. Cull, E. R. Braverman, and D. E. Comings. In *American Scientist, 84,* 132–145. Copyright © 1996 by *American Scientist.* Reprinted by permission.

Page 162: From "Genes, Environment, and Personality," by T. J. Bouchard Jr. Excerpted with permission from *Science, 264,* 1700–1701. Copyright © 1994, American Association for the Advancement of Science.

Page 167: From "Environment and Genes: Determinants of Behavior," by R. Plomin. In *American Psychologist, 44,* 105–111. Copyright © 1989 by the American Psychological Association. Adapted with permission.

Page 171: From "Sex Differences in Jealousy: Evolution, Physiology, and Psychology," By D. M. Buss, R. J. Larsen, D. Westen, and J. Semmelroth. In *Psychological Science, 3,* 251–255. Copyright © 1992 by the American Psychological Society. Reprinted with the permission of Blackwell Publishers.

Page 178: From "Male Sexual Proprietariness and Violence Against Wives," by M. I. Wilson and M. Daly. In *Current Directions in Psychological Science, 5,* 2–7. Copyright © 1996 by the American Psychological Society. Reprinted with the permission of Blackwell Publishers.

Page 186: From "The Origins of Sex Differences in Human Behavior: Evolved Dispositions Versus Social Roles," by A. H. Eagly and W. Wood. In *American Psychologist, 54,* 408–423. Copyright © 1999 by the American Psychological Association. Adapted with permission.

Page 205: "Exotic Becomes Erotic: A Developmental Theory of Sexual Orientation," by D. J. Bem. In *Psychological Review, 103,* 320–335. Copyright © 1996 by the American Psychological Association. Adapted with permission.

Page 227: From *Introductory Lectures on Psycho-analysis,* by Sigmund Freud, in *The Standard Edition of the Complete Works of Sigmund Freud,* translated by James Strachey, pp. 51–71. Translation © 1965, 1964, 1963 by James Strachey. Reprinted by permission of W. W. Norton & Company, Inc. and the Hogarth Press.

Page 236: From *Introductory Lectures on Psycho-analysis,* by Sigmund Freud, in *The Standard Edition of the Complete Works of Sigmund Freud,* translated by James Strachey, pp. 48–72. Translation © 1965, 1964, 1963 by James Strachey. Reprinted by permission of W. W. Norton & Company, Inc. and the Hogarth Press.

Page 245: From "Survey of Objective Studies of Psychoanalytic Concepts," by R. R. Sears. In *Social Research Council Bulletin, 51,* pp. 133–143. Reprinted by permission of the Social Science Research Council, 810 Seventh Ave., New York, NY 10019.

Page 250: From "Freudian Defense Mechanisms and Empirical Findings in Modern Social Psychology: Reaction Formation, Projection, Displacement, Undoing, Isolation, Sublimation, and Denial," by R. F. Baumeister, K. Dale, and K. L. Sommer. In *Journal of Personality, 66,* 1081–1124. Copyright © 1998 by the American Psychological Society. Reprinted with the permission of Blackwell Publishers.

Page 266: From "The Verdict on Freud," by F. Crews. In *Psychological Science, 7,* pp. 63–68. Copyright © 1996 by the American Psychological Society. Reprinted with the permission of Blackwell Publishers.

Page 272: From *Psychological Types,* by C. G. Jung, translated by R. Hull and H. Baynes, pp. 510–523. Copyright © 1971 by Princeton University Press. Reprinted by permission of Princeton University Press.

Page 277: From *Feminine Psychology,* by K. Horney, pp. 104–116. Copyright © 1967 by W. W. Norton & Company, Inc. Reprinted by permission of W. W. Norton & Company, Inc.

Page 283: From *Childhood and Society,* by E. H. Erikson, pp. 219–234. Copyright © 1950, 1963 by W. W. Norton & Company, Inc., renewed 1978, 1991, by Erik H. Erikson. Reprinted by permission of W. W. Norton & Company, Inc.

Page 295: From *Essays in Existentialism,* edited by W. Baskin, pp. 31–62. Copyright © 1965. All rights reserved. Published by arrangement with Citadel Press, Kensington Publishing Corporation.

Page 303: From "Existential Philosophy—What's in It for Us?" by A. H. Maslow. In *Existential Philosophy,* 2d ed., edited by R. May, pp. 49–57. New York: Random House. Copyright © 1969 by the McGraw-Hill Companies. Adapted with permission.

Page 308: From "Is the Concept of Self Necessary? The Proprium." In *Becoming: Basic Consideration for a Psychology of Personality,* by G. W. Allport (1955), pp. 36–65. New Haven, CT: Yale University Press. Copyright © 1955 by Yale University Press.

Page 315: From "A Theory of Human Motivation," in *Motivation and Personality,* by A. H. Maslow, pp. 80–106. Copyright © 1954 by Harper & Brothers. Copyright © 1970 by Abraham H. Maslow. Reprinted by permission of Addison-Wesley Educational Publishers.

Page 338: From "If We Are So Rich, Why Aren't We Happy?" by M. Csikszentmihalyi. In *American Psychologist, 54,* 821–827. Copyright © 1999 by the American Psychological Association. Adapted with permission.

Page 351: From "Body Ritual Among the Nacirema," by H. Miner. In *American Anthropologist, 58,* pp. 503–507.

Page 355: From "Exploring Implicit Personality Theories with Indigenous or Imported Constructs: The Chinese Case," by K. Yang and M. H. Bond. In *Journal of Personality and Social Psychology, 58,* 1087–1095. Copyright © 1990 by the American Psychological Association. Adapted with permission.

Page 365: From "A Collective Fear of the Collective: Implications for Selves and Theories of Selves," from H. R. Markus and S. Kitayama. In *Personality and Social Psychology Bulletin, 20,* 568–579. Copyright © 1994 by the Society for Personality and Social Psychology, Inc. Reprinted by permission of Sage Publications.

Page 378: From "The Self and Social Behavior in Differing Cultural Contexts," by H. C. Triandis. In *Psychological Review, 96,* 506–520. Copyright © 1989 by the American Psychological Association. Adapted with permission.

Page 394: From "Insult, Aggression, and the Southern Culture of Honor: An 'Experimental Ethnography,' " by D. Cohen, R. E. Nisbett, B. F. Bowdle, and N. Schwarz. In *Journal of Personality and Social Psychology, 70,* 945–960. Copyright © 1996 by the American Psychological Association. Adapted with permission.

Page 412: From "The O. J. Simpson Verdict: Predictors of Beliefs About Innocence or Guilt," by C. B. Murray, R. Kaiser, and S. Taylor. In *Journal of Social Issues, 53,* 455–475. Copyright © 1997 by the Ontario Institute for Studies in Education. Reprinted by permission of Blackwell Publishers.

Page 425: From *Science and Human Behavior,* by B. F. Skinner, pp. 23–42. Copyright © 1953. Adapted by permission of Prentice-Hall, Inc., Upper Saddle River, NJ.

Page 433: From "Whatever Happened to Psychology as the Science of Behavior?" by B. F. Skinner. In *American Psychologist, 42,* 780–786. Copyright © 1997. Adapted with permission of the American Psychological Association and the B. F. Skinner Foundation.

Page 439: From "An Introduction to Social Learning Theory," by J. B. Rotter. In *Applications of a Social Learning Theory of Personality,* edited by J. B. Rotter, J. E. Chance, and E. J. Phares, pp. 1–46. New York: Holt, Rinehart & Winston. Reprinted with permission of the authors.

Page 448: From "Imitation of Film-Mediated Aggressive Models," by A. Bandura, D. Ross, and S. A. Ross. In *Journal of Abnormal and Social Psychology, 66,* 3–11. Copyright © 1963 by the American Psychological Association. Adapted with permission.

Page 459: From "The Self System in Reciprocal Determinism," by A. Bandura. In *American Psychologist, 33,* 344–358. Copyright © 1978 by the American Psychological Association. Adapted with permission.

Page 472: From "Toward a Cognitive Social Learning Reconceptualization of Personality," by W. Mischel. In *Psychological Review, 80,* 252–283. Copyright © 1973 by the American Psychological Association. Adapted with permission.

Page 483: From "Cognitive Strategies as Personality: Effectiveness, Specificity, Flexibility, and Change," by J. K. Norem. In *Personality Psychology: Recent Trends and Emerging Directions,* edited by D. M. Buss and N. Cantor, pp. 45–60. New York: Springer-Verlag. Adapted with permission.

Page 494: From "Integration of the Cognitive and the Psychodynamic Unconscious," by S. Epstein. In *American Psychologist, 49,* 709–724. Copyright © 1994 by the American Psychological Association. Adapted with permission.

Page 507: From "Effects of Ruminative and Distracting Responses to Depressed Mood on Retrieval of Autobiographical Memories," by S. Lyubomirsky, N. D. Caldwell, and S. Nolen-Hoeksema. In *Journal of Personality and Social Psychology, 75,* 166–177. Copyright © 1998 by the American Psychological Association. Adapted with permission.

Page 520: From "Self-Knowledge of an Amnesic Patient: Toward a Neuropsychology of Personality and Social Psychology," by S. B. Klein, J. Loftus, and J. F. Kihlstrom. In *Journal of Experimental Psychology: General, 125,* 250–260. Copyright © 1996 by the American Psychological Association. Adapted with permission.

Disclaimer: Every effort has been made to contact the copyright holders of each of the selections. Rights holders of any selections not credited should contact W. W. Norton & Company, Inc., 500 Fifth Avenue, New York, NY 10110, in order for a correction to be made in the next reprinting of our work.